PENGUIN CLASSICS

EARLY AMERICAN WRITING

GILES GUNN is professor and Chair of the Department of English at the University of California, Santa Barbara. The author and editor of more than ten volumes, the most recent of which is *Thinking Across the American Grain: Ideology, Intellect, and the New Pragmatism* (1992), he has written and lectured widely on American literature and culture as well as on critical theory.

Early American Writing

Edited and
with an Introduction by
GILES GUNN

PENGUIN BOOKS

PENGUIN BOOKS
Published by the Penguin Group
Penguin Books USA Inc., 375 Hudson Street,
New York, New York 10014, U.S.A.
Penguin Books Ltd, 27 Wrights Lane, London W8 5TZ, England
Penguin Books Australia Ltd, Ringwood, Victoria, Australia
Penguin Books Canada Ltd, 10 Alcorn Avenue,
Toronto, Ontario, Canada M4V 3B2
Penguin Books (N.Z.) Ltd, 182–190 Wairau Road,
Auckland 10, New Zealand

Penguin Books Ltd, Registered Offices:
Harmondsworth, Middlesex, England

First published in Penguin Books 1994

9   10   8

LIBRARY OF CONGRESS CATALOGING IN PUBLICATION DATA
Early American writing/ edited and with an introduction by
Giles Gunn.
p. cm.
ISBN 0 14 03.9087 1
1. American literature—Colonial period, ca. 1600–1775.   2. United
States—history—Colonial period, ca. 1600–1775—Sources.
3. America—Discovery and exploration—Literary collections.
4. Indians of North America—Literary collections.   5. Great
Britain—Colonies—Literary collections.   I. Gunn, Giles B.
PS531.C65   1994
810.8'003—dc20   93–22916

Printed in the United States of America
Set in Sabon

In loving memory of Buckingham Willcox Gunn
(May 31, 1991–March 31, 1968) and
Janet Fargo Gunn (November 6, 1912–
January 18, 1988)

Do ut des

CONTENTS

Introduction   *xv*

Prefigurations (1):
Native American Mythology

Winnebago
  This Newly Created World   5
Cherokee
  How the World Was Made   6
Bering Strait Eskimo
  Raven Creation Myth   9
Hopi
  How the Spaniards Came to Shung-opovi, How
    They Built a Mission, and How the Hopi
    Destroyed the Mission   12
Iroquois
  Iroquois or Confederacy of the Five Nations   16

Prefigurations (2):
The Literature of
Imagination and Discovery

Anonymous
  from *The Saga of Eric the Red* (c. 1000)   23

Christopher Columbus (1451?–1506)
  from a *Letter to Lord Raphael Sanchez, Treasurer to
        Ferdinand and Isabella, King and Queen of Spain,
        on His First Voyage* (1493)   26
Amerigo Vespucci (1454–1512)
  from *Mundus Novus* (Letter on His Third Voyage to
        Lorenzo Pietro Francesco de Medici,
        1503)   33
Thomas More (1478–1535)
  from *Utopia* (1551)   37
Alvar Nuñez Cabeza de Vaca (1490?–1557?)
  from *The Narrative of Alvar Nuñez Cabeza de Vaca*
        (1542)   43
Pedro de Casteñeda (1510?–1570?)
  from *The Narrative of the Expedition of Coronado*
        (c. 1562)   48
Peter Martyr (1455–1526) and Richard Eden
        (1521–1576)
  from *The Decades of the New World or West India*
        (1555)   53
Michel de Montaigne (1533–1592)
  from *Of Cannibals* (1580)   56
Thomas Hariot (1560–1621)
  from *Brief and True Report of the New-found Land
        of Virginia* (1588)   61
Sir Walter Raleigh (1544–1618)
  from *The Discovery of Guiana* (1595)   66
Michael Drayton (1563–1631)
  To the Virginian Voyage (1606)   71
Richard Hakluyt (1552?–1616)
  from *The Famous Voyage of Sir Francis Drake*
        (1628)   75
William Shakespeare (1564–1616)
  from *The Tempest* (1611)   79
Francis Bacon (1561–1626)
  from *The New Atlantis* (1627)   81
Samuel de Champlain (1567–1635)
  from *The Voyages of Samuel de Champlain*
        (1604–1618)   86
George Herbert (1593–1633)
  from *The Church Militant* (1633)   90

The Literature of
Settlement and Colonization

John Smith (1580–1631)
  from A *True Relation of Such Occurences and Accidents of*
    Noate as Hath Hapned in Virginia Since the First
    Planting of That Collony (1608)   96
  from *A Description of New England* (1616)   97
John Cotton (1584–1652)
  from *God's Promise to His Plantations* (1630)   102
Alexander Whitaker (1585–1616?)
  from *Good Newes from Virginia* (1613)   105
John Winthrop (1587–1649)
  from *A Modell of Christian Charity* (1630)   108
  John Winthrop's Christian Experience (1637)   113
William Bradford (1590–1657)
  from *Of Plymouth Plantation* (1630–1651)
    from Chapter I [The Separatist Interpretation of
      the Reformation in England, 1550–1607]   120
    from Chapter II [Of Their Departure to Holland and
      the Troubles and Difficulties They Met with There.
      Anno 1608]   122
    from Chapter III [Of Their Settlement in Holland
      and Their Life There]   122
    from Chapter IV [On the Reasons and Causes
      of Their Removal]   123
    from Chapter IX [Of their Voyage, and How They
      Passed the Sea, and of Their Safe Arrival at Cape Cod]   126
    from Chapter XI [The Remainder of Anno 1620:
      Starving Time; Indian Relations]   129
    from Chapter XIX [Anno Domini 1628:
      Thomas Morton of Merry-mont]   132
    from Chapter XXXII [Anno Domini 1642:
      Wickedness Breaks Forth]   134
    from Chapter XXXIII [Anno Domini 1643:
      The Life and Death of Elder Brewster]   135
Thomas Morton (1579?–1647)
  from *The New English Canaan* (1637)   138
Thomas Hooker (1586?–1647)
  from *A True Sight of Sin* (1659)   148

Ann Hutchinson (1591–1643)
  from *The Examination of Mrs. Ann Hutchinson at
     the Court at Newtown* (1637)   *159*
Thomas Shepard (1605–1649)
  The Covenant of Grace (1651)   *171*
Anne Bradstreet (1612?–1672)
  The Prologue (1650)   *176*
  The Author to Her Book   *178*
  Before the Birth of One of Her Children   *178*
  Contemplations   *179*
  To My Dear and Loving Husband   *185*
  *A Letter to Her Husband, Absent upon
     Publick Employment*   *186*
  *In Memory of My Dear Grand-Child Elizabeth
     Bradstreet, Who Deceased August, 1655,
     Being a Year and a Half Old*   *186*
  *Here Follows Some Verses upon the Burning of
     Our House (July 10th, 1666)*   *187*
  To My Dear Children   *188*
Roger Williams (1613–1683)
  from *The Bloudy Tenent of Persecution* (1644)   *194*
  from *The Hireling Ministry None of Christs* (1652)   *195*
Samuel Danforth (1626–1674)
  from *A Brief Recognition of New England's Errand
     into the Wilderness* (1671)   *198*
Michael Wigglesworth (1631–1705)
  from *God's Controversy with New-England* (1662)   *209*
Mary Rowlandson (1635?–1678?)
  from *A Narrative of the Captivity and Restauration of
     Mrs. Mary Rowlandson* (1682)   *217*
Edward Taylor (1644?–1729)
  from *God's Determinations Concerning His Elect*
     (c. 1680)
    The Preface   *232*
    The Souls Groan to Christ for Succour   *233*
    Christ's Reply   *234*
  from *Preparatory Meditations*
    First Series Meditations (1, 8, 38, 39)   *237*
  from *Occasional Poems*
    Upon a Spider Catching a Fly   *241*
    Huswifery   *243*
    The Ebb & Flow   *243*

Contents   xi

Samuel Sewall (1652–1730)
  from *The Diary of Samuel Sewall* (1674–1729)   246
  from *Phaenomena quaedam Apocalyptica* (1697)   253
  from *The Selling of Joseph* (1700)   254
Cotton Mather (1633–1728)
  from *Magnalia Christi Americana* (1702)
    A General Introduction   259
    Galeacius Secundus: The Life of William
      Bradford, Esq., Governor of Plymouth Colony   261
Sarah Kemble Knight (1666–1727)
  from *The Journal of Madam Knight* (1704–1710)   269
Ebenezer Cook (1670–c. 1732)
  from *The Sot-Weed Factor; or, a Voyage to*
    Maryland, &c. (1708)   274
Robert Beverley (c. 1673–1722)
  from *The History and Present State of Virginia* (1705)
    Chapter I: Showing What Happened in the First
      Attempts to Settle Virginia, Before the Discovery
      of Chesapeake Bay   288
    Chapter II: Containing an Account of the First
      Settlement of Chesapeake Bay, in Virginia, by the
      Corporation of London Adventurers, and Their
      Proceedings During Their Government by a President
      and Council Elective   293
    Chapter III: Showing What Happened After
      the Alteration of the Government From an Elective
      President to a Commissionated Governor, Until the
      Dissolution of the Company   297
William Byrd II (1674–1744)
  from *The Secret Diary of William Byrd of Westover*
    (1719–1720)   301
Fray Carlos José Delgado (1677–c. 1750)
  Report made by Rev. Father Fray Carlos Delgado to our
    Reverend Father Ximeno concerning the abominable
    hostilities and tyrannies of the governors and alcaldes
    mayores toward the Indians, to the conster-
    nation of the custodia (1750)   304
Jonathan Edwards (1703–1758)
  Sarah Pierrepont (1723)   311
  from *Personal Narrative* (1740)   312
  Sinners in the Hands of an Angry God (1741)   320
  from *A Treatise Concerning Religious Affections* (1746)   333
  from *The Nature of True Virtue* (1765)   342

Benjamin Franklin (1706–1790)
  The Way to Wealth [Preface to *Poor Richard
      Improved*] (1758)   349
  *Address to the Public; from the Pennsylvania Society
      for Promoting the Abolition of Slavery, and the Relief
      of Free Negroes Unlawfully Held in Bondage* (1782)   354
  from *Information to Those Who Would Remove to
      America* (1784)   355
  Remarks Concerning the Savages of North America
      (1784)   358
  *Speech in the Convention at the Conclusion of Its
      Deliberations* (September 17, 1787)   362
  from *The Autobiography of Benjamin Franklin* (1784, 1788)   364
  Letter to Ezra Styles (March 9, 1790)   372
Elizabeth Ashbridge (1713–1755)
  from *Some Account of the Early Part of the Life of
      Elizabeth Ashbridge, . . . Written by Herself* (1807)   374
Jonathan Mayhew (1720–1766)
  from *A Discourse Concerning Unlimited Submission
      and Non-Resistance to the Higher Powers* (1750)   387
John Woolman (1720–1772)
  from *Some Considerations on the Keeping of
      Negroes* (1754)   391
Francisco Palou (1723–1789)
  from *Life of Junipero Serra* (1787)   397

Native American Literature
in the Colonial Period

North American Indian Oratory   405
Chief Powhatan (1609)   406
Chief Canassatego (1742)   407
Chief Logan (1774)   409
Chief Pachgantschilias (1787)   411
Chief Tecumseh (1810)   412

Literature of the
Early Republic

George Washington (1732–1799)
  from *The Farewell Address to the People of the United
      States* (September 17, 1796)   418

Thomas Jefferson (1734–1826)
  from *Autobiography* 431
  from *Notes on the State of Virginia* (1785)
    from Query IV. [A Notice of Its Mountains?] 437
    from Query V. [Its Cascades and Caverns?] 439
    from Query XI. [A Description of the Indians Established
      in that State?] 439
    from Query XVII. [Religion?] 440
  An Act for Establishing Religious Freedom in the State
    of Virginia (1786) 442
  First Inaugural Address (March 4, 1801) 443
  Letter to James Madison (December 20, 1787) 447
  Letter to Dr. Benjamin Rush (April 21, 1803) 451
  Letter to Peter Carr (August 19, 1785) 454
  Letter to Thomas Law, Esq. (June 13, 1814) 457
John Adams (1735–1826)
  from the Preface to *A Defense of the Constitutions of*
    Government (1787) 462
J. Hector St. Jean de Crevecoeur (1737–1818)
  from *Letters of an American Farmer* (1782)
    from Letter III. [What Is an American?] 473
    from Letter IX. [Thoughts on Slavery; On Physical
      Evil; A Melancholy Scene] 479
Thomas Paine (1737–1809)
  An Occasional Letter on the Female Sex (1775) 485
  from the Introduction to *Common Sense* (1776) 489
  from *Of the Religion of Deism Compared with the*
    Christian Religion, and the Superiority of the
    Former over the Latter (1804) 490
William Bartram (1739–1823)
  from *Travels Through North and South Carolina, Georgia,*
    East and West Florida (1791) 496
Abigail Adams (1744–1818)
  Letters to John Adams
    March 31, 1776 502
    April 5, 1776 504
    July 13, 1776 505
    August 14, 1776 505
    April 10, 1782 506
Gustavus Vassa [Olaudah Equiano] (1745–1797)
  from *The Interesting Narrative of the Life of Oloudah*

*Equiano, or Gustavus Vassa, the African, Written
      by Himself* (1789)   511
Hugh Henry Brackenridge (1748–1816)
  from *Modern Chivalry* (1792)
      Chapter I   524
      Chapter III   524
      Chapter V   529
John Trumbull
  "The Liberty Pole" from *M'Fingal* (1782)   532
The Federalist Papers (1787–1788)
      No. 1 [Alexander Hamilton] (1787)   538
      No. 10 [James Madison] (1787)   541
Judith Sargent Murray (1751–1820)
  On the Equality of the Sexes (1790)   548
Timothy Dwight (1752–1817)
  from *America* (1790)   556
Philip Freneau (1752–1832)
  On the Emigration to America (1784)   560
  The Wild Honey Suckle (1786)   561
  The Indian Burying Ground (1787)   562
  On Mr. Paine's Rights of Man (1791)   563
Phillis Wheatley (1753?–1784)
  On Being Brought from Africa to America (1773)   566
  On the Death of the Rev. Mr. George Whitfield (1770)   566
  *To S. M., A Young African Painter, on Seeing
      His Works* (1773)   567
  To His Excellency General Washington (1776)   568
Joel Barlow (1754–1812)
  From *Advise to the Privileged Orders in the Several
      States of Europe* (1792)   571
  The Hasty Pudding (1793)   577
Royall Tyler (1757–1826)
  Choice of a Wife (1796)   588
  Prologue to *The Contrast* (1787)   589
Hannah Webster Foster (1758–1840)
  from *The Coquette; or, The Life and Letters of Eliza Wharton*
      (1797)   592
Susanna Haswell Rowson (1762?–1824)
  Preface to *Charlotte Temple* (1794)   607

Explanatory Notes   609

INTRODUCTION

American literature is undergoing something like a seismic shift as new texts join the canon, older texts are being reinterpreted, unknown or forgotten writers are being discovered or reappropriated, and established reputations are being reassessed. This phenomenon would seem less notable if it were not so difficult to remember that the American literary canon has always been undergoing revision. The canon of 1920—or of 1950, or even of 1970—had a very different appearance than the canon of today, and the canon of today is far from stable. Literary canons, like cultures themselves, are always being contested and reconstructed, because they represent a culture's repository of narrative, lyrical, and discursive paradigms, its assemblage of the stories it tells itself about itself. The instability of the canon simply signifies, and at some moments actually mirrors, the debate that the culture is having with itself about what verbal shapings best describe those contours of experience that it imagines to be its own.

Nowhere is this more evident than in the field known as early American literature, the site of American culture's myths of origin. By "early" we used to mean a literature that began with the first evidence of sustained and purposeful European—and predominantly British—contact and settlement in what is now the United States at the beginning of the seventeenth century and that concluded sometime before the rise of nationalist aspirations around the middle of the eighteenth century. Now, however, it is accepted that early American literature originates in a period that antedates the commencement of English settlement along the Eastern seaboard, when the ideas that eventually inspired and nourished European contact with the New World were first achieving their initial Renaissance form. It is also generally conceded that no fair estimate can be made of the impact, fate, or effect of those ideas that the original European—and not just English—explorers, conquistadors, colonists, and settlers brought with them without at least some appreciation of the mythological framework and the conceptual mindset of the indigenous peoples who would be so violently displaced by them.

This means that the parameters of early American writing are now widely held to go back as far as the beginning of the early modern period in Europe and to include everything from narratives of discovery to utopian fantasies about the creation or recovery of Paradise and Amerindian legends about the founding of the world. Those parameters are now also understood to extend far enough forward not only to encompass the emergence of the new nation-state in part wrested out of the tensions and conflicts associated with that earlier, presettlement legacy but also to include some of the more consequential energies liberated by its early development. Where this literature was once thought to be the expression chiefly of men, we now realize that it was also shaped in significant ways by the sometimes different expressive talents of women. Where this literature was formerly considered the experiential record primarily of transplanted English citizens, we now know that Hispanic, French, African-American, and Native American peoples played a substantial role in its constitution and growth. And with an expanded sense of the various peoples who contributed to the complex formation of this literature has come as well a deepened understanding of the different kinds of writing that the colonization of the United States produced. In other words, we now know that the "America" that was brought into existence by the practice of early American writing was not "discovered," as the Mexican historian Edmundo O'Gorman has pointed out, so much as "invented," or "discovered" because it was "invented."

This is not to claim that there was nothing to be found on Friday, October 12, 1492, at around 2:00 A.M., when Christopher Columbus (1451?–1506) made landfall in the West Indies on the island of what is now called San Salvador; only that Columbus was mistaken about what he had come upon that fateful morning and that he then compounded the problem by resisting the corrections of experience. Looking for a sea passage to India, Columbus supposed that he had actually managed, as he'd intended, to reach the Orient, and then he steadfastly refused to relinquish this conviction despite three later voyages that at most never carried him farther west than the Paria peninsula of Venezuela. Convinced nonetheless that he had landed on the shores of Asia, he was therefore unaware that instead he had come upon a new landmass, leaving credit for that discovery to be claimed by another

Italian navigator named Amerigo Vespucci (1454–1512), whose report of a landfall achieved before Columbus's in the Southern hemisphere was most likely made up.

Columbus was certain instead that he had found a passage to India because he viewed everything before his eyes with a mental picture he had already constructed. This mental picture was derived chiefly from his reading of the Bible, together with his familiarity with the accounts of Marco Polo's overland journey to China and his knowledge of Ptolemaic geography. The ancient astronomer Ptolemy (fl. A.D. 130) had postulated that the earth was considerably smaller than we now know it to be and that the Asian landmass extended much farther into the ocean than it does. As it happens, this theory turned out to be admirably suited to Columbus's purposes, since it tended to confirm Marco Polo's speculations about the proximity of Japan's position relative to Portugal and was reinforced by certain prophetic claims found in the Bible. The apocryphal Book of Esdras (2:6), for example, held that the world was six parts land and only one part water. The Book of Ezekiel (5:5), in turn, maintained that Jerusalem was at the center of the world. Such assertions not only persuaded Columbus that the sea voyage from Portugal to Asia was comparatively short (2,700 miles, as opposed to the actual 12,000); they also assured him that in undertaking this expedition he was fulfilling the injunctions of Holy Scripture: "In carrying out this Enterprise of the Indies, neither reason nor mathematics nor maps were any use to me: fully accomplished were the words of Isaiah."

Vespucci, on the other hand, was prepared to steal credit for discovering a New World even if he had to fabricate his own account of it. According to his own account in *Mundus Novus*, or *The New World* (1503), Vespucci did not actually land on the coast of what is now Brazil until 1501, recording there that he and his company had come upon "a new land which . . . we observed to be a continent." But the validity of this achievement was immediately placed in jeopardy by the speculation that Columbus might have touched upon the coast of Venezuela during his third voyage in 1498. In his next book, Vespucci therefore changed his story to claim that, in fact, he had reached the South American mainland on a voyage made a year earlier—in 1497—than the one recorded in *Mundus Novus*. However, Vespucci's self-promotion as the first voyager to find a New World might still have come to nothing if his, as it turned out, fallacious claim had not caught the attention of a little-known German geographer named Martin Waldseemüller (1470?–1513?) who was preparing a new edition of Ptolemy. Deciding that the new continent ought to bear the name of its first discoverer, Waldseemüller wrote, "I do not see why anyone should rightly forbid naming it Amerigo, land of Americus as it were, after its discoverer Americus, a name of acute genius, or America, inasmuch as both Europe and Asia have received their names from women." Curiously enough, Waldseemüller himself was later to have second thoughts about this decision, and other interested parties, like the Spanish and Portuguese, were to object to it for centuries; but once attached to the newly delineated territory of Waldseemüller's 1507 world map, the name became ineradicable. From henceforth, and at the cost of no little misrepresentation, the New World was to be known as "America" (or, to the Spanish, "New Spain").

Both tales tell us something of what it means to say that America was invented as much as discovered. They tell us that the world that from this moment on was to realize itself within the compass of the name "America" was to be a world shaped as much by the energies of the imagination as by the substance of the actual; that it was to be defined as much by the ambiguities of desire as by the structures of the empirical. The world called "America," both North and South, would ever after be a world dominated and controlled by meanings as much as by facts; it would be a world where fantasy, fear, and fabrication would determine many of the contours of the real.

Nothing demonstrates this more vividly than the link we normally make between Christopher Columbus's name and the idea of America's "original" discovery. Whether Columbus reached the shores of this continent before Vespucci or Vespucci before Columbus, they were neither of them, as even they could see for themselves, America's first discoverers. That title instead belongs to the ancestors of those singular and, as Columbus and Vespucci themselves both reported, marvelous human specimens that confronted them on the beaches of the Americas, people who, as the Italian cleric Peter Martyr (1455–1526) described them, "go naked . . . know neither weights nor measures, nor that source of all misfortunes, money; living in a golden age, without laws, without lying judges, without books, satisfied with their life, and in no wise solicitous for the future." These natives, already in occupancy for centuries, if not millennia, of the lands Columbus and Vespucci claimed to have discovered for the first time, were descendants of nomadic peoples from Asia who first made their way across a land bridge the remnants of which now compose the Bering Strait nearly 22,000 years before the momentous journeys of Columbus and Vespucci. And whatever the motives of those genuinely original discoverers, their descendants over time were to work their way down and settle almost the whole of the Northern and Southern hemispheres, creating in the process some of the great civilizations of the ancient world: the Mayan in southern Mexico and Guatemala, the Incan in Peru, and the Aztec in Mexico. Indeed, so numerous had these disparate native descendants of America's first discoverers become by the time Columbus and Vespucci arrived at the end of the fifteenth century of the common era that, according to some estimates, there were then living in the Americas somewhere between 80 and 100 million people speaking as many as 2,200 different languages.

One can measure something of the sophistication and diversity of these various Native American peoples by the ruins of the many magnificent cities they left behind when disease, famine, natural disaster, and the genocidal policies of many of the Europeans took their toll: cities such as Palenque, Tikal, Tula, Monte Albán, Uxmal, and Chichén Itzá. On entering the Aztec capital of Tenochtitlan with the invading army of Hernando Cortés, one of his sergeants, Bernal Díaz del Castillo—who eventually recorded the history of the Spanish conquest in his great *Discovery and Conquest of Mexico* (published in 1632)—likened the amazement that overtook the soldiers to "the enchantments they tell of in the legend of Amadis" and noted that "some of the soldiers even asked whether the things that we saw were not a dream." Reflecting on the Aztec palaces, he could not help remarking,

> How spacious and well built they were, of beautiful stone work and cedar wood, and the wood of other sweet scented trees, with great rooms and courts, wonderful to behold, covered with awnings of cotton cloth. . . . And all was cemented and very splendid with many kinds of stone (monuments) with pictures on them. . . . I say again that I stood looking at it and thought that never in the world would there be discovered other lands such as these, for at that time there was no Peru [or knowledge of the great cities of Cuzco and Machu Picchu], nor any thought of it. Of all these wonders that I then beheld, today all is overthrown and lost, nothing left standing.

An even more dramatic indication of the achievements of Amerindian civilizations—in agriculture, economics, government, arts and crafts, and religion—is to be found in the way Europeans borrowed so heavily from them. From Native American agriculture, for example, the rest of the world's peoples acquired such staples as corn, potatoes, manioc, and sweet potatoes, as well as peanuts, squash, peppers, tomatoes, pumpkins, pineapples, avocados, cacao, and various kinds of legumes, to say nothing of cotton, tobacco, and a host of medicinal herbs. From Native American crafts and technology, they obtained such useful items as hammocks, canoes, toboggans, snowshoes, kayaks, and parkas. From Native American politics, and particularly the League of Iroquois, colonial leaders like Benjamin Franklin (1706–1790) derived some of their best ideas for constitutional government.

From Native American economies, early white settlers to the New World learned about the principles and practices of trade and barter. And not least, from Native American mythology and metaphysics, New World settlers heard, and sometimes learned, stories, poems, tales, and sayings that taught them, often for the very first time, about the ecological interdependence and unity of all life. Yet for all the sophistication and heterogeneity of their societies and cultures—while some Native Americans remained hunters and gatherers, others created written languages, became expert at engineering and astronomy, and even mastered the art of mathematical calculation—these infinitely various peoples were quickly, and tragically, lumped together by the name they received from Columbus when he mistook their homeland for Asia and thus called them "Indians."

But Native Americans were not the only people to have preceded Columbus and Vespucci to the New World. The earliest evidence of European discovery dates back to the beginning of the eleventh century, when Viking people reached the shores of Newfoundland and possibly attempted to establish settlements there, though there is some reason to believe that still earlier Chinese expeditions may have reached the coast of California. Archaeological evidence also suggests that African explorers may have landed in the Americas as early as the beginning of the fourteenth century, and we know for certain that English explorers sailed as far as North America at least a decade or more before Columbus's first voyage.

Nonetheless, it was the Spanish, the sponsors of Columbus, who led the parade of European explorers to the Americas, followed closely by the French. Inspired not just by the excitement of discovery but by dreams of conquest and wealth, Spanish explorers like Hernando Cortés (1486–1547), Francisco Pizarro (1470?–1541), and Francisco Vasquez de Coronado (1500?–1554) penetrated deep into Mexico, South America, and the southwestern territory of the United States in the early sixteenth century, often destroying or subduing and enslaving native populations as they went. Their expeditions into Central and South America were paralleled by expeditions mounted into North America by the French, where explorers like Jacques Cartier (1494–1557), Samuel de Champlain (1567–1635), and Robert de La Salle (1643–1687) opened up vast areas of Canada and the Mississippi Valley to settlement. By these standards the English were latecomers to the Americas; but when at the beginning of the seventeenth century they finally decided to come in numbers, they came for a somewhat different purpose. Originally inspired, like the Spanish and the French, by imperial dreams of wealth, conquest, and religious conversion, they soon readjusted their ambitions in order to complement colonization with community-building.

The cost of these "discoveries of America" to the indigenous people who were so quickly displaced by them and so often threatened
with extinction was unimaginably high. According to some calculations, if one assumes that there were as many as 80 to 100 million
inhabitants of the Northern and Southern hemispheres, somewhere
between 60 and 80 million Native American peoples died before the
beginning of the seventeenth century, either because of the genocidal
policies of the Spanish conquistadors or because of the diseases the
Europeans brought with them. During the seventeenth century, the
indigenous population of the Virginia colony declined from upwards
of 100,000 people to just 1,500 by 1697. In New England during the
same period, there was a comparable decline of 95 percent in the native population, and the same figures can be found almost everywhere.

The great Mayan codex of prophecies, chronicles, and mystical
speculations known as *The Book of Chilam Balam of Chumayel* reg-
isters the impact of this holocaust only years after the conquest of the
Americas had begun. Of the time before the Spanish arrived, the poem
speaks, no doubt with nostalgia, of the time before "The Beginning of
the Sickness":

> There was no sin;
> in the holy faith their lives were passed.
> There was then no sickness;
> they had then no aching bones;
> they had then no high fever;
> they had then no smallpox;
> they had then no burning chest;
> they had then no abdominal pains;
> they had then no consumption;
> they had then no headache.
> At that time the course of humanity was orderly.

When the Spanish arrived "from the east," all changed:

> Then Christianity also began. The fulfillment of its
> prophecy is ascribed to the east . . .
> Then with the true God, the true *Dios*,
> came the beginning of our misery.
> It was the beginning of tribute,
> the beginning of church dues,
> the beginning of strife by trampling on people,
> the beginning of robbery with violence,
> the beginning of forced debts,
> the beginning of debts enforced by false testimony,

                    the beginning of individual strife,
                    a beginning of vexation.

The earliest English experiments at settlement were fairly disastrous. The first attempt at colonization was made in 1584, when an
expedition to Roanoke Island off the coast of North Carolina organized by Sir Walter Raleigh (1552?–1618) was completely overrun and
destroyed by the native population. When a relief operation reached
the settlement in 1590, it found the colony in ruins and no trace of
survivors. A second attempt was made at Jamestown in 1607, and this
was more successful, thanks in part to the leadership provided by the
irrepressible Captain John Smith (1580–1631), then a young man of
only twenty-six years. Confronted with a colony composed mainly of
"poor gentlemen, tradesmen, serving-men, libertines, and such like ten
times more fit to spoil a commonwealth than . . . to begin one," Smith
helped rally his comrades against the threat of disease, weather, Indian
attack, and near starvation by establishing the policy that "he who
does not work shall not eat." However, it was not the resilience of the
settlers that finally enabled the colony to survive but their friendly
relations with the neighboring natives. Members of the Algonkian confederation which was led by Chief Powhatan, the father of Pocahontas,
they taught the colonists how to hunt and fish as well as how to grow
corn and to cultivate tobacco. In this they established a pattern that
would be repeated as often as relations remained amicable between
Europeans and Native Americans: a pattern of Native American assistance secured and supported by the opportunity for interracial trade.
    Through the English publication of his *Map of Virginia with a
Description of the Country* (1612) and his subsequent *Description of
New England* (1616), John Smith was instrumental in precipitating
the next wave of English emigration to North America. But the settlers
he later helped attract to the New World by his excited descriptions
of its topography and landscape were quite different from the adventurers first drawn to Jamestown. The members of the Jamestown expedition, however physically unprepared they were for the hardships
they were to encounter and however emotionally indisposed to meet
the challenges they were to face, were motivated chiefly by the desire
for personal gain and advancement. On the other hand, the members
of the 1620 *Mayflower* migration (an expedition that actually intended
to settle in Virginia but landed at Plymouth Rock in Massachusetts
instead), or the later and much larger company of immigrants that
settled in Massachusetts Bay in 1630, were drawn by motives of a very
different order. What the leaders of the Plymouth colony, like the leaders of the Massachusetts Bay colony, were seeking was not to satisfy
the needs of the flesh so much as to succor the needs of the spirit.

Their motives, in other words, were religious, not secular. Their ultimate aim, which they sought without complete success to instill in all
the members of their communities, was little less than the renewal of
Western Christendom itself, and to this end they saw themselves as
religious pilgrims journeying to what they hoped would be the promised land spoken of in the Hebrew scriptures and known to Christians
as the Old Testament.

This is not to suggest that the only motives behind the English
migrations to North America in the 1620s and 1630s were religious.
Since no more than approximately 30 percent of the company of the
Mayflower were confessing Christians, it is clear that other factors
fueled the English wave of immigration as well. Chief among them
were changes in the composition of English society, where a doubling
of the population between 1530 and 1680 placed severe pressures on
an already shaky economy, and tensions between the lower and mid-
dling classes were increasing. Add to this the political turbulence
caused by the aftereffects of the English Reformation, and the imaginative vistas opened up by New World exploration, and one can begin
to appreciate the complexity of factors that began to influence decisions to emigrate.

The English of this era were in some sense citizens of two different
cultural worlds. One was the world of the Renaissance, a world associated with a revival of interest in the classical ages of Greece and
Rome, with the dissemination of learning made possible by the invention of movable type, with the geographical expansion of the limits of
terrestrial life, with the discovery of lands and peoples never conceived
before, with advances in science and astronomy that defied tradition,
and with the development of new styles of dress, architecture, and
painting that placed as much emphasis on the perfectibility of this life
as on fulfillment in the next; this was a world capable of awakening
appetites difficult to satisfy, of arousing curiosities not easily exhausted. The other was the world of the Reformation, a world formally brought into being in 1517 when Martin Luther (1483–1546),
a German monk, nailed ninety-five theses to the door of a church in
Wittenburg to protest the Roman Catholic Church's sale of indul-
gences and thereby set in motion a chain of events that would soon
rend the body of Western Christendom in two and force England to
try to find a middle way between them, which eventually became
known as the Anglican Compromise.

Luther's original protest was to lead, as Roman Catholic resistance hardened, into a series of proposals for the reformation of Christian doctrine that would quickly become the basic theological profile
of Protestantism itself. These proposals were built around Luther's
conviction that justification before God is not possible through the

performance of good works but only through faith; that this faith, which is a function solely of divine grace rather than of human effort, cannot be mediated either by the Church through its possession of the sacraments or by tradition through the transmission of correct doctrine; that the sole authority for the spiritual deliverance this faith brings is not the Pope speaking for the Church visible but Holy Scripture, or what Luther called the Word itself, representing the Church invisible; that this faith turns all believers into de facto priests to themselves, whether or not they have been episcopally consecrated; and that, as a result, the Church is not a body of worshipers held together by apostolic authority but a communion of believers united in faith.

The Swiss theologian John Calvin (1509–1564) was later to systematize these beliefs and lend them further theological warrant in his two-volume *Institutes of the Christian Religion* (1536), which, through articulation of the related doctrines of Providence and Predestination, reinforced the Reformation assertion of God's sovereignty, unknowability, and unpredictability. By the doctrine of Providence, Calvin meant to protect and strengthen the view that the whole of history is in God's control and that nothing therefore happens in the world that does not, in some mysterious but definitive way, express His will. By the doctrine of Predestination, Calvin intended to carry the doctrine of Providence to its logical conclusion by maintaining that if all of life is obedient to God's will, then everything that happens in life, including the separation of the elect from the inelect—or who is to be saved from who is to be damned—must be known in advance by God himself.

Such theological refinements were to have momentous consequences when Protestantism crossed the Atlantic to take its place in what Cotton Mather (1663–1728) was to call "the American Strand," but they made almost no ripple at all when Protestantism merely traversed the English Channel. In England Protestantism became a major issue only when it provided Henry VIII, King of England (1509–1547), with an instrument to defy the Pope in Rome so that he could proceed with plans to divorce his wife, Catherine of Aragon, who had been unable to provide him with a male heir. The Protestantism Henry established in England was thus a far cry from the Protestantism conceived by Luther or installed in Geneva by Calvin. Though the Church of England followed the Reformed tradition in severing all ties with Rome, suppressing all monasteries, abolishing prayers for the dead, replacing altars with tables, and rewriting the liturgy in English, it simply replaced the Pope as its supreme head with the King, reaffirmed the doctrine of apostolic succession, maintained the episcopal hierarchy of bishops, priests, deacons, and laity, retained the sacraments of baptism and holy communion, continued the practice of vesting the clergy, and otherwise insisted on doctrinal orthodoxy.

These remnants of Romanism, and the abuses of episcopal power to which they led, were soon to generate religious opposition. This opposition, which until the outbreak of the English Civil War in 1642 was forced to suppress itself in the face of increasing persecution, was centered around the attempt to purify the English national church of its continuing medieval corruptions. These corruptions involved, at the very least, the King's supremacy over the Church, the hierarchy of the episcopate guaranteed by apostolic succession, the Book of Common Prayer, much church ritual, and even the celebration of Christmas. What the "Puritans," as they came to be called, wanted was a restoration of the kind of ecclesiastical and church order that was laid down, so they believed, in clear and definitive terms in the New Testament. To the great majority of English Puritans, this meant a replacement of the Church of England with a new national church organized along different lines. Following the model of John Calvin's system in Geneva, which had also been adopted with modifications by the Church of Scotland, the majority of Puritans wanted to substitute for the episcopal organization of church order a presbyterian form, where the presbytery of local churches, consisting of the minister and the elders, was organized into larger groups called synods that derived their authority from a national assembly.

Those Puritan settlers who came to the United States, however, were of a different persuasion. Insisting that each local church should be regarded as special and unique—composed, as it was, of people calling themselves "visible saints" who had united in the confession of their faith and had formally entered into a covenant with God—they proposed an alternative form of church organization known as Congregationalism. In this form of church organization, there were to be no compelling agencies above the individual congregation and no class of acceptable believers besides them. Each congregation was to be self-governing—able to choose its own pastors, administer its own rites, and accept or reject it own members—and all congregations were to enjoy the state's protection in keeping the unchurched in their place and in discouraging any competing heresies.

Lest it be concluded from this description that Congregationalism implied a more democratic form of church government than Presbyterianism, it should be remembered that the Puritans of New England, like those of Old England, possessed little sympathy for what we would now think of as representative governance. If their churches insisted on the right to select their own ministers, they never confused the freedom to elect the person with the duties proscribed for the office. Thus John Cotton (1584–1652) reminded Lord Say and Seal that if people were free to choose their governors, they were not by that fact free to determine how they would be governed. "In which respect it is," he added, "that church government is justly denied . . . to be democratical, though the people choose their owne officers and rulers."

Among Congregationalists, however, there was a further doctrinal turn that did affect the pattern of American colonization in the early seventeenth century. This was the dispute between those Puritans whose desire for congregational autonomy carried them to the point of wanting to separate themselves from the national church and those whose zeal clearly did not. The former merely conceived of themselves as carrying to its inevitable conclusion the notion of a convenanted church organized congregationally and were immediately branded as Separatists. Because the desire for separation from the national church struck the crown as seditious, some Separatists paid for this belief with their lives, and almost all Separatists in England suffered some form of persecution. One Separatist group in particular was so badly hounded by the ecclesiastical authorities that it fled to Holland, and when conditions there proved too difficult it then emigrated to the New World. This was the group known as the Pilgrims, who landed by mistake at Plymouth in New England. Ten years later the Pilgrims were followed by a much larger migration of Congregationalist Puritans of the non-separating kind, who landed in Massachusetts Bay in 1630.

If both groups were intent on returning Christianity to what they considered a more pristine—by which they meant more biblical— form, the theological project of each was to be affected not only by the extraordinary challenges of life in New England but also by political and religious developments in Old England. Until 1625, when Charles I (1600–1649) came to the throne, the English or Anglican Church tolerated a certain latitude of belief that protected all but Separatists and other radical sectarians. This policy was to change dramatically, however, after 1630, with the ascendancy of Archbishop Laud, who became so strict in the enforcement of religious conformity that by 1642 dissent was to boil over into Civil War, which resulted in Oliver Cromwell (1599–1658) and the Puritan Protectorate coming into power in 1649. But the Puritan Protectorate was extremely short-lived, and upon its overthrow in 1660, the Restoration of the Stuart line led to new waves of religious persecution that were only ended by the Glorious Revolution of 1688, when James II was expelled and a year later the Act of Toleration was established.

Dramatic as they were, these changes did not, for the most part, favor the religious ambitions of the early American Puritans. Having conceived themselves to be on a sacred errand to America not only to secure for themselves sufficient freedom to worship God in their own way but also—through the establishment of a theocratic state at once civil and ecclesiastical and organized according to scriptural ordinances—to serve as a kind of religious example to the rest of a fallen world, the Puritans quickly found themselves left behind by the accelerating course of English political developments and rendered somewhat irrelevant as a model for the continuing reformation of Western Christendom. While the circumstances confronting them in their new environment afforded them numerous opportunities to test their faith, alterations in the political fabric of English society left them alone in America to pursue their religious fate.

Needless to say, that fate was not—as John Cotton (1584–1652) pledged in his sermon "God's Promise to His Plantations" (1630) or Thomas Shepard (1605–1649) anticipated in his sermon "The Covenant of Grace" (1651)—triumphal. From the point of view of Puritanism itself, it was closer in some respects to tragic, inasmuch as it resulted in a decline of piety that seemed to increase in direct proportion to the growing spiritual rigidity of its adherents. But before the piety of Puritanism dissolved into something else—over the next two centuries really into many other things—it lent itself to a variety of different literary uses. This was due in part to the underlying cohesiveness of the Puritan view of experience, but it also derived from the fact that the Puritan view of experience was intensely dramatic and, at the same time, adaptable to the experience of a people conceiving of themselves as immigrants.

The doctrines the Puritans brought over with them from the Old World to the New had been systematically formalized at the Synod of Dort in Holland in 1619. Classically Calvinist, those doctrines were five in number. The first postulated that Adam and Eve's sin of disobedience in the Garden of Eden inaugurated the *total depravity* of humankind. The second affirmed that the stain of this corruption was capable of being removed because God's sacrifice of his own Son, Jesus Christ, had made available a *limited atonement*. The third insisted that God was prepared to offer those He deemed capable of accepting this limited atonement *unconditional election*. The fourth acknowledged that those fortunate enough to be predestined for election would be empowered to embrace it through God's *irresistible grace*. And the fifth emphasized that God's undeserved grace would override the effects of human depravity and contribute to the *perseverance of the saints* in their growth toward sanctity.

As tenets of belief, such doctrines were abstract and difficult to grasp. The Puritans rendered these doctrines more sensible, if not intelligible, by interpreting them within what they described as a covenantal view of history. This view of history presupposed that if the

Fall had all but destroyed the original bonds between God and his human creatures, still, God had not left human beings without evidence of His will. That evidence was to be found in the two covenants He had made with his people. The first was the covenant God had forged with Adam, based on works whose requirements were defined in the body of the Law, and particularly the Mosaic Law codified in the Ten Commandments. The second was the covenant God had made with Abraham and his seed—when Adam and his descendants had demonstrated time and again that they could not keep the Law—a new covenant based on grace and secured by faith. This new covenant that had been sealed by the Incarnation, Crucifixion, and Resurrection of Jesus Christ promised salvation to all those who, with divine assistance, were able to accept the truth of God's redeeming love.

Such doctrines nonetheless fail to capture the conviction, at the heart of Puritan spirituality, that God calls human beings to a radically new life. All of Puritan theology thus turned on the experience of conversion, which separated believer from unbeliever and brought with it a feeling that the communicant had been reborn. Just as this new birth separated the Puritan from the rest of humankind, so it separated the world of nature from the world of grace. The Puritans referred to that experience of shattering force in which the individual soul was confronted with the awful majesty of God's judging and salvific love and was compelled, in effect, to turn itself inside out as *regeneration*. But the decisiveness of this experience of regeneration carried with it no assurance that it would last, much less that those who underwent it could count on being among the elect. Hence the incessant scrutiny of one's life for signs of backsliding or indifference, the relentless discipline of self-accusation and renunciation, the ceaseless pursuit of moral perfection. Being a Puritan, in other words, was a lifetime project in self-study and personal reformation.

Yet such a spiritual project was not intended to immunize Puritans against every form of pleasure. They thought of alcohol, when used in moderation, as—in the words of Increase Mather—"a good creature of God, and to be received with thankfulness." Food and sport yielded them other delights, as did the world of print, which they employed for more than the production and perusal of sermons. Even sexuality had its place in their spiritual economy, at least for purposes of procreation; and to ease the problem of sexual restraint during courtship, they devised the substitute known as "bundling," where couples could of a cold evening share a bed with one another so long as a wooden bar or sword was placed between them. Thus the Puritans were not indifferent to the demands of the flesh, even when their attention was focused on less corporeal matters. As Anne Bradstreet (1612?–1672) and Samuel Sewall (1652–1730) variously attest, the bliss of the marriage bed offered a foretaste of that place where they looked for more permanent rest.

While it has sometimes been maintained—mistakenly, as it happens —that Puritanism produced a rigid uniformity of belief and practice in seventeenth-century New England, historians have reminded us that Puritans never constituted more than a minority, however influential, of the population of seventeenth-century New England society. Moreover, dissension within Puritan ranks was bound to spread as Puritan leaders struggled to retain their authority in the face of the increasing religious indifference among the majority of the white population, mounting hostility from the indigenous population, and the general expansion and differentiation of the economy. Two of the most important early voices of dissent came from Anne Hutchinson (1591– 1643) and Roger Williams (1603?–1683). Hutchinson challenged theocratic authority by questioning the clergy's right to legislate the covenant of grace God makes or may make with each individual. Williams called the church establishment to account not only for its intolerance of variant interpretations of Christianity but for its intrusion into state affairs. But dissent of a different order was also to erupt at the end of the century, when the spread of interest in the occult and magic, together with the increase of heretical ideas among the faithful and the growing insecurity of the Puritan establishment, culminated in 1692 in the reported outbreak of witchcraft in Salem, Massachusetts. Before the witchcraft trials were over, nineteen people would be hanged and numbers of others defamed and humiliated in what Samuel Sewall, the hanging judge at the trials, later referred to in his recantation as a shameful and sinful business.

But the Puritans were as deeply troubled by groups outside their communities as by those within. Disturbers of their religious peace included Anabaptists and Anglicans, and especially Quakers. Like the Anabaptists, Quakers belonged to the radical left wing of the Reformation and advocated reliance on what Christians had traditionally meant by the Third Person of the Trinity, or Holy Spirit, which they called the "Inner Light." Believing in the possibility of direct illumination by God's truth, which was sometimes accompanied by trembling or quaking (hence the name) and implied little need for trained clergy or the orthodox regulation of belief, the Quakers were almost immediately brought into conflict with the Puritan establishment. This conflict was exacerbated by the Quakers' simplification of religious ritual and the zeal with which some of their members witnessed to their faith. The Puritan reaction was predictable and severe. Many Quakers were imprisoned in New England, often after being whipped through the streets, and some were physically mutilated by having their ears cropped or their tongues severed. A hostility that was at times as much social as it was religious, its virulence was exceeded only by the treatment Puritans accorded Native Americans after the initial honeymoon of their early relations broke down.

Conflict between the two races was bound to follow from white encroachment on Indian lands, but it was aggravated by the religious predilection of so many Puritans, especially when their safety was threatened, to see the "savage" as Satanic and to view the American wilderness as the domain of the demonic. Fed by Indian raids like the one experienced by Mary Rowlandson (1635?–1687?), this predilection led her to describe her captors as "a company of hell-hounds, roaring, singing, ranting, and insulting, as if they would have torn our very hearts out." Yet the Lord's people, as Puritans typically thought of themselves, prevailed. And they prevailed not, as they also frequently supposed, because the Lord was on their side but because they possessed superiority in arms, supplies, and support. In the Pequot War of 1637, the colonists were finally able to corner what remained of their foe in Mystic, Connecticut, where they burned the Pequots alive in their wigwams or shot those attempting to escape. But final removal of the Indian threat in New England did not occur until 1675–1676, when the son of the friendly sachem Massasoit named Philip, who had by then become chief of the Wampanoags, attempted to organize five neighboring tribes into a confederation to obliterate white settlements. In the course of what came to be called King Philip's War, more than 3,000 Indians were killed and King Philip himself was captured, drawn, quartered, and beheaded. Puritan tactics and weaponry had carried the day, but the integrity of Puritan faith had received another wound.

The decline of Puritanism was most completely determined, however, by the pace, heterogeneity, and complexity of the process of colonial settlement itself. After the first generation and certainly by the second, the ranks of immigrants numbered fewer and fewer theological idealists and more and more people seeking anything but religious perfection. Instead, they looked for political liberty, commercial opportunity, physical adventure, the opportunity to work off one's indenture, forgetfulness, or any number of other things. The motives for migration were as mixed as the social habits of the immigrants, and this process of diversification only accelerated upon arrival as people were quickly caught up in an economic environment growing more variegated and secular by the day. Consider, for example, the spectacle recreated by the historian Edmund S. Morgan (in *The National Experience*, [1968], 61) of bustling and bewildering activity that awaited the eye of the colonial Puritan farmer, now settled in rural New England, paying a visit to the town of Boston around 1640, just ten years after the founding of the Massachusetts Bay Community:

> Swine roamed everywhere, feeding on the refuse; drovers herded sheep and cattle to the butchers. Elegant carriages rolled impatiently behind lumbering wagons as great packs of barking dogs worried the horses. Sailors reeled out of taverns, and over the roofs of the houses could be seen the swaying masts and spars of their ships. The farmer had been told that the city was a nursery of vice and prodigality. He now saw that it was so. Every shop had wares to catch his eye: exquisite fabrics, delicate chinaware, silver buckles, looking glasses, and other imported luxuries that never reached the cross-roads store. Putting up at the tavern, he found himself drinking too much rum. And there were willing girls, he heard, who had lost their virtue and would be glad to help him lose his. Usually he returned to the farm to warn his children as he had been warned. He seldom understood that the vice of the city, if not its prodigality, was mainly for transients like himself. Permanent residents had work to do.

That work was the building of a new society, and it proceeded at an equally rapid pace beyond Massachusetts. With another colony already established in Virginia as early as 1607, which was very quickly to develop a distinctive and much different way of life—one built around the cultivation and sale of tobacco and the exploitation of Virginia's network of tidewater rivers that facilitated the expansion of trade—additional colonies were to spring up all along the Eastern seaboard. Maryland was carved out of northern Virginia and founded as a refuge for Catholics in 1634. New Netherland had been founded by the Dutch some years earlier and was reclaimed by the English and named New York in 1664. That same year New Jersey came into being through a grant from the Duke of York; and less than twenty years later, William Penn (1644–1718), the man whom Cotton Mather wanted seized and sold into slavery, was awarded the territory now known as Pennsylvania, in which he immediately established the most liberal and religiously tolerant form of government in the Americas.

Not least among the institutions that, along with the general expansion of commerce, were to erode the hold of Puritan ideas over the minds of New Englanders was the printing press, which made its first appearance in the colonies at Cambridge, Massachusetts, in 1639 and which issued its first publication, *The Bay Psalm Book*, in 1640. A second institution whose development contributed over time to the weakening of Puritan ideas was the university. Harvard College was founded in 1636, followed by the establishment of the College of William and Mary in 1693 and of Yale College in 1701. Though created initially for the purpose of supplying the churches with clergy, these institutions became in time centers of learning that not only introduced their students to fresh ideas but soon began to encourage new thinking. But the gathering and dissemination of information that would weaken the appeal of the New England theocracy was perhaps most dramatically abetted by the creation at the beginning of the eighteenth century of that still more public institution known as the newspaper, which was in time to shape so decisively the career of someone like Benjamin Franklin.

Long before Puritanism went into sharp decline at the end of the seventeenth century, protests arose to try to halt it. These protests took a distinctive sermonic form known as the *jeremiad*, in which the spectacle of "declension," as it was termed, when carefully detailed, afforded the preacher an opportunity to remind his auditors and readers of the convenantal obligations that had been betrayed. Thus the jeremiad, as Samuel Danforth exhibited it in his Election Day sermon titled "A Brief Recognition of New England's Errand into the Wilderness" (1671), possessed a double focus and achieved a contradictory effect. Cataloging the sins that had led to New England's degeneration, at the same time it reiterated the terms of New England's originally transacted sacred mission. The reader or listener was therefore, as in Michael Wigglesworth's "God's Controversy with New England" (1662), simultaneously submerged under an inventory of misery, corruption, and perfidy and exalted by a reminder of the glorious future that awaited New England's fulfillment of its religious calling.

The dimming of religious intensity could not continue for long, however, without even more heroic exertions of religious renewal than those performed by the rhetoric of the jeremiad. Thus a Great Awakening occurred in the mid-1730s and early 1740s, centered in the ministry of the most theologically sophisticated of all Puritan-minded Christians, Jonathan Edwards (1703–1758), in Northampton, Massachusetts. Fueled by the preaching of the English itinerant Methodist minister George Whitefield (1715–1770)—whose voice, according to the calculations of Benjamin Franklin, could carry to a crowd of 30,000—the Great Awakening not only convulsed many of the churches of the New England colonies but spread as far south as Georgia. It was an impressive display of the pent-up energy of religious feeling, originally aroused and nourished by Puritan conceptions, that in the first third of the eighteenth century no longer found any forms —ecclesiastical, ceremonial, discursive—capable of by turns containing and releasing them. The same situation would repeat itself three-quarters of a century later, when an even more explosive charge of religious energy would burst through the rationalistic—and rationalizing—surface of American religious and cultural life in the early nineteenth century to form the Second Great Awakening. But it was already clear after the First Awakening, and particularly because of Jonathan Edwards's own need to embrace much of the new thinking of John Locke and Francis Hutcheson simply to keep the old faith alive, that Puritanism was not undergoing a revival so much as suffering a decline. The desire to build—as John Winthrop called it in "A Model of Christian Charity" (1630), the sermon he delivered aboard the *Arabella* before the ship dropped anchor in Massachusetts Bay—"a City on a Hill," a New Israel or New Jerusalem in the New World, would remain—indeed, would become—the motive force of the American myth of consensus; but the terms defining it would lose their specific theological coloring and begin to take on tints that were more generally metaphysical, political, social, legal, and economic.

English literature at the time of New World settlement was in a position to supply American writers with a variety of mythic paradigms and literary forms to record the meaning of their experience. Sir Philip Sidney's *Arcadia* (1590, 1593) furnished a name for the myth found as well in Edmund Spenser's *Fairie Queene* (1590, 1596) and William Shakespeare's *The Tempest* (1611), the myth about a pastoral world, often associated with a golden age, whose beauty and simplicity contrasts with the corruptions and complications of contemporary urban and court life. On the other hand, John Milton's *Paradise Lost* (1667) gave expression to the counter-myth, originating in the Bible, that nature and humankind had suffered a fall from grace that could only be overcome through the kind of spiritual pilgrimage of faith rendered, say, in John Bunyan's *Pilgrim's Progress* (1678). Still other works from the English Utopian tradition like Thomas More's *Utopia* (1551) and Francis Bacon's *New Atlantis* (1627), or from the tradition of country-house poems like Ben Jonson's "To Penshurst" (1616) and Andrew Marvell's "Upon Appleton House" (1652?), held out the possibility of nature's, and by extension humankind's, transformation by grace that inspired belief in America as potentially a new Eden, a new Israel, about to be restored in the American wilderness.

Even more significant, as Barbara Kiefer Lewalski has pointed out, were the literary modes and forms that English tradition made available to American writers. Chief among them, perhaps, was the sermon, followed closely in popularity by the theological manual. But Protestant poetics, drawing on the vast number of biblical genres and types, could supply an extraordinary set of literary models for American authors, from biblical epics and providential histories to spiritual and

secular autobiography, martyrology and hagiography, occasional and
deliberate meditations, and confessional lyrics. Thus Guillaume Sal-
luste De Bartas's unfinished epic, translated by Joshua Sylvester as *The
Divine Weekes and Workes* (1605, 1608), stimulated Michael Wigglesworth's *Day of Doom* (1662), Sir Walter Raleigh's *History of the
World* (1614), and Anne Bradstreet's uncompleted "Four Monarchies"
(1650). John Bunyan's *Grace Abounding to the Chief of Sinners*
(1666) furnished a model for John Winthrop's *Journal* (1630–1649)
and, at considerable remove, Benjamin Franklin's *Autobiography*
(1771, 1784). Joseph Hall's *Occasionall Meditations* (1630) and poems like Henry Vaughan's "Cock-Crowing" and "The Showre" were
echoed in Anne Bradstreet's famous lyric "Upon the Burning of Our
House" (1678) and her "Contemplations" (1678). More formal meditations like John Donne's "Holy Sonnets" and George Herbert's *The
Temple* (1633) had their American analogues in Edward Taylor's de-
votional poems. John Foxe's *Book of Martyrs* (1563, 1570) and Isaak
Walton's *Life of John Donne* (1640) provided a model for the sixty-
odd biographies of New England spiritual heroes in Cotton Mather's
Magnalia Christi Americana (1702).

But American colonial writers during the seventeenth and early
eighteenth centuries not only borrowed and imitated English models
but also adapted them in interesting ways. Promotional tracts like Alexander Whitaker's *Good Newes from Virginia* (1613) or Captain
John Smith's *A Description of New England* (1616) were soon to give
way to a kind of travel and nature writing that, in works like Samuel
Sewall's hymn to Plum Island in "Phaenomena" (1697), *The Journal
of Madam Knight* (1704), William Byrd's *The History of the Dividing
Line* (1728), and William Bartram's *Travels Through North and South
Carolina, Georgia, East and West Florida* (1791), was to evolve into
a distinctive American genre. Sermonic literature from the time of John
Winthrop's "A Model of Christian Charity" (1630) and Thomas
Hooker's "A True Sight of Sin" (1659) to Jonathan Edwards's "Sinners in the Hands of an Angry God" (1741) helped transform the
jeremiad into a rhetorical device for keeping alive a sense of national
destiny. Polemical tracts and treatises from Roger Williams's *The
Bloudy Tenent of Persecution* (1644) to Jonathan Mayhew's "Discourse Concerning Unlimited Submission" (1750) and John Woolman's "Some Considerations on the Keeping of Negroes" (1753)
opened within the rhetoric of disputation a public space for the consideration of ideas well beyond the range of their own focus. Histories
and biographies such as Bradford's *Plymouth Plantation* (1630–1651),
Thomas Morton's *New English Canaan* (1637), Cotton Mather's
Magnalia Christi Americana (1702), Fray Carlos José Delgado's *Re-*

port (1750), and Francisco Palou's *Life of Junipero Serra* (1787) performed a variety of kinds of cultural work all related to clarifying,
contesting, and critiquing the emergent terms of American national
identity. Diaries, memoirs, and autobiographies, from Jonathan Edwards's *Personal Narrative* (1765) and Anne Bradstreet's "To My
Dear Children" (1672) to Elizabeth Ashbridge's *Account of the Early
Life . . . Written by Herself* (1774), testified to the diverse ways of
adjusting to the many perils, and comparatively fewer pleasures, of life
in the colonial period, while also providing a set of forms for recording
the experiences of women. In this connection, one of the distinctive
genres that women would help to create in early American literature
—though it possesses crucial antecedents in Alva Nuñez Cabeza de
Vaca's *Relation* (1542) and John Smith's *A True Relation of Such
Occurences and Accidents of Noate as Hath Hapned in Virginia Since
the First Planting of that Collony* (1608)—is the captivity narrative,
such as the one written by Mary Rowlandson (1682). Finally, in poetry, early American writers like Taylor and Bradstreet contributed a
special kind of vernacular intensity and inwardness to the tradition of
English meditative verse that helped open the way for those even
deeper explorations of self that were to be undertaken two centuries
later in the verse of American authors like Walt Whitman and Emily
Dickinson.

Underlying all of these adaptations, modifications, and extensions
of British literary traditions was a situation the literature of England
had never been devised explicitly to confront. A situation that American writers could in no way manage to avoid and one that all of the
forms that slowly evolved from their need to give verbal expression to
their experiences on this continent somehow had to incorporate, it was
produced by the clash of diverse and often complex and always changing cultures and subcultures, which was to furnish American literature
for the next three centuries with some of its most enduring and explosive themes: European versus Native American, Puritan versus Anglican or Quaker, Calvinist versus Arminian or Antinomian, religious
versus secular, English versus French, city versus backwoods, first-
generation immigrant versus second- or third-generation, male versus
female, privileged versus marginalized, white versus black. This is not
to suggest that early American writers were always, or even frequently,
able to acknowledge and explore these oppositions and assymetries in
depth but merely to assert that they could evade them here only at the
risk of dismissing much of what was both so interesting and so prob-
lematic about their material. Such cultural differences and conflicts are
precisely what the experience of transplantation so often involved and
frequently magnified; they also helped to define many of the heuristic

or educative opportunities that the experience of transplantation potentially afforded.

Yet well before the seventeenth century had drawn to a close, life in the American colonies had begun to change even more rapidly and profoundly. If religion had held center stage in the 1600s, economics and politics would assume that role by the middle of the 1700s. Questions of theology, of church organization, of religious practice, would continue to remain paramount for many individual Americans, but they would no longer dominate cultural life. Within less than a century, America would declare its independence from England, fight a war to secure that freedom, and draw up and ratify a Constitution defining what was achieved thereby: the United States of America. In the meantime, the economy would diversify and expand, religious life would become much more pluralistic and heterogeneous, the population would explode, and new territories in the west would be opened up for exploration and additional settlement. Thus the world that the signers of the Constitution helped bring into being would operate according to very different assumptions, and be held together by very different structures of governance and feeling, than the world familiar to the first- and second-generation colonists in Massachusetts or even in Virginia. Some of the most consequential alterations marking these developments occurred in the realm of ideas. Nicolaus Copernicus (1473–1543) had already overturned the Ptolemaic notions that Christopher Columbus had carried in his head to the New World—notions supporting the medieval Christian conviction that humankind is at the center of the universe—by showing that the earth revolved around the sun rather than the sun and other heavenly bodies revolving around the earth. Sir Isaac Newton (1642–1727) had then used Copernicus's theory, together with discoveries made about the physics of motion by Galileo Galilei (1564–1642), to argue that the motions of the universe were susceptible to rational explanation. René Descartes (1596–1650) had then reinforced the possibility of such a claim by showing in his *Discourse on Method* (1637) that the attempt to place everything in doubt merely yielded the discovery that the one thing incapable of being doubted was the rational capacity of human beings. John Locke (1632–1704) subsequently determined, in *An Essay Concerning Human Understanding* (1690), that the ideas we think come not from the human mind itself but from the experience of our senses, which initially register their notional effects on a mental *tabula rasa*, or blank tablet. Having thus denied the view that the mind bears within itself, say, in the form of rationality, any image of its Divine Maker—or, for example, in its propensity for self-regard, any mark of original sin—Locke proceeded to show in his *Second Treatise on Civil Government*

(1690) that the only authority government can claim over individuals otherwise free and equal in the state of nature derives from the social contract in which they consent to enter for the sake of being governed. Baron Charles de Sedondant de Montesquieu (1689–1755) then extended these notions in his *The Spirit of Laws* (1748) by arguing that from the point of view of the governed the best government is one that separates its various powers by establishing a system of checks and balances against their various possible abuses.

Ideas such as these created an altogether different climate of opinion in the eighteenth century, a climate of opinion that we have come to associate with the Enlightenment. As a general term, the Enlightenment refers to all those European and American figures in the eighteenth century who had been sufficiently impressed by the scientific advances of the seventeenth century to share several general convictions about the nature of reason, the primacy of experience, and the possibility of human progress. First, they believed that the surest guide to understanding is provided by the natural human faculties, and particularly by our powers of common sense and rationality. Second, they held that reason finds its basic materials in experience itself—that is, in the discoveries yielded by the study of personal existence, of natural and human history, and of the structures of nature itself. Third, they tended to assume that the disciplined application of reason to the problems and potentialities of experience would lead to a progressive, though not necessarily an immediate or uninterrupted, relief of the human estate. Those who shared these convictions never constituted more than a small minority, mainly of learned men, but they were to have an enormous impact not only on the reconstitution of intellectual culture in the United States but also on the shaping of its political, social, and cultural institutions.

Historian Henry F. May maintains that there were actually four Enlightenments rather than one, or at least four phases or forms of a historical period in which the idea of Enlightenment took on paradigmatic force. The earliest was the Moderate or Rational Enlightenment, associated in England with Newton and Locke, which preached balance, order, and religious compromise. The second was the Skeptical Enlightenment, centered in France just before the French Revolution and linked with Voltaire (1694–1779) and Holbach (1723–1789)—though David Hume (1711–1776) presented another variant of it in Scotland—which was iconoclastic, materialist, and pragmatic. The third was the Revolutionary Enlightenment, which held out for the possibility of creating a new heaven and a new earth out of the destruction of the old and was associated in France with Jean Jacques Rousseau (1712–1778) and in America with Thomas Paine (1737–1809) and Thomas Jefferson (1734–1826). The fourth Enlightenment, inspired by Scottish Common Sense philosophers like Thomas Reid (1710–1796) and Francis Hutcheson (1694–1746), was Didactic, in that it tried to save from the Skeptical and Revolutionary Enlightenments what was left of the life of reason, the possibility of moral discrimination, a respect for law, and a sense of the intelligible universe. Despite their differences, however, it is clear that all the forms of the Enlightenment remained within the orbit of religious reflection. Their affirmations and agendas, like their denials and critiques, were all mounted from within an intellectual project whose continuing ambition was to better understand the way things hang together metaphysically, as part of a single, concatenated system of meaning, and they all shared the conviction that the furtherance of such understanding would only advance the course of human progress.

Little wonder, then, that one of the more interesting consequences of this many-sided movement known as the Enlightenment was the development of a distinctive theological position called Deism. Deism was less a doctrine or creed than a perspective that inflected Thomas Jefferson's *Notes on the State of Virginia* (1784) no less than Thomas Paine's enormously popular *Common Sense* (1776), the letters of Abigail Adams (1744–1818) no less than the poetry of Philip Freneau (1752–1832). It was nowhere more succinctly expressed than by Benjamin Franklin in his *Autobiography* when, in delineating what he deemed to be the essentials of every religion, and what he himself had never doubted, he confessed to his belief in "the existence of the Deity, that he made the world and governed it by his providence, that the most acceptable service of God was the doing good to man, that our souls are immortal, and that all crime will be punished and virtue rewarded either here or hereafter." But it was Thomas Jefferson, in his draft of the Declaration of Independence (1776), who inscribed the Deist faith in the very body of American public culture and life. When he wrote, "We hold these truths to be self evident: that all men are created equal; that they are endowed by their Creator with certain [inherent and] inalienable rights; that among these are life, liberty, and the pursuit of happiness," he made political Deists of all Americans, no matter what other faith they professed as Jews on Friday nights or as Christians on Sunday mornings. More to the point, he placed Deism in support of a revolutionary movement that would subsequently broaden the possibilities for literary expression in the republic soon to emerge, and eventually, but only after nearly a century and a half of political pressure and protest, begin to open the literary canon more fully to the writing of women and various minorities—racial, ethnic, and sexual.

The steps leading to the creation of that republic were manifold and diverse, beginning, perhaps, with the collapse of the Albany Plan of Union drafted by Benjamin Franklin in 1754 and designed to give the various colonies representation in a union whose president was to be appointed by the crown. They would include the French and Indian War (1755–1763), which was fought for control of the American continent and resulted in England's acquisition of almost the whole of Canada and the upper Mississippi Valley. They would then proceed to the Stamp Act crisis of 1765, which, like the taxation of tea that precipitated the Boston Tea Party in 1773, resulted from England's need for funds to support its enormous American empire. From there they would progress to the call of the first Continental Congress in Philadelphia in 1774, which issued a Declaration of Rights and Grievances; then on to the outbreak of conflict between the British regiments and American irregulars on the green at Lexington, Massachusetts, in 1775; next to the second Continental Congress in 1776, where the draft of a Declaration of Independence was prepared and approved on July 4; and finally to the revolutionary war itself, which lasted from 1776 to 1783. When the war itself was over, there was still to be drafted a Constitution to replace the loosely applied Articles of Confederation, which had held the country together since 1781; and once this was completed at the Philadelphia convention of 1787, then the debate over the Constitution could begin, with most of its important points being argued in the eighty-six papers of *The Federalist* (1787–1788), authored by Alexander Hamilton (1757–1804), James Madison (1751–1836), and John Jay (1745–1829). But the republic was not formally created until the Constitution was ratified in June 1788, though approval of the last state was not achieved until 1791.

During this momentous period almost all of the literature of the late eighteenth century was produced. Indeed, some of the most memorable instances of that literature, from Jefferson's "Act for Establishing Religious Freedom in the State of Virginia" (1786), John Adams's Preface to *A Defense of the Constitutions of Government* (1787), and Tom Paine's *Common Sense*, to *Federalist Paper* No. 10, by James Madison, played a crucial role in forwarding its motion. But it would be a mistake to suppose that this literature of historical moment constituted the only significant writing in the era of the early republic. In addition to writing that recorded or in some manner served these events, there was a large body of expression that either responded to various and sundry of their meanings or moved into the new personal as well as public spaces cleared by them. Hence if Abigail Adams wondered in her letters to her husband, John, about the Revolution's implications for, among other things, physical safety, education, and the possibility of retirement from public service, Judith Sargeant Murray (1751–1820), and before her Tom Paine, took up the question of women's equality in the emergent new order. Others like Timothy

Dwight (1752–1817) and Hugh Henry Brackenridge (1748–1816) either sought to celebrate or, respectively, to puncture some of the pretensions of the new order; or, like Philip Freneau and Phillis Wheatley, to colonize some of the new territories of the imagination to which it afforded them fresh access. Still others, like Oloudah Equiano (1745–1797) and various Native Americans, testified to what this new order, so often like the old, continued to defer or to betray.

At the end of the eighteenth century, then, American literature was still far from having achieved a distinctive voice or set of voices. But many of the notes that would eventually give American writing wider and deeper resonance had already been struck. If in the coming decades and even centuries what can already be heard in the pitch and tone of early American writing was to gravitate to an even richer, more reverbarative timbre—to what, almost three centuries later, Wallace Stevens was to call still "ghostlier demarcations, keener sounds"—many of the basic patterns of assonance and dissonance, of leitmotif and counterpoint, were by now distinctly in evidence and impressively varied. The seeds of American writing had been deeply planted; it now only awaited the chemistry of future experience to germinate them and set them free.

Prefigurations (1):
Native American
Mythology

NATIVE AMERICAN MYTHS

The difficulty with reading Native American myths is not that they are Native American but that they are myths. Like other narratives regarded by the people who tell and retell these tales to themselves in order to understand the meaning of their world and their place in it, they are constructed less to entertain or even inform the mind than to indicate in what directions and about what subjects and with what seriousness it should think. Myths therefore tend to dispense with the logic of stimulus and response, with the grammar of motive, and concentrate instead on the larger hierarchies of possibility that structure a given lifeworld.

This way of viewing narrative takes some readjustment. Modern readers are more apt to think of myths either as degenerate forms of fiction, what works of literature evolve into when one forgets that they are imaginative, or as stories about transcendent beings and supernatural events. They are rather more like classificatory schemes, as the social anthropologist Claude Levi-Strauss once called them, that at one and the same time help define and organize the constituents of the thinkable and also arouse, channel, release, and sometimes contain various feelings associated with them. They are thus the metaphysical and psychological building blocks, to go back to the earlier vocabulary, of a particular peoples' sense of being or lifeworld.

Such a lifeworld may well be prepared to admit the existence of other spheres of experience, other realms of being, than its own and even assume the easy passage between them. Indeed, in myth the domain of the real—which is often, as in the texts included here, realized in startlingly vivid detail and concreteness—can also be shifting, fluid, and susceptible to transformation. This may only mean that ancient peoples, for whom myth was sacred precisely because it was held to describe the way things truly are, acknowledged a much wider range of potential experience than modern peoples, but there is, in fact, more to it than this. Modern readers must understand that myths were originally communicated orally and then only later written down. As oral forms of literary expression, they were purposely kept schematic, not only so that the narrator might embellish them with gesture, inflection, and tone, but also in order that the auditor might be drawn more deeply into the tale. By having to fill in particulars of description and specifics of action, the auditor's experience of hearing the tale could simultaneously be transformed into an experience of creating the tale, which only then reinforced for its listeners its immediacy and authority.

But the reality, and thus the potentially sacred power, of the tale was ultimately secured through the practice of repetition. Myths were—and still are—generally constructed to be repeated in ritual circumstances, where the reiteration of the story is intended to sweep the listener back into that sacred time—in illo tempore—of which the story is record and template. Thus, as the historian of religion Mircea Eliade has written, the listener may relocate him- or herself within the sacred sphere but also reactualize the power resident in that sphere and extend it back over the more ephemeral world of the profane.

To fully understand the world of myth, it is necessary to grasp the sociocultural and emotional contexts in which its meanings were supposed to be efficacious. Short of that, however, it is still possible to learn from these stories how "belief," as the Irish poet William Butler Yeats put it, "makes the mind abundant."

Winnebago

This Newly Created World

Pleasant it looked,
this newly created world.
Along the entire length and breadth
of the earth, our grandmother,
extended the green reflection
of her covering
and the escaping odors
were pleasant to inhale.

Cherokee

How the World Was Made

The earth is a great island floating in a sea of water, and suspended at each of the four cardinal points by a cord hanging down from the sky vault, which is of solid rock. When the world grows old and worn out, the people will die and the cords will break and let the earth sink down into the ocean, and all will be water again. The Indians are afraid of this.

When all was water, the animals were above in Gălûñ'lătĭ,[1] beyond the arch; but it was very much crowded, and they were wanting more room. They wondered what was below the water, and at last Dâyuni'sĭ, "Beaver's Grandchild," the little Water-beetle, offered to go and see if it could learn. It darted in every direction over the surface of the water, but could find no firm place to rest. Then it dived to the bottom and came up with some soft mud, which began to grow and spread on every side until it became the island which we call the earth. It was afterward fastened to the sky with four cords, but no one remembers who did this.

At first the earth was flat and very soft and wet. The animals were anxious to get down, and sent out different birds to see if it was yet dry, but they found no place to alight and came back again to Gălûñ'lătĭ. At last it seemed to be time, and they sent out the Buzzard and told him to go and make ready for them. This was the Great Buzzard, the father of all the buzzards we see now. He flew all over the earth, low down near the ground, and it was still soft. When he reached the Cherokee country, he was very tired, and his wings began to flap and strike the ground, and wherever they struck the earth there was a valley, and where they turned up again there was a mountain. When the animals above saw this, they were afraid that the whole world would be mountains, so they called him back, but the Cherokee country remains full of mountains to this day.

When the earth was dry and the animals came down, it was still dark, so they got the sun and set it in a track to go every day across the island from east to west, just overhead. It was too hot this way, and Tsiska'gĭlĭ', the Red Crawfish, had his shell scorched a bright red, so that his meat was spoiled: and the Cherokee do not eat it. The conjurers put the sun another hand-breadth higher in the air, but it was still too hot. They raised it another time, and another, until it was seven hand-breadths high and just under the sky arch. Then it was right, and they left it so. This is why the conjurers call the highest place Gûlkwâ'gine Di'gălûñ'lătiyûn', "the seventh height," because it is seven hand-breadths above the earth. Every day the sun goes along under this arch, and returns at night on the upper side to the starting place.

There is another world under this, and it is like ours in every-thing—animals, plants, and people—save that the seasons are differ-ent. The streams that come down from the mountains are the trails by which we reach this underworld, and the springs at their heads are the doorways by which we enter it, but to do this one must fast and go to water and have one of the underground people for a guide. We know that the seasons in the underworld are different from ours, be-cause the water in the springs is always warmer in winter and cooler in summer than the outer air.

When the animals and plants were first made—we do not know by whom—they were told to watch and keep awake for seven nights, just as young men now fast and keep awake when they pray to their medicine. They tried to do this, and nearly all were awake through the first night, but the next night several dropped off to sleep, and the third night others were asleep, and then others, until, on the seventh night, of all the animals only the owl, the panther, and one or two more were still awake. To these were given the power to see and to go about in the dark, and to make prey of the birds and animals which must sleep at night. Of the trees only the cedar, the pine, the spruce, the holly, and the laurel were awake to the end, and to them it was given to be always green and to be greatest for medicine, but to the others it was said: "Because you have not endured to the end you shall lose your hair every winter."

Men came after the animals and plants. At first there were only a brother and sister until he struck her with a fish and told her to multiply, and so it was. In seven days a child was born to her, and thereafter every seven days another, and they increased very fast until there was danger that the world could not keep them. Then it was made that a woman should have only one child in a year, and it has been so ever since.

Bering Strait Eskimo

Raven Creation Myth

It was in the time when there were no people on the earth plain. During four days the first man lay coiled up in the pod of a beach-pea (*L. maritimus*). On the fifth day he stretched out his feet and burst the pod, falling to the ground, where he stood up, a full-grown man. He looked about him, and then moved his hands and arms, his neck and legs, and examined himself curiously. Looking back, he saw the pod from which he had fallen, still hanging to the vine, with a hole in the lower end, out of which he had dropped. Then he looked about him again and saw that he was getting farther away from his starting place, and that the ground moved up and down under his feet and seemed very soft. After a while he had an unpleasant feeling in his stomach, and he stooped down to take some water into his mouth from a small pool at his feet. The water ran down into his stomach and he felt better. When he looked up again he saw approaching, with a waving motion, a dark object which came on until just in front of him, when it stopped, and, standing on the ground, looked at him. This was a raven, and, as soon as it stopped, it raised one of its wings, pushed up its beak, like a mask, to the top of its head, and changed at once into a man. Before he raised his mask Raven had stared at the man, and after it was raised he stared more than ever, moving about from side to side to obtain a better view. At last he said: "What are you? Whence did you come? I have never seen anything like you." Then Raven looked at Man, and was still more surprised to find that this strange new being was so much like himself in shape.

Then he told Man to walk away a few steps, and in astonishment exclaimed again: "Whence did you come? I have never seen anything like you before." To this Man replied: "I came from the pea-pod." And he pointed to the plant from which he came. "Ah!" exclaimed Raven, "I made that vine, but did not know that anything like you would ever come from it. Come with me to the high ground over there; this ground I made later, and it is still soft and thin, but it is thicker and harder there."

In a short time they came to the higher land, which was firm under their feet. Then Raven asked Man if he had eaten anything. The latter answered that he had taken some soft stuff into him at one of the pools. "Ah!" said Raven, "you drank some water. Now wait for me here."

Then he drew down the mask over his face, changing again into a bird, and flew far up into the sky where he disappeared. Man waited where he had been left until the fourth day, when Raven returned, bringing four berries in his claws. Pushing up his mask, Raven became a man again and held out two salmonberries and two heathberries, saying, "Here is what I have made for you to eat. I also wish them to be plentiful over the earth. Now eat them." Man took the berries and placed them in his mouth one after the other and they satisfied his hunger, which had made him feel uncomfortable. Raven then led Man to a small creek near by and left him while he went to the water's edge and molded a couple of pieces of clay into the form of a pair of mountain sheep, which he held in his hand, and when they became dry he called Man to show him what he had done. Man thought they were very pretty, and Raven told him to close his eyes. As soon as Man's eyes were closed Raven drew down his mask and waved his wings four times over the images, when they became endowed with life and bounded away as full-grown mountain sheep. Raven then raised his mask and told Man to look. When Man saw the sheep moving away, full of life, he cried out with pleasure. Seeing how pleased Man was, Raven said, "If these animals are numerous, perhaps people will wish very much to get them." And Man said he thought they would. "Well," said Raven, "it will be better for them to have their home among the high cliffs, so that every one can not kill them, and there only shall they be found."

Then Raven made two animals of clay which he endowed with life as before, but as they were dry only in spots when they were given life, they remained brown and white, and so originated the tame reindeer with mottled coat. Man thought these were very handsome, and Raven told him that they would be very scarce. In the same way a pair of wild reindeer were made and permitted to get dry and white only on their bellies, then they were given life; in consequence, to this day the belly of the wild reindeer is the only white part about it. Raven told Man that these animals would be very common, and people would kill many of them.

"You will be very lonely by yourself," said Raven. "I will make you a companion." He then went to a spot some distance from where he had made the animals, and, looking now and then at Man, made an image very much like him. Then he fastened a lot of fine water grass on the back of the head for hair, and after the image had dried in his hands, he waved his wings over it as before and a beautiful young woman arose and stood beside Man. "There," cried Raven, "is a companion for you," and he led them back to a small knoll near by.

In those days there were no mountains far or near, and the sun never ceased shining brightly; no rain ever fell and no winds blew. When they came to the knoll, Raven showed the pair how to make a bed in the dry moss, and they slept there very warmly; Raven drew down his mask and slept near by in the form of a bird. Waking before the others, Raven went back to the creek and made a pair each of sticklebacks, graylings, and blackfish. When these were swimming about in the water, he called Man to see them. When the latter looked at them and saw the sticklebacks swim up the stream with a wriggling motion he was so surprised that he raised his hand suddenly and the fish darted away. Raven then showed him the graylings and told him that they would be found in clear mountain streams, while the sticklebacks would live along the seacoast and that both would be good for food. Next the shrew-mouse was made, Raven saying that it would not be good for food but would enliven the ground and prevent it from seeming barren and cheerless.

In this way Raven continued for several days making birds, fishes, and animals, showing them to Man, and explaining their uses. . . .

Hopi

How the Spaniards Came to
Shung-opovi, How They Built a
Mission, and How the Hopi
Destroyed the Mission

It may have taken quite a long time for these villages to be established. Anyway, every place was pretty well settled down when the Spanish came.[1] The Spanish were first heard of at Zuni and then at Awatovi. They came on to Shung-opovi, passing Walpi. At First Mesa, Si-kyatki was the largest village then, and they were called Si-kyatki, not Walpi. The Walpi people were living below the present village on the west side. When the Spaniards came, the Hopi thought that they were the ones they were looking for—their white brother, the Bahana, their savior.

The Spaniards visited Shung-opovi several times before the missions were established. The people of Mishongnovi welcomed them so the priest who was with the white men built the first Hopi mission at Mishongnovi. The people of Shung-opovi were at first afraid of the priests but later they decided he was really the Bahana,[2] the savior, and let him build a mission at Shung-opovi.

Well, about this time the Strap Clan were ruling at Shung-opovi and they were the ones that gave permission to establish the mission. The Spaniards, whom they called Castillia, told the people that they had much more power than all their chiefs and a whole lot more power than the witches. The people were very much afraid of them, particularly if they had much more power than their witches. They were so scared that they could do nothing but allow themselves to be made slaves. Whatever they wanted done must be done. Any man in power that was in this position the Hopi called To-ta-achi, which means a grouchy person that will not do anything himself, like a child. They couldn't refuse, or they would be slashed to death or punished in some way. There were two To-ta-achi.

The missionary did not like the ceremonies. He did not like the Kachinas and he destroyed the altars and the customs. He called it idol worship and burned up all the ceremonial things in the plaza.

When the Priests started to build the mission, the men were sent away over near the San Francisco peaks to get the pine or spruce beams. These beams were cut and put into shape roughly and were then left till the next year when they had dried out. Beams of that size were hard to carry and the first few times they tried to carry these beams on their backs, twenty to thirty men walking side by side under the beam. But this was rather hard in rough places and one end had to swing around. So finally they figured out a way of carrying the beam in between them. They lined up two by two with the beam between the lines. In doing this, some of the Hopis were given authority by the missionary to look after these men and to see if they all did their duty. If any man gave out on the way he was simply left to die. There was great suffering. Some died for lack of food and water, while others developed scabs and sores on their bodies.

It took a good many years for them to get enough beams to Shung-opovi to build the mission. When this mission was finally built, all the people in the village had to come there to worship, and those that did not come were punished severely. In that way their own religion was altogether wiped out, because they were not allowed to worship in their own way. All this trouble was a heavy burden on them and they thought it was on account of this that they were having a heavy drought at this time. They thought their gods had given them up because they weren't worshiping the way they should.

Now during this time the men would go out pretending they were going on a hunting trip and they would go to some hiding place, to make their prayer offerings. So today, a good many of these places are still to be found where they left their little stone bowls in which they ground their copper ore to paint the prayer sticks. These places are called Puwa-kiki, cave places. If these men were caught they were severely punished.

Now this man, To-ta-achi (the Priest)[3] was going from bad to worse. He was not doing the people any good and he was always figuring what he could do to harm them. So he thought out how the water from different springs or rivers would taste and he was always sending some man to these springs to get water for him to drink, but it was noticed that he always chose the men who had pretty wives. He tried to send them far away so that they would be gone two or three days, so it was not very long until they began to see what he was doing. The men were even sent to the Little Colorado River to get water for him, or to Moencopi. Finally, when a man was sent out he'd go out into the rocks and hide, and when the night came he would come home. Then, the priest, thinking the man was away, would come to visit his wife, but instead the man would be there when he came. Many men were punished for this.

All this time the priest, who had great power, wanted all the young girls to be brought to him when they were about thirteen or fourteen years old. They had to live with the priest. He told the people they would become better women if they lived with him for about three years. Now one of these girls told what the To-ta-achi were doing and a brother of the girl heard of this and he asked his sister about it, and he was very angry. This brother went to the mission and wanted to kill the priest that very day, but the priest scared him and he did nothing. So the Shung-opovi people sent this boy, who was a good runner, to Awatovi to see if they were doing the same thing over there, which they were. So that was how they got all the evidence against the priest.

Then the chief at Awatovi sent word by this boy that all the priests would be killed on the fourth day after the full moon. They had no calendar and that was the best way they had of setting the date. In order to make sure that everyone would rise up and do this thing on the fourth day the boy was given a cotton string with knots in it and each day he was to untie one of these knots until they were all out and that would be the day for the attack.[4]

Things were getting worse and worse so the chief of Shung-opovi went over to Mishongnovi and the two chiefs discussed their troubles. "He is not the savior and it is your duty to kill him," said the chief of Shung-opovi. The chief of Mishongnovi replied, "If I end his life, my own life is ended."

Now the priest would not let the people manufacture prayer offerings so they had to make them among the rocks in the cliffs out of sight, so again one day the chief of Shung-opovi went to Mishongnovi with tobacco and materials to make prayer offerings. He was joined by the chief of Mishongnovi and the two went a mile north to a cave. For four days they lived there heartbroken in the cave, making pahos. Then the chief of Mishongnovi took the prayer offerings and climbed to the top of the Corn Rock and deposited them in the shrine, for according to the ancient agreement with the Mishongnovi people it was their duty to do away with the enemy.

He then, with some of his best men, went to Shung-opovi, but he carried no weapons. He placed his men at every door of the priest's house. Then he knocked on the door and walked in. He asked the priest to come out but the priest was suspicious and would not come out. The chief asked the priest four times and each time the priest refused. Finally, the priest said, "I think you are up to something."

The chief said, "I have come to kill you." "You can't kill me," cried the priest, "you have no power to kill me. If you do, I will come to life and wipe out your whole tribe."

The chief returned, "If you have this power then blow me out into the air, my gods have more power than you have. My gods have put a heart into me to enter your home. I have no weapons. You have your weapons handy, hanging on the wall. My gods have prevented you from getting your weapons."

The old priest made a rush and grabbed his sword from the wall. The chief of Mishongnovi yelled and the doors were broken open. The priest cut down the chief and fought right and left but was soon over-powered, and his sword taken from him.

They tied his hands behind his back. Out of the big beams outside they made a tripod. They hung him on the beams, kindled a fire and burned him.

Iroquois

Iroquois or Confederacy of
the Five Nations

By the tradition of the Five Nations it appears that in their early history, they were frequently engaged in petty wars one with another, as well also with tribes living north of the lakes. The Five Nations, on account of their small numbers, suffered more by these wars than their neighbors, until there sprang up among the Onondagas a man more formidable in war than a whole tribe or nation. He consequently became the terror of all the surrounding nations, especially of the Cayugas and Senecas. This man, so formidable and whose cabin was as impregnable as a tower, is said to have had a head of hair, the ends of each terminating in a living snake; the ends of his fingers, and toes, his ears, nose & lips, eye brows & eye lashes all terminated in living snakes. He required in war, no bow and arrow, no battle axe or war club, for he had but to look upon his enemies, & they fell dead—so great was the power of the snakes that enshrouded him. He was a warrior by birth, and by his great power he had become the military despot of all the surrounding nations. And when he marched against his enemies they fled before his fatal sight.

Among the Onondagas there lived a man renowned for his wisdom, and his great love of peace. For a long time he had watched with great anxiety the increasing power of this military despot who on account of his snakey habilaments, was known by the applicable name Tadodahoh, or Atotahoh, signifying tangled because the snakes seemed to have tangled themselves into his hair; he saw bands of noble warriors fall before his fatal look. He revolved in his mind by what means he could take from the Tadodahoh his power, and also to divest him of his snakey appendages. He well knew that he could not wrest his power from him, unless he could put into his hands some means by which he could still exercise power and influence. He therefore concluded to call a general council, of the Five Nations, and to invite to this council the Tadodahoh, at which council he proposed to lay before the wise men a plan of Union that would secure not only amity and peace among themselves, and a perpetual existence as a confederacy but they would render themselves formidable & superior in power to any nation on the Continent. He accordingly called a council to be held upon the east bank of the Onondaga Lake, and to this council the Tadodahoh was invited, who it is said lived near the shores of Lake Ontario a short distance from Irondequoit Bay. He accepted the invitation and proceeded to the place. He occupied the council grounds alone, for no one would approach near to him, although great numbers had come to attend. The projector of the alliance alone proceeded to the grounds and into the presence of the Tadodahoh. He proceeded to divulge his plan when he was informed that his daughter had died whom he had left at home sick. He drew his robe about him, covering himself completely, and mourned for her. (His style of mourning was afterwards adopted by the Confederacy as the custom to mourn for sachems just before another was to be installed in his place.) He mourned night and day, and in his mourning which he did in a kind of song, he repeated the whole plan of Union. And when he had finished, no one of the wise men seemed to understand or comprehend his meaning and objects. Daganowedah, the projector of the plan of alliance, being provoked at their dullness of comprehension, which resulted more from their ignorance of civil matters than dullness of comprehension, arose in the night and travelled towards the east. He had not travelled far when he struck a small lake, and anyone could go around it sooner than to cross it in a canoe. Yet he chose to make a canoe of bark and go across it. It seems that he did not wish to deviate from a straight line. While he was crossing the lake, his canoe ran upon what he supposed to be a sand bar; he put his paddle down into the water to ascertain the cause of the stopping of the boat; in taking out his paddle he found a quantity of small shells, he took pains to put a sufficient quantity into his canoe, and after going ashore, he made a pouch of a young deer skin, and put these shells into it, after having first made a number of belts, and put the rest into strings of equal lengths. To this he gave the name of wampum, and the belts and strings he had made of the shells, he converted into the records of his wise sayings & the entire plan of his project of alliance.

He then proceeded on his journey, and he had not travelled far when he came to an Indian castle [a settlement]. Without calling a council he began to rehearse his plan of alliance, by means of his belts and strings of wampum. But the people of this castle were unable to comprehend the benefits of his project, and talked of him as crazy. When he heard what they were saying concerning him, he proceeded on his journey, sorrowing that he could not find a people who would listen to the words of wisdom. He at length came to another settlement, which was one of the Mohawk castles. Here again he rehearsed his plan of Union. Still his sayings were incomprehensible to that people. They however listened carefully for the purpose of ascertaining what it was that he could talk so long upon. All that they could understand of it, was the manner in which councils were to be called. A council was accordingly called and he invited to attend. They invited him for the purpose of giving him an opportunity to say in council and before a large number what he had been so long saying in the open fields. But after he had taken his seat in council and nothing was said or done, no exchange of wampum belts (for he had lent them a belt with which to call a council), he arose and again went into the fields and there repeated his speeches. He concluded by saying that they too were ignorant, and knew nothing about transacting civil matters. This was reported to the Grand Chief of the Mohawks and again he called another council and invited Daganowedah. When the council was opened and the wise man had taken his seat, the Mohawk Chief presented to him a belt of wampum, with a request that whatever he should have to say, should be said in open council. If he was a messenger from another tribe, they would hear in open council what were their wishes. He merely replied that he was the messenger of no one; that he had conceived a noble plan of alliance, but had not found a nation wise enough to comprehend its benefits, and thus he had travelled and should continue so to travel until he found support. He then rehearsed in open council his plan of Union, which though they could not comprehend it, was pronounced by all to be a noble project. Daganowedah the Onondaga wise man was immediately adopted into the Mohawk Nation, nor could the Onondagas afterwards claim him, since they first rejected his project of Alliance. He was also made a chief of the Mohawk Nation, and was to exercise equal power with the original Mohawk chief. They were to live in the same lodge, and to be, in every respect, equals.

But he had lived with the original chief but a short time, when he was ordered about as though he had been a mere servant. To this a free spirit will ever revolt, he therefore left him, and again went into the fields. He was asked why he left the house of his friend. He replied that he had not been treated as a friend or visitor, but as a slave. The original chief begged his pardon, and solicited him to return. He did, and was thenceforth treated with great regard. Daganowedah at length suggested the propriety of sending runners to the west, from whence he had come, to ascertain what may be doing from whence he had come. He wanted runners to go and seek the smoke of the council fire. The chief of the Mohawks at once called upon some runners to go towards the west in search of the smoke of a council fire. The guardian bird of the runners was the heron; they accordingly took upon themselves the form of herons. They went towards the west, but flying too high they did not see the smoke of the council fire of Onondaga. They proceeded as far west as Sandusky in Ohio, where they were unable to transform or change themselves again into men. Another set of runners were then sent out, who took upon them the form or shape of crows. They found the smoke of the council fire at Onondaga and so reported.

Daganowedah then proposed to send a few runners to the council to inform them that they had found a wise man of the Onondaga nation, who had conceived a plan of Union, and to request that he might be heard before the Great Tadodahoh. This was done; and as soon as the council at Onondaga heard where their wise man had gone, they sent a deputation to recall him. Daganowedah had in the mean time made arrangement with the Mohawk Chief to act as his spokesman when they should be in council. He was also to take the lead in the file, and to perform all the duties necessary to the completion of the Alliance, but he was to act as Daganowedah should direct. His reason for choosing a spokesman, was that he had not been heard when the council first opened, and that probably they might listen to a wise man of the Mohawks. To this arrangement the Mohawk agreed. He agreed also to divest Tadodahoh of his snakes, and to make him as other men, except that he should clothe him in civil power as the Head of the Confederacy that should be formed. They then proceeded with a delegation of the Mohawks to the council grounds at Onondaga. When they had arrived they addressed Tadodahoh the great military despot. The Mohawk divested him of his snakes, and for this reason he was styled Hayowenthah, or one who takes away or divests.

The plan of alliance was at first simple. It provided for the establishment of a confederacy, enjoying a democratic form of government. The civil and legislative power was to be vested in a certain number of wise men who should be styled civil sachems, and the military and executive power in another set of men who should be styled military sachems. The Union was to be established as a family organization, the Mohawks, Onondagas and Senecas to compose the Fathers and the Cayugas and Oneidas the children. This plan was adopted.

Prefigurations (2): The Literature of Imagination and Discovery

Anonymous

Eric the Red was the father of Leif Ericson—or, as he is sometimes called, "Leif the Lucky"—who was presumably the first European to discover America. Eric himself is celebrated in legend as the founder (in 985) of the earliest Scandinavian settlement in Greenland. This portion of the Saga he inspired treats of Leif's accidental landing on Newfoundland and suggests a number of motifs that will echo in much of the literature of discovery that follows and that will eventually swell into a set of dominant themes in subsequent American writing: the sense of destiny attached to exploration and colonization; the high purpose of exploration and settlement associated with the religious errand of American Christianity; the conception of the New World as a virgin paradise; the correlation of New World discovery with acts of deliverance and charity; and the underlying conviction that success in this missionary adventure is assured both by the beneficence of a favoring Providence and also by the resourcefulness and courage of human beings.

from *The Saga of Eric the Red*
(c. 1000)

Eric was married to a woman named Thorhild, and had two sons; one of these was named Thorstein, and the other Leif. They were both promising men. Thorstein lived at home with his father, and there was not at that time a man in Greenland who was accounted of so great promise as he. Leif had sailed to Norway, where he was at the court of King Olaf Tryggvason.[1] . . .

He was well received by the king, who felt that he could see that Leif was a man of great accomplishments. Upon one occasion the king came to speech with Leif, and asks him, "Is it thy purpose to sail to Greenland in the summer?" "It is my purpose," said Leif, "if it be your will." "I believe it will be well," answers the king, "and thither thou shalt go upon my errand, to proclaim Christianity there." Leif replied that the king should decide, but gave it as his belief that it would be difficult to carry this mission to a successful issue in Greenland. The king replied that he knew of no man who would be better fitted for this undertaking, "and in thy hands the cause will surely prosper." "This can only be," said Leif, "if I enjoy the grace of your protection." Leif put to sea when his ship was ready for the voyage. For a long time he was tossed about upon the ocean, and came upon lands of which he had previously had no knowledge. There were self-sown wheat fields and vines growing there. There were also those trees there which are called "mausur,"[2] and of all these they took specimens. Some of the timbers were so large that they were used in building. Leif found men upon a wreck, and took them home with him, and procured quarters for them all during the winter. In this wise he showed his nobleness and goodness, since he introduced Christianity into the country, and saved the men from the wreck; and he was called Leif the Lucky ever after.

Christopher Columbus
(1451?–1506)

Christopher Columbus attributed his discovery of the New World as much to divine Providence as to navigational genius or heroic courage. In 1502 he wrote to his patrons, King Ferdinand and Queen Isabella of Spain, "Neither reason nor mathematics nor maps were any use to me: fully accomplished were the works of Isaiah." (Isaiah 11:10–12 prophesies that God will gather the dispersed faithful remnant of his people into a new redeemed community.) This sense of providential direction for his epic mission, though obviously fed by Columbus's early imaginative response to tales of exploration and adventure and a strong personal sense of election, possessed at least a modest basis in fact. Born in Genoa, Italy, he arrived in Portugal after a miraculous escape from shipwreck that brought him ashore very close to the rock of Sagres, where Prince Henry the Navigator had established his famous academy of seamanship.

Columbus made four voyages to the New World between 1492 and 1502, all with the object of reaching the Indies. If the idea of sailing west to get to the East did not originate with Columbus—it was actually first suggested by Paolo Toscanelli, a Florentine cartographer—it was Columbus's obsession with this idea that finally allowed it to be tested. The story of the repeated rejection of his proposals, first by the king of Portugal and then by Ferdinand and Isabella, king and queen of what was then becoming Spain, before the latter reluctantly came to his aid, is only one of the many legendary elements of Columbus's biography. But the complex if not contrary motives that drove him—religious piety, dreams of wealth, the desire for glory, scientific curiosity, an extraordinary egotism, and much more—overcame all the obstacles set in his way, and the rest, as we say, is history. *While scholars continue to debate the nature of his motives and the significance of his accomplishments, there is no doubt that these four voyages helped redraw the boundaries of not only the European but also the Native American world.*

Though Columbus was so certain he had reached the Indies on his first voyage that he named the natives he encountered "Indians," his first landfall (on October 12, 1492) actually occurred on the island of San Salvador, from which he went on to discover the Bahamas, Cuba, and Haiti. The following selection constitutes his first report to Ferdinand and Isabella concerning his discovery.

from a *Letter to Lord Raphael Sanchez, Treasurer to Ferdinand and Isabella, King and Queen of Spain, on His First Voyage (1493)*

Sir, since I know that you will take pleasure at the great victory with which Our Lord has crowned my voyage, I write this to you, from which you will learn how in twenty[1] days I reached the Indies with the fleet which the most illustrious King and Queen, our lords, gave to me. And there I found very many islands filled with people without number, and of them all I have taken possession for their Highnesses, by proclamation and with the royal standard displayed, and nobody objected. To the first island which I found I gave the name *Sant Salvador*, in remembrance of His Heavenly Majesty, who marvelously hath given all this; the Indians call it *Guanahani*. To the second I gave the name *Isla de Santa Maria de Concepción*; to the third, *Ferrandina*; to the fourth, *La Isla Bella*; to the fifth, *La Isla Juana*; and so to each one I gave a new name.

When I reached Juana, I followed its coast to the westward, and I found it to be so long that I thought it must be the mainland, the province of Catayo.[2] And since there were neither towns nor cities on the coast, but only small villages, with the people of which I could not have speech because they all fled forthwith, I went forward on the same course, thinking that I should not fail to find great cities and towns. And, at the end of many leagues, seeing that there was no change and that the coast was bearing me to the north, which was contrary to my desire since winter was already beginning and I proposed to go thence to the south, and as moreover the wind was favorable, I determined not to wait for a change of weather and backtracked to a notable harbor;[3] and thence I sent two men upcountry to learn if there were a king or great cities. They traveled for three days and found an infinite number of small villages and people without number, but nothing of importance; hence they returned.

I understood sufficiently from other Indians, whom I had already taken, that continually this land was an island, and so I followed its coast eastwards 107 leagues up to where it ended. And from that cape I saw toward the east another island, distant 18 leagues from the former, to which I at once gave the name *La Española*. And I went there and followed its northern part, as I had in the case of Juana, to the eastward for 178 great leagues in a straight line. As Juana, so all the others are very fertile to an excessive degree, and this one especially. In it there are many harbors on the coast of the sea, incomparable to others which I know in Christendom, and numerous rivers, good and large, which is marvelous. Its lands are lofty and in it there are very many sierras and very high mountains, to which the island *Centrefrei*[4] is not comparable. All are most beautiful, of a thousand shapes, and all accessible and filled with trees of a thousand kinds and tall, and they seem to touch the sky; and I am told that they never lose their foliage, which I can believe, for I saw them as green and beautiful as they are in Spain in May, and some of them were flowering, some with fruit, and some in another condition, according to their quality. And there were singing the nightingale and other little birds of a thousand kinds in the month of November, there where I went. There are palm trees of six or eight kinds, which are a wonder to behold on account of their beautiful variety, and so are the other trees and fruits and herbs; therein are marvelous pine groves, and extensive champaign country; and there is honey, and there are many kinds of birds and a great variety of fruits. Upcountry there are many mines of metals, and the population is innumerable. *La Española* is marvelous, the sierras and the mountains and the plains and the champaigns and the lands are so beautiful and fat for planting and sowing, and for livestock of every sort, and for building towns and cities. The harbors of the sea here are such as you could not believe in without seeing them, and so the rivers, many and great, and good streams, the most of which bear gold. And the trees and fruits and plants have great differences from those of La Juana; in this there are many spices and great mines of gold and of other metals.

The people of this island and of all the other islands which I have found and seen, or have not seen, all go naked, men and women, as their mothers bore them, except that some women cover one place only with the leaf of a plant or with a net of cotton which they make for that. They have no iron or steel or weapons, nor are they capable of using them, although they are well-built people of handsome stature, because they are wonderfully timorous. They have no other arms than arms of canes, [cut] when they are in seed time, to the ends of which they fix a sharp little stick; and they dare not make use of these, for oftentimes it has happened that I have sent ashore two or three men to some town to have speech, and people without number have come out to them, and as soon as they saw them coming, they fled; even a father would not stay for his son; and this not because wrong has been done to anyone; on the contrary, at every point where I have been and have been able to have speech, I have given them of all that I had, such as cloth and many other things, without receiving anything for it; but they are like that, timid beyond cure. It is true that after they have been reassured and have lost this fear, they are so artless and so free with all they possess, that no one would believe it without having seen it. Of anything they have, if you ask them for it, they never say no; rather they invite the person to share it, and show as much love as if they were giving their hearts; and whether the thing be of value or of small price, at once they are content with whatever little thing of whatever kind may be given to them. I forbade that they should be given things so worthless as pieces of broken crockery and broken glass, and ends of straps, although when they were able to get them, they thought they had the best jewel in the world; thus it was ascertained that a sailor for a strap received gold to the weight of two and a half *castellanos*,[5] and others much more for other things which were worth much less; yea, for new *blancas*, for them they would give all that they had, although it might be two or three castellanos' weight of gold or an *arrova*[6] or two of spun cotton; they even took pieces of the broken hoops of the wine casks and, like animals, gave what they had, so that it seemed to me to be wrong and I forbade it, and I gave them a thousand good, pleasing things which I had brought, in order that they might be fond of us, and furthermore might be made Christians and be inclined to the love and service of their Highnesses and of the whole Castilian nation, and try to help us and to give us of the things which they have in abundance and which are necessary to us. And they know neither sect nor idolatry, with the exception that all believe that the source of all power and goodness is in the sky, and they believe very firmly that I, with these ships and people, came from the sky, and in this belief they everywhere received me, after they had overcome their fear. And this does not result from their being ignorant, for they are of a very keen intelligence and men who navigate all those seas, so that it is marvelous the good account they give of everything, but because they have never seen people clothed or ships like ours.

And as soon as I arrived in the Indies, in the first island which I found, I took by force some of them in order that they might learn [Castilian] and give me information of what they had in those parts;

it so worked out that they soon understood us, and we them, either by speech or signs, and they have been very serviceable. I still have them with me, and they are still of the opinion that I come from the sky, in spite of all the intercourse which they have had with me, and they were the first to announce this wherever I went, and the others went running from house to house and to the neighboring towns with loud cries of, "Come! Come! See the people from the sky!" Then all came, men and women, as soon as they had confidence in us, so that not one, big or little, remained behind, and all brought something to eat and drink, which they gave with marvelous love. In all the islands they have very many *canoas* like rowing *fustes*, some bigger and some smaller, and some are bigger than a *fusta*[7] of eighteen benches. They are not so broad, because they are made of a single log, but a *fusta* could not keep up with them by rowing, since they make incredible speed, and in these [canoes] they navigate all those islands, which are innumerable, and carry their merchandise. Some of these canoes I have seen with 70 and 80 men in them, each one with his oar.

In all these islands, I saw no great diversity in the appearance of the people or in their manners and language, but they all understand one another, which is a very singular thing, on account of which I hope that their Highnesses will determine upon their conversion to our holy faith, towards which they are much inclined.

I have already said how I went 107 leagues in a straight line from west to east along the coast of the island Juana, and as a result of that voyage I can say that this island is larger than England and Scotland together; for, beyond these 107 leagues, there remain to the westward two provinces where I have not been, one of which they call *Auau*, and there the people are born with tails. Those provinces cannot have a length of less than 50 or 60 leagues, as I could understand from those Indians whom I retain and who know all the islands. The other, *Española*, in circuit is greater than all Spain, from *Colunya* by the coast to *Fuenterauia* in Vizcaya, since I went along one side 188 great leagues in a straight line from west to east. It is a desirable land and, once seen, is never to be relinquished; and in it, although of all I have taken possession for their Highnesses and all are more richly supplied than I know or could tell, I hold them all for their Highnesses, which they may dispose of as absolutely as of the realms of Castile. In this *Española*, in the most convenient place and in the best district for the gold mines and for every trade both with this continent and with that over there belonging to the *Gran Can*[Grand Khan], where there will be great trade and profit, I have taken possession of a large town to which I gave the name *La Villa de Navidad*, and in it I have built a fort and defenses, which already, at this moment, will be all complete, and I have left in it enough people for such a purpose, with arms and artillery and provisions for more than a year, and a *fusta*, and a master of the sea in all arts to build others; and great friendship with the king of that land, to such an extent that he took pride in calling me and treating me as brother; and even if he were to change his mind and offer insult to these people, neither he nor his know the use of arms and they go naked, as I have already said, and are the most timid people in the world, so that merely the people whom I have left there could destroy all that land; and the island is without danger for their persons, if they know how to behave themselves.

In all these islands, it appears, all the men are content with one woman, but to their *Maioral*, or king, they give up to twenty. It appears to me that the women work more than the men. I have been unable to learn whether they hold private property, but it appeared true to me that all took a share in anything that one had, especially in victuals.

In these islands I have so far found no human monstrosities, as many expected; on the contrary, among all these people good looks are esteemed; nor are they Negroes, as in Guinea, but with flowing hair, and they are not born where there is excessive force in the solar rays; it is true that the sun there has great strength, although it is distant from the Equator 26 degrees. In these islands, where there are high mountains, the cold this winter was strong, but they endure it through habit and with the help of food which they eat with many and excessively hot spices. Thus I have neither found monsters nor had report of any, except in an island[8] which is the second at the entrance to the Indies, which is inhabited by a people who are regarded in all the islands as very ferocious and who eat human flesh; they have many canoes with which they range all the islands of India and pillage and take as much as they can; they are no more malformed than the others, except that they have the custom of wearing their hair long like women, and they use bows and arrows of the same stems of cane with a little piece of wood at the tip for want of iron, which they have not. They are ferocious toward these other people, who are exceeding great cowards, but I make no more account of them than of the rest. These are those who have intercourse with the women of *Matremonio*[9] which is the first island met on the way from Spain to the Indies, in which there is not one man. These women use no feminine exercises, but bows and arrows of cane, like the abovesaid; and they arm and cover themselves with plates of copper, of which they have plenty. In another island, which they assure me is larger than *Española*, the people have no hair. In this there is countless gold, and from it and from the other islands I bring with me Indios as evidence.

In conclusion, to speak only of that which has been accomplished on this voyage, which was so hurried, their Highnesses can see that I shall give them as much gold as they want if their Highnesses will render me a little help; besides spice and cotton, as much as their Highnesses shall command; and gum mastic, as much as they shall order shipped, and which, up to now, has been found only in Greece, in the island of Chios, and the Seignory[10] sells it for what it pleases; and aloe wood, as much as they shall order shipped, and slaves, as many as they shall order, who will be idolaters. And I believe that I have found rhubarb and cinnamon, and I shall find a thousand other things of value, which the people whom I have left there will have discovered, for I have not delayed anywhere, provided the wind allowed me to sail, except in the town of Navidad, where I stayed [to have it] secured and well seated. And the truth is I should have done much more if the ships had served me as the occasion required.

This is sufficient. And the eternal God, Our Lord, Who gives to all those who walk in His way victory over things which appear impossible, and this was notably one. For although men have talked or have written of these lands, all was conjecture, without getting a look at it, but amounted only to this, that those who heard for the most part listened and judged it more a fable than that there was anything in it, however small.

So, since our Redeemer has given this victory to our most illustrious King and Queen, and to their famous realms, in so great a matter, for this all Christendom ought to feel joyful and make great celebrations and give solemn thanks to the Holy Trinity with many solemn prayers for the great exaltation which it will have, in the turning of so many peoples to our holy faith, and afterwards for material benefits, since not only Spain but all Christians will hence have refreshment and profit. This is exactly what has been done, though in brief.

Done in the caravel, off the Canary Islands, on the fifteenth of February, year 1493.

At your service.

THE ADMIRAL

Amerigo Vespucci

(1454–1512)

An Italian merchant and navigator who acquired his experience as an explorer of the Western hemisphere in the service of Spain, Amerigo Vespucci is the man from whom the New World took its name. There is some question as to whether Vespucci made four voyages to the Western hemisphere or only two—in his Quatro Americi Navigationis, written in Lisbon in 1504 and printed in Florence the following year, he claimed four. His name was not directly associated with the "mundus novus" he claimed, in the following letter to Lorenzo de Medici, to have discovered on his third voyage until a Dutch humanist named Martin Waldseemüller reprinted the Quatro and proposed that it be so associated in an accompanying pamphlet of his own. Waldseemüller's proposal that Vespucci's discovery be called by his first name was given added impetus when Waldseemüller subsequently published a map or planisphere of the "world" on which the name "America" appeared for the first time (1507). It is worth noting, however, that on Waldseemüller's famous map Vespucci's name was applied only to the Southern hemisphere, not the Northern.

Vespucci's letter possesses considerable cultural as well as historical interest. Though he perpetuates Columbus's image of the New World as a virgin paradise whose people live in a state of nature, he does not paint an innocent or benign picture of that life. War is common in this primitive paradise and cannibalism an accepted practice. Furthermore, his description of the land implies its potential for exploitation and even, as history was to attest, destruction.

from *Mundus Novus (Letter on His Third Voyage to Lorenzo Pietro Francesco de Medici, 1503)*

Albericus Vespucius offers his best compliments to Lorenzo Pietro di Medici.

On a former occasion I wrote to you at some length concerning my return from those new regions which we found and explored with the fleet, at the cost, and by the command of this Most Serene King of Portugal. And these we may rightly call a new world. Because our ancestors had no knowledge of them, and it will be a matter wholly new to all those who hear about them. For this transcends the view held by our ancients, inasmuch as most of them hold that there is no continent to the south beyond the equator, but only the sea which they named the Atlantic; and if some of them did aver that a continent there was, they denied with abundant argument that it was a habitable land. But that this their opinion is false and utterly opposed to the truth, this my last voyage has made manifest; for in those southern parts I have found a continent more densely peopled and abounding in animals than our Europe or Asia or Africa, and, in addition, a climate milder and more delightful than in any other region known to us, as you shall learn in the following account wherein we shall set succinctly down only capital matters and the things more worthy of comment and memory seen or heard by me in this new world, as will appear below. . . .

It was on the seventh day of August, one thousand five hundred and one that we anchored off the shores of those parts, thanking our God with formal ceremonial and with the celebration of a choral mass. We knew that land to be a continent and not an island both because it stretches forth in the form of a very long and unbending coast, and because it is replete with infinite inhabitants. For in it we found innumerable tribes and peoples and species of all manner of wild beasts which are found in our lands and many others never seen by us concerning which it would take long to tell in detail. God's mercy shone upon us much when we landed at that spot, for there had come a shortage of fire-wood and water, and in a few days we might have ended our lives at sea. To Him be honor, glory, and thanksgiving. . . .

First then as to the people. We found in those parts such a multitude of people as nobody could enumerate (as we read in the Apocalypse), a race I say gentle and amenable. All of both sexes go about naked, covering no part of their bodies; and just as they spring from their mothers' wombs so they go until death. They have indeed large

square-built bodies, well formed and proportioned, and in color verg-
ing upon reddish. This I think has come to them, because, going about
naked, they are colored by the sun. They have, too, hair plentiful and
black. In their gait and when playing their games they are agile and
dignified. They are comely, too, of countenance which they nevertheless themselves destroy; for they bore their cheeks, lips, noses and ears.
Nor think those holes small or that they have one only. For some I
have seen having in a single face seven borings any one of which was
capable of holding a plum. They stop up these holes of theirs with
blue stones, bits of marble, very beautiful crystals of alabaster, very
white bones, and other things artificially prepared according to their
customs. But if you could see a thing so unwonted and monstrous,
that is to say a man having in his cheeks and lips alone seven stones
some of which are a span and a half in length, you would not be
without wonder. For I frequently observed and discovered that seven
such stones weighed sixteen ounces, aside from the fact that in their
ears, each perforated with three holes, they have other stones dangling
on rings; and this usage applies to the men alone. For women do not
bore their faces, but their ears only. They have another custom, very
shameful and beyond all human belief. For their women, being very
lustful, cause the private parts of their husbands to swell up to such a
huge size that they appear deformed and disgusting; and this is accomplished by a certain device of theirs, the biting of certain poisonous
animals. And in consequence of this many lose their organs which
break through lack of attention, and they remain eunuchs. They have
no cloth either of wool, linen or cotton, since they need it not; neither
do they have goods of their own, but all things are held in common.
They live together without king, without government, and each is his
own master. They marry as many wives as they please; and son co-
habits with mother, brother with sister, male cousin with female, and
any man with the first woman he meets. They dissolve their marriages
as often as they please, and observe no sort of law with respect to
them. Beyond the fact that they have no church, no religion and are
not idolaters, what more can I say? They live according to nature, and
may be called Epicureans rather than Stoics. There are no merchants
among their number, nor is there barter. The nations wage war upon
one another without art or order. The elders by means of certain ha-
rangues of theirs bend the youths to their will and inflame them to
wars in which they cruelly kill one another, and those whom they bring
home captives from war they preserve, not to spare their lives, but that
they may be slain for food; for they eat one another, the victors the
vanquished, and among other kinds of meat human flesh is a common
article of diet with them. Nay be the more assured of this fact because
the father has already been seen to eat children and wife, and I knew

a man whom I also spoke to who was reputed to have eaten more than three hundred human bodies. And I likewise remained twenty-seven days in a certain city where I saw salted human flesh suspended from beams between the houses, just as with us it is the custom to hang bacon and pork. I say further: they themselves wonder why we do not eat our enemies and do not use as food their flesh which they say is most savory. Their weapons are bows and arrows, and when they advance to war they cover no part of their bodies for the sake of protection, so like beasts are they in this matter. We endeavored to the extent of our power to dissuade them and persuade them to desist from these depraved customs, and they did promise us that they would leave off. The women as I have said go about naked and are very libidinous; yet they have bodies which are tolerably beautiful and cleanly. Nor are they so unsightly as one perchance might imagine; for, inasmuch as they are plump, their ugliness is the less apparent, which indeed is for the most part concealed by the excellence of their bodily structure. It was to us a matter of astonishment that none was to be seen among them who had a flabby breast, and those who had borne children were not to be distinguished from virgins by the shape and shrinking of the womb; and in the other parts of the body similar things were seen of which in the interest of modesty I make no mention. When they had the opportunity of copulating with Christians, urged by excessive lust, they defiled and prostituted themselves. They live one hundred and fifty years, and rarely fall ill, and if they do fall victims to any disease, they cure themselves with certain roots and herbs. These are the most noteworthy things I know about them. The climate there was very temperate and good, and as I was able to learn from their accounts, there was never there any pest or epidemic caused by corruption of the air; and unless they die a violent death they live long. This I take to be because the south winds are ever blowing there, and especially that which we call Eurus, which is the same to them as the Aquilo is to us. They are zealous in the art of fishing, and that sea is replete and abounding in every kind of fish. They are not hunters. This I deem to be because there are there many sorts of wild animals, and especially lions and bears and innumerable serpents and other horrid and ugly beasts, and also because forests and trees of huge size there extend far and wide; and they dare not, naked and without covering and arms, expose themselves to such hazards.

The land in those parts is very fertile and pleasing, abounding in numerous hills and mountains, boundless valleys and mighty rivers, watered by refreshing springs, and filled with broad, dense and well-nigh impenetrable forests full of every sort of wild animal. Trees grow to immense size without cultivation. Many of these yield fruits delectable to the taste and beneficial to the human body; some indeed do not, and no fruits there are like those of ours. Innumerable species of herbs and roots grow there too, of which they make bread and excellent food. They have, too, many seeds altogether unlike these of ours. They have there no metals of any description except gold, of which those regions have a great plenty, although to be sure we have brought none thence on this our first voyage. This the natives called to our attention, who averred that in the districts remote from the coast there is a great abundance of gold, and by them it is in no respect esteemed or valued. They are rich in pearls as I wrote you before. If I were to seek to recount in detail what things are there and to write concerning the numerous species of animals and the great number of them, it would be a matter all too prolix and vast. And I truly believe that our Pliny did not touch upon a thousandth part of the species of parrots and other birds and the animals, too, which exist in those same regions so diverse as to form and color; because Policletus, the master of painting in all its perfection, would have fallen short in depicting them. There all trees are fragrant and they emit each and all gum, oil, or some sort of sap. If the properties of these were known to us, I doubt not but that they would be salutary to the human body. And surely if the terrestrial paradise be in any part of this earth, I esteem that it is not far distant from those parts. Its situation, as I have related, lies toward the south in such a temperate climate that icy winters and fiery summers alike are never there experienced. . . .

Thomas More
(1478–1535)

A Christian humanist and statesman who eventually became Lord Chancellor of England, Sir Thomas More was executed by Henry VIII for refusing to accept the Act of Supremacy, which elevated the king to the position of supreme head of the Church of England. More "died the king's good servant," as he said on the scaffold, "but God's first." His Utopia, *which was written in Latin in 1516 but not translated into English until 1551, depicts an imaginary society governed entirely by reason. Inspired by descriptions of the New World provided by Amerigo Vespucci and by Peter Martyr, which More combined with the social and political views of such classical writers as Plato, Tacitus, and Pliny, More delineates a mode of life that is intended to present a stark contrast to the presiding conditions of English society. More defines egotism as the root of all moral and social evil and suggests that the only alternative is a communistic society, in which all goods are shared and pleasure is never pursued at the expense of others.*

from *Utopia* (1551)

In that part of philosophy which treats of manners and virtue, their reasons and opinions agree with ours. They dispute the good qualities of the soul, of the body, and of fortune; and whether the name of goodness may be applied to all these, or only to the endowments and gifts of the soul. They reason of virtue and pleasure. But the chief and principal question is in what thing, be it one or more, the felicity of man consists. But in this point they seem almost too much given and inclined to the opinion of those who defend pleasure, wherein they claim all or the chiefest part of man's felicity to rest. And (which is more to be marveled at) the defense of this so dainty and delicate an opinion they derive even from their grave, sharp, bitter, and rigorous religion. For they never dispute of felicity or blessedness but they join to the reasons of Philosophy certain principles taken out of religion; without which, for the investigation of true felicity, they think reason of itself weak and imperfect. Those principles are these and such like: That the soul is immortal, and by the bountiful goodness of God ordained to felicity; That to our virtues and good deeds rewards be appointed after this life, and to our evil deeds, punishments. Though these pertain to religion, yet they think it right that they should be believed and granted by proofs of reason. But if these principles were condemned and annulled, then without any delay they pronounce no man to be so foolish as not with all diligence to endeavor to obtain pleasure by right or wrong, only avoiding this inconvenience, that the less pleasure should not be a hindrance to the bigger, or that he labor for that pleasure which would bring after it displeasure, grief, and sorrow. For they judge it extreme madness to follow sharp and painful virtue, and not only to banish the pleasure of life but also willingly to suffer grief without any hope of profit thereof. For what profit can there be, if a man, when he has passed over all his life unpleasantly, that is to say, wretchedly, shall have no reward after his death?

But now, sir, they think felicity to rest not in all pleasure but only in that pleasure that is good and honest; that thereto, as to perfect blessedness, our nature is allured and drawn even by virtue, whereto only they that be of the contrary opinion attribute felicity. For they define virtue to be a life ordered according to nature; and that we be hereunto ordained of God; and that he doth follow the course of nature when in desiring and refusing things he is ruled by reason. Furthermore, that reason doth chiefly and principally kindle in men the love and veneration of the divine majesty, of whose goodness it is that we are, and that we possess the possibility of attaining felicity. And, that, secondarily, it moves and encourages us to lead our life free of care in joy and mirth, and to help all others, in respect of the society of nature, to obtain the same. For there was never a man so earnest and painstaking a follower of virtue, and hater of pleasure, that would so enjoin your labors, watchings, and fastings, but he would also exhort you to ease and lighten, as you are able, the lack and misery of others, praising the same as a deed of humanity and pity. Then if it be a point of humanity for man to bring health and comfort to man, and especially (which is a virtue most peculiarly belonging to man) to mitigate and assuage the grief of others, and by taking from them the

sorrow and heaviness of life, to restore them to joy, that is to say to
pleasure, why may it not then be said that nature doth provoke every
man to do the same to himself?

For a joyful life, that is to say, a pleasant life, is either evil; and
if it be so, then thou should not only help no man thereto, but rather,
as much as in thee lies, help all men from it, as troublous and hurtful;
or else, if thou not only may, but also of duty art bound to, procure
it to others, why not chiefly to thyself, to whom thou art bound to
show as much favor as to others? For when nature bids thee to be
good and gentle to others, she commands thee not to be cruel and
ungentle to thyself. Therefore even very nature (say they) prescribes to
us a joyful life, that is to say, pleasure, as the end of all our operations.
And they define virtue to be life ordered according to the prescript of
nature. But in that nature doth allure and provoke men to help one
another to live merrily (which surely she does not without a good
cause, for no man is so far above the love of man's state or condition,
that nature cares for him only, but equally favors all that can be comprehended under the communion of one shape, form, and passion),
verily she commands thee to use diligent circumspection, that thou do
not so seek for thine own commodities that thou procure for others
incommodities.

Wherefore their opinion is, that not only covenants and bargains
made among private men ought to be well and faithfully fulfilled, observed, and kept, but also common laws; which either a good prince
has justly published, or else the people, neither oppressed with tyranny,
nor deceived by fraud and guile, have by their common consent constituted and ratified, concerning the partition of the comforts of life,
—that is to say, the materials of pleasure. These laws not offended, it
is wisdom that thou look to thine own wealth. And to do the same
for the commonwealth is no less than thy duty, if thou barest any
reverent love or any natural zeal and affection to thy native country.
But to go about to keep another man from his pleasure, while procuring thine own, that is open wrong. Contrariwise, to withdraw
something from thyself to give to others, that is a mark of humanity
and gentleness; which never takes away so much commodity as it
brings again. For it is recompensed with return of benefits; and the
conscience of the good deed, with the remembrance of the thankful
love and benevolence of them to whom thou has done it brings more
pleasure to thy mind than that which thou hast witholden from thyself
could have brought to thy body. Finally (which to a godly-disposed
and religious mind is easy to be persuaded), God recompenses the gift
of a short and small pleasure with great and everlasting joy.

Therefore, the matter diligently weighed and considered, thus they
think: that all our actions, and in them the virtues themselves, be re-

ferred at the last to pleasure, as their end and felicity. Pleasure they call every motion and state of the body or mind wherein man naturally experiences delectation. Appetite they join to nature, and that not without a good cause. For as not only the senses but also right reason covets whatsoever is naturally pleasant, so long as it may be gotten without wrong or injury, not preventing or debarring a greater pleasure, nor causing painful labor; even so those things that men by vain imagination do feign against nature to be pleasant (as though it lay in their power to change the things as they do the names of things)—all such pleasures they believe to be of so small help and furtherance of felicity that they count them great trouble and hindrance, because those in whom they have once taken place, all his mind they possess with a false opinion of pleasure, so that there is no place left for true and natural delectations. For there may be many things, which of their own nature contain no pleasantness; yea, the most part of them much grief and sorrow; and yet, through the perverse and malicious flickering enticements of lewd and dishonest desires, be taken not only for special and sovereign pleasures, but also are counted among the chief causes of life.

In this counterfeit kind of pleasure they place them that I speak of before; where, the better gown men have on, the better they think of themselves. In the which thing they do twice err. For they be no less deceived in that they think their gown the better than they be in that they think themselves the better. For if you consider the profitable use of the garment, why should wool of a finer spun thread be thought better than the wool of a coarse spun thread? Yet they, as though the one did pass the other by nature, and not by their mistaking, advance themselves and think the price of their own persons thereby greatly increased. And therefore the honor, which in a coarse gown they dared not have looked for, they require, as if it were a duty, for their finer gown's sake. And if they be passed by without reverence, they take it angrily and disdainfully.

And again is it not a like madness to take pride in vain and unprofitable honors? For what natural or true pleasure dost thou take of another man's bare head or bowed knees? Will this ease the pain of thy knees, or remedy the frenzy of thy head? In this image of counterfeit pleasure, they be of a marvelous madness, which for the opinion of nobility rejoice much in their own conceit because it was their fortune to come of such ancestors whose stock of long time hath been counted rich (for now nobility is nothing else), especially rich in lands. And though their ancestors left them not one foot of land, or else they themselves have passed it against the walls, yet they think themselves not a hair's breadth the less noble. . . .

This is their judgement and opinion of virtue and pleasure. And they believe that by man's reason none can be found truer than this, unless any godlier be inspired into man from heaven. Wherein whether they believe well or no, neither the time doth suffer us to discuss, nor it is now necessary. For we have taken upon us to show and declare their laws and ordinances, and not to defend them.

But this thing I believe verily: however these decrees be, that there is in no place of the world either a more excellent people or a more flourishing commonwealth.

Alvar Nuñez Cabeza de Vaca
(1490?–1557?)

Alvar Nuñez Cabeza de Vaca was a member of a colonizing expedition led by Pánfilo de Nárvaez to the west coast of Florida in 1528. Due to the hostility of the natives and the hazards of the Florida wilderness, the expedition proved disastrous. Forced to flee to Mexico, the expedition was shipwrecked off the Texas coast near Galveston Island, and the survivors, now reduced from a company of three hundred to a group of only four individuals, were condemned to wander the Gulf Coast for eight years before finally making their way to Mexico City in 1536. Frequently taken prisoner by various Indian tribes during this period, Cabeza's Narrative constitutes, among other things, the first captivity narrative produced in the United States.

Like most captivity narratives, Cabeza's not only contains a wealth of information about natural as well as native conditions but also reflects an ambivalent attitude toward his various captors: He fears their strangeness, violence, and severity while respecting their fortitude and resourcefulness. Unlike many captivity narratives, however, Cabeza's refuses to demonize the Indians even when, as a Christian, he was inclined to feel spiritually superior to them. A man of extraordinary candor as well as courage, he was most interested in understanding them and in passing on that understanding to others.

from *The Narrative of Alvar Nuñez Cabeza de Vaca* (1542)

FROM CHAP. VII
THE CHARACTER OF THE COUNTRY.

The country where we came on shore to this town and region of Apalachen is for the most part level, the ground of sand and stiff earth. Throughout are immense trees and open woods, in which are walnut, laurel, and another tree called liquid-amber,[1] cedars, savins, evergreen oaks, pines, red-oaks, and palmitos like those of Spain. There are many lakes, great and small, over every part of it; some troublesome of fording, on account of depth and the great number of trees lying throughout them. Their beds are sand. The lakes in the country of Apalachen are much larger than those we found before coming there.

In this province are many maize fields; and the houses are scattered as are those of the Gelves. There are deer of three kinds, rabbits, hares, bears, lions, and other wild beasts. Among them we saw an animal with a pocket on its belly,[2] in which it carries its young until they know how to seek food, and if it happen that they should be out feeding and any one come near, the mother will not run until she has gathered them in together. The country is very cold. It has fine pastures for herds. Birds are of various kinds. Geese in great numbers. Ducks, mallards, royal-ducks, fly-catchers, night-herons and partridges abound. We saw many falcons, gerfalcons, sparrow-hawks, merlins, and numerous other fowl.

Two hours after our arrival at Apalachen, the Indians who had fled from there came in peace to us, asking for their women and children, whom we released; but the detention of a cacique by the Governor produced great excitement, in consequence of which they returned for battle early the next day, and attacked us with such promptness and alacrity that they succeeded in setting fire to the houses in which we were. As we sallied they fled to the lakes near by, because of which and the large maize fields we could do them no injury, save in the single instance of one Indian, whom we killed. The day following, others came against us from a town on the opposite side of the lake, and attacked us as the first had done, escaping in the same way, except one who was also slain.

We were in the town twenty-five days, in which time we made three incursions, and found the country very thinly peopled and difficult to travel for the bad passages, the woods and lakes. We inquired of the cacique we kept and the natives we brought with us, who were the neighbors and enemies of these Indians, as to the nature of the country, the character and condition of the inhabitants, of the food and all other matters concerning it. Each answered apart from the rest, that the largest town in all that region was Apalachen; the people beyond were less numerous and poorer, the land little occupied, and the inhabitants much scattered; that thenceforward were great lakes, dense forests, immense deserts and solitudes. We then asked touching the region towards the south, as to the towns and subsistence in it. They said that in keeping such a direction, journeying nine days, there was a town called Aute, the inhabitants whereof had much maize, beans, and pumpkins, and being near the sea they had fish, and that those people were their friends.

In view of the poverty of the land, the unfavorable accounts of the population and of everything else we heard, the Indians making continual war upon us, wounding our people and horses at the places where they went to drink, shooting from the lakes with such safety to themselves that we could not retaliate, killing a lord of Tescuco, named Don Pedro,[3] whom the commissary brought with him, we determined to leave that place and go in quest of the sea, and the town of Aute of which we were told. . . .

FROM CHAP. XXIV
CUSTOMS OF THE INDIANS
OF THAT COUNTRY.

From the Island of Malhado to this land,[4] all the Indians whom we saw have the custom from the time in which their wives find themselves pregnant, of not sleeping with them until two years after they have given birth. The children are suckled until the age of twelve years, when they are old enough to get support for themselves. We asked why they reared them in this manner; and they said because of the great poverty of the land, it happened many times, as we witnessed, that they were two or three days without eating, sometimes four, and consequently, in seasons of scarcity, the children were allowed to suckle, that they might not famish; otherwise those who lived would be delicate, having little strength.

If any one chance to fall sick in the desert, and cannot keep up with the rest, the Indians leave him to perish, unless it be a son or a brother; him they will assist, even to carrying on their back. It is common among them all to leave their wives when there is no conformity, and directly they connect themselves with whom they please. This is the course of the men who are childless; those who have children re-

main with their wives and never abandon them. When they dispute
and quarrel in their towns, they strike each other with the fists, fighting
until exhausted, and then separate. Sometimes they are parted by the
women going between them; the men never interfere. For no disaffec-
tion that arises do they resort to bows and arrows. After they have
fought, or had out their dispute, they take their dwellings and go into
the woods, living apart from each other until their heat has subsided.
When no longer offended and their anger is gone, they return. From
that time they are friends as if nothing had happened; nor is it necessary that any one should mend their friendships, as they in this way
again unite them. If those that quarrel are single, they go to some
neighboring people, and although these should be enemies, they receive
them well and welcome them warmly, giving them so largely of what
they have, that when their animosity cools, and they return to their
town, they go rich.

They are all warlike, and have as much strategy for protecting
themselves against enemies as they could have were they reared in
Italy in continual feuds. When they are in a part of the country where
their enemies may attack them, they place their houses on the skirt
of a wood, the thickest and most tangled they can find, and near it
make a ditch in which they sleep. The warriors are covered by small
pieces of stick through which are loop-holes; these hide them and present so false an appearance, that if come upon they are not discovered.
They open a very narrow way, entering into the midst of the wood,
where a spot is prepared on which the women and children sleep.
When night comes they kindle fires in their lodges, that should spies
be about, they may think to find them there; and before daybreak they
again light those fires. If the enemy comes to assault the houses, they
who are in the ditch make a sally; and from their trenches do much
injury without those who are outside seeing or being able to find them.
When there is no wood in which they can take shelter in this way,
and make their ambuscades,[5] they settle on open ground at a place
they select, which they invest with trenches covered with broken sticks,
having apertures whence to discharge arrows. These arrangements are
made for night.

While I was among the Aguenes, their enemies coming suddenly
at midnight, fell upon them, killed three and wounded many, so that
they ran from their houses to the fields before them. As soon as these
ascertained that their assailants had withdrawn, they returned to pick
up all the arrows the others had shot, and following after them in the
most stealthy manner possible, came that night to their dwellings without their presence being suspected. At four o'clock in the morning the
Aguenes attacked them, killed five, and wounded numerous others,
and made them flee from their houses, leaving their bows with all they

possessed. In a little while came the wives of the Quevenes to them
and formed a treaty whereby the parties became friends. The women,
however, are sometimes the cause of war. All these nations, when they
have personal enmities, and are not of one family, assassinate at night,
waylay, and inflict gross barbarities on each other.

FROM CHAP. XXV VIGILANCE OF THE
INDIANS IN WAR.

They are the most watchful in danger of any people I ever knew. If
they fear an enemy they are awake the night long, each with a bow
at his side and a dozen arrows. He that would sleep tries his bow, and
if it is not strung, he gives the turn necessary to the cord. They often
come out from their houses, bending to the ground in such manner
that they cannot be seen, looking and watching on all sides to catch
every object. If they perceive anything about, they are at once in the
bushes with their bows and arrows, and there remain until day, running from place to place where it is needful to be, or where they think
their enemies are. When the light has come, they unbend their bows
until they go out to hunt. The strings are the sinews of deer.

The method they have of fighting, is bending low to the earth,
and whilst shot at they move about, speaking and leaping from one
point to another, thus avoiding the shafts of their enemies. So effectual
is their manœuvring that they can receive very little injury from cross-
bow or arquebus;[6] they rather scoff at them; for these arms are of little
value employed in the open field, where the Indians move nimbly
about. They are proper for defiles[7] and in water; everywhere else the
horse will best subdue, being what the natives universally dread. Who-
soever would fight them must be cautious to show no fear, or desire
to have anything that is theirs; while war exists they must be treated
with utmost rigor; for if they discover any timidity or covetousness,
they are a race that will discern the opportunities for vengeance, and
gather strength from any weakness of their adversaries. When they use
arrows in battle and exhaust their store, each returns his own way,
without the one part following the other, although the one be many
and the other few, such being their custom. Oftentimes the body of
an Indian is traversed by the arrow; yet unless the entrails of the heart
be struck, he does not die but recovers from the wound.

I believe these people see and hear better, and have keener senses
than any other in the world. They are great in hunger, thirst, and cold,
as if they were made for the endurance of these more than other men,
by habit and nature.

This much I have wished to say, beyond the gratification of that desire men have to learn the customs and manners of each other, that those who hereafter at some time find themselves amongst these people, may have knowledge of their usages and artifices, the value of which they will not find inconsiderable in such event.

Pedro de Casteñeda
(1510?–1570?)

*Pedro de Casteñeda was a native of northern Spain who had come to
the New World and located himself in northwest Mexico at the time
Francisco Vasquez de Coronado organized his famous expedition into
New Mexico between 1540 and 1542, looking for the fabled City of
Gold. Writing twenty years after the expedition, Casteñeda recounted
Coronado's remarkable journey, which led him from Mexico across
northern Texas into Oklahoma and as far north as eastern Kansas.
During this same expedition, one of his scouting parties discovered the
Grand Canyon. Among the many remarkable features of this expedi-
tion are the depth of penetration it achieved and the motives for which
it was undertaken.*

from The Narrative of the
Expedition of Coronado
(c. 1562)

FROM CHAP. III:
OF HOW THEY KILLED THE
NEGRO ESTEVAN AT CIBOLA, AND
FRIAR MARCOS RETURNED
IN FLIGHT.

After Estevan had left the friars, he thought he could get all the reputation and honor himself, and that if he should discover those settlements with such famous high houses, alone, he would be considered

bold and courageous. So he proceeded with the people who had followed him, and attempted to cross the wilderness which lies between the country he had passed through and Cibola. He was so far ahead of the friars that, when these reached Chichilticalli[1] which is on the edge of the wilderness, he was already at Cibola, which is eighty leagues beyond. It is 220 leagues from Culiacan[2] to the edge of the wilderness, and eighty across the desert, which makes 300, or perhaps ten more or less. As I said, Estevan reached Cibola loaded with the large quantity of turquoises they had given him and some beautiful women whom the Indians who followed him and carried his things were taking with them and had given him. These had followed him from all the settlements he had passed, believing that under his protection they could traverse the whole world without any danger. But as the people in this country were more intelligent than those who followed Estevan, they lodged him in a little hut they had outside their village, and the older men and the governors heard his story and took steps to find out the reason he had come to that country. For three days they made inquiries about him and held a council. The account which the negro gave them of two white men who were following him, sent by a great lord, who knew about the things in the sky, and how these were coming to instruct them in divine matters, made them think that he must be a spy or a guide from some nations who wished to come and conquer them, because it seemed to them unreasonable to say that the people were white in the country from which he came and that he was sent by them, he being black. Besides these other reasons, they thought it was hard of him to ask them for turquoises and women, and so they decided to kill him. They did this, but they did not kill any of those who went with him, although they kept some young fellows and let the others, about sixty persons, return freely to their own country. As these, who were badly scared, were returning in flight, they happened to come upon the friars in the desert sixty leagues from Cibola, and told them the sad news, which frightened them so much that they would not even trust these folks who had been with the negro, but opened the packs they were carrying and gave away everything they had except the holy vestments for saying mass. They returned from here by double marches, prepared for anything, without seeing any more of the country except what the Indians told them.

FROM CHAP. IX:
OF HOW THE ARMY STARTED FROM
CULIACAN AND THE ARRIVAL OF THE
GENERAL AT CIBOLA, AND OF THE ARMY
AT SEÑORA AND OF OTHER THINGS
THAT HAPPENED.

The general, as has been said, started to continue his journey from the valley of Culiacan somewhat lightly equipped, taking with him the friars, since none of them wished to stay behind with the army. After they had gone three days, a regular friar who could say mass, named Friar Antonio Victoria, broke his leg, and they brought him back from the camp to have it treated. He stayed with the army after this, which was no slight consolation for all. The general and his force crossed the country without trouble, as they found everything peaceful, because the Indians knew Friar Marcos and some of the others who had been with Melchior Diaz when he went with Juan de Saldibar to investigate. After the general had crossed the inhabited region and came to Chichilticalli, where the wilderness begins, and saw nothing favorable, he could not help feeling somewhat downhearted, for, although the reports were very fine about what was ahead, there was nobody who had seen it except the Indians who went with the negro, and these had already been caught in some lies. Besides all this, he was much affected by seeing that the fame of Chichilticalli was summed up in one tumbledown house without any roof, although it appeared to have been a strong place at some former time when it was inhabited, and it was very plain that it had been built by a civilized and warlike race of strangers who had come from a distance. This building was made of red earth. From here they went on through the wilderness, and in fifteen days came to a river about eight leagues from Cibola which they called Red River,[3] because its waters were muddy and reddish. In this river they found mullets like those of Spain. The first Indians from that country were seen here—two of them, who ran away to give the news. During the night following the next day, about two leagues from the village, some Indians in a safe place yelled so that, although the men were ready for anything, some were so excited that they put their saddles on hind-side before; but these were the new fellows. When the veterans had mounted and ridden round the camp, the Indians fled. None of them could be caught because they knew the country.

The next day they entered the settled country in good order, and when they saw the first village, which was Cibola, such were the curses that some hurled at Friar Marcos that I pray God may protect him from them.

It is a little, crowded village, looking as if it had been crumpled all up together. There are haciendas in New Spain which make a better appearance at a distance. It is a village of about two hundred warriors, is three and four stories high, with the houses small and having only a few rooms, and without a courtyard. One yard serves for each section. The people of the whole district had collected here, for there are seven villages in the province, and some of the others are even larger and stronger than Cibola. These folks waited for the army, drawn up by divisions in front of the village. When they refused to have peace on the terms the interpreters extended to them, but appeared defiant, the Santiago⁴ was given, and they were at once put to flight. The Spaniards then attacked the village, which was taken with not a little difficulty, since they held the narrow and crooked entrance. During the attack they knocked the general down with a large stone, and would have killed him but for Don Garcia Lopez de Cardenas and Hernando de Alvarado, who threw themselves above him and drew him away, receiving the blows of the stones, which were not few. But the first fury of the Spaniards could not be resisted, and in less than an hour they entered the village and captured it. They discovered food there, which was the thing they were most in need of. After this the whole province was at peace. . . .

Peter Martyr
(1455–1526)
and Richard Eden
(1521–1576)

Peter Martyr (Pietro Martire D'Anghiera) was an Italian cleric who took up residence in Spain and made the acquaintance of many of the great New World explorers: Christopher Columbus, Vasco da Gama, Hernando Cortés, Ferdinand Magellan. Deeply moved by their tales of discovery, Peter Martyr decided to combine their information with official documents in order to compile a systematic account of what they had found. Martyr's letters were first published in De Orbe Novo (1516) but came to be called, when they were expanded and translated by Richard Eden in 1555, The Decades of the New World or West India.

Through Eden's translation, The Decades became an important textual event in the history of New World discovery. Initially making available for English readers a coherent account of the voyages of Columbus and others, it was augmented in 1589 by Richard Hakluyt (1553–1616), an English clergyman who compiled a more comprehensive record of all the English voyages of discovery known at the time, which was published as Principal Navigations, Voyages, Traffiques and Discoveries of the English Nation (later expanded into three volumes in 1598–1600). Hakluyt's Voyages was in turn further expanded by Samuel Purchas (1575–1626) into several books, including Hakluytus Posthumus or Purchas His Pilgrims (1625). Part of the interest of these accounts lies in the material they furnished for subsequent writers.

The present selection from Eden's translation of Peter Martyr's
Decades *is noteworthy for the approach it takes to its subject, namely,
the color of the New World's native inhabitants. Arguing that diversity
of color in human beings is a sign of divine omnipotence and wisdom,
Martyr broke with the theological view that whiteness of skin represented some sort of divine favor. Martyr's belief that variety of color
among New World peoples was—or should be—a source of religious
wonder and gratitude was as novel as the assumption on which it was
premised: that racial diversity is a blessing rather than a curse.*

from *The Decades of the New World or West India (1555)*

One of the marvellous things that God useth in the composition of
man is colour, which doubtless can not be considered without great
admiration in beholding one to be white, and another black, being
colours utterly contrary. Some likewise to be yellow, which is between
black and white, and other of other colours, as it were of divers liveries. And as these colours are to be marvelled at, even so is it to be
considered how they differ from another as it were by degrees, forasmuch as some men are white after divers sorts of whiteness, yellow
after divers manners of yellow, and black after divers sorts of black-
ness; and how from white they go to yellow by discolouring to brown
and red, and to black by ash colour, and murrey somewhat lighter
than black; and tawny like unto the West Indians which are altogether
in general either purple or tawny like unto sod quinces, or of the colour
of chestnuts or olives—which colour is to them natural and not by
their going naked, as many have thought, albeit their nakedness have
somewhat helped them thereunto. Therefore in like manner and with
such diversity as men are commonly white in Europe and black in
Africa, even with like variety are they tawny in these Indies, with divers
degrees diversely inclining more or less to black or white. No less
marvel is it to consider that men are white in Seville, and black at the
cape of Buena Speranza, and of chestnut colour at the river of Plata,
being all in equal degrees from the equinoctial line. Likewise that the
men of Africa and Asia that live under the burnt line (called *Zona
Torida*) are black, and not they that live beneath or on this side the
same line as in Mexico, Yucatan, Quauhtema, Lian, Nicaragua, Pan-
ama, Santo Domingo, Paria, Cape, Saint Augustine, Lima, Quito and
the other lands of Peru which touch in the same equinoctial. . . . It
may seem that such variety of colours proceedeth of man, and not of

the earth, which may well be although we be all born of Adam and
Eve, and know not the cause why God hath ordained it, otherwise
than to consider that his divine majesty hath done this as infinite other
to declare his omnipotence and wisdom in such diversity of colours as
appear not only in the nature of man, but the like also in beasts, birds
and flowers, where diverse and contrary colours are seen in one little
feather, or the leaves growing out of one little stalk. Another thing is
also to be noted as touching these Indians, and this is that their hair
is not curled as is the Moors' and Ethiopians' that inhabit the same
clime; neither are they bald except very seldom, and that but little. All
which things may give further occasion to philosophers to search the
secrets of nature and complexions of men with the novelties of the
new world. . . .

Michel de Montaigne
(1533–1592)

Michel de Montaigne was a French aristocrat and man of letters whose Essays have long been regarded as one of the great monuments of early modern culture. First published in 1580, Montaigne was to expand and revise The Essays continuously until his death.

In an age of volatile and diverse beliefs, Montaigne was remarkable for his breadth of perspective and general fairmindedness. Possessing, on the one hand, a classicist's respect for the past, its traditions and ideas, Montaigne exhibited, on the other, a radical's willingness to question existing institutions and to entertain new ideas. With a mind unusually free of prejudice and frequently skeptical of its own grounds, Montaigne's writing is as important for the quality of his thinking as the ideas with which he concerned himself.

In the following selection, Montaigne considers some typical reports about native inhabitants by New World discoverers and concludes that their treatment is deeply biased. Blinded by a sense of their spiritual superiority to their subjects, these European narrators are unable to provide a true perception of native facts. As he compares the evidence adduced to support the distinction between so-called "primitive" natives and so-called "civilized" Europeans, Montaigne finds the evidence betraying the distinction. Placing the facts held to epitomize the "primitive" against the facts assumed to represent "civility," he finds "civility" exhibited where one is supposed to discover "barbarism," nobility expressed in what is supposed to be the site of savagery, valor revealing itself in native behavior Europeans were expected to think of routinely as cunning and deceitful. Moreover, these perceptions gain in authority from Montaigne's exceptional moral realism, which justifies and supports the strength of his judgments.

from *Of Cannibals (1580)*

I long had a man in my house that lived ten or twelve years in the New World, discovered in these latter days, and in that part of it where Villegaignon landed,[1] which he called Antarctic France. This discovery of so vast a country seems to be of very great consideration. I cannot be sure, that hereafter there may not be another, so many wiser men than we having been deceived in this. I am afraid our eyes are bigger than our bellies, and that we have more curiosity than capacity; for we grasp at all, but catch nothing but wind. . . .

I find that there is nothing barbarous and savage in this nation, by anything that I can gather, excepting, that every one gives the title of barbarism to everything that is not in use in his own country. As, indeed, we have no other level of truth and reason, than the example and idea of the opinions and customs of the place wherein we live: there is always the perfect religion, there the perfect government, there the most exact and accomplished usage of all things. They are savages at the same rate that we say fruits are wild, which nature produces of herself and by her own ordinary progress; whereas in truth, we ought rather to call those wild, whose natures we have changed by our artifice, and diverted from the common order. In those, the genuine, most useful and natural virtues and properties are vigorous and sprightly, which we have helped to degenerate in these, by accommodating them to the pleasure of our own corrupted palate. And yet for all this, our taste confesses a flavour and delicacy, excellent even to emulation of the best of ours, in several fruits wherein those countries abound without art or culture. Neither is it reasonable that art should gain the pre-eminence of our great and powerful mother nature. We have so surcharged her with the additional orna-ments and graces we have added to the beauty and riches of her own works by our inventions, that we have almost smothered her; yet in other places, where she shines in her own purity and proper lustre, she marvellously baffles and disgraces all our vain and frivolous attempts.

> "Et veniunt hederæ sponte sua melius;
> Surgit et in solis formosior arbutus antris;
> Et volucres nulla dulcius arte canunt."[2]

Our utmost endeavours cannot arrive at so much as to imitate the nest of the least of birds, its contexture, beauty, and convenience: not so much as the web of a poor spider.

All things, says Plato, are produced either by nature, by fortune, or by art; the greatest and most beautiful by the one or the other of the former, the least and the most imperfect by the last.

These nations then seem to me to be so far barbarous, as having received but very little form and fashion from art and human invention, and consequently to be not much remote from their original simplicity. The laws of nature, however, govern them still, not as yet much vitiated with any mixture of ours: but 'tis in such purity, that I am sometimes troubled we were not sooner acquainted with these people, and that they were not discovered in those better times, when there were men much more able to judge of them than we are. I am sorry that Lycurgus and Plato had no knowledge of them; for to my apprehension, what we now see in those nations, does not only surpass all the pictures with which the poets have adorned the golden age, and all their inventions in feigning a happy state of man, but, moreover, the fancy and even the wish and desire of philosophy itself; so native and so pure a simplicity, as we by experience see to be in them, could never enter into their imagination, nor could they ever believe that human society could have been maintained with so little artifice and human patchwork. I should tell Plato, that it is a nation wherein there is no manner of traffic, no knowledge of letters, no science of numbers, no name of magistrate or political superiority; no use of service, riches or poverty, no contracts, no successions, no dividends, no properties, no employments, but those of leisure, no respect of kindred, but common, no clothing, no agriculture, no metal, no use of corn or wine; the very words that signify lying, treachery, dissimulation, avarice, envy, detraction, pardon, never heard of. How much would he find his imaginary Republic short of his perfection? "Viri a diis recentes."[3]

"Hos natura modos primum dedit."[4]

. . . They have continual war with the nations that live further within the mainland, beyond their mountains, to which they go naked, and without other arms than their bows and wooden swords, fashioned at one end like the head of our javelins. The obstinacy of their battles is wonderful, and they never end without great effusion of blood: for as to running away, they know not what it is. Every one for a trophy brings home the head of an enemy he has killed, which he fixes over the door of his house. After having a long time treated their prisoners very well, and given them all the regales they can think of, he to whom the prisoner belongs, invites a great assembly of his friends. They being come, he ties a rope to one of the arms of the prisoner, of which, at a distance, out of his reach, he holds the one end himself, and gives to the friend he loves best the other arm to hold after the same manner; which being done, they two, in the presence of all the assembly, despatch him with their swords. After that, they roast him, eat him amongst them, and send some chops to their absent friends. They do not do this, as some think, for nourishment, as the Scythians anciently did, but as a representation of an extreme revenge; as will appear by this: that having observed the Portuguese, who were in league with their enemies, to inflict another sort of death upon any of them they took prisoners, which was to set them up to the girdle in the earth, to shoot at the remaining part till it was stuck full of arrows, and then to hang them, they thought those people of the other world (as being men who had sown the knowledge of a great many vices amongst their neighbours, and who were much greater masters in all sorts of mischief than they) did not exercise this sort of revenge without a meaning, and that it must needs be more painful than theirs, they began to leave their old way, and to follow this. I am not sorry that we should here take notice of the barbarous horror of so cruel an action, but that, seeing so clearly into their faults, we should be so blind to our own. I conceive there is more barbarity in eating a man alive, than when he is dead; in tearing a body limb from limb by racks and torments, that is yet in perfect sense; in roasting it by degrees; in causing it to be bitten and worried by dogs and swine (as we have not only read, but lately seen, not amongst inveterate and mortal enemies, but among neighbours and fellow-citizens, and, which is worse, under colour of piety and religion), than to roast and eat him after he is dead. . . .

We may then call these people barbarous, in respect to the rules of reason: but not in respect to ourselves, who in all sorts of barbarity exceed them. Their wars are throughout noble and generous, and carry as much excuse and fair pretence, as that human malady is capable of; having with them no other foundation than the sole jealousy of valour. Their disputes are not for the conquest of new lands, for these they already possess are so fruitful by nature, as to supply them without labour or concern, with all things necessary, in such abundance that they have no need to enlarge their borders. And they are, moreover, happy in this, that they only covet so much as their natural necessities require: all beyond that, is superfluous to them: men of the same age call one another generally brothers, those who are younger, children; and the old men are fathers to all. These leave to their heirs in common the full possession of goods, without any manner of division, or other title than what nature bestows upon her creatures, in bringing them into the world. If their neighbours pass over the mountains to assault them, and obtain a victory, all the victors gain by it is glory only, and the advantage of having proved themselves the better in valour and virtue: for they never meddle with the goods of the conquered, but presently return into their own country, where they have no want of anything necessary, nor of this greatest of all goods, to know happily how to enjoy their condition and to be content. And those in turn do the same; they demand of their prisoners no other ransom, than acknowledgment that they are overcome: but there is not one found in an age, who will not rather choose to die than make such a confession, or either by word or look, recede from the entire grandeur of an invincible courage. There is not a man amongst them who had not rather be killed and eaten, than so much as to open his mouth to entreat he may not. They use them with all liberality and freedom, to the end their lives may be so much the dearer to them; but frequently entertain them with menaces of their approaching death, of the torments they are to suffer, of the preparations making in order to it, of the mangling their limbs, and of the feast that is to be made, where their carcass is to be the only dish. All which they do, to no other end, but only to extort some gentle or submissive word from them, or to frighten them so as to make them run away, to obtain this advantage that they were terrified, and that their constancy was shaken; and indeed, if rightly taken, it is in this point only that a true victory consists.

> "Victoria nulla est,
> Quam quæ confessos animo quoque subjugat hostes."[5]

. . . But to return to my story: these prisoners are so far from discovering the least weakness, for all the terrors that can be represented to them that, on the contrary, during the two or three months they are kept, they always appear with a cheerful countenance; importune their masters to make haste to bring them to the test, defy, rail at them, and reproach them with cowardice, and the number of battles they have lost against those of their country. I have a song made by one of these prisoners, wherein he bids them "come all, and dine upon him, and welcome, for they shall withal eat their own fathers and grandfathers, whose flesh has served to feed and nourish him. These muscles," says he, "this flesh and these veins, are your own: poor silly souls as you are, you little think that the substance of your ancestors' limbs is here yet; notice what you eat, and you will find in it the taste of your own flesh": in which song there is to be observed an invention that nothing relishes of the barbarian. Those that paint these people dying after this manner, represent the prisoner spitting in the faces of his executioners and making wry mouths at them. And 'tis most certain, that to the very last gasp, they never cease to brave and defy them both in word and gesture. In plain truth, these men are very savage in comparison of us; of necessity, they must either be absolutely so or else we are savages; for there is a vast difference betwixt their manners and ours. . . .

Three of these people, not foreseeing how dear their knowledge of the corruptions of this part of the world will one day cost their happiness and repose, and that the effect of this commerce will be their ruin, as I presuppose it is in a very fair way (miserable men to suffer themselves to be deluded with desire of novelty and to have left the serenity of their own heaven, to come so far to gaze at ours!) were at Rouen at the time that the late King Charles IX was there. The king himself talked to them a good while, and they were made to see our fashions, our pomp, and the form of a great city. After which, some one asked their opinion, and would know of them, what of all the things they had seen, they found most to be admired? To which they made answer, three things, of which I have forgotten the third, and am troubled at it, but two I yet remember. They said, that in the first place they thought it very strange, that so many tall men wearing beards, strong, and well armed, who were about the king ('tis like they meant the Swiss of his guard), should submit to obey a child, and that they did not rather choose out one amongst themselves to command. Secondly (they have a way of speaking in their language, to call men the half of one another), that they had observed, that there were amongst us men full and crammed with all manner of commodities, whilst, in the meantime, their halves were begging at their doors, lean, and half-starved with hunger and poverty; and they thought it strange that these necessitous halves were able to suffer so great an inequality and injustice, and that they did not take the others by the throats, or set fire to their houses.

I talked to one of them a great while together, but I had so ill an interpreter, and one who was so perplexed by his own ignorance to apprehend my meaning, that I could get nothing out of him of any moment. Asking him, what advantage he reaped from the superiority he had amongst his own people (for he was a captain, and our mariners called him king), he told me; to march at the head of them to war. Demanding of him further, how many men he had to follow him? he showed me a space of ground, to signify as many as could march in such a compass, which might be four or five thousand men; and putting the question to him, whether or no his authority expired with the war? he told me this remained: that when he went to visit the villages of his dependence, they plained him paths through the thick of their woods, by which he might pass at his ease. All this does not sound very ill, and the last was not at all amiss, for they wear no breeches.

Thomas Hariot
(1560–1621)

*Thomas Hariot was an English astronomer and mathematician who
served as scientific adviser for an expedition to the New World, and
specifically to Roanoke Island off the coast of North Carolina, organized by his friend Sir Walter Raleigh. Hariot's* Brief and True Report
*constitutes his record of that expedition; it was first reprinted in the
1600 edition of Richard Hakluyt's* Voyages.

Hariot's Report *contains one of the earliest detailed discussions
of the beliefs and practices of American Indian peoples in the New
World. Situated at the beginning of a continuing and voluminous
flow of observations—first by Europeans, then by their American
descendants—about the customs and traditions of Native Americans,
his remarks provide a good example of the kind of prejudices that a
European Christian brought to the interpretation of Amerindian religion. Hariot's comments also display something more than a grudging
respect for the "excellency of wit" represented by Indian technology
and the thirst for knowledge Indians express in response to what Europeans tell them about Christianity.*

from Brief and True Report of the New-found Land of Virginia (1588)

In respect of us they are a people poor, and for want of skill and
judgement in the knowledge and use of our things, do esteem our trifles
before things of greater value. Notwithstanding, in their proper man-

ner (considering the want of such means as we have), they seem very ingenious. For although they have no such tools, nor any such crafts, sciences, and arts as we, yet in those things they do, they show excellency of wit. And by how much they upon due consideration shall find our manner of knowledges and crafts to exceed theirs in perfection, and speed for doing or execution, by so much the more is it probable that they should desire our friendship and love, and have the greater respect for pleasing and obeying us. Whereby may be hoped, if means of good government be used, that they may in short time be brought to civility and the embracing of true religion.

Some religion they have already, which although it be far from the truth, yet being as it is, there is hope it may be the easier and sooner reformed.

They believe that there are many gods, which they call *Mantoac*, but of different sorts and degrees, one only chief and great god, which hath been from all eternity. Who, as they affirm, when he purposed to make the world, made first other gods of a principal order to be as means and instruments to be used in the creation and government to follow, and after the sun, moon, and stars as petty gods, and the instruments of the other order more principal. First, they say, were made waters, out of which by gods was made all diversity of creatures that are visible or invisible.

For mankind, they say a woman was made first which, by the working of one of the gods, conceived and brought forth children. And in such sort, they say, they had their beginning. But how many years or ages have passed since, they say they can make no relation, having no letters nor other such means as we to keep records of the particularities of times past, but only tradition from father to son.

They think that all the gods are of human shape, and therefore, they represent them by images in the forms of men, which they call *Kewasowok* (one alone is called *Kewas*). These they place in houses appropriate or temples, which they call *Machicomuck*, where they worship, pray, sing, and make many times offering unto them. In some *Machicomuck*, we have seen but one *Kewas*, in some two, and in other some three. The common sort think them to be also gods.

They believe also the immortality of the soul that, after this life as soon as the soul is departed from the body, according to the works it hath done, it is either carried to heaven, the habitat of gods, there to enjoy perpetual bliss and happiness, or else to a great pit or hole which they think to be in the furthest parts of their part of the world toward the sunset, there to burn continually. The place they call *Popogusso*.

For the confirmation of this opinion, they told me two stories of two men that had been lately dead and revived again. The one happened, but a few years before our coming into the country, of a wicked man, which having been dead and buried, the next day the earth of the grave being seen to move, was taken up again, who made declaration where his soul had been. That is to say, very near entering into *Popogusso*, had not one of the gods saved him, and gave him leave to return again and teach his friends what they should do to avoid that terrible place of torment. The other happened in the same year we were there, but in a town that was sixty miles from us, and it was told me for strange news, that one being dead, buried, and taken up again as the first, showed that although his body had lain dead in the grave, yet his soul was alive and had travelled far in a long broad way, on both sides whereof grew most delicate and pleasant trees, bearing more rare and excellent fruits than ever he had seen before or was able to express, and at length came to most brave and fair houses, near which he met his father that had been dead before, who gave him great charge to go back again and show his friends what good they were to do to enjoy the pleasures of that place, which when he had done he should after come again.

What subtlety soever be in the *Wiroances* and priests, this opinion worked so much in many of the common and simple sort of people, that it maketh them have great respect to their governors, and also great care what they do, to avoid torment after death, and to enjoy bliss, although notwithstanding there is punishment ordained for malefactors, as stealers, whoremongers, and other sort of wicked-doers, some punished with death, some with forfeitures, some with beating, according to the greatness of the facts.

And this is the sum of their religion, which I learned by having special familiarity with some of their priests. Wherein they were not so sure grounded, nor gave such credit to their traditions and stories, but through conversing with us they were brought into great doubts of their own, and no small admiration of ours, with earnest desire in many, to learn more than we had means for want of perfect utterance in their language to express.

Most things they saw with us, as mathematical instruments, sea compasses, the virtue of the lodestone [magnet] in drawing iron, a perspective glass [telescope] whereby was showed many strange sights, burning glasses [magnifying glass], wild fireworks, guns, hooks, writing and reading, spring-clocks that seem to go off themselves, and many other things that we had were so strange unto them, and so far exceeded their capacities to comprehend the reason and means how they should be made and done, that they thought they were rather the works of gods than of men, or at the leastwise, they had been given and taught by the gods. Which made many of them have such opinion of us, as that if they knew not the truth of God and religion already, it was rather to be had from us whom God so specially loved, than from a people that were so simple as they found themselves to be in comparison of us. Whereupon greater credit was given unto that we spoke of, concerning such matters.

Many times and in every town where I came, according as I was able, I made declaration of the contents of the Bible, that therein was set forth the true and only God, and his mighty works, that therein was contained the true doctrine of salvation through Christ, with many particulars of miracles and chief points of religion, as I was able then to utter, and thought fit for the time. And although I told them the book materially and of itself was not of any such virtue, as I thought they did conceive, but only the doctrine therein contained, yet would many be glad to touch it, to embrace it, to kiss it, to hold it to their breasts and heads, and stroke over all their body with it, to show their hungry desire of that knowledge which was spoken of.

Sir Walter Raleigh

(1544–1618)

Sir Walter Raleigh was a poet, courtier, adventurer, explorer, soldier, and statesman during the reign of Elizabeth I. Falling from favor when James I acceded to the throne after Elizabeth's death (1603), he was eventually tried for treason and beheaded. His unjust condemnation, however, together with the memory of his exploits, did little to hurt his reputation. Soon after his death Raleigh was transformed into a popular hero, even a figure of legend.

Two of the exploits that fed his legend concerned the New World. The first was an expedition he organized to America in 1584 (the first of its kind) to establish a colony on Roanoke Island, off the coast of what is now North Carolina. This ill-fated settlement soon had to be abandoned, leaving its remaining settlers to be destroyed by the Indians, but not before Raleigh had conferred upon this country, in honor of his queen, the name "Virginia." The second exploit that linked Raleigh's name with New World settlement was an expedition he later organized and led in 1595 to the Orinoco River in South America and which became the subject of The Discovery of Guiana. While this book largely failed to attract the financial support Raleigh hoped to secure for yet another expedition, it nevertheless helped to fuse in the early modern imagination of his English countrymen the image of New World settlement and vast economic gain. Indeed, no work produced during the age of exploration and discovery better represented what one scholar has described as "the shimmering mirage of gold and glory through which the sixteenth century saw the New World."

If Raleigh cannot be said exactly to have founded the literature of the "American dream," nonetheless he was surely among the first *in a long line of writers that runs from Thomas Morton, in* New English Canaan, *to F. Scott Fitzgerald, in* The Great Gatsby, *who have associated the lust for material wealth with the symbolism of sexual fulfillment. He was also among the first to identify America as a landmass whose wealth was more susceptible to assault and exploitation because it could be described in the imagery of a woman. In the following selection, Raleigh depicts the American continent as a virgin whose innocence remains intact but whose virtue can be violated by whichever nation first lays claims to her beauties. Thus it is hardly surprising that this book helped to inspire the conquistadors and set in motion the plunder of the New World and its peoples.*

from *The Discovery of Guiana* (1595)

. . . The Empire of Guiana is directly East from Peru towards the Sea, and lieth under the Equinoctial line, and it hath more abundance of golde than any part of Peru, and as many or more great Cities than ever Peru had when it flourished most: it is governed by the same lawes, and the Emperour and people observe the same religion, and the same forme and policies in government as were used in Peru, not differing in any part: and I have bene assured by such of the Spaniards as have seene Manoa the Imperial Citie of Guiana, which the Spaniards call El Dorado, that for the greatnesse, for the riches, and for the excellent seat, it farre exceedeth any of the world, at least of so much of the world as is knowen to the Spanish nation: it is founded upon a lake of salt water of 200. leagues long like unto Mare Caspium. And if we compare it to that of Peru, & but read the report of Francisco Lopez and others, it will seeme more than credible: and because we may judge of the one by the other, I thought good to insert part of the 120. Chapter of Lopez in his generall historie of the Indies, wherein he describeth the Court and magnificence of Guaynacapa, ancestour to the Emperour of Guiana, whose very wordes are these. . . .

All the vessels of his house, table and kitchin were of gold and silver, and the meanest of silver and copper for strength and hardnesse of metall. He had in his wardrobe hollow statues of gold which seemed giants, and the figures in proportion and bignesse of all the beasts, birds, trees, and hearbes, that the earth bringeth foorth: and of all the fishes that the sea or waters of his kingdome breedeth. He had also ropes, budgets, chestes and troughs of golde and silver, heapes of billets of gold, that seemed wood marked out to burne. Finally, there was nothing in his countrey, whereof he had not the counterfait in gold: Yea and they say, The Ingas had a garden of pleasure in an yland neere Puna, where they went to recreat themselves, when they would take the aire of the Sea, which had all kinde of garden-hearbs, flowers and trees of golde and silver, an invention, and magnificence till then never seene. Besides all this, he had an infinite quantitie of silver and golde unwrought in Cuzco which was lost by the death of Guascar, for the Indians hid it, seeing that the Spaniards tooke it, and sent it into Spaine.

And in the 117. chapter Francisco Pizarro caused the gold and silver of Atabalipa to be weyed after he had taken it, which Lopez setteth downe in these words following. . . . They found fiftie and two thousand markes of good silver, and one million, and three hundred twenty and sixe thousand and five hundred pezos of golde.

Now although these reports may seeme strange, yet if we consider the many millions which are dayly brought out of Peru into Spaine, wee may easily beleeve the same: for we finde that by the abundant treasure of that countrey the Spanish king vexeth all the princes of Europe, and is become, in a few yeeres, from a poore king of Castile, the greatest monarch of this part of the world, and likely every day to increase, if other princes forslow the good occasions offered, and suffer him to adde this empire to the rest, which by farre exceedeth all the rest: if his golde now indanger us, hee will then be unresistable. . . .

This Martinez was he that Christened the city of Manoa by the name of El Dorado, and as Berreo informed mee, upon this occasion: Those Guianians, and also the borderers, and all other in that tract which I have seene, are marvellous great drunkards; in which vice, I thinke no nation can compare with them: and at the times of their solemne feasts, when the emperour caroweth with his captaines, tributaries, and governours, the maner is thus: All those that pledge him are first stripped naked, and their bodies anointed all over with a kind of white balsamum (by them called curca) of which there is great plenty, and yet very deare amongst them, and it is of all other the most precious, whereof wee have had good experience: when they are anointed all over, certeine servants of the emperour, having prepared golde made into fine powder, blow it thorow hollow canes upon their naked bodies, untill they be all shining from the foot to the head: and in this sort they sit drinking by twenties, and hundreds, and continue in drunkennesse sometimes sixe or seven dayes together. The same is also confirmed by a letter written into Spaine, which was intercepted, which M. Robert Duddeley tolde me he had seene. Upon this sight, and for the abundance of golde which he saw in the city, the images of golde in their temples, the plates, armours, and shields of gold which they use in the warres, he called it El Dorado. . . .

I never saw a more beautifull countrey, nor more lively prospects, hils so raised here and there over the valleys, the river winding into divers branches, the plaines adjoyning without bush or stubble, all faire greene grasse, the ground of hard sand easie to march on, either for horse or foote, the deere crossing in every path, the birdes towards the evening singing on every tree with a thousand severall tunes, cranes and herons of white, crimson, and carnation pearching in the rivers side, the aire fresh with a gentle Easterly winde, and every stone that we stouped to take up, promised either golde or silver by his complexion. Your Lordship shall see of many sorts, and I hope some of them cannot bee bettered under the Sunne, and yet we had no meanes but with our daggers and fingers to teare them out here and there, the rockes being most hard of that minerall Sparre aforesaide, which is like a flint, and is altogether as hard or harder, and besides the veines lye a fathome or two deepe in the rockes. But we wanted all things requisite save onely our desires and good will to have performed more if it had pleased God. To be short, when both our companies returned, each of them brought also severall sorts of stones that appeared very faire, but were such as they found loose on the ground, and were for the most part but coloured, and had not any golde fixed in them, yet such as had no judgement or experience kept al that glistered, and would not be perswaded but it was rich because of the lustre, and brought of those, and of Marquesite with all, from Trinidad, and have delivered of those stones to be tried in many places, and have thereby bred an opinion that all the rest is of the same: yet some of these stones I shewed afterward to a Spaniard of the Caracas, who tolde mee that it was El Madre del oro, that is the mother of gold, and that the Mine was farther in the ground.

But it shall be found a weake policie in me, either to betray my selfe, or my countrey with imaginations, neither am I so farre in love with that lodging, watching, care, perill, diseases, ill savours, bad fare, and many other mischiefes that accompany these voyages, as to woo my selfe againe into any of them, were I not assured that the Sunne covereth not so much riches in any part of the earth. Captaine Whiddon, and our Chirurgion Nicholas Millechap brought mee a kinde of stones like Saphires, what they may prove I know not. I shewed them to some of the Orenoqueponi, and they promised to bring mee to a mountaine, that had of them very large pieces growing Diamond wise: whether it be Christall of the mountaine, Bristol-Diamond, or Saphire I doe not yet know, but I hope the best, sure I am that the place is as likely as those from whence all the rich stones are brought, and in the same height or very neere. . . .

For the rest, which my selfe have seene, I will promise these things that follow, which I know to be true. Those that are desirous to discover and to see many nations, may be satisfied within this river, which

bringeth foorth so many armes and branches leading to severall countries and provinces, above 2000 miles East and West, and 800 miles
South and North, and of these, the most eyther rich in golde, or in
other marchandizes. The common souldier shall here fight for golde,
and pay himselfe in steede of pence, with plates of halfe a foote broad,
whereas he breaketh his bones in other warres for provant and penury.
Those commanders and chieftaines that shoot at honour and abundance, shall finde there more rich and beautifull cities, more temples
adorned with golden images, more sepulchres filled with treasure, then
either Cortez found in Mexico, or Pizarro in Peru: and the shining
glory of this conquest will eclipse all those so farre extended beames
of the Spanish nation. There is no countrey which yeeldeth more pleasure to the inhabitants, either for those common delights of hunting,
hawking, fishing, fowling, or the rest, then Guiana doth. It hath so
many plaines, cleere rivers, abundance of Phesants, Partriges, Quailes,
Railes, Cranes, Herons, and all other fowle: Deere of all sorts, Porkes,
Hares, Lions, Tygers, Leopards, and divers other sortes of beastes,
either for chase, or food. It hath a kind of beast called Cama, or Anta,
as bigge as an English beefe, and in great plentie.

To speake of the severall sorts of every kind, I feare would be
troublesome to the Reader, and therefore I will omit them, and conclude that both for health, good ayre, pleasure, and riches I am resolved it cannot bee equalled by any region either in the East or West.
Moreover the countrey is so healthfull, as of an hundred persons &
more (which lay without shift most sluttishly, and were every day
almost melted with heate in rowing and marching, and suddenly wet
againe with great showers, and did eate of all sorts of corrupt fruits,
and made meales of fresh fish without seasoning, of Tortugas, of La-
gartos or Crocodiles, and of all sorts good and bad, without either
order or measure, and besides lodged in the open aire every night) we
lost not any one, nor had one ill disposed to my knowledge, nor found
any Calentura, or other of those pestilent diseases which dwell in all
hot regions, and so neere the Equinoctiall line.

Where there is store of gold, it is in effect needlesse to remember
other commodities for trade: but it hath towards the South part of the
river, great quantities of Brasil-wood, and diverse berries that die a
most perfect crimson and carnation: And for painting, all France, Italy,
or the East Indies yeelde none such: For the more the skin is washed,
the fairer the colour appeareth, and with which, even those browne
and tawnie women spot themselves, and colour their cheekes. All
places yeeld abundance of cotton, of silke, of balsamum, and of those
kindes most excellent, and never knowen in Europe, of all sortes of
gummes, of Indian pepper: and what else the countries may afford
within the land we knowe not, neither had we time to abide the triall,

and search. The soile besides is so excellent and so full of rivers, as it will carrie sugar, ginger, and all those other commodities, which the West Indies have.

The navigation is short, for it may be sayled with an ordinarie winde in sixe weekes, and in the like time backe againe, and by the way neither lee shore, enemies coast, rockes, nor sandes, all which in the voyages to the West Indies, and all other places we are subject unto, as the chanell of Bahama, comming from the West Indies, cannot well be passed in the Winter, & when it is at the best, it is a perilous and a fearefull place. The rest of the Indies for calmes, and diseases very troublesome, and the sea about the Bermudas a hellish sea for thunder, lightning, and stormes. . . .

To conclude, Guiana is a countrey that hath yet her maydenhead, never sackt, turned, nor wrought, the face of the earth hath not bene torne, nor the vertue and salt of the soyle spent by manurance, the graves have not bene opened for golde, the mines not broken with sledges, nor their Images puld downe out of their temples. It hath never bene entered by any armie of strength, and never conquered or possessed by any christian Prince. It is besides so defensible, that if two forts be builded in one of the Provinces which I have seene, the flood setteth in so neere the banke, where the channell also lyeth, that no ship can passe up but within a Pikes length of the artillerie, first of the one, and afterwards of the other: Which two Forts will be a sufficient guarde both to the Empire of Inga, and to an hundred other several kingdomes, lying within the said river, even to the citie of Quito in Peru.

Michael Drayton
(1563–1631)

*Michael Drayton was a minor English poet who was very conscious
of England's former glories. In "To the Virginian Voyage," he shows
himself concerned to protect and enhance the rich heritage of his nation. Sharing the typical early modern vision of the New World as
"Earth's onely paradise," Drayton sees the colonization of America as
an opportunity to revive England's diminished sense of national destiny and pride. The fresh challenges presented by the New World
should serve to create a new generation of English heroes whose exploits would be celebrated by New World poets.*

To the Virginian Voyage
(1606)

You brave heroique minds,
Worthy your countries name,
   That honour still pursue,
   Goe, and subdue,
Whilst loyt'ring hinds[1]
Lurke here at home, with shame.

Britans, you stay too long,
Quickly aboord bestow you,
   And with a merry gale
   Swell your stretch'd sayle,

With vowes as strong,
As the winds that blow you.

Your course securely steere,
West and by south forth keepe,
   Rocks, lee-shores, nor sholes,
    When Eolus² scowles,
You need not feare, So absolute the deepe.

And cheerefully at sea,
Successe you still intice,
   To get the pearle and gold,
   And ours to hold,
Virginia,
Earth's onely paradise.

Where nature hath in store,
Fowle, venison, and fish,
   And the fruitfull'st soyle,
   Without your toyle,
Three havests more,
All greater than you wish.

And the ambitious vine
Crownes with his purple masse,
   The Cedar reaching hie
   To kiss the sky,
The Cypresse, pine
And use-full Sassafras.

To whose, the golden age
Still natures lawes doth give,
   No other cares that tend,
But them to defend
From winters age,
That long there doth not live.

When as the lushious smell
Of that delicious land,
   Above the seas that flowes,
   The cleere wind throwes,
Your hearts to swell
Approching the deare strand.

In kenning[3] of the shore
(Thanks to God first given,)
   O you the happy'st men,
   Be frolike then,
Let cannons roare,
Frighting the wide heaven.

And in regions farre
Such heroes bring yee foorth,
   As those from whom we came,
   And plant our name,
Under that starre
Not knowne unto our north.

And as there plenty growes
Of lawrell every where,
   Apollo's sacred tree,
   You it may see,
A poets browes
To crowne, that may sing there.

Thy voyages attend,
Industrious Hackluit,
   Whose reading shall inflame
   Men to seeke fame,
And much commend
To after-times thy wit.

Richard Hakluyt
(1552?–1616)

Richard Hakluyt was a clergyman, geographer, and archivist who, beginning with his first book, Divers Voyages Touching the Discovery of America (1582), undertook to produce a comprehensive record of the European discovery, exploration, and colonization of the New World. Hakluyt carried this task of collecting, editing, and translating firsthand accounts much further in his Principal Navigations, Voyages, Traffiques and Discoveries of the English Nation, whose first edition appeared in 1589. Described as "the prose epic of [the] modern English nation," Hakluyt's Principal Navigations is an indispensable source of knowledge about the early modern age of exploration and discovery, though the need for secrecy about Sir Francis Drake's circumnavigation of the globe kept the account reprinted here out of Hakluyt's book until 1628.

This selection treats Drake's arrival on the coast of California and his initial contact with the Miwok Indians. Reminded of his native England by the white cliffs along the bay, Drake named the region "Nova Albion"—or, since "Albion" was the ancient name for Britain, "New England." Drake was not the first European explorer to reach the shores of North America. That honor presumably goes to the conquistador Hernando Cortés who, according to the sixteenth-century historian Antonia Herrera, was the first to reach the shores of what is now called the Baja peninsula. Subsequent expeditions by Spanish explorers such as Juan Rodriguez Cordillo would eventually be made *farther up the California coast itself, but it was Drake's landing in 1579 that initiated the first sustained European contact with the region.*

from *The Famous Voyage of Sir Francis Drake (1628)*

. . . The fifth of June [1579] being in 43 degrees towards the pole Arctic, we found the air so cold, that our men being grievously pinched with the same, complained of the extremity thereof; and the further we went, the more the cold increased upon us. Whereupon we thought it best for that time to seek the land, and did so; finding it not mountainous, but low plain land, till we came within 38 degrees towards the line. In which height it pleased God to send us into a fair and good bay, with a good wind to enter the same. In this bay we anchored; and the people of the country, having their houses close by the water's side, shewed themselves unto us, and sent a present to our General. When they came unto us, they greatly wondered at the things that we brought. But our General, according to his natural and accustomed humanity, courteously intreated them, and liberally bestowed on them necessary things to cover their nakedness; whereupon they supposed us to be gods, and would not be persuaded to the contrary. The presents which they sent to our General, were feathers, and cauls of network. Their houses are digged round about with earth, and have from the uttermost brims of the circle, clifts of wood set upon them, joining close together at the top like a spire steeple, which by reason of that closeness are very warm. Their bed is the ground with rushes strowed on it; and lying about the house, [they] have the fire in the midst. The men go naked; the women take bulrushes, and kemb them after the manner of hemp, and thereof make their loose garments, which being knit about their middles, hang down about their hips, having also about their shoulders a skin of deer, with the hair upon it. These women are very obedient and serviceable to their husbands.

After they were departed from us, they came and visited us the second time, and brought with them feathers and bags of *tabacco* for presents. And when they came to the top of the hill, at the bottom whereof we had pitched our tents, they stayed themselves; where one appointed for speaker wearied himself with making a long oration; which done, they left their bows upon the hill, and came down with their presents. In the meantime the women, remaining upon the hill, tormented themselves lamentably, tearing their flesh from their cheeks, whereby we perceived that they were about a sacrifice. In the meantime

our General with his company went to prayer, and to reading of the
Scriptures, at which exercise they were attentive, and seemed greatly
to be affected with it; but when they were come unto us, they restored
again unto us those things which before we bestowed upon them. The
news of our being there being spread through the country, the people
that inhabited round about came down, and amongst them the king
himself, a man of a goodly stature, and comely personage, with many
other tall and warlike men; before whose coming were sent two ambassadors to our General, to signify that their king was coming, in
doing of which message, their speech was continued about half an
hour. This ended, they by signs requested our General to send something by their hand to their king, as a token that his coming might be
in peace. Wherein our General having satisfied them, they returned
with glad tidings to their king, who marched to us with a princely
majesty, the people crying continually after their manner; and as they
drew near unto us, so did they strive to behave themselves in their
actions with comeliness. In the fore-front was a man of a goodly personage, who bare the sceptre or mace before the king; whereupon
hanged two crowns, a less and a bigger, with three chains of a marvellous length. The crowns were made of knit work, wrought artificially with feathers of divers colours. The chains were made of a bony
substance, and few be the persons among them that are admitted to
wear them; and of that number also the persons are stinted, as some
ten, some twelve, &c. Next unto him which bare the sceptre, was the
king himself, with his guard about his person, clad with coney skins,
and other skins. After them followed the naked common sort of people, every one having his face painted, some with white, some with
black, and other colours, and having in their hands one thing or another for a present. Not so much as their children, but they also
brought their presents.

In the meantime our General gathered his men together, and
marched within his fenced place, making, against their approaching,
a very warlike show. They being trooped together in their order, and
a general salutation being made, there was presently a general silence.
Then he that bare the sceptre before the king, being informed by another, whom they assigned to that office, with a manly and lofty voice
proclaimed that which the other spake to him in secret, continuing
half an hour. Which ended, and a general *Amen*, as it were, given, the
king with the whole number of men and women, the children excepted, came down without any weapon; who, descending to the foot
of the hill, set themselves in order. In coming towards our bulwarks
and tents, the sceptre-bearer began a song, observing his measures in
a dance, and that with a stately countenance; whom the king with his
guard, and every degree of persons, following, did in like manner sing

and dance, saving only the women, which danced and kept silence. The General permitted them to enter within our bulwark, where they continued their song and dance a reasonable time. When they had satisfied themselves, they made signs to our General to sit down; to whom the king and divers others made several orations, or rather supplications, that he would take their province and kingdom into his hand, and become their king, making signs that they would resign unto him their right and title of the whole land, and become his subjects. In which, to persuade us the better, the king and the rest, with one consent, and with great reverence, joyfully singing a song, did set the crown upon his head, enriched his neck with all their chains, and offered him many other things, honouring him by the name of *Hioh*, adding thereunto, as it seemed, a sign of triumph; which thing our General thought not meet to reject, because he knew not what honour and profit it might be to our country. Wherefore in the name, and to the use of her Majesty, he took the sceptre, crown, and dignity of the said country into his hands, wishing that the riches and treasure thereof might so conveniently be transported to the enriching of her kingdom at home, as it aboundeth in the same. . . .

Our necessary business being ended, our General with his company travelled up into the country to their villages, where we found herds of deer by a thousand in a company, being most large, and fat of body. We found the whole country to be a warren of a strange kind of coneys; their bodies in bigness as be the *Barbary* coneys, their heads as the heads of ours, the feet of a want [mole], and the tail of a rat, being of great length. Under her chin is on either side a bag, into the which she gathereth her meat, when she hath filled her belly abroad. The people eat their bodies, and make great account of their skins, for their king's coat was made of them. Our General called this country *Nova Albion*, and that for two causes; the one in respect of the white banks and cliffs, which lie towards the sea, and the other, because it might have some affinity with our country in name, which sometime was so called. There is no part of earth here to be taken up, wherein there is not some probable show of gold or silver.

At our departure hence our General set up a monument of our being there, as also of her Majesty's right and title to the same; namely a plate, nailed upon a fair great post, whereupon was engraved her Majesty's name, the day and year of our arrival there, with the free giving up of the province and people into her Majesty's hands, together with her Highness' picture and arms, in a piece of six pence of current English money, under the plate, whereunder was also written the name of our General. . . .

William Shakespeare
(1564–1616)

William Shakespeare, like so many Englishmen in the sixteenth century, was fascinated by the New World's symbolic as well as material importance. Sharing with many of his contemporaries a utopian perception of America as a site of Arcadian enchantment and possible spiritual regeneration, he also possessed a darker vision of this unknown, primitive, and vulnerable land. Sometimes called Shakespeare's "American fable" because it depicts the American wilderness as a pastoral landscape or garden with Edenic properties, The Tempest also contains glimpses of another America—later brought into clearer view by Jonathan Edwards, Herman Melville, Emily Dickinson, and others—that seems the anti-image of this first: a "hideous wilderness" where, to turn William Bradford's phrase around, the land becomes a scene of exploitation, treachery, betrayal, enslavement, and self-aggrandizement.

All of the following selections are taken from The Tempest. *The first is Prospero's speech reminding the spirit Ariel of what his life on the island had been like before Prospero came with his magic to rescue him from the clutches of "the foul witch Sycorax." The second passage is spoken by Caliban, Sycorax's "freckled whelp hag-born," whose bestiality is a reflection in human form not simply of the world without but also of a world predicated on the rule of domination. The third is Ferdinand's expression of wonder at hearing what seems to him to be the music of Nature itself. (All three are from Act I scene ii.) The fourth (III.ii.) shows that Caliban himself can be enthralled by the spirit of "Earth's onely paradise." The final selection (V.i.) is Miranda's exclamation of joyful amazement at her first sight of the court party.*

from *The Tempest* (1611)

Prospero: This blue-ey'd hag was hither brought with child
And here was left by th' sailors. Thou, my slave,
As thou report'st thyself, wast then her servant;
And, for thou wast a spirit too delicate
To act her earthy and abhorr'd commands,
Refusing her grand hests, she did confine thee,
By help of her more potent ministers
And in her most unmitigable rage,
Into a cloven pine; within which rift
Imprison'd thou didst painfully remain
A dozen years; within which space she died
And left thee there; where thou did'st vent thy groans
As fast as mill-wheels strike. Then was this island—
Save for the son that she did litter here,
A freckled whelp hag-born—not honour'd with
A human shape.

⦁ ⦁ ⦁

Caliban: This island's mine, by Sycorax my mother,
Which thou tak'st from me. When thou cam'st first,
Thou strok'st me and made much of me, wouldst give me
Water with berries in 't, and teach me how
To name the bigger light, and how the less,
That burn by day and night: and then I lov'd thee
And show'd thee all the qualities o' th' isle,
The fresh springs, brine-pits, barren place and fertile:
Curs'd be I that did so! All the charms
Of Sycorax, toads, beetles, bats, light on you!
For I am all the subjects that you have,
Which first was mine own king: and here you sty me
In this hard rock, whiles you do keep from me
The rest o' th' island.

⦁ ⦁ ⦁

Ferdinand: Where should this music be? i' th' air or th' earth?
It sounds no more: and, sure, it waits upon
Some god o' th' island. Sitting on a bank,
Weeping again the king my father's wrack,
This music crept by me upon the waters,
Allaying both their fury and my passion

With its sweet air: thence I have follow'd it,
Or it hath drawn me rather. But 'tis gone.
No, it begins again.

           •   •   •

Caliban: Be not afeard; the isle is full of noises,
Sounds and sweet airs, that give delight and hurt not.
Sometimes a thousand twangling instruments
Will hum about mine ears, and sometimes voices
That, if I then had wak'd after long sleep,
Will make me sleep again: and then, in dreaming,
The clouds methought would open and show riches
Ready to drop upon me, that, when I wak'd,
I cried to dream again.

           •   •   •

Miranda: *O, wonder!*
How many goodly creatures are there here!
How beauteous mankind is! O brave new world,
That has such people in 't!

Francis Bacon
(1561–1626)

Virtually no one living in his time understood as well as Francis Bacon that the Middle Ages had come to an end and that a new era had been inaugurated. Philosopher, scientist, metaphysician, man of letters, and statesman, Bacon gave expression to an idea central to this new era when he wrote in his Novum organum *(1620) that "Man, who is the servant and interpreter of nature, can act and understand no further than he has observed, either in operation or in contemplation, of the method and order of nature." In* The New Atlantis, *Bacon describes a utopian society where the scientific spirit has displaced all others. Not surprisingly, there is almost no institution more characteristic of this society than its college of science, known as "Salomon's House," which is dedicated to the empirical study of "the works and creatures of God." The purpose of this college, together with its chief instruments, components, functions, and special rites, is exhaustively described in the following selection. Something of the ethos of high seriousness this college attributes to the scientific calling can be discerned in the formal, stylized manner of the speaker, when he defines the college's function as seeking "the knowledge of causes, and secret motions of things; and the enlarging of the bounds of human empire, to the effecting of all things possible."*

from The New Atlantis (1627)

. . . God blesse thee, my Son; I will give thee the greatest Jewell I have: For I will impart unto thee, for the Love of God and Men, a Relation

of the true State of Salomon's House. Son, to make you know the true
state of Salomon's House, I will keep this order. First I will set forth
unto you the End of our Foundation. Secondly, the Preparations and
Instruments we have for our Works. Thirdly, the several Employments
and Functions wherto our Fellows are assigned. And fourthly, the Ordinances and Rites which we observe.

The End of our Foundation is the Knowledge of Causes, and Secret Motions of Things; And the Enlarging of the bounds of Humane
Empire, to the Effecting of all Things possible.

The Preparations and Instruments are these. We have large and
deep Caves of several Depths: The deepest are sunk 600 Fathom: And
some of them are digged and made under great Hills and Mountains:
So that if you reckon together the Depth of the Hill, and the Depth
of the Cave, they are (some of them) above three Miles deep. For we
find, that the Depth of a Hill, and the Depth of a Cave from the Flat,
is the same Thing; Both remote alike, from the Sun and Heaven's
Beames, and from the Open Aire. These Caves we call the Lower Region; And we use them for all Coagulations, Indurations, Refrigera-
tions, and Conservations of Bodies. We use them likewise for the
Imitation of Natural Mines; And the Producing also of New Artificial
Metals, by Compositions and Materials which we use, and lay there
for many years. We use them also sometimes, (which may seem
strange,) for Curing of some Diseases, and for Prolongation of Life,
in some Hermits that choose to live there, well accommodated of all
things necessarie, and indeed live very long; By whom also we learn
many things.

We have Burials in several Earths, where we put diverse Cements,
as the Chineses do their Porcellane. But we have them in greater Var-
ietie, and some of them more fine. We have also great variety of Com-
posts, and Soils, for the Making of the Earth Fruitful.

We have High Towers; The Highest about halfe a Mile in Heigth;
And some of them likewise set upon High Mountains: So that the
Vantage of the Hill with the Tower, is in the highest of them three
Miles at least. And these Places we call the Upper Region; Accounting
the Aire between the High Places, and the Low, as a Middle Region.
We use these Towers, according to their several Heights, and Situa-
tions, for Insolation, Refrigeration, Conservation; And for the View of
diverse Meteors; As Winds, Rain, Snow, Hail; And some of the Fiery
Meteors also. And upon them, in some Places, are Dwellings of Hermits, whom we visit sometimes, and instruct what to observe.

We have great Lakes, both Salt, and Fresh; wherof we have use
for the Fish, and Fowle. We use them also for Burials of some Natural
Bodies: For we find a Difference in Things buried in Earth, or in Air
below the Earth; and things buried in Water. We have also Pools, of

which some do strain Fresh Water out of Salt; And others by Art doe turn Fresh Water into Salt. . . .

We have also a Number of Artificial Wells, and Fountains, made in Imitation of the Natural Sources and Baths; As tincted upon Vitriol, Sulphur, Steel, Brass, Lead, Nitre, and other Minerals. And again we have little Wells for Infusions of many Things, where the Waters take the Virtue quicker and better, then in Vessels, or Basins. And amongst them we have a Water, which we call Water of Paradise, being, by that we do to it, made very Sovereigne for Health, and Prolongation of Life.

We have also Great and Spatious Houses, where we imitate and demonstrate Meteors. . . .

We have also certaine Chambers, which we call Chambers of Health, where wee qualifie the Aire as we think good and proper for the Cure of diverse Diseases, and Preservation of Health.

We have also faire and large Baths, of several Mixtures, for the Cure of Diseases, and the Restoring of Man's Body from Arefaction: And Others for the Confirming of it in Strength of Sinnews, Vital Parts, and the very Juice and Substance of the Body.

We have also large and various Orchards, and Gardens; Wherein we do not so much respect Beauty, as Variety of Ground and Soil, proper for diverse Trees, and Herbs. . . .

We have also Means to make diverse Plants rise by Mixtures of Earths without Seeds; And likewise to make diverse New Plants, differing from the Vulgar; and to make one Tree or Plant turn into another.

We have also Parks, and Enclosures of all Sorts, of Beasts, and Birds; which we use not only for View or Rareness, but likewise for Dissections, and Trials. . . .

We have also Particular Pools, where we make Trials upon Fishes, as we have said before of Beasts, and Birds.

We have also Places for Breed and Generation of those Kinds of Worms, and Flies, which are of Special Use; Such as are with you your Silkworms, and Bees.

I will not hold you long with recounting of our Brew-Houses, Bake-Houses, and Kitchens, where are made diverse Drinks, Breads, and Meats, Rare, and of special Effects. . . .

We have Dispensatories, or Shops of Medicines. Wherein you may easely think, if we have such Variety of Plants, and Living Creatures, more then you have in Europe, (for we know what you have,) the Simples, Drugs, and Ingredients of Medicines, must likewise be in so much the greater Variety. . . .

We have also diverse Mechanical Arts, which you have not; And Stuffs made by them; As Papers, Linen, Silks, Tissues; dainty

Works of Feathers of wonderful Lustre; excellent Dyes, and many others. . . .

We have also Furnaces of great Diversities, and that keep great Diversitie of Heats: Fierce and Quick; Strong and Constant; Soft and Mild; Blown, Quiet, Dry, Moist; And the like. . . .

We have also Perspective-Houses, where we make Demonstrations of all Lights, and Radiations: And of all Colours: And out of Things uncoloured and Transparent, we can represent unto you all several Colours; Not in Rain-Bows, (as it is in Gemms, and Prismes,) but of themselves Single. . . .

We have also Precious Stones of all kinds, many of them of great Beauty, and to you unknown. . . .

We have also Sound-Houses, where we practise and demonstrate all Sounds, and their Generation. We have Harmonies which you have not, of Quarter-Sounds, and lesser Slides of Sounds. Diverse Instruments of Music likewise to you unknown, some sweeter then any you have. . . .

We have also Perfume-Houses; wherwith we ioyne also Practices of Taste. . . .

We have also Engine-Houses, wher are prepared Engines and Instruments for all Sorts of Motions. . . .

We have also a Mathematical House, where are represented all Instruments, as well of Geometry, as Astronomy, exquisitely made.

We have also Houses of Deceits of the Senses; where we represent all manner of Feates of Jugling, False Apparitions, Impostures, and Illusions; And their Fallacies. And surely you will easily beleeve, that we, that have so many Things truely Natural, which induce Admiration, could in a World of Particulars deceive the Senses, if we would disguise those Things, and labour to make them seem more Miraculous. But we do hate all Impostures, and Lies: Insomuch as wee have severely forbidden it to all our Fellows, under pain of Ignominy and Fines, that they do not show any Natural work or Thing, Adorned or Swelling; but only Pure as it is, and without all Affectation of Strangeness.

These are (my Son) the Riches of Salomon's House.

For the several Employments and Offices of our Fellows; We have Twelve that Sail into Forraine Countries, under the Names of other Nations, (for our own we conceal;) Who bring us the Bookes, and Abstracts, and Patterns of Experiments of all other Parts. These wee call Merchants of Light.

We have Three that Collect the Experiments which are in all Books. These we call Depredatours.

We have Three that Collect the Experiments of all Mechanical

Arts; And also of Liberal Sciences; And also of Practices which are not Brought into Arts. These we call Mystery-Men.

We have Three that try New Experiments, such as themselves think good. These we call Pioners or Miners.

We have Three that Drawe the Experiments of the Former Four into Titles, and Tables, to give the better light, for the drawing of Observations and Axioms out of them. These we call Compilers.

We have Three that bend themselves, Looking into the Experiments of their Fellowes, and cast about how to draw out of them Things of Use, and Practice for Man's life. . . . These we call Dowry-men or Benefactours.

Then after diverse Meetings and Consults of our whole Number, to consider of the former Labours and Collections, we have Three that take care, out of them, to Direct New Experiments, of a Higher Light, more Penetrating into Nature then the Former. These we call Lamps. . . .

For our Ordinances and Rites: We have two very Long, and Fair Galleries: In one of these we place Patterns and Samples of all manner of the more Rare and Excellent Inventions: In the other we place the Statua's of all Principall Inventours. . . .

We have certain Hymns and Services, which we say dayly, of Laud and Thanks to God, for his Marveillous Works: And Forms of Prayers, imploring his Aide and Blessing, for the Illumination of our Labours, and the Turning of them into Good and Holy Uses.

Lastly, we have Circuits or Visits, of Divers Principal Cities of the Kingdom; where, as it commeth to pass, we do publish such New Profitable Inventions, as we think good. . . .

And when He had sayd this, He stood up: And I, as I had beene taught, kneeled down, and He laid his Right Hand upon my Head, and said; God bless thee, my Son; And God bless this Relation, which I have made. I give thee leave to Publish it, for the Good of other Nations; For we here are in God's Bosome, a Land unknown. And so he left me; Having assigned a Valew of about two Thousand Duckets, for a Bounty to me and my Fellows. For they give great Largesses, where they come, upon all occasions.

Samuel de Champlain
(1567–1635)

Samuel de Champlain was a French explorer of the Canadian wilderness who helped found the French colony at Quebec in 1608. He also made several expeditions to what is now coastal New England, charting the area as far south as Cape Cod and Martha's Vineyard fifteen years before the Pilgrims landed at Plymouth.

Allying himself with Algonquin, Huron, and Montagnais Indians in their quarrel with neighboring Iroquois, Champlain participated in a raid in the spring of 1609 near what is now Fort Ticonderoga. During this raid, the Iroquois were fired upon for the first time with muskets, and they consequently developed a deep enmity against the French, which lasted for many years.

The episode related below took place in the fall of 1615, during which time Champlain was in the company of a band of Huron Indians in Ontario, northern Canada.

from The Voyages
of Samuel de Champlain
(1604–1618)

LOST IN THE WOODS

. . . When they first went out hunting, I lost my way in the woods, having followed a certain bird that seemed to me peculiar. It had a beak like that of a parrot, and was of the size of a hen. It was entirely yellow, except the head which was red, and the wings which were blue, and it flew by intervals like a partridge. The desire to kill it led me to pursue it from tree to tree for a very long time, until it flew away in good earnest. Thus losing all hope, I desired to retrace my steps, but found none of our hunters, who had been constantly getting ahead, and had reached the enclosure. While trying to overtake them, and going, as it seemed to me, straight to where the enclosure was, I found myself lost in the woods, going now on this side now on that, without being able to recognize my position. The night coming on, I was obliged to spend it at the foot of a great tree, and in the morning set out and walked until three o'clock in the afternoon, when I came to a little pond of still water. Here I noticed some game, which I pursued, killing three or four birds, which were very acceptable, since I had had nothing to eat. Unfortunately for me there had been no sunshine for three days, nothing but rain and cloudy weather, which increased my trouble. Tired and exhausted I prepared to rest myself and cook the birds in order to alleviate the hunger which I began painfully to feel, and which by God's favor was appeased.

When I had made my repast I began to consider what I should do, and to pray God to give me the will and courage to sustain patiently my misfortune if I should be obliged to remain abandoned in this forest without counsel or consolation except the Divine goodness and mercy, and at the same time to exert myself to return to our hunters. Thus committing all to His mercy I gathered up renewed courage, going here and there all day, without perceiving any foot-print or path, except those of wild beasts, of which I generally saw a good number. I was obliged to pass here this night also. Unfortunately I had forgotten to bring with me a small compass which would have put me on the right road, or nearly so. At the dawn of day, after a brief repast, I set out in order to find, if possible, some brook and follow it, thinking that it must of necessity flow into the river on the border of which our hunters were encamped. Having resolved upon this plan, I carried it out so well that at noon I found myself on the border of a little lake, about a league and a half in extent, where I killed some game, which was very timely for my wants; I had likewise remaining some eight or ten charges of powder, which was a great satisfaction.

I proceeded along the border of this lake to see where it discharged, and found a large brook, which I followed until five o'clock in the evening, when I heard a great noise, but on carefully listening failed to perceive clearly what it was. On hearing the noise, however, more distinctly, I concluded that it was a fall of water in the river which I was searching for. I proceeded nearer, and saw an opening, approaching which I found myself in a great and far-reaching meadow, where there was a large number of wild beasts, and looking to my right I perceived the river, broad and long. I looked to see if I could not recognize the place, and walking along on the meadow I noticed a little path where the savages carried their canoes. Finally, after careful observation, I recognized it as the same river, and that I had gone that way before.

I passed the night in better spirits than the previous ones, supping on the little I had. In the morning I re-examined the place where I was, and concluded from certain mountains on the border of the river that I had not been deceived, and that our hunters must be lower down by four or five good leagues. This distance I walked at my leisure along the border of the river, until I perceived the smoke of our hunters, where I arrived to the great pleasure not only of myself but of them, who were still searching for me, but had about given up all hopes of seeing me again. They begged me not to stray off from them any more, or never to forget to carry with me my compass, and they added: If you had not come, and we had not succeeded in finding you, we should never have gone again to the French, for fear of their accusing us of having killed you. After this he was very careful of me when I went hunting, always giving me a savage as companion, who knew how to find again the place from which he started so well that it was something very remarkable. . . .

George Herbert
(1593–1633)

George Herbert—along with John Donne, Thomas Crashaw, and Henry Vaughan among religious writers and John Cleveland, Andrew Marvell, and Abraham Cowley among secular writers—was one of those poets described by Dr. Samuel Johnson as affecting a common poetic style and way of thinking he described as "metaphysical." Modeled after the rhythms and diction of actual speech and frequently organized in dramatic or rhetorical forms that simulated the dialectic and irony of argument, this style was thought to more closely resemble the full complex grammar of human emotions. As Herbert confessed on his deathbed to his friend and editor Nicholas Ferrar, he desired to present in his poetry "a picture of the many spiritual conflicts that . . . passed between God and my soul, before I could subject mine to the will of Jesus my Master, in whose service I have now found perfect freedom."

In "The Church Militant," written in the year of Herbert's death, he seems reconciled with God and His plan for history. In the following selection, Herbert portrays religion fleeing the corruption of the Old World to the unsullied purity of the New, while at the same time acknowledging that sin and darkness will inevitably follow the Church into the West and corrupt it there. Yet he finds consolation in the realization that as the Church moves west into the American wilderness, "symbolically" it also moves "east," to the time and place where final redemption is promised.

Several important themes in later colonial American writing emerge in this passage. One the one hand, Herbert foreshadows such Puritan figures as William Bradford and John Winthrop in his belief that America will provide religion with the possibility of continuing *reformation and even a new beginning. On the other, he anticipates the view that America will initiate a new and potentially decisive period of testing for religion; that transplantation will produce a time of new reckonings and perhaps new deliverances for the whole inheritance of Western Christendom.*

from *The Church Militant* (1633)

Religion stands on tip-toe in our land,
Readie to passe to the *American* strand.
When height of malice and prodigious lusts,
Impudent sinning, witchcrafts, and distrusts
(The marks of future bane) shall fill our cup
Unto the brimme and make our measure up;
When *Sein* shall swallow *Tiber*, and the *Thames*
By letting in them both pollutes her streams,
When *Italie* of us shall have her will,
And all her calender of sinnes fulfill;
Whereby one may fortell what sinnes next yeare
Shall both in *France* and *England* domineer;
Then shall Religion to *America* flee.
They have their times of Gospel ev'n as we.
My God, thou dost prepare for them a way
By carrying first their gold from them away;
For gold and grace did never yet agree.
Religion alwaies sides with povertie.
We think we rob them, but we think amisse;
We are more poore, and they more rich by this.
Thou wilt revenge their quarrell, making grace
To pay our debts, and leave our ancient place
To go to them, while that which now their nation
But lends to us shall be our desolation.
Yet as the Church shall thither westward flie,
So Sinne shall trace and dog her instantly.
They have their period also and set times
Both for their vertuous actions and their crimes.
And where of old the Empire and the Arts
Usher'd the Gospel ever in men's hearts,
Spain hath done one; when Arts perform the other,
The Church shall come, and Sinne the Church shall smother.
That when they have accomplished the round,

And met in th' east their first and ancient sound,
Judgement may meet them both and search them round.
Thus do both lights, as well in Church as Sunne,
Light one another and together runne.
Thus also Sinne and Darknesse follow still
The Church and Sunne with all their power and skill.
But as the Sunne still goes both west and east,
So also did the Church by going west
Still eastward go; because it drew more neare
To time and place where judgement shall appeare.
How deare to me, O God, thy counsels are!
              Who may with thee compare?

The Literature of
Settlement and
Colonization

John Smith
(1580–1631)

*Explorer, mercenary, entrepreneur, geographer, colonial promoter,
Captain John Smith is best known for his capture by Chesapeake Indians during his participation in the 1607 expedition that founded the
colony at Jamestown and his subsequent rescue from certain death at
the hands of their King Powhatan by his daughter Pocohantas.
Whether fact or fiction (Smith suppressed this incident in his first account of the expedition), its histrionics should not be permitted to
overshadow a fair estimate of Smith's achievements, dramatic and daring as they often were. Representative of a new breed of explorers and
colonists as equally interested in financial gain as in personal fame,
Smith was a tough, disciplined, courageous man whose leadership of
the Jamestown colony from September 1608 to August 1609 almost
certainly saved the colonists from starvation even as it earned him their
hostility. Returning to England to recover from a wound caused by
the accidental explosion of his gunpowder bag, he made a second visit
in 1614, this time to New England, and became so enamored of the
region that he devoted two of his next books (*A Description of New
England *[1616] and* Advertisements for the Unexperienced Planters of
New England, or Anywhere *[1631]) to promoting its virtues and encouraging its colonization.*

*Before they set out from Holland, Smith offered to lead the Pil-
grims to Virginia. When they rejected his offer—and, as subsequent
history records, landed in what would become Massachusetts instead—he contented himself, after a lifetime of travel, with remaining
in England, where he compiled narratives of his adventures. His* Advertisements *was addressed to the Puritans who made their way to
Massachusetts Bay in 1630.*

from *A True Relation of Such Occurences and Accidents of Noate as Hath Hapned in Virginia Since the First Planting of That Collony (1608)*

... The next night I lodged at a hunting town of *Powhatams*, and the next day arrived at *Waranacomoco* upon the river of *Pamauncke*, where the great king is resident. By the way we passed by the top of another little river, which is betwixt the two, called *Payankatank*. The most of this Country [is] th[r]ough Desert, yet exceeding fertil; good timber, most[ly] hils and dales, in each valley a cristall spring.

Arriving at *Weramocomoco* [?*on or about 5 January 1608*], their Emperour proudly lying uppon a Bedstead a foote high, upon tenne or twelve Mattes, richly hung with manie Chaynes of great Pearles about his necke, and covered with a great Covering of *Rahaughcums.* [racoon skins] At [his] heade sat a woman, at his feete another; on each side sitting uppon a Matte upon the ground, were raunged his chiefe men on each side the fire, tenne in a ranke, and behinde them as many yong women, each [with] a great Chaine of white Beades over their shoulders, their heades painted in redde: and [*Powhatan*] with such a grave and Maiesticall countenance, as drave me into admiration to see such state in a naked Salvage.

Hee kindly welcomed me with good wordes, and great Platters of sundrie Victuals, assuring mee his friendship, and my libertie within foure days. ...

After good deliberation, hee began to describe [to] mee the Countreys beyonde the Falles, with many of the rest. ...

I requited his discourse (seeing what pride hee had in his great and spacious Dominions, seeing that all hee knewe were under his Territories) in describing to him, the territories of *Europe*, which was subject to our great King whose subject I was, the innumerable multitude of his ships, I gave him to understand the noyse of Trumpets, and terrible manner of fighting [that] were under captain *Newport* my father: whom I intituled the *Meworames*, which they call the King of all the waters. At his greatnesse, he admired: and not a little feared. He desired mee [*i.e., the English*] to forsake *Paspahegh* [*i.e., James Town*], and to live with him upon his River, a Countrie called *Capa Howasicke*. Hee promised to give me Corne, Venison, or what I wanted to feede us: Hatchets and Copper wee should make him, and none should disturbe us.

This request I promised to performe: and thus, having with all the kindnes hee could devise, sought to content me, hee sent me home, with 4. men: one that usually carried my Gowne and Knapsacke after me, two other loded with bread, and one to accompanie me. . . .

The Empereur *Powhatan*, each weeke once or twice, sent me many presents of Deare, bread, *Raugroughcuns*; halfe alwayes for my father [*Captaine Newport*] whom he much desired to see, and halfe for me: and so continually importuned by messengers and presents, that I would come to fetch the corne, and take the Countrie their King had given me, as at last Captaine *Newport* resolved to go [to] see him.

Such acquaintance I had amongst the *Indians*, and such confidence they had in me, as neare the Fort they would not come till I came to them; every of them calling me by my name, would not sell any thing till I had first received their presents, and what they had that I liked, they deferred to my discretion: but after acquaintance, they usually came into the Fort at their pleasure: The President and the rest of the Councell, they knewe not; but Captaine *Newports* greatnesse I had so described, as they conceyved him the chiefe, the rest his children, Officers, and servants. . . .

from *A Description of New England* (1616)

. . . But it is not a worke for every one, to manage such an affaire as makes a discoverie, and plants a Colony. It requires all the best parts of Art, Judgement, Courage, Honesty, Constancy, Diligence, and Industrie, to doe but neere well. Some are more proper for one thing then another; and therein are to be imployed: and nothing breedes more confusion then misplacing and misimploying men in their undertakings. *Columbus, Cortez, Pitzara, Soto, Magellanes*, and the rest served more than a prentiship to learne how to begin their most memorable attempts in the *West Ind[i]es*: which to the wonder of all ages successfully they effected, when many hundreds of others, farre above them in the worlds opinion, beeing instructed but by relation, came to shame and confusion in actions of small moment, who doubtlesse in other matters, were both wise, discreet, generous, and couragious. I say not this to detract any thing from their incomparable merits, but to answer those questionlesse questions that keep us back from imitating the worthinesse of their brave spirits that advanced themselves from poore Souldiers to great Captaines, their posterity to great Lords, their King to be one of the greatest Potentates on earth, and the fruites of their labours, his greatest glory, power, and renowne. . . .

That part wee call *New England* is betwixt the degrees of 41. and

45; but that parte this discourse speaketh of, stretcheth but from *Pennobscot* to *Cape Cod*, some 75 leagues by a right line distant each from other: within which bounds I have seene at least 40. severall habitations upon the Sea Coast, and sounded about 25 excellent good Harbours; [8] in many whereof there is anc[h]orage for 500. sayle of ships of any burden; in some of them for 5000. And more than 200 Iles overgrowne with good timber, of divers sorts of wood, which doe make so many harbours as requireth a longer time then I had, to be well discovered. . . .

Who can desire more content, that hath small meanes; or but only his merit to advance his fortune, then to tread, and plant that ground hee hath purchased by the hazard of his life? If he have but the taste of virtue and magnanimitie, what to such a minde can bee more pleasant, then planting and building a foundation for his Posteritie, gotte from the rude earth, by Gods blessing and his owne industrie, without preiudice to any? If hee have any graine of faith or zeale in Religion, what can hee doe lesse hurtfull to any: or more agreeable to God, then to seeke to convert those poore Savages to know Christ, and humanitie, whose labors with discretion will triple requite thy charge and paines? What so truely su[i]tes with honour and honestie, as the discovering things unknowne? erecting Townes, peopling Countries, informing the ignorant, reforming things unjust, teaching virtue; and gaine to our Native mother-countrie a kingdom to attend her: finde imployment for those that are idle, because they know not what to doe: so farre from wronging any, as to cause Posteritie to remember thee; and remembring thee, ever honour that remembrance with praise? . . .

I have not beene so ill bred, but I have tasted of *Plenty* and *Pleasure*, as well as *Want* and *Miserie*: nor doth necessitie yet, or occasion of discontent, force me to these endeavors: nor am I ignorant what small thanke I shall have for my paines; or that many would have the Worlde imagine them to be of great iudgement, that can but blemish these my designes, by their witty obiections and detractions: yet (I hope) my reasons with my deeds, will so prevaile with some, that I shall not want imployment in these affaires, to make the most blinde see his owne senselessnesse, and incredulity; Hoping that gaine will make them affect that, which Religion, Charity, and the Common good cannot. It were but a poore device in me, To deceive my selfe; much more the King, State, my Friends and Countrey, with these inducements: which, seeing his Maiestie hath given permission, I wish all sorts of worthie, honest, industrious spirits, would understand: and if they desire any further satisfaction, I will doe my best to give it: Not to perswade them to goe onely; but goe with them: Not leave them there; but live with them there.

I will not say, but by ill providing and undue managing, such courses may be taken, [that] may make us miserable enough: But if I may have the execution of what I have proiected; if they want to eate, let them eate or never digest Me. If I performe what I say, I desire but that reward out of the gaines [which] may su[i]te my paines, quality, and condition. And if I abuse you with my tongue, take my head for satisfaction. If any dislike at the yeares end, defraying their charge, by my consent they should freely returne. I feare not want of companie sufficient, were it but knowne what I know of those Countries; and by the proofe of that wealth I hope yearely to returne, if God please to blesse me from such accidents, as are beyond my power in reason to prevent: For, I am not so simple to thinke, that ever any other motive then wealth, will ever erect there a Commonweale; or draw companie from their ease and humours at home, to stay in *New England* to effect my purposes.

And lest any should think the toile might be insupportable, though these things may be had by labour, and diligence: I assure my selfe there are who delight extreamly in vaine pleasure, that take much more paines in *England*, to enioy it, then I should doe heere [*New England*] to gaine wealth sufficient: and yet I thinke they should not have halfe such sweet content: for, our pleasure here is still gaines; in *England* charges and losse. Heer nature and liberty affords vs that freely, which in *England* we want, or it costeth vs dearely. What pleasure can be more, then (being tired with any occasion a-shore, in planting Vines, Fruits, or Hearbs, in contriving their owne Grounds, to the pleasure of their owne mindes, their Fields, Gardens, Orchards, Buildings, Ships, and other works, &c.) to recreate themselves before their owne doores, in their owne boates upon the Sea; where man, woman and childe, with a small hooke and line, by angling, may take diverse sorts of excellent fish, at their pleasures? And is it not pretty sport, to pull up two pence, six pence, and twelve pence, as fast as you can ha[u]le and veare a line? He is a very bad fisher [that] cannot kill in one day with his hooke and line, one, two, or three hundred Cods: which dressed and dried, if they be sould there for ten shillings the hundred, though in England they will give more than twentie, may not both the servant, the master, and marchant, be well content with this gaine? If a man worke but three dayes in seaven, he may get more then hee can spend, unlesse he will be excessive. Now that Carpenter, Mason, Gardiner, Taylor, Smith, Sailer, Forgers, or what other, may they not make this a pretty recreation though they fish but an houre in a day, to take more then they eate in a weeke? or if they will not eate it, because there is so much better choice; yet sell it, or change it, with the fisher men, or marchants, for any thing they want. And what sport doth yeeld a more pleasing content, and lesse hurt or charge then angling with a hooke; and crossing the sweete ayre from Ile to Ile, over the silent streames of a calme Sea? Wherein the most curious may finde pleasure, profit, and content. ·

Thus, though all men be not fishers: yet all men, whatsoever, may in other matters doe as well. For necessity doth in these cases so rule a Commonwealth, and each in their severall functions, as their labours in their qualities may be as profitable, because there is a necessary mutuall use of all.

For Gentlemen, what exercise should more delight them, then ranging dayly those unknowne parts, using fowling and fishing, for hunting and hawking? and yet you shall see the wilde-haukes give you some pleasure, in seeing them stoope (six or seaven after one another) an houre or two together, at the skuls of fish in the faire harbours, as those a-shore at a foule; and never trouble nor torment yourselves, with watching, mewing, feeding, and attending them: nor kill horse and man with running and crying, *See you not a hawk?* For hunting also: the woods, lakes, and rivers affoord not onely chase sufficient, for any that delights in that kinde of toyle, or pleasure; but such beasts to hunt, that besides the delicacy of their bodies for food, their skins are so rich, as may well recompence thy dayly labour, with a Captains pay.

For labourers, if those that sowe hemp, rape, turnups, parsnips, carrats, cabidge, and such like; giue 20, 30, 40, 50 shillings yearely for an acre of ground, and meat drinke and wages to use it, and yet grow rich; when better, or at least as good ground, may be had, and cost nothing but labour; it seems strange to me, any such should there grow poore.

My purpose is not to perswade children from their parents; men from their wives; nor servants from their masters: onely, such as with free consent may be spared: But that each parish, or village, in Citie or Countrey, that will but apparell their fatherlesse children, of thirteene or fourteene years of age, or young mar[r]ied people, that have small wealth to live on; heere by their labour may live exceeding well: provided alwaies that first there bee a sufficient power to command them, houses to receive them, meanes to defend them, and meet provisions for them; for, any place may bee overlain: and it is most necessarie to have a fortresse (ere this grow to practice) and sufficient masters (as, Carpenters, Masons, Fishers, Fowlers, Gardiners, Husbandmen, Sawyers, Smiths, Spinsters, Taylors, Weavers, and such like) to take ten, twelve, or twentie, or as ther is occasion, for Apprentises. The Masters by this may quicklie growe rich; these may learne their trades themselves, to doe the like; to a generall and an incredible benefit, for King, and Countrey, Master, and Servant. . . .

John Cotton
(1584–1652)

John Cotton, former dean of Emmanuel College, Cambridge University, emigrated to America in 1633. He quickly became a prominent figure in the Massachusetts Bay Colony. Best known, perhaps, for his eventual opposition (he was initially one of her supporters) to Ann Hutchinson and the Antinomians, who resisted his belief in the authority of the Church and in its responsibility to act as an intermediary between God and the individual believer, as well as for his later clash with Roger Williams, who challenged his undemocratic views of civil and religious government in The Bloudy Tenent of Persecution, Cotton was nonetheless an extremely able and widely respected, though sometimes reactionary, defender of New England Congregationalism.

Cotton wrote "God's Promise to His Plantations" while still in England. His central image of "planting" is significant in several respects. This rich metaphor opens up what would become for many of Cotton's seventeenth-century contemporaries a treasury of apt biblical references to describe God's work in the New World and particularly to define the meaning of the Puritan "errand," as Samuel Danforth called it in a well-known Election Day sermon, into the wilderness. It also anticipates the way subsequent generations of writers, beginning with the early nineteenth-century Transcendentalists, would turn again and again to Nature for images to describe their sense of the meaning and mission of North American culture.

from *God's Promise to His Plantations (1630)*

Quest. What is it for God to plant a people?

Answr. It is a Metaphor taken from young Impes; I will plant them, that is, I will make them to take roote there; and that is, where they and their soyle agree well together, when they are well and sufficiently provided for, as a plant suckes nourishment from the soyle that fitteth it.

Secondly, When hee causeth them to grow as plants doe, in *Psal.* 80. 8, 9, 10, 11. When a man growes like a tree in tallnesse and strength, to more firmnesse and eminency, then hee may be said to be planted.

Thirdly, When God causeth them to *fructifie. Psal.* 1.5.

Fourthly, When he establisheth them there, then he plants, and rootes not up.

But here is something more especiall in this planting; for they were planted before in this land, and yet he promiseth here againe, that he will plant them in their owne land; which doth imply first, That whatever former good estate they had already, he would prosper it, and increase it.

Secondly, God is said to plant a people more especially when they become *Trees of righteousnesse, Isay.* 61.3: That they may be called trees of righteousnesse, the planting of the Lord. So that there is implyed not onely a continuance of their former good estate, but that hee would make them a good people, a choice generation; which he did, first, by planting the Ordinances of God amongst them in a more glorious manner, as he did in *Salomons* time.

2. He would give his people *a naile*, and *a place in his Tabernable, Isay.* 56.5. And that is to give us part in Christ; for so the Temple typified. So then hee plants us when hee gives us roote in Christ.

Thirdly, When he giveth us to *grow up in him as Calves in the stall. Mal.* 4.2, 3.

Fourthly, & to *bring forth much fruit,* Joh. 15.1, 2.

Fifthly, and to continue and abide in the state of grace. This is to plant us in his holy Sanctuary, he not rooting us up.

Reasons. This is taken from the kinde acceptance of *Davids* purpose to build God an house, because he saw it was done in the honesty of his heart, therefore he promiseth to give his people a place wherein they should abide forever as in a house of rest.

Secondly, it is taken from the office God takes upon him, when he is our planter, hee becomes our husbandman; and *if he plants us, who shall plucke us up? Isay.* 27.1, 2. *Job.* 34.29. When he giveth quiet, who can make trouble? If God be the Gardiner, who shall plucke up what he sets down? Every plantation that he hath not planted shall be plucked up, and what he hath planted shall surely be established.

Thirdly, from the nature of the blessing hee conferres upon us: When he promiseth to plant a people, their dayes shall be as the dayes of a Tree, *Isay.* 65.22: As the Oake is said to be an hundred yeares in growing, and an hundred yeares in decaying.

Alexander Whitaker

(1585–1616?)

An Anglican clergyman who came to the newly established colony of Virginia in 1611, Alexander Whitaker served two parishes near James-town until his untimely death by drowning. Good Newes from Virginia was originally prepared as a sermon and constitutes Whitaker's only known published work. Like many colonial sermons that were composed in part to be also read by an audience back in England, it is designed to broaden support for the American colony by providing a favorable description of the country. Indeed, Whitaker's sermon helps inaugurate what one historian has called the "celebrationist tradition" of American writing.

The following selection is particularly notable because of the attitude it displays toward Indian peoples. Urging their conversion to Christianity, it nonetheless sees them as something more than mere subjects for proselytization. While believing them to be "servants of sinne and slaves of the divell," he thinks this only marks their solidarity with the rest of humankind, with whom they share the same common parentage. But rather than dwell exclusively on the miserable condition of these other "sonnes of Adam," whose plight in any case deserves the compassion rather than the contempt of his listeners, Whitaker finds much to admire about American Indians, from their physical prowess, dexterity at arms, and inventions to their enlightened form of government. Possessing "reasonable soules and intellectuall faculties as well as wee," they bear abundant traces of the divine image in which all human beings were made and are thus fully capable of receiving the gospel.

from *Good Newes from Virginia*
(1613)

. . . Let the miserable condition of these naked slaves of the divell move you to compassion toward them. They acknowledge that there is a great good God, but know him not, having the eyes of their understanding as yet blinded: wherefore they serve the divell for feare, after a most base manner, sacrificing sometimes (as I have heere heard) their owne Children to him. I have sent one Image of their god to the Counsell in England, which is painted upon one side of a toad-stoole, much like unto a deformed monster. Their Priests (whom they call Quiokosoughs) are no other but such as our English Witches are. They live naked in bodie, as if their shame of their sinne deserved no covering: Their names are as naked as their bodie: they esteeme it a vertue to lie, deceive and steale as their master the divell teacheth them. Much more might be said of their miserable condition, but I refer the particular narration of these things to some other season. If this bee their life, what thinke you shall become of them after death? but to be partakers with the divell and his angels in hell for evermore. Wherefore my brethren, put on the bowels of compassion, and let the lamentable estate of these miserable people enter in your consideration: One God created us, they have reasonable soules and intellectuall faculties as well as wee; we all have Adam for our common parent: yea, by nature the condition of us both is all one, the servants of sinne and slaves of the divell. Oh remember (I beseech you) what was the state of England before the Gospell was preached in our Countrey? How much better were we then, and concerning our soules health, then these now are? Let the word of the Lord sound out that it may be heard in these parts; and let your faith which is toward God spread it selfe abroad, and shew forth the charitable fruits of it in these barren parts of the world: And let him know that he which hath converted a sinner from going a stray out of his way, shall save a soule from death, and hide a multitude of sinnes.

But if any of us should misdoubt that this barbarous people is uncapable of such heavenly mysteries, let such men know that they are farre mistaken in the nature of these men, for besides the promise of God, which is without respect of persons, made as well to unwise men after the flesh, as to the wise &c. let us not thinke that these men are so simple as some have supposed them: for they are of bodie lustie, strong, and very nimble: they are a very understanding generation, quicke of apprehension, suddaine in their dispatches, subtile in their dealings, exquisite in their inventions, and industrious in their labour.

I suppose the world hath no better markemen with their bow and arrowes then they be; they will kill birds flying, fishes swimming and beasts running; they shoote also with mervailous strength, they shot one of our men being unarmed quite through the bodie, and nailed both his armes to his bodie with one arrow: one of their Children also, about the age of 12. or 13. yeares, killed a bird with his arrow in my sight. The service of their God is answerable to their life, being performed with great feare and attention, and many strange dumb shewes used in the same, stretching forth their limbes and straining their bodie, much like to the counterfeit women in England who faine themselves bewitched, or possessed of some evill spirit.

They stand in great awe of their Quiokosoughs or Priests, which are a generation of vipers even of Sathans owne brood. The manner of their life is much like to the popish Hermits of our age; for they live alone in the woods, in houses sequestred from the common course of men, neither may any man bee suffered to come into their house or to speake with them, but when this Priest doth call him. He taketh no care for his victuals, for all such kinde of things both bread and water, &c. are brought unto a place neere unto his cottage and there are left, which hee fetcheth for his proper neede. If they would have raine, or have lost any thing, they have their recourse to him, who conivreth for them, and many times prevaileth. If they be sicke, he is their Physition, if they bee wounded he sucketh them. At his command they make warre and peace, neither doe they any thing of moment without him. I will not bee teadious in these strange Narrations, when I have more perfectly entered into their secrets, you shall know all. Finally, there is a civill governement amongst them which they strictly observe, and shew thereby that the law of Nature dwelleth in them: for they have a rude kinde of Common-wealth, and rough government, wherein they both honour and obey their Kings, Parents, and Governours, both greater and lesse, they observe the limits of their owne possessions, and incroach not upon their neighbours dwellings. Murther is a capitall crime scarce heard of among them: adultery is the most severely punished, and so are their other offences. These unnurtured grounds of reason in them, may serve to incourage us: to instruct them in the knowledge of the true God, the rewarder of all righteousnesse, not doubting but that he that was powerfull to save us by his word, when we were nothing, will be mercifull also to these sonnes of Adam in his appointed time, in whom there bee remaining so many footsteps of Gods image. . . .

John Winthrop
(1587–1649)

John Winthrop was the first governor of the colony established at
Massachusetts Bay in 1630. Trained as a barrister in England and
eventually appointed attorney to the Court of Wards and Liveries before losing his position to the enmity Charles I bore to Puritans, Winthrop immediately became one of a small group of first-generation
leaders whose strong religious principles greatly influenced the formation of the early American commonwealth and its character. From
Winthrop's Journal it is clear that he saw himself as a latter-day Moses
leading his people to a New World Canaan.

Though not published until 1838, "A Modell of Christian Charity" was delivered as a sermon aboard the Puritans' flagship Arabella
just before the landing in Boston harbor. Its purpose was to define the
social and theological ideal that the Puritans hoped to realize in the
New World. Winthrop saw the Puritan exodus to the New World as
an attempt to build a "City upon a Hill" that might serve as an example to the rest of Western Christendom. This "City," organized as
faithfully as possible according to biblical precept and supported by
the covenant God had originally made with the people of Israel, was
designed to serve as a beacon of hope and inspiration in a world still
struggling to fulfill the injunctions of the Protestant Reformation. Not
least among the distinctive features of this sermon is the claim Winthrop makes for the importance of love itself as the adhesive in this
experiment in community-building. Winthrop argues that the only
force that can knit the people of God together with one another and
their Lord in a community strong and vital enough to become a model
for the rest of the world is the power of charity.

from *A Modell of Christian Charity*
(1630)

A MODELL HEREOF.

God Almightie in his most holy and wise providence hath soe disposed of the Condicion of mankinde, as in all times some must be rich some poore, some highe and eminent in power and dignitie; others meane and in subjeccion.

THE REASON HEREOF.

1. REAS: *First*, to hold conformity with the rest of his workes, being delighted to shewe forthe the glory of his wisdome in the variety and differance of the Creatures and the glory of his power, in ordering all these differences for the preservacion and good of the whole, and the glory of his greatnes that as it is the glory of princes to have many officers, soe this great King will have many Stewards counting himselfe more honoured in dispenceing his guifts to man by man, then if hee did it by his owne immediate hand.

2. REAS: *Secondly*, That he might have the more occasion to manifest the worke of his Spirit: first, upon the wicked in moderateing and restraineing them: soe that the riche and mighty should not eate upp the poore, nor the poore, and dispised rise upp against theire superiours, and shake off theire yoake; 2ly in the regenerate in exerciseing his graces in them, as in the greate ones, theire love mercy, gentlenes, temperance etc., in the poore and inferiour sorte, theire faithe patience, obedience etc:

3. REAS: Thirdly, That every man might have need of other, and from hence they might be all knitt more nearly together in the Bond of brotherly affeccion: from hence it appeares plainely that noe man is made more honourable then another or more wealthy etc., out of any perticuler and singuler respect to himselfe but for the glory of his Creator and the Common good of the Creature, Man; Therefore God still reserves the propperty of these guifts to himselfe as Ezek: 16. 17. he there calls wealthe his gold and his silver etc. Prov: 3.9. He claimes theire service as his due honour the Lord with thy riches etc. All men being thus (by divine providence) rancked into two sortes, riche and poore; under the first, are comprehended all such as are able to live comfortably by theire owne meanes duely improved; and all others,

are poore according to the former distribution. There are two rules whereby wee are to walke one towards another: JUSTICE and MERCY. These are allwayes distinguished in theire Act and in theire obiect, yet may they both concurre in the same Subiect in eache respect; as sometimes there may be an occasion of shewing mercy to a rich man, in some sudden danger of distresse, and allsoe doeing of meere Justice to a poor man in regard of some perticuler contract etc. There is likewise a double Lawe by which wee are regulated in our conversacion one towardes another: in both the former respects, the lawe of nature and the lawe of grace, or the morrall lawe or the lawe of the gospell, to omitt the rule of Justice as not propperly belonging to this purpose otherwise then it may fall into consideracion in some perticuler Cases: By the first of these lawes man as he was enabled soe withall [is] commaunded to love his neighbour as himselfe[1] upon this ground stands all the precepts of the morrall lawe, which concernes our dealings with men. To apply this to the works of mercy this lawe requires two things first that every man afford his help to another in every want or distresse Secondly, That hee performe this out of the same affeccion, which makes him carefull of his owne good according to that of our Saviour Math: [7.12] Whatsoever ye would that men should doe to you. This was practised by Abraham and Lott in entertaineing the Angells and the old man of Gibea.[2]

The Lawe of Grace or the Gospell hath some differance from the former as in these respectes first the lawe of nature was given to man in the estate of innocency; this of the gospell in the estate of regeneracy; 2ly, the former propounds one man to another, as the same fleshe and Image of god, this as a brother in Christ allsoe, and in the Communion of the same spirit and soe teacheth vs to put a difference betweene Christians and others. Doe good to all especially to the household of faith;[3] upon this ground the Israelites were to putt a difference betweene the brethren of such as were strangers though not of the Canaanites. 3ly. The Lawe of nature could give noe rules for dealeing with enemies for all are to be considered as freinds in the estate of innocency, but the Gospell commaunds love to an enemy. proofe. If thine Enemie hunger feede him; Love your Enemies doe good to them that hate you Math: 5.44.

This Lawe of the Gospell propoundes likewise a difference of seasons and occasions there is a time when a christian must sell all and give to the poore as they did in the Apostles times.[4] There is a tyme allsoe when a christian (though they give not all yet) must give beyond theire abillity, as they of Macedonia. Cor: 2.6[5] likewise community of perills calls for extraordinary liberallity and soe doth Community in some speciall service for the Churche. Lastly, when there is noe other meanes whereby our Christian brother may be releived in this distresse, wee must help him beyond our ability, rather then tempt God, in putting him upon help by miraculous or extraordinary meanes. . . .

From hence wee may frame these Conclusions.

1 first all true Christians are of one body in Christ 1. Cor. 12. 12. 13. 17. [27.] Ye are the body of Christ and members of [your?] parte.

2ly. The ligamentes of this body which knitt together are love.

3ly. Noe body can be perfect which wants its propper ligamentes.

4ly. All the partes of this body being thus united are made soe contiguous in a speciall relacion as they must needes partake of each others strength and infirmity, ioy, and sorrowe, weale and woe. 1 Cor: 12. 26. If one member suffers all suffer with it, if one be in honour, all reioyce with it.

5ly. This sensiblenes and Sympathy of each others Condicions will necessarily infuse into each parte a native desire and endeavour, to strengthen defend preserve and comfort the other.

To insist a little on this Conclusion being the product of all the former the truthe hereof will appeare both by precept and patterne i. John. 3. 10. yee ought to lay downe your lives for the brethren Gal: 6. 2. beare ye one anothers burthens and soe fulfill the lawe of Christ. . . .

It rests now to make some application of this discourse by the present designe which gave the occasion of writeing of it. Herein are 4 things to be propounded: first the persons, 2ly, the worke, 3ly, the end, 4ly the meanes.

1. For the persons, wee are a Company professing our selves fellow members of Christ, In which respect onely though wee were absent from eache other many miles, and had our imploymentes as farre distant, yet wee ought to account our selves knitt together by this bond of love, and live in the excercise of it, if wee would have comforte of our being in Christ, this was notorious in the practise of the Christians in former times, as is testified of the Waldenses[6] from the mouth of one of the adversaries Aeneas Sylvius,[7] mutuo [solent amare] penè antequam norint, they use to love any of theire owne religion even before they were acquainted with them.

2ly. for the worke wee have in hand, it is by a mutuall consent through a speciall overruleing providence, and a more then an ordinary approbation of the Churches of Christ to seeke out a place of Cohabitation and Consorteshipp under a due forme of Goverment both civill and ecclesiasticall. In such cases as this the care of the publique must oversway all private respects, by which not onely conscience, but meare Civill pollicy doth binde us; for it is a true rule that perticuler estates cannott subsist in the ruine of the publique.

3ly. The end is to improve our lives to doe more service to the Lord the comforte and encrease of the body of christe whereof wee are members that our selves and posterity may be the better preserved from the Common corrupcions of this evill world to serve the Lord and worke out our Salvacion under the power and purity of his holy Ordinances.

4ly for the meanes whereby this must bee effected, they are 2fold, a Conformity with the worke and end wee aime at, these wee see are extraordinary, therefore wee must not content our selves with usuall ordinary meanes whatsoever wee did or ought to have done when wee lived in England, the same must wee doe and more allsoe where wee goe: That which the most in theire Churches maineteine as a truthe in profession onely, wee must bring into familiar and constant practise, as in this duty of love wee must love brotherly without dissimulation, wee must love one another with a pure hearte fervently wee must beare one anothers burthens, wee must not looke onely on our owne things, but allsoe on the things of our brethren, neither must wee think that the lord will beare with such faileings at our hands as hee dothe from those among whome wee have lived. . . .

Thus stands the cause betweene God and us, wee are entered into Covenant with him for this worke, wee have taken out a Commission, the Lord hath given us leave to drawe our owne Articles wee have professed to enterprise these Accions upon these and these ends, wee have hereupon besought him of favour and blessing: Now if the Lord shall please to heare us, and bring us in peace to the place wee desire, then hath hee ratified this Covenant and sealed our Commission, [and] will expect a strickt performance of the Articles contained in it, but if wee shall neglect the observacion of these Articles which are the ends wee have propounded, and dissembling with our God, shall fall to embrace this present world and prosecute our carnall intencions, seekeing great things for our selves and our posterity, the Lord will surely breake out in wrathe against us be revenged of such a periured people and make us knowe the price of the breache of such a Covenant.

Now the onely way to avoyde this shipwracke and to provide for our posterity is to followe the Counsell of Micah, to doe Justly, to love mercy, to walke humbly with our God,[8] for this end, wee must be knitt together in this worke as one man, wee must entertaine each other in brotherly Affeccion, wee must be willing to abridge our selves of our superfluities, for the supply of others necessities, wee must uphold a familiar Commerce together in all meekenes, gentlenes, patience and liberallity, wee must delight in eache other, make others Condicions our owne reioyce together, mourne together, labour, and suffer together, allwayes haveing before our eyes our Commission and Community in the worke, our Community as members of the same body, soe shall wee keepe the unitie of the spirit in the bond of peace,[9] the Lord will be our God and delight to dwell among us, as his owne people and will commaund a blessing upon us in all our wayes, soe that wee shall see much more of his wisdome power goodnes and truthe then formerly wee have beene acquainted with, wee shall finde that the God of Israell is among us, when tenn of us shall be able to resist a thousand of our enemies, when hee shall make us a prayse and glory, that men shall say of succeeding plantacions: the lord make it like that of New England: for wee must Consider that wee shall be as a Citty upon a Hill,[10] the eies of all people are uppon us; soe that if wee shall deale falsely with our god in this worke wee have undertaken and soe cause him to withdrawe his present help from us, wee shall be made a story and a by-word through the world, wee shall open the mouthes of enemies to speake evill of the wayes of god and all professours for Gods sake; wee shall shame the faces of many of gods worthy servants, and cause theire prayers to be turned into Cursses upon us till wee be consumed out of the good land whether wee are goeing: And to shutt upp this discourse with that exhortacion of Moses that faithfull servant of the Lord in his last farewell to Israell Deut. 30. Beloved there is now sett before us life, and good, deathe and evill in that wee are Commaunded this day to love the Lord our God, and to love one another to walke in his wayes and to keepe his Commaundements and his Ordinance, and his lawes, and the Articles of our Covenant with him that wee may live and be multiplyed, and that the Lord our God may blesse us in the land whether wee goe to possesse it: But if our heartes shall turne away soe that wee will not obey, but shall be seduced and worshipp [serve *cancelled*] other Gods our pleasures, and proffitts, and serve them; it is propounded unto us this day, wee shall surely perishe out of the good Land whether wee passe over this vast Sea to possesse it;

> Therefore lett us choose life,
>   that wee, and our Seede,
>   may live; by obeyeing his
> voyce, and cleaveing to him,
>   for he is our life, and
>   our prosperity.

John Winthrop's Christian Experience (1637)

In my youth I was very lewdly disposed, inclining unto and attempting (so far as my yeares enabled mee) all kind of wickednesse, except swearing and scorning religion, which I had no temptation unto in regard of my education. About ten years of age, I had some notions of God, for in some great frighting or danger, I have prayed unto God, and have found manifest answer; the remembrance whereof many yeares after made mee think that God did love mee, but it made mee no whit the better:

After I was 12. yeares old, I began to have some more savour of Religion, and I thought I had more understanding in Divinity then many of my yeares; for in reading of some good books I conceived, that I did know divers of those points before, though I knew not how I should come by such knowledge (but since I perceived it was out of some logicall principles, whereby out of some things I could conclude others) yet I was still very wild, and dissolute, and as years came on my lusts grew stronger, but yet under some restraint of my naturall reason; whereby I had the command of my self that I could turne into any form. I would as occasion required write letters etc. of meer vanity; and if occasion were I could write others of savory and godly counsell.

About 14 years of age, being in Cambridge[1] I fell into a lingring feaver, which took away the comfort of my life. For being there neglected, and despised, I went up and down mourning with myself; and being deprived of my youthfull joyes, I betook my self to God whom I did believe to bee very good and mercifull, and would welcome any that would come to him, especially such a yongue soule, and so well qualifyed as I took my self to bee; so as I took pleasure in drawing neer to him. But how my heart was affected with my sins, or what thoughts I had of Christ I remember not. But I was willing to love God, and therefore I thought hee loved mee. But so soon as I recovered my perfect health, and met with somewhat els to take pleasure in, I forgot my former acquaintance with God, and fell to former lusts, and grew worse then before. Yet some good moodes I had now, and then, and sad checks of my naturall Conscience, by which the Lord preserved mee from some foule sins, which otherwise I had fallen into. But my lusts were so masterly as no good could fasten upon mee, otherwise then to hold mee to some task of ordinary dutyes for I cared for nothing but how to satisfy my voluptuous heart.

About 18 yeares of age (being a man in stature, and in understanding as my parents conceived mee) I married into a family under

Mr. Culverwell his ministry in Essex; and living there sometimes I first found the ministry of the word to come to my heart with power (for in all before I found onely light) and after that I found the like in the ministry of many others. So as there began to bee some change which I perceived in my self, and others took notice of. Now I began to come under strong excersises of Conscience: (yet by fits only) I could no longer dally with Religion. God put my soule to sad tasks sometimes, which yet the flesh would shake off, and outweare still. I had withall many sweet invitations which I would willingly have intertained, but the flesh would not give up her interest. The mercifull Lord would not thus bee answered, but notwithstanding all my stubbornesse, and unkind rejections of mercy, hee left mee not till hee had overcome my heart to give up itself to him, and to bid farewell to all the world, and untill my heart could answer, Lord what wilt thou have mee to doe?

Now came I to some peace and comfort in God and in his wayes, my cheif delight was therein, I loved a Christian, and the very ground hee went upon. I honoured a faythfull minister in my heart and could have kissed his feet: Now I grew full of zeal (which outranne my knowledge and carried mee sometimes beyond my calling) and very liberall to any good work. I had an unsatiable thirst after the word of God and could not misse a good sermon, though many miles off, especially of such as did search deep into the conscience. I had also a great striveing in my heart to draw others to God. It pittyed my heart to see men so little to regard their soules, and to despise that happines which I knew to bee better then all the world besides, which stirred mee up to take any opportunity to draw men to God, and by successe in my endeavors I took much encouragement hereunto. But those affections were not constant but very unsetled. By these occasions I grew to bee of some note for religion (which did not a little puffe me up) and divers would come to mee for advice in cases of conscience; and if I heard of any that were in trouble of mind I usually went to comfort them; so that upon the bent of my spirit this way and the successe I found of my endeavors, I gave up my selfe to the study of Divinity, and intended to enter into the ministry, if my friends had not diverted mee.

But as I grew into employment and credit thereby; so I grew also in pride of my guifts, and under temptations which sett mee on work to look to my evidence more narrowly then I had done before (for the great change which God had wrought in mee, and the generall approbation of good ministers and other Christians, kept mee from makeing any great question of my good estate, though my secrett corruptions, and some tremblings of heart (which was greatest when I was among the most Godly persons) put me to some plunges; but especially when I perceived a great decay in my zeale and love, etc.) And hearing sometimes of better assurance by the seale of the spirit, which I also knew by the word of God, but could not, nor durst say that ever I had it; and finding by reading of Mr. Perkins[2] and other books that a reprobate might (in appearance) attaine to as much as I had done: finding withall much hollownes and vaine glory in my heart, I began to grow very sad, and knew not what to doe, I was ashamed to open my case to any minister that knew mee; I feared it would shame my self and religion also, that such an eminent professour as I was accounted, should discover such corruptions as I found in my selfe, and had in all this time attained no better evidence of salvation; and I should prove a hypocrite it was too late to begin anew: I should never repent in truth having repented, so oft as I had done. It was like hell to mee to think of that in Hebr: 6. Yet I should sometimes propound questions afarre off to such of the most Godly ministers as I mett, which gave mee ease for the present, but my heart could not find where to rest; but I grew very sad, and melancholy; and now to hear others applaud mee was a dart through my liver; for still I feared I was not sound at the root, and sometimes I had thoughts of breaking from my profession, and proclaiming myself an Hipocrite. But those troubles came not all at once but by fits, for sometimes I should find refreshing in prayer, and sometimes in the love that I had had to the Saints: which though it were but poor comfort (for I durst not say before the Lord that I did love them in truth) yet the Lord upheld mee, and many times outward occasions put these feares out of my thoughts. And though I had knowne long before the Doctrine of free Justification by Christ and had often urged it upon my owne soul and others, yet I could not close with Christ to my satisfaction. I have many times striven to lay hold upon Christ in some promise and have brought forth all the arguments that I had for my part in it. But instead of finding it to bee mine, I have lost sometimes the fayth of the very general truth of the promise, sometimes after much striveing by prayer for fayth in Christ, I have thought I had received some power to apply Christ unto my soule: but it was so doubtfull as I could have little comfort in it, and it soon vanished.

Upon these and the like troubles, when I could by no meanes attaine sure and setled peace; and that which I did get was still broken off upon every infirmity; I concluded there was no way to help it, but by walking more close with God and more strict observation of all dutyes; and hereby though I put myself to many a needlesse task, and deprived my self of many lawfull comforts, yet my peace would fayle upon every small occasion, and I was held long under great bondage to the Law (sinne, and humble myself; and sinne, and to humiliation again, and so day after day) yet neither got strength to my Sanctification nor betterd my Evidence, but was brought to such bondage, as

I durst not use any recreation, nor meddle with any worldly businesse etc.: for feare of breaking my peace (which even such as it was, was very preteous to mee) but this would not hold neither, for then I grew very melancholy and mine own thoughts wearied mee, and wasted my spirits.

While I wandred up and downe in this sad and doubtful estate (wherein yet I had many intermissions, for the flesh would often shake off this yoake of the law, but was still forced to come under it again) wherein my greatest troubles were not the sense of Gods wrath or fear of damnation, but want of assurance of salvation, and want of strength against my corruptions; I knew that my greatest want was fayth in Christ, and faine would I have been united to Christ but I thought I was not holy enough. I had many times comfortable thoughts about him in the word prayer, and meditation, but they gave mee no satisfaction but brought mee lower in mine own eyes, and held mee still to a constant use of all meanes, in hope of better thinges to come. Sometimes I was very confident that hee had given mee a hungring and thirsting soule after Christ and therefore would surely satisfy mee in his good time. Sometimes againe I was ready to entertaine secret murmurings that all my paines and prayers etc. should prevayle no more: but such thoughts were soon rebuked: I found my heart still willing to justify God. Yea I was perswaded I should love him though hee should cast mee off.

Being in this condition it pleased the Lord in my family exercise to manifest unto mee the difference between the Covenant of grace, and the Covenant of workes (but I took the foundation of that of workes to have been with man in innocency, and onely held forth in the law of Moses to drive us to Christ). This Covenant of grace began to take great impression in mee and I thought I had now enough: To have Christ freely, and to bee justifyed freely was very sweet to mee; and upon sound warrant (as I conceived) but I could not say with any confidence, it had been sealed to mee, but I rather took occasion to bee more remisse in my spirituall watch, and so more loose in my conversation.

I was now about 30 yeares of age, and now was the time come that the Lord would reveale Christ unto mee whom I had long desired, but not so earnestly as since I came to see more clearly into the covenant of free grace. First therefore hee laid a sore affliction upon mee wherein hee laid mee lower in myne owne eyes then at any time before, and showed mee the emptines of all my guifts, and parts; left mee neither power nor will, so as I became as a weaned child. I could now no more look at what I had been or what I had done nor bee discontented for want of strength or assurance mine eyes were onely upon his free mercy in Jesus Christ. I knew I was worthy of nothing for I knew I could doe nothing for him or for my selfe. I could only mourn, and weep to think of free mercy to such a vile wretch as I was. Though I had no power to apply it yet I felt comfort in it. I did not long continue in this estate, but the good spirit of the Lord breathed upon my soule, and said I should live. Then every promise I thought upon held forth Christ unto me saying I am thy salvation. Now could my soule close with Christ, and rest there with sweet content, so ravished with his love, as I desired nothing nor feared anything, but was filled with joy unspeakable, and glorious and with a spirit of Adoption. Not that I could pray with more fervency or more enlargement of heart than sometimes before, but I could now cry my father with more confidence. Mee thought this condition and that frame of heart which I had after, was in respect of the former like the reigne of Solomon, free, peaceable, prosperous and glorious, the other more like that of Ahaz, full of troubles, feares and abasements. And the more I grew thus acquainted with the spirit of God the more were my corruptions mortifyed, and the new man quickened: the world, the flesh and Satan were for a time silent, I heard not of them: but they would not leave mee so. This Estate lasted a good time (divers months), but not alwayes alike, but if my comfort, and joy slackened a while, yet my peace continued, and it would returne with advantage. I was now growne familiar with the Lord Jesus Christ, hee would oft tell mee he loved mee, I did not doubt to believe him; If I went abroad hee went with mee, when I returned hee came home with mee. I talked with him upon the way, hee lay down with mee and usually I did awake with him. Now I could goe into any company and not loose him: and so sweet was his love to mee as I desired nothing but him in heaven or earth.

This Estate would not hold neither did it decline suddainly but by degrees. And though I found much spirituall strength in it, yet I could not discerne but my hunger after the word of God, and my love to the Saints had been as great (if not more) in former times. One reason might bee this, I found that the many blemishes and much hollow heartednesse which I discerned in many professors, had weakned the esteem of a Christian in my heart. And for my comfort in Christ, as worldly imployments, and the love of temporall things did steal away my heart from him so would his sweet countenance bee withdrawne from mee. But in such a condition hee would not long leave mee, but would still recall mee by some word or affliction or in prayer or meditation, and I should then bee as a man awakened out of a dreame or as if I had been another man. And then my care was (not so much to get pardon for that was sometimes sealed to mee while I was purposing to goe seek it, and yet sometimes I could not obtaine it without seeking and wayteing also but) to mourn for my ingratitude towards my God, and his free, and rich mercy. The consideration whereof would break my heart more, and wring more teares from myne eyes, then ever the fear of Damnation or any affliction had done; so as many times and to this very day a thought of Christ Jesus, and free grace bestowed on mee melts my heart that I cannot refraine.

Since this time I have gone under continuall conflicts between the flesh and the spirit, and sometimes with Satan himself (which I have more discerned of late then I did formerly) many falls I have had, and have lyen long under some, yet never quite forsaken of the Lord. But still when I have been put to it by any suddaine danger or fearefull temptation, the good spirit of the Lord hath not fayled to beare witnesse to mee, giveing mee comfort, and courage in the very pinch, when of my self I have been very fearefull, and dismayed. My usuall falls have been through dead heartedness, and presumptuousnesse, by which Satan hath taken advantage to wind mee into other sinnes. When the flesh prevayles the spirit withdrawes, and is sometimes so greived as hee seemes not to acknowledge his owne work. Yet in my worst times hee hath been pleased to stirre, when hee would not speak, and would yet support mee that my fayth hath not fayled utterly. . . .

William Bradford
(1590–1657)

William Bradford was among the first group of Pilgrims who arrived
in America aboard the Mayflower in 1620. Undisputed leader of the
Plymouth colony during much of its early history, he served for almost
thirty years as its governor. Bradford began to write his history of the
plantation about 1630, but he did not complete it until 1651. The text
was subsequently lost and did not turn up until the nineteenth century.

Of Plymouth Plantation is a theological history of the first New
England settlement. To Bradford the destiny of the colony was guided
by divine Providence, and he believed that the history of the colony
would arouse in the minds and hearts of his readers the same sense of
inspiration and thanksgiving that had filled the hearts and minds of
its principal actors. His narrative includes many striking and representative images: the plight of the Pilgrims waiting in Holland for an
opportunity to sail, as circumstances became more and more difficult
and time began to grow short for the older members of the community; the mixture of hope and dread with which the Pilgrims faced the
prospect of a dangerous crossing to an unknown land; the courageous
realism of the Pilgrims in assessing their chances of survival and success; the unwelcoming aspect of their new home when they first
reached the shores of America; the heavy toll in suffering and death
endured during the earliest months in the New World; the quiet her-
oism and devotion of the few unstricken Pilgrims who nursed the colony through its first winter of sickness and despair; the decency and
cordiality of their first contacts with the indigenous population, etc.
The book also furnishes some counter-images of Pilgrim intolerance
and confusion, as in Bradford's severe response to the carnivalesque

*atmosphere of Thomas Morton's experiment at Merrymount and his
distress at the spectacle of wickedness breaking out in the community.
Nevertheless, with his vivid and moving account of the Pilgrims' arrival in America, Bradford planted some of the most durable images
in terms of which Americans have defined themselves and their cultural
project: of America itself as a kind of last chance for mankind; of the
American adventure as a voyage into the unknown and the untried;
of the American people as a community knit together by suffering and
upheld by a sense of hope tempered with an understanding of always
threatening defeat; and of the American experience itself as a grappling
with adversity and dissension.*

from *Of Plymouth Plantation*
(1630–1651)

And first of the occasion and inducements thereunto; the which that I
may truly unfold, I must begin at the very root and rise of the same.
The which I shall endeavor to manifest in a plain style, with singular
regard unto the simple truth in all things, at least as near as my slender
judgement can attain the same.

FROM CHAPTER I
[THE SEPARATIST INTERPRETATION OF
THE REFORMATION IN ENGLAND,
1550–1607]

But that I may come more near my intendment; when as by the travail
and diligence of some godly and zealous preachers, and God's blessing
on their labors, as in other places of the land, so in the North parts,
many became enlightened by the word of God, and had their ignorance
and sins discovered unto them, and began by his grace to reform their
lives, and make conscience of their ways, the work of God was no
sooner manifest in them, but presently they were both scoffed and
scorned by the profane multitude, and the ministers urged with the
yoke of subscription, or else must be silenced; and the poor people
were so vexed with apparitors, and pursuants,[1] and the commissary
courts, as truly their affliction was not small; which, notwithstanding,

they bore sundry years with much patience, till they were occasioned (by the continuance and increase of these troubles, and other means which the Lord raised up in those days) to see further into things by the light of the world of God. How not only these base and beggarly ceremonies were unlawful, but also that the lordly and tyrannous power of the prelates ought not to be submitted unto; which thus, contrary to the freedom of the gospel, would load and burden men's consciences, and by their compulsive power make a profane mixture of persons and things in the worship of God. . . .

So many therefore of these professors as saw the evil of these things, in these parts, and whose hearts the Lord had touched with heavenly zeal for his truth, they shook off this yoke of antichristian bondage, and as the Lord's free people, joined themselves (by a covenant of the Lord) into a church estate, in the fellowship of the gospel, to walk in all his ways, made known, or to be made known, unto them, according to their best endeavors, whatsoever it would cost them, the Lord assisting them. And that it cost them something this ensuing history will declare. . . .

But after these things they could not long continue in any peaceable condition, but were hunted and persecuted on every side, so as their former afflictions were but as flea-bittings in comparison of these which now came upon them. For some were taken and clapped up in prison, others had their houses beset and watched night and day, and hardly escaped their hands; and the most were fain to fly and leave their houses and habitations, and the means of their livelihood. Yet these and many other sharper things which afterward befell them, were no other than they looked for, and therefore were the better prepared to bear them by the assistance of God's grace and spirit. Yet seeing themselves thus molested, and that there was no hope of their continuance there, by a joint consent they resolved to go into the Low Countries, where they hear was freedom of Religion for all men; as also how sundry from London, and other parts of the land, had been exiled and persecuted for the same cause, and were gone thither, and lived at Amsterdam, and in other places of the land. So after they had continued together about a year, and kept their meetings every Sabbath in one place or other, exercising the worship of God amongst themselves, notwithstanding all the diligence and malice of their adversaries, they seeing they could no longer continue in the condition, they resolved to get over into Holland as they could. . . .

FROM CHAPTER II
[OF THEIR DEPARTURE TO HOLLAND
AND THE TROUBLES AND DIFFICULTIES
THEY MET WITH THERE. ANNO 1608]

Being thus constrained to leave their native soil and country, their lands and livings, and all their friends and familiar acquaintance, it was much, and thought marvelous by many. But to go into a country they knew not (but by hearsay), where they must learn a new language, and get their livings they knew not how, it being a dear place, and subject to the miseries of war, it was by many thought an adventure almost desperate, a case intolerable, and a misery worse than death. Especially seeing they were not acquainted with trades nor traffic, (by which the country doth subsist,) but had only been used to a plain country life, and the innocent trade of husbandry. But these things did not dismay them (though they did sometimes trouble them) for their desires were set on the ways of God, and to enjoy his ordinances; but they rested on his providence, and knew whom they had believed. Yet this was not all, for though they could not say, yet were they not suffered to go, but the ports and havens were shut against them, so as they were fain to seek secret means of conveyance, and to bribe and fee the mariners, and give extraordinary rates for their passages. And yet were they often times betrayed (many of them), and both they and their goods intercepted and surprised, and thereby put to great trouble and charge, of which I will given an instance or two, and omit the rest. . . .

FROM CHAPTER III
[OF THEIR SETTLEMENT IN HOLLAND
AND THEIR LIFE THERE]

Being now come into the Low Countries, they saw many goodly and fortified cities, strongly walled and guarded with troops of armed men. Also they heard a strange and uncouth language, and beheld them different manners and customs of the people, with their strange fashions and attires; all so far differing from that of their plain country villages (wherein they were bred, and had so long lived) as it seemed they were come into a new world. But these were not the things they most looked on, nor long took up their thoughts; for they had other work in hand, and an other kind of war to wage and maintain. For though they saw fair and beautiful cities, flowing with abundance of all sort of wealth and riches, yet it was not long before they saw the grim and grizzly face of poverty coming upon them like an armed man,[2] with whom they must buckle and encounter, and from whom they could not fly; but they were armed with faith and patience against him, and all his encounters; and though they were sometimes foiled, yet by God's assistance they prevailed and got the victory. . . .

FROM CHAPTER IV
[ON THE REASONS AND CAUSES
OF THEIR REMOVAL]

After they had lived in this city[3] about some 11 or 12 years (which is the more observable being the whole time of that famous truce between that state and the Spaniards,)[4] and sundry of them were taken away by death, and many others began to be well striken in years, the grave mistress Experience having taught them many things, those prudent governors with sundry of the sagest members began both deeply to apprehend their present dangers, and wisely to foresee the future and think of timely remedy. In the agitation of their thoughts, and much discourse of things hereabout, at length they began to incline to this conclusion, of removal to some other place. Not out of any newfangledness, or other such like giddy humor, by which men are oftentimes transported to their great hurt and danger, but for sundry weighty and solid reasons; some of the chief of which I hear briefly touch.

And first, they saw and found by experience the hardness of their place and country to be such, as few in comparison would come to them, and fewer what would bide it out, and continue with them. For many that came to them, and many more that desired to be with them, could not endure that great labor and hard fare, with other inconveniences which they underwent and were contented with. But though they loved their persons, approved their cause, and honored their sufferings, yet they left them as it were weeping, as Orpah did her mother-in-law Naomi,[5] or as those Romans did Cato in Utica, who desired to be excused and borne with, though they could not all be Catoes. For many, though they desired to enjoy the ordinances of God in their purity, and the liberty of the gospel with them, yet, alas, they admitted of bondage, with danger of conscience, rather than to endure these hardships; yea some preferred and chose the prisons in England, rather than this liberty in Holland, with these afflictions. But it was thought that if a better and easier place of living could be had, it would draw many, and take away these discouragements. Yea, their pastor would often say, that many of those who both wrote and preached now against them, if they were in a place where they might have liberty and live comfortably, they would then practise as they did.

Secondly; they say that though the people generally bore all these difficulties very cheerfully, and with a resolute courage, being in the best and strength of their years, yet old age began to steal on many of them, (and their great and continual labors, with other crosses and sorrows, hastened it before the time,) so as it was not only probably thought, but apparently seen, that within a few years more they would be in danger to scatter, by necessities pressing then, or sink under their burdens, or both. And therefore according to the divine proverb, let a wiser man seeth the plague when it cometh, and hideth himself, Proverbs xxii.3, so they like skillful and beaten [experienced] soldiers were fearful either to be entrapped or surrounded by their enemies, so as they should neither be able to fight nor fly; and therefore thought it better to dislodge betimes to some place of better advantage and less danger, if any such could be found.

Thirdly; as necessity was a taskmaster over them, so they were forced to be such, not only to their servants, but in a sort, to their dearest children; the which as it did not a little wound the tender hearts of many a loving father and mother, so it produced likewise sundry sad and sorrowful effects. For many of their children, that were of best dispositions and gracious inclinations, having learned to bear the yoke of their youth,[6] and willing to bear part of their parents burden, were, oftentimes, so oppressed with the heavy labors, that though their minds were free and willing, yet their bodies bowed under the weight of the same, and became decrepit in their early youth; the vigor of nature being consumed in their very bud as it were. But that which was more lamentable, and of all sorrows most heavy to be borne, was that many of their children, by these occasions, and the great licentiousness of youth in that country, and the manifold temptations of the place, were drawn away by evil examples into extravagant and dangerous courses, getting the reins off their necks, and departing from their parents. Some became soldiers, others took upon them far voyages by sea, and others some worse courses, tending to dissoluteness and the danger of their souls, to the great grief of their parents and dishonor of God. So that they saw their posterity would be in danger to degenerate and be corrupted.

Lastly, (and which was not least), a great hope and inward zeal they had of laying some good foundation, or at least to make some way thereunto, for the propagations and advancing the gospel of the kingdom of Christ in those remote parts of the world; yea, though they should be but even as stepping-stones unto others for the performing of so great a work.

These, and some other like reasons, moved them to undertake this resolution of their removal; the which they afterward prosecuted with so great difficulties, as the sequel will appear.

The place they had thoughts on was some of those vast and unpeopled countries of America, which are fruitful and fit for habitation, being devoid of all civil inhabitants, where there are only savage and brutish men, which range up and down, little otherwise than the wild beasts of the same. This proposition being made public and coming to the scanning of all, it raised many variable opinions amongst men, and caused many fears and doubts amongst themselves. Some, from their reasons and hopes conceived, labored to stir up and encourage the rest to undertake and prosecute the same; others, again, out of their fears, objected against it, and sought to divert from it, alleging many things, and those neither unreasonable nor unprobable; as that it was a great design, and subject to many unconceivable perils and dangers; as, besides the casualties of the seas (which none can be free from) the length of the voyage was such, as the weak bodies of women and other persons worn out with age and travail (as many of them were) would never be able to endure. And yet if they should, the miseries of the land which they should be exposed unto, would be hard to be borne; and likely, some or all of them together, to consume and utterly to ruinate them. For there they should be liable to famine, and nakedness and the want, in a manner, of all things. The change of air, diet, and drinking of water, would infect their bodies with sore sicknesses, and grievous diseases. And also those which should escape and overcome these difficulties, should yet be in continual danger of the savage people, who are cruel, barbarous, and most treacherous, being more furious in their rage, and merciless where they overcome; not being content only to kill, and take away life, but delight to torment men in their most bloody manner that may be; flaying some alive with the shells of fishes, cutting of the members and joints of others by piecemeal, and broiling on the coals, eat the collops [fatty folds] of their flesh in their sight whilst they live; with other cruelties horrible to be related. And surely it could not be thought but the very hearing of these things could not but move the very bowels of men to grate within them, and make the weak to quake and tremble. It was further objected, that it would require greater sums of money to furnish such a voyage, and to fit them with necessaries, than their consumed estates would amount to; and yet they must as well look to be seconded with supplies, as presently to be transported. Also many precedents of ill success, and lamentable miseries befallen others in the like designs, were easy to be found, and not forgotten to be alleged; and besides their own experience, in their former troubles and hardships in their removal into Holland, and how hard a thing it was for them to live in that strange place, though it was a neighbor country, and a civil and rich commonwealth.

It was answered, that all great and honorable actions are accompanied with great difficulties, and must be both enterprised and overcome with answerable courages. It was granted the dangers were great, but not desperate; the difficulties were many, but not invincible. For though their were many of them likely, yet they were not certain; it might be sundry of the things feared might never befall; others by provident care and the use of good means, might in a great measure be prevented; and all of them, through the help of God, by fortitude and patience, might either be borne, or overcome. True it was, that such attempts were not to be made and undertaken without good ground and reason; not rashly or lightly as many have done for curiosity or hope of gain, etc. But their condition was not ordinary; their ends were good and honorable; their calling lawful, and urgent; and therefore they might expect the blessing of God in their proceeding. Yea, though they should lose their lives in this action, yet might they have comfort in the same, and their endeavors would be honorable. They lived here but as men in exile, and in a poor condition; as great miseries might possibly befall them in this place, for the 12 years of truce were not out, and there was nothing but beating of drums, and preparing for war, the events whereof are always uncertain. The Spaniard might prove as cruel as the savages of America, and the famine and pestilence as sore here as there, and their liberty less to look out for remedy. After many other particular things answered and alleged on both sides, it was fully concluded by the major part, to put this design in execution, and to prosecute it by the best means they could.

FROM CHAPTER IX
[OF THEIR VOYAGE,
AND HOW THEY PASSED THE SEA,
AND OF THEIR SAFE ARRIVAL
AT CAPE COD]

Sept. 6. These troubles being blown over, and now all being compact together in one ship, they put to sea again with a prosperous wind, which continued divers days together, which was some encouragement unto them; yet according to the usual manner many were afflicted with sea-sickness. And I may not omit here a special work of God's providence. There was a proud and very profane young man, one of the sea-men, of a lusty, able body, which made him the more haughty; he would always be contemning the poor people in their sickness, and cursing them daily with grievous execrations, and did not let to tell them, that he hoped to help to cast half of them overboard before they came to their journeys end, and to make merry with what they had; and if he were by any gently reproved, he would curse and swear most bitterly. But it pleased God before they came half seas over, to smite this young man with a grievous disease, of which he died in a desperate manner, and so was himself the first that was thrown overboard. Thus his curses light on his own head; and it was an astonishment to all his fellows, for they noted it to be the just hand of God upon him.

After they had enjoyed fair winds and weather for a season, they were encountered many times with cross winds, and met with many fierce storms, with which the ship was shrewdly shaken, and her upper works made very leaky; and one of the main beams in the mid ships was bowed and cracked, which put them in some fear that the ship could not be able to perform the voyage. So some of the chief of the company, perceiving the mariners to fear the sufficiency of the ship, as appeared by their mutterings, they entered into serious consultation with the master and other officers of the ship, to consider in time of the danger; and rather to return than to cast themselves into a desperate and inevitable peril. And truly there was great distraction and difference of opinion amongst the mariners themselves; fain would they do what could be done for their wages' sake, (being now half the sea over,) and on the other hand they were loath to hazard their lives too desperately. But in examining of all opinions, the master and others affirmed they knew the ship to be strong and firm under water; and for the buckling of the main beam, there was a great iron screw the passengers brought out of Holland, which would raise the beam into his place; the which being done, the carpenter and the master affirmed that with a post put under it, set firm in the lower deck, and otherways bound, he would make it sufficient. And as for the decks and upper works they would caulk them as well as they could, and thought with the working of the ship they would not long keep staunch [watertight] yet there would otherwise be no great danger, if they did not overpress her with sails. So they committed themselves to the will of God, and resolved to proceed. . . .

But to omit other things (that I may be brief,) after long beating at sea they fell with that land which is called Cape Cod; the which being made and certainly known to be it, they were not a little joyful. After some deliberation had amongst themselves and with the master of the ship, they tacked about and resolved to stand for the southward (the wind and weather being fair) to find some place about Hudson's River for their habitation. But after they had sailed the course about half the day, they fell amongst dangerous shoals and roaring breakers, and they were so far entangled therewith as they conceived themselves in great danger; and the wind shrinking upon them withal, they resolved to bear up again for the Cape, and thought themselves happy to get out of those dangers before night overtook them, as by God's providence they did. And the next day they got into the Cape-harbor[7] where they rid in safety. . . .

Being thus arrived in good harbor and brought safe to land, they fell upon their knees and blessed the God of heaven, who had brought them over the vast and furious ocean, and delivered them from all the perils and miseries thereof, again to set their feet on the firm and stable earth, their proper element. And no marvel if they were thus joyful, seeing wise Seneca[8] was so affected with sailing a few miles on the coast of his own Italy; as he affirmed, that he had rather remain twenty years on his way by land, than pass by sea to any place in a short time; so tedious and dreadful was the same unto him.

But here I cannot but stay and make a pause, and stand half amazed at this poor peoples present condition; and so I think will the reader too, when he well considers the same. Being thus passed the vast ocean, and a sea of troubles before in their preparation (as may be remembered by the which went before), they had now no friends to welcome them, nor inns to entertain or refresh their weather-beaten bodies, no houses or much less towns to repair to, to seek for succor. It is recorded in Scripture as a mercy to the apostle and his shipwrecked company, that the barbarians shewed them no small kindness in refreshing them, but these savage barbarians, when they met with them (as after will appear) were readier to fill their sides full of arrows than otherwise. And for the season it was winter, and they that know the winters of that country know them to be sharp and violent, and subject to cruel and fierce storms, dangerous to travel to known places, much more to search an unknown coast. Besides, what could they see but a hideous and desolate wilderness, full of wild beasts and wild men? And what multitudes there might be of them they knew not. Nether could they, as it were, go up to the top of Pisgah,[9] to view from this wilderness a more goodly country to feed their hopes; for which way soever they turned their eyes (save upward to the heavens) they could have little solace or content in respect of any outward objects. For summer being done, all things stand upon them with a weather-beaten face; and the whole country, full of woods and thickets, represented a wild and savage hue. If they looked behind them, there was the mighty ocean which they had passed, and was now as a main bar and gulf to separate them from all the civil parts of the world. If it be said they had a ship to succor them, it is true; but what heard they daily from the master and company? But that with speed they should look out a place with their shallop,[10] where they would be at some near distance; for the season was such as he would not stir from thence till a safe harbor was discovered by them, where they could be, and he might go without danger; and that victuals consumed apace, but he must and would keep sufficient for themselves and their return. Yea, it was uttered by some, that if they got not a place in time, they would turn them and their goods ashore and leave them. Let it also be considered what weak hopes of supply and succor they left behind them, that might bear up their minds in this sad condition and trial they were under; and they could not but be very small. It is true, indeed, the affection and love of their brethren at Leyden was cordial and entire towards them, but they had little power to help them, or themselves; and how the case stood between them and the merchants at their coming away, hath already been declared. What could now sustain them but the spirit of God and his grace? May not and ought not the children of these fathers rightly say: "Our fathers were Englishmen which came over this great ocean, and were ready to perish in this wilderness; but they cried unto the Lord, and he heard their voice, and looked on their adversity, etc." "Let them therefore praise the Lord, because he is good, and his mercies endure forever. Yea, let them which have been redeemed of the Lord, show how he has delivered them from the hand of the oppressor. When they wandered in the desert wilderness out of the way, and found no city to dwell in, both hungry, and thirsty, their soul was overwhelmed in them. Let them confess before the Lord his loving-kindness, and his wonderful works before the sons of men."[11]

FROM CHAPTER XI
[THE REMAINDER OF ANNO 1620]

I shall return back and begin with a combination made by them before they came ashore, being the first foundation of their government in this place;[12] occasioned partly by the discontented and mutinous speeches that some of the strangers amongst them had let fall from them in the ship—That when they came ashore they would use their own liberty; for none had power to command them, the patent they had being for Virginia, and not for New England, which belonged to an other Government, with which the Virginia Company had nothing to do. And partly what such an act by them done (this their condition considered) might be as firm as any patent, and in some respects more sure.

The form was as followeth.

In the name of god, Amen. We whose names are underwritten, the loyal subjects of our dread sovereign Lord, King James, by the grace of God, of Great Britain, France, and Ireland king, defender of the faith, etc., having undertaken, for the glory of God, and advancement of the Christian faith, and honor of our kind and country, a voyage to plant the first colony in the Northern parts of Virginia, do by these presents solemnly and mutually in the presence of God, and one of another, covenant and combine ourselves together into a civil body politic, for our better ordering and preservation and furtherance of the ends aforesaid; and by virtue hereof to enact, constitute, and frame such just and equal laws, ordinances, acts, constitutions, and offices, from time to time, as shall be thought most meet and convenient and the general good of the Colony, unto which we promise all due submission and obedience. In witness whereof we have hereunder subscribed our names at Cape Cod the 11th of November, in the year of the reign of our sovereign lord, King James, of England, France, and Ireland the eighteenth, and of Scotland the fifty fourth. Anno Domini 1620.

After this they chose, or rather confirmed, Mr. John Carver (a man godly and well approved amongst them) their Governor for that year. And after they had provided a place for their goods, or common store, (which were long in unloading for want of boats, foulness of winter weather, and sickness of divers,) and begun some small cottages for their habitation, as time would admit, they met and consulted of laws and orders, both for their civil and military Government, as the necessity of their condition did require, still adding thereunto as urgent occasion in several times, and as cases did require.

[STARVING TIME]

In these hard and difficult beginnings they found some discontents and murmurings arise amongst some, and mutinous speeches and carriages in others; but they were soon quelled and overcome by the wisdom, patience, and just and equal carriage of things by the Governor and better part, which clove faithfully together in the main. But that which was most sad and lamentable was, that in 2 or 3 months' time half of their company died, especially in January: and February, being the depth of winter, and wanting houses and other comforts; being infected with the scurvy and other diseases, which this long voyage and their inaccommodate condition had brought upon them; so as there died some times 2 or 3 of a day, in the foresaid time; that of 100 and odd persons, scarce 50 remained. And of these in the time of most distress, there was but 6 or 7 persons, who, to their great commendations be it spoken, spared no pains, night nor day, but with abundance of toil and hazard of their own health, fetched them wood, made them fires, dressed them meat, made their beds, washed their loathsome clothes, clothed and unclothed them; in a word, did all the homely and necessary offices for them which dainty and queasy stomachs cannot endure to hear named; and all this willingly and cheerfully, without any grudging in the least, showing herein their true love unto their friends and brethren. A rare example and worthy to be remembered. Two of these 7 were Mr. William Brewster, their reverend Elder, and Myles Standish, their Captain and military commander, until whom myself and many others, were much beholden in our low and sick condition. And yet the Lord so upheld these persons, as in this general calamity they were not at all infected with sickness or lameness. And what I have said of these, I may say of many others who died in this general visitation, and others yet living, that whilst they had health, yea, or any strength continuing, they were not wanting to any that had need of them. And I doubt not but their recompense is with the Lord. . . .

[INDIAN RELATIONS]

All this while the Indians came skulking about them, and would sometimes show themselves aloof off, but when any approached near them, they would run away. And once they stole away their tools where they had been at work, and were gone to dinner. But about the 16th of March a certain Indian came boldly amongst them, and spoke to them in broken English, which they could well understand, but marveled at it. At length they understood by discourse with him, that he was not of these parts, but belonged to the eastern parts, where some English ships came to fish, with whom he was acquainted, and could name sundry of them by their names, amongst whom he had got his language. He became profitable to them in acquainting them with many things concerning the state of the country in the east parts where he lived, which was afterwards profitable unto them; as also of the people here, of their names, number, and strength; of their situation and distance from this place, and who was chief amongst them. His name was *Samaset*; he told them also of another Indian whose name was *Squanto*, a native of this place, who had been in England and could speak better

English than himself. Being, after some time of entertainment and gifts, dismissed, a while after he came again, and 5 more with him, and they brought again all the tools that were stolen away before, and made way for the coming of their great Sachem, called *Massasoyt*; who, about 4 or 5 days after, came with the chief of his friends and other attendance, with the aforesaid *Squanto*. With whom, after friendly entertainment, and some gifts given him, they made a peace with him (which hath now continued this 24 years) in these terms.

1. That neither he nor any of his should injure or do hurt to any of their people.

2. That if any of his did any hurt to any of theirs, he would send the offender, that they might punish him.

3. That if anything were taken away from any of theirs, he should cause it to be restored; and they should do the like to his.

4. If any did unjustly war against him, they would aid him; if any did war against them, he should aid them.

5. He should send to his neighbors confederates, to certify them of this, that they might not wrong them, but might be likewise comprised in the conditions of peace.

6. That when their men came to them, they should leave their bows and arrows behind them.

After these things he returned to his place called *Sowams*, some 40 mile from this place, but *Squanto* continued with them, and was their interpreter, and was a special instrument sent of God for their good beyond their expectation. He directed them how to set their corn, where to take fish, and to procure other commodities, and was also their pilot to bring them to unknown places for their profit, and never left them till he died. He was a *native of this place*, and scarce any left alive besides himself. He was carried away with divers others by one *Hunt*, a master of a ship, who thought to sell them for slaves in Spain; but he got away for England, and was entertained by a merchant in London, and employed to Newfoundland and other parts, and lastly brought hither into these parts by one Mr. *Dermer*, a gentleman employed by Sir Ferdinando Gorges and others, for discovery, and other designs in these parts. . . .

FROM CHAPTER XIX
[ANNO DOMINI 1628:
THOMAS MORTON OF MERRY-MOUNT]

About some 3 or 4 years before this time, there came over one Captain Wollaston, (a man of pretty parts,) and with him 3 or 4 more of some eminence, who brought with them a great many servants, with provisions and other implements for to begin a plantation; and pitched themselves in a place within the Massachusetts, which they called, after their Captain's name, Mount-Wollaston. Amongst whom was one Mr. Morton, who, it should seem, had some small adventure (of his own or other men's) amongst them; but had little respect amongst them, and was slighted by the meanest servants. Having continued there some time, and not finding things to answer their expectations, nor profit to arise as they looked for, Captain Wollaston takes a great part of the servants, and transports them to Virginia, where he puts them off at good rates, selling their time to other men; and writes back to one Mr. Rasdall, one of his chief partners, and accounted their merchant, to bring another part of them to Virginia likewise, intending to put them off there as he had done the rest. And he, with the consent of the said Rasdall, appointed one Fitcher to be his Lieutenant, and govern the remains of the plantation, till he or Rasdall returned to take further order thereabout. But this Morton abovesaid, having more craft than honesty, (who had been a kind of pettifogger, of Furnival's Inn,) in the others absence, watches an opportunity, (commons being but hard amongst them,) and got some strong drink and other junkets, and made them a feast; and after they were merry, he began to tell them, would give them good counsel. You see (saith he) that many of your fellows are carried to Virginia; and if you stay till this Rasdall return, you will also be carried away and sold for slaves with the rest. Therefore I would advise you to thrust out this Lieutenant Fitcher; and I, having a part in the plantation, will receive you as my partners and consociates; and so may you be free from service, and we will converse, trade, plant, and live together as equals, and support and protect one another, or to like effect. This counsel was easily received; so they took opportunity, and thrust Lieutenant Fitcher out o' doors, and would suffer him to come no more amongst them, but forced him to seek bread to eat, and other relief from his neighbors, till he could get passage for England.

After this they fell to great licentiousness, and led a dissolute life, pouring out themselves into all profaneness. And Morton became lord of misrule, and maintained (as it were) a school of Atheism. And after they had got some good into their hands, and got much by trading with the Indians, they spent it as vainly, in quaffing and drinking both wine and strong waters in great excess, and, as some reported, 10 pounds worth in the morning. They also set up a May-pole, drinking and dancing about it many days together, inviting the Indian women, for their consorts, dancing and drinking together, (like so many fairies, or furies rather,) and worse practices. As if they had anew revived and celebrated the feasts of the Roman Goddess Flora, or the beastly prac-

tices of the mad Bacchanalians. Morton likewise (to shew his poetry)
composed sundry rimes and verses, some tending to lasciviousness, and
others to the detraction and scandal of some persons, which he affixed
to this idle or idol Maypole. They changed also the name of their place,
and instead of calling it Mount Wollaston, they call it Merry-mount,
as if this jollity would have lasted ever. But this continued not long,
for after Morton was sent for England, (as follows to be declared,)
shortly after came over that worthy gentleman, Mr. John Endecott,
who brought over a patent under the broad seal, for the government
of the Massachusetts, who visiting those parts cause the Maypole to
be cut down, and rebuked them for their profaneness, and admon-
ished them to look there should be better walking; so they now, or
others, changed the name of their place again, and called it Mount-
Dagon.[13] . . .

FROM CHAPTER XXXII
[ANNO DOMINI 1642:
WICKEDNESS BREAKS FORTH]

Marvelous it may be to see and consider how some kind of wickedness did grow and break forth here, in a land where the same was so
much witnessed against, and so narrowly looked unto, and severely
punished when it was known; as in no place more, or so much, that
I have known or heard of; insomuch as they have been somewhat
censured, even by moderate and good men, for their severity in punishments. And yet all this could not suppress the breaking out of
sundry notorious sins, (as this year, besides other, gives us too many
sad precedents and instances,) especially drunkenness and uncleanness;
not only incontinency between persons unmarried, for which many
both men and women have been punished sharply enough, but some
married persons also. But that which is worse, even sodomy and bug-
gery, (things fearful to name,) have broke forth in this land, oftener
than once.

I say it may justly be marveled at, and cause us to fear and tremble
at the consideration of our corrupt natures, which are so hardly bri-
dled, subdued, and mortified; nay, cannot by any other means but the
powerful work and grace of God's spirit. But (besides this) one reason
may be, that the Devil may carry a greater spite against the churches
of Christ and the gospel here, by how much the more they endeavor
to preserve holiness and purity amongst them, and strictly punish the
contrary when it arise either in church or commonwealth; that he

might cast a blemish and stain upon them in the eyes of [the] world, who used to be rash in judgment. I would rather think thus, than that Satan hath more power in these heathen lands, as some have thought, than in more Christian nations, especially over God's servants in them.

2. An other reason may be, that it may be in this case as it is with waters when their streams are stopped or damned up, when they get passage they flow with more violence, and make more noise and disturbance, than when they are suffered to run quietly in their own channels. So wickedness being here more stopped by strict laws, and the same more nearly looked unto so as it cannot run in a common road of liberty as it would, and is inclined, it searches everywhere, and at last breaks out where it gets vent.

3. A third reason may be, here (as I am verily persuaded) is not more evils in this kind, nor nothing near so many by proportion, as in other places; but they are here more discovered and seen, and made public by due search, inquisition, and due punishment; for the churches look narrowly to their members, and the magistrates over all, more strictly than in other places. Besides, here the people are but few in comparison of other places, which are full and populous, and lie hid, as it were, in a wood or thicket, and many horrible evils by this means are never seen nor known; whereas here, they are, as it were, brought into the light, and set in the plain field, or rather on a hill, made conspicuous to the view of all. . . .

FROM CHAPTER XXXIII
[ANNO DOMINI 1643: THE LIFE AND DEATH OF ELDER BREWSTER]

I am to begin this year with that which was a matter of great sadness and mourning unto them all. About the 18th of April died their Reverend Elder, and my dear and loving friend, Mr. William Brewster; a man that had done and suffered much for the Lord Jesus and the gospel's sake, and had bore his part in weal and woe with this poor persecuted church above 36 years in England, Holland, and in this wilderness, and done the Lord and them faithful service in his place and calling. And notwithstanding the many troubles and sorrows he passed through, the Lord upheld him to a great age. He was near fourscore years of age (if not all out) when he died. He had this blessing added by the Lord to all the rest, to die in his bed, in peace, amongst the midst of his friends, who mourned and wept over him and ministered what help and comfort they could unto him, and he again re-comforted them whilest he could. His sickness was not long, and till the last day thereof he did not wholly keep his bed. His speech continued till somewhat more than half a day, and then failed him; and about 9 or 10 o'clock that evening he died, without any pangs at all. A few hours before, he drew his breath short, and some few minutes before his last, he drew his breath long, as a man fallen into a sound sleep, without any pangs or gaspings, and so sweetly departed this life unto a better. . . .

For his personal abilities, he was qualified above many; he was wise and discreet and well spoken, having a grave and deliberate utterance, of a very cheerful spirit, very sociable and pleasant amongst his friends, of an humble and modest mind, of a peaceable disposition, undervaluing himself and his own abilities, and some time overvaluing others; inoffensive and innocent in his life and conversations, which gained him the love of those without, as well as those within; yet he would tell them plainly of their faults and evils, both publicly and privately, but in such a manner as usually was well taken from him. He was tender-hearted, and compassionate of such as were in miseries, but especially of such as had been of good estate and rank, and were fallen unto want and poverty, either for goodness and religion's sake, or by the injury and oppression of others; he would say, of all men these deserved to be pitied most. And none did more offend and displease him than such as would haughtily or proudly carry and lift up themselves, being risen from nothing, and having little riches more than others.

In teaching, he was very moving and stirring of affections, also very plain and distinct in what he taught; by which means he became the more profitable to the hearers. He had a singular good gift in prayer, both public and private, in ripping up the heart and conscience before God, in the humble confession of sin, and begging the mercies of God in Christ for the pardon of the same. He always thought it were better for ministers to pray oftener, and divide their prayers, than be long and tedious in the same (except upon solemn and special occasions, as in days of humiliation and the like). His reason was, that the heart and spirits of all, especially the weak, could hardly continue and stand bent (as it were) so long towards God, as they ought to do in that duty, without flagging and falling off. For the government of the church (which was most proper to his office,) he was careful to preserve good order in the same, and to preserve purity, both in the doctrine and communion of the same; and to suppress any error or contention that might begin to rise up amongst them; and accordingly God gave good success to his endeavors herein all his days, and he saw the fruit of his labours in that behalf. But I must brake off, having only thus touched a few, as it were, heads of things.

Thomas Morton
(1579?–1647)

Thomas Morton, reputed to have been an English "petiefogger" or lawyer (though the record is unclear), came to Massachusetts as a fur trader in 1622. Soon finding himself in conflict with the Separatist colony of Pilgrims at Plymouth, just a few miles south of his own trading post on Quincy Bay, Morton increased the friction by selling liquor and arms to the Indians. But hostilities would not have broken out if the Anglican Morton had not attracted a group of rowdies to his home at Merry Mount and decided, in 1627, to erect an eighty-foot maypole, topped with goat horns, around which he and his companions centered their revels, drinking and dancing with Indian maidens and composing licentious poems to Eros. The Puritans at Plymouth were outraged by these practices, as William Bradford records in his history of Plymouth Plantation, and quickly moved against this self-styled "Lord of Misrule," not only imprisoning him but twice sending him back to England.

During one period of exile, Morton set down his own spiritedly unorthodox views of America and published them in The New English Canaan, *where, in addition to satirizing his Puritan opponents, he provides an interesting account of the Indians and a description of New England itself. However at variance his morals were with those of his Puritan-Separatist neighbors, it is clear that Morton's provocative behavior was motivated at least as strongly by religious and political concerns. Writing his book at a time when the pro-Catholic Charles I was on the English throne, Morton hoped that he might help get the charter of the Massachusetts Bay Company revoked by portraying the Puritans as anti-Anglican.*

from *The New English Canaan (1637)*

FROM BOOK II
FROM CHAPTER I.
THE GENERAL SURVEY OF
THE COUNTRY

In the month of June, *Anno Salutis*[1] 1622, it was my chance to arrive in the parts of New England with 30 servants and provisions of all sorts fit for a plantation; and while our houses were building, I did endeavor to take a survey of the country. The more I looked, the more I liked it. And when I had more seriously considered of the beauty of the place, with all her fair endowments, I did not think that in all the known world it could be paralleled for so many goodly groves of trees, dainty fine round rising hillocks, delicate fair large plains, sweet crystal fountains, and clear running streams that twine in fine meanders through the meads, making so sweet a murmuring noise to hear as would even lull the senses with delight asleep, so pleasantly do they glide upon the pebble stones, jetting most jocundly where they do meet, and hand in hand run down to Neptune's court, to pay the yearly tribute which they owe to him as sovereign lord of all the springs. Contained within the volume of the land, [are] fowls in abundance, [and] fish in multitude. And [I] discovered, besides, millions of turtledoves on the green boughs, which sat pecking of the full ripe pleasant grapes that were supported by the lusty trees, whose fruitful load did cause the arms to bend: [among] which here and there dispersed, you might see lilies and of [sic] the Daphnean-tree,[2] which made the land to me seem paradise. For mine eye t'was Nature's masterpiece, her chiefest magazine of all where lives her store. If this land be not rich, then is the whole world poor. . . .

FROM BOOK III
CHAPTER XIV.
OF THE REVELS OF NEW CANAAN

[The Maypole of Merry Mount]

The inhabitants of Passonagessit[3] (having translated the name of their habitation from that ancient savage name to Ma-re Mount[4] and being resolved to have the new name confirmed for a memorial to after ages) did devise amongst themselves to have it performed in a solemn man-

ner, with revels and merriment after the old English custom; [they]
prepared to set up a Maypole upon the festival day of Philip and
Jacob,[5] and therefore brewed a barrel of excellent beer and provided
a case of bottles to be spent, with other good cheer, for all comers of
that day. And because they would have it in a complete form, they
had prepared a song fitting to the time and present occasion. And upon
May Day they brought the Maypole to the place appointed, with
drums, guns, pistols, and other fitting instruments for that purpose,
and there erected it with the help of savages that came thither of purpose to see the manner of our revels. A goodly pine tree of eighty feet
long was reared up, with a pair of buck's horns nailed on somewhat
near unto the top of it, where it stood as a fair sea mark for directions
how to find out the way to mine host[6] of Ma-re Mount.

And because it should more fully appear to what end it was placed
there, they had a poem in readiness made, which was fixed to the
Maypole to show the new name confirmed upon that plantation,
which, although it were made according to the occurrence of the time,
it being enigmatically composed, puzzled the Separatists[7] most pitifully
to expound it, which (for the better information of the reader) I have
here inserted.

The Poem

Rise Oedipus, and, if thou canst, unfold
What means Charybdis underneath the mold,
When Scylla solitary on the ground
(Sitting in form of Niobe) was found,
Till Amphitrite's darling did acquaint
Grim Neptune with the tenor of her plaint,
And caused him send forth Triton with the sound
Of trumpet loud, at which the seas were found
So full of protean forms that the bold shore
Presented Scylla a new paramour
So strong as Samson and so patient
As Job himself, directed thus, by fate,
To comfort Scylla so unfortunate.
I do profess, by Cupid's beauteous mother,
Here's Scogan's choice for Scylla, and none other;
Though Scylla's sick with grief, because no sign
Can there be found of virtue masculine.
Asclepius come; I know right well
His labor's lost when you may ring her knell.
The fatal sisters' doom none can withstand,
Nor Cytherea's power, who points to land

> With proclamation that the first of May
> At Ma-re Mount shall be kept holiday.

The setting up of this Maypole was a lamentable spectacle to the precise Separatists that lived at New Plymouth. They termed it an idol; yea, they called it the Calf of Horeb[8] and stood at defiance with the place, naming it Mount Dagon, threatening to make it a woeful mount and not a merry mount.

The riddle, for want of Oedipus, they could not expound, only they made some explication of part of it and said it was meant by Samson Job, the carpenter of the ship that brought over a woman to her husband that had been there long before and thrived so well that he sent for her and her children to come to him where shortly after he died, having no reason but because of the sound of those two words, when as (the truth is) the man they applied it to was altogether unknown to the author.

There was likewise a merry song made which (to make their revels more fashionable) was sung with a chorus, every man bearing his part, which they performed in a dance, hand in hand about the Maypole, while one of the company sang and filled out the good liquor, like Ganymede[9] and Jupiter.

The Song

Chorus.
Drink and be merry, merry, merry boys;
Let all your delight be in the Hymen's[10] joys;
Io[11] to Hymen, now the day is come,
About the merry Maypole take a room.
  Make green garlands, bring bottles out
  And fill sweet nectar freely about.
  Uncover thy head and fear no harm.
  For here's good liquor to keep it warm.
Then drink and be merry, &c.
Io to Hymen, &c.
  Nectar is a thing assigned
  By the Deity's own mind
  To cure the heart oppressed with grief,
  And of good liquors is the chief.
Then drink, &c.
Io to Hymen, &c.
  Give to the melancholy man
  A cup or two of't now and then;

> This physic will soon revive his blood,
> And make him be of a merrier mood.
> Then drink, &c.
> Io to Hymen, &c.
> Give to the nymph that's free from scorn
> No Irish stuff nor Scotch over worn.
> Lasses in beaver coats come away,
> Ye shall be welcome to us night and day.
> To drink and be merry, &c.
> Io to Hymen, &c.

This harmless mirth made by young men (that lived in hope to have wives brought over to them, that would save them a labor to make a voyage to fetch any over) was much distasted of the precise Separatists that keep much ado about the tithe of mint and cummin,[12] troubling their brains more than reason would require about things that are indifferent, and from that time sought occasion against my honest host of Ma-re Mount, to overthrow his undertakings and to destroy his plantation quite and clean. But because they presumed, with their imaginary gifts (which they have out of Phaon's box[13]), they could expound hidden mysteries, to convince them of blindness as well in this as in other matters of more consequence, I will illustrate the poem according to the true intent of the authors of these revels, so much distasted by those moles.

Oedipus is generally received for the absolute reader of riddles, who is invoked; Scylla and Charybdis are two dangerous places for seamen to encounter, near unto Venice, and have been by poets formerly resembled to man and wife. The like license the author challenged for a pair of his nomination, the one lamenting for the loss of the other as Niobe for her children. Amphitrite is an arm of the sea, by which the news was carried up and down of a rich widow, now to be taken up or laid down. By Triton is the fame spread that caused the suitors to muster (as it had been to Penelope of Greece); and, the coast lying circular, all our passage to and fro is made more convenient by sea than land. Many aimed at this mark, but he that played Proteus best and could comply with her humor must be the man that would carry her; and he had need have Samson's strength to deal with a Delilah, and as much patience as Job that should come there, for a thing that I did observe in the lifetime of the former.

But marriage and hanging (they say) come by destiny, and Scogan's choice is better [than] none at all. He that played Proteus (with the help of Priapus) put their noses out of joint, as the proverb is.

And this the whole company of the revelers at Ma-re Mount knew to be the true sense and exposition of the riddle that was fixed to the Maypole which the Separatists were at defiance with. Some of them affirmed that the first institution thereof was in memory of a whore, not knowing that it was a trophy erected at first in honor of Maia, the Lady of Learning which they despise, vilifying the two universities with uncivil terms, accounting what is there obtained by study is but unnecessary learning, not considering that learning does enable men's minds to converse with elements of a higher nature than is to be found within the habitation of the mole.

CHAPTER XV.
OF A GREAT MONSTER SUPPOSED TO BE
AT MA-RE MOUNT; AND THE
PREPARATION MADE TO DESTROY IT

[Puritan Arrest of Morton by "Outragious Riot"]

The Separatists, envying the prosperity and hope of the plantation at Ma-re Mount (which they perceived began to come forward and to be in a good way for gain in the beaver trade), conspired together against mine host especially (who was the owner of that plantation) and made up a party against him and mustered up what aid they could, accounting of him as of a great monster.

Many threatening speeches were given out both against his person and his habitation, which they divulged should be consumed with fire. And taking advantage of the time when his company (which seemed little to regard their threats) were gone up unto the inlands to trade with the savages for beaver, they set upon my honest host at a place called Wessaguscus, where, by accident, they found him. The inhabitants there were in good hope of the subversion of the plantation at Ma-re Mount (which they principally aimed at) and the rather because mine host was a man that endeavored to advance the dignity of the Church of England, which they (on the contrary part) would labor to vilify with uncivil terms, inveighing against the sacred Book of Common Prayer and mine host that used it in a laudable manner amongst his family as a practice of piety.

There he would be a means to bring sacks to their mill (such is the thirst after beaver) and helped the conspirators to surprise mine host (who was there all alone), and they charged him (because they would [like to] seem to have some reasonable cause against him, to set a gloss upon their malice) with criminal things, which indeed had been done by such a person, but was of their conspiracy. Mine host demanded of the conspirators who it was that was author of that information that seemed to be their ground for what they now intended. And because they answered they would not tell him, he as peremptorily replied that he would not say whether he had or he had not done as they had been informed.

The answer made no matter (as it seemed), whether it had been negatively or affirmatively made, for they had resolved what he would suffer, because, (as they boasted), they were now become the greater number: they had shaken off their shackles of servitude and were become masters and masterless people.

It appears they were like bears' whelps in former time when mine host's plantation was of as much strength as theirs, but now (theirs being stronger) they (like over grown bears) seemed monstrous. In brief, mine host must endure to be their prisoner until they could contrive it so that they might send him for England (as they said), there to suffer according to the merit of the fact which they intended to father upon him, supposing (belike) it would prove a heinous crime.

Much rejoicing was made that they had gotten their capital enemy (as they concluded him) whom they purposed to hamper in such sort that he should not be able to uphold his plantation at Ma-re Mount.

The conspirators sported themselves at my honest host, that meant them no hurt, and were so jocund that they feasted their bodies and fell to tippling as if they had obtained a great prize, like the Trojans when they had the custody of Epeios' pinetree horse.

Mine host feigned grief and could not be persuaded either to eat or drink, because he knew emptiness would be a means to make him as watchful as the geese kept in the Roman Capital; whereon, the contrary part, the conspirators would be so drowsy that he might have an opportunity to give them a slip instead of a tester.[14] Six persons of the conspiracy were set to watch him at Wessaguscus. But he kept waking, and in the dead of the night (one lying on the bed for further surety), up gets mine host and got to the second door that he was to pass, which, notwithstanding the lock, he got open and shut it after him with such violence that it affrighted some of the conspirators.

The word which was given with an alarm was, "O he's gone, he's gone, what shall we do, he's gone!" The rest (half asleep) start up in amaze and like rams, ran their heads one at another full butt in the dark.

Their grand leader, Captain Shrimp,[15] took on most furiously and tore his clothes for anger, to see the empty nest and their bird gone.

The rest were eager to have torn their hair from their heads, but it was so short that it would give them no hold. Now Captain Shrimp thought in the loss of this prize (which he accounted his masterpiece) all his honor would be lost forever.

In the meantime mine host was got home to Ma-re Mount through the woods, eight miles round about the head of the river Mon-atoquit that parted the two plantations, finding his way by the help of the lightning (for it thundered as he went terribly), and there he prepared powder, three pounds dried, for his present employment, and four good guns for him and the two assistants left at his house, with bullets of several sizes, three hundred or thereabouts, to be used if the conspirators should pursue him thither; and these two persons promised their aids in the quarrel and confirmed that promise with health in good *rosa solis.*[16]

Now Captain Shrimp, the first captain in the land (as he supposed), must do some new act to repair this loss and to vindicate his reputation, who had sustained blemish by this oversight, begins now to study how to repair or survive his honor; in this manner, calling of council, they conclude.

He takes eight persons more to him, and (like the nine worthies of New Canaan) they embark with preparation against Ma-re Mount where this monster of a man, as their phrase was, had his den; the whole number, had the rest not been from home, being but seven, would have given Captain Shrimp (a *quondam* [former] drummer) such a welcome as would have made him wish for a drum as big as Diogenes' tub, that he might have crept into it out of sight.

Now the nine worthies are approached, and mine host prepared, having intelligence by a savage that hastened in love from Wessaguscus to give him notice of their intent.

One of mine host's men proved a craven; the other had proved his wits to purchase a little valor, before mine host had observed his posture.

The nine worthies coming before the den of this supposed monster (this seven-headed hydra, as they termed him) and began, like Don Quixote against the windmill, to beat a parley and to offer quarter if mine host would yield, for they resolved to send him to England and bade him lay by his arms.

But he (who was the son of a soldier), having taken up arms in his just defense, replied that he would not lay by those arms because they were so needful at sea, if he should be sent over. Yet, to save the effusion of so much worthy blood as would have issued out of the veins of these nine worthies of New Canaan if mine host should have played upon them out at his portholes (for they came within danger like a flock of wild geese, as if they had been tailed one to another, as colts to be sold at a fair), mine host was content to yield upon quarter and did capitulate with them in what manner it should be for more certainty, because he knew what Captain Shrimp was.

He expressed that no violence should be offered to his person, none to his goods, nor any of his household but that he should have his arms and what else was requisite for the voyage: which their herald returns, it was agreed upon and should be performed.

But mine host no sooner had set open the door and issued out, but instantly Captain Shrimp and the rest of the worthies stepped to him, laid hold of his arms, and had him down; and so eagerly was every man bent against him (not regarding any agreement made with such a carnal man), that they fell upon him as if they would have eaten him; some of them were so violent that they would have a slice with scabbard, and all for haste, until an old soldier (of the Queen's, as the proverb is) that was there by accident, clapped his gun under the weapons and sharply rebuked these worthies for their unworthy practices. So the matter was taken into more deliberate consideration.

Captain Shrimp and the rest of the nine worthies made themselves (by this outrageous riot) masters of mine host of Ma-re Mount and disposed of what he had at his plantation.

This, they knew (in the eye of the savages), would add to their glory and diminish the reputation of mine honest host, whom they practiced to be rid of upon any terms, as willingly as if he had been the very hydra of the time.

CHAPTER XVI.
HOW THE NINE WORTHIES PUT MINE HOST OF MA-RE MOUNT INTO THE ENCHANTED CASTLE AT PLYMOUTH AND TERRIFIED HIM WITH THE MONSTER BRIAREUS[17]

The nine worthies of New Canaan having now the law in their own hands (there being no general governor in the land, nor none of the separation that regarded the duty they owe their sovereign, whose natural born subjects they were, though translated out of Holland from whence they had learned to work all to their own ends, and make a great show of religion but no humanity), for they were now to sit in council on the cause.

And much it stood mine honest host upon to be very circumspect, and to take Eacus[18] to task; for that his voice was more allowed of than both the other; and had not mine host confounded all the arguments that Eacus could make in their defense, and confuted him that swayed the rest, they would have made him unable to drink in such manner of merriment any more. So that following this private counsel, given him by one that knew who ruled the roost, the hurricane ceased that else would split his pinnace.

A conclusion was made and sentence given that mine host should be sent to England a prisoner. But when he was brought to the ships for that purpose, no man durst be so foolhardy as to undertake [to] carry him. So these worthies set mine host upon an island, without gun, powder, or shot, or dog, or so much as a knife to get anything to feed upon, or any other clothes to shelter him with at winter than a thin suit which he had on at that time. Home he could not get to Ma-re Mount. Upon this island he stayed a month at least, and was relieved by savages that took notice that mine host was a sachem [chief] of Passonagessit, and would bring bottles of strong liquor to him and unite themselves into a league of brotherhood with mine host, so full of humanity are these infidels before those Christians.

From this place for England sailed mine host in a Plymouth ship (that came into the land to fish upon the coast) that landed him safe in England at Plymouth; and he stayed in England until the ordinary time for shipping to set forth for these parts, and then returned, no man being able to tax him of anything.

But the worthies (in the meantime) hoped they had been rid of him.

Thomas Hooker
(1586?–1647)

Thomas Hooker possessed one of the most remarkable theological
minds among the first generation of Puritan colonists. Trained at Emmanuel College, Cambridge, he quickly became noted as a preacher
who excelled in the exercise known as the "preparation" of the heart
to receive the news of deliverance brought by the Gospel. But because
of his Puritan sympathies, Hooker was prevented by the English Anglican establishment from winning a pulpit commensurate with his
abilities and therefore decided to emigrate to America, just managing
to escape arrest before he set out in 1633. Soon after reaching Massachusetts, he and his congregation found themselves sufficiently at
odds with the autocracy of the Massachusetts Puritan establishment
to warrant a move farther west. Settling in Hartford, Hooker immediately became the Connecticut colony's leader and proceeded to shape
the new community in a more liberal direction. Though no democrat,
Hooker shows how in literary terms Puritanism often helped prepare
a receptive environment for such views, as when he described his Survey of the Summe of Church Discipline (1647) as a book that "comes
out of the wilderness" and that, being written in a "plain style," will
not cater to "the niceness of men's palates" but will let those "that
covet more sauce than meat . . . [to] find cooks to their [own] mind."
Part of what Hooker meant by "meat" can be seen in the two conditions he held to be requisite in the selection below for "a true sight
of sin": to see it clearly, without interference or embellishment, and to
fathom by feeling the full power or force of it.

from *A True Sight of Sin (1659)*

Wherein this true sight and apprehension of sin properly discovers itself:

I answer, a true sight of sin hath two conditions attending upon it, or it appears in two things: we must see sin (1) clearly; (2) convictingly—what it is in itself and what it is to us, not in the appearance and paint of it, but in the power of it; not to fathom it in the notion and conceit only, but to see it with application.

We must see it clearly in its own nature, its native color and proper hue. It's not every slight conceit, not every general and cursory, confused thought or careless consideration that will serve the turn or do the work here. We are all sinners: it is my infirmity, I cannot help it; my weakness, I cannot be rid of it. No man lives without faults and follies, the best have their failings, "In many things we offend all." But alas! all this wind shakes no corn, it costs more to see sin aright than a few words of course. It's one thing to say sin is thus and thus, another thing to see it to be such; we must look wisely and steadily upon our distempers, look sin in the face and discern it to the full. The want whereof is the cause of our mistaking our estates and not redressing of our hearts and ways: (Gal. 6. 4) "Let a man prove his own work." Before the goldsmith can sever and see the dross asunder from the gold, he must search the very bowels of the metal, and try it by touch, by taste, by hammer and by fire; and then he will be able to speak by proof what it is. So here: we perceive sin in the crowd and by hearsay, when we attend some common and customary expressions taken up by persons in their common converse, and so report what others speak, and yet never knew the truth, what either others or we say; but we do not single out our corruptions and survey the loathsomeness of them, as they come naked in their own natures.

This we ought to do. There is great odds betwixt the knowledge of a traveler, that in his own person hath taken a view of many coasts, passed through many countries and hath there taken up his abode some time, and by experience hath been an eyewitness of the extreme cold and scorching heats, hath surveyed the glory and beauty of the one, the barrenness and meanness of the other—he hath been in the wars, and seen the ruin and desolation wrought there—and another that sits by his fireside and happily reads the story of these in a book, or views the proportion of these in a map. The odds is great, and the difference of their knowledge more than a little: the one saw the country really, the other only in the story; the one hath seen the very place, the other only in the paint of the map drawn. The like difference is there in the right discerning of sin. The one hath surveyed the compass of his whole course, searched the frame of his own heart, and examined the windings and turnings of his own ways. He hath seen what sin is and what it hath done, how it hath made havoc of his peace and comfort, ruinated and laid waste the very principles of reason and nature and morality, and made him a terror to himself. When he hath looked over the loathsome abominations that lie in his bosom, that he is afraid to approach the presence of the Lord to bewail his sins and to crave pardon, lest he could be confounded for them while he is but confessing of them—afraid and ashamed lest any man living should know but the least part of that which he knows by himself, and could count it happy that himself was not, that the remembrance of those hideous evils of his might be no more. Another happily hears the like preached or repeated, reads them writ or recorded in some authors, and is able to remember and relate them. The odds is marvelous great! The one sees the history of sin, the other the nature of it; the one knows the relation of sin as it is mapped out and recorded, the other the poison, as by experience he hath found and proved it. It's one thing to see a disease in the book or in a man's body, another thing to find and feel it in a man's self. There is the report of it, here the malignity and venom of it.

But how shall we see clearly the nature of sin in his naked hue?

This will be discovered, and may be conceived in the particulars following. Look we at it: first, as it respects God; secondly, as it concerns ourselves.

As it hath reference to God, the vileness of the nature of sin may thus appear:

It would dispossess God of that absolute supremacy which is indeed His prerogative royal, and doth in a peculiar manner appertain to Him, as the diamond of His crown and diadem of His deity; so the Apostle, "He is God over all blessed for ever" (Rom. 9. 5). All from Him and all for Him, He is the absolute first being, the absolute last end, and herein is the crown of His glory. All those attributes of wisdom, goodness, holiness, power, justice, mercy, the shine and concurrency of all these meeting together, is to set out the inconceivable excellency of His glorious name, which exceeds all praise: "Thine is the kingdom, the power and the glory," the right of all and so the rule of all and the glory of all belongs to Him.

Now herein lies the inconceivable heinousness of the hellish nature of sin: it would jostle the Almighty out of the throne of His glorious sovereignty, and indeed be above Him. For the will of man being the chiefest of all His workmanship, all for his body, the body of the soul, the mind to attend upon the will, the will to attend upon God and to make choice of Him and His will, that is next to Him and He only above that: and that should have been His throne and temple or chair of state in which He would have set his sovereignty forever. He did in a special manner intend to meet with man, and to communicate Himself to man in His righteous law, as the rule of His holy and righteous will, by which the will of Adam should have been ruled and guided to Him and made happy in Him; and all creatures should have served God in man, and been happy by or through him, serving of God being happy in him. But when the will went from under the government of his rule, by sin, it would be above God and be happy without Him, for the rule of the law, in each command of it, holds forth a threefold expression of sovereignty from the Lord, and therein the sovereignty of all the rest of His attributes.

1. The powerful supremacy of His just will, as that He hath right to dispose of all and authority to command all at His pleasure: "What if God will?" (Rom. 9. 22); "My counsel shall stand and I will do all my pleasure" (Isa. 46. 10). And as it's true of what shall be done upon us, so His will hath sovereignty of command in what should be done by us; we are to say, "The will of the Lord be done." David's warrant was to do all God's will (Acts 13. 22), and our saviour himself professeth (John 6. 38) that "He came not to do his own will but the will of Him that sent him." And therefore His wrath and jealousy and judgment will break out in case that be disobeyed.

2. There is also a fullness of wisdom in the law of God revealed to guide and direct us in the way we should walk: (Psal. 19. 7) "The law of God makes wise the simple"; (II Tim. 3. 15) "It's able to make us wise unto salvation."

3. There's a sufficiency of God to content and satisfy us. "Blessed are they who walk in His ways and blessed are they that keep His testimonies" (Psal. 119. 1, 2). "Great prosperity have they that love the law, and nothing shall offend them" (verse 16). And in truth there can be no greater reward for doing well than to be enabled to do well; he that hath attained his last end he cannot go further, he cannot be better.

Now by sin we jostle the law out of its place and the Lord out of His glorious sovereignty, pluck the crown from His head and the scepter out of His hand; and we say and profess by our practice, there is not authority and power there to govern, nor wisdom to guide, nor good to content me, but I will be swayed by mine own will and led by mine own deluded reason and satisfied with my own lusts. This is the guise of every graceless heart in the commission of sin; so Pharaoh: "Who is the Lord? I know not the Lord nor will I let Israel go" (Exod. 5. 2). In the time of their prosperity, see how the Jews turn their backs and shake off the authority of the Lord: "We are lords," say they, "we will come no more at Thee" (Jer. 2. 31), and "Our

tongues are our own, who shall be lord over us" (Psal. 12. 4)? So for
the wisdom of the world, see how they set light by it as not worth the
looking after it: (Jer. 18. 12) "We will walk after our own devices and
we will every one do the imagination of his own evil heart." Yea, they
set up their own traditions, their own idols and delusions, and lord it
over the law: "Making the command of God of none effect" (Matt.
15. 8, 9). So for the goodness of the word: (Job 22. 17; Matt. 3. 14)
"It is in vain to serve God and what profit is there that we have kept
his ordinances, yea, His commandments are ever grievous." It's a
grievous thing to the loose person, he cannot have his pleasures but
he must have his guilt and gall with them; it's grievous to the worldling
that he cannot lay hold on the world by unjust means but conscience
lays hold upon him as breaking the law. Thou that knowest and kee-
pest thy pride and stubbornness and thy distempers, know assuredly
thou dost jostle God out of the throne of His glorious sovereignty,
and thou dost profess, not God's will but thine own (which is above
His) shall rule thee. Thy carnal reason and the folly of thy mind is
above the wisdom of the Lord, and that shall guide thee; to please
thine own stubborn crooked perverse spirit is a greater good than to
please God and enjoy happiness, for this more contents thee. That
when thou considerest but thy course, dost thou not wonder that the
great and terrible God doth not pash such a poor insolent worm to
powder and send thee packing to the pit every moment?

It smites at the essence of the Almighty and the desire of the
sinner, in not only that God should not be supreme but that indeed
He should not be at all; and therefore it would destroy the being of
Jehovah (Psal. 81. 15). Sinners are called the haters of the Lord:
(John 15. 24) "They hated both me and my Father." Now he that
hates endeavors, if it be possible, the annihilation of the thing hated,
and it's most certain, were it in their power, they would pluck God
out of Heaven, the light of His truth out of their consciences and the
law out of the societies and assemblies where they live, that they might
have elbow room to live as they list. Nay, whatever they hate most,
and intend and plot more evil against in all the world, they hate God
most of all, and intend more evil against Him than against all their
enemies besides, because they hate all for His sake. Therefore wicked
men are said to destroy the law (Psal. 126, 119). The adulterer loathes
that law that condemns uncleanness; the earthworm would destroy
that law that forbids covetousness, they are said to hate the light (John
3. 21), to hate the saints and servants of the Lord: (John 15. 18) "The
world hates you." He that hates the lantern for the light's sake, he
hates the light much more; he that hates the faithful because of the
image of God and the grace that appears there, he hates the God of
all grace and holiness, most of all. So God to Sennacherib: (Isa. 37.

28) "I know thy going out and thy coming in, and thy rage against me." Oh! it would be their content if there was no God in the world to govern them, no law to curb them, no justice to punish, no truth to trouble them. Learn therefore to see how far your rebellions reach. It is not arguments you gainsay, not the counsel of a minister you reject, the command of a magistrate ye oppose, evidence of rule or reason ye resist, but be it known to you, you fly in the very face of the Almighty. And it is not the gospel of grace ye would have destroyed, but the spirit of grace, the author of grace, the Lord Jesus, the God of all grace that ye hate.

It crosseth the whole course of providence, perverts the work of the creation and defaceth the beautiful frame and that sweet correspondence and orderly usefulness the Lord first implanted in the order of things. The heavens deny their influence, the earth her strength, the corn her nourishment: thank sin for that. Weeds come instead of herbs, cockle and darnel instead of wheat: thank sin for that, (Rom. 8. 22) "The whole creature" (or creation) "groans under vanity"—either cannot do what it would or else misseth of that good and end it intended, breeds nothing but vanity, brings forth nothing but vexation. It crooks all things so as that none can straighten them, makes so many wants that none can supply them (Eccles. 1. 15). This makes crooked servants in a family, no man can rule them, crooked inhabitants in towns, crooked members in congregations; there's no ordering nor joining of them in that comely accord and mutual subjection: "Know," they said, "the adversary sin hath done all this." Man was the mean betwixt God and the creature, to convey all good with all the constancy of it; and therefore when man breaks, heaven and earth breaks all asunder: the conduit being cracked and displaced, there can be no conveyance from the fountain.

In regard of ourselves, see we and consider nakedly the nature of sin, in four particulars:

It's that which makes a separation between God and the soul, breaks that union and communion with God for which we were made, and in the enjoyment of which we should be blessed and happy: (Isa. 59. 1, 2) "God's ear is not heavy that it cannot hear nor His hand that it cannot help, but your iniquities have separated betwixt God and you and your sins have hid His face that He will not hear." For He professeth, (Psal. 5. 4) that He is a God that wills not wickedness, neither shall iniquity dwell with him. "Into the new Jerusalem shall no unclean thing enter, but without shall be dogs" (Rev. 21. 27). The dogs to their kennel, and hogs to their sty and mire; but if an impenitent wretch should come into heaven, the Lord would go out of heaven: Iniquity shall not dwell with sin. That then that deprives me of my greatest good for which I came into the world, and for which

I live and labor in the world, and without which I had better never to have been born—nay, that which deprives me of an universal good, a good that hath all good in it—that must needs be an evil, but have all evil in it. But so doth sin deprive me of God as the object of my will, and that wills all good, and therefore it must bring in truth all evil with it. Shame takes away my honor, poverty my wealth, persecution my peace, prison my liberty, death my life, yet a man may still be a happy man, lose his life, and live eternally. But sin takes away my God, and with Him all good goes; prosperity without God will be my poison, honor without Him my bane; nay, the word without God hardens me, my endeavor without Him profits nothing at all for my good. A natural man hath no God in anything, and therefore hath no good.

It brings an incapability in regard of myself to receive good, and an impossibility in regard of God Himself to work my spiritual good, while my sin continues, and I continue impenitent in it. An incapability of a spiritual blessing: "Why transgress ye the commandment of the Lord that ye cannot prosper do what ye can" (II Chron. 24. 20). And he that being often reproved hardens his heart, shall be consumed suddenly and there is no remedy, he that spills the physic that should cure him, the meat that should nourish him, there is no remedy but he must needs die: so that the commission of sin makes not only a separation from God, but obstinate resistance and continuance in it maintains an infinite and everlasting distance between God and the soul. So that so long as the sinful resistance of thy soul continues, God cannot vouchsafe the comforting and guiding presence of His grace, because it's cross to the Covenant of Grace He hath made, which He will not deny, and His oath which He will not alter. So that should the Lord save thee and thy corruption, carry thee and thy proud unbelieving heart to heaven He must nullify the Gospel (Heb. 5. 9): "He's the author of salvation to them that obey Him," and forswear Himself (Heb. 3. 18): "He hath sworn unbelievers shall not enter into His rest"; He must cease to be just and holy, and so to be God. As Saul said to Jonathan concerning David (I Sam. 20. 30, 31), "So long as the son of Jesse lives, thou shalt not be established, nor thy kingdom." So do thou plead against thyself, and with thy own soul: so long as these rebellious distempers continue, grace and peace and the kingdom of Christ can never be established in thy heart. For this obstinate resistance differs nothing from the plagues of the state of the damned, when they come to the highest measure, but that it is not yet total and final, there being some kind of abatement of the measure of it and stoppage of the power of it. Imagine thou sawest the Lord Jesus coming in the clouds, and heardest the last trump blow, "Arise, ye dead, and come to judgment"; imagine thou sawest the Judge of all the world

sitting upon the throne, thousands of angels before Him and ten
thousands ministering unto Him, the sheep standing on His right hand
and the goats at the left; suppose thou heardest that dreadful sentence, and final doom pass from the Lord of life (whose word made
heaven and earth, and will shake both) "Depart from me, ye cursed":
how would thy heart shake and sink, and die within thee in the
thought thereof, wert thou really persuaded it was thy portion? Know,
that by thy daily continuance in sin, thou dost to the utmost of thy
power execute that sentence upon thy soul. It's thy life, thy labor, the
desire of thy heart, and thy daily practice to depart away from the
God of all grace and peace, and turn the tombstone of everlasting
destruction upon thine own soul.

It's the cause which brings all other evils of punishment into the
world and without this they are not evil, but so far as sin is in them.
The sting of a trouble, the poison and malignity of a punishment and
affliction, the evil of the evil of any judgment, it is the sin that brings
it, or attends it: (Jer. 2. 19) "Thine own wickedness shall correct thee,
and thy backslidings shall reprove thee, know therefore that it is an
evil, and bitter thing that thou has forsaken the Lord"; (Jer. 4. 18)
"Thy ways and doings have procured these things unto thee, therefore it is bitter, and reacheth unto the heart." Take miseries and
crosses without sin, they are like to be without a sting, the serpent
without poison; ye may take them, and make medicines of them. So
Paul (I Cor. 15. 55), he plays with death itself, sports with the grave:
"Oh death, where is thy sting? Oh grave, where is thy victory?" The
sting of death is sin. All the harmful annoyance in sorrows and punishments, further than either they come from sin or else tend to it, they
are rather improvements of what we have than parting with anything
we do enjoy; we rather lay out our conveniences than seem to lose
them, yea, they increase our crown and do not diminish our comfort.
"Blessed are ye when men revile you, and persecute you, and speak all
manner of evil of you for my sake, for great is your reward in Heaven"
(Matt. 5. 11). There is a blessing in persecutions and reproaches when
they be not mingled with the deserts of our sins; yea, our momentary
short affliction for a good cause and a good conscience works an excessive exceeding weight of glory. If then sin brings all evils, and makes all
evils indeed to us, then is it worse than all those evils.

It brings a curse upon all our comforts, blasts all our blessings,
the best of all our endeavors, the use of all the choicest of all God's
ordinances: it's so evil and vile, that it makes the use of all good things,
and all the most glorious, both ordinances and improvements, evil to
us (Hag. 2. 13, 14). When the question was made to the priest, "If
one that is unclean by a dead body touch any of the holy things, shall
it be unclean?" And he answered, "Yea. So is this people, and so is

this nation before me, saith the Lord; and so is every work of their hands, and that which they offer is unclean." If any good thing a wicked man had, or any action he did, might be good, or bring good to him, in reason it was the services and sacrifices wherein he did approach unto God and perform service to Him, and yet "the sacrifice of the wicked is an abomination to the Lord" (Prov. 28. 9 and Tit. 1. 15) "To the pure all things are pure; but to the unbelieving there is nothing pure, but their very consciences are defiled." It is a desperate malignity in the temper of the stomach that should turn our meat and diet into diseases, the best cordials and preservatives into poisons, so that what in reason is appointed to nourish a man should kill him. Such is the venom and malignity of sin, makes the use of the best things become evil, nay, the greatest evil to us many times: (Psal. 109. 7) "Let his prayer be turned into sin." That which is appointed by God to be the choicest means to prevent sin is turned into sin out of the corrupt distemper of these carnal hearts of ours.

Hence then it follows that sin is the greatest evil in the world, or indeed that can be. For, that which separates the soul from God, that which brings all evils of punishment and makes all evils truly evil, and spoils all good things to us, that must needs be the greatest evil. But this is the nature of sin, as hath already appeared.

But that which I will mainly press is, sin is only opposite to God, and cross as much as can be to that infinite goodness and holiness which is in His blessed majesty. It's not the miseries or distresses that men undergo that the Lord distastes them for, or estrangeth Himself from them; He is with Joseph in the prison, with the three children in the furnace, with Lazarus when he lies among the dogs and gathers the crumbs from the rich man's table, yea, with Job upon the dunghill, but He is not able to bear the presence of sin. Yea, of this temper are His dearest servants: the more of God is in them, the more opposite they are to sin wherever they find it. It was that He commended in the church of Ephesus, "That she could not bear those that were wicked" (Rev. 2. 3). As when the stomach is of a pure temper and good strength, the least surfeit or distemper that befalls, it presently distastes and disburdens itself with speed. So David noted to be "a man after God's own heart." He professeth: (Psal. 101. 3, 7) "I hate the work of them that turn aside, he that worketh deceit shall not dwell in my house; he that telleth lies, shall not tarry in my sight." But when the heart becomes like the stomach, so weak it cannot help itself nor be helped by physic, desperate diseases and dissolution of the whole follows, and in reason must be expected. Hence see how God looks at the least connivance or a faint and feeble kind of opposition against sin as that in which He is most highly dishonored; and He follows it with most hideous plagues, as that indulgent carriage

of Eli towards the vile behavior of his sons for their grosser evils:
(I Sam. 2. 23, 24) "Why do you such things? It's not well, my sons,
that I hear such things." It is not well, and is that all? Why, had they
either out of ignorance not known their duty or out of some sudden
surprisal of a temptation neglected it, it had not been well; but for
them so purposely to proceed on in the practice of such gross evils,
and for him so faintly to reprove, the Lord looks at it as a great sin
thus feebly to oppose sin. And therefore (verse 29). He tells him that
he honored his sons above God, and therefore He professeth, "Far be
it from me to maintain thy house and comfort, for he that honors me
I will honor, and he that despiseth me shall be lightly esteemed" (verse
30). Hence it is the Lord Himself is called "the holy one of Israel,"
(Hab. 1. 12) "who is of purer eyes than to behold evil, and cannot
look upon iniquity"—no, not in such as profess themselves saints,
though most dear unto Him; no, nor in His son the Lord Jesus, not
in his saints. (Amos 8. 7) The Lord hath sworn by Himself, "I abhor
the excellency of Jacob"; whatever their excellencies, their privileges
are, if they do not abhor sin, God will abhor them: (Jer. 22. 24)
"Though Coniah was as the signet of my right hand, thence would I
pluck Him." Nay, He could not endure the appearance of it in the
Lord Christ, for when but the reflection of sin (as I may so say) fell
upon our savior, even the imputation of our transgressions to him,
though none iniquity was ever committed by him, the Father withdrew
His comforting presence from him, and let loose His infinite displeasure against him, forcing him to cry out, "My God, my God, why hast
thou forsaken me?"

    Yea, sin is so evil (that though it be in nature, which is the good
creation of God) that there is no good in it, nothing that God will
own; but in the evil of punishment it is otherwise, for the torments of
the devils, and punishments of the damned in hell, and all the plagues
inflicted upon the wicked upon earth, issue from the righteous and
revenging justice of the Lord, and He doth own such execution as His
proper work: (Isa. 45. 7) "Is there any evil in the city," *viz.* of punishment, "and the Lord hath not done it? I make peace, I create evil,
I the Lord do all these things." It issues from the justice of God that
He cannot but reward everyone according to His own ways and
works; those are a man's own, the holy one of Israel hath no hand in
them. But he is the just executioner of the plagues that are inflicted
and suffered for these; and hence our blessed savior becoming our
surety, and standing in our room, he endured the pains of the second
death, even the fierceness of the fury of an offended God, and yet it
was impossible he could commit the least sin, or be tainted with the
least corrupt distemper. And it's certain it's better to suffer all plagues
without any one sin than to commit the least sin and to be freed from

all plagues. Suppose that all miseries and sorrows that ever befell all the wicked in earth and hell should meet together in one soul, as all waters gathered together in one sea; suppose thou heardest the devil's roaring, and sawest hell gaping, and flames of everlasting burnings flashing before thine eyes? It's certain it were better for thee to be cast into those inconceivable torments than to commit the least sin against the Lord. Thou dost not think so now, but thou wilt find it so one day.

Ann Hutchinson
(1591–1643)

Ann Hutchinson, a strong-minded and courageous woman who emigrated to Massachusetts in 1634, quickly came into conflict with the religious and political authorities of the new colony when she began holding weekly meetings at her home, mostly for women, to discuss sermons heard the previous Sunday. An ardent disciple of John Cotton, the Massachusetts Bay colony's foremost minister during the first generation, who emphasized the Puritan view that God's grace is wholly unmerited and that salvation is possible only because it is given freely, without conditions, Hutchinson insisted that the "covenant of grace" represented an unmediated relationship with God based on an individual's direct intuition or apprehension of His will. Further, Hutchinson believed that those clergy who, unlike Cotton, preached that "the covenant of grace" was somehow conditional upon an individual's response or effort were, in fact, preaching what to all radical Protestants since the Reformation was a detested "covenant of works." Such views were held to be Antinominian (literally, "against the law") and precipitated a crisis of grave magnitude, during which Hutchinson was brought to trial for "traducing the ministers and their ministry."

Though Hutchinson was originally supported in her ideas by her mentor, Cotton eventually joined the rest of the male court during the trial in condemning her. Governor John Winthrop, who presided over this sorry business, then banished her and her family to Rhode Island *in 1638. By 1642 the Hutchinsons had moved on to New York, where all but one of them were killed in an Indian raid a year later. In the following transcript of the trial, Hutchinson is as eloquent in her silences as in her speeches, and throughout the whole of the proceedings, which are excerpted here, she maintains an extraordinary poise and clear-headedness.*

from *The Examination of Mrs. Ann Hutchinson at the Court at Newtown (1637)*

MR. WINTHROP, GOVERNOR. Mrs. Hutchinson, you are called here as one of those that have troubled the peace of the commonwealth and the churches here; you are known to be a woman that hath had a great share in the promoting and divulging of those opinions that are causes of this trouble, and to be nearly joined not only in affinity and affection with some of those the court had taken notice of and passed censure upon, but you have spoken divers things as we have been informed very prejudicial to the honour of the churches and ministers thereof, and you have maintained a meeting and an assembly in your house that hath been condemned by the general assembly as a thing not tolerable nor comely in the sight of God nor fitting for your sex, and notwithstanding that was cried down you have continued the same, therefore we have thought good to send for you to understand how things are, that if you be in an erroneous way we may reduce you that so you may become a profitable member here among us, otherwise if you be obstinate in your course that then the court may take such course that you may trouble us no further, therefore I would intreat you to express whether you do not assent and hold in practice to those opinions and factions that have been handled in court already, that is to say, whether you do not justify Mr. Wheelwright's sermon and the petition.

MRS. HUTCHINSON. I am called here to answer before you but I hear no things laid to my charge.

GOV. I have told you some already and more I can tell you.

MRS. H. Name one Sir.

GOV. Have I not named some already?

Mrs. H. What have I said or done?

Gov. Why for your doings, this you did harbour and countenance those that are parties in this faction that you have heard of.

Mrs. H. That's matter of conscience, sir.

Gov. Your conscience you must keep or it must be kept for you.

Mrs. H. Must not I then entertain the saints because I must keep my conscience.

Gov. Say that one brother should commit felony or treason and come to his brother's house, if he knows him guilty and conceals him he is guilty of the same. It is his conscience to entertain him, but if his conscience comes into act in giving countenance and entertainment to him that hath broken the law he is guilty too. So if you do countenance those that are transgressors of the law you are in the same fact.

Mrs. H. What law do they transgress?

Gov. The law of God and of the state.

Mrs. H. In what particular?

Gov. Why in this among the rest, whereas the Lord doth say honour thy father and thy mother.

Mrs. H. Ey Sir in the Lord.

Gov. This honour you have broke in giving countenance to them.

Mrs. H. In entertaining those did I entertain them against any act (for there is the thing) or what God hath appointed?

Gov. You knew that Mr. Wheelwright did preach this sermon and those that countenance him in this do break a law.

Mrs. H. What law have I broken?

Gov. Why the fifth commandment.

Mrs. H. I deny that for he saith in the Lord.

Gov. You have joined with them in the faction.

Mrs. H. In what faction have I joined with them?

Gov. In presenting the petition.

Mrs. H. Suppose I had set my hand to the petition what then?

Gov. You saw that case tried before.

Mrs. H. But I had not my hand to the petition.

Gov. You have councelled them.

Mrs. H. Wherein?

Gov. Why in entertaining them.

Mrs. H. What breach of law is that Sir?

Gov. Why dishonouring of parents.

Mrs. H. But put the case Sir that I do fear the Lord and my parents, may not I entertain them that fear the Lord because my parents will not give me leave?

Gov. If they be the fathers of the commonwealth, and they of another religion, if you entertain them then you dishonour your parents and are justly punishable.

Mrs. H. If I entertain them, as they have dishonoured their parents I do.

Gov. No but you by countenancing them above others put honor upon them.

Mrs. H. I may put honor upon them as the children of God and as they do honor the Lord.

Gov. We do not mean to discourse with those of your sex but only this; you do adhere unto them and do endeavor to set forward this faction and so you do dishonour us.

Mrs. H. I do acknowledge no such thing neither do I think that I ever put any dishonour upon you.

Gov. Why do you keep such a meeting at your house as you do every week upon a set day?

Mrs. H. It is lawful for me so to do, as it is all your practices and can you find a warrant for yourself and condemn me for the same thing? The ground of my taking it up was, when I first came to this land because I did not go to such meetings as those were, it was presently reported that I did not allow of such meetings but held them unlawful and therefore in that regard they said I was proud and did despise all ordinances, upon that a friend came unto me and told me of it and I to prevent such aspersions took it up, but it was in practice before I came therefore I was not the first.

Gov. For this, that you appeal to our practice you need no confutation. If your meeting had answered to the former it had not been offensive, but I will say that there was no meeting of women alone, but your meeting is of another sort for there are sometimes men among you.

Mrs. H. There was never any man with us.

Gov. Well, admit there was no man at your meeting and that you was sorry for it, there is no warrant for your doings, and by what warrant do you continue such a course?

Mrs. H. I conceive there lyes a clear rule in Titus, that the elder women should instruct the younger and then I must have a time wherein I must do it.

Gov. All this I grant you, I grant you a time for it, but what is this to the purpose that you Mrs. Hutchinson must call a company together from their callings to come to be taught of you?

Mrs. H. Will it please you to answer me this and to give me a rule for them I will willingly submit to any truth. If any come to my house to be instructed in the ways of God what rule have I to put them away?

Gov. But suppose that a hundred men come unto you to be instructed will you forbear to instruct them?

Mrs. H. As far as I conceive I cross a rule in it.

Gov. Very well and do you not so here?

Mrs. H. No Sir for my ground is they are men.

Gov. Men and women all is one for that, but suppose that a man should come and say Mrs. Hutchinson I hear that you are a woman that God hath given his grace unto and you have knowledge in the word of God I pray instruct me a little, ought you not to instruct this man?

Mrs. H. I think I may.——Do you think it not lawful for me to teach women and why do you call me to teach the court?

Gov. We do not call you to teach the court but to lay open yourself.

Mrs. H. I desire you that you would then set me down a rule by which I may put them away that come unto me and so have peace in so doing.

Gov. You must shew your rule to receive them.

Mrs. H. I have done it.

Gov. I deny it because I have brought more arguments than you have.

Mrs. H. I say, to me it is a rule.

• • •

Dep. Gov. I would go a little higher with Mrs. Hutchinson. About three years ago we were all in peace. Mrs. Hutchinson from that time she came hath made a disturbance, and some that came over with her in the ship did inform me what she was as soon as she was landed. I being then in place dealt with the pastor and teacher of Boston and desired them to enquire of her, and then I was satisfied that she held nothing different from us, but within half a year after, she had vented divers of her strange opinions and had made parties in the country, and at length it comes that Mr. Cotton and Mr. Vane were of her judgment, but Mr. Cotton hath cleared himself that he was not of that mind, but now it appears by this woman's meeting that Mrs. Hutchinson hath so forestalled the minds of many by their resort to her meeting that now she hath a potent party in the country. Now if all these things have endangered us from that foundation and if she in particular hath disparaged all our ministers in the land that they have preached a covenant of works, and only Mr. Cotton a covenant of grace, why this is not to be suffered, and therefore being driven to the foundation and it being found that Mrs. Hutchinson is she that hath depraved all the ministers and hath been the cause of what is fallen out, why we must take away the foundation and the building will fall.

MRS. H. I pray Sir prove it that I said they preached nothing but a covenant of works.

DEP. GOV. Nothing but a covenant of works, why a Jesuit may preach truth sometimes.

MRS. H. Did I ever say they preached a covenant of works then?

DEP. GOV. If they do not preach a covenant of grace clearly, then they preach a covenant of works.

MRS. H. No Sir, one may preach a covenant of grace more clearly than another, so I said.

D. GOV. We are not upon that now but upon position.

MRS. H. Prove this then Sir that you say I said.

D. GOV. When they do preach a covenant of works do they preach truth?

MRS. H. Yes Sir, but when they preach a covenant of works for salvation, that is not truth.

D. GOV. I do but ask you this, when the ministers do preach a covenant of works do they preach a way of salvation?

MRS. H. I did not come hither to answer to questions of that sort.

D. GOV. Because you will deny the thing.

MRS. H. Ey, but that is to be proved first.

D. GOV. I will make it plain that you did say that the ministers did preach a covenant of works.

MRS. H. I deny that.

D. GOV. And that you said they were not able ministers of the new testament, but Mr. Cotton only.

MRS. H. If ever I spake that I proved it by God's word.

COURT. Very well, very well.

MRS. H. If one shall come unto me in private, and desire me seriously to tell then what I thought of such an one. I must either speak false or true in my answer.

D. GOV. Likewise I will prove this that you said the gospel in the letter and words holds forth nothing but a covenant of works and that all that do not hold as you do are in a covenant of works.

MRS. H. I deny this for if I should so say I should speak against my own judgment.

MR. ENDICOT. I desire to speak seeing Mrs. Hutchinson seems to lay something against them that are to witness against her.

GOVER. Only I would add this. It is well discerned to the court that Mrs. Hutchinson can tell when to speak and when to hold her tongue. Upon the answering of a question which we desire her to tell her thoughts if she desires to be pardoned.

MRS. H. It is one thing for me to come before a public magistracy and there to speak what they would have me to speak and another when a man comes to me in a way of friendship privately there is difference in that.

• • •

The next morning.

GOV. We proceeded the last night as far as we could in hearing of this cause of Mrs. Hutchinson. There were divers things laid to her charge, her ordinary meetings about religious exercises, her speeches in derogation of the ministers among us, and the weakening of the hands and hearts of the people towards them. Here was sufficient proof made of that which she was accused of in that point concerning the ministers and their ministry, as that they did preach a covenant of works when others did preach a covenant of grace, and that they were not able ministers of the new testament, and that they had not the seal of the spirit, and this was spoken not as was pretended out of private conference, but out of conscience and warrant from scripture alledged the fear of man is a snare and seeing God had given her a calling to it she would freely speak. Some other speeches she used, as that the letter of the scripture held forth a covenant of works, and this is offered to be proved by probable grounds. If there be any thing else that the court hath to say they may speak.

MRS. H. The ministers come in their own cause. Now the Lord hath said that an oath is the end of all controversy; though there be a sufficient number of witnesses yet they are not according to the word, therefore I desire they may speak upon oath.

GOV. Well, it is in the liberty of the court whether they will have an oath or no and it is not in this case as in case of a jury. If they be satisfied they have sufficient matter to proceed.

MRS. H. I have since I went home perused some notes out of what Mr. Wilson did then write and I find things not to be as hath been alledged.

GOV. Where are the writings?

MRS. H. I have them not, it may be Mr. Wilson hath.

GOV. What are the instructions that you can give, Mr. Wilson?

MR. WILSON. I do say that Mr. Vane desired me to write the

discourse out and whether it be in his own hands or in some body's else I know not. For my own copy it is somewhat imperfect, but I could make it perfect with a little pains.

Gov. For that which you alledge as an exception against the elders it is vain and untrue, for they are no prosecutors in this cause but are called to witness in the cause.

Mrs. H. But they are witnesses of their own cause.

Gov. It is not their cause but the cause of the whole country and they were unwilling that it should come forth, but that it was the glory and honour of God.

Mrs. H. But it being the Lord's ordinance that an oath should be the end of all strife, therefore they are to deliver what they do upon oath.

Mr. Bradstreet. Mrs. Hutchinson, these are but circumstances and adjuncts to the cause, admit they should mistake you in your speeches you would make them to sin if you urge them to swear.

Mrs. H. That is not the thing. If they accuse me I desire it may be upon oath.

• • •

Gov. Let us state the case and then we may know what to do. That which is laid to Mrs. Hutchinson's charge is this, that she hath traduced the magistrates and ministers of this jurisdiction, that she hath said the ministers preached a covenant of works and Mr. Cotton a covenant of grace, and that they were not able ministers of the gospel, and she excuses it that she made it a private conference and with a promise of secrecy, &c. now this is charged upon her, and they therefore sent for her seeing she made it her table talk, and then she said the fear of man was a snare and therefore she would not be affeared of them.

Mrs. H. This that your self hath spoken, I desire that they may take their oaths upon.

Gov. That that we should put the reverend elders unto is this that they would deliver upon oath that which they can remember themselves.

Mr. Shepard.[1] I know no reason of the oath but the importunity of this gentlewoman.

Mr. Endicot.[2] You lifted up your eyes as if you took God to witness that you came to entrap none and yet you will have them swear.

Mr. Harlakenden.[3] Put any passage unto them and see what they say.

Mrs. H. They say I said the fear of man is a snare, why should

I be afraid. When I came unto them, they urging many things unto me and I being backward to answer at first, at length this scripture came into my mind 29th Prov. 15. The fear of man bringeth a snare, but whoso putteth his trust in the Lord shall be safe.

·   ·   ·

MRS. H. If you please to give me leave I shall give you the ground of what I know to be true. Being much troubled to see the falseness of the constitution of the church of England, I had like to have turned separatist; whereupon I kept a day of solemn humiliation and pondering of the thing; this scripture was brought unto me—he that denies Jesus Christ to be come in the flesh is antichrist—This I considered of and in considering found that the papists did not deny him to be come in the flesh, nor we did not deny him—who then was antichrist? Was the Turk antichrist only? The Lord knows that I could not open scripture; he must by his prophetical office open it unto me. So after that being unsatisfied in the thing, the Lord was pleased to bring this scripture out of the Hebrews. He that denies the testament denies the testator, and in this did open unto me and give me to see that those which did not teach the new covenant had the spirit of antichrist, and upon this he did discover the ministry unto me and ever since, I bless the Lord, he hath let me see which was the clear ministry and which the wrong. Since that time I confess I have been more choice and he hath left me to distinguish between the voice of my beloved and the voice of Moses, the voice of John Baptist and the voice of antichrist, for all those voices are spoken of in scripture. Now if you do condemn me for speaking what in my conscience I know to be truth I must commit myself unto the Lord.

MR. NOWEL.[4] How do you know that that was the spirit?

MRS. H. How did Abraham know that it was God that bid him offer his son, being a breach of the sixth commandment?

DEP. GOV. By an immediate voice.

MRS. H. So to me by an immediate revelation.

DEP. GOV. How! an immediate revelation.

MRS. H. By the voice of his own spirit to my soul. I will give you another scripture, Jer. 46. 27, 28—out of which the Lord shewed me what he would do for me and the rest of his servants.—But after he was pleased to reveal himself to me I did presently like Abraham run to Hagar. And after that he did let me see the atheism of my own heart, for which I begged of the Lord that it might not remain in my heart, and being thus, he did shew me this (a twelvemonth after) which

I told you of before. Ever since that time I have been confident of what he hath revealed unto me.

[*Obliterated*] another place out of Daniel chap. 7. and he and for us all, wherein he shewed me the sitting of the judgment and the standing of all high and low before the Lord and how thrones and kingdoms were cast down before him. When our teacher came to New England it was a great trouble unto me, my brother Wheelwright being put by also. I was then much troubled concerning the ministry under which I lived, and then that place in the 30th of Isaiah was brought to my mind. Though the Lord give thee bread of adversity and water of affliction yet shall not thy teachers be removed into corners any more, but thine eyes shall see thy teachers. The Lord giving me this promise and they being gone there was none then left that I was able to hear, and I could not be at rest but I must come hither. Yet that place of Isaiah did much follow me, though the Lord give thee the bread of adversity and water of affliction. This place lying I say upon me then this place in Daniel was brought unto me and did shew me that though I should meet with affliction yet I am the same God that delivered Daniel out of the lion's den, I will also deliver thee.——— Therefore I desire you to look to it, for you see this scripture fulfilled this day and therefore I desire you that as you tender the Lord and the church and commonwealth to consider and look what you do. You have power over my body but the Lord Jesus hath power over my body and soul, and assure yourselves thus much, you do as much as in you lies to put the Lord Jesus Christ from you, and if you go on in this course you begin you will bring a curse upon you and your posterity, and the mouth of the Lord hath spoken it.

DEP. GOV. What is the scripture she brings?

MR. STOUGHTON.[5] Behold I turn away from you.

MRS. H. But now having seen him which is invisible I fear not what man can do unto me.

GOV. Daniel was delivered by miracle do you think to be deliver'd so too?

MRS. H. I do here speak it before the court. I look that the Lord should deliver me by his providence.

MR. HARLAKENDEN. I may read scripture and the most glorious hypocrite may read them and yet go down to hell.

MRS. H. It may be so.

• • •

Here now was a great whispering among the ministers, some drew back others were animated on.

MR. ELIOT.[6] If the court calls us out to swear we will swear.

GOV. Any two of you will serve.

MR. STOUGHTON. There are two things that I would look to discharge my conscience of, 1st to hear what they testify upon oath and 2dly to——

GOV. It is required of you Mr. Weld and Mr. Eliot.

MR. WELD[7] AND MR. ELIOT. We shall be willing.

GOV. We'll give them their oaths. [Mr. Peters held up his hand also.] You shall swear to the truth and nothing but the truth as far as you know. So help you God. What you do remember of her speak, pray speak.

MR. ELIOT. I do remember and I have it written, that which she spake first was, the fear of man is a snare, why should she be afraid but would speak freely. The question being asked whether there was a difference between Mr. Cotton and us, she said there was a broad difference. I would not stick upon words—the thing she said—and that Mr. Cotton did preach a covenant of grace and we of works and she gave this reason—to put a work in point of evidence is a revealing upon a work. We did labour then to convince her that our doctrine was the same with Mr. Cotton's: She said no, for we were not sealed. This is all I shall say.

GOV. What say you Mr. Weld?

MR. WELD. I will speak to the things themselves—these two things I am fully clear in—she did make a difference in three things, the first I was not so clear in, but that she said this I am fully sure of, that we were not able ministers of the new testament and that we were not clear in our experience because we were not sealed.

MR. ELIOT. I do further remember this also, that she said we were not able ministers of the gospel because we were but like the apostles before the ascension.

MR. CODDINGTON. This was I hope no disparagement to you.

GOV. Well, we see in the court that she doth continually say and unsay things.

MR. PETERS.[8] I was much grieved that she should say that our ministry was legal. Upon which we had a meeting as you know and this was the same she told us that there was a broad difference between Mr. Cotton and us. Now if Mr. Cotton do hold forth things more clearly than we, it was our grief we did not hold it so clearly as he did, and upon those grounds that you have heard.

MR. CODDINGTON. What wrong was that to say that you were not able ministers of the new testament or that you were like the apostles—me-thinks the comparison is very good.

GOV. Well, you remember that she said but now that she should be delivered from this calamity.

MR. COTTON. I remember she said she should be delivered by God's providence, whether now or at another time she knew not.

MR. PETERS. I profess I thought Mr. Cotton would never have took her part.

MR. STOUGHTON. I say now this testimony doth convince me in the thing, and I am fully satisfied the words were pernicious, and the frame of her spirit doth hold forth the same.

GOV. The court hath already declared themselves satisfied concerning the things you hear, and concerning the troublesomness of her spirit and the danger of her course amongst us, which is not to be suffered. Therefore if it be the mind of the court that Mrs. Hutchinson for these things that appear before us is unfit for our society, and if it be the mind of the court that she shall be banished out of our liberties and imprisoned till she be sent away, let them hold up their hands.

All but three.

Those that are contrary minded hold up yours,

Mr. Coddington and Mr. Colborn, only.

MR. JENNISON.[9] I cannot hold up my hand one way or the other, and I shall give my reason if the court require it.

GOV. Mrs. Hutchinson, the sentence of the court you hear is that you are banished from out of our jurisdiction as being a woman not fit for our society, and are to be imprisoned till the court shall send you away.

MRS. H. I desire to know wherefore I am banished?

GOV. Say no more, the court knows wherefore and is satisfied.

Thomas Shepard
(1605–1649)

Thomas Shepard was a Cambridge-educated clergyman banned for his Puritan views in England who emigrated to Massachusetts in 1635. Soon after his arrival he became minister of the church in Cambridge and a leader in the new colony. Active in the founding of Harvard University as well as in the conversion of Indian peoples, Shepard not only helped draft the basic statement of New England Congregationalism known as the Cambridge Platform in 1648 but also served in the synod that condemned Ann Hutchinson and the Antinominians eleven years earlier, in 1637. Author of numerous works that include his Autobiography (publ. 1832) and the popular Sincere Convert (1641), Shepard captured the essence of what Puritans meant by the "Covenant of Grace" in the sermon printed below.

    The Covenant of Grace sealed by the coming of Jesus Christ, though originally made with Abraham and his seed, was intended to supplant the Covenant of Works that God had originally established with Adam and his descendants. After Adam failed to live up to the Covenant of Works, God established a new relation with his creatures in which salvation would no longer depend on fulfilling the requirements of the Law given to Moses on Mount Sinai and inscribed in the heart but only on accepting God's freely given, though wholly unmerited, grace, which was now made historically available and physically palpable in the Incarnation. The Covenant of Grace did not alter the fact that God was free to choose to save only those whom He elected to save, nor did it mean that those chosen to be saved or wishing to be saved should not work to prepare themselves. It simply meant that the grace of God made manifest in salvation had nothing to do with human accomplishment and could not be reduced to a human *arrangement. The Covenant of Grace was merely the "intelligible medium," as one historian has put it, "between the absolute and undecipherable mystery of God's original purposes and His ultimate performance."*

The Covenant of Grace
(1651)

The blessed God hath evermore delighted to reveal and communicate Himself by way of Covenant. He might have done good to man before his fall, as also since his fall, without binding Himself in the bond of Covenant; Noah, Abraham, and David, Jews, Gentiles, might have had the blessings intended, without any promise or Covenant. But the Lord's heart is so full of love (especially to His own) that it cannot be contained so long within the bounds of secrecy—*viz.* from God's eternal purpose to the actual accomplishment of good things intended—but it must aforehand overflow and break out into the many streams of a blessed Covenant. The Lord can never get near enough to His people, and thinks He can never get them near enough unto Himself, and therefore unites and binds and fastens them close to Himself, and Himself unto them, by the bonds of a Covenant. And therefore when we break our Covenant, and that will not hold us, He takes a faster bond and makes a sure and everlasting Covenant, according to Grace, not according to Works; and that shall hold His people firm unto Himself, and hold Himself close and fast unto them, that He may never depart from us.

Oh! the depth of God's grace herein: that when sinful man deserves never to have the least good word from Him, that He should open His whole heart and purpose to him in a Covenant; that when he deserves nothing else but separation from God, and to be driven up and down the world as a vagabond, or as dried leaves fallen from our God, that yet the Almighty God cannot be content with it, but must make Himself to us, and us to Himself, more sure and near than ever before! And is not this Covenant then (Christian reader) worth thy looking into and searching after? Surely never was there a time wherein the Lord calls His people to more serious searching into the nature of the Covenant than in these days.

For are there not some who cut off the entail to children of those in Covenant, and so lessen and shorten the riches of grace in the Lord's free Covenant, and that in the time of more grace under the Gospel than He was wont to dispense under the Law? Are there not others who preach a new, or rather another Gospel or Covenant—*viz.* that actual remission of sins and reconciliation with God (purchased indeed in redemption by Christ's death) is without, nay, before faith . . . ? Is it not time for the people of God now to pry into the secret of God's Covenant—which He reveals to them that fear Him (Psal. 25. 14)—when, by clipping of it and distinguishing about it, the beautiful countenance of it begins to be changed and transformed by those angels of "new light" [from that] which once it had when it began to be published in the simplicity of it by the Apostles of Christ (II Cor. 11. 3)? Nay, is not the time come wherein the Lord of hosts seems to have a quarrel against all the world, and especially His churches and people, whom He goes on to waste by the sharpest sword that (almost) was ever drawn out? And is it not the duty of all that have the least spark of holy fear and trembling to ask and search diligently what should be the reason of this sore anger and hot displeasure, before they and theirs be consumed in the burning flames of it?

Search the scriptures, and there we shall find the cause, and see God Himself laying His finger upon that which is the sore and the wound of such times: for so it is said (Isa. 24. 1–5), "Behold, the Lord maketh the earth empty and waste, and turns it upside down, and scattereth abroad the inhabitants thereof; and it shall be as with the people, so with the priest; and the land shall be utterly spoiled." Why? "For the earth is defiled under the inhabitants thereof." Why so? "Because they have transgressed the laws, changed the ordinance, and broken the everlasting Covenant." And therefore when the Lord shall have wasted His church, and hath made it as Adnah and Zeboim, when heathen nations shall ask, "Wherefore hath the Lord done all this against this land? What meaneth the heat of His great anger?", the answer is made by the Lord Himself expressly (Deut. 29. 25): *viz.* "Because they have forsaken the Covenant of the Lord God of their fathers." And no wonder, for they that reject the Covenant of Grace, they break the league of peace between God and themselves. And hence, if acts of hostility in desolating kingdoms, churches, families and persons break out from a long-suffering God, they may easily see the cause, and that the cause and quarrel of God herein is just.

As all good things are conveyed to God's people not barely by common providence but by special Covenant (Isa. 16. 8, 9), so all the evils they meet with in this world (if in them the face of God's anger appears), upon narrow search, will be found to arise from breach of Covenant, more or less. So that if it be the great cause of all the public calamities of the church and people of God, and those calamities are already begun, and God's hand is stretched out still—was there then ever a more seasonable time and hour to study the Covenant, and so see the sin, repent of it, and at last to lay hold of God's rich grace and bowels in it, lest the Lord go on and fulfill the word of His servants, and expose most pleasant lands to the doleful lamentation of a very little remnant, reserved as a few coals in the ashes, when all else is consumed?

As particular persons, when they break their Covenant, the Lord therefore breaks out against them: so, when whole churches forsake their Covenant, the Lord therefore doth sorely visit them. Sins of ignorance the Lord Jesus pities (Heb. 5. 2) and many times winks at, but sins against light He cannot endure (II Pet. 2. 21). Sins against light are great, but sins against the purpose and Covenant, nay God's Covenant, are by many degrees worse, for the soul of man rusheth most violently and strongly against God when it breaks through all the light of the mind and purposes of the will that stand in his way to keep him from sin. And is not this done by breach of Covenant? And therefore no wonder if the Lord makes His people's chain heavy by sore affliction, until they come to consider and behold this sin, and learn more fear (after they are bound to their good behavior) of breaking Covenant with God again.

It is true, the Covenant effectually made can never be really broke, yet externally it may. But suppose God's churches were in greatest peace, and had a blessed rest from all their labors round about them: yet what is the child's position, but his legacy left him, written with the finger of God his father, in the New Covenant, and the blood of Jesus Christ his redeemer, in His last will and testament? What is a Christian's comfort, and where doth it chiefly lie, but in this: that the Lord hath made with him an everlasting Covenant, in all things stablished and sure? Which were the last breathing of the sweet singer of Israel, and the last bubblings up of the joy of his heart (II Sam. 23. 5).

God the Father's eternal purposes are sealed secrets, not immediately seen, and the full and blessed accomplishments of those purposes are not yet experimentally felt. The Covenant is the midst between both God's purposes and performances, by which and in which we come to see the one before the world began, and by a blessed faith (which makes things absent, present) to enjoy the other, which shall be our glory when this world shall be burned up and all things in it shall have an end. For in God's Covenant we see with open face God's secret purpose for time past—God's purposes toward His people being, as it were, nothing else but promises concealed, and God's promises in the Covenant being nothing else but His purposes revealed. As also, in the same Covenant and promises we see performances for [the] future, as if they were accomplishments at present. Where then is a Christian's comfort but in that Covenant, wherein two eternities (as it were) meet together, and whereby he may see accomplishments (made sure to him) of eternal glory, arising from blessed purposes of eternal grace? In a word, wherein he fastens upon God, and hath Him from everlasting to everlasting, comprehended at hand near and obvious in His words of a gracious Covenant?

The Church of God is therefore bound to bless God much for this food in season, and for the holy judicious and learned labors of this aged, experienced and precious servant of Christ Jesus, who hath taken much pains to discover—and that not in words and allegories but in the demonstration and evidence of the Spirit—the great mystery of godliness wrapped up in the Covenant, and hath now fully opened sundry knotty questions concerning the same, which happily have not been brought so fully to light until now. Which cannot but be of singular and seasonable use, to prevent apostasies from the simplicity of the Covenant and Gospel of Christ. The sermons were preached in the remote ends of the earth and, as it were, set under a bushel, a church more remote from the numerous society of others of the saints; if now, therefore, the light be set upon a hill, 'tis where it should stand, and where Christ surely would have it put. The good Lord enlighten the minds of all those who seek for the truth by this and such like helps; and the Lord enlighten the whole world with His glory, even with the glory of His Covenant, grace and love, that His people hereby may be sealed up daily unto all fulness of assurance and peace, in these evil times.

Anne Bradstreet
(1612?–1672)

Anne Bradstreet, along with Simon, her husband of two years, and her parents, sailed to the New World and Massachusetts Bay aboard the Arabella and undoubtedly heard John Winthrop deliver his famous sermon "A Modell of Christian Charity." But upon landing in New England, Bradstreet reports that her heart initially "rose up" against her surroundings and was to become reconciled to them only with difficulty. Having left behind in England a life of relative comfort and modest privilege—her father, Thomas Dudley, was a financial officer in the house of Lord Lincoln and had taken pains to expose his daughter to the intellectual wealth of this Puritan nobleman's library —she found her circumstances in the New World far ruder and more primitive than she had imagined, learning to accept them only when she became convinced that her transplantation was part of God's plan.

Arriving in Salem, the family quickly moved to Newtowne (present-day Cambridge), where they resided for just over a decade before setting out for the Massachusetts frontier in Ipswich. The physical hardships of life in Ipswich were offset by a remarkable intellectual community that joined the Bradstreets there, a group that included John Winthrop, Jr., the owner of another good library, and Nathaniel Ward, author of The Simple Cobbler at Aggawam (1646?). It was in Ipswich that Bradstreet began to write poetry in earnest, though much of her best-known verse and prose was written after the family had *moved yet again fifteen miles farther west, and still deeper into the American wilderness, to [North] Andover.*

While her earlier poetry concerned itself with formal, often classical, subjects, such as the four elements or the cycles of history, her later poems addressed more personal and domestic issues, such as her husband's frequent absences from home on the colony's business, or the death of one of her grandchildren, or the burning of her house. Less learned or artistically ambitious than her first poems—at the outset Bradstreet clearly wanted to establish a place for herself in the ranks of English poetry—her later poems develop the tension between her need to take the full emotional measure of her experiences, many of them daunting, and her need to submit to what she believed to be the will of God for her life. This tension in her later verse makes for a poetry of unusual candor and immediacy as she struggles with the difference between writing what she thought she ought to feel and writing what she actually did feel.

In 1650, partly in response to the interest her work had aroused among family and friends, her brother-in-law, unbeknownst to her, carried thirteen of her earlier poems to England, where they were published under the title The Tenth Muse Lately Sprung up in America. *Somewhat abashed that poems intended for private circulation had now received public exposure—*The Tenth Muse *is the first book of poetry published by an "American" writer—she later recorded her surprise and embarrassment over the publication of what she referred to as her "ill-formed offspring" in "The Author to Her Book." The great bulk of her poetry that we now value more highly was published in 1678, six years after her death.*

The Prologue
(1650)

To sing of Wars, of Captains, and of Kings,
Of Cities founded, Common-wealths begun,
For my mean pen are too superiour things:
Or how they all, or each their dates have run
Let Poets and Historians set these forth,
My obscure Lines shall not so dim their worth.

But when my wondring eyes and envious heart
Great *Bartas*[1] sugar'd lines, do but read o're
Fool I do grudg the Muses did not part
'Twixt him and me that overfluent store;

A *Bartas* can, do what a *Bartas* will
But simple I according to my skill.

From school-boyes tongue no rhet'rick we expect
Nor yet a sweet Consort from broken strings,
Nor perfect beauty, where's a main defect:
My foolish, broken, blemish'd Muse so sings
And this to mend, alas, no Art is able,
'Cause nature, made it so irreparable.

Nor can I, like that fluent sweet tongu'd Greek,[2]
Who lisp'd at first, in future times speak plain
By Art he gladly found what he did seek
A full requital of his, striving pain
Art can do much, but this maxime's most sure
A weak or wounded brain admits no cure.

I am obnoxious to each carping tongue
Who says my hand a needle better fits,
A Poets pen all scorn I should thus wrong,
For such despite they cast on Female wits:
If what I do prove well, it won't advance,
They'l say it's stoln, or else it was by chance.

But sure the Antique Greeks were far more mild
Else of our Sexe, why feigned they those Nine
And poesy made, *Calliope's* own Child;
So 'mongst the rest they placed the Arts Divine,
But this weak knot, they will full soon untie,
The Greeks did nought, but play the fools & lye.

Let Greeks be Greeks, and women what they are
Men have precedency and still excell,
It is but vain unjustly to wage warre;
Men can do best, and women know it well
Preheminence in all and each is yours;
Yet grant some small acknowledgement of ours.

And oh ye high flown quills that soar the Skies,
And ever with your prey still catch your praise,
If e're you daigne these lowly lines your eyes
Give Thyme or Parsley wreath, I ask no bayes,
This mean and unrefined ore of mine
Will make you glistring gold, but more to shine.

The Author to Her Book (1678)

Thou ill-form'd offspring of my feeble brain,
Who after birth did'st by my side remain,
Till snatcht from thence by friends, less wise than true
Who thee abroad, expos'd to publick view,
Made thee in raggs, halting to th' press to trudge,
Where errors were not lessened (all may judge)
At thy return my blushing was not small,
My rambling brat (in print) should mother call,
I cast thee by as one unfit for light,
Thy Visage was so irksome in my sight;
Yet being mine own, at length affection would
Thy blemishes amend, if so I could:
I wash'd thy face, but more defects I saw,
And rubbing off a spot, still made a flaw.
I stretcht thy joynts to make thee even feet,
Yet still thou run'st more hobling then is meet;
In better dress to trim thee was my mind,
But nought save home-spun Cloth, i'th' house I find
In this array, 'mongst Vulgars¹ mayst thou roam
In Critick's hands, beware thou dost not come;
And take thy way where yet thou art not known,
If for thy Father askt, say, thou hadst none:
And for thy Mother, she alas is poor,
Which caus'd her thus to send thee out of door.

Before the Birth of One of
Her Children (1678)

All things within this fading world hath end,
Adversity doth still our joyes attend;
No tyes so strong, no friends so dear and sweet,
But with deaths parting blow is sure to meet.
The sentence past is most irrovocable,
A common thing, yet oh inevitable;
How soon, my Dear, death may my steps attend,
How soon't may be thy Lot to lose thy friend,
We both are ignorant, yet love bids me
These farewell lines to recommend to thee,

That when that knot's unty'd that made us one,
I may seem thine, who in effect am none.
And if I see not half my dayes that's due,
What nature would, God grant to yours and you;
The many faults that well you know I have,
Let be interr'd in my oblivion's grave;
If any worth or virtue were in me,
Let that live freshly in thy memory
And when thou feel'st no grief, as I no harms,
Yet love thy dead, who long lay in thine arms:
And when thy loss shall be repaid with gains
Look to my little babes my dear remains.
And if thou love thy self, or loved'st me
These O protect from step Dames¹ injury.
And if chance to thine eyes shall bring this verse,
With some sad sighs honour my absent Herse;²
And kiss this paper for thy love's dear sake,
Who with salt tears this last Farewel did take.

Contemplations *(1678)*

Some time now past in the Autumnal Tide,
When *Phœbus* wanted but one hour to bed,
The trees all richly clad, yet void of pride,
Where gilded o're by his rich golden head.
Their leaves & fruits seem'd painted, but was true
Of green, of red, of yellow, mixed hew,
Rapt were my fences at this delectable view.

I wist not what to wish, yet sure thought I,
If so much excellence abide below;
How excellent is he that dwells on high?
Whose power and beauty by his works we know.
Sure he is goodness, wisdom, glory, light,
That hath this under world so richly dight:¹
More Heaven then Earth was here no winter & no night.

Then on a stately Oak I cast mine Eye,
Whose ruffling top the Clouds seem'd to aspire;
How long since thou wast in thine Infancy?
Thy strength, and stature, more thy years admire,

Hath hundred winters past since thou wast born?
Or thousand since thou brakest thy shell of horn,[2]
If so, all these as nought, Eternity doth scorn.

Then higher on the glistering Sun I gaz'd,
Whose beams was shaded by the leafie Tree,
The more I look'd, the more I grew amaz'd,
And softly said, what glory's like to thee?
Soul of this world, this Universe's Eye,
No wonder, some made thee a Deity:
Had I not better known, (alas) the fame had I.

Thou as a Bridegroom from thy Chamber rushes,
And as a strong man, joyes to run a race,[3]
The morn doth usher thee, with smiles & blushes,
The Earth reflects her glances in thy face.
Birds, insects, Animals with Vegative,
Thy heart from death and dulness doth revive:
And in the darksome womb of fruitful nature dive.

Thy swift Annual, and diurnal Course,
Thy daily streight, and yearly oblique path,
Thy pleasing fervor, and thy scorching force,
All mortals here the feeling knowledge hath.
Thy presence makes it day, thy absence night,
Quaternal Seasons caused by thy might:
Hail Creature, full of sweetness, beauty & delight.

Art thou so full of glory, that no Eye
Hath strength, thy shining Rayes once to behold?
And is thy splendid Throne erect so high?
As to approach it, can no earthly mould.
How full of glory then must thy Creator be?
Who gave this bright light luster unto thee:
Admir'd, ador'd for ever, be that Majesty.

Silent alone, where none or saw, or heard,
In pathless paths I lead my wandring feet,
My humble Eyes to lofty Skyes I rear'd
To sing some Song, my mazed Muse thought meet.
My great Creator I would magnifie,
That nature had, thus decked liberally:
But Ah, and Ah, again, my imbecility!

I heard the merry grashopper then sing,
The black clad Cricket, bear a second part,
They kept one tune, and plaid on the same string,
Seeming to glory in their little Art.
Shall Creatures abject, thus their voices raise?
And in their kind resound their makers praise:
Whilst I as mute, can warble forth no higher layes.

When present times look back to Ages past,
And men in being fancy those are dead,
It makes things gone perpetually to last,
And calls back moneths and years that long since fled
It makes a man more aged in conceit,
Then was *Methuselah*, or's grand-sire great:
While of their persons & their acts his mind doth treat.

Sometimes in *Eden* fair, he seems to be,
Sees glorious *Adam* there made Lord of all,
Fancyes the Apple, dangle on the Tree,
That turn'd his Sovereign to a naked thrall.
Who like a miscreant's driven from that place,
To get his bread with pain, and sweat of face:
A penalty impos'd on his backsliding Race.

Here sits our Grandame in retired place,
And in her lap, her bloody *Cain* new born,
The weeping Imp oft looks her in the face,
Bewails his unknown hap,[4] and fate forlorn;
His Mother sighs, to think of Paradise,
And how she lost her bliss, to be more wife,
Believing him that was, and is, Father of lyes.

Here *Cain* and *Abel* come to sacrifice,
Fruits of the Earth, and Fatlings each do bring,
On *Abels* gift the fire descends from Skies,
But no such sign on false *Cain's* offering;
With sullen hateful looks he goes his wayes.
Hath thousand thoughts to end his brothers dayes,
Upon whose blood his future good he hopes to raise

There *Abel* keeps his sheep, no ill he thinks,
His brother comes, then acts his fratricide,
The Virgin Earth, of blood her first draught drinks

But since that time she often hath been cloy'd;
The wretch with gastly face and dreadful mind,
Thinks each he sees will serve him in his kind,
Though none on Earth but kindred near then could he find.

Who fancyes not his looks now at the Barr,[5]
His face like death, his heart with horror fraught,
Nor Male-factor ever felt like warr,
When deep dispair, with wish of life hath fought,
Branded with guilt, and crusht with treble woes,
A Vagabond to Land of *Nod*[6] he goes.
A City builds, that walls might him secure from foes.

Who thinks not oft upon the Father's ages.
Their long descent, how nephews' sons they saw,
The starry observations of those Sages,
And how their precepts to their sons were law,
How Adam sigh'd to see his Progeny,
Cloath'd all in his black sinfull Livery,
Who neither guilt, nor yet the punishment could fly.

Our Life compare we with their length of dayes
Who to the tenth of theirs doth now arrive?
And though thus short, we shorten many wayes,
Living so little while we are alive;
In eating, drinking, sleeping, vain delight
So unawares comes on perpetual night,
And puts all pleasures vain unto eternal flight.

When I behold the heavens as in their prime,
And then the earth (though old) still clad in green,
The stones and trees, insensible of time,
Nor age nor wrinkle on their front are seen;
If winter come, and greeness then do fade,
A Spring returns, and they more youthfull made;
But Man grows old, lies down, remains where once he's laid.

By birth more noble then those creatures all,
Yet seems by nature and by custom curs'd,
No sooner born, but grief and care makes fall
That state obliterate he had at first:
Nor youth, nor strength, nor wisdom spring again
Nor habitations long their names retain,
But in oblivion to the final day remain.

Shall I then praise the heavens, the trees, the earth
Because their beauty and their strength last longer
Shall I wish there, or never to had birth,
Because they're bigger, & their bodyes stronger?
Nay, they shall darken, perish, fade and dye,
And when unmade, so ever shall they lye,
But man was made for endless immortality.

Under the cooling shadow of a stately Elm
Close sat I by a goodly Rivers side,
Where gliding streams the Rocks did overwhelm;
A lonely place, with pleasures dignifi'd.
I once that lov'd the shady woods so well,
Now thought the rivers did the trees excel,
And if the sun would ever shine, there would I dwell.

While on the stealing stream I fixt mine eye,
Which to the long'd for Ocean held its course,
I markt, nor crooks, nor rubs that there did lye
Could hinder ought, but still augment its force:
O happy Flood, quoth I, that holds thy race
Till thou arrive at thy beloved place,
Nor is it rocks or shoals that can obstruct thy pace

Nor is't enough, that thou alone may'st slide,
But hundred brooks in thy cleer waves do meet,
So hand in hand along with thee they glide
To *Thetis* house,[7] where all imbrace and greet:
Thou Emblem true, of what I count the best,
O could I lead my Rivolets to rest,
So may we press to that vast mansion, ever blest.

Ye Fish which in this liquid Region 'bide,
That for each season, have your habitation,
Now salt, now fresh where you think best to glide
To unknown coasts to give a visitation,
In Lakes and ponds, you leave your numerous fry,
So nature taught, and yet you know not why,
You watry folk that know not your felicity.

Look how the wantons frisk to taste the air,
Then to the colder bottom streight they dive,
Estsoon[8] to *Neptun*'s[9] glassie Hall repair

To see what trade they great ones there do drive,
Who forrage o're the spacious sea-green field,
And take the trembling prey before it yield,
Whose armour is their scales, their spreading fins their shield.

While musing thus with contemplation fed,
And thousand fancies buzzing in my brain,
The sweet-tongu'd Philomel[10] percht ore my head,
And chanted forth a most melodious strain
Which rapt me so with wonder and delight,
I judg'd my hearing better then my sight,
And wisht me wings with her a while to take my flight.

O merry Bird (said I) that fears no snares,
That neither toyles nor hoards up in thy barn,
Feels no sad thoughts, nor cruciating[11] cares
To gain more good, or shun what might thee harm
Thy cloaths ne're wear, thy meat is every where,
Thy bed a bough, thy drink the water cleer,
Reminds not what is past, nor what's to come dost fear

The dawning morn with songs thou dost prevent,
Sets hundred notes unto thy feathered crew,
So each one tunes his pretty instrument,
And warbling out the old, begin anew,
And thus they pass their youth in summer season,
Then follow thee into a better Region,
Where winter's never felt by that sweet airy legion

Man at the best a creature frail and vain,
In knowledge ignorant, in strength but weak,
Subject to sorrows, losses, sickness, pain,
Each storm his state, his mind, his body break,
From some of these he never finds cessation,
But day or night, within, without, vexation,
Troubles from foes, from friends, from dearest, near'st
   Relation

And yet this sinfull creature, frail and vain,
This lump of wretchedness, of sin and sorrow,
This weather-beaten vessel wrackt with pain,
Joyes not in hope of an eternal morrow;
Nor all his losses, crosses and vexation,

In weight, in frequency and long duration
Can make him deeply groan for that divine Translation.

The Mariner that on smooth waves doth glide,
Sings merrily, and steers his Barque with ease,
As if he had command of wind and tide,
And now become great Master of the seas;
But suddenly a storm spoiles all the sport,
And makes him long for a more quiet port,
Which 'gainst all adverse winds may serve for fort.

So he that saileth in this world of pleasure,
Feeding on sweets, that never bit of th' sour,
That's full of friends, of honour and of treasure,
Fond fool, he takes this earth ev'n for heav'ns bower.
But sad affliction comes & makes him see
Here's neither honour, wealth, nor safety;
Only above is found all with security.

O Time the fatal wrack of mortal things,
That draws oblivions curtains over kings,
Their sumptuous monuments, men know them not,
Their names without a Record are forgot,
Their parts, their ports, their pomp's all laid in th' dust
Nor wit nor gold, nor buildings scape time's rust;
But he whose name is grav'd in the white stone[12]
Shall last and shine when all of these are gone.

To My Dear and Loving Husband
(1678)

If ever two were one, then surely we.
If ever man were lov'd by wife, then thee;
If ever wife was happy in a man,
Compare with me ye women if you can.
I prize thy love more then whole Mines of gold,
Or all the riches that the East doth hold.
My love is such that Rivers cannot quench,
Nor ought but love from thee, give recompence.
Thy love is such I can no way repay,
The heavens reward thee manifold I pray.
Then while we live, in love let's so persever,[1]
That when we live no more, we may live ever.

A Letter to Her Husband,
Absent upon Publick Employment
(1678)

My head, my heart, mine Eyes, my life, nay more,
My joy, my Magazine of earthly store,
If two be one, as surely thou and I,
How stayest thou there, whilst I at *Ipswich*[1] lye?
So many steps, head from the heart to sever
If but a neck, soon should we be together:
I like the earth this season, mourn in black,
My Sun is gone so far in's Zodiack,
Whom whilst I 'joy'd, nor storms, nor frosts I felt,
His warmth such frigid colds did cause to melt.
My chilled limbs now nummed lye forlorn;
Return, return sweet *Sol* from *Capricorn*;[2]
In this dead time, alas, what can I more
Than view those fruits which through thy heat I bore?
Which sweet contentment yield me for a space,
True living Pictures of their Fathers face.
O strange effect! now thou art *Southward* gone,
I weary grow, the tedious day so long;
But when thou *Northward* to me shalt return,
I wish my Sun may never set, but burn
Within the Cancer[3] of my glowing breast,
The welcome house of him my dearest guest.
Where ever, ever stay, and go not thence,
Till natures sad decree shall call thee hence;
Flesh of thy flesh, bone of thy bone,[4]
I here, thou there, yet both but one.

In Memory of My Dear
Grand-Child Elizabeth Bradstreet,
Who Deceased August, 1665,
Being a Year and Half Old
(1678)

Farewell dear babe, my hearts too much content,
Farewell sweet babe, the pleasure of mine eye,
Farewell fair flower that for a space was lent,

Then ta'en away unto Eternity.
Blest babe why should I once bewail thy fate,
Or sigh the dayes so soon were terminate;
Sith[1] thou art settled in an Everlasting state.

By nature Trees do rot when they are grown.
And Plumbs and Apples throughly ripe do fall,
And Corn and grass are in their season mown,
And time brings down what is both strong and tall.
But plants new set to be eradicate,
And buds new blown, to have so short a date,
Is by his hand alone that guides nature and fate.

Here Follows Some Verses upon the Burning of Our House
(July 10th, 1666)

Copied Out of a Loose Paper

In silent night when rest I took
For sorrow near I did not look
I wakened was with thund'ring noise
And piteous shrieks of dreadful voice.
That fearful sound of "Fire!" and "Fire!"
Let no man know is my desire.
I, starting up, the light did spy,
And to my God my heart did cry
To strengthen me in my distress
And not to leave me succorless.
Then, coming out, beheld a space
The flame consume my dwelling place.
And when I could no longer look,
I blest His name that gave and took,
That laid my goods now in the dust.
Yea, so it was, and so 'twas just.
It was His own, it was not mine,
Far be it that I should repine;
He might of all justly bereft
But yet sufficient for us left.
When by the ruins oft I past
My sorrowing eyes aside did cast,

And here and there the places spy
Where oft I sat and long did lie:
Here stood that trunk, and there that chest,
There lay that store I counted best.
My pleasant things in ashes lie,
And them behold no more shall I.
Under thy roof no guest shall sit,
Nor at thy table eat a bit.
No pleasant tale shall e'er be told,
Nor things recounted done of old.
No candle e'er shall shine in thee,
Nor bridegroom's voice e'er heard shall be.
In silence ever shall thou lie,
Adieu, Adieu, all's vanity.
Then straight I 'gin my heart to chide,
And did thy wealth on earth abide?
Didst fix thy hope on mold'ring dust?
The arm of flesh didst make thy trust?
Raise up thy thoughts above the sky
That dunghill mists away may fly.
Thou hast an house on high erect,
Framed by that mighty Architect,
With glory richly furnished,
Stands permanent though this be fled.
It's purchased and paid for too
By Him who hath enough to do.
A price so vast as is unknown
Yet by His gift is made thine own;
There's wealth enough, I need no more,
Farewell, my pelf,[1] farewell my store.
The world no longer let me love,
My hope and treasure lies above.

To My Dear Children

This book by any yet unread,
I leave for you when I am dead,
That being gone, here you may find
What was your living mother's mind.
Make use of what I leave in love,
And God shall bless you from above.

                                             A. B.

MY DEAR CHILDREN,

I, knowing by experience that the exhortations of parents take most effect when the speakers leave to speak, and those especially sink deepest which are spoke latest, and being ignorant whether on my death bed I shall have opportunity to speak to any of you, much less to all, thought it the best, whilst I was able, to compose some short matters (for what else to call them I know not) and bequeath to you, that when I am no more with you, yet I may be daily in your remembrance (although that is the least in my aim in what I now do), but that you may gain some spiritual advantage by my experience. I have not studied in this you read to show my skill, but to declare the truth, not to set forth myself, but the glory of God. If I had minded the former, it had been perhaps better pleasing to you, but seeing the last is the best, let it be best pleasing to you.

The method I will observe shall be this: I will begin with God's dealing with me from my childhood to this day.

In my young years, about 6 or 7 as I take it, I began to make conscience of my ways, and what I knew was sinful, as lying, disobedience to parents, etc., I avoided it. If at any time I was overtaken with the like evils, it was as a great trouble, and I could not be at rest 'till by prayer I had confessed it unto God. I was also troubled at the neglect of private duties though too often tardy that way. I also found much comfort in reading the Scriptures, especially those places I thought most concerned my condition, and as I grew to have more understanding, so the more solace I took in them.

In a long fit of sickness which I had on my bed I often communed with my heart and made my supplication to the most High who set me free from that affliction.

But as I grew up to be about 14 or 15, I found my heart more carnal, and sitting loose from God, vanity and the follies of youth take hold of me.

About 16, the Lord laid His hand sore upon me and smote me with the smallpox. When I was in my affliction, I besought the Lord and confessed my pride and vanity, and He was entreated of me and again restored me. But I rendered not to Him according to the benefit received.

After a short time I changed my condition and was married, and came into this country, where I found a new world and new manners, at which my heart rose. But after I was convinced it was the way of God, I submitted to it and joined to the church at Boston.

After some time I fell into a lingering sickness like a consumption together with a lameness, which correction I saw the Lord sent to humble and try me and do me good, and it was not altogether ineffectual.

It pleased God to keep me a long time without a child, which was a great grief to me and cost me many prayers and tears before I obtained one, and after him gave me many more of whom I now take the care, that as I have brought you into the world, and with great pains, weakness, cares, and fears brought you to this, I now travail in birth again of you till Christ be formed in you.

Among all my experiences of God's gracious dealings with me, I have constantly observed this, that He hath never suffered me long to sit loose from Him, but by one affliction or other hath made me look home, and search what was amiss; so usually thus it hath been with me that I have no sooner felt my heart out of order, but I have expected correction for it, which most commonly hath been upon my own person in sickness, weakness, pains, sometimes on my soul, in doubts and fears of God's displeasure and my sincerity towards Him; sometimes He hath smote a child with a sickness, sometimes chastened by losses in estate, and these times (through His great mercy) have been the times of my greatest getting and advantage; yea, I have found them the times when the Lord hath manifested the most love to me. Then have I gone to searching and have said with David, "Lord, search me and try me, see what ways of wickedness are in me, and lead me in the way everlasting," and seldom or never but I have found either some sin I lay under which God would have reformed, or some duty neglected which He would have performed, and by His help I have laid vows and bonds upon my soul to perform His righteous commands.

If at any time you are chastened of God, take it as thankfully and joyfully as in greatest mercies, for if ye be His, ye shall reap the greatest benefit by it. It hath been no small support to me in times of darkness when the Almighty hath hid His face from me that yet I have had abundance of sweetness and refreshment after affliction and more circumspection in my walking after I have been afflicted. I have been with God like an untoward child, that no longer than the rod has been on my back (or at least in sight) but I have been apt to forget Him and myself, too. Before I was afflicted, I went astray, but now I keep Thy statutes.

I have had great experience of God's hearing my prayers and returning comfortable answers to me, either in granting the thing I prayed for, or else in satisfying my mind without it, and I have been confident it hath been from Him, because I have found my heart through His goodness enlarged in thankfulness to Him.

I have often been perplexed that I have not found that constant joy in my pilgrimage and refreshing which I supposed most of the servants of God have, although He hath not left me altogether without the witness of His holy spirit, who hath oft given me His word and set to His seal that it shall be well with me. I have sometimes tasted of that hidden manna that the world knows not, and have set up my Ebenezer, and have resolved with myself that against such a promise, such tastes of sweetness, the gates of hell shall never prevail; yet have I many times sinkings and droopings, and not enjoyed that felicity that sometimes I have done. But when I have been in darkness and seen no light, yet have I desired to stay myself upon the Lord, and when I have been in sickness and pain, I have thought if the Lord would but lift up the light of His countenance upon me, although He ground me to powder, it would be but light to me; yea, oft have I thought were I in hell itself and could there find the love of God toward me, it would be a heaven. And could I have been in heaven without the love of God, it would have been a hell to me, for in truth it is the absence and presence of God that makes heaven or hell.

Many times hath Satan troubled me concerning the verity of the Scriptures, many times by atheism how I could know whether there was a God; I never saw any miracles to confirm me, and those which I read of, how did I know but they were feigned? That there is a God my reason would soon tell me by the wondrous works that I see, the vast frame of the heaven and the earth, the order of all things, night and day, summer and winter, spring and autumn, the daily providing for this great household upon the earth, the preserving and directing of all to its proper end. The consideration of these things would with amazement certainly resolve me that there is an Eternal Being. But how should I know He is such a God as I worship in Trinity, and such a Saviour as I rely upon? Though this hath thousands of times been suggested to me, yet God hath helped me over. I have argued thus with myself. That there is a God, I see. If ever this God hath revealed himself, it must be in His word, and this must be it or none. Have I not found that operation by it that no human invention can work upon the soul, hath not judgments befallen divers who have scorned and contemned it, hath it not been preserved through all ages maugre all the heathen tyrants and all of the enemies who have opposed it? Is there any story but that which shows the beginnings of times, and how the world came to be as we see? Do we not know the prophecies in it fulfilled which could not have been so long foretold by any but God Himself?

When I have got over this block, then have I another put in my way, that admit this be the true God whom we worship, and that be his word, yet why may not the Popish religion be the right? They have the same God, the same Christ, the same word. They only enterpret it one way, we another.

This hath sometimes stuck with me, and more it would, but the vain fooleries that are in their religion together with their lying miracles and cruel persecutions of the saints, which admit were they as they term them, yet not so to be dealt withal.

The consideration of these things and many the like would soon turn me to my own religion again.

But some new troubles I have had since the world has been filled with blasphemy and sectaries, and some who have been accounted sincere Christians have been carried away with them, that sometimes I have said, "Is there faith upon the earth?" and I have not known what to think; but then I have remembered the works of Christ that so it must be, and if it were possible, the very elect should be deceived. "Behold," saith our Saviour, "I have told you before." That hath stayed my heart, and I can now say, "Return, O my Soul, to thy rest, upon this rock Christ Jesus will I build my faith, and if I perish, I perish"; but I know all the Powers of Hell shall never prevail against it. I know whom I have trusted, and whom I have believed, and that He is able to keep that I have committed to His charge.

Now to the King, immortal, eternal and invisible, the only wise God, be honour, and glory for ever and ever, Amen.

This was written in much sickness and weakness, and is very weakly and imperfectly done, but if you can pick any benefit out of it, it is the mark which I aimed at.

Roger Williams
(1613–1683)

Often described as the father of religious tolerance in America, Roger Williams emigrated to New England in 1631. He was soon banished from the Massachusetts Bay colony for his democratic views of church government. He eventually made his way to present-day Rhode Island, where he established the first settlement at Providence in 1636, finally succeeding in obtaining a charter for the new colony in 1644. Famous for his work among the Indians, in 1643 Williams published the first book on their language, A Key into the Language of America. *Williams continued to move toward the religious left, from Separatist to Baptist and finally to "Seeker"—repudiating all orthodox creeds without abandoning his basic allegiance to the Christian faith.*

The first selection that follows is taken from Williams's most celebrated work, The Bloudy Tenent of Persecution, *which was written in protest against the doctrine that God requires uniformity in religious belief and practice. Williams insisted that all religious groups and individuals were entitled to religious liberty as a natural right. He thus anticipated such Enlightenment thinkers as Benjamin Franklin and Thomas Jefferson, who would call for the separation of church and state and insist on the state's civil responsibility to protect religious freedom. In the second selection, from* The Hireling Ministry None of Christs, *Williams contends that freedom of belief will in fact assist rather than impede the spread of Christianity in America.*

from *The Bloudy Tenent of Persecution*
(1644)

First, That the blood of so many hundred thousand soules of *Protestants* and *Papists*, spilt in the *Wars* of *present* and *former Ages*, for their respective *Consciences*, is not *required* nor *accepted* by *Jesus Christ* the *Prince* of *Peace*.

Secondly, Pregnant *Scriptures* and *Arguments* are throughout the Worke proposed against the *Doctrine* of *persecution* for for *cause* of *Conscience*.

Thirdly, Satisfactorie Answers are given to *Scriptures*, and objections produced by Mr. *Calvin, Beza*, Mr. *Cotton*, and the Ministers of the New English Churches and others former and later, tending to prove the *Doctrine of persecution* for cause of *Conscience*.

Fourthly, The *Doctrine of persecution* for cause of *Conscience*, is proved guilty of all the *blood* of the *Soules* crying for *vengeance* under the *Altar*.

Fifthly, All *Civill States* with their *Officers* of *justice* in their respective *constitutions* and *administrations* are proved *essentially Civill*, and therefore not *Judges, Governours* or *Defendours* of the *Spirituall* or *Christian State* and *Worship*.

Sixtly, It is the will and command of *God*, that (since the comming of his Son the *Lord Jesus*) a *permission* of the most *Paganish, Jewish, Turkish*, or *Antichristian consciences* and *worships*, be granted to *all* men in all *Nations* and *Countries*: and they are onely to bee *fought* against with that *Sword* which is only (in *Soule matters*) *able* to *conquer*, to wit, the *Sword of Gods Spirit*, the *Word* of *God*.

Seventhly, The *state* of the Land of *Israel*, the *Kings* and *people* thereof in *Peace & War*, is proved *figurative* and *ceremoniall*, and no *patterne* nor *precident* for any *Kingdome* or *civill state* in the *world* to follow.

Eightly, *God* requireth not an *uniformity* of *Religion* to be *inacted* and *inforced* in any *civill state*; which inforced *uniformity* (sooner or later) is the greatest occasion of *civill Warre, ravishing* of *conscience, persecution* of *Christ Jesus* in his servants, and of the *hypocrisie* and *destruction* of *millions* of *souls*.

Ninthly, In holding an inforced *uniformity* of *Religion* in a *civill state*, wee must necessarily *disclaime* our desires and hopes of the *Jewes conversion* to *Christ*.

Tenthly, An inforced *uniformity* of *Religion* throughout a *Nation* or *civill state*, confounds the *Civill* and *Religious*, denies the principles of Christianity and civility, and that *Jesus Christ* is come in the Flesh.

Eleventhly, The permission of other *consciences* and *worships* then a state professeth, only can (according to God) procure a firme and lasting *peace*, (good *assurance* being taken according to the *wisedome* of the *civill state* for *uniformity* of *civill obedience* from all forts.)

Twelfthly, lastly, true *civility* and *Christianity* may both flourish in a *state* or *Kingdome*, notwithstanding the *permission* of divers and contrary *consciences*, either of *Jew* or *Gentile*.

The Hireling Ministry
None of Christs
(1652)

What is then the express duty of the Civill Magistrate, as to *Christ Jesus* his *Gospell* and *Kingdome*?

I answer, I know how wofully that Scripture, *Kings shall be thy nursing Fathers, &c.* hath been abused, and elswhere I have at large discussed that, and other such *Objections*: At present, I humbly conceive, that the great *Duty* of the *Magistrate*, as to *spirituals*, will turne upon these two *Hinges*.

First, In removing the Civill *Bars, Obstructions, Hinderances*, in taking of those *Yoaks*, that pinch the very *Soules* and *consciences* of men, such as yet are the *payments* of *Tithes*, and the *Maintenance* of *Ministers*, they have no faith in: Such are the inforced *Oaths*, and some *ceremonies* therein, in all the Courts of *Justice*, such are the holy *Marryings*, holy *buryings, &c.*

Secondly, In a free and absolute *permission* of the *consciences* of all men, in what is meerly spirituall, nor the very *consciences* of the *Jews*, nor the *consciences* of the *Turkes* or *Papists*, or *Pagans* themselves excepted.

But how will this *Propagate* the *Gospell* of *Christ Jesus*?

I answer thus, The first grand *Design* of *Christ Jesus* is, to destroy and consume his *Mortal enemy Antichrist*. This must be done by the *breath* of his *Mouth* in his *Prophets* and *Witnesses*: Now the *Nations* of the *World*, have impiously *stopt* this heavenly *breath*, and *stifled* the *Lord Jesus* in his *servants*: Now if it shall please the *civill State* to remove the *state bars*, set up to resist the holy *Spirit* of God in his *servants* (whom yet finally to resist, is not in all the powers of the *world*) I humbly conceive that the *civill state* hath made a fair progresse in promoting the *Gospel* of *Jesus Christ*.

This *Mercy* and *freedome* is due to the (meerly) religious *con-*

sciences of all men in the *world*. Is there no more due from the *Magistrate* to *Christ Jesus* his *saints* and *Kingdome*?

I answer, While I pleade the *Conscience* of All men to be at *Liberty*, doubtlesse I must plead the *Liberty* of the *Magistrates conscience* also, and therefore were his *bounties* and *donations* to his *Bishops* and *Ministers*, as large as those of *Constantine*; who, but the holy *Spirit* of *God* in the mouths of his Prophets can restrain him? Onely let not *Cæsar*, (as *Constantine* in his setled *prosperity* did) rob the *God* of Heaven of his *Rights*, the *consciences* of his *subjects* their heavenly *Rights* and *Liberties*. . . .

The *Summa totalis* of all the former *particulars* is this, First, since the people of this *Nation* have been forc't into a *Nationall way* of *Worship*, both *Popish* and *Protestant* (as the *Wheels* of *times* revolutions, by *Gods* mighty *providence* and *permission* have turned about) The *civill state* is bound before *God* to take of that *bond* and *yoak* of *Soul-oppression*, and to proclaime free and impartiall *Liberty* to all the *people* of the three *Nations*, to choose and maintaine what *Worship* and *Ministry* their *Soules* and *Consciences* are perswaded of: which *Act*, as it will prove an *Act* of *mercy* and *righteousnesse* to the inslaved *Nations*, so is it of a binding force to ingage the whole and every *Interest* and *Conscience*, to preserve the *Common-freedom* and *peace*. However, an *Act* most suiting with the *piety* and *Christianity* of the holy *Testament* of *Christ Jesus*.

Secondly, The *civill state* is humbly to be implored, to provide in their high *Wisdome* for the *security* of all the respective *consciences*, in their respective *meetings, assemblings, worshippings, preachings, Disputings, &c.* and that *civil peace*, and the *beauty* of *civility* and *humanity* be maintained among the chiefe *opposers* and *dissenters*.

Thirdly, It is the *duty* of all that are in *Authority*, and of all that are *able*, to *countenance, incourage*, and *supply* such true *Voluntiers* as give and devote themselves to the *service* and *Ministry* of *Christ Jesus* in any kind: although it be also the *duty*, and will be the practise of all such whom the *Spirit* of *God* sends upon any *work* of *Christs*, rather to work as *Paul* did, among the *Corinthians* and *Thessalonians*, then the work and service of their *Lord* and *Master*, should be neglected.

Such true *Christian* worthies (whether endowed with *humane Learning*, or without it) will alone be found that despised *modell* which the *God* of *Heaven* will onely bless; that poor *handfull* and three hundred out of *Israels* thirty two thousand by whom the *work* of the *God* of *Israel* must be effected. And if this course be effected in the three *Nations*, the *bodies* and *soules* of the three *Nations* will be more and more at peace, and in a fairer way then ever, to that peace which is *Eternall* when this *World* is gone.

Samuel Danforth
(1626–1674)

Samuel Danforth served for most of his life with the more famous John Eliot as a pastor of the church at Roxbury, Massachusetts. Known by his first biographer, Cotton Mather, for his earnestness as a student at Harvard and then for his moral vigilance as the pastor of his flock at Roxbury, Danforth is best remembered today for the sermon he preached on Election Day in 1671.

"Election sermons," such as the one Arthur Dimmesdale delivers at the end of Nathaniel Hawthorne's The Scarlet Letter, were typically devoted to measuring the difference between public conduct and the high purposes of the Puritan errand. Focusing on lapses in personal and collective behavior, preachers used these occasions to remind the community of their covenanted responsibilities. Election Day sermons thus frequently took the form of "jeremiads," which rehearsed the details of "declension," as it was called, chiefly for the purpose of recalling the people to their religious vocation and helping them to reclaim the covenant.

As the historian Perry Miller was the first to realize, this traditional aim actually propelled Danforth into a theological paradox of real and lasting cultural consequences. Having served heretofore to remind communicants of the purpose for which they had come to New England—to establish a society at once civil and ecclesiastical that might be a model for the continuing reformation of Western Christendom—Election Day sermons, once centered around the original Puritan errand and its subsequent betrayal, had by 1671 been rendered somewhat moot because the English Puritans had accepted toleration. The American Puritans were thus left with no other purpose for their "errand into the wilderness" but to perfect themselves.

But as the literary critic Sacvan Bercovitch has pointed out, this paradox was even graver than Miller realized. For if the Puritans were deprived of the purpose for which their errand had originally been run—to perform a mission essentially for someone else—and were compelled to content themselves with running it for their own self-realization, then every mode of self-criticism could be seen as potentially a mode as well of self-affirmation. Which may be why, Bercovitch reasons, American writers have subsequently turned the jeremiad into the preeminent national literary form: Repeated citations of cultural dissensus are the way Americans keep alive the myth of cultural consensus.

from *A Brief Recognition of New England's Errand into the Wilderness* (1671)

"What went ye out into the wilderness to see? A reed shaken with the wind?

"But what went ye out for to see? A man clothed in soft raiment? Behold, they that wear soft clothing are in kings' houses.

"But what went ye out for to see? A prophet? Yea, I say unto you, and more than a prophet" (Matt. 11. 7–9).

These words are our Saviour's proem to His illustrious encomium of John the Baptist. John began his ministry not in Jerusalem nor in any famous city of Judea, but in the wilderness, i.e., in a woody, retired, and solitary place, thereby withdrawing himself from the envy and preposterous zeal of such as were addicted to their old traditions and also taking the people aside from the noise and tumult of their secular occasions and businesses, which might have obstructed their ready and cheerful attendance unto his doctrine. The ministry of John at first was entertained by all sorts with singular affection: There "went out to him Jerusalem, and all Judea, and all the region round about Jordan" (Matt. 3. 5); but after awhile the people's fervor abated, and John being kept under restraint divers months, his authority and esteem began to decay and languish (John 5. 35). Wherefore our Saviour, taking occasion from John's messengers coming to Him, after their departure gives an excellent e[u]logy and commendation of John to the intent that he might ratify and confirm his doctrine and administration and revive his authority and estimation in the hearts and consciences of the people.

This e[u]logy our Saviour begins with an elegant dialogism which the rhetorician calleth communication, gravely deliberating with His hearers and seriously enquiring to what purpose they went out into the wilderness and what expectation drew them thither. Wherein we have: 1. The general question and main subject of His inquisition; 2. the particular enquiries; 3. the determination of the question.

The general question is, "What went ye out into the wilderness to see?" He saith not, "Whom went ye out to hear," but "What went ye out to see?"

The meaning then of this first enquiry is, "Went ye out into the wilderness to see a light, vain, and inconstant man, one that could confess and deny and deny and confess the same truth?" This interrogation is to be understood negatively and ironically, q.d., "Surely ye went not into the desert to behold such a ludicrous and ridiculous sight, a man like unto a reed shaken with the wind." Under the negation of the contrary levity our Saviour sets forth one of John's excellencies, viz., his eminent constancy in asserting the truth. The winds of various temptations both on the right hand and on the left blew upon him, yet he wavered not in his testimony concerning Christ; "he confessed, and denied not; but confessed" the truth [John 1. 20].

Doctrine. *Such as have sometime left their pleasant cities and habitations to enjoy the pure worship of God in a wilderness are apt in time to abate and cool in their affection thereunto; but then the Lord calls upon them seriously and thoroughly to examine themselves, what it was that drew them into the wilderness, and to consider that it was not the expectation of ludicrous levity nor of courtly pomp and delicacy, but of the free and clear dispensation of the Gospel and kingdom of God.*

This doctrine consists of two distinct branches; let me open them severally.

Branch I. Such as have sometime left their pleasant cities and habitations to enjoy the pure worship of God in a wilderness are apt in time to abate and cool in their affection thereunto. To what purpose did the children of Israel leave their cities and houses in Egypt and go forth into the wilderness? Was it not to "hold a feast to the Lord," and to "sacrifice to the God of their fathers"? That was the only reason which they gave of their motion to Pharaoh (Exod. 5. 1, 3); but how soon did they forget their errand into the wilderness and corrupt themselves in their own inventions? Within a few months after their coming out of Egypt, "they make a calf in Horeb, and worship the molten image, and change their glory into the similitude of an ox that eateth grass" (Psal. 106. 19, 20; Exod. 32. 7, 8). Yea, for the space of forty years in the wilderness, while they pretended to sacrifice to the Lord, they indeed worshipped the stars and the host of heaven and together with the Lord's tabernacle carried about with them the tabernacle of Moloch (Amos 5. 25, 26; Acts 7. 42, 43). And how did they spend their time in the wilderness but in tempting God and in murmuring against their godly and faithful teachers and rulers, Moses and Aaron (Psal. 95. 8)? To what purpose did the children of the captivity upon Cyrus his proclamation, leave their houses which they had built and their vineyards and oliveyards which they had planted in the province of Babylon and return to Judea and Jerusalem, which were now become a wilderness? Was it not that they might build the house of God at Jerusalem and set up the temple-worship? But how shamefully did they neglect that great and honorable work for the space of above forty years? They pretended that God's time was not come to build his house because of the rubs and obstructions which they met with, whereas all their difficulties and discouragements hindered not their building of stately houses for themselves (Hag. 1. 2–4). To what purpose did Jerusalem and all Judea and all the region round about Jordan leave their several cities and habitations and flock into the wilderness of Judea? Was it not to see that burning and shining light which God had raised up? To hear his heavenly doctrine and partake of that new sacrament which he administered? O how they were affected with his rare and excellent gifts! with his clear, lively, and powerful ministry! The kingdom of heaven pressed in upon them with a holy violence and the violent, the zealous, and affectionate hearers of the gospel took it by force (Matt. 11. 12; Luke 16. 16). They leapt over all discouragements and impediments, whether outward, as legal rites and ceremonies, or inward, the sense of their own sin and unworthiness, and pressed into the kingdom of God as men rush into a theater to see a pleasant sight or as soldiers run into a besieged city to take the spoil thereof; but their hot fit is soon over, their affection lasted but for an hour, i.e., a short season (John 5. 35).

Branch II. When men abate and cool in their affection to the pure worship of God which they went into the wilderness to enjoy, the Lord calls upon them seriously and thoroughly to examine themselves, what it was that drew them into the wilderness, and to consider that it was not the expectation of ludicrous levity nor of courtly pomp and delicacy, but of the free and clear dispensation of the Gospel and kingdom of God. Our Saviour knowing that the people had lost their first love and singular affection to the revelation of His grace by the ministry of His herald John, He is very intense in examining them, what expectation drew them into the wilderness. He doth not once nor twice but thrice propound that question, "What went ye out into the wilderness to see?" Yea in particular He enquires whether it were to see a man that was like to "a reed shaken with the wind," or whether it were to see "a man clothed like a courtier," or whether it were to see a "prophet," and then determines the question, concluding that it was to see a great and excellent prophet and that had not they seen rare and admirable things in him they would never have gone out into the wilderness unto him.

The reason is because the serious consideration of the inestimable grace and mercy of God in the free and clear dispensation of the Gospel and kingdom of God is a special means to convince men of their folly and perverseness in undervaluing the same, and a sanctified remedy to recover their affections thereunto. The Lord foreseeing the defection of Israel after Moses his death, commands him to write that prophetical song recorded in Deuteronomy 32 as a testimony against them, wherein the chief remedy which he prescribes for the prevention and healing of their apostasy is their calling to remembrance God's great and signal love in manifesting Himself to them in the wilderness, in conducting them safely and mercifully, and giving them possession of their promised inheritance (ver. 7–14). And when Israel was apostatized and fallen, the Lord, to convince them of their ingratitude and folly, brings to their remembrance His deliverance of them out of Egypt, His leading them through the wilderness for the space of forty years, and not only giving them possession of their enemies' land but also raising up even of their own sons, prophets, faithful and eminent ministers, and of their young men. Nazarites, who being separated from worldly delights and encumbrances were patterns of purity and holiness—all which were great and obliging mercies. Yea the Lord appeals to their own consciences whether these his favors were not real and signal (Amos 2. 10, 11). The prophet Jeremiah, that he might reduce the people from their backsliding, cries in the ears of Jerusalem with earnestness and boldness, declaring unto them that the Lord remembered how well they stood affected towards him when he first chose them to be his people and espoused them to himself; how they followed him in the wilderness and kept close to him in their long and wearisome passage through the uncultured desert; how they were then consecrated to God and set apart for his worship and service, as the first fruits are wont to be sequestered and devoted to God; and thereupon expostulates with them for their forsaking the Lord, and following after their idols (Jer. 2. 2, 3, 5, 6). Surely our Saviour's dialogism with His hearers in my text is not a mere rhetorical elegancy to adorn His testimony concerning John, but a clear and strong conviction of their folly in slighting and despising that which they sometime so highly pretended unto, and a wholesome admonition and direction how to recover their primitive affection to his doctrine and administration.

Use I. Of solemn and serious inquiry to us all in this general assembly is whether we have not in a great measure forgotten our errand into the wilderness. You have solemnly professed before God, angels, and men that the cause of your leaving your country, kindred, and fathers' houses and transporting yourselves with your wives, little ones, and substance over the vast ocean into this waste and howling wilderness, was your liberty to walk in the faith of the Gospel with all good conscience according to the order of the Gospel, and your enjoyment of the pure worship of God according to His institution without human mixtures and impositions. Now let us sadly consider whether our ancient and primitive affections to the Lord Jesus, His glorious Gospel, His pure and spiritual worship, and the order of His house, remain, abide, and continue firm, constant, entire, and inviolate. Our Saviour's reiteration of this question, "What went ye out into the wilderness to see?" is no idle repetition but a sad conviction of our dullness and backwardness to this great duty and a clear demonstration of the weight and necessity thereof. It may be a grief to us to be put upon such an inquisition, as it is said of Peter, "Peter was grieved because He said unto him the third time, Lovest thou me?" (John 21. 17); but the Lord knoweth that a strict and rigid examination of our hearts in this point is no more than necessary. Wherefore let us call to remembrance the former days and consider whether "it was not then better with us than it is now" [Hos. 2. 7].

In our first and best times the kingdom of heaven brake in upon us with a holy violence and every man pressed into it. What mighty efficacy and power had the clear and faithful dispensation of the Gospel upon your hearts? How affectionately and zealously did you entertain the kingdom of God? How careful were you, even all sorts, young and old, high and low, to take hold of the opportunities of your spiritual good and edification, ordering your secular affairs (which were wreathed and twisted together with great variety) so as not to interfere with your general calling, but that you might attend upon the Lord without distraction? How diligent and faithful in preparing your hearts for the reception of the Word, "laying apart all filthiness and superfluity of naughtiness," that you might "receive with meekness the ingraffed[1] word, which is able to save your souls" [Jas. 1. 21], "and purging out all malice, guile, hypocrisies, envies, and all evil speakings, and as newborn babes, desiring the sincere milk of the Word, that ye might grow thereby" [I Pet. 2. 1, 2]? How attentive in hearing the everlasting Gospel, "watching daily at the gates of wisdom, and waiting at the posts of her doors, that ye might find eternal life, and obtain favor of the Lord" [Prov. 8. 34, 35]? Gleaning day by day in the field of God's ordinances, even among the sheaves, and gathering up handfuls, which the Lord let fall of purpose for you, and at night going home and beating out what you had gleaned, by meditation, repetition, conference, and therewith feeding yourselves and your families. How painful were you in recollecting, repeating, and discoursing of what you heard, whetting the Word of God upon the hearts of your children, servants, and neighbors? How fervent in prayer to almighty God for His divine blessing upon the seed sown, that it might take root and fructify? O what a reverent esteem had you in those days of Christ's faithful ambassadors that declared unto you the word of reconciliation! "How beautiful" were "the feet of them that preached the Gospel of peace, and brought the glad tidings of salvation!" [Rom. 10. 15]. You "esteemed them highly in love for their work's sake" [I Thess. 5. 13]. Their persons, names, and comforts were precious in your eyes; you counted yourselves blessed in the enjoyment of a pious, learned, and orthodox ministry; and though you ate the bread of adversity and drank the water of affliction, yet you rejoiced in this, that your eyes saw your teachers, they were not removed into corners, and your ears heard a word behind you saying, "This is the way, walk ye in it," when you turned to the right hand and when your turned to the left (Isa. 30. 20, 21). What earnest and ardent desires had you in those days after communion with Christ in the holy sacraments? With desire you desired to partake of the seals of the covenant. You thought your evidences for heaven not sure nor authentic unless the broad seals of the kingdom were annexed. What solicitude was there in those days to "seek the Lord after the right order" [I Chron. 15. 13]? What searching of the holy Scriptures, what collations among your leaders, both in their private meetings and public councils and synods, to find out the order which Christ hath constituted and established in His house? What fervent zeal was there then against sectaries and heretics and all manner of heterodoxies? "You could not bear them that were evil" [Rev. 2. 2] but tried them that pretended to new light and revelations, and found them liars.[2] What pious care was there of sister churches, that those that wanted breasts might be supplied and that those that wanted peace, their dissensions might be healed? What readiness was there in those days to call for the help of neighbor elders and brethren in case of any difference or division that could not be healed at home? What reverence was there then of the sentence of a council as being decisive and issuing the controversy, according to that ancient proverbial saying, "They shall surely ask counsel of Abel: and so they ended the matter" (II Sam. 20. 18)? What holy endeavors were there in those days to propagate religion to your children and posterity, training them up in the nurture and admonition of the Lord, keeping them under the awe of government, restraining their enormities and extravagancies, charging them to know the God of their fathers and serve Him with a perfect heart and willing mind, and publicly asserting and maintaining their interest in the Lord and in His holy covenant and zealously opposing those that denied the same?

And then had the churches "rest" throughout the several colonies and were "edified; and walking in the fear of the Lord, and in the comfort of the Holy Ghost, were multiplied" [Acts 9. 31]. O how your faith grew exceedingly! You proceeded from faith to faith, from a less to a greater degree and measure, growing up in Him who is our head and receiving abundance of grace and of the gift of righteousness, that you might reign in life by Jesus Christ. O how your love and charity towards each other abounded! O what comfort of love! What bowels[3] and mercies! What affectionate care was there one of another! What a holy sympathy in crosses and comforts, weeping with those that wept and rejoicing with those that rejoiced!

But who is there left among you that saw these churches in their first glory and how do you see them now? Are they not in your eyes in comparison thereof as nothing? "How is the gold become dim! how is the most fine gold changed!" [Lam. 4. 1]. Is not the temper, complexion, and countenance of the churches strangely altered? Doth not a careless, remiss, flat, dry, cold, dead frame of spirit grow in upon us secretly, strongly, prodigiously? They that have ordinances are as though they had none; and they that hear the Word as though they heard it not; and they that pray as though they prayed not; and they that receive sacraments as though they received them not; and they that are exercised in the holy things using them by the by as matters of custom and ceremony, so as not to hinder their eager prosecution of other things which their hearts are set upon. Yea and in some particular congregations amongst us is there not instead of a sweet smell, a stink; and instead of a girdle, a rent; and instead of a stomacher, a girding with sackcloth; and burning instead of beauty?[4] Yea "the vineyard is all overgrown with thorns, and nettles cover the face thereof, and the stone wall thereof is broken down" (Prov. 24. 31). Yea and that which is the most sad and certain sign of calamity approaching: "Iniquity aboundeth, and the love of many waxeth cold" (Matt. 24. 12). Pride, contention, worldliness, covetousness, luxury, drunkenness, and uncleanness break in like a flood upon us and good men grow cold in their love to God and to one another. If a man be cold in his bed let them lay on the more clothes that he may get heat; but we are like to David in his old age: "They covered him with clothes, but he gat no heat" (I Kings 1. 1). The Lord heaps mercies, favors, blessings upon us and loads us daily with His benefits, but all His love and bounty cannot heat and warm our hearts and affections. Well the furnace is able to heat and melt the coldest iron; but how oft hath the Lord cast us into the hot furnace of affliction and tribulation and we have been scorched and burnt, yet not melted but hardened thereby (Isa. 63. 17)? How long hath God kept us in the furnace day after day, month after month, year after year? But all our afflictions, crosses, trials have not been able to keep our hearts in a warm temper.

Now let me freely deliberate with you what may be the causes and grounds of such decays and languishings in our affections to, and estimation of, that which we came into the wilderness to enjoy. Is it because "there is no bread, neither is there any water; and our soul loatheth this light bread" (Num. 21. 5)? "Our soul is dried away: and there is nothing at all, besides this manna, before our eyes" (Num. 11. 6). What, is manna no bread? Is this angelical food light bread which cannot satisfy but starves the soul? Doth our soul loathe the bread of heaven? The Lord be merciful to us; the full soul loatheth the honeycomb (Prov. 27. 7).

But though unbelief be the principal yet it is not the sole cause of our decays and languishings; inordinate worldly cares, predominant lusts, and malignant passions and distempers stifle and choke the Word and quench our affections to the kingdom of God (Luke 8. 14). The manna was gathered early in the morning; when the sun waxed hot, it melted (Exod. 16. 21). It was a fearful judgment on Dathan and Abiram that the earth opened its mouth and swallowed them up.[5] How many professors of religion are swallowed up alive by earthly affections? Such as escape the lime pit of Pharisaical hypocrisy fall into the coal pit of Sadducean atheism and epicurism. Pharisaism and Sadduceism do almost divide the professing world between them. Some split upon the rock of affected ostentation of singular piety and holiness and others are drawn into the whirlpool, and perish in the gulf of sensuality and luxury.

If any question how seasonable such a discourse may be upon such a day as this, let him consider Haggai 2. 10–14:

> In the four and twentieth day of the ninth month, in the second year of Darius, came the word of the Lord by Haggai the prophet, saying, "Thus saith the Lord of hosts; Ask now the priests concerning the law, saying, 'If one bear holy flesh in the skirt of his garment, and with his skirt do touch bread, or pottage, or wine, or oil, or any meat, shall it be holy?'" And the priests answered and said, "No." Then said Haggai, "If one that is unclean by a dead body touch any of these, shall it be unclean?" And the priests answered and said, "It shall be unclean." Then answered Haggai, and said, "So is this people, and so is this nation before me," saith the Lord; "and so is every work of their hands; and that which they offer there is unclean."

It was an high and great day wherein the prophet spake these words and an holy and honorable work which the people were employed in. For this day they laid the foundation of the Lord's temple (ver. 18). Nevertheless, the Lord saw it necessary this very day to represent and declare unto them the pollution and uncleanness both of their persons and of their holy services, that they might be deeply humbled before God and carry on their present work more holily and purely. What was their uncleanness? Their eager pursuit of their private interests took off their hearts and affections from the affairs of the house of God. It seems they pleased themselves with this, that the altar stood upon its bases and sacrifices were daily offered thereon and the building of the Temple was only deferred until a fit opportunity were afforded, free from disturbance and opposition; and having now gained such a season they are ready to build the Temple. But the Lord convinceth them out of the Law that their former negligence was not expiated by their daily sacrifices, but the guilt thereof rendered both the nation and this holy and honorable work which they were about vile and unclean in the sight of God. And having thus shown them their spiritual uncleanness, He encourageth them to go on with the work in hand, the building of the Temple, promising them from this day to bless them (ver. 19).

Use II. Of exhortation, to excite and stir us all up to attend and prosecute our errand into the wilderness. To what purpose came we into this place and what expectation drew us hither? Surely not the expectation of ludicrous levity. We came not hither to see "a reed shaken with the wind." Then let not us be reeds—light, empty, vain, hollow-hearted professors, shaken with every wind of temptation—but solid, serious, and sober Christians, constant and steadfast in the profession and practice of the truth, "trees of righteousness, the planting of the Lord, that He may be glorified" [Isa. 61. 3], holding fast the profession of our faith without wavering.

"Alas there is such variety and diversity of opinions and judgments that we know not what to believe."

Were there not as various and different opinions touching the person of Christ even in the days of his flesh? Some said that He was John the Baptist, some Elias, others Jeremias, or one of the old prophets. Some said He was a gluttonous man and a wine-bibber, a friend of publicans and sinners; others said He was a Samaritan and had a devil; yet the disciples knew what to believe. "Whom say ye that I am? Thou art Christ, the Son of the living God" (Matt. 16. 15, 16). The various heterodox opinions of the people serve as a foil or tinctured leaf to set off the luster and beauty of the orthodox and apostolical faith. This is truly commendable, when in such variety and diversity of apprehensions you are not biased by any sinister respects, but discern, embrace, and profess the truth as it is in Christ Jesus.

But to what purpose came we into the wilderness and what expectation drew us hither? Not the expectation of courtly pomp and delicacy. We came not hither to see men clothed like courtiers. The affectation of courtly pomp and gallantry is very unsuitable in a wilderness. Gorgeous attire is comely in princes' courts if it exceed not the limits of Christian sobriety; but excess in kings' houses escapes not divine vengeance. "I will punish the princes, and the kings' children, and all such as are clothed with strange apparel" (Zeph. 1. 8). The pride and haughtiness of the ladies of Zion in their superfluous ornaments and stately gestures brought wrath upon themselves, upon their husbands, and upon their children, yea and upon the whole land (Isa. 3. 16–26). How much more intolerable and abominable is excess of this kind in a wilderness, where we are so far removed from the riches and honors of princes' courts?

To what purpose then came we into the wilderness and what expectation drew us hither? Was it not the expectation of the pure and faithful dispensation of the Gospel and kingdom of God? The times were such that we could not enjoy it in our own land, and therefore having obtained liberty and a gracious patent from our sovereign, we left our country, kindred, and fathers' houses, and came into these wild woods and deserts where the Lord hath planted us and made us "dwell in a place of our own, that we might move no more, and that the children of wickedness might not afflict us any more" (II Sam. 7. 10). What is it that distinguisheth New England from other colonies and plantations in America? Not our transportation over the Atlantic Ocean, but the ministry of God's faithful prophets and the fruition of his holy ordinances. Did not the Lord bring "the Philistines from Caphtor, and the Assyrians from Kir" as well as "Israel from the land of Egypt" (Amos 9. 7)? But "by a prophet the Lord brought Israel out of Egypt, and by a prophet was he preserved" (Hos. 12. 13). What, is the price and esteem of God's prophets and their faithful dispensations now fallen in our hearts?

The hardships, difficulties, and sufferings which you have exposed yourselves unto that you might dwell in the house of the Lord and leave your little ones under the shadow of the wings of the God of Israel, have not been few nor small. And shall we now withdraw ourselves and our little ones from under those healing wings and lose that full reward which the Lord hath in His heart and hand to bestow upon us? Did we not with Mary choose this for our part, "to sit at Christ's feet, and hear His word" [Luke 10. 39]? And do we now repent of our choice and prefer the honors, pleasures, and profits of the world before it? "You did run well; who doth hinder you that you should not obey the truth?" (Gal. 5. 7).

Michael Wigglesworth

(1631–1705)

Michael Wigglesworth is best known as the author of The Day of Doom *(1662), in its time a hugely popular sermon in verse of 224 stanzas that treated, as its subtitle states, "the Great and Last Judgment." Its ballad form and its lack of literary ornamentation, together with its Calvinist obsession with the end of time when the evil "goats" will be separated from the good "sheep," served to turn it into the first American best-seller. But Wigglesworth, a minister and physician who combined a tormented conscience with a broad, classical education, was also capable of writing verse of a more subtle nature.*

Of his two other long poems, God's Controversy with New-England *(1662) is far more memorable than* Meat Out of the Eater *(1670). Composed as a jeremiad, the former poem intends to recall a backsliding people to their obligations under the Covenant by detailing the nature of God's present controversy with them. Mincing no words in detailing the reasons for New England's "declension," God's Controversy nonetheless keeps alive, as the intellectual historian Perry Miller first observed, a sense of New England's high religious calling. Indeed, the denunciatory tone that is struck during most of the poem gives way at the very end to a note of celebration whose meanings would not be fully understood until Samuel Sewall made his lyric outburst to Plum Island several decades later in* Phaenomena quaedam Apocalyptica *(1697).*

from *God's Controversy with New-England*
(1662)

Beyond the great Atlantick flood
   There is a region vast,
A country where no English foot
   In former ages past:
A waste and howling wilderness,
   Where none inhabited
But hellish fiends, and brutish men
   That Devils worshiped.

This region was in darkness plac't
Far off from heavens light,
Amidst the shaddows of grim death
   And of eternal night.
For there the Sun of righteousness
   Had never made to shine
The light of his sweet countenance,
   And grace which is divine:

Until the time drew nigh wherein
   The glorious Lord of hostes
Was pleasd to lead his armies forth
   Into those forrein coastes.
At whose approach the darkness sad
   Soon vanished away,
And all the shaddows of the night
   Were turnd to lightsome day.

The stubborn he in pieces brake,
   Like vessels made of clay:
And those that sought his peoples hurt
   He turned to decay.
Those curst Amalekites,[1] that first
   Lift up their hand on high
To fight against Gods Israel,
   Were ruin'd fearfully.

Thy terrours on the Heathen folk,
   O Great Jehovah, fell:

The fame of thy great acts, o Lord,
  Did all the nations quell.
Some hid themselves for fear of thee
  In forrests wide and great:
Some to thy people croutching came,
For favour to entreat.

Some were desirous to be taught
  The knowledge of thy wayes,
And being taught, did soon accord
  Therein to spend their dayes.
Thus were the fierce and barbarous
  Brought to civility,
And those that liv'd like beasts (or worse)
  To live religiously.

O happiest of dayes wherein
  The blind received sight,
And those that had no eyes before
  Were made to see the light.[2]
The wilderness hereat rejoyc't,
  The woods for joy did sing,
The vallys and the little hills
  Thy praises ecchoing.

· · ·

Our temp'rall blessings did abound:
  But spirituall good things
Much more abounded, to the praise
  Of that great King of Kings.
Gods throne was here set up; here was
  His tabernacle pight.[3]
This was the place, and these the folk
  In whom he took delight.

Our morning starrs shone all day long:
  Their beams gave forth such light,
As did the noon-day sun abash,
  And 's glory dazle quite.
Our day continued many yeers,
  And had no night at all:
Yea many thought the light would last,
  And be perpetuall.

Such, o New-England, was thy first,
  Such was thy best estate:
But, Loe! a strange and suddain change
  My courage did amate.
The brightest of our morning starrs
  Did wholly disappeare:
And those that tarried behind
  With sack-cloth covered were.

Moreover, I beheld and saw
  Our welkin overkest,[4]
And dismal clouds for sun-shine late
  O'respread from east to west.
The air became tempestuous;
  The wilderness gan quake:
And from above with awfull voice
  Th' Almighty thundring spake.

Are these the men that erst at my command
  Forsook their ancient seats and native soile,
To follow me into a desart land,
  Contemning all the travell and the toile,
  Whose love was such to purest ordinances[5]
As made them set at nought their fair inheritances?

Are these the men that prized libertee
  To walk with God according to their light,
To be as good as he would have them bee,
  To serve and worship him with all their might,
  Before the pleasures which a fruitful field,
And country flowing-full of all good things, could yield?

Are these the folk whom from the brittish Iles,
  Through the stern billows of the watry main,
I safely led so many thousand miles,
  As if their journey had been through a plain?
  Whom having from all enemies protected,
And through so many deaths and dangers well directed,

I brought and planted on the western shore,
  Where nought but bruits and salvage wights[6] did swarm
(Untaught, untrain'd, untam'd by vertue's lore)
  That sought their blood, yet could not do them harm?
  My fury's flaile them thresht, my fatall broom
Did sweep them hence, to make my people Elbow-room.

Are these the men whose gates with peace I crown'd,
To whom for bulwarks I salvation gave,
Whilst all things else with rattling tumults sound,
And mortall frayes send thousands to the grave?
Whilest their own brethren bloody hands embrewed
In brothers blood, and Fields with carcases bestrewed?

Is this the people blest with bounteous store,
By land and sea full richly clad and fed,
Whom plenty's self stands waiting still before,
And powreth out their cups well tempered?
For whose dear sake an howling wildernes
I lately turned into a fruitful paradeis?

Are these the people in whose hemisphere
Such bright-beam'd, glist'ring, sun-like starrs I placed,
As by their influence did all things cheere,
As by their light blind ignorance defaced,
As errours into lurking holes did fray,
As turn'd the late dark night into a lightsome day?

Are these the folk to whom I milked out
And sweetnes stream'd from consolations brest;
Whose soules I fed and strengthened throughout
With finest spirituall food most finely drest?
On whom I rained living bread[7] from Heaven,
Withouten Errour's bane, or Superstition's leaven?

With whom I made a Covenant of peace,
And unto whom I did most firmly plight
My faithfulness, If whilst I live I cease
To be their Guide, their God, their full delight;
Since them with cords of love to me I drew,
Enwrapping in my grace such as should then ensew.

Are these the men, that now mine eyes behold,
Concerning whom I thought, and whilome spake,
First Heaven shall pass away together scrold,[8]
Ere they my lawes and righteous wayes forsake,
Or that they slack to runn their heavenly race?
Are these the same? or are some others come in place?

If these be they, how is it that I find
In stead of holiness Carnality,

In stead of heavenly frames an Earthly mind,
For burning zeal luke-warm Indifferency,
For flaming Love, key-cold Dead-heartedness,
For temperance (in meat, and drinke, and cloaths) excess?

Whence cometh it, that Pride, and Luxurie
Debate, Deceit, Contention and Strife,
False-dealing, Covetousness, Hypocrisie
(With such like Crimes) amongst them are so rife,
That one of them doth over-reach another?
And that an honest man can hardly trust his Brother?

How is it, that Security, and Sloth,
Amongst the best are Common to be found?
That grosser sinns, in stead of Graces growth,
Amongst the many more and more abound?
I hate dissembling shews of Holiness.
Or practise as you talk, or never more profess.

Judge not, vain world, that all are hypocrites
That do profess more holiness then thou:
All foster not dissembling, guilefull sprites,
Nor love their lusts, though very many do.
Some sin through want of care and constant watch,
Some with the sick converse, till they the sickness catch.

Some, that maintain a reall root of grace,
Are overgrown with many noysome weeds,
Whose heart, that those no longer may take place,
The benefit of due correction needs.
And such as these however gone astray
I shall by stripes reduce into a better way.

Moreover some there be that still retain
Their ancient vigour and sincerity;
Whom both their own, and others sins, constrain
To sigh, and mourn, and weep, and wail, and cry:
And for their sakes I have forborn to powre
My wrath upon Revolters to this present houre.

To praying Saints I always have respect,
And tender love, and pittifull regard:
Nor will I now in any wise neglect
Their love and faithful service to reward;

Although I deal with others for their folly,
And turn their mirth to tears that have been too too jolly.

For thinke not, O Backsliders, in your heart,
That I shall still your evill manners beare:
Your sinns me press as sheaves do load a cart,[9]
And therefore I will plague you for this geare[10]
Except you seriously, and soon, repent,
Ile not delay your pain and heavy punishment.

And who be those themselves that yonder shew?
The seed of such as name my dreadfull Name!
On whom whilere compassions skirt I threw
Whilest in their blood they were, to hide their shame!
Whom my preventing love did neer me take!
Whom for mine own I mark't, lest they should me forsake!

I look't that such as these to vertue's Lore
(Though none but they) would have Enclin'd their ear:
That they at least mine image should have bore,
And sanctify'd my name with awfull fear.
Let pagan's Bratts pursue their lusts, whose meed
Is Death: For christians children are an holy seed.

But hear O Heavens! Let Earth amazed stand;
Ye Mountaines melt, and Hills come flowing down:
Let horror seize upon both Sea and Land;
Let Natures self be cast into a stown.
I children nourisht, nurtur'd and upheld:
But they against a tender Father have rebell'd.

What could have been by me performed more?
Or wherein fell I short of your desire?
Had you but askt, I would have op't my store,
And given what lawfull wishes could require.
For all this bounteous cost I lookt to see
Heaven-reaching-hearts, and thoughts, Meekness,
 Humility.

But lo, a sensuall Heart all void of grace,
An Iron neck, a proud presumptuous Hand;
A self-conceited, stiff, stout, stubborn Race,
That fears no threats, submitts to no command:

Self-will'd, perverse, such as can beare no yoke;
A Generation even ripe for vengeance stroke.

· · ·

Ah dear New-England! dearest land to me;
Which unto God hast hitherto been dear,
And mayst be still more dear than formerlie,
If to his voice thou wilt incline thine ear.

Consider wel and wisely what the rod,
Wherewith thou art from yeer to yeer chastized,
Instructeth thee. Repent, and turn to God,
Who wil not have his nurture be despized.

Thou still hast in thee many praying saints,
Of great account, and precious with the Lord,
Who dayly powre out unto him their plaints,
And strive to please him both in deed and word.

Cheer on, sweet souls, my heart is with you all,
And shall be with you, maugre[11] sathan's might:
And whereso'ere this body be a Thrall,
Still in New-England shall be my delight.

Mary Rowlandson
(1635?–1678?)

Mary Rowlandson was the wife of a Congregational minister in Lancaster, Massachusetts. On February 10, 1675, during the Narragansett Indian uprising known as King Philip's War, Lancaster was attacked and burned and Mrs. Rowlandson was taken captive, together with three of her children. She was a prisoner for nearly three months before she and her two surviving children were ransomed and freed. Her captivity was harrowing. Not only did Mrs. Rowlandson have to witness the death of one of her children; she was forced throughout her captivity to endure the hardships and hazards of numerous "removals," as she calls them, as well as the rigors of daily existence among a hostile people in the American wilderness. Her "captivity narrative," published soon after her death, quickly became the most famous of many similar accounts and one of the most widely read books in late-seventeenth-century America.

Mrs. Rowlandson wrote her narrative in gratitude for her deliverance and in hopes that she might testify to the providential meaning of her trials. She was confident that her sufferings possessed a divine purpose and that she had survived them only because God intended for them to be instructive. But in providing one of the earliest detailed pictures of native American life, her narrative also suggests, somewhat unintentionally, what kinds of accommodations, spiritual as well as physical, she was obliged to make to what she called "this Wilderness-condition." The narrative thus anticipates what later writers would come to imagine as the archetypal pattern of American acculturation: the violent confrontation between self and its moral "other," in which the self survives only by taking on some of the attributes of that "other."

from A Narrative of the Captivity and Restauration of Mrs. Mary Rowlandson (1682)

On the tenth of February 1675,[1] Came the Indians with great numbers upon Lancaster: Their first coming was about Sun-rising; hearing the noise of some Guns, we looked out; several Houses were burning, and the Smoke ascending to Heaven. There were five persons[2] taken in one house, the Father, and the Mother and a sucking Child, they knockt on the head; the other two they took and carried away alive. Their were two others, who being out of their Garison upon some occasion were set upon; one was knockt on the head, the other escaped: Another their was who running along was shot and wounded, and fell down; he begged of them his life, promising them Money (as they told me) but they would not hearken to him but knockt him in head, and stript him naked, and split open his Bowels. Another seeing many of the Indians about his Barn, ventured and went out, but was quickly shot down. There were three others belonging to the same Garison who were killed; the Indians getting up upon the roof of the Barn, had advantage to shoot down upon them over their Fortification. Thus these murtherous wretches went on, burning, and destroying before them.

At length they came and beset our own house, and quickly it was the dolefullest day that ever mine eyes saw. The House stood upon the edg of a hill; some of the Indians got behind the hill, others into the Barn, and others behind any thing that could shelter them; from all which places they shot against the House, so that the Bullets seemed to fly like hail; and quickly they wounded one man among us, then another, and then a third. About two hours (according to my observation, in that amazing time) they had been about the house before they prevailed to fire it (which they did with Flax and Hemp, which they brought out of the Barn, and there being no defence about the House, only two Flankers[3] at two opposite corners and one of them not finished) they fired it once and one ventured out and quenched it, but they quickly fired it again, and that took. Now is the dreadfull hour come, that I have often heard of (in time of War, as it was the case of others) but now mine eyes see it. Some in our house were fighting for their lives, others wallowing in their blood, the House on fire over our heads, and the bloody Heathen ready to knock us on the head, if we stirred out. Now might we hear Mothers and Children crying out for themselves, and one another, Lord, What shall we do? Then I took my Children (and one of my sisters, hers) to go forth and leave the house: but as soon as we came to the dore and appeared, the Indians shot so thick that the bulletts rattled against the House, as if one had taken an handfull of stones and threw them, so that we were fain to give back. We had six stout Dogs belonging to our Garrison, but none of them would stir, though another time, if any Indian had come to the door, they were ready to fly upon him and tear him down. The Lord hereby would make us the more to acknowledge his hand, and to see that our help is always in him. But out we must go, the fire increasing, and coming along behind us, roaring, and the Indians gaping before us with their Guns, Spears and Hatchets to devour us. No sooner were we out of the House, but my Brother in Law (being before wounded, in defending the house, in or near the throat) fell down dead, wherat the Indians scornfully shouted, and hallowed, and were presently upon him, stripping off his cloaths, the bulletts flying thick, one went through my side, and the same (as would seem) through the bowels and hand of my dear Child in my arms. One of my elder Sisters Children, named William, had then his Leg broken, which the Indians perceiving, they knockt him on head. Thus were we butchered by those merciless Heathen, standing amazed, with the blood running down to our heels. My eldest Sister being yet in the House, and seeing those wofull sights, the Infidels haling Mothers one way, and Children another, and some wallowing in their blood: and her elder Son telling her that her Son William was dead, and my self was wounded, she said, And, Lord, let me dy with them; which was no sooner said, but she was struck with a Bullet, and fell down dead over the threshold. I hope she is reaping the fruit of her good labours, being faithfull to the service of God in her place. In her younger years she lay under much trouble upon spiritual accounts, till it pleased God to make that precious Scripture take hold of her heart, 2 Cor. 12. 9. *And he said unto me, my Grace is sufficient for thee.* More then twenty years after I have heard her tell how sweet and comfortable that place was to her. But to return: The Indians laid hold of us, pulling me one way, and the Children another, and said, Come go along with us; I told them they would kill me: they answered, If I were willing to go along with them, they would not hurt me.

  Oh the dolefull sight that now was to behold at this House! *Come, behold the works of the Lord, what dissolations he has made in the Earth.*[4] Of thirty seven persons who were in this one House, none escaped either present death, or a bitter captivity, save only one,[5] who might say as he, Job 1. 15, *And I only am escaped alone to tell the News.* There were twelve killed, some shot, some stab'd with their Spears, some knock'd down with their Hatchets. When we are in prosperity, Oh the little that we think of such dreadfull sights, and to see our dear Friends, and Relations ly bleeding out their heart-blood upon the ground. There was one who was chopt into the head with a

Hatchet, and stript naked, and yet was crawling up and down. It is a solemn sight to see so many Christians lying in their blood, some here, and some there, like a company of Sheep torn by Wolves, All of them stript naked by a company of hell-hounds, roaring, singing, ranting and insulting, as if they would have torn our very hearts out; yet the Lord by his Almighty power preserved a number of us from death, for there were twenty-four of us taken alive and carried Captive.

I had often before this said, that if the Indians should come, I should chuse rather to be killed by them then taken alive but when it came to the tryal my mind changed; their glittering weapons so daunted my spirit, that I chose rather to go along with those (as I may say) ravenous Beasts, then that moment to end my dayes; and that I may the better declare what happened to me during that grievous Captivity, I shall particularly speak of the severall Removes we had up and down the Wilderness.

THE FIRST REMOVE.

Now away we must go with those Barbarous Creatures, with our bodies wounded and bleeding, and our hearts no less than our bodies. About a mile we went that night, up upon a hill within sight of the Town, where they intended to lodge. There was hard by a vacant house (deserted by the English before, for fear of the Indians). I asked them whither I might not lodge in the house that night to which they answered, what will you love English men still? this was the dolefullest night that ever my eyes saw. Oh the roaring, and singing and danceing, and yelling of those black creatures in the night, which made the place a lively resemblance of hell. And as miserable was the wast that was there made, of Horses, Cattle, Sheep, Swine, Calves, Lambs, Roasting Pigs, and Fowl (which they had plundered in the Town) some roasting, some lying and burning, and some boyling to feed our merciless Enemies; who were joyful enough though we were disconsolate. To add to the dolefulness of the former day, and the dismalness of the present night: my thoughts ran upon my losses and sad bereaved condition. All was gone, my Husband gone (at least separated from me, he being in the Bay,[6] and to add to my grief, the Indians told me they would kill him as he came homeward) my Children gone, my Relations and Friends gone, our House and home and all our comforts within door, and without, all was gone, (except my life) and I knew not but the next moment that might go too. There remained nothing to me but one poor wounded Babe, and it seemed at present worse than death that it was in such a pitiful condition, bespeaking Compassion, and I had no refreshing for it, nor suitable things to revive it. Little do many think what is the savageness and bruitishness of this barbarous Enemy, Ay, even those that seem to profess more than others among them, when the English have fallen into their hands.

Those seven that were killed at Lancaster the summer before upon a Sabbath day,[7] and the one that was afterward killed upon a week day, were slain and mangled in a barbarous manner, by one-ey'd John, and Marlborough's Praying Indians, which Capt. Mosely brought to Boston, as the Indians told me.

THE SECOND REMOVE[8]

But now, the next morning, I must turn my back upon the Town, and travel with them into the vast and desolate Wilderness, I knew not whither. It is not my tongue, or pen can express the sorrows of my heart, and bitterness of my spirit, that I had at this departure: but God was with me, in a wonderfull manner, carrying me along, and bearing up my spirit, that it did not quite fail. One of the Indians carried my poor wounded Babe upon a horse, it went moaning all along, I shall dy, I shall dy. I went on foot after it, with sorrow that cannot be exprest. At length I took it off the horse, and carried it in my armes till my strength failed, and I fell down with it: Then they set me upon a horse with my wounded Child in my lap, and there being no furniture upon the horse back, as we were going down a steep hill, we both fell over the horses head, at which they like inhumane creatures laught, and rejoyced to see it, though I thought we should there have ended our dayes, as overcome with so many difficulties. But the Lord renewed my strength still, and carried me along, that I might see more of his Power; yea, so much that I could never have thought of, had I not experienced it.

After this it quickly began to snow, and when night came on, they stopt: and now down I must sit in the snow, by a little fire, and a few boughs behind me, with my sick Child in my lap; and calling much for water, being now (through the wound) fallen into a violent Fever. My own wound also growing so stiff, that I could scarce sit down or rise up; yet so it must be, that I must sit all this cold winter night upon the cold snowy ground, with my sick Child in my armes, looking that every hour would be the last of its life; and having no Christian friend near me, either to comfort or help me. Oh, I may see the wonderfull power of God, that my Spirit did not utterly sink under my affliction: still the Lord upheld me with his gracious and mercifull Spirit, and we were both alive to see the light of the next morning.

THE THIRD REMOVE[9]

The morning being come, they prepared to go on their way. One of the Indians got up upon a horse, and they set me up behind him, with my poor sick Babe in my lap. A very wearisome and tedious day I had of it; what with my own wound, and my Childs being so exceeding sick, and in a lamentable condition with her wound. It may be easily judged what a poor feeble condition we were in, there being not the least crumb of refreshing that came within either of our mouths, from Wednesday night to Saturday night, except only a little cold water. This day in the afternoon, about an hour by Sun, we came to the place where they intended, *viz.* an Indian Town, called Wenimesset, Norward of Quabaug. When we were come, Oh the number of Pagans (now merciless enemies) that there came about me, that I may say as David, Psal. 27. 13, *I had fainted, unless I had believed,* etc. The next day was the Sabbath: I then remembered how careless I had been of Gods holy time, how many Sabbaths I had lost and mispent, and how evily I had walked in Gods sight; which lay so close unto my spirit, that it was easie for me to see how righteous it was with God to cut off the thread of my life, and cast me out of his presence for ever. Yet the Lord still shewed mercy to me, and upheld me; and as he wounded me with one hand, so he healed me with the other. This day there came to me one Robbert Pepper (a man belonging to Roxbury) who was taken in Captain Beers his Fight,[10] and had been now a considerable time with the Indians; and up with them almost as far as Albany, to see king Philip, as he told me, and was now very lately come into these parts. Hearing, I say, that I was in this Indian Town, he obtained leave to come and see me. He told me, he himself was wounded in the leg at Captain Beers his Fight; and was not able some time to go, but as they carried him, and as he took Oaken leaves and laid to his wound, and through the blessing of God he was able to travel again. Then I took Oaken leaves and laid to my side, and with the blessing of God it cured me also; yet before the cure was wrought, I may say, as it is in Psal. 38. 5, 6. *My wounds stink and are corrupt, I am troubled, I am bowed down greatly, I go mourning all the day long.* I sat much alone with a poor wounded Child in my lap, which moaned night and day, having nothing to revive the body, or cheer the spirits of her, but in stead of that, sometimes one Indian would come and tell me one hour, that your Master will knock your Child in the head, and then a second, and then a third, your Master will quickly knock your Child in the head.

This was the comfort I had from them, miserable comforters are

ye all, as he said.¹¹ Thus nine dayes I sat upon my knees, with my
Babe in my lap, till my flesh was raw again; my Child being even ready
to depart this sorrowfull world, they bade me carry it out to another
Wigwam (I suppose because they would not be troubled with such
spectacles) Whither I went with a very heavy heart, and down I sat
with the picture of death in my lap. About two houres in the night,
my sweet Babe like a Lambe departed this life, on Feb. 18, 1675. It
being about six yeares, and five months old. It was nine dayes from
the first wounding, in this miserable condition, without any refreshing
of one nature or other, except a little cold water. I cannot, but take
notice, how at another time I could not bear to be in the room where
any dead person was, but now the case is changed; I must and could
ly down by my dead Babe, side by side all the night after. I have
thought since of the wonderfull goodness of God to me, in preserving
me in the use of my reason and senses, in that distressed time, that I
did not use wicked and violent means to end my own miserable life.
In the morning, when they understood that my child was dead they
sent for me home to my Masters Wigwam: (by my Master in this
writing, must be understood Quanopin,¹² who was a Saggamore, and
married King Phillips wives Sister; not that he first took me, but I was
sold to him by another Narrhaganset Indian, who took me when first
I came out of the Garison). I went to take up my dead child in my
arms to carry it with me, but they bid me let it alone: there was no
resisting, but goe I must and leave it. When I had been at my masters
wigwam, I took the first opportunity I could get, to go look after my
dead child: when I came I askt them what they had done with it? then
they told me it was upon the hill: then they went and shewed me where
it was, where I saw the ground was newly digged, and there they told
me they had buried it: There I left that Child in the Wilderness, and
must commit it, and my self also in this Wilderness-condition, to him
who is above all. God having taken away this dear Child, I went to
see my daughter Mary, who was at this same Indian Town, at a Wigwam not very far off, though we had little liberty or opportunity to
see one another. She was about ten years old, and taken from the door
at first by a Praying Ind and afterward sold for a gun. When I came
in sight, she would fall a weeping; at which they were provoked, and
would not let me come near her, but bade me be gone; which was a
heart-cutting word to me. I had one Child dead, another in the Wilderness, I knew not where, the third they would not let me come near
to: *Me* (as he said) *have ye bereaved of my Children, Joseph is not,
and Simeon is not, and ye will take Benjamin also, all these things are
against me.*¹³ I could not sit still in this condition, but kept walking
from one place to another. And as I was going along, my heart was
even ·overwhelm'd with the thoughts of my condition, and that I

should have Children, and a Nation which I knew not ruled over them. Whereupon I earnestly entreated the Lord, that he would consider my low estate, and shew me a token for good, and if it were his blessed will, some sign and hope of some relief. And indeed quickly the Lord answered, in some measure, my poor prayers: for as I was going up and down mourning and lamenting my condition, my Son came to me, and asked me how I did; I had not seen him before, since the destruction of the Town, and I knew not where he was, till I was informed by himself, that he was amongst a smaller percel of Indians, whose place was about six miles off; with tears in his eyes, he asked me whether his Sister Sarah was dead; and told me he had seen his Sister Mary; and prayed me, that I would not be troubled in reference to himself. The occasion of his coming to see me at this time, was this: There was, as I said, about six miles from us, a smal Plantation of Indians, where it seems he had been during his Captivity: and at this time, there were some Forces of the Ind. gathered out of our company, and some also from them (among whom was my Sons master) to go to assault and burn Medfield: In this time of the absence of his master, his dame brought him to see me. I took this to be some gracious answer to my earnest and unfeigned desire. The next day, *viz.* to this, the Indians returned from Medfield, all the company, for those that belonged to the other smal company, came thorough the Town that now we were at. But before they came to us, Oh! the outragious roaring and hooping that there was: They began their din about a mile before they came to us. By their noise and hooping they signified how many they had destroyed (which was at that time twenty three.) Those that were with us at home, were gathered together as soon as they heard the hooping, and every time that the other went over their number, these at home gave a shout, that the very Earth rung again: And thus they continued till those that had been upon the expedition were come up to the Sagamores Wigwam; and then, Oh, the hideous insulting and triumphing that there was over some Englishmens scalps that they had taken (as their manner is) and brought with them. I cannot but take notice of the wonderfull mercy of God to me in those afflictions, in sending me a Bible. One of the Indians that came from Medfield fight, had brought some plunder, came to me, and asked me, if I would have a Bible, he had got one in his Basket. I was glad of it, and asked him, whether he thought the Indians would let me read? he answered, yes: So I took the Bible, and in that melancholy time, it came into my mind to read first the 28. Chap. of Deut., which I did, and when I had read it, my dark heart wrought on this manner, That there was no mercy for me, that the blessings were gone, and the curses come in their room, and that I had lost my opportunity. But the Lord helped me still to go on reading till I came to Chap. 30 the seven first verses, where I found, There was mercy promised again, if we would return to him by repentance; and though we were scatered from one end of the Earth to the other, yet the Lord would gather us together, and turn all those curses upon our Enemies. I do not desire to live to forget this Scripture, and what comfort it was to me.

Now the Ind. began to talk of removing from this place, some one way, and some another. There were now besides my self nine English Captives in this place (all of them Children, except one Woman). I got an opportunity to go and take my leave of them; they being to go one way, and I another, I asked them whether they were earnest with God for deliverance, they told me, they did as they were able, and it was some comfort to me, that the Lord stirred up Children to look to him. The Woman *viz.* Goodwife Joslin told me, she should never see me again, and that she could find in her heart to run away; I wisht her not to run away by any means, for we were near thirty miles from any English Town, and she very big with Child, and had but one week to reckon; and another Child in her Arms, two years old, and bad Rivers there were to go over, and we were feeble, with our poor and course entertainment. I had my Bible with me, I pulled it out, and asked her whether she would read; we opened the Bible and lighted on Psal. 27, in which Psalm we especially took notice of that, *ver. ult., Wait on the Lord, Be of good courage, and he shall strengthen thine Heart, wait I say on the Lord.*[14]

THE FOURTH REMOVE[15]

And now I must part with that little Company I had. Here I parted from my Daughter Mary, (whom I never saw again till I saw her in Dorchester, returned from Captivity), and from four little Cousins and Neighbours, some of which I never saw afterward: the Lord only knows the end of them. Amongst them also was that poor Woman before mentioned, who came to a sad end, as some of the company told me in my travel: She having much grief upon her Spirit, about her miserable condition, being so near her time, she would be often asking the Indians to let her go home; they not being willing to that, and yet vexed with her importunity, gathered a great company together about her, and stript her naked, and set her in the midst of them; and when they had sung and danced about her (in their hellish manner) as long as they pleased, they knockt her on head, and the child in her arms with her: when they had done that, they made a fire and put them both into it, and told the other Children that were with them, that if they attempted to go home, they would serve them in like manner: The Children said, she did not shed one tear, but prayed all the while. But to return to my own Journey; we travelled about half a day or little more, and came to a desolate place in the Wilderness, where there were no Wigwams or Inhabitants before; we came about the middle of the afternoon to this place, cold and wet, and snowy, and hungry, and weary, and no refreshing, for man, but the cold ground to sit on, and our poor Indian cheer.

Heart-aking thoughts here I had about my poor Children, who were scattered up and down among the wild beasts of the forrest: My head was light and dissey (either through hunger or hard lodging, or trouble or altogether) my knees feeble, my body raw by sitting double night and day, that I cannot express to man the affliction that lay upon my Spirit, but the Lord helped me at that time to express it to himself. I opened my Bible to read, and the Lord brought that precious Scripture to me, Jer. 31. 16. *Thus saith the Lord, refrain thy voice from weeping, and thine eyes from tears, for thy work shall be rewarded, and they shall come again from the land of the Enemy.* This was a sweet Cordial to me, when I was ready to faint, many and many a time have I sat down, and weept sweetly over this Scripture. At this place we continued about four dayes. . . .

THE SEVENTH REMOVE[16]

After a restless and hungry night there, we had a wearisome time of it the next day. The Swamp by which we lay, was, as it were, a deep Dungeon, and an exceeding high and steep hill before it. Before I got to the top of the hill, I thought my heart and legs, and all would have broken, and failed me. What through faintness, and soreness of body, it was a grievous day of travel to me. As we went along, I saw a place where English Cattle had been: that was comfort to me, such as it was: quickly after that we came to an English Path, which so took with me, that I thought I could have freely lyen down and dyed. That day, a little after noon, we came to Squaukheag, where the Indians quickly spread themselves over the deserted English Fields, gleaning what they could find; some pickt up ears of Wheat that were crickled down, some found ears of Indian Corn, some found Ground-nuts, and others sheaves of Wheat that were frozen together in the shock, and went to threshing of them out. My self got two ears of Indian Corn, and whilst I did but turn my back, one of them was stolen from me, which much troubled me. There came an Indian to them at that time, with a basket of Horse-liver. I asked him to give me a piece: What, says he, can you eat Horse-liver? I told him, I would try, if he would give a piece, which he did, and I laid it on the coals to rost; but before it was half ready they got half of it away from me, so that I was fain to take the rest and eat it as it was, with the blood about my mouth, and yet a savoury bit it was to me: *For to the hungry Soul every bitter thing is sweet.*[17] A solemn sight methought it was, to see Fields of wheat and Indian Corn forsaken and spoiled: and the remainders of them to be food for our merciless Enemies. That night we had a mess of wheat for our Supper.

THE TWENTIETH REMOVE[18]

It was their usual manner to remove, when they had done any mischief, lest they should be found out: and so they did at this time. We went about three or four miles, and there they built a great Wigwam, big enough to hold an hundred Indians, which they did in preparation to a great day of Dancing. . . .

On Tuesday morning they called their General Court (as they call it) to consult and determine, whether I should go home or no: And they all as one man did seemingly consent to it, that I should go home; except Philip, who would not come among them.

But before I go any further, I would take leave to mention a few remarkable passages of providence, which I took special notice of in my afflicted time.

1. Of the fair opportunity lost in the long March, a little after the Fort-fight, when our English Army was so numerous, and in pursuit of the Enemy, and so near as to take several and destroy them: and the Enemy in such distress for food, that our men might track them by their rooting in the earth for Ground-nuts, whilest they were flying for their lives. I say, that then our Army should want Provision, and be forced to leave their pursuit and return homeward: and the very next week the Enemy came upon our Town, like Bears bereft of their whelps, or so many ravenous Wolves, rending us and our Lambs to death. But what shall I say? God seemed to leave his People to themselves, and order all things for his own holy ends. *Shal there be evil in the City and the Lord hath not done it?*[19] *They are not grieved for the affliction of Joseph, therefore shal they go Captive, with the first that go Captive.*[20] It is the Lords doing, and it should be marvelous in our eyes.

2. I cannot but remember how the Indians derided the slowness, and dulness of the English Army, in its setting out. For after the desolations at Lancaster and Medfield, as I went along with them, they asked me when I thought the English Army would come after them?

I told them I could not tell: It may be they will come in May, said they. Thus did they scoffe at us, as if the English would be a quarter of a year getting ready.

3. Which also I have hinted before, when the English Army with new supplies were sent forth to pursue after the enemy, and they understanding it, fled before them till they came to Baquaug River, where they forthwith went over safely: that that River should be impassable to the English. I can but admire to see the wonderfull providence of God in preserving the heathen for farther affliction to our poor Countrey. They could go in great numbers over, but the English must stop: God had an over-ruling hand in all those things.

4. It was thought, if their Corn were cut down, they would starve and dy with hunger: and all their Corn that could be found, was destroyed, and they driven from that little they had in store, into the Woods in the midst of Winter; and yet how to admiration did the Lord preserve them for his holy ends, and the destruction of many still amongst the English! strangely did the Lord provide for them; that I did not see (all the time I was among them) one Man, Woman, or Child, die with hunger.

Though many times they would eat that, that a Hog or a Dog would hardly touch; yet by that God strengthened them to be a scourge to his People. . . .

But to return again to my going home, where we may see a remarkable change of Providence: At first they were all against it, except my Husband would come for me; but afterwards they assented to it, and seemed much to rejoyce in it; some askt me to send them some Bread, others some Tobacco, others shaking me by the hand, offering me a Hood and Scarfe to ride in; not one moving hand or tongue against it. Thus hath the Lord answered my poor desire, and the many earnest requests of others put up unto God for me. In my travels an Indian came to me, and told me, if I were willing, he and his Squaw would run away, and go home along with me: I told him No: I was not willing to run away, but desired to wait Gods time, that I might go home quietly, and without fear. And now God hath granted me my desire. O the wonderfull power of God that I have seen, and the experience that I have had: I have been in the midst of those roaring Lyons, and Salvage Bears, that feared neither God, nor Man, nor the Devil, by night and day, alone and in company: sleeping all sorts together, and yet not one of them ever offered me the least abuse of unchastity to me, in word or action. Though some are ready to say, I speak it for my own credit; But I speak it in the presence of God, and to his Glory. Gods Power is as great now, and as sufficient to save, as when he preserved Daniel in the Lions Den; or the three Children in the fiery Furnace. I may well say as his Psal. 107. 12, *Oh give thanks*

unto the Lord for he is good, for his mercy endureth for ever. Let the
Redeemed of the Lord say so, whom he hath redeemed from the hand
of the Enemy, especially that I should come away in the midst of so
many hundreds of Enemies quietly and peacably, and not a Dog moving his tongue. So I took my leave of them, and in coming along my
heart melted into tears, more then all the while I was with them, and
I was almost swallowed up with the thoughts that ever I should go
home again. About the Sun going down, Mr. Hoar, and my self, and
the two Indians came to Lancaster, and a solemn sight it was to me.
There had I lived many comfortable years amongst my Relations and
Neighbours, and now not one Christian to be seen, nor one house left
standing. We went on to a Farm house[21] that was yet standing, where
we lay all night: and a comfortable lodging we had, though nothing
but straw to ly on. The Lord preserved us in safety that night, and
raised us up again in the morning, and carried us along, that before
noon, we came to Concord. Now was I full of joy, and yet not without
sorrow: joy to see such a lovely sight, so many Christians together,
and some of them my Neighbours: There I met with my Brother, and
my Brother in Law, who asked me, if I knew where his Wife was?
Poor heart! he had helped to bury her, and knew it not; she being shot
down by the house was partly burnt: so that those who were at Boston
at the desolation of the Town, and came back afterward, and buried
the dead, did not know her. Yet I was not without sorrow, to think
how many were looking and longing, and my own Children amongst
the rest, to enjoy that deliverance that I had now received, and I did
not know whither ever I should see them again. Being recruited with
food and raiment we went to Boston that day, where I met with my
dear Husband, but the thoughts of our dear Children, one being dead,
and the other we could not tell where, abated our comfort each to
other. I was not before so much hem'd in with the merciless and cruel
Heathen, but now as much with pittiful, tender-hearted and compassionate Christians. In that poor, and destressed, and beggerly condition
I was received in, I was kindly entertained in severall Houses: so much
love I received from several (some of whom I knew, and others I knew
not) that I am not capable to declare it. . . .

Our Family being now gathered together (those of us that were
living) the South Church in Boston hired an House for us: Then we
removed from Mr. Shepards, those cordial Friends, and went to Boston, where we continued about three quarters of a year: Still the Lord
went along with us, and provided graciously for us. I thought it somewhat strange to set up House-keeping with bare walls; but as Solomon
says, *Mony answers all things,*[22] and that we had through the benevolence of Christian-friends, some in this Town, and some in that, and
others: And some from England, that in a little time we might look,

and see the House furnished with love. The Lord hath been exceeding good to us in our low estate, in that when we had neither house nor home, nor other necessaries; the Lord so moved the hearts of these and those towards us, that we wanted neither food, nor raiment for our selves or ours, Prov. 18. 24. *There is a Friend which sticketh closer than a Brother*. And how many such Friends have we found, and now living amongst? And truly such a Friend have we found him to be unto us, in whose house we lived, *viz.* Mr. James Whitcomb, a Friend unto us near hand, and afar off.

I can remember the time, when I used to sleep quietly without workings in my thoughts, whole nights together, but now it is other wayes with me. When all are fast about me, and no eye open, but his who ever waketh, my thoughts are upon things past, upon the awfull dispensation of the Lord towards us; upon his wonderfull power and might, in carrying of us through so many difficulties, in returning us in safety, and suffering none to hurt us. I remember in the night season, how the other day I was in the midst of thousands of enemies, and nothing but death before me: It is then hard work to perswade my self, that ever I should be satisfied with bread again. But now we are fed with the finest of the Wheat, and, as I may say, With honey out of the rock: In stead of the Husk, we have the fatted Calf: The thoughts of these things in the particulars of them, and of the love and goodness of God towards us, make it true of me, what David said of himself, Psal. 6. 5.[23] *I watered my Couch with my tears*. Oh! the wonderfull power of God that mine eyes have seen, affording matter enough for my thoughts to run in, that when others are sleeping mine eyes are weeping.

I have seen the extreme vanity of this World: One hour I have been in health, and wealth, wanting nothing: But the next hour in sickness and wounds, and death, having nothing but sorrow and affliction.

Before I knew what affliction meant, I was ready sometimes to wish for it. When I lived in prosperity, having the comforts of the World about me, my relations by me, my Heart chearfull, and taking little care for any thing; and yet seeing many, whom I preferred before my self, under many tryals and afflictions, in sickness, weakness, poverty, losses, crosses, and cares of the World, I should be sometimes jealous least I should have my portion in this life, and that Scripture would come to my mind, Heb. 12. 6. *For whom the Lord loveth he chasteneth, and scourgeth every Son whom he receiveth*. But now I see the Lord had his time to scourge and chasten me. The portion of some is to have their afflictions by drops, now one drop and then another; but the dregs of the Cup, the Wine of astonishment, like a sweeping rain that leaveth no food, did the Lord prepare to be my portion. Affliction I wanted, and affliction I had, full measure (I thought) pressed down and running over; yet I see, when God calls a Person to any thing, and through never so many difficulties, yet he is fully able to carry them through and make them see, and say they have been gainers thereby. And I hope I can say in some measure, As David did, *It is good for me that I have been afflicted.* The Lord hath shewed me the vanity of these outward things. That they are the Vanity of vanities, and vexation of spirit; that they are but a shadow, a blast, a bubble, and things of no continuance. That we must rely on God himself, and our whole dependance must be upon him. If trouble from smaller matters begin to arise in me, I have something at hand to check my self with, and say, why am I troubled? It was but the other day that if I had had the world, I would have given it for my freedom, or to have been a Servant to a Christian. I have learned to look beyond present and smaller troubles, and to be quieted under them, as Moses said, Exod. 14. 13. *Stand still and see the salvation of the Lord.*

Edward Taylor
(1644?–1729)

Although Edward Taylor's poems remained unpublished until 1939, two years after his manuscript book had been found in Yale University Library, he is now regarded as the colonial period's finest poet. Often associated with the tradition of English metaphysical poets that included John Donne, George Herbert, Francis Quarles, Henry Vaughan, and Richard Crashaw, the only poet known to be collected in Taylor's own library was his American compatriot Anne Bradstreet, and much of Taylor's interest in wordplay, wit, the juxtaposition of contrary feeling, and elaborate poetic figures, all of which have placed him in the company of the metaphysicals, he undoubtedly derived from the Bible, and particularly the Song of Songs.

Upon graduation from Harvard, where he was the roommate of Samuel Sewall, he immediately accepted the call to a frontier parish in western Massachusetts at Westfield, where he served as minister from 1671 to 1729. There he wrote all the poetry that took up 400 pages of his manuscript book. Chief among those poems were those included in Preparatory Meditations, *which he began writing in secret in 1679, spiritual exercises of an often curiously non-Puritan character designed to prepare him to deliver the sacrament of holy communion to those members of his church who were willing to confess publicly to the presence of God's grace in their lives. In addition to these poems, Taylor wrote occasional verse on miscellaneous subjects whose central interest for the Puritan always lies in their revelation of God's design or purpose. Taylor also tried his hand at the long poem, his most successful called* God's Determinations Concerning His Elect. *Composed of thirty-five poems that portray a merciful deity observing the battle between Christ and Satan over God's elect, some critics have*

*thought this poem might have been written as Taylor's answer to
Michael Wigglesworth's* Day of Doom. *If Taylor's richly symbolic,
often densely realized, poems reveal little else, they demonstrate that
art was not for the Puritan inimical to faith, that meditative poetry
could deepen religious experience.*

from *God's Determinations Concerning His Elect (c. 1680)*

The Preface

   Infinity, when all things it beheld
In Nothing, and of Nothing all did build,
Upon what Base was fixt the Lath, wherein
He turn'd this Globe, and riggalld[1] it so trim?
Who blew the Bellows of his Furnace Vast?
Or held the Mould wherein the world was Cast?
Who laid its Corner Stone?[2] Or whose Command?
Where stand the Pillars upon which it stands?
Who Lac'de and Fillitted[3] the earth so fine,
With Rivers like green Ribbons Smaragdine?[4]
Who made the Sea's its Selvedge, and it locks
Like a Quilt Ball[5] within a Silver Box?
Who Spread its Canopy? Or Curtains Spun?
Who in this Bowling Alley bowld the Sun?
Who made it always when it rises set
To go at once both down, and up to get?
Who th'Curtain rods made for this Tapistry?
Who hung the twinckling Lanthorns in the Sky?
Who? who did this? or who is he? Why, know
Its Onely Might Almighty this did doe.
His hand hath made this noble worke which Stands
His Glorious Handywork not made by hands.
Who spake all things from nothing; and with ease
Can speake all things to nothing, if he please.
Whose Little finger at his pleasure Can
Out mete[6] ten thousand worlds with halfe a Span:
Whose Might Almighty can by half a looks
Root up the rocks and rock the hills by th'roots.
Can take this mighty World up in his hande,
And shake it like a Squitchen[7] or a Wand.[8]

Whose single Frown will make the Heavens shake
Like as an aspen leafe the Winde makes quake.
Oh! what a might is this Whose single frown
Doth shake the world as it would shake it down?
Which All from Nothing fet,[9] from Nothing, All:
Hath All on Nothing set, lets Nothing fall.
Gave All to nothing Man indeed, whereby
Through nothing man all might him Glorify.
In Nothing then imbosst the brightest Gem
More pretious than all pretiousness in them.
But Nothing man did throw down all by Sin:
And darkened that lightsom Gem in him.
   That now his Brightest Diamond is grown
   Darker by far than any Coalpit Stone.

The Souls Groan to Christ for Succour

Good Lord, behold this Dreadfull Enemy
   Who makes me tremble with his fierce assaults,
I dare not trust, yet feare to give the ly,
   For in my soul, my soul finds many faults.
   And though I justify myselfe to's face:
   I do Condemn myselfe before thy Grace.

He strives to mount my sins, and them advance
   Above thy Merits, Pardons, or Good Will
Thy Grace to lessen, and thy Wrath t'inhance
   As if thou couldst not pay the sinners bill.
   He Chiefly injures thy rich Grace, I finde
   Though I confess my heart to sin inclin'de.

Those Graces which thy Grace enwrought in mee,
   He makes as nothing but a pack of Sins.
He maketh Grace no grace, but Crueltie,
   Is Graces Honey Comb, a Comb of Stings?
   This makes me ready leave thy Grace and run.
   Which if I do, I finde I am undone.

I know he is thy Cur, therefore I bee
   Perplexed lest I from thy Pasture stray.
He bayghs, and barks so veh'mently at mee.
   Come rate[10] this Cur, Lord, breake his teeth I pray.
   Remember me I humbly pray thee first.
   Then halter up this Cur that is so Curst.

Christ's Reply

Peace, Peace, my Hony, do not Cry,
My Little Darling, wipe thine eye,
   Oh Cheer, Cheer up, come see.
Is anything too deare, my Dove,[11]
Is anything too good, my Love
   To get or give for thee?

If in the severall thou art
This Yelper fierce will at thee bark:
   That thou art mine this shows.
As Spot barks back the sheep again
Before they to the Pound are ta'ne,
   So he and hence 'way goes.

But yet this Cur that bayghs so sore
Is broken tootht, and muzzled sure,
   Fear not, my Pritty Heart.
His barking is to make thee Cling
Close underneath thy Saviours Wing.
   Why did my sweeten start?

And if he run an inch too far,
I'le Check his Chain, and rate the Cur.
   My Chick, keep clost to mee.
The Poles shall sooner kiss, and greet[12]
And Paralells shall sooner meet
   Than thou shalt harmed bee.

He seeks to aggrivate thy sin
And screw[13] them to the highest pin,[14]
   To make thy faith to quaile.
Yet mountain Sins like mites should show
And then these mites for naught should goe
   Could he but once prevaile.

I smote thy sins upon the Head.[15]
They Dead'ned are, though not quite dead:
   And shall not rise again.
I'l put away the Guilt thereof,
And purge its Filthiness cleare off:
   My Blood doth out the stain.

And though thy judgment was remiss
Thy Headstrong Will too Wilfull is.
  I will Renew the same.
And though thou do too frequently
Offend as heretofore hereby
  I'l not severly blaim.

And though thy senses do inveagle
Thy Noble Soul to tend the Beagle,
  That t'hunt her games forth go.
I'le Lure her back to me, and Change
Those fond Affections that do range
  As yelping beagles doe.

Although thy sins increase their race,
And though when thou hast sought for Grace,
  Thou fallst more than before
If thou by true Repentence Rise,
And Faith makes me thy Sacrifice,
  I'l pardon all, though more.

Though Satan strive to block thy way
By all his Stratagems he may:
  Come, come though through the fire.
For Hell that Gulph of fire for sins,
Is not so hot as t'burn thy Shins.
  Then Credit not the Lyar.

Those Cursed Vermin Sins that Crawle
All ore thy Soul, both Greate, and small
  Are onely Satans own:
Which he in his Malignity
Unto thy Souls true Sanctity
  In at the doors hath thrown.

And though they be Rebellion high.
Ath'ism or Apostacy:
  Though blasphemy it bee:
Unto what Quality, or Sise
Excepting one, so e're it rise.
  Repent, I'le pardon thee.

Although thy Soule was once a Stall
Rich hung with Satans nicknacks all;

If thou Repent thy Sin,
A Tabernacle in't I'le place
Fild with Gods Spirit, and his Grace.
   Oh Comfortable thing!

I dare the World therefore to show
A God like me, to anger slow:
   Whose wrath is full of Grace.
Doth hate all Sins both Greate, and small:
Yet when Repented, pardons all.
   Frowns with a Smiling Face.

As for thy outward Postures each,
Thy Gestures, Actions, and thy Speech,
   I Eye and Eying spare,
If thou repent. My Grace is more
Ten thousand times still tribled ore
   Than thou canst want, or ware.

As for the Wicked Charge he makes,
That he of Every Dish first takes
   Of all thy holy things.
Its false, deny the same, and say,
That which he had he stool away
   Out of thy Offerings.

Though to thy Griefe, poor Heart, thou finde
In Pray're too oft a wandring minde,
   In Sermons Spirits dull.
Though faith in firy furnace[16] flags,
And Zeale in Chilly Seasons lags.
   Temptations powerfull.

These faults are his, and none of thine
So far as thou dost them decline.
   Come then receive my Grace.
And when he buffits thee therefore
If thou my aid, and Grace implore
   I'le shew a pleasant face.

But still look for Temptations Deep,
Whilst that thy Noble Sparke doth keep
   Within a Mudwald Cote.
These White Frosts and the Showers that fall

Are but to whiten thee withall.
   Not rot the Web they smote.

If in the fire where Gold is tride
Thy Soule is put, and purifide
   Wilt thou lament thy loss?
If silver-like this fire refine
Thy Soul and make it brighter shine:
   Wilt thou bewaile the Dross?

Oh! fight my Field: no Colours fear:
I'l be thy Front, I'l be thy reare.
   Fail not: my Battells fight.
Defy the Tempter, and his Mock.
Anchor thy heart on mee thy Rock.[17]
   I do in thee Delight.

from *Preparatory Meditations (1939)*

"Meditation 1"

What Love is this of thine, that Cannot bee
   In thine Infinity, O Lord, Confinde,
Unless it in thy very Person see,
   Infinity, and Finity Conjoyn'd?
   What hath thy Godhead, as not satisfide
   Marri'de our Manhood, making it its Bride?

Oh, Matchless Love! filling Heaven to the brim!
   O're running it: all running o're beside.
This World! Nay Overflowing Hell; wherein
   For thine Elect, there rose a mighty Tide!
   That there our Veans might through thy Person bleed,
   To quench those flames, that else would on us feed.

Oh! that thy Love might overflow my Heart!
   To fire the same with Love: for Love I would.
But oh! my streight'ned Breast! my Lifeless Sparke!
   My Fireless Flame! What Chilly Love, and Cold?
   In measure small! In Manner Chilly! See.
   Lord blow the Coal: Thy Love Enflame in mee.

"Meditation 8"

John 6.51. I am the Living Bread

I kening[1] through Astronomy Divine
    The World's bright Battlement, wherein I spy
A Golden Path my Pensill cannot line,
    From that bright Throne unto my Threshold ly.
    And while my puzzled thoughts about it pore
    I finde the Bread of Life in't at my doore.

When that this Bird of Paradise put in
    This Wicker Cage (my Corps) to tweedle praise
Had peckt the Fruite forbad: and so did fling
    Away its Food; and lost its golden dayes;
    It fell into Celestiall Famine sore:
    And never could attain a morsell more.

Alas! alas! Poore Bird, what wilt thou doe?
    The Creatures field no food for Souls e're gave.
And if thou knock at Angells dores they show
    An Empty Barrell: they no soul bread have.
    Alas! Poore Bird, the Worlds White Loafe is done.
    And cannot yield thee here the smallest Crumb.

In this sad state, Gods Tender Bowells run
    Out streams of Grace: And he to end all strife
The Purest Wheate in Heaven, his deare-dear Son
    Grinds, and kneads up into this Bread of Life.
    Which Bread of Life from Heaven down came and stands
    Disht on thy Table up by Angells Hands.

Did God mould up this Bread in Heaven, and bake,
    Which from his Table came, and to thine goeth?
Doth he bespeake thee thus, This Soule Bread take.
    Come Eate thy fill of this thy God's White Loafe?
    Its Food too fine for Angells, yet come, take
    And Eate thy fill. Its Heavens Sugar Cake.

What Grace is this knead in this Loafe? This thing
    Souls are but petty things it to admire.
Yee Angells, help: This fill would to the brim
    Heav'ns whelm'd-down Chrystall meele Bowle, yea and higher.

This Bread of Life dropt in thy mouth, doth Cry.
Eate, Eate me, Soul, and thou shalt never dy.

"Meditation 38" (1690)

1 John 2.1 An Advocate with the Father.

Oh! what a thing is man? Lord, who am I?
   That Thou shouldst give him law (Oh! golden line)
To regulate his thoughts, words, life thereby.
     And judge him wilt thereby too in Thy time.
     A court of justice Thou in heaven hold'st
     To try his case while he's here housed on mold.[2]

How do Thy angels lay before Thine eye
   My deeds both white and black I daily do?
How doth Thy court Thou Panelist there them try?
     But flesh complains. What right for this? let's know.
     For right, or wrong I can't appear unto't.
     And shall a sentence pass on such a suite?

Soft; blemish not this golden bench, or place.
   Here is no bribe, nor colorings to hide
Nor pettifogger[3] to befog the case
     But justice hath her glory here well tried.
     Her spotless law all spotted cases tends.
     Without respect or disrespect them ends.

God's judge Himself: and Christ attorney is,
   The Holy Ghost registerer is found.
Angels the sergeants are, all creatures kiss
     The book, and do as Evidences[4] abound.
     All cases pass according to pure law
     And in the sentence is no fret, nor flaw.

What sayst, my soul? Here all thy deeds are tried.
   Is Christ thy advocate to plead thy cause?
Art thou His client? Such shall never slide.
     He never lost His case: He pleads such laws
     As carry do the same, nor doth refuse
     The vilest sinner's case that doth Him choose.

This is His honor, not dishonor: nay,
   No habeas-corpus against His clients came

For all their fines His purse doth make down pay.
  He non-suits Satan's suit or casts[5] the same.
  He'll plead thy case, and not accept a fee.
  He'll plead sub forma pauperis[6] for thee.

My case is bad. Lord, be my advocate.
  My sin is red: I'm under God's arrest.
Thou hast the hint of pleading; plead my state.
    Although it's bad Thy plea will make it best.
    If Thou wilt plead my case before the King:
    I'll wagonloads of love and glory bring.

"Meditation 39"

  1 John 2.1 If any man sin, we have an Advocate.

My Sin! my Sin, My God, these Cursed Dregs,
  Green, Yellow, Blew streakt Poyson hellish, ranck,
Bubs[7] hatcht in natures nest on Serpents Eggs,
    Yelp, Cherp and Cry; they set my Soule a Cramp.
    I frown, Chide, strik and fight them, mourn and Cry
    To Conquour them, but cannot them destroy.

I cannot kill nor Coop them up: my Curb
  'S less than a Snaffle[8] in their mouth: my Rains
They as a twine thrid, snap: by hell they're spurd:
    And load my Soule with swagging loads of pains.
    Black Imps, young Divells, snap, bite, drag to bring
    And pick mee headlong hells dread Whirle Poole in.

Lord, hold thy hand: for handle mee thou may'st
  In Wrath: but, oh, a twinckling Ray of hope
Methinks I spie thou graciously display'st.
    There is an Advocate: a doore is ope.
    Sin's poyson swell my heart would till it burst,
    Did not a hope hence creep in't thus, and nurse't.

Joy, joy, Gods Son's the Sinners Advocate
  Doth plead the Sinner guiltless, and a Saint.
But yet Atturnies pleas spring from the State
    The Case is in: if bad its bad in plaint.
    My Papers do contain no pleas that do
    Secure mee from, but knock me down to, woe.

I have no plea mine Advocate to give:
  What now? He'l anvill Arguments greate Store
Out of his Flesh and Blood to make thee live.
  O Deare bought Arguments: Good pleas therefore.
  Nails made of heavenly Steel, more Choice than gold
  Drove home, Well Clencht, eternally will hold.

Oh! Dear bought Plea, Deare Lord, why buy't so deare?
  What with thy blood purchase thy plea for me?
Take Argument out of thy Grave t'appeare
  And plead my Case with, me from Guilt to free.
  These maule both Sins, and Divells, and amaze
  Both Saints, and Angells; Wreath their mouths with praise.

What shall I doe, my Lord? what do, that I
  May have thee plead my Case? I fee thee will
With Faith, Repentance, and obediently
  Thy Service gainst Satanick Sins fulfill.
  I'l fight thy fields while Live I do, although
  I should be hackt in pieces by thy foe.

Make me thy Friend, Lord, be my Surety: I
  Will be thy Client, be my Advocate:
My Sins make thine, thy Pleas make mine hereby.
  Thou wilt mee save, I will thee Celebrate.
  Thou'lt kill my Sins that cut my heart within:
  And my rough Feet shall thy smooth praises sing.

from *Occasional Poems*[1]

Upon a Spider Catching a Fly (1680–1682)

  Thou Sorrow, venom Elfe.
      Is this thy ploy,
To Spin a web out of thyselfe
      To Catch a Fly?
              For Why?

  I saw a pettish wasp
      Fall foule therein.
Whom yet thy whorlepins[2] did not [clasp]

Lest he should fling
His Sting.

But as affraid, remote
Didst Stand hereat
And with thy little fingers stroke
And gently tap
His back.

Thus gently him didst treate
Lest he Should pet,
And in a froppish,³ waspish heate
Should greatly fret
Thy net.

Whereas the Silly Fly,
Caught by its leg
Thou by the throate tookst hastily
And 'hinde the head
Bite Dead.

This goes to pot, that not
Nature doth call.
Strive not above what strength hath got
Lest in the brawle
Thou fall.

This Frey seems thus to us
Hells Spider gets
His intrails Spun to whip Cords thus
And wove to nets
And sets.

To tangle Adams race
In's Stratigems
To their Destructions, Spoil'd made base
By venom things
Damn'd Sins.

But mighty, Gracious Lord
Communicate
Thy Grace to breake the Cord afford
Us Glorys Gate
And State.

We'l Nightingaile Sing like
　　When pearcht on high
In Glories Cage, thy glory, bright,
　　　[And] thankfully,
　　　　　　　　For joy.

Huswifery (1682–1683)

Make mee, O Lord, thy Spining Wheele compleat.
　　Thy Holy Words my Distaff[4] make for mee.
Make mine Affections thy Swift Flyers[5] neate
　　And make my Soule thy holy Spoole to bee.
　　My Conversation make to be thy Reele[6]
　　And reele the yarn there on Spun of thy Wheele.

Make me thy Loome then, knit therein this Twine:
　　And make thy Holy Spirit, Lord, winde quills:[7]
Then weave the Web thyselfe. The yarn is fine.
　　Thine Ordinances make my Fulling Mills.[8]
　　Then dy the same in Heavenly Colours Choice,
　　All pinkt[9] with Varnisht Flowers of Paradise.

Then cloath therewith mine Understanding, Will,
　　Affections, Judgment, Conscience, Memory
My Words, & Actions, that their Shine may fill
　　My wayes with glory and thee glorify.
　　Then mine apparell shall display before yee
　　That I am Cloathd in Holy robes for glory.

The Ebb & Flow

When first thou on me Lord, wrought'st thy Sweet Print,
　　My heart was made thy tinder box.
　　My 'ffections were thy tinder in't.
　　Where fell thy Sparkes by drops.
Those holy Sparks of Heavenly Fire that came
Did ever catch & often out would flame.

But now my Heart is made thy Censar[10] trim,
　　Full of thy golden Altars fire,
　　To offer up Sweet Incense in
　　Unto thyselfe intire:
I finde my tinder scarce thy Sparks can feel
That drop out from thy Holy flint & Steel.

Hence doubts out bud for feare thy fire in mee
   'S a mocking Ignis Fatuus,[11]
   Or lest thine Altars fire out bee,
   Its hid in ashes thus.
Yet when the bellows of thy Spirit blow
Away mine ashes, then thy fire doth glow.

Samuel Sewall
(1652–1730)

Originally known as the hanging judge at the Salem witchcraft trials, Samuel Sewall has subsequently emerged, thanks to the publication of his Diary, *as a Puritan of considerable moral character who was not above recanting in public his own responsibility for that miserable affair. This impression has been enhanced by the discovery that in* The Selling of Joseph, *published in 1710, Sewall also wrote one of the first antislavery tracts.*

Fleeing religious persecution during the Restoration, Sewall arrived in America in 1661 and settled with his family in Boston, where he would remain for the rest of his life. Initially enrolling at Harvard to study for the ministry, Sewall decided instead on a career in business and politics, and by the early 1690s he had achieved remarkable success in a number of fields from banking, publishing, and international trade to the judiciary. But Sewall's Diary, *which he began in 1673 and did not suspend until 1729, shows that he remained a devout Puritan throughout, using the discipline of his* Diary *to monitor, as any Puritan should, his spiritual life. If the* Diary *details Sewall's religious experience, however, it also provides an extraordinarily full record of colonial existence during a period of rapid change, when coastal New England was being transformed from a backward, semireligious society into a more secular, cosmopolitan world.*

from *The Diary of Samuel Sewall*
(1674–1729)

[WITCHCRAFT TRIALS: INVOLVEMENT,
1692, AND RECANTATION, 1697]

April 11, 1692. Went to Salem, where, in the meeting-house, the persons accused of witchcraft were examined; was a very great assembly; 'twas awful to see how the afflicted persons were agitated. Mr. Noyes pray'd at the beginning, and Mr. Higginson concluded.

August 19, 1692. This day George Burrough, John Willard, John Procter, Martha Carrier and George Jacobs were executed at Salem, a very great number of spectators being present. Mr. Cotton Mather was there, Mr. Sims, Hale, Noyes, Chiever, &c. All of them said they were innocent, Carrier and all. Mr. Mather says they all died by a righteous sentence. Mr. Burrough by his speech, prayer, protestation of his innocence, did much move unthinking persons, which occasions their speaking hardly concerning his being executed.

August 25. Fast at the old [*First*] Church, respecting the witchcraft, drought, &c.

Monday, September 19, 1692. About noon, at Salem, Giles Corey was press'd to death for standing mute; much pains was used with him two days, one after another, by the Court and Capt. Gardner of Nantucket who had been of his acquaintance: but all in vain.[1]

September 20. Now I hear from Salem that about 18 years ago, he [Giles Corey] was suspected to have stampd and press'd a man to death, but was cleared. 'Twas not remembered till Anne Putnam was told of it by said Corey's spectre the sabbath-day night before execution.

September 21. A petition is sent to town in behalf of Dorcas Hoar, who now confesses: accordingly an order is sent to the sheriff to forbear her execution, notwithstanding her being in the warrant to die tomorrow. This is the first condemned person who has confess'd.[2]

Thursday, September 22, 1692. William Stoughton, Esqr., John Hathorne, Esqr., Mr. Cotton Mather, and Capt. John Higginson, with my Brother St., were at our house, speaking about publishing some Trials of the Witches.[3]

January 14, 1697. Copy of the bill I put up on the fast day;[4] giving it to Mr. Willard as he pass'd by, and standing up at the reading of it, and bowing when finished; in the afternoon.

"Samuel Sewall, sensible of the reiterated strokes of God upon himself and family; and being sensible, that as to the guilt contracted, upon the opening of the late Commission of Oyer and Terminer[5] at Salem (to which the order for this day relates) he is, upon many accounts, more concerned than any that he knows of, desires to take the blame and shame of it, asking pardon of men, and especially desiring prayers that God, who has an unlimited authority, would pardon that sin and all other his sins; personal and relative: And according to his infinite benignity, and sovereignty, not visit the sin of him, or of any other, upon himself or any of his, nor upon the land: But that He would powerfully defend him against all temptations to sin, for the future; and vouchsafe him the efficacious, saving conduct of his word and spirit."

[COURTSHIP OF MADAM WINTHROP, 1720]

September 5 [1720]. Going to son Sewall's I there meet with Madam Winthrop, told her I was glad to meet her there, had not seen her a great while; gave her Mr. Homes's *Sermon.*[6]

[September 30]. Mr. Colman's lecture: Daughter Sewall acquaints Madam Winthrop that if she pleas'd to be within at 3. p.m. I would wait on her. She answer'd she would be at home.

[October] 1. *Saturday,* I dine at Mr. Stoddard's: from thence I went to Madam Winthrop's just at 3. Spake to her, saying, my loving wife died so soon and suddenly, 'twas hardly convenient for me to think of marrying again; however I came to this resolution, that I would not make my court to any person without first consulting with her. Had a pleasant discourse about 7 single persons sitting in the fore-seat [September] 29th, viz. Madm Rebekah Dudley, Catharine Winthrop, Bridget Usher, Deliverance Legg, Rebekah Loyd, Lydia Colman, Elizabeth Bellingham. She propounded one and another for me; but none would do, said Mrs. Loyd was about her age.

October 3. Waited on Madam Winthrop again; 'twas a little while before she came in. Her daughter Noyes being there alone with me. I said, I hoped my waiting on her mother would not be disagreeable to her. She answer'd she should not be against that that might be for her comfort. I saluted her, and told her I perceiv'd I must shortly wish her a good time; (her mother had told me, she was with child, and within a month or two of her time). By and by in came Mr. Ayers, Chaplain of the Castle, and hang'd up his hat, which I was a little startled at, it seeming as if he was to lodge there. At last Madam Winthrop came in. After a considerable time, I went up to her and said, if it might not be inconvenient I desired to speak with her. She assented, and spake of going into another room; but Mr. Ayers and Mrs. Noyes presently rose up, and went out, leaving us there alone. Then I usher'd in discourse from the names in the fore-seat; at last I pray'd that Katharine [*Mrs. Winthrop*] might be the person assign'd for me. She instantly took it up in way of denial, as if she had catch'd at an opportunity to do it, saying she could not do it before she was asked. Said that was her mind unless she should change it, which she believed she should not; could not leave her children. I express'd my sorrow that she should do it so speedily, pray'd her consideration, and ask'd her when I should wait on her again. She setting no time, I mention'd that day sennight.[7] Gave her Mr. Willard's *Fountain* open'd with the little print and verses; saying, I hop'd if we did well read that book, we should meet together hereafter, if we did not now. She took the book, and put it in her pocket. Took leave.

[*October*] 6. A little after 6 p.m. I went to Madam Winthrop's. She was not within. . . . After awhile Dr. Noyes came in with his mother; and quickly after his wife came in. They sat talking, I think, till eight a-clock. I said I fear'd I might be some interruption to their business. Dr. Noyes reply'd pleasantly: He fear'd they might be an interruption to me, and went away. Madam seem'd to harp upon the same string. Must take care of her children; could not leave that house and neighbourhood where she had dwelt so long. I told her she might do her children as much or more good by bestowing what she laid out in house-keeping, upon them. Said her son would be of age the 7th of August. I said it might be inconvenient for her to dwell with her daughter-in-law, who must be mistress of the house. I gave her a piece of Mr. Belcher's cake and ginger-bread wrapped up in a clean sheet of paper; told her of her father's kindness to me when treasurer, and I constable. My daughter Judith was gone from me and I was more lonesome—might help to forward one another in our journey to Canaan.—Mr. Eyre came within the door; I saluted him, ask'd how Mr. Clark did, and he went away. I took leave about 9 o'clock. I told [*her*] I came now to refresh her memory as to Monday-night; said she had not forgot it. In discourse with her, I ask'd leave to speak with her sister; I meant to gain Madam Mico's[8] favour to persuade her sister. She seem'd surpris'd and displeas'd, and said she was in the same condition!

[*October*] 11. I writ a few lines to Madam Winthrop to this purpose: "Madam, these wait on you with Mr. Mayhew's Sermon, and account of the state of the Indians on Martha's Vinyard. I thank you for your unmerited favours of yesterday; and hope to have the happiness of waiting on you to-morrow before eight a-clock after noon. I pray GOD to keep you, and give you a joyfull entrance upon the two hundred and twenty ninth year of Christopher Columbus his discovery; and take leave, who am, Madam, your humble Servt. S.S.

Sent this by Deacon Green, who deliver'd it to Sarah Chickering, her mistress not being at home.

[*October*] *12.* . . . Mrs. Anne Cotton came to door (twas before 8.) said Madam Winthrop was within, directed me into the little room, where she was full of work behind a stand; Mrs. Cotton came in and stood. Madam Winthrop pointed to her to set me a chair. Madam Winthrop's countenance was much changed from what 'twas on Monday, look'd dark and lowering. At last, the work, (black stuff or silk) was taken away, I got my chair in place, had some converse, but very cold and indifferent to what 'twas before. Ask'd her to acquit me of rudeness if I drew off her glove. Enquiring the reason, I told her 'twas great odds between handling a dead goat, and a living lady. Got it off. I told her I had one petition to ask of her, that was, that she would take off the negative she laid on me the third of October; She readily answer'd she could not, and enlarg'd upon it; She told me of it so soon as she could; could not leave her house, children, neighbours, business. I told her she might do some good to help and support me. . . . Sarah fill'd a glass of wine; she drank to me, I to her. She sent Juno home with me with a good lantern, I gave her 6d and bid her thank her Mistress. In some of our discourse, I told her I had rather go to the stone-house^9 adjoining to her, than to come to her against her mind. Told her the reason why I came every other night was lest I should drink too deep draughts of pleasure. She had talk'd of canary,^{10} her kisses were to me better than the best canary. Explain'd the expression concerning Columbus.

[*October*] *17. Monday,* . . . In the evening I visited Madam Winthrop, who treated me courteously, but not in clean linen as sometimes. She said, she did not know whether I would come again, or no. I ask'd her how she could so impute inconstancy to me. (I had not visited her since Wednesday night being unable to get over the indisposition received by the treatment received that night, and *I must* in it seem'd to sound like a made piece of formality.) Gave her this day's *Gazette.* . . .

[*October*] *18.* Visited Madam Mico, who came to me in a splendid dress. I said, "It may be you have heard of my visiting Madam Winthrop," her sister. She answered, Her sister had told her of it. I ask'd her good will in the affair. She answer'd. If her sister were for it, she should not hinder it. I gave her Mr. Homes's *Sermon.* She gave me a glass of canary, entertain'd me with good discourse, and a respectful remembrance of my first wife. I took leave.

[*October*] 19. Midweek, visited Madam Winthrop; Sarah told me she was at Mr. Walley's, would not come home till late. I gave her Hannah's 3 oranges with her duty, not knowing whether I should find her or no. Was ready to go home: but said if I knew she was there, I would go thither. Sarah seem'd to speak with pretty good courage. She would be there. I went and found her there, with Mr. Walley and his wife in the little room below. At 7 a-clock I mentioned going home; at 8. I put on my coat, and quickly waited on her home. She found occasion to speak loud to the servant, as if she had a mind to be known. Was courteous to me; but took occasion to speak pretty earnestly about my keeping a coach: I said 'twould cost £100. per annum: she said 'twould cost but £40. Spake much against John Winthrop, his false-heartedness. . . . Came away somewhat late.

[*October*] 20. . . . Madam Winthrop not being at lecture, I went thither first; found her very serene with her daughter Noyes, Mrs. Dering, and the widow Shipreev sitting at a little table, she in her arm'd chair. She drank to me, and I to Mrs. Noyes. After awhile pray'd the favour to speak with her. She took one of the candles, and went into the best room, clos'd the shutters, sat down upon the couch. She told me Madam Usher had been there, and said the coach must be set on wheels, and not by rusting. She spake something of my needing a wig. Ask'd me what her sister said to me. I told her: She said, If her sister were for it, she would not hinder it. But I told her, she did not say she would be glad to have me for her brother. Said, I shall keep you in the cold, and ask her if she would be within tomorrow night, for we had had but a running feast. She said she could not tell whether she should, or no. I took leave. As were drinking at the Governour's, he said: In England the ladies minded little more than that they might have money, and coaches to ride in. I said, And New-England brooks its name. At which Mr. Dudley smiled. Govr said they were not quite so bad here.

[*October*] 21. *Friday*, My son, the minister, came to me p.m. by appointment and we pray one for another in the old chamber; more especially respecting my courtship. About 6. a-clock I go to Madam Winthrop's; Sarah told me her mistress was gone out, but did not tell me whither she went. She presently order'd me a fire; so I went in, having Dr. Sibb's *Bowels*[11] with me to read. I read the two first Sermons, still no body came in: at last about 9. a-clock Mr. John Eyre came in; I took the opportunity to say to him as I had done to Mrs. Noyes before, that I hoped my visiting his mother would not be disagreeable to him; he answered me with much respect. When 'twas after 9. a-clock he of himself said he would go and call her, she was but at one of his brothers. A while after I heard Madam Winthrop's voice, enquiring something about John. After a good while and clapping the

garden door twice or thrice, she came in. I mention'd something of
the lateness; she banter'd me, and said I was later. She receiv'd me
courteously. I ask'd when our proceedings should be made public: She
said they were like to be no more public than they were already. Offer'd me no wine that I remember. I rose up at 11 a-clock to come
away, saying I would put on my coat. She offer'd not to help me. I
pray'd her that Juno might light me home, she open'd the shutter, and
said twas pretty light abroad; Juno was weary and gone to bed. So I
came home by star-light as well as I could. At my first coming in, I
gave Sarah five shillings. I wrote Mr. Eyre his name in his book with
the date October 21, 1720. It cost me 8s. Jehovah jireh![12] Madam told
me she had visited M. Mico, Wendell, and Wm Clark of the South
[*Church*].

October 24. I went in the hackny coach through the Common,
stopped at Madam Winthrop's (had told her I would take my departure from thence). Sarah came to the door with Katie in her arms: but
I did not think to take notice of the child. Call'd her mistress. I told
her, being encourag'd by David Jeffries loving eyes, and sweet words,
I was come to enquire whether she could find in her heart to leave
that house and neighbourhood, and go and dwell with me at the south
end; I think she said softly, Not yet. I told her It did not lie in my
hands to keep a coach. If I should, I should be in danger to be brought
to keep company with her neighbour Brooker, (he was a little before
sent to prison for debt). Told her I had an antipathy against those who
would pretend to give themselves; but nothing of their estate. I would
a proportion of my estate with my self. And I suppos'd she would do
so. As to a Periwig, my best and greatest friend, I could not possibly
have a greater, began to find me with hair before I was born, and had
continued to do so ever since; and I could not find in my heart to go
to another. She commended the book I gave her, Dr. Preston, the
Church's Marriage; quoted him saying 'twas inconvenient keeping out
of a fashion commonly used. I said the time and tide did circumscribe
my visit. She gave me a dram of black-cherry brandy, and gave me a
lump of the sugar that was in it. She wish'd me a good journey. I
pray'd God to keep her, and came away. Had a very pleasant journey
to Salem.

[*October*] 31. . . . At night I visited Madam Winthrop about 6.
p.m. They told me she was gone to Madam Mico's. I went thither and
found she was gone; so return'd to her house, read the Epistles to the
Galatians, Ephesians in Mr. Eyre's Latin Bible. After the clock struck
8, I began to read the 103. Psalm. Mr. Wendell came in from his
warehouse. Ask'd me if I were alone? Spake very kindly to me, offer'd
me to call Madam Winthrop. I told him, She would be angry, had
been at M. Mico's; he help'd me on with my coat and I came home:

left the *Gazette* in the Bible, which told Sarah of, bid her present my service to M. Winthrop, and tell her I had been to wait on her if she had been at home.

November 1. I was so taken up that I could not go if I would.

November 2. Midweek, went again, and found Mrs. Alden there, who quickly went out. Gave her[13] about ½ pound of sugar almonds, cost 3s per £. Carried them on Monday. She seem'd pleas'd with them, ask'd what they cost. Spake of giving her a hundred pounds per annum if I died before her. Ask'd her what sum she would give me, if she should die first? Said I would give her time to consider of it. She said she heard as if I had given all to my children by deeds of gift. I told her 'twas a mistake, Point-Judith was mine &c. That in England, I own'd, my father's desire was that it should go to my eldest son; 'twas 20£ per annum; she thought 'twas forty. I think when I seem'd to excuse pressing this, she seem'd to think 'twas best to speak of it; a long winter was coming on. Gave me a glass or two of Canary.

November 4. Friday, Went again about 7. a-clock; found there Mr. John Walley and his wife: sat discoursing pleasantly. I shew'd them Isaac Moses's [*an Indian*] writing. Madam W. serv'd comfits to us. After a while a table was spread, and supper was set. I urg'd Mr. Walley to crave a blessing; but he put it upon me. About 9, they went away. I ask'd Madam what fashioned neck-lace I should present her with; she said, "None at all." I ask'd her whereabout we left off last time; mention'd what I had offer'd to give her; ask'd her what she would give me. She said she could not change her condition. She had said so from the beginning; could not be so far from her children, the lecture. Quoted the Apostle Paul affirming that a single life was better than a married. I answer'd, that was for the present distress. Said she had not pleasure in things of that nature as formerly; I said, you are the fitter to make me a wife. If she held in that mind, I must go home and bewail my rashness in making more haste than good speed. However, considering the supper, I desired her to be within next Monday night, if we liv'd so long. Assented. She charg'd me with saying, that she must put away Juno, if she came to me: I utterly deny'd it; it never came in my heart; yet she insisted upon it; saying it came in upon discourse about the Indian woman that obtained her freedom this court. About 10, I said I would not disturb the good orders of her house, and came away. She not seeming pleas'd with my coming away. Spake to her about David Jeffries, had not seen him.

Monday, November 7. My son pray'd in the old chamber. Our time had been taken up by son and daughter Cooper's visit; so that I only read the 130th and 143. Psalm. 'Twas on the account of my courtship. I went to Mad. Winthrop; found her rocking her little Katie in the cradle. I excus'd my coming so late (near eight). She set me an arm'd chair and cushion; and so the cradle was between her arm'd chair and mine. Gave her the remnant of my almonds; she did not eat of them as before, but laid them away; I said I came to enquire whether she had alter'd her mind since Friday, or remained of the same mind still. She said, "Thereabouts." I told her I loved her, and was so fond[14] as to think that she loved me: she said [she] had a great respect for me. I told her, I had made her an offer, without asking any advice; she had so many to advise with, that twas a hindrance. The fire was come to one short brand besides the block, which brand was set up in end; at last it fell to pieces, and no recruit was made.[15] She gave me a glass of wine. I think I repeated again that I would go home and bewail my rashness in making more haste than good speed. I would endeavour to contain myself, and not go on to solicit her to do that which she could not consent to. Took leave of her. As came down the steps she bid me have a care. Treated me courteously. Told her she had enter'd the 4th year of her widowhood. I had given her the News-Letter before: I did not bid her draw off her glove as sometime I had done. Her dress was not so clean as sometime it had been. Jehovah jireh!

Midweek, [November] 9. Dine at Bro^r Stoddard's: were so kind as to enquire of me if they should invite M^m Winthrop; I answer'd, "No." Thank'd my sister Stoddard for her courtesy. . . . She sent her servant home with me with a lantern. Madam Winthrop's shutters were open as I pass'd by.

November 11. Went not to Madam Winthrop's. This is the 2nd withdraw.

from *Phaenomena quaedam Apocalyptica* (1697)

[PLUM ISLAND]

Captain John Smith, in his *History* published *anno* 1624, affirms that he found New England well inhabited with a goodly, strong and well-proportioned people. And the proverb is, "Show me the man and not the meat." And if men can be contented with the food and raiment intended in 1 Tim. 6. 8, they need not fear subsisting where ash, chestnut, hazel, oak and walnut do naturally and plentifully grow. But for this, let Mr. Morden be consulted, to whom New England is beholden for the fair character given them in his *Geography*. It is remarkable that Mr. Parker, who was a successful schoolmaster at Newbury in

Barkshire in the happy days of Dr. Twisse, was much about this time
preaching and proving at Ipswich in Essex that the passengers came
over upon good grounds, and that God would multiply them as He
did the children of Israel. His text was Exod. 1. 7. As Mr. Nicholas
Noyes, who was an auditor and is yet living, lately informed me, Mr.
Parker was at this time (1634) principally concerned in beginning
Newbury, where the learned and ingenious Mr. Benjamin Wood-
bridge, Dr. Twisse's successor, had part of his education under his
uncle Parker. Mary Brown (now Godfry) the first-born of Newbury is
yet alive, and is become the mother and grandmother of many children. And so many have been born after her in the town that they
make two assemblies, wherein God is solemnly worshiped every Sabbath day.

   And as long as Plum Island shall faithfully keep the commanded
post, notwithstanding all the hectoring words and hard blows of the
proud and boisterous ocean; as long as any salmon or sturgeon shall
swim in the streams of Merrimac, or any perch or pickerel in Crane
Pond; as long as the sea-fowl shall know the time of their coming, and
not neglect seasonably to visit the places of their acquaintance; as long
as any cattle shall be fed with the grass growing in the meadows which
do humbly bow down themselves before Turkey Hill; as long as any
sheep shall walk upon Old Town Hill, and shall from thence pleasantly
look down upon the river Parker and the fruitful marshes lying beneath; as long as any free and harmless doves shall find a white oak
or other tree within the township to perch or feed or build a careless
nest upon, and shall voluntarily present themselves to perform the
office of gleaners after barley harvest; as long as nature shall not grow
old and dote, but shall constantly remember to give the rows of Indian
corn their education by pairs: so long shall Christians be born there,
and being first made meet, shall from thence be translated, to be made
partakers of the Inheritance of the saints in light.

from *The Selling of Joseph*[1] (1700)

[*Fourth-day, June 19, 1700.* . . . Having been long and much dissat-
isfied with the trade of fetching Negroes from Guinea; at last I had a
strong inclination to write something about it; but it wore off. At last
reading Bayne, *Ephes*[2] about servants, who mentions blackamoors,[3] I
began to be uneasy that I had so long neglected doing any thing. When
I was thus thinking, in came Brother Belknap to shew me a petition
he intended to present to the General Court for the freeing a Negro

and his wife, who were unjustly held in bondage. And there is a motion by a Boston Committee to get a law that all importers of Negroes shall pay 40s *per* head, to discourage the bringing of them. And Mr. C. Mather resolves to publish a sheet to exhort masters to labour their conversion. Which makes me hope that I was call'd of God to write this apology for them; Let His blessing accompany the same.]

[AGAINST SLAVERY]

Foreasmuch as liberty is in real value next unto life: none ought to part with it themselves, or deprive others of it, but upon most mature considerations.

The numerousness of slaves at this day in the province, and the uneasiness of them under their slavery, hath put many upon thinking whether the foundation of it be firmly and well laid, so as to sustain the vast weight that is built upon it. It is most certain that all men, as they are the sons of Adam, are coheirs, and have equal right unto liberty, and all other outward comforts of life.

"God hath given the earth [with all its commodities] unto the sons of Adam," Psalm 115:16; "And hath made of one blood all nations of men for to dwell on all the face of the earth, and hath determined the times before appointed, and the bounds of their habitation, that they should seek the Lord. Forasmuch then as we are the offspring of God," etc., Acts 17: 26, 27, 29.

Now although the title given by the last Adam doth infinitely better men's estates respecting God and themselves, and grants them a most beneficial and inviolable lease under the broad seal of heaven, who were before only tenants at will: yet through the indulgence of God to our first parents after the Fall, the outward estate of all and every of their children remains the same, as to one another.

So that originally, and naturally, there is no such thing as slavery. Joseph was rightfully no more a slave to his brethren, than they were to him; and they had no more authority to sell him than they had to slay him. And if they had nothing to do to sell him, the Ishmaelites bargaining with them, and paying down twenty pieces of silver, could not make a title. Neither could Potiphar have any better interest in him than the Ishmaelites had. Gen. 37:20, 27, 28. For he that shall in this case plead alteration of property, seems to have forefeited a great part of his own claim to humanity. There is no proportion between twenty pieces of silver and liberty. The commodity itself is the claimer. If Arabian gold be imported in any quantities, most are afraid to meddle with it, though they might have it at easy rates, lest if it should

have been wrongfully taken from the owners, it should kindle a fire
to the consumption of their whole estate. 'Tis pity there should be
more caution used in buying a horse, or a little lifeless dust, than there
is in purchasing men and women: whenas they are the offspring of
God, and their liberty is,

> . . . *auro pretiosior omni.*[4]

And seeing God hath said, "He that stealeth a man and selleth
him, or if he be found in his hand, he shall surely be put to death."
Exod. 21:16. This law being of everlasting equity, wherein man-steal-
ing is ranked among the most atrocious of capital crimes, what louder
cry can there be made of that celebrated warning,

> CAVEAT EMPTOR![5]

And all things considered, it would conduce more to the welfare
of the province, to have white servants for a term of years, than to
have slaves for life. Few can endure to hear of a negro's being made
free; and indeed they can seldom use their freedom well; yet their
continual aspiring after their forbidden liberty renders them unwilling
servants. And there is such a disparity in their conditions, color and
hair, that they can never embody with us and grow up into orderly
families, to the peopling of the land: but still remain in our body politic
as a kind of extravasate[6] blood. As many negro men as there are
among us, so many empty places there are in our train bands, and the
places taken up of men that might make husbands for our daughters.
And the sons and daughters of New England would become more like
Jacob and Rachel, if this slavery were thrust quite out of doors. Moreover, it is too well known what temptations masters are under, to
connive at the fornication of their slaves; lest they should be obliged
to find them wives or pay their fines. It seems to be practically pleaded
that they might be lawless; 'tis thought much of, that the law should
have satisfaction for their thefts and other immoralities; by which
means, holiness to the Lord is more rarely engraven upon this sort of
servitude. It is likewise most lamentable to think how, in taking negroes out of Africa and selling of them here, that which God has joined
together men do boldly rend asunder; men from their country, husbands from their wives, parents from their children. How horrible is
the uncleanness, immorality, if not murder, that the ships are guilty of
that bring great crowds of these miserable men and women. Methinks,
when we are bemoaning the barbarous usage of our friends and kins-
folk in Africa,[7] it might not be unseasonable to inquire whether we

are not culpable in forcing the Africans to become slaves among ourselves. And it may be a question whether all the benefit received by negro slaves will balance the account of cash laid out upon them; and for the redemption of our own enslaved friends out of Africa. Besides all the persons and estates that have perished there.

Cotton Mather
(1633–1728)

Cotton Mather was the last of a family of famous New England divines that included his father, Increase Mather, and his grandfather, Richard Mather. A man of inexhaustible energy and prodigious learning, Cotton Mather produced over 450 works in the course of an active life fraught with controversy. Too often remembered in connection with his support of the Salem witchcraft trials—though he recommended that those possessed of demons be treated with prayer and fasting rather than hanging—he is better understood as perhaps the last embattled defender of the old Puritan ideal in a time of rapid social, political, and religious change.

Mather's crowning intellectual achievement was an ecclesiastical history of New England, which chronicles what it describes as the mighty acts of God in the New World from the time of the Plymouth landing to the end of the seventeenth century. As the first of the "celebrationist" histories of America, Magnalia Christi Americana occupies an important place not only in Puritan spirituality but also in American historiography. The two selections reprinted below come from the justly famous "Introduction" and the book devoted to the life of William Bradford, first governor of Plymouth colony.

from *Magnalia Christi Americana; or, The Ecclesiastical History of New-England (1702)*

A GENERAL INTRODUCTION

Dicam hoc propter utilitatem eorum qui Lecturi sunt hoc opus. Theodoret[1]

1. I WRITE the *Wonders* of the CHRISTIAN RELIGION, flying from the Depravations of *Europe*, to the *American Strand*.[2] And, assisted by the Holy Author of that *Religion*, I do, with all Conscience of *Truth*, required therein by Him, who is the *Truth* itself, Report the *Wonderful Displays* of His Infinite Power, Wisdom, Goodness, and Faithfulness, wherewith His Divine Providence hath *Irradiated* an *Indian Wilderness*.

I Relate the *Considerable Matters*, that produced and attended the First Settlement of COLONIES, which have been Renowned for the Degree of REFORMATION, Professed and Attained by *Evangelical Churches*, erected in those *Ends of the Earth*: And a *field* being thus prepared, I proceed unto a Relation of the *Considerable Matters* which have been acted thereupon.

I first introduce the *Actors*, that have, in a more exemplary manner served those *Colonies*; and give *Remarkable Occurrences*, in the exemplary LIVES of many *Magistrates*, and more *Ministers*, who so *Lived*, as to leave unto Posterity, *Examples* worthy of *Everlasting Remembrance*.

I add hereunto, the *Notables* of the only *Protestant University*,[3] that ever *shone* in that Hemisphere of the *New World*; with particular Instances of *Criolians*,[4] in our *Biography*, provoking the *whole World*, with vertuous Objects of Emulation.

I introduce then, the *Actions* of a more Eminent Importance, that have signalized those *Colonies*; Whether the *Establishments*, directed by their *Synods*; with a Rich Variety of *Synodical* and *Ecclesiastical* Determinations; or, the *Disturbances*, with which they have been from all sorts of *Temptations* and *Enemies* Tempestuated; and the *Methods* by which they have still weathered out each *Horrible Tempest*.

And into the midst of these *Actions*, I interpose an entire *Book*, wherein there is, with all possible Veracity, a *Collection* made, of *Memorable Occurrences*, and amazing *Judgments* and *Mercies*, befalling many *particular Persons* among the People of *New-England*.

Let my Readers expect all that I have promised them, in this *Bill*

of Fare; and it may be they will find themselves entertained with yet
many other Passages, above and beyond their Expectation, deserving
likewise a room in *History*: In all which, there will be nothing, but the
Author's too mean way of preparing so great Entertainments, to Reproach the Invitation . . .

3. It is the History of these PROTESTANTS, that is here attempted: PROTESTANTS that highly honoured and affected *The
Church of* ENGLAND, and humbly Petition to be a *Part* of it: But by
the Mistake of a few powerful *Brethren*, driven to seek a place for the
Exercise of the *Protestant Religion*, according to the Light of their
Consciences, in the Desarts of *America*. And in this Attempt I have
proposed, not only to preserve and secure the Interest of *Religion*, in
the Churches of that little Country *NEW-ENGLAND*, so far as the
Lord Jesus Christ may please to Bless it for that End, but also to offer
unto the Churches of the *Reformation*, abroad in the World, some
small *Memorials*, that may be serviceable unto the Designs of *Reformation*, whereto, I believe, they are quickly to be awakened . . . Tho'
the *Reformed Churches* in the *American Regions*, have, by very Injurious Representations of their Brethren (all which they desire to Forget
and Forgive!) been many times thrown into a *Dung-Cart*; yet, as they
have been a *precious Odour to God in Christ*, so, I hope, they will be
a *precious Odour* unto *His People*; and not only *Precious*, but *Useful*
also, when the *History* of them shall come to be considered. A *Reformation of the Church* is coming on, and I cannot but thereupon say,
with the dying *Cyrus* to his Children in *Xenophon*[5] . . . *Learn from
the things that have been done already, for this is the best way of
Learning.* The Reader hath here an Account of *The Things that have
been done already.* . . . Thus I do not say, That the Churches of *New-
England* are the most *Regular* that can be; yet I do say, and am sure,
That they are very like unto those that were in the *First Ages* of Christianity. And if I assert, That in the *Reformation* of the Church, the
State of it in those *First Ages*, is to be not a little considered, the Great
Peter Ramus,[6] among others, has emboldened me. . . . In short, *The
First Age* was the *Golden Age*: To return unto *That*, will make a Man
a *Protestant*, and I may add, a *Puritan*. 'Tis possible, That our Lord
Jesus Christ carried some Thousands of *Reformers* into the Retirements of an *American Desart*, on purpose, that, with an opportunity
granted unto many of his Faithful Servants, to enjoy the precious *Liberty* of their *Ministry*, tho' in the midst of many *Temptations* all their
days, He might there, *To* them first, and then *By* them, give a *Specimen*
of many Good Things, which He would have His Churches elsewhere
aspire and arise unto: And *This* being done, He knows whether there
be not *All done*, that *New-England* was planted for; and whether the
Plantation may not, soon after this, *Come to Nothing*. Upon that Ex-

pression in the Sacred Scripture, *Cast the unprofitable Servant into Outer Darkness*,[7] it hath been imagined by some, That the *Regiones Exteræ* of *America*, are the *Tenebræ Exteriores*, which the *Unprofitable* are there condemned unto. No doubt, the Authors of those Ecclesiastical Impositions and Severities, which drove the English Christians into the *Dark Regions* of *America*, esteemed those *Christians* to be a very *unprofitable* sort of Creatures. But behold, ye *European* Churches, There are *Golden Candlesticks* [more than *twice Seven times Seven*!] in the midst of this *Outer Darkness*: Unto the *upright* Children of *Abraham*, here hath arisen *Light in Darkness*. And let us humbly speak it, it shall be *Profitable* for you to consider the *Light*, which from the midst of this *Outer Darkness*, is now to be Darted over unto the other side of the *Atlantick Ocean*. But we must therewithal ask your Prayers, that these *Golden Candlesticks* may not *quickly* be *Removed out of their place!*

4. But whether *New England* may *Live* any where else or no, it must *Live* in our *History!* . . .

GALEACIUS SECUNDUS:[8]
THE LIFE OF WILLIAM BRADFORD, ESQ.,
GOVERNOR OF PLYMOUTH COLONY

> Omnium Somnos illius vigilantia defendit; omnium otium, illius Labor; omnium Delitias, illius Industria; omnium vacationem, illius occupatio.[9]

1. It has been a matter of some observation, that although Yorkshire be one of the largest shires in England; yet, for all the *fires* of martyrdom which were kindled in the days of Queen Mary, it afforded no more *fuel* than one poor *Leaf*; namely, John Leaf, an apprentice, who suffered for the doctrine of the Reformation at the same time and stake with the famous John Bradford.[10] But when the reign of Queen Elizabeth would not admit the Reformation of worship to proceed unto those degrees, which were proposed and pursued by no small number of the faithful in those days, Yorkshire was not the least of the shires in England that afforded suffering *witnesses* thereunto. The Churches there gathered were quickly molested with such a raging persecution, that if the spirit of separation in them did carry them unto a further *extream* than it should have done, one blameable cause thereof will be found in the *extremity* of that persecution. Their troubles made that *cold* country too *hot* for them, so that they were under a necessity to *seek* a retreat in the Low Countries; and yet the watchful malice

and fury of their adversaries rendred it almost impossible for them to *find* what they sought. For them to leave their native soil, their lands and their friends, and go into a strange place, where they must hear foreign language, and live meanly and hardly, and in other imployments than that of husbandry, wherein they had been educated, *these* must needs have been such discouragements as could have been conquered by none, save those who "sought first the kingdom of God, and the righteousness thereof." But that which would have made these discouragements the more unconquerable unto an ordinary faith, was the terrible zeal of their enemies to guard all ports, and search all ships, that none of them should be carried off. I will not relate the sad things of this kind then *seen* and *felt* by this people of God; but only exemplifie those trials with one short story. Divers of this people having hired a Dutchman, then lying at Hull, to carry them over to Holland, he promised faithfully to take them in between Grimsly and Hill; but they coming to the place a day or two too soon, the appearance of such a multitude alarmed the officers of the town adjoining, who came with a great body of soldiers to seize upon them. Now it happened that one boat full of men had been carried aboard, while the women were yet in a bark that lay aground in a creek at low water. The Dutchman perceiving the storm that was thus beginning ashore, swore by the sacrament that he would stay no longer for any of them; and so taking the advantage of a fair wind then blowing, he put out to sea for Zealand. The women thus left near Grimsly-common, bereaved of their husbands, who had been hurried from them, and forsaken of their neighbours, of whom none durst in this fright stay with them, were a very rueful spectacle; some crying for *fear*, some shaking for *cold*, all dragged by troops of armed and angry men from one Justice to another, till not knowing what to do with them, they even dismissed them to shift as well as they could for themselves. But by their singular *afflictions*, and by their Christian *behaviours*, the *cause* for which they exposed themselves did gain considerably. In the mean time, the men at sea found reason to be glad that their families were not with them, for they were surprized with an horrible tempest, which held them for fourteen days together, in seven whereof they saw not sun, moon or star, but were driven upon the coast of Norway. The mariners often despaired of life, and once with doleful shrieks gave over all, as thinking the vessel was foundred: but the vessel rose again, and when the mariners with sunk hearts often cried out, "We sink! we sink!" the passengers, without such distraction of mind, even while the water was running into their mouths and ears, would cheerfully shout, "Yet, Lord, thou canst save! Yet, Lord, thou canst save!" And the Lord accordingly brought them at last safe unto their desired haven: and not long after helped their distressed relations thither after them, where indeed they found upon almost all accounts a *new world*, but a world in which they found that they must live like strangers and pilgrims.

2. Among those devout people was our William Bradford, who was born *Anno 1588*, in an obscure village called Ansterfield, where the people were as unacquainted with the Bible, as the Jews do seem to have been with *part* of it in the days of Josiah; a most ignorant and licentious *people*, and *like unto their priest*. Here, and in some other places, he had a comfortable inheritance left him of his honest parents, who died while he was yet a child, and cast him on the education, first of his grand parents, and then of his uncles, who devoted him, like his ancestors, unto the affairs of husbandry. Soon a long sickness kept him, as he would afterwards thankfully say, from the *vanities of youth*, and made him the fitter for what he was afterwards to undergo. When he was about a dozen years old, the reading of the Scriptures began to cause great impressions upon him; and those impressions were much assisted and improved, when he came to enjoy Mr. Richard Clifton's illuminating ministry, not far from his abode; he was then also further befriended, by being brought into the company and fellowship of such as were then called professors; though the young man that brought him into it did after become a prophane and wicked *apostate*. Nor could the wrath of his uncles, nor the scoff of his neighbours, now turned upon him, as one of the *Puritans*, divert him from his pious inclinations.

3. At last, beholding how fearfully the evangelical and apostolical *church-form* whereinto the churches of the primitive times were cast by the good spirit of God, had been *deformed* by the apostacy of the succeeding times; and what little progress the Reformation had yet made in many parts of Christendom towards its recovery, he set himself by reading, by discourse, by prayer, to learn whether it was not his duty to withdraw from the communion of the parish-assemblies, and engage with some society of the faithful, that should keep close unto the *written word* of God, as the *rule* of their worship. And after many distresses of mind concerning it, he took up a very deliberate and understanding resolution, of doing so; which resolution he chearfully prosecuted, although the provoked rage of his friends tried all the ways imaginable to reclaim him from it, unto all whom his answer was:

"Were I like to endanger my life, or consume my estate by any ungodly courses, your counsels to me were very seasonable; but you know that I have been diligent and provident in my calling, and not only desirous to augment what I have, but also to enjoy it in your company; to part from which will be as great a cross as can befal me. Nevertheless, to keep a good conscience, and walk in such a way as God has prescribed in his Word, is a thing which I must prefer before you all, and above life it self. Wherefore, since 'tis for a good cause that I am like to suffer the disasters which you lay before me, you have no cause to be either angry with me, or sorry for me; yea, I am not only willing to part with every thing that is dear to me in this world for this cause, but I am also thankful that God has given me an heart to do, and will accept me so to suffer for him."

Some lamented him, some derided him, *all* disswaded him: nevertheless, the more they did it, the more fixed he was in his purpose to seek the ordinances of the gospel, where they should be dispensed with most of the *commanded purity*; and the sudden deaths of the chief relations which thus lay at him, quickly after convinced him what a folly it had been to have quitted his profession, in expectation of any satisfaction from them. So to Holland he attempted a removal.

4. Having with a great company of Christians hired a ship to transport them for Holland, the master perfidiously betrayed them into the hands of those persecutors, who rifled and ransacked their goods, and clapped their persons into prison at Boston,[11] where they lay for a month together. But Mr. Bradford being a young man of about eighteen, was dismissed sooner than the rest, so that within a while he had opportunity with some others to get over to Zealand, through *perils*, both by *land* and *sea* not inconsiderable; where he was not long ashore ere a viper seized on his hand—that is, an officer—who carried him unto the magistrates, unto whom an envious passenger had accused him as having *fled* out of England. When the magistrates understood the true cause of his coming thither, they were well satisfied with him; and so he repaired joyfully unto his brethren at Amsterdam, where the difficulties to which he afterwards stooped in learning and serving of a Frenchman at the working of silks, were abundantly compensated by the delight wherewith he sat under the shadow of our Lord, in his purely dispensed ordinances. At the end of two years, he did, being of age to do it, convert his estate in England into money; but setting up for himself, he found some of his designs by the *providence* of God frowned upon, which he judged a *correction* bestowed by God upon him for certain decays of *internal piety*, whereinto he had fallen; the consumption of his *estate* he thought came to prevent a consumption in his *virtue*. But after he had resided in Holland about half a score years, he was one of those who bore a part in that hazardous and generous enterprise of removing into New-England, with part of the English church at Leyden, where, at their first landing, his dearest consort accidentally falling overboard, was drowned in the harbour; and the rest of his days were spent in the service, and the temptations, of that American wilderness.

5. Here was Mr. Bradford, in the year 1621, unanimously chosen the governour of the plantation: the difficulties whereof were such,

that if he had not been a person of more than ordinary piety, wisdom and courage, he must have sunk under them. He had, with a laudable industry, been laying up a treasure of experiences, and he had now occasion to use it: indeed, nothing but an *experienced* man could have been suitable to the necessities of the people. The potent nations of the Indians, into whose country they were come, would have cut them off, if the blessing of God upon *his* conduct had not quelled them; and if his prudence, justice and moderation had not over-ruled them, they had been ruined by their own distempers. One specimen of his demeanour is to this day particularly spoken of. A company of young fellows that were newly arrived, were very unwilling to comply with the governour's order for working abroad on the publick account; and therefore on Christmas-day, when he had called upon them, they excused themselves, with a pretence that it was against their conscience to *work* on such a day. The governour gave them no answer, only that he would spare them till they were better informed; but by and by he found them all at *play* in the street, sporting themselves with various diversions; whereupon commanding the instruments of their games to be taken from them, he effectually gave them to understand. *"That it was against his conscience that they should play whilst others were at work*: and that if they had any devotion to the day, they should show it at home in the exercises of religion, and not in the streets with pasttime and frolicks,"* and this gentle reproof put a final stop to all such disorders for the future.

6. For two years together after the beginning of the colony, whereof he was now governour, the poor people had a great experiment of "man's not living by bread alone;"[12] for when they were left all together without one morsel of bread for many months one after another, still the good providence of God relieved them, and supplied them, and this for the most part out of the *sea*. In this low condition of affairs, there was no little exercise for the prudence and patience of the governour, who chearfully bore his part in all: and, that industry might not flag, he quickly set himself to settle *propriety* among the new-planters; foreseeing that while the whole country laboured upon a common stock, the husbandry and business of the plantation could not flourish, as Plato and others long since dreamed that it would, if a *community* were established. Certainly, if the spirit which dwelt in the old puritans, had not inspired these new-planters, they had sunk under the burden of these difficulties; but our Bradford had a double portion of that spirit.

7. The plantation was quickly thrown into a storm that almost overwhelmed it, by the unhappy actions of a minister sent over from England by the adventurers concerned for the plantation; but by the blessing of Heaven on the conduct of the governour, they weathered

out that storm. Only the adventurers hereupon breaking to pieces, threw up all their concealments with the infant-colony; whereof they gave this as one reason, "That the planters dissembled with his Majesty and their friends in their petition, wherein they declared for a church-discipline, agreeing with the French and others of the reforming churches in Europe."[13] Whereas 'twas now urged, that they had admitted into their communion a person who at his admission utterly renounced the Churches of England, (which person, by the way, was *that* very man who had made the complaints against them,) and therefore, though they denied the *name* of Brownists,[14] yet they were the thing. In answer hereunto, the very words written by the governour were these:

"Whereas you tax us with dissembling about the *French discipline*, you do us wrong, for we both hold and practice the *discipline* of the French and other Reformed Churches (as they have published the same in the Harmony of Confessions) according to our means, in effect and substance. But whereas you would tie us up to the French *discipline* in every circumstance, you derogate from the *liberty* we have in Christ Jesus. The Apostle Paul would have none to *follow him* in any thing, but wherein he *follows* Christ; much less ought any Christian or church in the world to do it. The French may err, we may err, and other churches may err, and doubtless do in many *circumstances*. That honour therefore belongs only to the *infallible Word of God*, and *pure Testament of Christ*, to be propounded and followed as the only rule and pattern for direction herein to all churches and Christians. And it is too great arrogancy for any man or church to think that he or they have so sounded the Word of God unto the bottom, as precisely to set down the church's discipline without error in substance or circumstances, that no other without blame may digress or differ in any thing from the same. And it is not difficult to shew that the Reformed Churches differ in many *circumstances* among themselves."

By which words it appears how far he was free from that rigid spirit of separation, which broke to pieces the Separatists themselves in the Low Countries, unto the great scandal of the reforming churches. He was indeed a person of a well-tempered spirit, or else it had been scarce possible for him to have kept the affairs of Plymouth in so good a temper for thirty-seven years together; in every one of which he was chosen their governour, except the three years wherein Mr. Winslow, and the two years wherein Mr. Prince, at the choice of the people, took a turn with him.

8. The leader of a people in a wilderness had need be a Moses; and if a Moses had not led the people of Plymouth Colony, when this worthy person was their governour, the people had never with so much unanimity and importunity still called him to lead them. Among

many instances thereof, let this one piece of self-denial be told for a memorial of him, wheresoever this History shall be considered: The Patent of the Colony was taken in his name, running in these terms: "To William Bradford his heirs, associates, and assigns." But when the number of the freemen was much increased, and many new townships erected, the General Court there desired of Mr. Bradford, that he would make a surrender of the same into their hands, which he willingly and presently assented unto, and confirmed it according to their desire by his hand and seal, reserving no more for himself than was his proportion, with others, by agreement. But as he found the providence of Heaven many ways recompensing his many acts of self-denial, so he gave this testimony to the faithfulness of the divine promises: "That he had forsaken friends, houses and lands for the sake of the gospel, and the Lord gave them him again." Here he prospered in his estate; and besides a worthy son which he had by a former wife, he had also two sons and a daughter by another, whom he married in this land.

9. He was a person for study as well as action; and hence, notwithstanding the difficulties through which he passed in his youth, he attained unto a notable skill in languages: the Dutch tongue was become almost as vernacular to him as the English; the French tongue he could also manage; the Latin and the Greek he had mastered; but the Hebrew he most of all studied, "Because," he said, "he would see with his own eyes the ancient oracles of God in their native beauty." He was also well skilled in History, in Antiquity, and in Philosophy; and for Theology he became so versed in it, that he was an irrefragable disputant against the *errors*, especially those of Anabaptism,[15] which with trouble he saw rising in his colony; wherefore he wrote some significant things for the confutation of those errors. But the *crown* of all was his holy, prayerful, watchful, and fruitful walk with God, wherein he was very exemplary.

10. At length he fell into an indisposition of body, which rendred him unhealthy for a whole winter; and as the spring advanced, his health yet more declined; yet he felt himself not what he counted sick, till one day; in the night after which, the God of heaven so filled his mind with ineffable consolations, that he seemed little short of Paul, rapt up unto the unutterable entertainments of Paradise.[16] The next morning he told his friends, "That the good Spirit of God had given him a pledge of his happiness in another world, and the first-fruits of his eternal glory;" and on the day following he died, May 9, 1657, in the 69th year of his age—lamented by all the colonies of New-England, as a common blessing and father to them all.

O mihi si Similis Contingat Clausula Vitæ![17]

Plato's brief description of a governour, is all that I will now leave as his character, in an

EPITAPH[18]
MEN are but FLOCKS: BRADFORD beheld their need,
And long did them at once both rule and feed.

Sarah Kemble Knight
(1666–1727)

Sarah Kemble Knight, often known as "Madam Knight," was apparently employed in legal as well as business affairs that necessitated the journey that is recorded in her Journal. *Asked to settle an estate for a friend, she set out on a journey from Boston to New Haven, and eventually beyond to New York, that would keep her absent for some six months. A hazardous and arduous trip by any measure, it was particularly difficult and unusual for a woman. In addition to the physical obstacles—rugged topography, inclement weather, unfamiliar forests, unpredictable rivers, inhospitable neighbors, crude lodgings, bad food—there were the problems of a woman traveling alone. Madam Knight coped with these last by following the postal routes and hiring male companions when the way proved dangerous. But despite these trials, Madam Knight was not easily daunted. A sharp observer of local incongruities and banalities, she also brought to her journey an intrepid interest in the world around her and a delight in independent judgment.*

from The Journal of Madam Knight
(1704–1710)

MONDAY, OCTB'R THE SECOND, 1704.

About three o'clock afternoon, I begun my Journey from Boston to New-Haven; being about two Hundred Mile. My Kinsman, Capt.

Robert Luist, waited on me as farr as Dedham, where I was to meet
the Western post.

WEDNESDAY, OCTOBER 4TH.

About four in the morning, we set out for Kingston (for so was the
Town called) with a french Docter in our company. Hee and the Post
put on very furiously, so that I could not keep up with them, only as
now and then they'd stop till they see mee. This Rode was poorly
furnished with accommodations for Travellers, so that we were forced
to ride 22 miles by the post's account, but neerer thirty by mine, before
wee could bait so much as our Horses, which I exceedingly complained
of. But the post encourag'd mee, by saying wee should be well accommodated anon at mr. Devills, a few miles further. But I questioned
whether we ought to go to the Devil to be helpt out of affliction.
However, like the rest of Deluded souls that post to the Infernal denn,
Wee made all posible speed to this Devil's Habitation; where alliting,
in full assurance of good accommodation, wee were going in. But
meeting his two daughters, as I suposed twins, they so neerly resembled each other, both in features and habit, and look't as old as the
Divel himselfe, and quite as Ugly, We desired entertainm't, but could
hardly get a word out of 'um, till with our Importunity, telling them
our necesity, &c. they call'd the old Sophister, who was as sparing of
his words as his daughters had bin, and no, or none, was the reply's
hee made us to our demands. Hee differed only in this from the old
fellow in to'ther Country: hee let us depart. However, I thought it
proper to warn poor Travailers to endeavor to Avoid falling into circumstances like ours, which at our next Stage I sat down and did as
followeth:

> May all that dread the cruel feind of night
> Keep on, and not at this curs't Mansion light.
> 'Tis Hell; 'tis Hell! and Devills here do dwell:
> Here dwells the Devill—surely this's Hell.
> Nothing but Wants: a drop to coll yo'r Tongue
> Cant be procur'd these cruel Feinds among.
> Plenty of horrid Grins and looks sevear,
> Hunger and thirst, but pitty's bannish'd here—
> The Right hand keep, if Hell on Earth you fear!

Thus leaving this habitation of cruelty, we went forward; and arriving
at an Ordinary about two mile further, found tollerable accommo-

dation. But our Hostes, being a pretty full mouth'd old creature, entertain'd our fellow travailer, the french Docter with Inumirable complaints of her bodily infirmities; and whisperd to him so lou'd, that all the House had as full a hearing as hee: which was very divirting to the company, (of which there was a great many,) as one might see by their sneering. But poor weary I slipt out to enter my mind in my Jornal, and left my Great Landly with her Talkative Guests to themselves.

From hence we proceeded (about ten forenoon) through the Narragansett country, pretty Leisurely; and about one afternoon come to Paukataug River, which was about two hundred paces over, and now very high, and no way over to to'ther side but this. I darid not venture to Ride thro, my courage at best in such cases but small, And now at the Lowest Ebb, by reason of my weary, very weary, hungry and uneasy Circumstances. So takeing leave of my company, tho' with no little Reluctance, that I could not proceed with them on my Jorny, Stop at a little cottage Just by the River, to wait the Waters falling, which the old man that lived there said would be in a little time, and he would conduct me safe over. This little Hutt was one of the wretchedest I ever saw a habitation for human creatures. It was suported with shores enclosed with Clapbords, laid on Lengthways, and so much asunder, that the Light come throu' every where; the doore tyed on with a cord in the place of hinges; The floor the bear earth; no windows but such as the thin covering afforded, nor any furniture but a Bedd with a glass Bottle hanging at the head on't; an earthen cupp, a small pewter Bason, A Bord with sticks to stand on, instead of a table, and a block or two in the corner instead of chairs. The family were the old man, his wife and two Children; all and every part being the picture of poverty. Notwithstanding both the Hutt and its Inhabitance were very clean and tydee: to the crossing the Old Proverb, that bare walls make giddy hows-wifes.

I Blest myselfe that I was not one of this misserable crew; and the Impressions their wretchedness formed in me caused mee on the very Spott to say:

> Tho' Ill at ease, A stranger and alone,
> All my fatigu's shall not extort a grone.
> These Indigents have hunger with their ease:
> Their best is wors behalfe than my disease.
> Their Misirable hutt which Heat and Cold
> Alternately without Repulse do hold;
> Their Lodgings thyn and hard, their Indian fare,
> The mean Apparel which the wretches wear,
> And their ten thousand ills which can't be told,

> Makes nature er'e 'tis midle age'd look old.
> When I reflect, my late fatigues do seem
> Only a notion or forgotten Dreem.

I had scarce done thinking, when an Indian-like Animal come to the door, on a creature very much like himselfe, in mien and feature, as well as Ragged cloathing; and having 'litt, makes an Awkerd Scratch with his Indian shoo, and a Nodd, sitts on the block, fumbles out his black Junk, dipps it in the Ashes, and presents it piping hott to his muscheeto's, and fell to sucking like a calf, without speaking, for near a quarter of an hower. At length the old man said how do's Sarah do? who I understood was the wretches wife, and Daughter to the old man: he Replyed—as well as can be expected, &c. So I remembred the old say, and suposed I knew Sarah's case. Butt hee being, as I understood, going over the River, as ugly as hee was, I was glad to ask him to show me the way to Saxtons, at Stoningtown; which he promising, I ventur'd over with the old mans assistance; who having rewarded to content, with my Tattertailed guide, I Ridd on very slowly thro' Stoningtown, where the Rode was very Stony and uneven. I asked the fellow, as we went, divers questions of the place and way, &c. I being arrived at my country Saxtons, at Stoningtown, was very well accommodated both as to victuals and Lodging, the only Good of both I had found since my setting out. Here I heard there was an old man and his Daughter to come that way, bound to N. London; and being now destitute of a Guide, gladly waited for them, being in so good a harbour, and accordingly . . .

THIRSDAY, OCTOBER THE 5TH,

about 3 in the afternoon, I sat forward with neighbor Polly and Jemima, a Girl about 18 Years old, who hee said he had been to fetch out of the Narragansetts, and said they had Rode thirty miles that day, on a sory lean Jade, with only a Bagg under her for a pillion, which the poor Girl often complain'd was very uneasy.

Wee made Good speed along, which made poor Jemima make many a sow'r face, the mare being a very hard trotter; and after many a hearty and bitter Oh, she at length Low'd out: Lawful Heart father! this bare mare hurts mee Dingeely, I'me direfull sore I vow; with many words to that purpose: poor Child sais Gaffer—she us't to serve your mother so. I don't care how mother us't to do, quoth Jemima, in a pasionate tone. At which the old man Laught, and kik't his Jade o' the side, which made her Jolt ten times harder.

About seven that Evening, we come to New London Ferry: here, by reason of a very high wind, we mett with great difficulty in getting over—the Boat tos't exceedingly, and our Horses capper'd at a very surprizing Rate, and set us all in a fright; especially poor Jemima, who desired her father to say so jack to the Jade, to make her stand. But the careless parent, taking no notice of her repeated desires, She Rored out in a Passionate manner: Pray suth father, Are you deaf? Say so Jack to the Jade, I tell you. The Dutiful Parent obey's; saying so Jack, so Jack, as gravely as if hee'd bin to saying Catechise after Young Miss, who with her fright look't of all coullors in the RainBow.

Being safely arrived at the house of Mrs. Prentices in N. London, I treated neighbour Polly and daughter for their divirting company, and bid them farewell; and between nine and ten at night waited on the Rev^d Mr. Gurdon Saltonstall, minister of the town, who kindly Invited me to Stay that night at his house, where I was very handsomely and plentifully treated and Lodg'd; and made good the Great Character I had before heard concerning him: *viz*. that hee was the most affable, courteous, Genero's and best of men.

Ebenezer Cooke
(1670–c. 1732)

Though born in Maryland, where his family were landowners, Ebenezer Cooke followed the practice of two generations of his forebears by living much of the time in England. A prolific writer, he nonetheless also gained firsthand experience on the eastern shore as a sot-weed factor, or tobacco merchant.

The poem by which he has become famous was little known until the contemporary novelist John Barth borrowed its title for his 1960 comic novel of the same name. Written in a hudibrastic style of grotesque, imperfect doggerel—named after Samuel Butler's satire Hudibras (1663–1678)—full of burlesque, epigram, and mock epic, Cooke adopts the mask of the sot-weed factor to ridicule plantation life and customs in Maryland. But there is some reason to think that Cooke may also have as another of his targets the snobbish view held in England that America is a land of bumpkins and boors, since the colonists often come off better than their British counterparts.

from The Sot-Weed[1] Factor; or, a Voyage to Maryland, &c. (1708)

Condemn'd by Fate to way-ward Curse,
Of Friends unkind, and empty Purse;
Plagues worse than fill'd *Pandora*'s Box,
I took my leave of *Albion*'s Rocks:
With heavy Heart, concern'd that I

Was forc'd my Native Soil to fly,
And the *Old World* must bid good-buy.
But Heav'n ordain'd it should be so,
And to repine is vain we know:
Freighted with Fools, from *Plymouth* sound,
To *Mary-Land* our Ship was bound;
Where we arriv'd in dreadful Pain,
Shock'd by the Terrours of the Main;
For full three Months, our wavering Boat,
Did thro' the surley Ocean float,
And furious Storms and threat'ning Blasts,
Both tore our Sails and sprung our Masts:
Wearied, yet pleas'd, we did escape,
Such Ills, we anchor'd at the *Cape*,[2]
But weighing soon, we plough'd the *Bay*,
To Cove[3] it in *Piscato-way*,[4]
Intending there to open Store,
I put myself and Goods a-shore:
Where soon repair'd a numerous Crew,
In Shirts and Drawers of *Scotch-cloth* Blue.[5]
With neither Stockings, Hat, nor Shooe.
These *Sot-weed* Planters Crowd the Shoar,
In Hue as tawny as a Moor:
Figure so strange, no God design'd,
To be a part of Humane Kind:
But wanton Nature, void of Rest,
Moulded the brittle Clay in Jest,
At last a Fancy very odd
Took me, this was the Land of *Nod*;
Planted at first, when Vagrant *Cain*,
His Brother had unjustly slain:
Then conscious of the Crime he'd done,
From Vengeance dire, he hither run;
And in a Hut supinely dwelt,
The first in *Furs* and *Sot-weed* dealt.
And ever since his Time, the Place,
Has harbour'd a detested Race;
Who when they cou'd not live at Home,
For Refuge to these Worlds did roam;
In hopes by Flight they might prevent,
The Devil and his fell intent;
Obtain from Tripple Tree[6] reprieve,
And Heav'n and Hell alike deceive:
But e're their Manners I display,

I think it fit I open lay
My Entertainment by the way;
That Strangers well may be aware on,
What homely Diet they must fare on.
To touch that Shoar, where no good Sense is found,
But Conversation's lost, and Maners drown'd.
I crost unto the other side,
A River whose impetuous Tide,
The Savage Borders does divide;
In such a shining odd invention,
I scarce can give its due Dimention.
The *Indians* call this watry Waggon
Canoo, a Vessel none can brag on;[7]
Cut from a *Popular-Tree*, or *Pine*,
And fashion'd like a Trough for Swine:
In this most noble Fishing-Boat,
I boldly put myself a-float;
Standing Erect, with Legs stretch'd wide,
We paddled to the other side:
Where being Landed safe by hap,
As *Sol* fell into *Thetis* Lap.
A ravenous Gang bent on the stroul,
Of Wolves for Prey, began to howl;[8]
This put me in a pannick Fright,
Least I should be devoured quite:
But as I there a musing stood,
And quite benighted in a Wood,
A Female Voice pierc'd thro' my Ears,
Crying, *You Rogue drive home the Steers.*
I listen'd to th' attractive sound,
And straight a Herd of Cattel found
Drove by a Youth, and homewards bound:
Cheer'd with the sight, I straight thought fit,
To ask where I a Bed might get.
The surley Peasant bid me stay,
And ask'd from whom I'de run away.[9]
Surprized at such a saucy Word,
I instantly lugg'd out my Sword;
Swearing I was no Fugitive,
But from *Great-Britain* did arrive,
In hopes I better there might Thrive.
To which he mildly made reply,
I beg your Pardon, Sir, *that I*
Should talk to you Unmannerly;

> *But if you please to go with me,*
> *To yonder House, you'll welcome be.*

Encountering soon the smoaky Seat,
The Planter old did thus me greet:
"Whether you come from Gaol or Colledge,
"You're welcome to my certain Knowledge;
"And if you please all Night to stay,
"My Son shall put you in the way."
Which offer I most kindly took,
And for a Seat did round me look;
When presently amongst the rest,
He plac'd his unknown *English* Guest,
Who found them drinking for a whet,
A Cask of Syder on the Fret,[10]
Till Supper came upon the Table,
On which I fed whilst I was able.
So after hearty Entertainment,
Of Drink and Victuals without Payment;
For Planters Tables, you must know,
Are free for all that come and go.
While Pon[11] and Milk, with Mush[12] well stoar'd,
In wooden Dishes grac'd the Board;
With Homine and Syder-pap,[13]
(Which scarce a hungry Dog wou'd lap)
Well stuff'd with Fat, from Bacon fry'd,
Or with *Molossus* dulcify'd.

   Then out our Landlord pulls a Pouch
As greasy as the Leather Couch
On which he sat, and straight begun,
To load with Weed his *Indian* Gun;[14]
In length, scarce longer than ones Finger,
Or that for which the Ladies linger.
His Pipe smoak'd out with aweful Grace,
with aspect grave and solemn pace;
The reverend Sire walks to a Chest,
Of all his Furniture the best,
Closely confin'd within a Room,
Which seldom felt the weight of Broom;
From thence he lugs a Cag of Rum,
And nodding to me, thus begun:
I find, says he, you don't much care,
for this our *Indian* Country Fare;
But let me tell you, Friend of mine,
You may be glad of it in time,

Tho' now your Stomach is so fine;
And if within this Land you stay,
You'll find it true what I do say.
This said, the Rundlet up he threw,
And bending backwards strongly drew:
I pluck'd as stoutly for my part,
Altho' it made me sick at Heart,
and got so soon into my Head
I scarce cou'd find my way to Bed;
Where I was instantly convey'd
By one who pass'd for Chamber-Maid;
Tho' by her loose and sluttish Dress,
She rather seem'd a *Bedlam-Bess*:
Curious to know from whence she came,
I prest her to declare her Name.
She Blushing, seem'd to hide her Eyes,
And thus in Civil Terms replies;
In better Times, e'er to this Land,
I was unhappily Trapann'd;
Perchance as well I did appear,
As any Lord or Lady here,
Not then a Slave for twice two Year.[15]
My Cloaths were fashionably new,
Nor were my Shifts of Linnen Blue;
But things are changed now at the Hoe,
I daily work, and Bare-foot go,
In weeding Corn or feeding Swine,
I spend my melancholy Time.
Kidnap'd and Fool'd, I hither fled,
To shun a hated Nuptial Bed,[16]
And to my cost already find,
Worse Plagues than those I left behind.
Whate'er the Wanderer did profess,
Good-faith I cou'd not choose but guess
The Cause which brought her to this place,
Was supping e'er the Priest said Grace.
Quick as my Thoughts, the Slave was fled,
(Her Candle left to shew my Bed)
Which made of Feathers soft and good,
Close in the Chimney-corner stood;[17]
I threw me down expecting Rest,
To be in golden Slumbers blest:
But soon a noise disturb'd my quiet,
And plagu'd me with nocturnal Riot;

A Puss which in the ashes lay,
With grunting Pig began a Fray;
And prudent Dog, that Feuds might cease,
Most strongly bark'd to keep the Peace.
This Quarrel scarcely was decided,
By stick that ready lay provided;
But *Reynard* arch and cunning Loon,
Broke into my Appartment soon;
In hot pursuit of Ducks and Geese,
With fell intent the same to seize:
Their Cackling Plaints with strange surprize,
Chac'd Sleeps thick Vapours from my Eyes:
Raging I jump'd upon the Floar,
And like a Drunken Saylor Swore;
With Sword I fiercely laid about,
And soon dispers'd the Feather'd Rout:
The Poultry out of Window flew,
And *Reynard* cautiously withdrew:
The Dogs who this Encounter heard,
Fiercely themselves to aid me rear'd,
And to the Place of Combat run,
Exactly as the Field was won.
Fretting and hot as roasting Capon,
And greasy as a Flitch of Bacon;
I to the Orchard did repair,
To Breathe the cool and open Air;
Expecting there the rising Day,
Extended on a Bank I lay;
But Fortune here, that saucy Whore,
Disturb'd me worse and plagu'd me more,
Than she had done the night before.
Hoarse croaking Frogs did 'bout me ring,[18]
Such Peals the Dead to Life wou'd bring,
A Noise might move their Wooden King.[19]
I stuff'd my Ears with Cotten white
For fear of being deaf out-right,
And curst the melancholy Night:
But soon my Vows I did recant,
And Hearing as a Blessing grant;
When a confounded Rattle-Snake,
With hissing made my Heart to ake:
Not knowing how to fly the Foe,
Or whether in the Dark to go;
By strange good Luck, I took a Tree,

Prepar'd by Fate to set me free;
Where riding on a Limb astride,
Night and the Branches did me hide,
And I the Devil and Snake defy'd.
Not yet from Plagues exempted quite,
The curst Muskitoes did me bite;
Till rising Morn' and blushing Day,
Drove both my Fears and Ills away;
And from Night's Errors set me free.
Discharg'd from hospitable Tree;
I did to Planters Booth repair,
And there at Breakfast nobly Fare,
On rashier broil'd of infant Bear:
I thought the Cub delicious Meat,
Which ne'er did ought but Chestnuts eat;
Nor was young Orsin's flesh the worse,
Because he suck'd a Pagan Nurse.[20]
Our Breakfast done, my Landlord stout,
Handed a Glass of Rum about;
Pleas'd with the Treatment I did find,
I took my leave of Oast so kind;
Who to oblige me, did provide,
His eldest Son to be my Guide,
And lent me Horses of his own,
A skittish Colt, and aged Rhoan,
The four-leg'd prop of his Wife *Joan*.
Steering our Barks in Trot or Pace,
We sail'd directly for a place
In *Mary-Land* of high renown,
Known by the Name of *Battle-Town*.

· · ·

My Guide starts up, and in amaze,
With blood-shot Eyes did round him gaze;
At length with many a sigh and groan,
He went in search of aged Rhoan;
But Rhoan, tho' seldome us'd to faulter,
Had fairly this time slipt his Halter;
And not content all Night to stay
Ty'd up from Fodder, ran away:
After my Guide to ketch him ran,
And so I lost both Horse and Man;
Which Disappointment, tho' so great,

Did only Mirth and Jests create:
Till one more Civil than the rest,
In Conversation for the best,
Observing that for want of Rhoan,
I should be left to walk alone;
Most readily did me intreat,
To take a Bottle at his Seat;
A Favour at that time so great,
I blest my kind propitious Fate;
And finding soon a fresh supply,
Of Cloaths from Stoar-house kept hard by,
I mounted streight on such a Steed,
Did rather curb, than whipping need;
And straining at the usual rate,
With spur of Punch which lay in Pate,
E'er long we lighted at the Gate:
Where in an antient *Cedar* House,
Dwelt my new Friend, a Cokerouse;[21]
Whose Fabrick, tho' 'twas built of Wood,
Had many Springs and Winters stood;
When sturdy Oaks, and lofty Pines
Were level'd with Musmelion Vines,[22]
And Plants eradicated were,
By Hurricanes in the air;
There with good Punch and apple Juice,
We spent our Hours without abuse:
Till Midnight in her sable Vest,
Persuaded Gods and Men to rest;
And with a pleasing kind surprize,
Indulg'd soft Slumbers to my Eyes.
Fierce Ælthon courser of the Sun.[23]
Had half his Race exactly run;
And breath'd on me a fiery Ray,
Darting hot Beams the following Day,
When snug in Blanket white I lay:
But Heat and *Chinces*[24] rais'd the Sinner,
Most opportunely to his Dinner;
Wild Fowl and Fish delicious Meats,
As good as *Neptune's* Doxy eats,
Began our Hospitable Treat;
Fat Venson follow'd in the Rear,
And Turkies[25] wild Luxurious Chear:
But what the Feast did most commend,
Was hearty welcom from my Friend.

Thus having made a noble Feast,
And eat as well as pamper'd Priest,
Madera strong in flowing Bowls,
Fill'd with extream, delight our Souls;
Till wearied with a purple Flood,
Of generous Wine (the Giant's blood,
As Poets feign) away I made,
For some refreshing verdant Shade;
Where musing on my Rambles strange,
And Fortune which so oft did change;
In midst of various Contemplations
Of Fancies odd, and Meditations,
I slumber'd long————————
Till hazy Night with noxious Dews,
Did Sleep's unwholsom Fetters lose:
With Vapours chil'd, and misty air,
To fire-side I did repair:
Near which a jolly Female Crew,
Were deep engag'ed at *Lanctre-Looe*;²⁶
In Nightrails white, with dirty Mein,
Such Sights are scarce in *England* seen:
I thought them first some Witches bent,
On Black Designs in dire Convent.
Till one who with affected air,
Had nicely learn'd to Curse and Swear:
Cry'd Dealing's lost is but a flam,
And vow'd by G–d she'd keep her *Pam*.²⁷
When dealing through the board had run,
They ask'd me kindly to make one;
Not staying often to be bid,
I sat me down as others did:
We scarce had play'd a Round about,
But that these *Indian* Froes fell out.
D–m you, says one, tho' now so brave,
I knew you late a Four-Years Slave;
What if for Planters Wife you go,
Nature design'd you for the Hoe.
Rot you replies the other streight,
The Captain kiss'd you for his Freight;
And if the Truth was known aright,
And how you walk'd the Streets by night,
You'd blush (if one cou'd blush) for shame,
Who from *Bridewell* or *Newgate* came.
From Words they fairly fell to Blows,

And being loath to interpose,
Or meddle in the Wars of Punk,[28]
Away to Bed in hast I slunk.
Waking next day, with aking Head,
And Thirst, that made me quit my Bed;
I rigg'd myself, and soon got up.
To cool my Liver with a Cup
Of *Succahana* fresh and clear,[29]
Not half so good as *English* Beer;
Which ready stood in Kitchin Pail,
And was in fact but *Adam's* Ale;
For Planters Cellars you must know,
Seldom with good *October* flow,
But Perry Quince and Apple Juice,
Sprout from the Tap like any Sluce;
Untill the Cask's grown low and stale,
They're forc'd again to Goad and Pail:[30]
The soathing drought scarce down my Throat,
Enough to put a Ship a float,
With Cockerouse as I was sitting,
I felt a Feaver Intermitting;
A fiery Pulse beat in my Veins,
From Cold I felt resembling Pains:
This cursed seasoning I remember,
Lasted from *March* to cold *December*;
Nor would it then its *Quarters* shift
Until by *Cardus*[31] turn'd a drift,
And had my Doctress wanted skill,
Or Kitchin Physick at her will,
My Father's Son had lost his Lands,
And never seen the *Goodwin-Sands*:
But thanks for Fortune and a Nurse
Whose Care depended on my Purse,
I saw myself in good Condition,
Without the help of a Physitian:
At length the shivering ill relieved,
Which long my Head and Heart have grieved;
I then began to think with Care,
How I might sell my *British* Ware,
That with my Freight I might comply,
Did on my Charter party lie:
To this intent, with Guide before,
I tript it to the Eastern Shoar;
While riding near a Sandy Bay,

I met a *Quaker, Yea* and *Nay*;
A Pious Conscientious Rogue,
As e'er woar Bonnet or a Brogue,
Who neither Swore nor kept his Word,
But cheated in the Fear of God;
And when his Debts he would not pay,
By Light within he ran away.
With this sly Zealot soon I struck
A Bargain for my *English* Truck,
Agreeing for ten thousand weight,
Of *Sot-weed* good and fit for freight,
Broad *Oronooko* bright and sound,
The growth and product of his ground;
In Cask that should contain compleat,
Five hundred of Tobacco neat.
The Contract thus betwixt us made,
Not well acquainted with the Trade,
My Goods I trusted to the Cheat,
Whose crop was then aboard the Fleet;
And going to receive my own,
I found the Bird was newly flown:
Cursing this execrable Slave,
This damn'd pretended Godly Knave;
On due Revenge and Justice bent,
I instantly to Counsel went,
Unto an ambodexter *Quack*,[32]
Who learnedly had got the knack,
Of giving Glisters, making Pills,
Of filling Bonds, and forging Wills;
And with a stock of Impudence,
Supply'd his want of Wit and Sense;
With Looks demure, amazing People,
No wiser than a Daw in Steeple;
My Anger flushed in my Face,
I stated the preceeding Case:
And of my Money was so lavish,
That he'd have poyson'd half the Parish,
And hang'd his Father on a Tree,
For such another tempting Fee;
Smiling, said he, the Cause is clear,
I'll manage him you need not fear;
The Case is judg'd, good Sir, but look
In *Galen*, No—in my Lord *Cook*,
I vow to God I was mistook:

I'll take out a Provincial Writ,
And Trounce him for his Knavish Wit;
Upon my life we'll win the Case,
With all the ease I cure the *Yaws*:[33]
Resolv'd to plague the holy Brother,
I set one Rogue to catch another;
To try the Cause, then fully bent,
Up to *Annapolis*[34] I went,
A City Situate on a Plain,
Where scarce a House will keep out Rain;
The Buildings fram'd with Cyprus rare,
Resembles much our *Southwark* Fair:
But Stranger here will scarcely meet
With Market-place, Exchange, or Street;
And if the Truth I may report,
'Tis not so large as *Tottenham Court*.
St. Mary's once was in repute,
Now here the Judges try the Suit,
And lawyers twice a Year dispute.
As oft the Bench most gravely meet,
Some to get Drunk, and some to eat
A swinging share of Country Treat.
But as for Justice right or wrong,
Not one amongst the numerous throng,
Knows what they mean, or has the Heart,
To give his Verdict on a Stranger's part:
Now Court being call'd by beat of Drum,
The Judges left their Punch and Rum,
When Pettifogger Doctor draws,
His Paper forth, and opens Cause:
And least I shou'd the better get,
Brib'd *Quack* supprest his Knavish Wit.
So Maid upon the downy Field,
Pretends a Force, and Fights to yield:
The Byast Court without delay,
Adjudg'd my Debt in Country Pay;
In Pipe staves, Corn, or Flesh of Boar,[35]
Rare Cargo for the *English* Shoar:
Raging with Grief, full speed I ran,
To joyn the Fleet at *Kicketan*;[36]
Embarqu'd and waiting for a Wind,
I left this dreadful Curse behind.
May Canniballs transported o'er the Sea
Prey on these Slaves, as they have done on me;

May never Merchant's, trading Sails explore
This Cruel, this Inhospitable Shoar;
But left abandon'd by the World to starve,
May they sustain the Fate they well deserve:
May they turn Savage, or as *Indians* Wild,
From Trade, Converse, and Happiness exil'd;
Recreant to Heaven, may they adore the Sun,
And into Pagan Superstitions run
For Vengence ripe————————————————
May Wrath Divine then lay those Regions wast
Where no Man's[37] Faithful, nor a Woman Chast.

Robert Beverley
(c. 1673–1722)

Robert Beverly was a Virginia gentleman, born in America but edu-cated in England, who returned to take up various colonial offices that eventually led to his election to the House of Burgesses as Jamestown's representative. Disputes with local officials eventually forced him to retire to the plantation he inherited in Virginia known as Beverley Park, but this leisure also furnished him with the opportunity to write his History.

Tradition has it that Beverley undertook The History and Present State of Virginia *to correct misrepresentations that were soon to be published in a book Beverley had seen in manuscript by John Old-mixon titled* The British Empire in America *(1708). But the chief in-terest of Beverley's work is its decidedly Virginian perspective, which seems so different from the New England viewpoint. Here the empha-sis is on this world, its "Native Beauty, Riches, and Value"—as Bev-erley wrote about the "incomparable book" on "the history of the world" by one of his heroes, "the Learned and Valiant Sir Walter Raleigh"—not on any world beyond. Beverley's tone is ironic and cosmopolitan, his style bemused by the spectacle of people gullible enough to believe that the country could have been founded by indi-viduals whose motives were unselfish.*

from *The History and Present State*
of Virginia (1705)

CHAPTER I. SHOWING WHAT HAPPENED
IN THE FIRST ATTEMPTS TO SETTLE
VIRGINIA, BEFORE THE DISCOVERY OF
CHESAPEAKE BAY

1. The learned and valiant Sir *Walter Raleigh* having entertained some deeper and more serious considerations upon the state of the earth, than most other men of his time, as may sufficiently appear by his incomparable book, *The History of the World*: and having laid together the many stories then in *Europe* concerning *America*; the native beauty, riches, and value of this part of the world; and the immense profits the *Spaniards* drew from a small settlement or two thereon made; resolved upon an adventure for further discoveries.

According to this purpose, in the year of our Lord, 1583, he got several men of great value and estate to join with him in an expedition of this nature; and for their encouragement obtained Letters Patents from Queen *Elizabeth*, bearing date the 25th of *March*, 1584, for turning their discoveries to their own advantage.

2. In *April* following they set out two small vessels under the command of Capt. *Philip Amidas*, and Capt. *Arthur Barlow*; who, after a prosperous voyage, anchored at the inlet by *Roanoke*, at present under the government of North *Carolina*. They made good profit of the *Indian* truck, which they bought for things of much inferior value, and returned. Being over-pleased with their profits, and finding all things there entirely new, and surprising; they gave a very advantageous account of matters; by representing the country so delightful, and desirable; so pleasant, and plentiful; the climate, and air, so temperate, sweet, and wholesome; the woods, and soil, so charming and fruitful; and all other things so agreeable, that paradise itself seemed to be there, in its first native luster.

They gave particular accounts of the variety of good fruits, and some whereof they had never seen the like before; but above all, that there were grapes in such abundance, as was never known in the world: stately tall large oaks, and other timber; red cedar, cypress, pines, and other evergreens, and sweetwoods; for tallness and largeness exceeding all they had ever heard of; wild fowl, fish, deer, and other game in such plenty, and variety; that no epicure could desire more than this New World did seem naturally to afford.

And, to make it yet more desirable, they reported the native *In-*

dians (which were then the only inhabitants) so affable, kind, and
good-natured; so uncultivated in learning, trades, and fashions; so
innocent, and ignorant of all manner of politics, tricks, and cunning;
and so desirous of the company of the *English*: that they seemed rather
to be like soft wax, ready to take any impression, than any ways likely
to oppose the settling of the *English* near them: they represented it as
a scene laid open for the good and gracious Q. *Elizabeth*, to propagate
the Gospel in, and extend her dominions over: as if purposely reserved
for Her Majesty, by a peculiar direction of Providence, that had
brought all former adventures in this affair to nothing: and to give a
further taste of their discovery, they took with them, in their return
for *England*, two men of the native *Indians*, named *Wanchese* and
Manteo.

3. Her Majesty accordingly took the hint, and espoused the project, as far as her present engagements in war with *Spain* would let
her; being so well pleased with the account given, that as the greatest
mark of honor she could do the discovery, she called the country by
the name of *Virginia*; as well, for that it was first discovered in her
reign, a virgin queen; as that it did still seem to retain the virgin purity
and plenty of the first creation, and the people their primitive innocence: for they seemed not debauched nor corrupted with those pomps
and vanities, which had depraved and enslaved the rest of mankind;
neither were their hands hardened by labor, nor their minds corrupted
by the desire of hoarding up treasure: they were without boundaries
to their land; and without property in cattle; and seemed to have escaped, or rather not to have been concerned in the first curse, *of getting
their bread by the sweat of their brows*: for, by their pleasure alone,
they supplied all their necessities; namely, by fishing, fowling and hunting; skins being their only clothing; and these too, five-sixths of the
year thrown by: living without labor, and only gathering the fruits of
the earth when ripe, or fit for use: neither fearing present want, nor
solicitous for the future, but daily finding sufficient afresh for their
subsistence.

4. This report was backed, nay much advanced, by the vast riches
and treasure mentioned in several merchants' letters from *Mexico* and
Peru, to their correspondents in *Spain*; which letters were taken with
their ships and treasure, by some of ours in Her Majesty's service, in
prosecution of the *Spanish* wars: this was encouragement enough for
a new adventure, and set people's invention at work, till they had
satisfied themselves, and made sufficient essays for the further discovery of the country. Pursuant whereunto Sir *Richard Grenville*, the chief
of Sir *Walter Raleigh's* associates, having obtained seven sail of ships,
well laden with provision, arms, ammunition, and spare men to make
a settlement, set out in person with them early in the spring of the

succeeding year, to make further discoveries, taking back the two *Indians* with him; and according to his wish, in the latter end of *May*, arrived at the same place, where the *English* had been the year before: there he made a settlement, sowed beans and peas, which he saw come up and grow to admiration while he stayed, which was about two months; and having made some little discoveries more in the *sound* to the southward, and got some treasure in skins, furs, pearls, and other rarities of the country, for things of inconsiderable value, he returned for *England*, leaving one hundred and eight men upon *Roanoke* Island, under the command of Mr. *Ralph Lane*, to keep possession.

5. As soon as Sir *Richard Grenville* was gone, they, according to order and their own inclination, set themselves earnestly about discovering the country, and ranged about a little too indiscreetly up the rivers, and into the land backward from the rivers, which gave the *Indians* a jealousy of their meaning: for they cut off several stragglers of them, and had laid designs to destroy the rest, but were happily prevented. This put the *English* upon the precaution of keeping more within bounds, and not venturing themselves too defenseless abroad, who till then had depended too much upon the natives' simplicity and innocence.

After the *Indians* had done this mischief, they never observed any real faith towards those *English*: for being naturally suspicious and revengeful themselves, they never thought the *English* could forgive them; and so by this jealousy, caused by the cowardice of their nature, they were continually doing mischief.

The *English*, notwithstanding all this, continued their discoveries, but more carefully than they had done before, and kept the *Indians* in some awe, by threatening them with the return of their companions again with a greater supply of men and goods: and, before the cold of the winter became uneasy, they had extended their discoveries near an hundred miles along the sea coast to the northward; but not reaching the southern cape of *Chesapeake* Bay in *Virginia*, they had as yet found no good harbor.

6. In this condition they maintained their settlement all the winter, and till *August* following; but were much distressed for want of provisions, not having learned to gather food, as the *Indians* did, nor having conveniences like them of taking fish and fowl: besides, being now fallen out with the *Indians*, they feared to expose themselves to their contempt and cruelty; because they had not received the supply they talked of, and which had been expected in the spring.

All they could do under these distresses, and the despair of the recruits promised them this year, was only to keep a good looking out to seaward, if, perchance, they might find any means of escape, or recruit. And, to their great joy and satisfaction, in *August* aforesaid, they happened to espy, and make themselves be seen to Sir *Francis Drake's* fleet, consisting of twenty-three sail, who being sent by Her Majesty upon the coast of *America*, in search of the *Spanish* treasures, had orders from Her Majesty to take a view of this plantation, and see what assistance or encouragement it wanted: their first petition to him was to grant them a fresh supply of men and provisions, with a small vessel, and boats to attend them; that so if they should be put to distress for want of relief, they might embark for *England*. This was as readily granted by Sir *Francis Drake* as asked by them; and a ship was appointed them, which ship they began immediately to fit up, and supply plentifully with all manner of stores for a long stay; but while they were a doing this, a great storm arose, and drove that very ship (with some others) from her anchor to sea, and so she was lost for that occasion.

Sir *Francis* would have given them another ship, but this accident coming on the back of so many hardships which they had undergone, daunted them, and put them upon imagining that Providence was averse to their designs: and now having given over, for that year, the expectation of their promised supply from *England*, they consulted together, and agreed to desire Sir *Francis Drake* to take them along with him, which he did.

Thus their first intention of settlement fell, after discovering many things of the natural growth of the country, useful for the life of man, and beneficial to trade, they having observed a vast variety of fish, fowl and beasts; fruits, seeds, plants, roots, timber-trees, sweet-woods and gums: they had likewise attained some little knowledge in the language of the *Indians*, their religion, manners, and ways of correspondence one with another; and been made sensible of their cunning and treachery towards themselves.

7. While these things were thus acting in *America*, the adventurers in *England* were providing, tho' too tediously, to send them recruits. And tho' it was late before they could dispatch them (for they met with several disappointments, and had many squabbles among themselves). However, at last they provided four good ships, with all manner of recruits suitable for the colony, and Sir *Walter Raleigh* designed to go in person with them.

Sir *Walter* got his ship ready first, and fearing the ill consequence of a delay, and the discouragement it might be to those that were left to make a settlement, he set sail by himself. And a fortnight after him Sir *Richard Grenville* sailed with the three other ships.

Sir *Walter* fell in with the land at Cape *Hatteras*, a little to the southward of the place, where the 108 men had been settled, and after search not finding them, he returned: however, Sir *Richard*, with his ships, found the place where he had left the men, but entirely deserted,

which was at first a great disheartening to him, thinking them all destroyed, because he knew not that Sir *Francis Drake* had been there,
and taken them off; but he was a little better satisfied by *Manteo's*
report, that they were not cut off by the *Indians*, tho' he could give
no good account what was become of them. However, notwithstanding this seeming discouragement, he again left fifty men in the same
island of *Roanoke*, built them houses necessary, gave them two years'
provision, and returned.

8. The next summer, being *Anno* 1587. Three ships more were
sent, under the command of Mr. *John White*, who himself was to settle
there as governor with more men, and some women, carrying also
plentiful recruits of provisions.

In the latter end of *July* they arrived at *Roanoke* aforesaid, where
they again encountered the uncomfortable news of the loss of these
men also; who (as they were informed by *Manteo*) were secretly set
upon by the *Indians*, some cut off, and the others fled, and not to be
heard of, and their place of habitation now all grown up with weeds.
However, they repaired the houses on *Roanoke*, and sat down there
again.

The 13th of *August* they christened *Manteo*, and styled him Lord
of *Dassamonpeak*, an *Indian* nation so called, in reward of the fidelity
he had shown to the *English* from the beginning; who being the first
Indian that was made a Christian in that part of the world, I thought
it not amiss to remember him.

On the same occasion also may be mentioned the first child there
born of Christian parentage, *viz.* a daughter of Mr. *Ananias Dare*. She
was born the 18th of the same *August* upon *Roanoke*, and, after the
name of the country, was christened *Virginia*.

This seemed to be a settlement prosperously made, being carried
on with much zeal and unanimity among themselves. The form of
government consisted of a governor and twelve counselors, incorporated by the name of the governor and assistants of the city of *Raleigh*
in *Virginia*.

Many nations of the *Indians* renewed their peace, and made firm
leagues with the corporation: the chief men of the *English* also were
so far from being disheartened at the former disappointments, that
they disputed for the liberty of remaining on the spot; and by mere
constraint compelled Mr. *White*, their governor, to return for *England*,
to negotiate the business of their recruits and supply, as a man the
most capable to manage that affair, leaving at his departure one hundred and fifteen in the corporation.

9. It was above two years before Mr. *White* could obtain any
grant of supplies; and then, in the latter end of the year 1589 he set
out from *Plymouth* with three ships, and sailed round by the *Western*

and *Carribbee* Islands, they having hitherto not found any nearer way: for tho' they were skilled in navigation, and understood the use of the globes, yet did example so much prevail upon them, that they chose to sail a thousand leagues about, rather than attempt a more direct passage.

Towards the middle of *August*, 1590 they arrived upon the coast, at Cape *Hatteras*, and went to search upon *Roanoke* for the people; but found, by letters on the trees, that they were removed to *Croatan*, one of the islands forming the *sound*, and southward of *Roanoke* about twenty leagues, but no sign of distress. Thither they designed to sail to them in their ships; but a storm arising in the meanwhile, lay so hard upon them, that their cables broke; they lost three of their anchors, were forced to sea; and so returned home, without ever going near those poor people again for sixteen years following: and it is supposed, that the *Indians* seeing them forsaken by their country, and unfurnished of their expected supplies, cut them off: for to this day they were never more heard of.

Thus, after all this vast expense and trouble, and the hazard and loss of so many lives, Sir *Walter Raleigh*, the great projector and furtherer of these discoveries and settlements, being under trouble, all thoughts of further prosecuting these designs, lay dead for about twelve years following. . . .

CHAPTER II.

CONTAINING AN ACCOUNT OF THE FIRST
SETTLEMENT OF CHESAPEAKE BAY, IN
VIRGINIA, BY THE CORPORATION OF
LONDON ADVENTURERS, AND THEIR
PROCEEDINGS DURING THEIR
GOVERNMENT BY A PRESIDENT AND
COUNCIL ELECTIVE

13. The merchants of *London*, *Bristol*, *Exeter* and *Plymouth*, soon perceived what great gains might be made of a trade this way, if it were well managed, and colonies could be rightly settled; which was sufficiently evinced by the great profits some ships had made, which had not met with ill accidents. Encouraged by this prospect, they joined together in a petition to King *James* the First; showing forth, that it would be too much for any single person to attempt the settling of colonies, and to carry on so considerable a trade: they therefore prayed His Majesty to incorporate them, and enable them to raise a

joint stock for that purpose, and to countenance their undertaking.

His Majesty did accordingly grant their petition, and by letters patents bearing date the 10th of *April*, 1606, did in one patent incorporate them into two distinct companies to make two separate colonies, *viz.* "Sir *Tho. Gates*, Sir *George Summers*, Knights; Mr. *Richard Hackluit*, Clerk Prebend of *Westminster*, and *Edward-Maria Wingfield*, Esq; adventurers of the City of *London*, and such others as should be joined unto them of that colony, which should be called, *the First Colony*; with liberty to begin their first plantation and seat, at any place upon the coast of *Virginia*, where they should think fit and conve[ni]ent between the degrees of 34 and 41 of northern latitude: and that they should extend their bounds from the said first seat of their plantation and habitation, fifty *English* miles along the sea coast each way; and include all the lands within an hundred miles directly over-against the same seacoast, and also back into the mainland one hundred miles from the seacoast: and that no other should be permitted or suffered to plant or inhabit behind, or on the back of them towards the mainland, without the express license of the council of that colony thereunto in writing first had and obtained. And for the second colony, to *Tho. Hanham, Rawleigh Gilbert, William Parker*, and *George Popham*, Esqs; of the town of *Plymouth*, and all others who should be joined to them of that colony; with liberty to begin their first plantation and seat at any place upon the coast of *Virginia*, where they should think fit, between the degrees of 38 and 45 of northern latitude, with the like liberties and bounds as the first colony: provided they did not seat within an hundred miles of them."

14. By virtue of this patent, Capt. *John Smith* was sent by the *London* Company in *December*, 1606, on his voyage with three small ships; and a commission was given to him, and to several other gentlemen, to establish a colony, and to govern by a president, to be chosen annually, and council, who should be invested with sufficient authorities and powers. And now all things seemed to promise a plantation in good earnest. Providence seemed likewise very favorable to them: for tho' they designed only for that part of *Virginia* where the hundred and fifteen were left, and where there is no security of harbor: yet, after a tedious voyage of passing the old way again, between the *Carribbee* Islands and the main, he, with two of his vessels, luckily fell in with *Virginia* itself, that part of the continent now so called, anchoring in the mouth of the Bay of *Chesapeake*: and the first place they landed upon, was the southern cape of that bay, which they named Cape *Henry*, and the northern Cape *Charles*, in honor of the King's two eldest sons; and the first great river they searched whose *Indian* name was *Powhatan*, they called *James* River, after the King's own name.

15. Before they would make any settlement here, they made a full search of *James* River; and then by an unanimous consent pitched upon a *peninsula* about fifty miles up the river; which, besides the goodness of the soil, was esteemed as most fit, and capable to be made a place both of trade and security, two-thirds thereof being environed by the main river, which affords good anchorage all along, and the other third by a small narrow river, capable of receiving many vessels of an hundred tons, quite up as high as till it meets within thirty yards of the main river again, and where generally in springtides it overflows into the main river: by which means the land they chose to pitch their town upon, has obtained the name of an island. In this back river ships and small vessels may ride lashed to one another, and moored ashore secure from all wind and weather whatsoever.

The town, as well as the river, had the honor to be called by King *James's* name. The whole island thus enclosed contains about two thousand acres of high land, and several thousands of very good and firm marsh, and is an extraordinary good pasture as any in that country.

By means of the narrow passage, this place was of great security to them from the *Indian* enemy: and if they had then known of the biting of the worm in the salts, they would have valued this place upon that account also, as being free from that mischief.

16. They were no sooner settled in all this happiness and security, but they fell into jars and dissensions among themselves, by a greedy grasping at the *Indian* treasures, envying and overreaching one another in that trade.

After five weeks' stay before this town, the ships returned home again, leaving one hundred and eight men settled in the form of government before spoken of.

After the ships were gone, the same sort of feuds and disorders happened continually among them, to the unspeakable damage of the plantation.

The *Indians* were the same there as in all other places; at first very fair and friendly, tho' afterwards they gave great proofs of their deceitfulness. However, by the help of the *Indian* provisions, the *English* chiefly subsisted till the return of the ships the next year; when two vessels were sent thither full-freighted with men and provisions for supply of the plantation, one of which only arrived directly, and the other being beat off to the *Carribbee* Islands, did not arrive till the former was sailed hence again.

17. In the interval of these ships returning from *England*, the *English* had a very advantageous trade with the *Indians*; and might have made much greater gains of it, and managed it both to the greater satisfaction of the *Indians*, and the greater ease and security of them-

selves; if they had been under any rule, or subject to any method in trade, and not left at liberty to outvie or outbid one another; by which they not only cut short their own profit, but created jealousies and disturbances among the *Indians*, by letting one have a better bargain than another: for they being unaccustomed to barter, such of them as had been hardest dealt by in their commodities, thought themselves cheated and abused; and so conceived a grudge against the *English* in general, making it a national quarrel: and this seems to be the original cause of most of their subsequent misfortunes by the *Indians*.

What also gave a greater interruption to this trade, was an object that drew all their eyes and thoughts aside, even from taking the necessary care for their preservation, and for the support of their lives; which was this; they found in a neck of land, on the back of *Jamestown Island*, a fresh stream of water springing out of a small bank, which washed down with it a yellow sort of dust isinglass, which being cleansed by the fresh streaming of the water, lay shining in the bottom of that limpid element, and stirred up in them an unseasonable and inordinate desire after riches: for they, taking all to be gold that glistened, run into the utmost distraction, neglecting both the necessary defense of their lives from the *Indians*, and the support of their bodies by securing of provisions; absolutely relying, like *Midas*, upon the almighty power of gold, thinking, that where this was in plenty nothing could be wanting: but they soon grew sensible of their error; and found that if this gilded dirt had been real gold, it could have been of no advantage to them. For, by their negligence, they were reduced to an exceeding scarcity of provisions, and that little they had, was lost by the burning of their town, while all hands were employed upon this imaginary golden treasure; so that they were forced to live for some time upon the wild fruits of the earth, and upon crabs, muscles, and such like, not having day's provision beforehand; as some of the laziest *Indians*, who have no pleasure in exercise, and won't be at the pains to fish and hunt: and, indeed, not so well as they neither; for by this careless neglecting of their defense against the *Indians*, many of 'em were destroyed by that cruel people; and the rest durst not venture abroad, but were forced to be content with what fell just into their mouths.

18. In this condition they were, when the first ship of the two beforementioned came to their assistance, but their golden dreams overcame all difficulties: they spoke not, nor thought of any thing but gold, and that was all the lading that most of them were willing to take care for; accordingly they put into this ship all the yellow dirt they had gathered, and what skins and furs they had trucked for; and filling her up with cedar, sent her away.

After she was gone, the other ship arrived, which they stowed likewise with this supposed gold dust, designing never to be poor again; filling her up with cedar and clapboard.

Those two ships being thus dispatched, they made several discoveries in *James* River, and up *Chesapeake* Bay, by the undertaking and management of Capt. *John Smith*: and the year 1608 was the first year in which they gathered *Indian* corn of their own planting.

While these discoveries were making by Capt. *Smith*, matters run again into confusion in *Jamestown*; and several uneasy people, taking advantage of his absence, attempted to desert the settlement, and run away with the small vessel that was left to attend upon it; for Capt. *Smith* was the only man among them that could manage the discoveries with success, and he was the only man too that could keep the settlement in order. Thus the *English* continued to give themselves as much perplexity by their own distraction, as the *Indians* did by their watchfulness and resentments.

19. *Anno* 1609, *John Laydon* and *Anna Burrows* were married together, the first Christian marriage in that part of the world: and the year following the plantation was increased to near five hundred men.

This year *Jamestown* sent out people, and made two other settlements; one at *Nansamond* in *James River*, above thirty miles below *Jamestown*, and the other at *Powhatan*, six miles below the falls of *James River* (which last was bought of *Powhatan* for a certain quantity of copper), each settlement consisting of about a hundred and twenty men. Some small time after another was made at *Kiquotan* by the mouth of *James River*.

CHAPTER III. SHOWING WHAT HAPPENED AFTER THE ALTERATION OF THE GOVERNMENT FROM AN ELECTIVE PRESIDENT TO A COMMISSIONATED GOVERNOR, UNTIL THE DISSOLUTION OF THE COMPANY

20. In the meanwhile the treasurer, council, and company of *Virginia* adventurers in *London*, not finding that return and profit from the adventures they expected; and rightly judging that this disappointment, as well as the idle quarrels in the colony, proceeded from a mismanage[ment] of the government; petitioned His Majesty, and got a new patent with leave to appoint a governor.

Upon this new grant they sent out nine ships, and plentiful supplies of men and provisions; and made three joint commissioners or governors in equal power, *viz.* Sir *Thomas Gates*, Sir *George Summers*, and Capt. *Newport*. They agreed to go all together in one ship.

This ship, on board of which the three governors had embarked, being separated from the rest, was put to great distress in a severe storm; and after three days and nights constant baling and pumping, was at last cast ashore at *Bermudas*, and there staved, but by good providence the company was preserved.

Notwithstanding this shipwreck, and extremity they were put to, yet could not this common misfortune make them agree. The best of it was, they found plenty of provisions in that island, and no *Indians* to annoy them: but still they quarrelled amongst themselves, and none more than the two knights; who made their parties, built each of them a cedar vessel, one called the *Patience*, the other the *Deliverance*, and used what they gathered of the furniture of the old ship for rigging, and fish oil, and hogs' grease mixed with lime and ashes instead of pitch and tar: for they found great plenty of *Spanish* hogs in this island, which are supposed to have swam ashore from some wrecks, and there afterwards increased.

21. While these things were acting in *Bermudas*, Capt. *Smith* being very much burnt by the accidental firing of some gunpowder, as he was upon a discovery in his boat, was forced for his cure sake, and the benefit of a surgeon, to take his passage for *England* in a ship that was then upon the point of sailing.

Several of the nine ships that came out with the three governors arrived, with many of the passengers; some of which in their humors would not submit to the government there, pretending the new commission destroyed the old one; that governors were appointed instead of a president, and that they themselves were to be of the council; and so would assume an independent power, inspiring the people with disobedience; by which means they became frequently exposed in great parties to the cruelty of the *Indians*; all sorts of discipline was laid aside, and their necessary defense neglected; so that the *Indians* taking advantage of those divisions, formed a stratagem to destroy them root and branch, and indeed they did cut many of 'em off, by massacring whole companies at a time; so that all the out-settlements were deserted, and the people that were not destroyed took refuge in *Jamestown*, except the small settlement at *Kiquotan*, where they had built themselves a little fort, and called it *Algernoon* Fort: and yet, for all this, they continued their disorders, wasting their old provisions, and neglecting to gather others; so that they who remained alive were all near famished, having brought themselves to that pass, that they durst not stir from their own doors to gather the fruits of the earth, or the crabs and mussels from the waterside: much less to hunt or catch wild beasts, fish or fowl, which were found in great abundance there. They continued in these scanty circumstances till they were at last reduced to such extremity, as to eat the very hides of their horses, and the bodies of the *Indians* they had killed; and sometimes also upon a pinch they would not disdain to dig them up again to make a homely meal of after they had been buried. And that time is to this day remembered by the name of the *Starving Time*.

Thus a few months' indiscreet management brought such an infamy upon the country, that to this day it cannot be wiped away: and the sicknesses occasioned by this bad diet, or rather want of diet are unjustly remembered to the disadvantage of the country, as a fault in the climate; which was only the foolishness and indiscretion of those who assumed the power of governing. I call it assumed because the new commission mentioned, by which they pretended to be of the council, was not in all this time arrived, but remained in *Bermudas* with the new governors.

Here I can't but admire the care, labor, courage and understanding that Capt. *John Smith* showed in the time of his administration; who not only founded, but also preserved all these settlements in good order, while he was amongst them. And without him, they had certainly all been destroyed, either by famine, or the enemy long before; tho' the country naturally afforded subsistence enough, even without any other labor than that of gathering and preserving its spontaneous provisions.

For the first three years that Capt. *Smith* was with them, they never had in that whole time above six months' *English* provisions. But as soon as he had left 'em to themselves, all went to ruin; for the *Indians* had no longer any fear for themselves, or friendship for the *English*. And six months after this gentleman's departure, the 500 men that he left were reduced to three-score; and they too must of necessity have starved, if their relief had been withheld a week longer.

William Byrd II
(1674–1744)

William Byrd, a Virginia landowner of great wealth, was sent to England for fourteen years to be educated and "finished" before returning to America to take over the management of his family's immense land holdings (the city of Richmond was eventually laid out on some of his property). In addition to owning a library of 4,000 volumes that was reputed to be the largest in the colonies, Byrd became a member of the Royal Society and served as a colonial agent in England on two separate occasions for periods of eight or more years. But Byrd's literary reputation is based on a commission he received to survey the boundary between North Carolina and Virginia, which is reported in his History of the Dividing Line. In addition to two other narratives of frontier expeditions, Journey in the Land of Eden and Progress to the Mines, he also composed The Secret History of the Dividing Line, which reported what one "smart lass" they encountered on their travels described not as "the good" Byrd's survey team accomplished but "the evil," and the private diary excerpted here that he kept during part of his adult life.

Though none of his writing was intended for publication, we would have a much poorer understanding of the sentiments and customs of the Virginia gentry during the early years of the eighteenth century without Byrd's candid accounts, particularly in the two secret volumes. Witty and urbane as well as, for all his religious observance, secular, vain, and lusty, The Secret Diary of William Byrd of Westover (Another Secret Diary was discovered and published in 1942 and a London Diary found and published in 1958) provides an unusual glimpse into the daily life of one of colonial America's richest as well as most self-possessed and, within limits, cosmopolitan men.

from *The Secret Diary of William Byrd of Westover (1719–1720)*

[IN LONDON, MAY 1719]

25. I rose about 7 o'clock and read a chapter in Hebrew and some Greek in Lucian. I said no prayers but had milk for breakfast. The weather continued very warm and clear, the wind southeast. I wrote abundance of Hebrew till 2 o'clock and then read some English till three when I ate some roast chicken. After dinner I put several things in order and took a nap till four. Then I read English till five and then went into the City to Mr. Dick Perry's where was Mrs. C-r-d-k and we played at cards and I lost ten shillings. About nine we went to supper and I ate some ham and cold chicken and drank some rack punch. About eleven we took leave and I walked home where I said my prayers.

26. I rose about 7 o'clock and read a chapter in Hebrew and some Greek in Lucian. I said no prayers, but had milk for breakfast. The weather was clear and very hot, the wind still southeast. I wrote some Hebrew till 11 o'clock and then went to Mr. J-n-n but he was from home. Then to my Lord Islay's but he was from home. Then to my Lord Orrery's, but he was from home; then to Mrs. Southwell's and sat with her about an hour and then went to the Cockpit and saw Mr. Beake and then went home and ate some battered eggs. After dinner I put several things in order and read some French till 5 o'clock and then went to visit Mrs. Pierson; then I went to Will's Coffeehouse and saw my Lord Orrery and then took a walk to Mrs. S-t-r-d but she was from home. Then I picked up a woman and carried her to the tavern and ate some roast lamb. I was very wanton till 12 o'clock and then walked home and said my prayers. This was the hottest day I ever felt at the time of year.

27. I rose about 7 o'clock and read a chapter in Hebrew and some Greek in Lucian. I said my prayers and had milk for breakfast. The weather was much cooler. However, it was warm and clear, the wind northeast. I danced my dance. About 11 o'clock I went to my Lord Orrery's where I drank a dish of chocolate and about twelve went with my Lord Orrery and Lord B-n-l-y to see the [burning glass]. Then I went to the Council office and found my business was not yet done. Then I went to St. James's Coffeehouse and there had a jelly. About two I went to my Lord Orrery's where I dined with my Lord B-n-l-y and ate some fish. After dinner we drank a bottle of champagne and about 5 o'clock went to see the anatomy of wax and stayed there two

hours and then went to Will's and from thence to St. James's Park with Mr. Ashley where I walked till ten and joined Mrs. [Andrews]. Then I walked home and said my prayers.

28. I rose about 7 o'clock and read a chapter in Hebrew and some Greek. I neglected my prayers, but had milk for breakfast. The weather was still warm and clear and very dry, the wind north. About eleven came Annie Wilkinson but I would not speak with her. I was disappointed in the coming of Mrs. B-s who wrote me word she would come and breakfast with me, so I read some English and ate some bread and butter because I was to dine late and about 3 o'clock went to dine with Sir Wilfred Lawson and ate some mutton. After dinner we talked a little and about 6 o'clock went to Kensington in Sir Wilfred's coach where there was a ball in the gardens and several ladies and among the rest Miss Perry whom I stuck most to and she complained I squeezed her hand. Here I stayed till 1 o'clock and then came home and neglected my prayers.

29. I rose about 8 o'clock and read a chapter in Hebrew and some Greek in Lucian. I said my prayers, and had milk for breakfast. The weather continued hot but was a little cloudy. I read some English till 11 o'clock and then came Colonel Blakiston and stayed about half an hour and then I went to Mrs. S-t-r-d-x to inquire after my little daughter and found she was better. Then I went into the City to Garraway's Coffeehouse where I read the news and then went to Mr. Lindsay's to dinner and ate some fish. After dinner we played at faro and I won forty shillings. About 6 o'clock I went to Will's Coffeehouse, and from thence to Lady Guise's and then returned to Will's where Margaret G-t-n called on me and I went with her to the bagnio where I rogered her three times with vigor, twice at night and once in the morning. I neglected my prayers.

[IN VIRGINIA, JUNE 1720]

20. I rose about 5 o'clock and read a chapter in Hebrew and some Greek. I said my prayers, and had boiled milk for breakfast. The weather continued very hot. However, about 8 o'clock I went to Mrs. Harrison's in a boat and ate some milk there. We played at piquet and shot with bows and I won five bits. Sometimes we romped and sometimes talked and complained of the heat till dinner and then I ate some hashed lamb. After dinner we romped again and drank abundance of water. We played at piquet again and I stayed till 8 o'clock and then took leave and walked home and found everything well, thank God.

I talked with my people and said my prayers and then retired and slept but indifferently because of the exceedingly great heat.

21. I rose about 5 o'clock and read a chapter in Hebrew and some Greek. I neglected to say my prayers, but had milk for breakfast. The weather continued very hot and we began to cut down our wheat. About 9 o'clock came Frank Lightfoot and we played at billiards and then at piquet and I won two bits. Then we sat and talked till dinner when I ate some beans and bacon. After dinner we agreed to take a nap and slept about an hour and then I received a letter from New Kent that told me William R-s-t-n was run away. Then Mr. Lightfoot and I played again at piquet till the evening and then walked about the garden till night and then he went away and I gave my people a bowl of punch and they had a fiddle and danced and I walked in the garden till ten and then committed uncleanness with Annie. I said my prayers.

Fray Carlos José Delgado
(1677–c. 1750)

During the early years of the eighteenth century, a series of conflicts broke out between civil and religious colonial authorities seeking to gain influence, if not control, over native populations. One site of these conflicts was central and northern New Mexico where, in the mideighteenth century, there remained considerable numbers of Indian people who still lived outside the realm of Spanish dominion. Fray Delgado was a Franciscan priest assigned to the pueblo of San Augustin de la Isleta who undertook missionary work first among the Moqui Indians and then among the Navajo where, in 1744, he reported the miraculous conversion of 5,000 souls. His letter to the Reverend Father Ximeno details some of the cruelties he observed Indian people suffering at the hands of Spanish civil authorities when he sought to extend his missionary work in northeastern New Mexico in 1750.

Report made by Reverend Father Fray Carlos Delgado to our Reverend Father Ximeno concerning the abominable hostilities and tyrannies of the governors and alcaldes mayores toward the Indians, to the consternation of the custodia. (1750)

Very Reverend Father and our Minister Provincial: I, Fray Carlos José Delgado, preacher general, commissary, notary, and censor of the

Holy Office, apostolic notary, and missionary in the *custodia*[1] of the conversion of San Pablo of this province of El Santo Evangelio in the kingdom of New Mexico, appear before your reverence only for the purpose of lamenting before your paternal love the grave extortions that we, the ministers of these missions, are suffering, at the hands of the governors and alcaldes of that kingdom. I declare, that of the eleven governors and many *alcaldes mayores* whom I have known in the long period of forty years that I have served at the mission called San Augustin de la Isleta, most of them have hated, and do hate to the death, and insult and persecute the missionary religious, causing them all the troubles and annoyances that their passion dictates, without any other reason or fault than the opposition of the religious to the very serious injustices which the said governors and alcaldes inflict upon the helpless Indians recently received into the faith, so that the said converts shall not forsake our holy law and flee to the heathen, to take up anew their former idolatries. This is experienced every day, not without grave sorrow and heartfelt tears on the part of those evangelical sowers, who, on seeing that their work is wasted and that the fecund seed of their preaching to those souls is lost and bears no fruit, cry out to heaven and sorrowfully ask a remedy for this great evil. In order that your reverence's exalted understanding may regard as just the reasons which support the said missionaries in their opposition to the aforesaid extortions, even though it should be at the cost of their lives, and also in order that you may come to their aid with the measures best fitted for the total abolition of the said injuries and injustices, I shall specify them in the following manner:

The first annoyance with which the persons mentioned molest the Indians is to send agents every year (contrary to the royal ordinances, and especially to a decree of the most excellent señor, Don Francisco Fernández de la Cueva Henriquez, Duke of Albuquerque, and viceroy of New Spain, issued in this City of Mexico on May 18, 1709, whose content I present, the original being kept in the archive of the *custodia* mentioned) at the time of the harvest, to all the pueblos of the kingdom, under the pretext of buying maize for the support of their households, though most of it is really to be sold in the nearest villages. The said agents take from all the pueblos and missions eight hundred or a thousand *fanegas*, and compel the Indians to transport them to the place where the governor lives. Besides not paying them anything for the said transportation, they do not pay them for the maize at once, and when the date arrives which they have designated for the payment, if the maize is worth two pesos a *fanega* they give them only one. Even this amount is not in coin or in any article that can be useful to the Indians, but in baubles, such as *chuchumater*, which are glass beads, ill-made knives, relics, awls, and a few handfuls of common tobacco, the value of which does not amount even to a tenth part of what the maize is worth which they extract from them by force, and this even though as has been said, they pay them only half the proper price that is charged throughout the kingdom. From this manifest injustice two very serious evils result: first, the unhappy Indians are left without anything to eat for the greater part of the year; and second, in order not to perish of hunger they are forced to go to the mountains and hunt for game or to serve on the ranches or farms for their food alone, leaving the missions abandoned.

The second oppression that the Indians frequently suffer at the hands of the governors is being compelled arbitrarily and by force, for the small price of an awl or other similar trifle, to work on the buildings that they need, whatever they may be and whether they require little or much time. The Indians also are required to drive cattle as far as the villa of Chihuahua,[2] which is more than two hundred leagues distant from the place where the governors live. They receive in payment for this service only a little ground corn, which they call *pinole*, and the Indian cattle drivers are compelled to pay for those [animals] that are lost or die for want of care or by any other accident. A pernicious evil arises from this cattle driving, for the Indians must abandon their families and leave their lands uncultivated, and, as a consequence, be dying of hunger during the greater part of the year.

The third oppression, and the most grievous and pernicious, from which originate innumerable evils and sins against God, and manifest injuries against the missionaries and Indians, is the wicked dissimulation of the governors in regard to the acts of the *alcaldes mayores*, for it is publicly known throughout the realm that when they give them their *varas*, or wands of office, they tell and advise them to make the Indians work without pity.

With such express license, your reverence can imagine how many disturbances will be caused by men who usually take the employment of *alcaldes mayores* solely for the purpose of advancing their own interests and acquiring property with which to make presents to the governors, so that the latter will countenance their unjust proceedings, even though they be denounced before them, and perhaps will even promote them in office. Every year they make the Indians weave four hundred blankets, or as many woolen sheets; they take from all the pueblos squads of thirty or forty Indians and work them the greater part of the year in planting maize and wheat, which they care for until it is placed in the granaries; they send them among the heathen Indians to trade indigo, knives, tobacco, and *chuchumates*, for cattle and for deer hides. Not even the women are exempt from this tyranny, for if the officials cannot make use of their work in any other way they compel them to spin almost all the wool needed for the said sheets and blankets. And the most lamentable thing about all this is that they recompense them for these tasks with only a handful of tobacco, which is divided among eighteen or twenty.

The most grievous thing for the heathen Indians is that the alcaldes and even some of the governors, mix with their wives and daughters, often violating them, and this so openly that with a very little effort the violation of their consorts comes to the knowledge of the husbands, and as a result it often happens that they repudiate their wives and will not receive them until the missionary fathers labor to persuade them. The shameless way in which the officials conduct themselves in this particular is proved by an occasion when a certain governor was in conversation with some missionaries, and an Indian woman came into their presence to charge him with the rape of her daughter, and he, without changing countenance, ordered that she should be paid by merely giving her a buffalo skin that he had at hand.

Yet all that I have hitherto related does not drive the Indians to the limits of desperation or cause them to fall away from our holy faith so much as when the said alcaldes compel them to deliver to them a quantity of deer skins, lard, sheaves [of grain], chickens, and other things that their desires dictate, saying that they are for the governors, who ask for them. The Indian has to submit to this injustice, for they either take it from him without asking, or, if he does not have what the alcaldes ask for or does not give it promptly enough when he has it, he suffers either spoliation or punishment.

These punishments are so cruel and inhuman that sometimes for a slight offence, sometimes because the Indian resists the outrages that they inflict upon him, or sometimes because they are slow in doing what the alcaldes order, they are put in jail for many days, are confined in the stocks, or—and I cannot say it without tears—the officials flog them so pitilessly that, their wrath not being appeased by seeing them shed their blood, they inflict such deep scars upon them that they remain for many years. It is a proof of this second point that when I went among the heathens to reduce the apostates there were among them some who, with an aggrieved air, showed me their scars, thus giving me to understand that the reason why they fled and did not return to the pale of the church was their fear of these cruel punishments.

A further distressing proof of this practice is what was done in the past year at El Paso by a captain to a Catholic Indian of the Zuma nation, sacristan of the mission of El Real. A servant of the captain of El Paso had hidden three ears of corn which he had stolen from his master. The sacristan took them from him, and, without any more proof or reason than having found him with them in his hands, and because the said servant, to escape punishment, said that the innocent

Indian often stole corn from the granaries, the said captain became so angered that, in violation of all natural and divine laws, he ordered six soldiers to take the Indian out and kill him in the fields.

They carried out the order, and when the unfortunate Zuma cried aloud for confession they did not yield to his entreaties, but gave him a violent death, perhaps being fearful that the missionary religious, whose duty it was to administer the holy sacrament to him, would prevent the execution of that unjust order, even though it might be at the cost of his life.

The outrage did not stop here, for when the Zuma Indians of the mission of El Real learned of the death of their countryman, they began to rise up, all crying out: "Why, since we are Christians, do they not permit us to confess at the hour of death? Let us flee to the mountains!" They did not flee, our father, either because the soldiers restrained them or because the fathers appealed to them. A still greater injury, however, arose from the remedy, for the governor having ordered a large troop of Zumas of both sexes to come to this city, simply because an Indian woman and two men were not able to travel as fast as the others, having crippled feet, the corporal who was leading them ordered them to be beheaded at a place called El Gallego, where he left the bodies unburied, to the intense grief of their companions and relatives, whose sorrow was not lessened on seeing that the said corporal and the rest of the escort robbed them of their little children in order to sell them as slaves in various places along the road.

Nor is it only the sad alcaldes and governors that ill-treat the Indians in the manner described, but even the judges who enter to conduct the *residencias*[3] of the alcaldes and governors who have completed their terms of offices, inflict upon the Indians as much injury and hardship as may conduce to the advancement of their own interests and the success of their ambitious desires. It is public knowledge throughout the kingdom that such persons seek to conduct these *residencias* more for what they gain by unjust and violent spoliation of the Indians than for what they receive from the office that they exercise.

Finally, to such an extreme do the iniquities reach that are practiced against the Indians by governors and *alcaldes mayores*, as well as by the judges of *residencia*, that, losing patience and possessed by fear, they turn their backs to our holy mother, the Church, abandon their pueblos and missions, and flee to the heathen, there to worship the devil, and, most lamentable of all, to confirm in idolatries those who have never been illuminated by the light of our holy faith, so that they will never give ear or credit to the preaching of the gospel. Because of all this, every day new conversions become more difficult, and the zealous missionaries who in the service of both Majesties are anxiously seeking the propagation of the gospel, most often see their work wasted and do [not] accomplish the purpose of their extended wanderings.

Although it cannot be denied that those barbarous nations are stiffnecked, yet there have been many instances where thousands of them have entered joyfully through the requisite door of the holy sacrament of baptism, and most of the apostates would return to the bosom of the Church if they did not fear, with such good reason, the punishments and extortions that I have already spoken of. They have told me this on most of the occasions when I have entered in fulfillment of my obligation to reduce apostates and convert the heathen. In the year 1742, when, at the cost of indescribable labor and hardships, I reduced four hundred and forty odd among apostates and heathen in the province of Moqui, innumerable souls would have come to the bosom of our holy Church had they not been deterred by the reason that I have stated.

Although the missionary religious ought to oppose themselves to these grave injuries and their pernicious consequences, they often do not do it; first, because they never succeed in attaining their purpose, but on the contrary are insulted, disrespected, and held to be disturbers of the peace; second, because the governors and alcaldes impute and charge them with crimes that they have never committed, which they proceed to prove with false witnesses whom they have suborned before the father custodian, and compel the latter to proceed against the religious whom they calumniate. And although the said custodians know very well that the denunciations are born of hatred, they proceed against the missionaries, changing them from one mission to another, in order to prevent the said governors from committing the excess of using their power to expel the missionaries from the kingdom, as has often happened; and also because, when the custodians do not agree to what the governors ask, the latter refuse to certify the allowance for the administration of the religious, which certification is necessary in order that the most excellent señor viceroy may issue the honorariums that his Majesty (whom may God preserve) assigns for the maintenance of the missionary religious. It has seemed to me that all that I have said ought to be presented before the charitable zeal of your reverence, so that, having it before you as father of those faithful sons, your apostolic missionaries, you may put into execution the means that your discretion may decide upon, with the purpose of ending this great abuse, of redeeming all those helpless people, and consoling your sorrowing sons. It is indisputable that whatever I have said is public, notorious, certain and true, as I swear *in verbo sacerdotis tacto pectore*, at this hospice of Santa Bárbara of the pueblo of Tlatelolco,[4] on March 27, 1750. Our very reverend father, your humblest subject, Fray CARLOS JOSÉ DELGADO, who venerates you, places himself at your feet.

Jonathan Edwards
(1703–1758)

Jonathan Edwards is widely regarded as the United States' greatest native-born theologian. This estimation is based not only on the range, subtlety, and consistency of his thinking, but also on its passion, power, and originality. Virtually alone among his contemporaries and near-contemporaries, Edwards saw clearly the cancerous growth of self-regard that lay beneath the religious platitudes and theological formulas by which men and women of his age justified themselves to their God. Edwards did not content himself with merely exposing this spiritual cancer, for he believed that the critique of faith must be followed by its renewal—a renewal not only in the head but also in the heart. Edwards thus undertook to reform the whole edifice of Puritan—really Calvinist—spirituality by awakening a fresh understanding of religion's seat in the life of the feelings.

Though Edwards's life was comparatively short, his literary output was prodigious, especially in view of his active and frequently controversial ministry. He helped touch the match to the religious conflagration of the 1730s and 1740s, which became known as the First Great Awakening. Later he became embroiled in the bitter controversy in Northampton, Massachusetts, that would eventually cost him his parish there. Refusing to compromise on standards of church membership, he was finally sent packing to the wilderness of western Massachusetts to serve as a missionary to the Indians. Despite these distractions, Edwards's pen was always active, producing everything from spiritual biography and autobiography to narratives of the religious awakening; from treatises on morality and the will to his great works on original sin and the purpose of Creation; from miscellaneous journals and notebooks to sermons like "A Divine and Supernatural

Light" and his more famous, if uncharacteristic, "Sinners in the Hands
of an Angry God." Edwards died soon after he was appointed first
president of the new college being founded in Princeton, New Jersey,
as a result of a smallpox vaccination for which he volunteered to serve
as a guinea pig.

The following selections reflect some of the diversity of Edwards's
writing as well as its underlying unity. "Sarah Pierrepont," which takes
for its subject the woman who was to become Edwards's wife, reveals
his fascination with religious biography. The selection from Personal
Narrative, in addition to exposing his talents as an autobiographer,
illuminates his interest in the whole process of spiritual regeneration
and his willingness to use a language to describe it consistent with the
form of experience in which it occurs. The selection from A Treatise
Concerning Religious Affections demonstrates Edwards's capacity to
reason about, as well as from, the heart and his intellectual commit-
ment to re-situate the understanding of religious experience in the
changes it works in the whole life of human desire. Finally, the selection from The Nature of True Virtue shows Edwards moving from
the theological language of grace and depravity to the philosophical
language of being and consent to make the point that love is the axis
of Creation and the source of goodness.

Sarah Pierrepont (1723)

They say there is a young lady in [New Haven] who is beloved of that
Great Being, who made and rules the world, and that there are certain
seasons in which this Great Being, in some way or other invisible,
comes to her and fills her mind with exceeding sweet delight; and that
she hardly cares for any thing, except to meditate on him—that she
expects after a while to be received up where he is, to be raised up
out of the world and caught up into heaven; being assured that he
loves her too well to let her remain at a distance from him always.
There she is to dwell with him, and to be ravished with love and
delighted forever. Therefore, if you present all the world before her,
with the richest of its treasures, she disregards it and cares not for it,
and is unmindful of any pain or affliction; is most just and conscientious in all her conduct; and you could not persuade her to do any
thing wrong or sinful, if you would give her all the world, lest she
should offend this Great Being. She is of a wonderful sweetness, calm-
ness, and universal benevolence of mind; especially after this Great
God has manifested himself to her mind. She will sometimes go about

from place to place, singing sweetly; and seems to be always full of joy and pleasure; and no one knows for what. She loves to be alone, walking in the fields and groves, and seems to have some one invisible always conversing with her.

from *Personal Narrative (1740)*

I had a variety of concerns and exercises about my soul, from my childhood; but I had two more remarkable seasons of awakening, before I met with that change, by which I was brought to those new dispositions, and that new sense of things, that I have since had. The first time was when I was a boy, some years before I went to college, at a time of remarkable awakening in my father's congregation. I was then very much affected for many months, and concerned about the things of religion, and my soul's salvation; and was abundant in religious duties. I used to pray five times a day in secret, and to spend much time in religious conversation with other boys; and used to meet with them to pray together. I experienced I know not what kind of delight in religion. My mind was much engaged in it, and had much self-righteous pleasure; and it was my delight to abound in religious duties. I, with some of my school-mates, joined together, and built a booth in a swamp, in a very retired spot, for a place of prayer.—And besides, I had particular secret places of my own in the woods, where I used to retire by myself; and was from time to time much affected. My affections seemed to be lively and easily moved, and I seemed to be in my element, when engaged in religious duties. And I am ready to think, many are deceived with such affections, and such a kind of delight as I then had in religion, and mistake it for grace.

But, in process of time, my convictions and affections wore off; and I entirely lost all those affections and delights, and left off secret prayer, at least as to any constant preference of it; and returned like a dog to his vomit, and went on in the ways of sin.[1] Indeed, I was at times very uneasy, especially towards the latter part of my time at college; when it pleased God, to seize me with a pleurisy; in which he brought me nigh to the grave, and shook me over the pit of hell. And yet, it was not long after my recovery, before I fell again into my old ways of sin. But God would not suffer me to go on with any quietness; I had great and violent inward struggles, till, after many conflicts with wicked inclinations, repeated resolutions, and bonds that I laid myself under by a kind of vows to God, I was brought wholly to break off all former wicked ways, and all ways of known outward sin; and to apply myself to seek salvation, and practise many religious duties; but without that kind of affection and delight which I had formerly experienced. My concern now wrought more, by inward struggles, and conflicts, and self-reflections. I made seeking my salvation, the main business of my life. But yet, it seems to me, I sought it after a miserable manner; which has made me sometimes since to question, whether such miserable seeking ever succeeded. I was indeed brought to seek salvation, in a manner that I never was before; I felt a spirit to part with all things in the world, for an interest in Christ. My concern continued and prevailed, with many exercising thoughts and inward struggles; but yet it never seemed to be proper, to express that concern by the name of terror.

From my childhood up, my mind had been full of objections against the doctrine of God's sovereignty, in choosing whom he would to eternal life, and rejecting whom he pleased; leaving them eternally to perish, and be everlastingly tormented in hell. It used to appear like a horrible doctrine to me. But I remember the time very well, when I seemed to be convinced, and fully satisfied, as to this sovereignty of God, and his justice in thus eternally disposing of men, according to his sovereign pleasure. But never could give an account, how, or by what means, I was thus convinced, not in the least imagining at the time, nor a long time after, that there was any extraordinary influence of God's Spirit in it; but only that now I saw further, and my reason apprehended the justice and reasonableness of it. However, my mind rested in it; and it put an end to all those cavils and objections. And there has been a wonderful alteration in my mind, with respect to the doctrine of God's sovereignty, from that day to this; so that I scarce ever have found so much as the rising of an objection against it, in the most absolute sense, in God shewing mercy to whom he will shew mercy, and hardening whom he will.[2] God's absolute sovereignty and justice, with respect to salvation and damnation, is what my mind seems to rest assured of, as much as of any thing that I see with my eyes; at least it is so at times. But I have often, since the first conviction, had quite another kind of sense of God's sovereignty than I had then. I have often since had not only a conviction, but a *delightful* conviction. The doctrine has very often appeared exceedingly pleasant, bright, and sweet. Absolute sovereignty is what I love to ascribe to God. But my first conviction was not so.

The first instance, that I remember, of that sort of inward, sweet delight in God and divine things, that I have lived much in since, was on reading those words, 1 Tim. i. 17. *Now unto the King eternal, immortal, invisible, the only wise god, be honour and glory for ever and ever, Amen.* As I read the words, there came into my soul, and was as it were diffused through it, a sense of the glory of the Divine

Being; a new sense, quite different from any thing I ever experienced before. Never any words of Scripture seemed to me as these words did. I thought with myself, how excellent a Being that was, and how happy I should be, if I might enjoy that God, and be rapt up to him in heaven, and be as it were swallowed up in him for ever! I kept saying, and as it were singing, over these words of scripture to myself; and went to pray to God that I might enjoy him, and prayed in a manner quite different from what I used to do; with a new sort of affection. But it never came into my thought, that there was any thing spiritual, or of a saving nature in this.

From about that time, I began to have a new kind of apprehensions and ideas of Christ, and the work of redemption, and the glorious way of salvation by him. An inward, sweet sense of these things, at times, came into my heart; and my soul was led away in pleasant views and contemplations of them. And my mind was greatly engaged to spend my time in reading and meditating on Christ, on the beauty and excellency of his person, and the lovely way of salvation by free grace in him. I found no books so delightful to me, as those that treated of these subjects. Those words Cant³ ii. 1. used to abundantly with me, *I am the Rose of Sharon, and the Lily of the valleys*. The words seemed to me, sweetly to represent the loveliness and beauty of Jesus Christ. The whole book of Canticles used to be pleasant to me, and I used to be much in reading it, about that time; and found, from time to time, an inward sweetness, that would carry me away, in my contemplations. This I know not how to express otherwise, than by a calm, sweet abstraction of soul from all the concerns of this world; and sometimes a kind of vision, or fixed ideas and imaginations, of being alone in the mountains, or some solitary wilderness far from all mankind, sweetly conversing with Christ, and wrapt and swallowed up in God. The sense I had of divine things, would often of a sudden kindle up, as it were, a sweet burning in my heart; an ardour of soul, that I know not how to express.

Not long after I first began to experience these things, I gave an account to my father of some things that had passed in my mind. I was pretty much affected by the discourse we had together; and when the discourse was ended, I walked abroad alone, in a solitary place in my father's pasture, for contemplation. And as I was walking there, and looking upon the sky and clouds, there came into my mind so sweet a sense of the glorious *majesty* and *grace* of God, as I know not how to express.—I seemed to see them both in a sweet conjunction; majesty and meekness joined together; it was a sweet, and gentle, and holy majesty; and also a majestic meekness; an awful sweetness, a high, and great, and holy gentleness.

After this my sense of divine things gradually increased, and became more and more lively, and had more of that inward sweetness. The appearance of every thing was altered; there seemed to be, as it were, a calm, sweet, cast, or appearance of divine glory, in almost every thing. God's excellency, his wisdom, his purity and love, seemed to appear in every thing; in the sun, moon and stars; in the clouds and blue sky; in the grass, flowers, trees; in the water and all nature; which used greatly to fix my mind. I often used to sit and view the moon for a long time; and in the day, spent much time in viewing the clouds and sky, to behold the sweet glory of God in these things: in the meantime, singing forth, with a low voice, my contemplations of the Creator and Redeemer. And scarce any thing, among all the works of nature, was so sweet to me as thunder and lightning; formerly nothing had been so terrible to me. Before, I used to be uncommonly terrified with thunder, and to be struck with terror when I saw a thunder-storm rising; but now, on the contrary, it rejoiced me. I felt God, if I may so speak, at the first appearance of a thunder storm; and used to take the opportunity to view the clouds, and see the lightnings play, and hear the majestic and awful voice of God's thunder, which oftentimes was exceedingly entertaining, leading me to sweet contemplations of my great and glorious God. While thus engaged, it always seemed natural for me to sing, or chant forth my meditations; or, to speak my thoughts in soliloquies with a singing voice.

I felt then great satisfaction, as to my good estate; but that did not content me. I had vehement longings of soul after God and Christ, and after more holiness, wherwith my heart seemed to be full, and ready to break; which often brought to my mind the words of the Psalmist, Psal. cxix. 28. *My soul breaketh for the longing it hath*. I often felt a mourning and lamenting in my heart, that I had not turned to God sooner, that I might have had more time to grow in grace. My mind was greatly fixed on divine things; almost perpetually in the contemplation of them. I spent most of my time in thinking of divine things, year after year; often walking alone in the woods, and solitary places, for meditation, soliloquy, and prayer, and converse with God; and it was always my manner, at such times, to sing forth my contemplations. I was almost constantly in ejaculatory prayer, wherever I was. Prayer seemed to be natural to me, as the breath by which the inward burnings of my heart had vent. The delights which I now felt in the things of religion, were of an exceedingly different kind from those before-mentioned, that I had when a boy; and what then I had no more notion of, that one born blind has of pleasant and beautiful colours. They were of a more inward, pure, soul-animating and refreshing nature. Those former delights never reached the heart; and did not arise from any sight of the divine excellency of the things or God; of any taste of the soul-satisfying and life-giving good there is in them.

Since I came to Northampton, I have often had sweet complacency in God, in views of his glorious perfections, and of the excellency of Jesus Christ. God has appeared to me a glorious and lovely Being, chiefly on account of his holiness. The holiness of God has always appeared to me the most lovely of all his attributes. The doctrines of God's absolute sovereignty, and free grace, in shewing mercy to whom he would shew mercy; and man's absolute dependence on the operations of God's Holy spirit, have very often appeared to me as sweet and glorious doctrines. These doctrines have been much my delight. God's sovereignty has ever appeared to me, a great part of his glory. It has often been my delight to approach God, and adore him as a sovereign god, and ask sovereign mercy of him.

I have loved the doctrines of the gospel; they have been to my soul like green pastures. The gospel has seemed to me the richest treasure; the treasure that I have most desired, and longed that it might dwell richly in me. The way of salvation by Christ, has appeared, in a general way, glorious and excellent, most pleasant and most beautiful. It has often seemed to me, that it would, in a great measure, spoil heaven, to receive it in any other way. That text has often been affecting and delightful to me, Isa. xxxii, 2, *A man shall be an hiding place from the wind, and a covert from the tempest, &c.*

It has often appeared to me delightful, to be united to Christ; to have him for my head, and to be a member of his body; also to have Christ for my teacher and prophet. I very often think with sweetness, and longings, and pantings of soul, of being a little child, taking hold of Christ, to be led by him through the wilderness of this world. That text, Matt. xviii. 3, has often been sweet to me, *Except ye be converted and become as little children, &c.* I love to think of coming to Christ, to receive salvation of him, poor in spirit, and quite empty of self, humbly exalting him alone; cut off entirely from my own root, in order to grow into, and out of Christ: to have god in Christ to be all in all; and to live by faith on the Son of God, a life of humble, unfeigned confidence in him. That Scripture has often been sweet to me, Psal. cxv. 1, *Not unto us, O Lord, not unto us, but unto thy name give glory, for thy mercy, and for thy truth's sake.* And those words of Christ, Luke x. 21, *In that hour Jesus rejoiced in spirit, and said, I thank thee, O Father, Lord of heaven and earth, that thou hast hid these things from the wise and prudent, and hast revealed them unto babes: even so, Father, for so it seemed good in thy sight.* That sovereignty of God, which Christ rejoiced in, seemed to me worthy of such joy; and that rejoicing seemed to show the excellency of Christ, and of what spirit he was.

Sometimes, only mentioning a single word, caused my heart to burn within me; or only seeing the name of Christ, or the name of some attribute of God. And God has appeared glorious to me, on account of the Trinity. It has made me have exalting thoughts of God, that he subsists in three persons: Father, Son, and Holy Ghost. The sweetest joys and delights I have experienced, have not been those that have arisen from a hope of my own good estate; but in a direct view of the glorious things of the gospel. When I enjoy this sweetness, it seems to carry me above the thoughts of my own estate; it seems, at such times, a loss that I cannot bear, to take off my eye from the glorious, pleasant object I behold without me, to turn my eye in upon myself, and my own good estate.

My heart has been much on the advancement of Christ's kingdom in the world. The histories of the past advancement of Christ's kingdom have been sweet to me. When I have read histories of past ages, the pleasantest thing, in all my reading, has been, to read of the kingdom of Christ being promoted. And when I have expected, in my reading, to come to any such thing, I have rejoiced in the prospect, all the way as I read. And my mind has been much entertained and delighted with the scripture promises and prophecies, which relate to the future glorious advancement of Christ's kingdom upon earth.

I have sometimes had a sense of the excellent fulness of Christ, and his meetness and suitableness as a Saviour; whereby he has appeared to me, far above all, the chief of ten thousands.[4] His blood and atonement have appeared sweet, and his righteousness sweet; which was always accompanied with ardency of spirit; and inward strugglings and breathings, and groanings that cannot be uttered, to be emptied of myself, and swallowed up in Christ.

Once, as I rode out into the woods for my health, in 1737, having alighted from my horse in a retired place, as my manner commonly has been, to walk for divine contemplation and prayer, I had a view, that for me was extraordinary, of the glory of the Son of God, as Mediator between God and man, and his wonderful, great, full, pure and sweet grace and love, and meek and gentle condescension. This grace that appeared so calm and sweet, appeared also great above the heavens. The person of Christ appeared ineffably excellent, with an excellency great enough to swallow up all thought and conception— which continued, as near as I can judge, about an hour; which kept me the greater part of the time, in a flood of tears, and weeping aloud. I felt an ardency of soul to be, what I know not otherwise how to express, emptied and annihilated; to lie in the dust, and to be full of Christ alone; to love him with a holy and pure love; to trust in him;

to live upon him; to serve and follow him; and to be perfectly sanctified and made pure, with a divine and heavenly purity. I have, several other times, had views very much of the same nature, and which have had the same effects.

I have, many times, had a sense of the glory of the Third Person in the Trinity, in his office of Sanctifier; in his holy operations, communicating divine light and life to the soul. God in the communications of his holy spirit, has appeared as an infinite fountain of divine glory and sweetness; being full and sufficient to fill and satisfy the soul; pouring forth itself in sweet communications; like the sun in its glory, sweetly and pleasantly diffusing light and life. And I have sometimes had an affecting sense of the excellency of the word of God as a word of life; as the light of life; a sweet, excellent, life-giving word; accompanied with a thirsting after that word, that it might dwell richly in my heart.

Often, since I lived in this town, I have had very affecting views of my own sinfulness and vileness; very frequently to such a degree, as to hold me in a kind of loud weeping, sometimes for a considerable time together; so that I have often been forced to shut myself up. I have had a vastly greater sense of my own wickedness, and the badness of my heart, than ever I had before my conversion. It has often appeared to me, that if God should mark iniquity against me, I should appear the very worst of all mankind; of all that have been, since the beginning of the world, to this time: and that I should have by far the lowest place in hell. When others, that have come to talk with me about their soul-concerns, have expressed the sense they have had of their own wickedness, by saying, that it seemed to them, that they were as bad as the devil himself; I thought their expressions seemed exceeding faint and feeble, to represent my wickedness.

My wickedness, as I am in myself, has long appeared to me perfectly ineffable, and swallowing up all thought and imagination; like an infinite deluge, or mountains over my head. I know not how to express better what my sins appear to me to be, than by heaping infinite upon infinite, and multiplying infinite by infinite. Very often, for these many years, these expressions are in my mind, and in my mouth, "Infinite upon infinite—Infinite upon infinite!" When I look into my heart, and take a view of my wickedness, it looks like an abyss, infinitely deeper than hell. And it appears to me, that were it not for free grace, exalted and raised up to the infinite height of all the fulness and glory of the great Jehovah, and the arm of his power and grace stretched forth in all the majesty of his power, and in all the glory of his sovereignty, I should appear sunk down in my sins below hell itself; far beyond the sight of every thing, but the eye of sovereign grace, that can pierce even down to such a depth. And yet, it seems to me that my conviction of sin is exceedingly small, and faint; it is enough to amaze me, that I have no more sense of my sin. I know certainly, that I have very little sense of my sinfulness. When I have had turns of weeping and crying for my sins, I thought I knew at the time, that my repentance was nothing to my sin.

I have greatly longed of late, for a broken heart, and to lie low before God; and, when I ask for humility, I cannot bear the thoughts of being no more humble than other christians. It seems to me, that though their degrees of humility may be suitable for them, yet it would be a vile self-exaltation in me, not to be the lowest in humility of all mankind. Others speak of their longing to be "humbled to the dust;" that may be a proper expression for them, but I always think of myself, that I ought, and it is an expression that has long been natural for me to use in prayer, "to lie infinitely low before God." And it is affecting to think, how ignorant I was, when a young christian, of the bottomless, infinite depths of wickedness, pride, hypocrisy and deceit, left in my heart.

I have a much greater sense of my universal, exceeding dependance on God's grace and strength, and mere good pleasure, of late, than I used formerly to have; and have experienced more of an abhorrence of my own righteousness. The very thought of any joy arising in me, on any consideration of my own amiableness, performances, or experiences, or any goodness of heart, or life, is nauseous and detestable to me. And yet, I am greatly afflicted with a proud and self-righteous spirit, much more sensibly than I used to be formerly. I see that serpent rising and putting forth its head continually, every where, all around me.

Though it seems to me, that in some respects, I was a far better christian, for two or three years after my first conversion, than I am now; and lived in a more constant delight and pleasure; yet of late years, I have had a more full and constant sense of the absolute sovereignty of God, and a delight in that sovereignty; and have had more of a sense of the glory of Christ, as a Mediator revealed in the gospel. On one Saturday night, in particular, I had such a discovery of the excellency of the gospel above all other doctrines, that I could not but say to myself, "This is my chosen light, my chosen doctrine": and of Christ, "This is my chosen Prophet." It appeared sweet, beyond all expression, to follow Christ, and to be taught, and enlightened, and instructed by him; to learn of him, and live to him. Another Saturday night, (*Jan.* 1739) I had such a sense, how sweet and blessed a thing it was to walk in the way of duty; to do that which was right and meet to be done, and agreeable to the holy mind of God; that it caused me to break forth into a kind of loud weeping, which held me some time, so that I was forced to shut myself up, and fasten the doors. I could not but, as it were, cry out, "How happy are they, who do that which is right in the sight of God! They are blessed indeed, *they* are the happy ones!" I had, at the same time, a very affecting sense, how meet and suitable it was that God should govern the world, and order all things according to his own pleasure; and I rejoiced in it, that God reigned, and that his will was done.

Sinners in the Hands of an Angry God (1741)

THEIR FOOT SHALL SLIDE IN DUE TIME.
(DEUT. XXXII. 35)

In this verse is threatened the vengeance of God on the wicked unbelieving Israelites, who were God's visible people, and who lived under the means of grace; but who, notwithstanding all God's wonderful works towards them, remained (as ver. 28.) void of counsel,[1] having no understanding in them. Under all the cultivations of heaven, they brought forth bitter and poisonous fruit: as in the two verses next preceding the text.—The expression I have chosen for my text, *Their foot shall slide in due time*, seems to imply the following things, relating to the punishment and destruction to which these wicked Israelites were exposed.

1. That they were always exposed to *destruction*; as one that stands or walks in slippery places is always exposed to fall. This is implied in the manner of their destruction coming upon them, being represented by their foot sliding. The same is expressed. Psalm lxxiii. 18. "Surely thou didst set them in slippery places; thou castedst them down into destruction."

2. It implies, that they were always exposed to sudden unexpected destruction. As he that walks in slippery places is every moment liable to fall, he cannot foresee one moment whether he shall stand or fall the next; and when he does fall, he falls at once without warning: Which is also expressed in Psalm lxxiii. 18, 19. "Surely thou didst set them in slippery places; thou castedst them down into destruction: How are they brought into desolation as in a moment!"

3. Another thing implied is, that they are liable to fall of *themselves*, without being thrown down by the hand of another; as he that stands or walks on slippery ground needs nothing but his own weight to throw him down.

4. That the reason why they are not fallen already, and do not

fall now, is only that God's appointed time is not come. For it is said, that when that due time, or appointed times comes, *their foot shall slide*. Then they shall be left to fall, as they are inclined by their own weight. God will not hold them up in these slippery places any longer, but will let them go; and then, at that very instant, they shall fall into destruction; as he that stands on such slippery declining ground, on the edge of a pit, he cannot stand alone, when he is let go he immediately falls and is lost.

The observation from the words that I would now insist upon is this.—"There is nothing that keeps wicked men at any one moment out of hell, but the mere pleasure of God"—By the *mere* pleasure of God, I mean his *sovereign* pleasure, his arbitrary will, restrained by no obligation, hindered by no manner of difficulty, any more than if nothing else but God's mere will had in the least degree, or in any respect whatsoever, any hand in the preservation of wicked men one moment.—The truth of this observation may appear by the following considerations.

1. There is no want of *power* in God to cast wicked men into hell at any moment. Men's hands cannot be strong when God rises up. The strongest have no power to resist him, nor can any deliver out of his hands.—He is not only able to cast wicked men into hell, but he can most easily do it. Sometimes an earthly prince meets with a great deal of difficulty to subdue a rebel, who has found means to fortify himself, and has made himself strong by the numbers of his followers. But it is not so with God. There is no fortress that is any defence from the power of God. Though hand join in hand, and vast multitudes of God's enemies combine and associate themselves, they are easily broken in pieces. They are as great heaps of light chaff before the whirlwind; or large quantities of dry stubble before devouring flames. We find it easy to tread on and crush a worm that we see crawling on the earth; so it is easy for us to cut or singe a slender thread that any thing hangs by: thus easy is it for God, when he pleases, to cast his enemies down to hell. What are we, that we should think to stand before him, at whose rebuke the earth trembles, and before whom the rocks are thrown down?

2. They *deserve* to be cast into hell; so that divine justice never stands in the way, it makes no objection against God's using his power at any moment to destroy them. Yea, on the contrary, justice calls aloud for an infinite punishment of their sins. Divine justice says of the tree that brings forth such grapes of Sodom, "Cut it down, why cumbereth it the ground?" Luke xiii. 7. The sword of divine justice is every moment brandished over their heads, and it is nothing but the hand of arbitrary mercy, and God's mere will, that holds it back.

3. They are already under a sentence of *condemnation* to hell.

They do not only justly deserve to be cast down thither, but the sentence of the law of God, that eternal and immutable rule of righteousness that God has fixed between him and mankind, is gone out against them, and stands against them; so that they are bound over already to hell. John iii. 18. "He that believeth not is condemned already." So that every unconverted man properly belongs to hell; that is his place; from thence he is, John viii. 23. "Ye are from beneath:" And thither he is bound; it is the place that justice, and God's word, and the sentence of his unchangeable law assign to him.

4. They are now the objects of that very same *anger* and wrath of God, that is expressed in the torments of hell. And the reason why they do not go down to hell at each moment, is not because God, in whose power they are, is not then very angry with them; as he is with many miserable creatures now tormented in hell, who there feel and bear the fierceness of his wrath. Yea, God is a great deal more angry with great numbers that are now on earth: yea, doubtless, with many that are now in this congregation, who it may be are at ease, than he is with many of those who are now in the flames of hell.

So that it is not because God is unmindful of their wickedness and does not resent it, that he does not let loose his hand and cut them off. God is not altogether such an one as themselves though they may imagine him to be so. The wrath of God burns against them, their damnation does not slumber; the pit is prepared, the fire is made ready, the furnace is now hot, ready to receive them; the flames do now rage and glow. The glittering sword is whet, and held over them, and the pit hath opened its mouth under them.

5. The *devil* stands ready to fall upon them, and seize them as his own, at what moment God shall permit him. They belong to him; he has their souls in his possession, and under his dominion. The scripture represents them as his goods, Luke xi. 12. The devils watch them; they are ever by them at their right hand; they stand waiting for them, like greedy hungry lions that see their prey, and expect to have it, but are for the present kept back. If God should withdraw his hand, by which they are restrained, they would in one moment fly upon their poor souls. The old serpent is gaping for them; hell opens its mouth wide to receive them; and if God should permit it, they would be hastily swallowed up and lost.

6. There are in the souls of wicked men those hellish *principles* reigning, that would presently kindle and flame out into hell fire, if it were not for God's restraints. There is laid in the very nature of carnal men, a foundation for the torments of hell. There are those corrupt principles, in reigning power in them, and in full possession of them, that are seeds of hell fire. These principles are active and powerful, exceeding violent in their nature, and if it were not for the restraining

hand of God upon them, they would soon break out, they would flame out after the same manner as the same corruptions, the same enmity does in the hearts of damned souls, and would beget the same torments as they do in them. The souls of the wicked are in scripture compared to the troubled sea, Isa, lvii. 20. For the present, God restrains their wickedness by his mighty power, as he does the raging waves of the troubled sea, saying, "Hitherto shalt thou come, but no further;"[2] but if God should withdraw that restraining power, it would soon carry all before it. Sin is the ruin and misery of the soul; it is destructive in its nature; and if God should leave it without restraint, there would need nothing else to make the soul perfectly miserable. The corruption of the heart of man is immoderate and boundless in its fury; and while wicked men live here, it is like fire pent up by God's restraints, whereas if it were let loose, it would set on fire the course of nature; and as the heart is now a sink of sin, so if sin was not restrained, it would immediately turn the soul into a fiery oven, or a furnace of fire and brimstone.

7. It is no security to wicked men for one moment, that there are no visible means of death at hand. It is no security to a natural man, that he is now in health, and that he does not see which way he should now immediately go out of the world by any accident, and that there is no visible danger in any respect in his circumstances. The manifold and continual experience of the world in all ages, shows this is no evidence, that a man is not on the very brink of eternity, and that the next step will not be into another world. The unseen, unthought-of ways and means of persons going suddenly out of the world are innumerable and inconceivable. Unconverted men walk over the pit of hell on a rotten covering, and there are innumerable places in this covering so weak that they will not bear their weight, and these places are not seen. The arrows of death fly unseen at noonday; the sharpest sight cannot discern them.[3] God has so many different unsearchable ways of taking wicked men out of the world and sending them to hell, that there is nothing to make it appear, that God had need to be at the expence of a miracle, or go out of the ordinary course of his providence, to destroy any wicked man, at any moment. All the means that there are of sinners going out of the world, are so in God's hands, and so universally and absolutely subject to his power and determination, that it does not depend at all the less on the mere will of God, whether sinners shall at any moment go to hell, than if means were never made use of, or at all concerned in the case.

8. Natural men's prudence and care to preserve their own lives, or the care of others to preserve them, do not secure them a moment. To this, divine providence and universal experience do also bear testimony. There is this clear evidence that men's own wisdom is no

security to them from death; that if it were otherwise we should see some difference between the wise and politic men of the world, and others, with regard to their liableness to early and unexpected death: but how is it in fact? Eccles. ii. 16. "How dieth the wise man? even as the fool."

9. All wicked men's pains and *contrivance* which they use to escape hell, while they continue to reject Christ, and so remain wicked men, do not secure them from hell one moment. Almost every natural man that hears of hell, flatters himself that he shall escape it; he depends upon himself for his own security; he flatters himself in what he has done, in what he is now doing, or what he intends to do. Every one lays out matters in his own mind how he shall avoid damnation, and flatters himself that he contrives well for himself, and that his schemes will not fail. They hear indeed that there are but few saved, and that the greater part of men that have died heretofore are gone to hell; but each one imagines that he lays out matters better for his own escape than others have done. He does not intend to come to that place of torment; he says within himself, that he intends to take effectual care, and to order matters so for himself as not to fail.

But the foolish children of men miserably delude themselves in their own schemes, and in confidence in their own strength and wisdom; they trust to nothing but a shadow. The greater part of those who heretofore have lived under the same means of grace, and are now dead, are undoubtedly gone to hell; and it was not because they were not as wise as those who are now alive: it was not because they did not lay out matters as well for themselves to secure their own escape. If we could speak with them, and inquire of them, one by one, whether they expected, when alive, and when they used to hear about hell, ever to be the subjects of that misery: we doubtless, should hear one and another reply, "No, I never intended to come here: I had laid out matters otherwise in my mind; I thought I should contrive well for myself: I thought my scheme good. I intended to take effectual care; but it came upon me unexpected; I did not look for it at that time, and in that manner; it came as a thief: Death outwitted me: God's wrath was too quick for me. Oh, my cursed foolishness! I was flattering myself, and pleasing myself with vain dreams of what I would do hereafter; and when I was sayin, Peace and safety, then suddenly destruction came upon me."

10. God has laid himself under *no obligation*, by any promise to keep any natural man out of hell one moment. God certainly has made no promises either of eternal life, or of any deliverance or preservation from eternal death, but what are contained in the covenant of grace, the promises that are given in Christ, in whom all the promises are yea and amen. But surely they have no interest in the promises of the

covenant of grace who are not the children of the covenant, who do not believe in any of the promises, and have no interest in the Mediator of the covenant.

So that, whatever some have imagined and pretended about promises made to natural men's earnest seeking and knocking, it is plain and manifest, that whatever pains a natural man takes in religion, whatever prayers he makes, till he believes in Christ, God is under no manner of obligation to keep him a moment from eternal destruction.

So that, thus it is that natural men are held in the hand of God, over the pit of hell; they have deserved the fiery pit, and are already sentenced to it; and God is dreadfully provoked, his anger is as great towards them as to those that are actually suffering the executions of the fierceness of his wrath in hell, and they have done nothing in the least to appease or abate that anger, neither is God in the least bound by any promise to hold them up one moment; the devil is waiting for them, hell is gaping for them, the flames gather and flash about them, and would fain lay hold on them, and swallow them up; the fire pent up in their own hearts is struggling to break out: and they have no interest in any Mediator, there are no means within reach that can be any security to them. In short, they have no refuge, nothing to take hold of; all that preserves them every moment is the mere arbitrary will, and uncovenanted, unobliged forbearance of an incensed God.

APPLICATION

The use of this awful subject may be for awakening unconverted persons in this congregation. This that you have heard is the case of every one of you that are out of Christ.—That world of misery, that lake of burning brimstone, is extended abroad under you. There is the dreadful pit of the glowing flames of the wrath of God; there is hell's wide gaping mouth open; and you have nothing to stand upon, nor any thing to take hold of; there is nothing between you and hell but the air; it is only the power and mere pleasure of God that holds you up.

You probably are not sensible of this; you find you are kept out of hell, but do not see the hand of God in it; but look at other things, as the good state of your bodily constitution, your care of your own life, and the means you use for your own preservation. But indeed these things are nothing; if God should withdraw his hand, they would avail no more to keep you from falling, than the thin air to hold up a person that is suspended in it.

Your wickedness makes you as it were heavy as lead, and to tend downwards with great weight and pressure towards hell; and if God should let you go, you would immediately sink and swiftly descend and plunge into the bottomless gulf, and your healthy constitution, and your own care and prudence, and best contrivance, and all your righteousness, would have no more influence to uphold you and keep you out of hell, than a spider's web would have to stop a fallen rock. Were it not for the sovereign pleasure of God, the earth would not bear you one moment; for you are a burden to it; the creation groans with you; the creature is made subject to the bondage of your corruption, not willingly; the sun does not willingly shine upon you to give you light to serve sin and Satan; the earth does not willingly yield her increase to satisfy your lusts; nor is it willingly a stage for your wickedness to be acted upon; the air does not willingly serve you for breath to maintain the flame of life in your vitals, while you spend your life in the service of God's enemies. God's creatures are good, and were made for men to serve God with, and do not willingly subserve to any other purpose, and groan when they are abused to purposes so directly contrary to their nature and end. And the world would spew you out, were it not for the sovereign hand of him who hath subjected it in hope. There are black clouds of God's wrath now hanging directly over your heads, full of the dreadful storm, and big with thunder; and were it not for the restraining hand of God, it would immediately burst forth upon you. The sovereign pleasure of God, for the present, stays his rough wind; otherwise it would come with fury, and your destruction would come like a whirlwind, and you would be like the chaff of the summer threshing floor.

The wrath of God is like great waters that are dammed for the present; they increase more and more, and rise higher and higher, till an outlet is given; and the longer the stream is stopped, the more rapid and mighty is its course, when once it is let loose. It is true, that judgment against your evil works has not been executed hitherto; the floods of God's vengeance have been withheld; but your guilt in the mean time is constantly increasing, and you are every day treasuring up more wrath; the waters are constantly rising, and waxing more and more mighty; and there is nothing but the mere pleasure of God, that holds the waters back, that are unwilling to be stopped, and press hard to go forward. If God should only withdraw his hand from the floodgate, it would immediately fly open, and the fiery floods of the fierceness and wrath of God, would rush forth with inconceivable fury, and would come upon you with omnipotent power; and if your strength were ten thousand times greater than it is, yea, ten thousand times greater than the strength of the stoutest, sturdiest devil in hell, it would be nothing to withstand or endure it.

The bow of God's wrath is bent, and the arrow made ready on the string, and justice bends the arrow at your heart, and strains the bow, and it is nothing but the mere pleasure of God, and that of an angry God, without any promise or obligation at all, that keeps the arrow one moment from being made drunk with your blood. Thus all you that never passed under a great change of heart, by the mighty power of the Spirit of God upon your souls; all you that were never born again, and made new creatures, and raised from being dead in sin, to a state of new, and before altogether unexperienced light and life, are in the hands of an angry God. However you may have reformed your life in many things, and may have had religious affections, and may keep up a form of religion in your families and closets, and in the house of God, it is nothing but his mere pleasure that keeps you from being this moment swallowed up in everlasting destruction. However unconvinced you may now be of the truth of what you hear, by and by you will be fully convinced of it. Those that are gone from being in the like circumstances with you, see that it was so with them; for destruction came suddenly upon most of them; when they expected nothing of it, and while they were saying, Peace and safety: now they see, that those things on which they depended for peace and safety, were nothing but thin air and empty shadows.

The God that holds you over the pit of hell, much as one holds a spider, or some loathsome insect over the first, abhors you, and is dreadfully provoked: his wrath towards you burns like fire; he looks upon you as worthy of nothing else, but to be cast into the fire; he is of purer eyes than to bear to have you in his sight; you are ten thousand times more abominable in his eyes, than the most hateful venomous serpent is in ours. You have offended him infinitely more than ever a stubborn rebel did his prince; and yet it is nothing but his hand that holds you from falling into the fire every moment. It is to be ascribed to nothing else, that you did not go to hell the last night; that you was suffered to awake again in this world, after you closed your eyes to sleep. And there is no other reason to be given, why you have not dropped into hell since you arose in the morning, but that God's hand has held you up. There is no other reason to be given why you have not gone to hell, since you have sat here in the house of God, provoking his pure eyes by your sinful wicked manner of attending his solemn worship. Yea, there is nothing else that is to be given as a reason why you do not this very moment drop down into hell.

O sinner! Consider the fearful danger you are in: it is a great furnace of wrath, a wide and bottomless pit, full of the fire of wrath, that you are held over in the hand of that God, whose wrath is provoked and incensed as much against you, as against many of the damned in hell. You hang by a slender thread, with the flames of divine wrath flashing about it, and ready every moment to singe it, and burn it asunder; and you have no interest in any Mediator, and nothing to lay hold of to save yourself, nothing to keep off the flames of wrath, nothing of your own, nothing that you ever have done, nothing that you can do, to induce God to spare you one moment.—And consider here more particularly,

1. *Whose* wrath it is: it is the wrath of the infinite God. If it were only the wrath of man, though it were of the most potent prince, it would be comparatively little to be regarded. The wrath of kings is very much dreaded, especially of absolute monarchs, who have the possessions and lives of their subjects wholly in their power, to be disposed of at their mere will. Prov. xx. 2. "The fear of a king is as the roaring of a lion: Whoso provoketh him to anger, sinneth against his own soul." The subject that very much enrages an arbitrary prince, is liable to suffer the most extreme torments that human art can invent, or human power can inflict. But the greatest earthly potentates in their greatest majesty and strength, and when clothed in their greatest terrors, are but feeble, despicable worms of the dust, in comparison of the great and almighty Creator and King of heaven and earth. It is but little that they can do, when most enraged, and when they have exerted the utmost of their fury. All the kings of the earth, before God, are as grasshoppers; they are nothing, and less than nothing: both their love and their hatred is to be despised. The wrath of the great King of kings, is as much more terrible than theirs, as his majesty is greater. Luke xii. 4, 5. "And I say unto you, my friends, Be not afraid of them that kill the body, and after that, have no more that they can do. But I will forewarn you whom you shall fear: fear him, which after he hath killed, hath power to cast into hell: yea, I say unto you, Fear him."

2. It is the *fierceness* of his wrath that you are exposed to. We often read of the fury of God; as in Isaiah lix. 18. "According to their deeds, accordingly he will repay fury to his adversaries." So Isaiah lxvi. 15. "For behold, the Lord will come with fire, and with his chariots like a whirlwind, to render his anger with fury, and his rebuke with flames of fire." And in many other places. So, Rev. xix. 15. we read of "the wine press of the fierceness and wrath of Almighty God." The words are exceeding terrible. If it had only been said, "the wrath of God," the words would have implied that which is infinitely dreadful: but it is "the fierceness and wrath of God." The fury of God! the fierceness of Jehovah! Oh, how dreadful must that be! Who can utter or conceive what such expressions carry in them! But it is also "the fierceness and wrath of *Almighty* God." As though there would be a very great manifestation of his almighty power in what the fierceness of his wrath should inflict, as though omnipotence should be as it were enraged, and exerted, as men are wont to exert their strength in the

fierceness of their wrath. Oh! then, what will be the consequence. What will become of the poor worms that shall suffer it! Whose hands can be strong? And whose heart can endure? To what a dreadful, inexpressible, inconceivable depth of misery must the poor creature be sunk who shall be the subject of this!

Consider this, you that are here present, that yet remain in an unregenerate state. That God will execute the fierceness of his anger, implies, that he will inflict wrath without any pity. When God beholds the ineffable extremity of your case, and sees your torment to be so vastly disproportioned to your strength, and sees how your poor soul is crushed, and sinks down, as it were, into an infinite gloom; he will have no compassion upon you, he will not forbear the executions of his wrath, or in the least lighten his hand; there shall be no moderation or mercy, nor will God then at all stay his rough wind; he will have no regard to your welfare, nor be at all careful lest you should suffer too much in any other sense, than only that you shall *not suffer beyond what strict justice requires.* Nothing shall be withheld, because it is so hard for you to bear. Ezek. viii. 18. "Therefore will I also deal in fury: mine eye shall not spare, neither will I have pity; and though they cry in mine ears with a loud voice, yet I will not hear them." Now God stands ready to pity you; this is a day of mercy; you may cry now with some encouragement of obtaining mercy. But when once the day of mercy is past, your most lamentable and dolorous cries and shrieks will be in vain; you will be wholly lost and thrown away of God, as to any regard to your welfare. God will have no other use to put you to, but to suffer misery; you shall be continued in being to no other end; for you will be a vessel of wrath fitted to destruction; and there will be no other use of this vessel, but to be filled full of wrath. God will be so far from pitying you when you cry to him, that it is said he will only "laugh and mock," Prov. i. 25, 26, &c.

How awful are those words, Isa. lxiii. 3, which are the words of the great God. "I will tread them in mine anger, and will trample them in my fury, and their blood shall be sprinkled upon my garments, and I will stain all my raiment." It is perhaps impossible to conceive of words that carry in them greater manifestations of these three things, *viz.* contempt, and hatred, and fierceness of indignation. If you cry to God to pity you, he will be so far from pitying you in your doleful case, or showing you the least regard or favour, that instead of that, he will only tread you under foot. And though he will know that you cannot bear the weight of omnipotence treading upon you, yet he will not regard that, but he will crush you under his feet without mercy: he will crush out your blood, and make it fly, and it shall be sprinkled on his garments, so as to stain all his raiment. He will not only hate you, but he will have you, in the utmost contempt: no place shall be thought fit for you, but under his feet to be trodden down as the mire of the streets.

3. The *misery* you are exposed to is that which God will inflict to that end, that he might show what that wrath of Jehovah is. God hath had it on his heart to show to angels and men, both how excellent his love is, and also how terrible his wrath is. Sometimes earthly kings have a mind to show how terrible their wrath is, by the extreme punishments they would execute on those that would provoke them. Nebuchadnezzar, that mighty and haughty monarch of the Chaldean empire, was willing to show his wrath when enraged with Shadrach, Meshech, and Abednego.⁴ and accordingly gave orders that the burning fiery furnace should be heated seven times hotter than it was before; doubtless, it was raised to the utmost degree of fierceness that human art could raise it. But the great God is also willing to show his wrath, and magnify his awful majesty and mighty power in the extreme sufferings of his enemies. Rom. ix. 22. "What if God, willing to show his wrath, and to make his power known, endure with much long-suffering the vessels of wrath fitted to destruction?" And seeing this is his design, and what he has determined, even to show how terrible the unrestrained wrath, the fury and fierceness of Jehovah is, he will do it to effect. There will be something accomplished and brought to pass that will be dreadful with a witness. When the great and angry God hath risen up and executed his awful vengeance on the poor sinner, and the wretch is actually suffering the infinite weight and power of his indignation, then will God call upon the whole universe to behold that awful majesty and mighty power that is to be seen in it. Isa. xxxiii. 12–14. "And the people shall be as the burnings of lime, as thorns cut up shall they be burnt in the fire. Hear ye that are far off, what I have done; and ye that are near, acknowledge my might. The sinners in Zion are afraid; fearfulness hath surprised the hypocrites," &c.

Thus it will be with you that are in an unconverted state, if you continue in it; the infinite might, and majesty, and terribleness of the omnipotent God shall be magnified upon you, in the ineffable strength of your torments. You shall be tormented in the presence of the holy angels, and in the presence of the Lamb; and when you shall be in this state of suffering, the glorious inhabitants of heaven shall go forth and look on the awful spectacle, that they may see what the wrath and fierceness of the Almighty is; and when they have seen it, they will fall down and adore that great power and majesty. Isa. lxvi. 23, 24. "And it shall come to pass, that from one new moon to another, and from one sabbath to another, shall all flesh come to worship before me, saith the Lord. And they shall go forth and look upon the carcasses of the men that have transgressed against me; for their worm shall not die, neither shall their fire be quenched, and they shall be an abhorring unto all flesh."

4. It is *everlasting* wrath. It would be dreadful to suffer this fierceness and wrath of Almighty God one moment; but you must suffer it to all eternity. There will be no end to this exquisite horrible misery. When you look forward, you shall see a long for ever, a boundless duration before you, which will swallow up your thoughts, and amaze your soul; and you will absolutely despair of ever having any deliverance, any end, any mitigation, any rest at all. You will know certainly that you must wear out long ages, millions of millions of ages, in wrestling and conflicting with this almighty merciless vengeance; and then when you have so done, when so many ages have actually been spent by you in this manner, you will know that all is but a point to what remains. So that your punishment will indeed be infinite. Oh, who can express what the state of a soul in such circumstances is! All that we can possibly say about it, gives but a very feeble, faint representation of it; it is inexpressible and inconceivable: For "who knows the power of God's anger?"⁵

How dreadful is the state of those that are daily and hourly in the danger of this great wrath and infinite misery! But this is the dismal case of every soul in this congregation that has not been born again, however moral and strict, sober and religious, they may otherwise be. Oh that you would consider it, whether you be young or old! There is reason to think, that there are many in this congregation now hearing this discourse, that will actually be the subjects of this very misery to all eternity. We know not who they are, or in what seats they sit, or what thoughts they now have. It may be they are now at ease, and hear all these things without much disturbance, and are now flattering themselves that they are not the persons, promising themselves that they shall escape. If we knew that there was one person, and but one, in the whole congregation, that was to be the subject of this misery, what an awful thing would it be to think of! If we knew who it was, what an awful sight would it be to see such a person! How might all the rest of the congregation lift up a lamentable and bitter cry over him! But, alas! instead of one, how many is it likely will remember this discourse in hell? And it would be a wonder, if some that are now present should not be in hell in a very short time, even before this year is out. And it would be no wonder if some persons, that now sit here, in some seats of this meeting-house, in health, quiet and secure, should be there before to-morrow morning. Those of you that finally continue in a natural condition, that shall keep out of hell longest will be there in a little time! your damnation does not slumber; it will come swiftly, and, in all probability, very suddenly upon many of you. You have reason to wonder that you are not already in hell. It is doubtless the case of some whom you have seen and known, that never deserved hell more than you, and that heretofore appeared as likely to have been now alive as you. Their case is past all hope; they are crying in extreme misery and perfect despair; but here you are in the land of the living and in the house of God, and have an opportunity to obtain salvation. What would not those poor damned hopeless souls give for one day's opportunity such as you now enjoy!

And now you have an extraordinary opportunity, a day wherein Christ has thrown the door of mercy wide open, and stands in calling and crying with a loud voice to poor sinners; a day wherein many are flocking to him, and pressing into the kingdom of God. Many are daily coming from the east, west, north and south; many that were very lately in the same miserable condition that you are in, are now in a happy state, with their hearts filled with love to him who has loved them, and washed them from their sins in his own blood, and rejoicing in hope of the glory of God. How awful is it to be left behind at such a day! To see so many others feasting, while you are pining and perishing! To see so many rejoicing and singing for joy of heart, while you have cause to mourn for sorrow of heart, and howl for vexation of spirit! How can you rest one moment in such a condition? Are not your souls as precious as the souls of the people at Suffield,[6] where they are flocking from day to day to Christ?

Are there not many here who have lived long in the world, and are not to this day born again? and so are aliens from the commonwealth of Israel, and have done nothing ever since they have lived, but treasure up wrath against the day of wrath? Oh, sirs, your case, in an especial manner, is extremely dangerous. Your guilt and hardness of heart is extremely great. Do you not see how generally persons of your years are passed over and left, in the present remarkable and wonderful dispensation of God's mercy? You had need to consider yourselves, and awake thoroughly out of sleep. You cannot bear the fierceness and wrath of the infinite God.—And you, young men, and young women, will you neglect this precious season which you now enjoy, when so many others of your age are renouncing all youthful vanities, and flocking to Christ? You especially have now an extraordinary opportunity; but if you neglect it, it will soon be with you as with those persons who spent all the precious days of youth in sin, and are now come to such a dreadful pass in blindness and hardness.—And you, children, who are unconverted, do not you know that you are going down to hell, to bear the dreadful wrath of that God, who is now angry with you every day and every night? Will you be content to be the children of the devil, when so many other children in the land are converted, and are become the holy and happy children of the King of kings?

And let every one that is yet of Christ, and hanging over the pit of hell, whether they be old men and women, or middle aged, or young people, or little children, now hearken to the loud calls of God's word and providence. This acceptable year of the Lord, a day of such great favours to some, will doubtless be a day of as remarkable vengeance to others. Men's hearts harden, and their guilt increases apace at such a day as this, if they neglect their souls; and never was there so great danger of such persons being given up to hardness of heart and blindness of mind. God seems now to be hastily gathering in his elect in all parts of the land: and probably the greater part of adult persons that ever shall be saved, will be brought in now in a little time, and that it will be as it was on the great out-pouring of the Spirit upon the Jews in the apostles' days; the election will obtain, and the rest will be blinded. If this should be the case with you, you will eternally curse this day, and will curse the day that ever you was born, to see such a season of the pouring out of God's Spirit, and will wish that you had died and gone to hell before you had seen it. Now undoubtedly it is, as it was in the days of John the Baptist, the axe is in an extraordinary manner laid at the root of the trees, that every tree which brings not forth good fruit, may be hewn down and cast into the fire.[7]

Therefore, let every one that is out of Christ, now awake and fly from the wrath to come. The wrath of Almighty God is now undoubtedly hanging over a great part of this congregation: Let every one fly out of Sodom: "Haste and escape for your lives, look not behind you, escape to the mountain, lest you be consumed."[8]

from *A Treatise Concerning Religious Affections (1746)*

1 PETER i. 8: *Whom having not seen, ye love; in whom though now ye see him not, yet believing, ye rejoice with joy unspeakable and full of glory.*

SECT. I.
INTRODUCTORY REMARKS RESPECTING THE AFFECTIONS

In these words, the apostle represents the state of the Christians to whom he wrote, under persecutions. To these persecutions he has respect, in the two preceding verses, when he speaks of *the trial of their faith*, and of *their being in heaviness through manifold temptations*.

Such *trials* are of threefold benefit to true religion. Hereby the *truth* of it is manifested, it appears to be indeed *true religion*. Trials, above all other things, have a tendency to distinguish true religion and false, and to cause the difference between them evidently to appear. Hence they are called by the name of *trials*, in the verse preceding the text, and innumerable other places.—They try the faith and religion of professors, of what sort it is, as apparent gold is tried in the fire, and manifested, whether it be true gold or not. And the faith of true Christians, being thus tried and proved to be true, is *found to praise, and honour, and glory*.

And then, these trials not only manifest the *truth* of true religion, but they make its genuine *beauty* and *amiableness* remarkably to appear. True virtue never appears so lovely, as when it is most oppressed: and the divine excellency of real Christianity, is never exhibited with such advantage, as when under the greatest trials. Then it is that true faith appears much more precious than gold; and upon this account, is *found to praise, and honour, and glory*.

Again, another benefit of such trials to true religion, is that they *purify* and *increase* it. They not only manifest it to be *true*, but also tend to *refine* it, and deliver it from those mixtures of what is false, which encumber and impede it; that nothing may be left but that which is true. They not only shew the amiableness of true religion to the best advantage, but they tend to increase its beauty by establishing and confirming it; making it more lively and vigourous, and purifying it from those things that obscured its lustre and glory. As gold that is tried in the fire is purged from its alloy, and all remainders of dross, and comes forth more beautiful; so true faith being tried as gold is tried in the fire, becomes more precious; and thus also is *found unto praise, and honour, and glory*. The apostle seems to have respect to each of these benefits in the verse preceding the text.

And, in the text, the apostle observes how true religion *operated* in these Christians under their persecitions, whereby these benefits appeared in them; or what manner of operation it was, whereby their religion, under persecution, was manifested to be *true* religion in its genuine *beauty* and *amiableness*, and also appeared to be *increased* and *purified*, and so was like to be *found unto praise, and honour, and glory, at the appearing of Jesus Christ*. And there were two kinds of operation, or exercise of true religion, in them, under their sufferings, that the apostle takes notice of in the text, wherein these benefits appeared.

1. *Love to Christ. Whom having not seen, ye love.* The world was ready to wonder, what strange principle it was, that influenced them

to expose themselves to so great sufferings, to forsake the things that were seen, and renounce all that was dear and pleasant, which was the object of sense. They seemed to the men of the world as if they were beside themselves, and to act as though they hated themselves; there was nothing in *their* view, that could induce them thus to suffer, or to support them under, and carry them through such trials. But although there was nothing that the world saw, or that the Christians themselves ever saw with their bodily eyes, that thus influenced and supported them, yet they had a supernatural principle of love to something *unseen*; they loved Jesus Christ, for they saw him spiritually, whom the world saw not, and whom they themselves had never seen with bodily eyes.

2. *Joy in Christ.* Though their outward sufferings were very grevious, yet their inward spiritual joys were greater than their sufferings; and these supported them, and enabled them to suffer with cheerfulness.

There are two things which the apostle takes notice of in the text concerning this joy. 1. The manner in which it rises, the way in which Christ, though unseen, is the foundation of it, *viz.* by *faith*; which is the evidence of things not seen; *In whom, though now ye see him not, yet* BELIEVING, *ye rejoice.* 2. The *nature* of this joy; *unspeakable, and full of glory. Unspeakable* in the *kind* of it; very different from worldly joys, and carnal delights; of a vastly more pure, sublime, and heavenly nature, being something supernatural, and truly divine, and so ineffably excellent! the sublimity and exquisite sweetness of which, there were no words to set forth. Unspeakable also in *degree*; it having pleased God to give them this holy joy with a liberal hand, in their state of persecution.

Their joy was *full of glory.* Although the joy was unspeakable, and no words were sufficient to describe it; yet something might be said of it, and no words more fit to represent its excellency than these, that it was *full of glory*; or, as it is in the original, *glorified joy.* In rejoicing with this joy, their minds were filled, as it were, with a glorious brightness, and their natures exalted and perfected. It was a most worthy, noble rejoicing, that did not corrupt and debase the mind, as many carnal joys do; but did greatly beautify and dignify it. It was a prelibation of the joy of heaven, that raised their minds to a degree of heavenly blessedness; it filled their minds with the light of God's glory, and made themselves to shine with some communication of that glory.

Hence the proposition or doctrine, that I would raise from these words is this, TRUE RELIGION, IN GREAT PART, CONSISTS IN HOLY AFFECTIONS.

We see that the apostle, in remarking the operations and exercises of religion in these Christians, when it had its greatest trial by persecution, as gold is tried in the fire—and when it not only proved true, but was most pure from dross and mixtures—and when it appeared in them most in its genuine excellency and native beauty, and was found to praise, and honour, and glory—he singles out the religious affections of *love* and *joy*, as those exercises, wherein their religion did thus appear *true, pure* and *glorious*.

Here it may be inquired, what the *affections* of the mind are?— I answer, The affections are no other than the more vigorous and *sensible exercises of the inclination and will* of the soul.

God has endued the soul with two principal faculties: The one, that by which it is capable of *perception* and speculation, or by which it discerns, and judges of things; which is called the *understanding*. The other, that by which the soul is some way *inclined* with respect to the things it views or considers: or it is the faculty by which the soul beholds things—not as an indifferent unaffected spectator, but— either as liking or disliking, pleased or displeased, approving or rejecting. This faculty is called by various names: it is sometimes called the *inclination*; and, as it respects the actions determined and governed by it, the *will*: and the *mind*, with regard to the exercises of this faculty, is often called the *heart*.

The *exercises* of this last faculty are of two sorts; either those by which the soul is carried out towards the things in view in *approving* them, being pleased with, and inclined to them; or, those in which the soul opposes the things in view, in *disapproving* them; and in being displeased with, averse from, and rejecting them. And as the exercises of the inclination are various in their *kinds*, so they are much more various in their *degrees*. There are some exercises of pleasedness or displeasedness, inclination or disinclination, wherein the soul is carried but a little beyond a state of perfect indifference. And there are other degrees, wherein the approbation or dislike, pleasedness or aversion, are stronger; wherein we may rise higher and higher, till the soul comes to act vigorously and sensibly, and its actings are with that strength, that (through the laws of union which the Creator has fixed between soul and body) the motion of the blood and animal spirits begins to be sensibly altered: whence oftentimes arises some bodily sensation, especially about the *heart* and vitals, which are the fountain of the fluids of the body. Whence it comes to pass, that the *mind*, with regard to the exercises of this faculty, perhaps in all nations and ages, is called *the heart*. And it is to be noted, that they are these more vigorous and sensible exercises of this faculty, which are called the *affections*.

The *will*, and the *affections* of the soul, are not two faculties; the affections are not essentially distinct from the will, nor do they differ from the mere *actings* of the will and inclination, but only in the liveliness and sensibility of exercise.—It must be confessed, that language is here somewhat imperfect, the meaning of words in a considerable measure loose and unfixed, and not precisely limited by custom which governs the use of language. In some sense, the affection of the soul differs nothing at all from the will and inclination, and the will never is in any exercise further than it is *affected*; it is not moved out of a state of perfect indifference, any otherwise than as it is *affected* one way or another. But yet there are many actings of the will and inclination, that are not so commonly called *affections*. In every thing we do, wherein we act voluntarily, there is an exercise of the will and inclination. It is our inclination that governs us in our actions; but *all the actings* of the inclination and will, are not ordinarily called affections. Yet, what are commonly called affections are not essentially different from them, but only in the *degree* and *manner* of exercise. In every act of the will whatsoever, the soul either likes or dislikes, is either inclined or disinclined to what is in view. These are not *essentially* different from the affections of *love* and *hatred*. A liking or inclination of the soul to a thing, if it be in a high degree vigorous and lively, is the very same thing with the affection of *love*: and a disliking and disinclining, if in a great degree, is the very same with *hatred*. In every act of the will *for,* or *towards* something not present, the soul is in some degree *inclined* to that thing; and that inclination, if in a considerable degree, is the very same with the affection of *desire*. And in every degree of an act of the will, wherein the soul approves of something present, there is a degree of pleasedness; and that pleasedness, if it be in a considerable degree, is the very same with the affection of *joy* or *delight*. And if the will disapproves of what is present, the soul is in some degree displeased, and if that displeasedness be great, it is the very same with the affection of *grief* or *sorrow*.

Such seems to be our nature, and such the laws of the union of soul and body, that there never is in any case whatsoever, any lively and vigorous exercise of the inclination, without some effect upon the body, in some alteration of the motion of its fluids, and especially of the animal spirits. And, on the other hand, from the same laws of union, over the consitution of the body, and the motion of its fluids, may promote the exercise of the affections. But yet, it is not the body, but the mind only, that is the proper seat of the affections. The body of man is no more capable of being really the subject of love or hatred, joy or sorrow, fear or hope, than the body of a tree, or than the same body of man is capable of thinking and understanding. As it is the soul only that has ideas, so it is the soul only that is pleased or displeased with its ideas. As it is the soul only that thinks, so it is the soul only that loves or hates, rejoices or is grieved at what it thinks of. Nor are these motions of the animal spirits, and fluids of the body, any thing properly belonging to the *nature* of the affections; though

they always *accompany* them in the present state; but are only effects
or concomitants of the affections, which are entirely distinct from the
affections themselves, and no way essential to them; so that an un-
bodied spirit may be as capable of love and hatred, joy or sorrow,
hope or fear, or other affections, as one that is united to a body.

The *affections* and *passions* are frequently spoken of as the same;
and yet, in the more common use of speech, there is in some respect
a difference. *Affection* is a word, that in its ordinary signification,
seems to be something more extensive than *passion*, being used for all
vigorous lively actings of the will or inclination; but *passion* is used
for those that are more sudden, and whose effects on the animal spirits
are more violent, the mind being more overpowered, and less in its
own command.

As all the exercises of inclination and will are concerned either in
approving and liking, or disapproving and rejecting; so the affections
are of two sorts; they are those by which the soul is carried out to
what is in view, cleaving *to* it, or *seeking* it; or those by which it is
averse *from* it, and *opposes* it. Of the former sort are *love, desire,
hope, joy, gratitude, complacence.* Of the latter kind, are *hatred, fear,
anger, grief,* and such like; which it is needless now to stand particularly to define.

And there are some affections wherein there is a *composition* of
each of the aforementioned kinds of actings of the will; as in the affection of *pity*, there is something of the *former kind*, towards the
person suffering, and something of the *latter*, towards what he suffers.
And so in *zeal*, there is in it high *approbation* of some person or thing,
together with vigorous *opposition* to what is conceived to be contrary
to it.

SEC. II.
TRUE RELIGION, IN GREAT PART,
CONSISTS IN THE AFFECTIONS

1. What has been said of the *nature* of the affections makes this evident; and may be sufficient, without adding any thing further, to put
this matter out of doubt; for who will deny that true religion consists,
in a great measure, in vigorous and lively actings of the *inclination*
and *will* of the soul, or the fervent exercises of the *heart*? That religion
which God requires, and will accept, does not consist in weak, dull,
and lifeless wishes, raising us but a little above a state of indifference.
God, in his word, greatly insists upon it, that we be in good earnest,
fervent in spirit, and our hearts vigorously engaged in religion: Rom.

xii. 11. *Be ye fervent in spirit, serving the Lord.* Deut. x. 12. *And now Israel, what doth the Lord thy God require of thee, but to fear the Lord the God, to walk in all his ways, and to love him, and to serve the Lord thy God with all thy heart, and with all thy soul?* And chap. vi. 4, 5. *Hear, O Israel, the Lord our God is one Lord; and thou shalt love the Lord thy God with all thy heart, and with all thy soul, and with all thy might.* It is such a fervent, vigorous engagedness of the heart in religion, that is the fruit of a real circumcision of the heart, or true regeneration, and that has the promises of life; Deut. xxx. 6. *And the Lord thy God will circumcise thine heart, and the heart of thy seed, to love the Lord thy God with all thy heart, and with all thy soul, that thou mayest live.*

If we be not in good earnest in religion, and our wills and inclinations be not strongly exercised, we are nothing. The things of religion are so great, that there can be no suitableness in the exercises of our hearts, to their nature and importance, unless they be lively and powerful. In nothing is vigour in the actings of our inclinations so requisite, as in religion; and in nothing is lukewarmness so odious. True religion is evermore a powerful thing; and the power of it appears, in the first place, in its exercises in the heart, its principal and original seat. Hence true religion is called the *power of godliness*, in distinction from external appearances, which are *the form* of it, 2 Tim. iii. 5. *Having a form of godliness, but denying the power of it*. The Spirit of God, in those who have sound and solid religion, is a spirit of powerful holy affection; and, therefore, God is said *to have given them the Spirit of power, and of love, and of a sound mind*, (2 Tim. i. 7.) And such, when they receive the Spirit of God in his sanctifying and saving influences, are said to be *baptized with the Holy Ghost, and with fire*; by reason of the power and fervour of those exercises which the Spirit of God excites in them, and whereby *their hearts*, when grace is in exercise, may be said to *burn within them*. (Luke xxiv. 32.)

The business of *religion* is, from time to time, compared to those *exercises*, wherein men are wont to have their hearts and strength greatly exercised and engaged; such as running, wrestling or agonizing for a great prize or crown, and fighting with strong enemies that seek our lives, and warring as those that by violence take a city or kingdom. Though true grace has various degrees, and there are some who are but babes in Christ, in whom the exercise of the inclination and will towards divine and heavenly things, is comparatively weak; yet every one that has the power of godliness, has his inclinations and heart exercised towards God and divine things with such strength and vigour, that these holy exercises prevail in him above all carnal or natural affections, and are effectual to overcome them; for every true disciple

of Christ, *loves him above father or mother, wife and children, brethren and sisters, houses and lands, yea more than his own life.* Hence
it follows, that wherever true religion is, there are vigorous exercises
of the inclination and will towards divine objects: but by what was
said before, the vigorous, lively, and sensible exercises of the will, are
no other than the *affections* of the soul.

2. The Author of our nature has not only given us affections, but
has made them very much the spring of actions. As the *affections* not
only necessarily belong to the *human nature*, but are a very *great part*
of it; so (inasmuch as by regeneration persons are renewed in the whole
man) *holy affections* not only necessarily belong to *true religion*, but
are a very great part of such religion. And as true religion is practical,
and God hath so constituted the human nature, that the affections are
very much the spring of men's actions, this also shews, that true religion must consist very much in the affections.

Such is man's nature, that he is very inactive, any otherwise than
he is influenced by either *love* or *hatred, desire, hope, fear*, or some
other affection. These affections we see to be the moving springs in all
the affairs of life, which engage men in all their pursuits; and especially
in all affairs wherein they are earnestly engaged, and which they pursue with vigour. We see the world of mankind exceedingly busy and
active; and their affections are the springs of motion; take away all
love and *hatred*, all *hope* and *fear*, all *anger, zeal*, and affectionate
desire, and the world would be, in a great measure, motionless and
dead: there would be no such thing as activity amongst mankind, or
any earnest pursuit whatsoever. It is affection that engages the covet-
ous man, and him that is greedy of worldly profits; it is by the affections that the ambitious man is put forward in his pursuit of worldly
glory; and the affections also actuate the voluptuous man, in his pleasure and sensual delights. The world continues, from age to age, in a
continual commotion and agitation, in pursuit of these things; but take
away affection, and the *spring* of all this motion would be gone; the
motion itself would cease. And as in worldly things, worldly affections
are very much the spring of men's motion and action; so in religious
matters, the spring of their actions are very much religious affections:
he that has doctrinal knowledge and speculation only, without affection, never is *engaged* in the business of religion.

3. Nothing is more manifest *in fact*, than that the things of religion take hold of men's souls no further than they *affect* them. There
are multitudes who often hear the word of God, things infinitely great
and important, and which most nearly concern them, yet all seems to
be wholly ineffectual upon them, and to make no alteration in their
disposition or behaviour; the reason is, they are not *affected* with what

they hear. There are many who often hear of the glorious perfections of God, his almighty power, boundless wisdom, infinite majesty, and that holiness by which he is of purer eyes than to behold evil, and cannot look on iniquity; together with his infinite goodness and mercy. They hear of the great works of God's wisdom, power, and goodness, wherein there appear the admirable manifestations of these perfections. They hear particularly of the unspeakable love of God and Christ, and what Christ has done and suffered. They hear of the great things of another world, of eternal misery, in bearing the fierceness and wrath of almighty God; and of endless blessedness and glory in the presence of God, and the enjoyment of his love. They also hear the peremptory commands of God, his gracious counsels and warnings, and the sweet invitations of the gospel. Yet they remain as before, with no sensible alteration, either in heart or practice, because they are not affected with what they hear. I am bold to assert, that there never was any considerable change wrought in the mind or conversation of any person, by any thing of a religious nature that ever he read, heard or saw, who had not his affections moved. Never was a natural man engaged earnestly to seek his salvation; never were any such brought to cry after wisdom, and lift up their voice for understanding, and to wrestle with God in prayer for mercy; and never was one humbled, and brought to the foot of God, from any thing that ever he heard or imagined of his own unworthiness and deservings of God's displeasure: nor was ever one induced to fly for refuge unto Christ, while his heart remained *unaffected*. Nor was there ever a saint awakened out of a cold, lifeless frame, or recovered from a declining state in religion, and brought back from a lamentable departure from God, without having his heart *affected*. And, in a word, there never was any thing *considerable* brought to pass in the heart or life of any man living, by the things of religion, that had not his heart *deeply affected* by those things.

4. The holy scriptures every where place religion very much in the affections; such as fear, hope, love, hatred, desire, joy, sorrow, gratitude, compassion, and zeal.

The scriptures place much of religion in godly *fear*; insomuch that an experience of it is often spoken of as the character of those who are truly religious persons. *They tremble at God's word, they fear before him, their flesh trembles for fear of him, they are afraid of his judgments, his excellency makes them afraid, and his dread falls upon them, & c.* An appellation commonly given the saints in scripture, is, *fearers of God*, or *they that fear the Lord*. And because this is a great part of true godliness, hence true godliness in general is very commonly called *the fear of God*.

So *hope* in God, and in the promises of his word, is often spoken of in the scripture, as a very considerable *part of true religion*. It is mentioned as one of the three great things of which religion consists, 1 Cor. xiii. 13. Hope in the Lord is also frequently mentioned as the *character of the saints*: Psal. cxlvi. 5. *Happy is he that hath the God of Jacob for his help, whose* HOPE *is in the Lord his God*. Jer. xvii. 7. *Blessed is the man that trusteth in the Lord, and whose* HOPE *the Lord is*. Psal. xxxi 24. *Be of good courage, and he shall strengthen your heart, all ye that* HOPE *in the Lord*. And the like in many other places. Religious fear and hope are, once and again, joined together, as jointly constituting the character of the true saints; Psal. xxxiii. 18. *Behold, the eye of the Lord is upon them that* FEAR *him, upon them that* HOPE *in his mercy*. Psal. cxlvii. 11. *The Lord taketh pleasure in them that* FEAR *him, in those that* HOPE *in his mercy*. Hope is so great a part of true religion, that the apostle says *we are saved by* HOPE, Rom. viii. 24. And this is spoken of as *the helmet* of the Christian soldier, 1 Thess. v. 8. *And for an helmet the* HOPE *of salvation*; and the sure and steadfast *anchor* of the soul, which preserves it from being cast away by the storms of this evil world, Heb. vi. 19. *Which* HOPE *we have as an anchor of the soul, both sure and steadfast, and which entereth into that within the veil*. It is spoken of as a great benefit which true saints receive by Christ's resurrection, 1 Pet. i. 3. *Blessed by the God and Father of our Lord Jesus Christ, which, according to his abundant mercy, hath begotten us again unto a lively* HOPE, *by the resurrection of Jesus Christ from the dead*.

The scriptures place religion very much in the affection of *love*; love to God, and the Lord Jesus Christ; love to the people of God, and to mankind. The texts in which this is manifest, both in the Old Testament and New, are innumerable. But of this more afterwards. . . .

from *The Nature of True Virtue (1765)*

CHAPTER I.
SHEWING WHEREIN THE ESSENCE OF
TRUE VIRTUE CONSISTS.

Whatever controversies and variety of opinions there are about the nature of virtue, yet all (excepting some sceptics, who deny any real difference between virtue and vice) mean by it, something *beautiful*, or rather some kind of *beauty*, or excellency. . . . It is not *all* beauty, that is called virtue; for instance, not the beauty of a building, of a flower, or of the rainbow: But some beauty belonging to Beings that have *perception* and *will*. . . . It is not all beauty of *mankind*, that is called virtue; for instance, not the external beauty of the countenance, or shape, gracefulness of motion, or harmony of voice: But it is a beauty that has its original seat in the mind. . . . But yet perhaps not *every* thing that may be called a beauty of mind, is properly called virtue. There is a beauty of understanding and speculation. There is something in the ideas and conceptions of great philosophers and statesmen, that may be called beautiful; which is a different thing from what is most commonly meant by virtue. But virtue is the beauty of those qualities and acts of the mind, that are of a *moral* nature, i. e. such as are attended with desert or worthiness of *praise*, or *blame*. Things of this sort, it is generally agreed, so far as I know, are not any thing belonging merely to speculation; but to the *disposition* and *will*, or (to use a general word, I suppose commonly well understood) the *heart*. Therefore I suppose, I shall not depart from the common opinion, when I say, that virtue is the beauty of the qualities and exercises of the heart, or those actions which proceed from them. So that when it is inquired, what is the nature of true *virtue*? This is the same as to inquire, what that is which renders any habit, disposition, or exercise of the heart truly *beautiful*? I use the phrase *true* virtue, and speak of things *truly* beautiful, because I suppose it will generally be allowed, that there is a distinction to be made between some things which are truly virtuous, and others which only seem to be virtuous, through a partial and imperfect view of things: That some actions and dispositions appear beautiful, if considered partially and superficially, or with regard to some things belonging to them, and in some of their circumstances and tendencies, which would appear otherwise in a more extensive and comprehensive view, wherein they are seen clearly in their whole nature and the extent of their connexions in the universality of things. . . . There is a general and a particular beauty. By a *particular* beauty, I mean that by which a thing appears beautiful when considered only with regard to its connexion with, and tendency to some particular things within a limited, and as it were, a private sphere. And a *general* beauty is that by which a thing appears beautiful when viewed most perfectly, comprehensively and universally, with regard to all its tendencies, and its connexions with every thing it stands related to. . . . The former may be without and against the latter. As, a few notes in a tune, taken only by themselves, and in their relation to one another, may be harmonious; which, when considered with respect to all the notes in the tune, or the entire series of sounds, they are connected with, may be very discordant and disagreeable. (Of which more afterwards). . . . *That only* therefore, is what I mean by true virtue, which is *that*, belonging to the *heart* of an intelligent Being, that is beautiful by a *general* beauty, or beautiful in a comprehensive view as it is in itself, and as related to every thing that it stands in connexion with. And therefore when we are inquiring concerning the nature of true virtue, viz. wherein this true and general beauty of the heart does most essentially consist. . . . this is my answer to the inquiry. . . .

True virtue most essentially consists in benevolence to Being in general. Or perhaps to speak more accurately, it is that consent, propensity and union of heart to Being in general, that is immediately exercised in a general good will.

The things which were before observed of the nature of true virtue, naturally lead us to such a notion of it. If it has its seat in the heart, and is the general goodness and beauty of the disposition and exercise of that, in the most comprehensive view, considered with regard to its universal tendency, and as related to every thing that it stands in connexion with; what can it consist in, but a consent and good will to being in general?. . . . Beauty does not consist in discord and dissent, but in consent and agreement. And if every intelligent Being is some way related to Being in general, and is a part of the universal system of existence; and so stands in connexion with the whole; what can its general and true beauty be, but its union and consent with the great whole.

If any such thing can be supposed as an union of heart to some particular Being, or number of Beings, disposing it to benevolence to a private circle or system of Beings, which are but a small part of the whole; not implying a tendency to an union with the great system, and not at all inconsistent with enmity towards Being in general; this I suppose not to be of the nature of true virtue: Although it may in some respects be good, and may appear beautiful in a confined and contracted view of things. . . . But of this more afterwards.

It is abundantly plain by the holy scriptures, and generally allowed, not only by Christian divines, but by the more considerable deists,[1] that virtue most essentially consists in love. And I suppose, it is owned by the most considerable writers, to consist in general love of benevolence, or kind affection: Though it seems to me, the meaning of some in this affair is not sufficiently explained which perhaps occasions some error or confusion in discourses on this subject.

When I say, true virtue consists in love to being in general, I shall not be likely to be understood, that no one act of the mind or exercise of love is of the nature of true virtue, but what has Being in general, or the great system of universal existence, for its direct and immediate object: So that no exercise of love or kind affection to any one particular Being, that is but a small part of this whole, has any thing of the nature of true virtue. But, that the nature of true virtue consists in a disposition to benevolence towards Being in general. Though, from such a disposition may arise exercises of love to particular Beings, as objects are presented and occasions arise. No wonder, that he who is of a generally benevolent disposition, should be more disposed than another to have his heart moved with benevolent affection to particular persons, whom he is acquainted and conversant with, and from whom arise the greatest and most frequent occasions for exciting his benevolent temper. But my meaning is, that no affections towards particular persons, or Beings, are of the nature of true virtue, but such as arise from a generally benevolent temper, or from that habit or frame of mind, wherein consists a disposition to love Being in general.

And perhaps it is needless for me to give notice to my readers, that when I speak of an intelligent Being's having a heart united and benevolently disposed to Being in general, I thereby mean *intelligent* Being in general. Not inanimate things, or Beings that have no perception or will, which are not properly capable objects of benevolence.

Love is commonly distinguished into love of benevolence and love of complacence. Love of *benevolence* is that affection or propensity of the heart to any Being, which causes it to incline to its well being, or disposes it to desire and take pleasure in its happiness. And if I mistake not, it is agreeable to the common opinion, that beauty in the object is not always the ground of this propensity: But that there may be such a thing as benevolence, or a disposition to the welfare of those that are not considered as beautiful; unless mere existence be accounted a beauty. And benevolence or goodness in the divine Being is generally supposed, not only to be prior to the beauty of many of its objects, but to their existence: So as to be the ground both of their existence and their beauty, rather than they the foundation of God's benevolence; as it is supposed that it is God's goodness which moved him to give them both Being and beauty. So that if all virtue primarily consists in that affection of heart to Being, which is exercised in benevolence, or an inclination to its good, then God's virtue is so extended as to include a propensity, not only to Being actually existing, and actually beautiful, but to possible Being, so as to incline him to give Being, beauty and happiness. But not now to insist particularly on this. What I would have observed at present, is, that it must be allowed, benevolence doth not necessarily presuppose beauty in its object.

What is commonly called love of *complacence*, presupposes beauty. For it is no other than delight in beauty; or complacence in the person or Being beloved for his beauty.

If virtue be the beauty of an intelligent Being, and virtue consists in love, then it is a plain inconsistence, to suppose that virtue primarily consists in any love to its object *for its beauty*; either in a love of complacence, which is delight in a Being for his beauty, or in a love of benevolence, that has the beauty of its object for its foundation. For that would be to suppose, that the beauty of intelligent Beings primarily consists in love to beauty; or, that their virtue first of all consists in their love to virtue. Which is an inconsistence, and going in a circle. Because it makes virtue, or beauty of mind, the foundation or first motive of that love wherein virtue originally consists, or wherein the very first virtue consists; or, it supposes the first virtue to be the consequence and effect of virtue. So that virtue is originally the foundation and exciting cause of the very beginning or first Being of virtue. Which makes the first virtue, both the ground, and the consequence, both cause and effect of itself. Doubtless virtue primarily consists in something else besides any effect or consequence of virtue. If virtue consists primarily in love to virtue, then virtue, the thing loved, is the love of virtue: So that virtue must consist in the love of the love of virtue. And if it be inquired, what that virtue is, which virtue consists in the love of the love of, it must be answered, it is the love of virtue. So that there must be the love of the love of the love of virtue, and so on *in infinitum*. For there is no end of going back in a circle. We never come to any beginning, or foundation. For it is without beginning and hangs on nothing.

Therefore if the essence of virtue or beauty of mind lies in love, or a disposition to love, it must primarily consist in something *different* both from complacence, which is a delight in beauty, and also from any benevolence that has the beauty of its object for its foundation. Because it is absurd, to say that virtue is primarily and first of all the consequence of itself. For this makes virtue primarily prior to itself.

Nor can virtue primarily consist in *gratitude*; or one Being's benevolence to another for his benevolence to him. Because this implies the same inconsistence. For it supposes a benevolence prior to gratitude, that is the cause of gratitude. Therefore the first benevolence, or that benevolence which has none prior to it, cannot be gratitude.

Therefore there is room left for no other conclusion than that the primary object of virtuous love is Being, simply considered; or, that true virtue primarily consists, not in love to any particular Beings, because of their virtue or beauty, nor in gratitude, because they love us; but in a propensity and union of heart to Being simply considered; exciting absolute benevolence (if I may so call it) to Being in general. . . . I say, true virtue *primarily* consists in this.

CHAPTER II.

SHEWING HOW THAT LOVE, WHEREIN TRUE VIRTUE CONSISTS, RESPECTS THE DIVINE BEING AND CREATED BEINGS.

From what has been said, it is evident, that true virtue must chiefly consist in love to God; the Being of Beings, infinitely the greatest and best of Beings. This appears, whether we consider the primary or secondary ground of virtuous love. It was observed, that the *first* objective ground of that love, wherein true virtue consists, is Being, simply considered: And as a necessary consequence of this, that Being who has the most of Being, or the greatest share of universal existence, has proportionably the greatest share of virtuous benevolence, so far as such a Being is exhibited to the faculties of our minds, other things being equal. But God has infinitely the greatest share of existence, or is infinitely the greatest Being. So that all other Being, even that of all created things whatsoever, throughout the whole universe, is as nothing in comparison of the divine Being.

And if we consider the *secondary* ground of love, viz. beauty, or moral excellency, the same thing will appear. For as God is infinitely the greatest Being, so he is allowed to be infinitely the most beautiful and excellent: And all the beauty to be found throughout the whole creation, is but the reflection of the diffused beams of that Being who hath an infinite fulness of brightness and glory. . . .

Benjamin Franklin
(1706–1790)

No figure from the past seems quite so thoroughly American as Benjamin Franklin. An apostle of the Protestant work ethic and a precursor of Ralph Waldo Emerson's image of the self-reliant individual, Franklin seems the epitome of the self-made man and thus one of the classic American types. But this printer turned businessman, inventor, maxim-maker, humorist, scientist, statesman, autobiographer, student of manners, nation-builder, and philosopher, whose spectacular financial success permitted him to retire at the age of forty so that he could devote the rest of his life to public service and private intellectual pursuits, was far more various and complex than he is usually credited with being. Yankee entrepreneur, Puritan workaholic, free-thinking Deist, Enlightenment moralist, and experimental scientist: Franklin has been called all these things and much more, but he may well remain most himself in his capacity to elude any simple—or, for that matter, compound—definition. In his novel Israel Potter, Herman Melville probably came closest to capturing something of the distinctiveness of Franklin by describing him simply as a "Jack of all trades, master of each and mastered by none—the type and genius of this land."

The various selections reprinted here—which include Franklin's Preface to the twenty-fifth edition of his immensely popular book of advice on how, among other things, to become wealthy (as a precondition, Franklin would have added, to pursuing the nature of true virtue), his realistic assessment of what might recommend America to prospective settlers, his speech to the Constitutional Convention of 1787 urging a spirit of compromise as a recognition of human fallibility, the Autobiography he began in 1771 and that was left unfin-

ished at his death, his astute and fair-minded observations about the customs and morals of his native American neighbors, his recommendations about the kinds of policies that should be implemented following the abolition of what he regarded as the detestable practice of slavery, and his thoughtful letters to friends and correspondents such as Ezra Stiles—suggest only a portion of his diversity and largeness. But perhaps the most indicative measure of the man is to be found in the plan he devised for attempting to arrive at moral perfection, the never-completed project he conceived for creating a national society for the spread of virtue, and the nonsectarian creed he based it on, which contained, as he thought, "the essentials of every known religion." What is most striking about Franklin's creed, as can be seen from the portion of the Autobiography *reprinted here, is the "doctrine," to use his own word, that lay at its heart. This was a "doctrine" that turned exactly inside out the principle on which the religious America of Franklin's time had staked its own future: "vicious actions are not hurtful because they are forbidden, but forbidden because they are hurtful."*

The Way to Wealth (Preface to Poor Richard Improved) (1758)

COURTEOUS READER

I have heard that nothing gives an Author so great Pleasure, as to find his Works respectfully quoted by other learned Authors. This Pleasure I have seldom enjoyed; for tho' I have been, if I may say it without Vanity, an *eminent Author* of Almanacks annually now a full Quarter of a Century, my Brother Authors in the same Way, for what Reason I know not, have ever been very sparing in their Applauses, and no other Author has taken the least Notice of me, so that did not my Writings produce me some solid *Pudding*, the great Deficiency of *Praise* would have quite discouraged me.

I concluded at length, that the People were the best Judges of my Merit; for they buy my Works; and besides, in my Rambles, where I am not personally known, I have frequently heard one or other of my Adages repeated, with, *as Poor Richard says*, at the End on 't; this gave me some Satisfaction, as it showed not only that my Instructions were regarded, but discovered likewise some Respect for my Authority; and I own, that to encourage the Practice of remembering and repeating those wise Sentences, I have sometimes *quoted myself* with great Gravity.

Judge, then how much I must have been gratified by an Incident I am going to relate to you. I stopt my Horse lately where a great Number of People were collected at a Vendue of Merchant Goods. The Hour of Sale not being come, they were conversing on the Badness of the Times and one of the Company call'd to a plain clean old Man, with white Locks, "Pray, Father Abraham, what think you of the Times? Won't these heavy Taxes quite ruin the Country? How shall we be ever able to pay them? What would you advise us to?" Father *Abraham* stood up, and reply'd, "If you'd have my Advice, I'll give it you in short, for *A Word to the Wise is enough*, and *many Words won't fill a Bushel*, as *Poor Richard* says." They join'd in desiring him to speak his Mind, and gathering round him, he proceeded as follows;

"Friends," says he, and Neighbours, "the Taxes are indeed very heavy, and if those laid on by the Government were the only Ones we had to pay, we might more easily discharge them; but we have many others, and much more grievous to some of us. We are taxed twice as much by our *Idleness*, three times as much by our *Pride*, and four times as much by our *Folly*; and from these Taxes the Commissioners cannot ease or deliver us by allowing an Abatement. However let us hearken to good Advice, and something may be done for us; *God helps them that help themselves*, as *Poor Richard* says, in his Almanack of 1733.

It would be thought a hard Government that should tax its People one-tenth Part of their *Time*, to be employed in its Service. But *Idleness* taxes many of us much more, if we reckon all that is spent in absolute *Sloth*, or doing of nothing, with that which is spent in idle Employments or Amusements, that amount to nothing. *Sloth*, by bringing on Diseases, absolutely shortens Life. *Sloth, like Rust, consumes faster than Labour wears; while the used Key is always bright*, as *Poor Richard* says. *But dost thou love Life, then do not squander Time, for that's the stuff Life is made of*, as *Poor Richard* says. How much more than is necessary do we spend in sleep, forgetting that *The sleeping Fox catches no Poultry*, and that *There will be sleeping enough in the Grave*, as *Poor Richard* says.

If Time be of all Things the most precious, wasting Time must be, as *Poor Richard* says, *the greatest Prodigality*; since, as he elsewhere tells us, *Lost Time is never found again; and what we call Time enough, always proves little enough*: Let us then up and be doing, and doing to the Purpose; so by Diligence shall we do more with less Perplexity. *Sloth makes all Things difficult, but Industry all easy*, as *Poor Richard* says; and *He that riseth late must trot all Day, and shall scarce overtake his Business at Night*; while *Laziness travels so slowly, that Poverty soon overtakes him*, as we read in *Poor Richard*, who adds, *Drive thy Business, let not that drive thee*; and *Early to Bed, and early to rise, makes a Man healthy, wealthy, and wise.*

So what signifies *wishing* and *hoping* for better Times. We may make these Times better, if we bestir ourselves. *Industry need not wish*, as *Poor Richard* says, *and he that lives upon Hope will die fasting. There are no Gains without Pains; then Help Hands, for I have no Lands*, or if I have, they are smartly taxed. And, as *Poor Richard* likewise observes, *He that hath a Trade hath an Estate; and he that hath a Calling, hath an Office of Profit and Honour*; but then the *Trade* must be worked at, and the *Calling* well followed, or neither the *Estate* nor the *Office* will enable us to pay our Taxes. If we are industrious, we shall never starve; for, as *Poor Richard* says, *At the working Man's House Hunger looks in, but dares not enter.* Nor will the Bailiff or the Constable enter, for *Industry pays Debts, while Despair encreaseth them*, says *Poor Richard.* What though you have found no Treasure, nor has any rich Relation left you a Legacy, *Diligence is the Mother of Good-luck* as *Poor Richard* says *and God gives all Things to Industry. Then plough deep, while Sluggards sleep, and you shall have Corn to sell and to keep*, says *Poor Dick.* Work while it is called To-day, for you know not how much you may be hindered To-morrow, which makes *Poor Richard* say, *One to-day is worth two To-morrows*, and farther, *Have you somewhat to do To-morrow, do it To-day.* If you were a Servant, would you not be ashamed that a good Master should catch you idle? Are you then your own Master, *be ashamed to catch yourself idle*, as *Poor Dick* says. When there is so much to be done for yourself, your Family, your Country, and your gracious King, be up by Peep of Day; *Let not the Sun look down and say, Inglorious here he lies.* Handle your Tools without Mittens; remember that *The Cat in Gloves catches no Mice*, as *Poor Richard* says. 'Tis true there is much to be done, and perhaps you are weak-handed, but stick to it steadily; and you will see great Effects, for *Constant Dropping wears away Stones*, and by *Diligence and Patience the Mouse ate in two the Cable*; and *Little Strokes fell great Oaks*, as *Poor Richard* says in his Almanack, the Year I cannot just now remember.

Methinks I hear some of you say, *Must a Man afford himself no Leisure?* I will tell thee, my friend, what *Poor Richard* says, *Employ thy Time well, if thou meanest to gain Leisure; and, since thou art not sure of a Minute, throw not away an Hour.* Leisure, is Time for doing something useful; this Leisure the diligent Man will obtain, but the lazy Man never; so that, as *Poor Richard* says *A Life of Leisure and a Life of Laziness are two Things.* Do you imagine that Sloth will afford you more Comfort than Labour? No, for as *Poor Richard* says,

*Trouble springs from Idleness, and grievous Toil from needless Ease.
Many without Labour, would live by their Wits only, but they break
for want of Stock.* Whereas Industry gives Comfort, and Plenty, and
Respect: *Fly Pleasures, and they'll follow you. The diligent Spinner has
a large Shift; and now I have a Sheep and a Cow, everyBody bids me
good Morrow;* all which is well said by *Poor Richard.*

But with our Industry, we must likewise be *steady, settled,* and
careful, and oversee our own Affairs *with our own Eyes,* and not trust
too much to others; for, as *Poor Richard* says

> *I never saw an oft-removed Tree,*
> *Nor yet an oft-removed Family,*
> *That throve so well as those that settled be.*

And again, *Three Removes is as bad as a Fire;* and again, *Keep thy
Shop, and thy Shop will keep thee;* and again, *If you would have your
Business done, go; if not, send.* And again,

> *He that by the Plough would thrive,*
> *Himself must either hold or drive.*

And again, *The Eye of a Master will do more Work than both his
Hands;* and again, *Want of Care does us more Damage than Want of
Knowledge;* and again, *Not to oversee Workmen, is to leave them your
Purse open.* Trusting too much to others' Care is the Ruin of many;
for, as the Almanack says, *In the Affairs of this World, Men are saved,
not by Faith, but by the Want of it;* but a Man's own Care is profitable;
for, saith *Poor Dick, Learning is to the Studious,* and *Riches to the
Careful,* as well as *Power to the Bold,* and *Heaven to the Virtuous,*
And farther, *If you would have a faithful Servant, and one that you
like, serve yourself.* And again, he adviseth to Circumspection and
Care, even in the smallest Matters, because sometimes *A little Neglect
may breed great Mischief;* adding, *for want of a Nail the Shoe was
lost; for want of a Shoe the Horse was lost; and for want of a Horse
the Rider was lost, being overtaken and slain by the Enemy;* all for
want of Care about a Horse-shoe Nail.

So much for Industry, my Friends, and Attention to one's own
Business; but to these we must add *Frugality,* if we would make our
Industry more certainly successful. A Man may, if he knows not how
to save as he gets, *keep his Nose all his Life to the Grindstone,* and

die not worth a *Groat* at last. *A fat Kitchen makes a lean Will*, as *Poor Richard* says; and

> *Many Estates are spent in the Getting,*
> *Since Women for Tea forsook Spinning and Knitting,*
> *And Men for Punch forsook Hewing and Splitting.*

If you would be wealthy, says he, in another Almanack, *think of Saving as well as of Getting: The Indies have not made Spain rich, because her Outgoes are greater than her Incomes.*

Away then with your expensive Follies, and you will not then have so much Cause to complain of hard Times, heavy Taxes, and chargeable Families; for, as *Poor Dick* says,

> *Women and Wine, Game and Deceit,*
> *Make the Wealth small and the Wants great.*

And farther, *What maintains one Vice, would bring up two Children.* You may think perhaps, that a *little* Tea, or a *little* Punch now and then, Diet a *little* more costly, Clothes a *little* finer, and a *little* Entertainment now and then, can be no *great* Matter; but remember what *Poor Richard* says, *Many a Little makes a Mickle*; and farther, Beware of little *Expences; A small Leak will sink a great Ship*; and again, *Who Dainties love, shall Beggars prove*; and moreover, *Fools make Feasts, and wise Men eat them.* . . .

And now to conclude, *Experience keeps a dear School, but Fools will learn in no other, and scarce in that*; for it is true, *we may give Advice, but we cannot give Conduct*, as *Poor Richard* says: However, remember this, *They that won't be counselled, can't be helped*, as *Poor Richard* says: and farther, That, *if you will not hear Reason, she'll surely rap your Knuckles.*"

Thus the old Gentleman ended his Harangue. The People heard it, and approved the Doctrine, and immediately practised the contrary, just as if it had been a common Sermon; for the Vendue opened, and they began to buy extravagantly, notwithstanding, his Cautions and their own Fear of Taxes. I found the good Man had thoroughly studied my Almanacks, and digested all I had dropt on these Topicks during the Course of Five and twenty Years. The frequent Mention he made of me must have tired any one else, but my Vanity was wonderfully delighted with it, though I was conscious that not a tenth Part of the Wisdom was my own, which he ascribed to me, but rather the *Gleanings* I had made of the Sense of all Ages and Nations. However, I resolved to be the better for the Echo of it; and though I had at first determined to buy Stuff for a new Coat, I went away resolved to wear my old One a little longer. *Reader*, if thou wilt do the same, thy Profit will be as great as mine. I *am, as ever, thine to serve thee,*

RICHARD SAUNDERS.

July 7, 1757.

An Address to the Public; from the Pennsylvania Society for Promoting the Abolition of Slavery, and the Relief of Free Negroes Unlawfully Held in Bondage (1782)

It is with peculiar satisfaction we assure the friends of humanity, that, in prosecuting the design of our association our endeavours have proved successful, far beyond our most sanguine expectations.

Encouraged by this success, and by the daily progress of that luminous and benign spirit of liberty, which is diffusing itself throughout the world, and humbly hoping for the continuance of the divine blessing on our labours, we have ventured to make an important addition to our original plan, and to therefore earnestly solicit the support and assistance of all who can feel the tender emotions of sympathy and compassion, or relish the exalted pleasure of beneficence.

Slavery is such an atrocious debasement of human nature, that its very extirpation, if not performed with solicitous care, may sometimes open a source of serious evils.

The unhappy man, who has long been treated as a brute animal, too frequently sinks beneath the common standard of the human species. The galling chains, that bind his body, to also fetter his intellectual faculties, and impair the social affections of his heart. Accustomed to move like a mere machine, by the will of a master, reflection is suspended; he has not the power of choice; and reason and conscience have but little influence over his conduct, because he is chiefly governed by the passion of fear. He is poor and friendless; perhaps worn out by extreme labour, age, and disease.

Under such circumstances, freedom may often prove a misfortune to himself, and prejudicial to society.

Attention to emancipated black people, it is therefore to be hoped, will become a branch of our national policy; but, as far as we contribute to promote this emancipation, so far that attention is evidently a serious duty incumbent on us, and which we mean to discharge to the best of our judgment and abilities.

To instruct, to advise, to qualify those, who have been restored to freedom, for the exercise and enjoyment of civil liberty, to promote in them habits of industry, to furnish them with employments suited to their age, sex, talents, and other circumstances, and to procure their children an education calculated for their future situation in life; these are the great outlines of the annexed plan, which we have adopted and which we conceive will essentially promote the public good, and the happiness of these our hitherto too much neglected fellow-creatures.

A plan so extensive cannot be carried into execution without considerable pecuniary resources, beyond the present ordinary funds of the Society. We hope much from the generosity of enlightened and benevolent freemen, and will gratefully receive any donations or subscriptions for this purpose, which may be made to our treasurer, James Starr, or to James Pemberton, chairman of our committee of correspondence.

from *Information to Those Who Would Remove to America (1784)*

Many persons in Europe, having directly or by Letters, express'd to the Writer of this, who is well acquainted with North America, their Desire of transporting and establishing themselves in that Country; but who appear to have formed, thro' Ignorance, mistaken Ideas and Expectations of what is to be obtained there; he thinks it may be useful, and prevent inconvenient, expensive, and fruitless Removals and Voyages of improper Persons, if he gives some clearer and truer Notions of that part of the World, than appear to have hitherto prevailed.

He finds it is imagined by Numbers, that the Inhabitants of North America are rich, capable of rewarding, and dispos'd to reward, all sorts of Ingenuity; that they are at the same time ignorant of all the Sciences, and, consequently, that Strangers, possessing Talents in the Belles-Lettres, fine Arts, &c., must be highly esteemed, and so well paid, as to become easily rich themselves; that there are also abundance of profitable Offices to be disposed of, which the Natives are not qualified to fill; and that, having few Persons of Family among them, Strangers of Birth must be greatly respected, and of course easily obtain the best of those Offices, which will make all their Fortunes; that the Governments too, to encourage Emigrations from Europe, not only pay the Expence of personal Transportation, but give Lands gratis to Strangers, with Negroes to work for them, Utensils of Husbandry, and Stocks of Cattle. These are all wild Imaginations; and those who go to America with Expectations founded upon them will surely find themselves disappointed.

The Truth is, that though there are in that Country few People so miserable as the Poor of Europe, there are also very few that in Europe would be called rich; it is rather a general happy Mediocrity that prevails. There are few great Proprietors of the Soil, and few Tenants; most People cultivate their own Lands, or follow some Handicraft or Merchandise; very few rich enough to live idly upon their Rents or Incomes, or to pay the high Prices given in Europe for Paintings, Statues, Architecture, and the other Works of Art, that are more curious than useful. Hence the natural Geniuses, that have arisen in America with such Talents, have uniformly quitted that Country for Europe, where they can be more suitably rewarded. It is true, that Letters and Mathematical Knowledge are in Esteem there, but they are at the same time more common than is apprehended: there being already existing nine Colleges or Universities viz. four in New England, and one in each of the Provinces of New York, New Jersey, Pensilvania, Maryland, and Virginia, all furnish'd with learned Professors; besides a number of smaller Academies; these educate many of their Youth in the Languages, and those Sciences that qualify men for the Professions of Divinity, Law, or Physick. Strangers indeed are by no means excluded from exercising those Professions; and the quick Increase of Inhabitants everywhere gives them a Chance of Employ, which they have in common with the Natives. Of civil Offices, or Employments, there are few; no superfluous Ones, as in Europe; and it is a Rule establish'd in some of the States, that no Office should be so profitable as to make it desirable. The 36th Article of the Constitution of Pennsilvania, runs expressly in these Words; "As every Freeman, to preserve his Independence, (if he has not a sufficient Estate) ought to have some Profession, Calling, Trade, or Farm, whereby he may honestly subsist, there can be no Necessity for, nor Use in, establishing Offices of Profit; the usual Effects of which are Dependance and Servility, unbecoming Freemen, in the Possessors and Expectants; Faction, Contention, Corruption, and Disorder among the People. Wherefore, whenever an Office, thro' Increase of Fees or otherwise, becomes so profitable, as to occasion many to apply for it, the Profits ought to be lessened by the Lagislature."

These Ideas prevailing more or less in all the United States, it cannot be worth any Man's while, who has a means of Living at home, to expatriate himself, in hopes of obtaining a profitable civil Office in America; and, as to military Offices, they are at an End with the War, the Armies being disbanded. Much less is it adviseable for a Person to go thither, who has no other Quality to recommend him but his Birth. In Europe it has indeed its Value; but it is a Commodity that cannot be carried to a worse Market than that of America, where people do not inquire concerning a Stranger, *What is he?* but, *What can he do?* If he has any useful Art, he is welcome; and if he exercises it, and behaves well, he will be respected by all that know him; but a mere Man of Quality, who, on that Account, wants to live upon the Public, by some Office or Salary, will be despis'd and disregarded. The Husbandman is in honor there, and even the Mechanic, because their Employments are useful. The People have a saying, that God Almighty is himself a Mechanic, the greatest in the Univers; and he is respected and admired more for the Variety, Ingenuity, and Utility of his Handyworks, than for the Antiquity of his Family. They are pleas'd with the Observation of a Negro, and frequently mention it, that *Boccarorra* (meaning the White men) *make de black man workee, make de Horse workee, make de Ox workee, make ebery ting workee; only de Hog. He, de hog, no workee; he eat, he drink, he walk about, he go to sleep when he please, he libb like a Gentleman.* According to these Opinions of the Americans, one of them would think himself more oblig'd to a Genealogist, who could prove for him that his Ancestors and Relations for ten Generations had been Ploughmen, Smiths, Carpenters, Turners, Weavers, Tanners, or even Shoemakers, and consequently that they were useful Members of Society; than if he could only prove that they were Gentlemen, doing nothing of Value, but living idly on the Labour of others, mere *jruges consumere nati,*[1] and otherwise *good for nothing,* till by their Death their Estates, like the Carcass of the Negro's Gentleman-Hog, come to be *cut up.*

With regard to Encouragements for Strangers from Government, they are really only what are derived from good Laws and Liberty. Strangers are welcome, because there is room enough for them all, and therefore the old Inhabitants are not jealous of them; the Laws protect them sufficiently, so that they have no need of the Patronage of Great Men; and every one will enjoy securely the Profits of his Industry. But, if he does not bring a Fortune with him, he must work and be industrious to live. One or two Years' residence gives him all the Rights of a Citizen; but the government does not at present, whatever it may have done in former times, hire People to become Settlers, by Paying their Passages, giving Land, Negroes, Utensils, Stock, or any other kind of Emolument whatsoever. In short, America is the Land of Labour, and by no means what the English call *Lubberland,* and the French *Pays de Cocagne,* where the streets are said to be pav'd with half-peck Loaves, the Houses til'd with Pancakes, and where the Fowls fly about ready roasted, crying, *Come eat me!*

Remarks Concerning the Savages of
North America (1784)

Savages we call them, because their manners differ from ours, which
we think the perfection of civility; they think the same of theirs.

Perhaps, if we could examine the manners of different nations
with impartiality, we should find no people so rude, as to be without
any rules of politeness; nor any so polite, as not to have some remains
of rudeness.

The Indian men, when young, are hunters and warriors; when
old, counselors; for all their government is by counsel of the sages;
there is no force, there are no prisons, no officers to compel obedience,
or inflict punishment. Hence they generally study oratory, the best
speaker having the most influence. The Indian women till the ground,
dress the food, nurse and bring up the children, and preserve and hand
down to posterity the memory of public transactions. These employments of men and women are accounted natural and honorable.
Having few artificial wants, they have abundance of leisure for improvement by conversation. Our laborious manner of life, compared
with theirs, they esteem slavish and base; and the learning, on which
we value ourselves, they regard as frivolous and useless. An instance
of this occurred at the Treaty of Lancaster, in Pennsylvania, *anno*
1744, between the government of Virginia and the Six Nations.[1] After
the principal business was settled, the commissioners from Virginia
acquainted the Indians by a speech, that there was at Williamsburg a
college, with a fund for educating Indian youth; and that, if the chiefs
of the Six Nations would send down half a dozen of their sons to that
college,[2] the government would take care that they should be well
provided for, and instructed in all the learning of the white people. It
is one of the Indian rules of politeness not to answer a public proposition the same day that it is made; they think it would be treating it
as a light matter, and that they show it respect by taking time to
consider it, as of a matter important. They therefore deferred their
answer till the day following; when their speaker began, by expressing
their deep sense of the kindness of the Virginia government, in making
them that offer; "for we know," says he, "that you highly esteem the
kind of learning taught in those Colleges, and that the maintenance of
our young men, while with you, would be very expensive to you. We
are convinced, therefore, that you mean to do us good by your proposal, and we thank you heartily. But you, who are wise, must know
that different nations have different conceptions of things; and you
will therefore not take it amiss, if our ideas of this kind of education

happen not to be the same with yours. We have had some experience of it. Several of our young people were formerly brought up at the colleges of the northern provinces; they were instructed in all your sciences; but, when they came back to us, they were bad runners, ignorant of every means of living in the woods, unable to bear either cold or hunger, knew neither how to build a cabin, take a deer, or kill an enemy, spoke our language imperfectly, were therefore neither fit for hunters, warriors, nor counselors; they were totally good for nothing. We are however not the less obliged by your kind offer, though we decline accepting it; and, to show our grateful sense of it, if the gentlemen of Virginia will send us a dozen of their sons, we will take great care of their education, instruct them in all we know, and make *men* of them."

Having frequent occasions to hold public councils, they have acquired great order and decency in conducting them. The old men sit in the foremost ranks, the warriors in the next, and the women and children in the hindmost. The business of the women is to take exact notice of what passes, imprint it in their memories, for they have no writing, and communicate it to their children. They are the records of the council, and they preserve tradition of the stipulations in treaties a hundred years back; which, when we compare with our writings, we always find exact. He that would speak, rises. The rest observe a profound silence. When he has finished and sits down, they leave him 5 or 6 minutes to recollect, that, if he has omitted anything he intended to say, or has anything to add, he may rise again and deliver it. To interrupt another, even in common conversation, is reckoned highly indecent. How different this is from the conduct of a polite British House of Commons, where scarce a day passes without some confusion that makes the speaker hoarse in calling *to order*; and how different from the mode of conversation in many polite companies of Europe, where, if you do not deliver your sentence with great rapidity, you are cut off in the middle of it by the impatient loquacity of those you converse with, and never suffered to finish it.

The politeness of these savages in conversation is indeed carried to excess, since it does not permit them to contradict or deny the truth of what is asserted in their presence. By this means they indeed avoid disputes, but then it becomes difficult to know their minds, or what impression you make upon them. The missionaries who have attempted to convert them to Christianity, all complain of this as one of the great difficulties of their mission. The Indians hear with patience the truths of the Gospel explained to them, and give their usual tokens of assent and approbation; you would think they were convinced. No such matter. It is mere civility.

A Swedish minister, having assembled the chiefs of the Susquehanah Indians, made a sermon to them, acquainting them with the principal historical facts on which our religion is founded; such as the fall of our first parents by eating an apple, the coming of Christ to repair the mischief, His miracles and suffering, &c. When he had finished, an Indian orator stood up to thank him. "What you have told us," says he, "is all very good. It is indeed bad to eat apples. It is better to make them all into cider. We are much obliged by your kindness in coming so far to tell us those things which you have heard from your mothers. In return, I will tell you some of those we have heard from ours.

"In the beginning, our fathers had only the flesh of animals to subsist on; and if their hunting was unsuccessful, they were starving. Two of our young hunters, having killed a deer, made a fire in the woods to broil some parts of it. When they were about to satisfy their hunger, they beheld a beautiful young woman descend from the clouds, and seat herself on that hill, which you see yonder among the blue mountains. They said to each other, it is a spirit that has smelled our broiling venison, and wishes to eat of it; let us offer some to her. They presented her with the tongue. She was pleased with the taste of it, and said, 'Your kindness shall be rewarded. Come to this place after thirteen moons, and you shall find something that will be of great benefit in nourishing you and your children to the latest generations.' They did so, and, to their surprise, found plants they had never seen before, but which, from that ancient time, have been constantly cultivated among us, to our great advantage. Where her right hand had touched the ground, they found maize; where her left hand had touched it, they found kidney-beans; and where her backside had sat on it, they found tobacco." The good missionary, disgusted with this idle tale, said, "What I delivered to you were sacred truths; but what you tell me is mere fable, fiction, and falsehood." The Indian, offended, replied, "My brother, it seems your friends have not done you justice in your education; they have not well instructed you in the rules of common civility. You saw that we, who understand and practice those rules, believed all your stories; why do you refuse to believe ours?"

When any of them come into our towns, our people are apt to crowd round them, gaze upon them, and incommode them, where they desire to be private; this they esteem great rudeness, and the effect of the want of instruction in the rules of civility and good manners. "We have," say they, "as much curiosity as you, and when you come into our towns, we wish for opportunities of looking at you; but for this purpose we hide ourselves behind bushes, where you are to pass, and never intrude ourselves into your company."

Their manner of entering one another's village has likewise its rules. It is reckoned uncivil in traveling strangers to enter a village abruptly, without giving notice of their approach. Therefore, as soon as they arrive within hearing, they stop and hollow,³ remaining there till invited to enter. Two old men usually come out to them, and lead them in. There is in every village a vacant dwelling, called the strangers' house. Here they are placed, while the old men go round from hut to hut acquainting the inhabitants that strangers are arrived, who are probably hungry and weary; and every one sends them what he can spare of victuals, and skins to repose on. When the strangers are refreshed, pipes and tobacco are brought; and then, but not before, conversation begins, with inquiries who they are, whither bound, what news, &c.; and it usually ends with offers of service, if the strangers have occasion of guides, or any necessaries for continuing their journey; and nothing is exacted for the entertainment.

The same hospitality, esteemed among them as a principal virtue, is practiced by private persons; of which Conrad Weiser, our interpreter, gave me the following instances. He had been naturalized among the Six Nations, and spoke well the Mohawk language. In going through the Indian country, to carry a message from our Governor to the Council at Onondaga, he called at the habitation of Canassatego, an old acquaintance, who embraced him, spread furs for him to sit on, placed before him some boiled beans and venison, and mixed some rum and water for his drink. When he was well refreshed, and had lit his pipe, Canassatego began to converse with him, asked how he had fared the many years since they had seen each other, whence he then came, what occasioned the journey, &c. Conrad answered all his questions; and when the discourse began to flag, the Indian, to continue it, said, "Conrad, you have lived long among the white people, and know something of their customs; I have been sometimes at Albany, and have observed that once in seven days they shut up their shops and assemble all in the great house; tell me what it is for? What do they do there?" "They meet there," says Conrad, "to hear and learn *good things.*" "I do not doubt," says the Indian, "that they tell you so; they have told me the same; but I doubt the truth of what they say, and I will tell you my reasons. I went lately to Albany to sell my skins and buy blankets, knives, powder, rum, &c. You know I used generally to deal with Hans Hanson; but I was a little inclined this time to try some other merchant. However, I called first upon Hans, and asked him what he would give for beaver. He said he could not give any more than four shillings a pound; 'but,' says he, 'I cannot talk on business now; this is the day when we meet together to learn *good things,* and I am going to the meeting.' So I thought to myself, 'Since we cannot do any business today, I may as well go to the meeting too,' and I went with him. There stood up a man in black, and began to talk to the people very angrily. I did not understand what he said; but, perceiving that he looked much at me and at Hanson, I imagined he was angry at seeing me there; so I went out, sat down near the house, struck fire, and lit my pipe, waiting till the meeting should break up. I thought too, that the man had mentioned something of beaver, and I suspected it might be the subject of their meeting. So, when they came out, I accosted my merchant. 'Well, Hans,' says I, 'I hope you have agreed to give more than four shillings a pound.' 'No,' says he, 'I cannot give so much; I cannot give more than three shillings and sixpence.' I then spoke to several other dealers, but they all sung the same song, three and sixpence, three and sixpence. This made it clear to me, that my suspicion was right; and, that whatever they pretended of meeting to learn *good things*, the real purpose was to consult how to cheat Indians in the price of beaver. Consider but a little, Conrad, and you must be of my opinion. If they met so often to learn *good things*, they would certainly have learned some before this time. But they are still ignorant. You know our practice. If a white man, in traveling through our country, enters one of our cabins, we all treat him as I treat you; we dry him if he is wet, we warm him if he is cold, and give him meat and drink that he may allay his thirst and hunger; and we spread soft furs for him to rest and sleep on. We demand nothing in return.[4] But, if I go into a white man's house at Albany, and ask for victuals and drink, they say, 'Where is your money?' and if I have none, they say, 'Get out, you Indian dog.' You see they have not yet learned those little *good things*, that we need no meetings to be instructed in, because our mothers taught them to us when we were children. And therefore it is impossible their meetings should be, as they say, for any such purpose, or have any such effect; they are only to contrive *the cheating of Indians in the price of beaver*."

Speech in the Convention at the Conclusion of Its Deliberations
(September 17, 1787)

MR. PRESIDENT,

I confess, that I do not entirely approve of this Constitution at present; but, Sir, I am not sure I shall never approve it; for, having lived long, I have experienced many instances of being obliged, by better information or fuller consideration, to change my opinions even on important subjects, which I once thought right, but found to be otherwise. It is therefore that, the older I grow, the more apt I am to doubt my own judgment of others. Most men, indeed, as well as most sects in religion, think themselves in possession of all truth, and that wherever others differ from them, it is so far error. Steele, a Protestant, in a dedication, tells the Pope, that the only difference between our two churches in their opinions of the certainty of their doctrine, is, the Romish Church is *infallible*, and the Church of England is *never in the wrong*. But, though many private Persons think almost as highly of their own infallibility as of that of their Sect, few express it so naturally as a certain French Lady, who, in a little dispute with her sister, said, "But I meet with nobody but myself that is *always* in the right." *"Je ne trouve que moi qui aie toujours raison."*

In these sentiments, Sir, I agree to this Constitution, with all its faults,—if they are such; because I think a general Government necessary for us, and there is no *form* of government but what may be a blessing to the people, if well administered; and I believe, farther, that this is likely to be well administered for a course of years, and can only end in despotism, as other forms have done before it, when the people shall become so corrupted as to need despotic government, being incapable of any other. I doubt, too, whether any other Convention we can obtain, may be able to make a better constitution; for, when you assemble a number of men, to have the advantage of their joint wisdom, you inevitably assemble with those men all their prejudices, their passions, their errors of opinion, their local interests, and their selfish views. From such an assembly can a *perfect* production be expected? It therefore astonishes me, Sir, to find this system approaching so near to perfection as it does; and I think it will astonish our enemies, who are waiting with confidence to hear, that our councils are confounded like those of the builders of Babel, and that our States are on the point of separation, only to meet hereafter for the purpose of cutting one another's throats. Thus I consent, Sir, to this Constitution, because I expect no better, and because I am not sure that it is not the best. The opinions I have had of its *errors* I sacrifice to the public good. I have never whispered a syllable of them abroad. Within these walls they were born, and here they shall die. If every one of us, in returning to our Constituents, were to report the objections he has had to it, and endeavour to gain Partisans in support of them, we might prevent its being generally received, and thereby lose all the salutary effects and great advantages resulting naturally in our favour among foreign nations, as well as among ourselves, from our real or apparent unanimity. Much of the strength and efficiency of any government, in procuring and securing happiness to the people, depends on *opinion*, on the general opinion of the goodness of that government, as well as of the wisdom and integrity of its governors. I hope, therefore, for our own sakes, as a part of the people, and for the sake

of our posterity, that we shall act heartily and unanimously in recommending this Constitution, wherever our Influence may extend, and
turn our future thoughts and endeavours to the means of having it
well administered.

On the whole, Sir, I cannot help expressing a wish, that every
member of the Convention who may still have objections to it, would
with me on this occasion doubt a little of his own infallibility, and, to
make *manifest* our *unanimity*, put his name to this Instrument.

[Then the motion was made for adding the last formula, viz.
"Done in convention by the Unanimous Consent," &c.; which was
agreed to and added accordingly.]

from *The Autobiography of Benjamin Franklin (1784, 1788)*

. . . I had been religiously educated as a Presbyterian; and tho' some
of the dogmas of that persuasion, such as *the eternal decrees of God,
election, reprobation, etc.*, appeared to me unintelligible, others doubtful, and I early absented myself from the public assemblies of the sect,
Sunday being my studying day, I never was without some religious
principles. I never doubted, for instance, the existence of the Deity;
that he made the world, and govern'd it by his Providence; that the
most acceptable service of God was the doing good to man; that our
souls are immortal; and that all crime will be punished, and virtue
rewarded, either here or hereafter. These I esteem'd the essentials of
every religion; and, being to be found in all the religions we had in
our country, I respected them all, tho' with different degrees of respect,
as I found them more or less mix'd with other articles, which, without
any tendency to inspire, promote, or confirm morality, serv'd principally to divide us, and make us unfriendly to one another. This respect
to all, with an opinion that the worst had some good effects, induc'd
me to avoid all discourse that might tend to lessen the good opinion
another might have of his own religion; and as our province increas'd
in people, and new places of worship were continually wanted, and
generally erected by voluntary contribution, my mite for such purpose,
whatever might be the sect, was never refused.

Tho' I seldom attended any public worship, I had still an opinion
of its propriety, and of its utility when rightly conducted, and I regu-
larly paid my annual subscription for the support of the only Presbyterian minister or meeting we had in Philadelphia. He us'd to visit me
sometimes as a friend, and admonish me to attend his administrations,

and I was now and then prevail'd on to do so, once for five Sundays successively. Had he been in my opinion a good preacher, perhaps I might have continued, notwithstanding the occasion I had for the Sunday's leisure in my course of study; but his discourses were chiefly either polemic arguments, or explications of the peculiar doctrines of our sect, and were all to me very dry, uninteresting, and unedifying, since not a single moral principle was inculcated or enforc'd, their aim seeming to be rather to make us Presbyterians than good citizens.

At length he took for his text that verse of the fourth chapter of Philippians, *"Finally, brethren, whatsoever things are true, honest, just, pure, lovely, or of good report, if there be any virtue, or any praise, think on these things."*[1] And I imagin'd, in a sermon on such a text, we could not miss of having some morality. But he confin'd himself to five points only, as meant by the apostle, viz.: 1. Keeping holy the Sabbath day. 2. Being diligent in reading the holy Scriptures. 3. Attending duly the publick worship. 4. Partaking of the Sacrament. 5. Paying a due respect to God's ministers. These might be all good things; but, as they were not the kind of good things that I expected from that text, I despaired of ever meeting with them from any other, was disgusted, and attended his preaching no more. I had some years before compos'd a little Liturgy, or form of prayer, for my own private use (viz., in 1728), entitled, *Articles of Belief and Acts of Religion.* I return'd to the use of this, and went no more to the public assemblies. My conduct might be blameable, but I leave it, without attempting further to excuse it; my present purpose being to relate facts, and not to make apologies for them.

It was about this time I conceiv'd the bold and arduous project of arriving at moral perfection. I wish'd to live without committing any fault at any time; I would conquer all that either natural inclination, custom, or company might lead me into. As I knew, or thought I knew, what was right and wrong, I did not see why I might not always do the one and avoid the other. But I soon found I had undertaken a task of more difficulty than I had imagined. While my care was employ'd in guarding against one fault, I was often surprised by another; habit took the advantage of inattention; inclination was sometimes too strong for reason. I concluded, at length, that the mere speculative conviction that it was our interest to be completely virtuous, was not sufficient to prevent our slipping; and that the contrary habits must be broken, and good ones acquired and established, before we can have any dependence on a steady, uniform rectitude of conduct. For this purpose I therefore contrived the following method.

In the various enumerations of the moral virtues I had met with in my reading, I found the catalogue more or less numerous, as different writers included more or fewer ideas under the same name.

Temperance, for example, was by some confined to eating and drinking, while by others it was extended to mean the moderating every other pleasure, appetite, inclination, or passion, bodily or mental, even to our avarice and ambition. I propos'd to myself, for the sake of clearness, to use rather more names, with fewer ideas annex'd to each, than a few names with more ideas; and I included under thirteen names of virtues all that at that time occurr'd to me as necessary or desirable, and annexed to each a short precept, which fully express'd the extent I gave to its meaning.

These names of virtues, with their precepts, were:

1. TEMPERANCE. Eat not to dullness; drink not to elevation.

2. SILENCE. Speak not but what may benefit others or yourself; avoid trifling conversation.

3. ORDER. Let all your things have their places; let each part of your business have its time.

4. RESOLUTION. Resolve to perform what you ought; perform without fail what you resolve.

5. FRUGALITY. Make no expense but to do good to others or yourself; *i.e.*, waste nothing.

6. INDUSTRY. Lose no time; be always employ'd in something useful; cut off all unnecessary actions.

7. SINCERITY. Use no hurtful deceit; think innocently and justly, and, if you speak, speak accordingly.

8. JUSTICE. Wrong none by doing injuries, or omitting the benefits that are your duty.

9. MODERATION. Avoid extreams; forbear resenting injuries so much as you think they deserve.

10. CLEANLINESS. Tolerate no uncleanliness in body, cloaths, or habitation.

11. TRANQUILITY. Be not disturbed at trifles, or at accidents common or unavoidable.

12. CHASTITY. Rarely use venery but for health or offspring, never to dullness, weakness, or the injury of your own or another's peace or reputation.

13. HUMILITY. Imitate Jesus and Socrates.

My intention being to acquire the *habitude* of all these virtues, I judg'd it would be well not to distract my attention by attempting the whole at once, but to fix it on one of them at a time; and, when I should be master of that, then to proceed to another, and so on, till I should have gone thro' the thirteen; and, as the previous acquisition of some might facilitate the acquisition of certain others, I arrang'd them with that view, as they stand above. Temperance first, as it tends to procure that coolness and clearness of head, which is so necessary where constant vigilance was to be kept up, and guard maintained against the unremitting attraction of ancient habits, and the force of perpetual temptations. This being acquir'd and establish'd, Silence would be more easy; and my desire being to gain knowledge at the same time that I improv'd in virtue, and considering that in conversation it was obtain'd rather by the use of the ears than of the tongue, and therefore wishing to break a habit I was getting into of prattling, punning, and joking, which only made me acceptable to trifling company, I gave *Silence* the second place. This and the next, *Order*, I expected would allow me more time for attending to my project and my studies. *Resolution*, once become habitual, would keep me firm in my endeavors to obtain all the subsequent virtues; *Frugality* and Industry freeing me from my remaining debt, and producing affluence and independence, would make more easy the practice of Sincerity and Justice, etc., etc. Conceiving then, that, agreeably to the advice of Pythagoras[2] in his Golden Verses, daily examination would be necessary, I contrived the following method for conducting that examination.

I made a little book, to which I allotted a page for each of the virtues. I rul'd each page with red ink, so as to have seven columns, one for each day of the week, marking each column with a letter for the day. I cross'd these columns with thirteen red lines, marking the beginning of each line with the first letter of one of the virtues, on which line, and in its proper column, I might mark, by a little black spot, every fault I found upon examination to have been committed respecting that virtue upon that day. . . .

In truth, I found myself incorrigible with respect to Order; and now I am grown old, and my memory bad, I feel very sensibly the want of it. But, on the whole, tho' I never arrived at the perfection I had been so ambitious of obtaining, but fell far short of it, yet I was, by the endeavour, a better and a happier man than I otherwise should have been if I had not attempted it; as those who aim at perfect writing by imitating the engraved copies, tho' they never reach the wish'd-for excellence of those copies, their hand is mended by the endeavor, and is tolerable while it continues fair and legible.

It may be well my posterity should be informed that to this little artifice, with the blessing of God, their ancestor ow'd the constant felicity of his life, down to his 79th year, in which this is written. What reverses may attend the remainder is in the hand of Providence; but, if they arrive, the reflection on past happiness enjoy'd ought to help his bearing them with more resignation. To Temperance he ascribes his long-continued health, and what is still left to him of a good constitution; to Industry and Frugality, the early easiness of his circumstances and acquisition of his fortune, with all that knowledge that enabled him to be a useful citizen, and obtained for him some degree of reputation among the learned; to Sincerity and Justice, the confidence of his country, and the honorable employs it conferred upon him; and to the joint influence of the whole mass of the virtues, even in the imperfect state he was able to acquire them, all that evenness of temper, and that cheerfulness in conversation, which makes his company still sought for, and agreeable even to his younger acquaintance. I hope, therefore, that some of my descendants may follow the example and reap the benefit.

It will be remark'd that, tho' my scheme was not wholly without religion, there was in it no mark of any of the distinguishing tenets of any particular sect. I had purposely avoided them; for, being fully persuaded of the utility and excellency of my method, and that it might be serviceable to people in all religions, and intending some time or other to publish it, I would not have anything in it that should prejudice any one, of any sect, against it. I purposed writing a little comment on each virtue, in which I would have shown the advantages of possessing it, and the mischiefs attending its opposite vice; and I should have called my book THE ART OF VIRTUE, because it would have shown the means and manner of obtaining virtue, which would have distinguished it from the mere exhortation to be good, that does not instruct and indicate the means, but is like the apostle's man of verbal charity, who only without showing to the naked and hungry how or where they might get clothes or victuals, exhorted them to be fed and clothed. James ii. 15, 16.

But it so happened that my intention of writing and publishing this comment was never fulfilled. I did, indeed, from time to time, put down short hints of the sentiments, reasonings, etc., to be made use of in it, some of which I have still by me; but the necessary close attention to private business in the earlier part of my life, and public business since, have occasioned my postponing it; for, it being connected in my mind with *a great and extensive project*, that required the whole man to execute, and which an unforeseen succession of employs prevented my attending to, it has hitherto remain'd unfinish'd.

In this piece it was my design to explain and enforce this doctrine, that vicious actions are not hurtful because they are forbidden, but forbidden because they are hurtful, the nature of man alone considered; that it was, therefore, every one's interest to be virtuous who wish'd to be happy even in this world; and I should, from this circumstance (there being always in the world a number of rich merchants, nobility, states, and princes, who have need of honest instruments for the management of their affairs, and such being so rare), have endeavored to convince young persons that no qualities were so likely to make a poor man's fortune as those of probity and integrity.

My list of virtues contain'd at first but twelve; but a Quaker friend having kindly informed me that I was generally thought proud; that my pride show'd itself frequently in conversation; that I was not content with being in the right when discussing any point, but was overbearing, and rather insolent, of which he convinc'd me by mentioning several instances; I determined endeavouring to cure myself, if I could, of this vice or folly among the rest, and I added *Humility* to my list, giving an extensive meaning to the word.

I cannot boast of much success in acquiring the *reality* of this virtue, but I had a good deal with regard to the *appearance* of it. I made it a rule to forbear all direct contradiction to the sentiments of others, and all positive assertion of my own. I even forbid myself, agreeably to the old laws of our Junto, the use of every word or expression in the language that imported a fix'd opinion, such as *certainly, undoubtedly*, etc., and I adopted, instead of them, *I conceive, I apprehend*, or *I imagine* a thing to be so or so; or it *so appears to me at present*. When another asserted something that I thought an error, I deny'd myself the pleasure of contradicting him abruptly, and of showing immediately some absurdity in his proposition; and in answering I began by observing that in certain cases or circumstances his opinion would be right, but in the present case there *appear'd* or *seem'd* to me some difference, etc. I soon found the advantage of this change in my manner; the conversations I engag'd in went on more pleasantly. The modest way in which I propos'd my opinions procur'd them a readier reception and less contradiction; I had less mortification when I was found to be in the wrong, and I more easily prevail'd with others to give up their mistakes and join with me when I happened to be in the right.

And this mode, which I at first put on with some violence to natural inclination, became at length so easy, and so habitual to me, that perhaps for these fifty years past no one has ever heard a dogmatical expression escape me. And to this habit (after my character of integrity) I think it principally owing that I had early so much weight with my fellow-citizens when I proposed new institutions, or alterations in the old, and so much influence in public councils when I became a member; for I was but a bad speaker, never eloquent, subject to much hesitation in my choice of words, hardly correct in language, and yet I generally carried my points.

In reality, there is, perhaps, no one of our natural passions so hard to subdue as *pride*. Disguise it, struggle with it, beat it down, stifle it, mortify it as much as one pleases, it is still alive, and will every now and then peep out and show itself; you will see it, perhaps, often in this history; for, even if I could conceive that I had compleatly overcome it, I should probably be proud of my humility.

[Thus far written at Passy, 1784.]

["I am now about to write at home, August, 1788, but can not have the help expected from my papers, many of them being lost in the war. I have, however, found the following."]

Having mentioned *a great and extensive project* which I had conceiv'd, it seems proper that some account should be here given of that project and its object. Its first rise in my mind appears in the following little paper, accidentally preserv'd, viz.:

Observations on my reading history, in Library, May 19th, 1731.

"That the great affairs of the world, the wars, revolutions, etc., are carried on and affected by parties.

"That the view of these parties is their present general interest, or what they take to be such.

"That the different views of these different parties occasion all confusion.

"That while a party is carrying on a general design, each man has his particular private interest in view.

"That as soon as a party has gain'd its general point, each member becomes intent upon his particular interest; which, thwarting others, breaks that party into divisions, and occasions more confusion.

"That few in public affairs act from a mere view of the good of their country, whatever they may pretend; and, tho' their actings bring real good to their country, yet men primarily considered that their own and their country's interest was united, and did not act from a principle of benevolence.

"That fewer still, in public affairs, act with a view to the good of mankind.

"There seems to me at present to be great occasion for raising a United Party for Virtue, by forming the virtuous and good men of all nations into a regular body, to be govern'd by suitable good and wise rules, which good and wise men may probably be more unanimous in their obedience to, than common people are to common laws.

"I at present think that whoever attempts this aright, and is well qualified, can not fail of pleasing God, and of meeting with success. B. F."

Revolving this project in my mind, as to be undertaken hereafter, when my circumstances should afford me the necessary leisure, I put down from time to time, on pieces of paper, such thoughts as occurr'd to me respecting it. Most of these are lost; but I find one purporting to be the substance of an intended creed, containing, as I thought, the essentials of every known religion, and being free of every thing that might shock the professors of any religion. It is express'd in these words, viz.:

"That there is one God, who made all things.

"That he governs the world by his providence.

"That he ought to be worshipped by adoration, prayer, and thanksgiving.

"But that the most acceptable service of God is doing good to man.

"That the soul is immortal.

"And that God will certainly reward virtue and punish vice, either here or hereafter."

My ideas at that time were, that the sect should be begun and spread at first among young and single men only; that each person to be initiated should not only declare his assent to such creed, but should have exercised himself with the thirteen weeks' examination and practice of the virtues, as in the before-mention'd model; that the existence of such a society should be kept a secret, till it was become considerable, to prevent solicitations for the admission of improper persons, but that the members should each of them search among his acquaintance for ingenuous, well-disposed youths, to whom, with prudent caution, the scheme should be gradually communicated; that the members should engage to afford their advice, assistance, and support to each other in promoting one another's interests, business, and advancement in life; that, for distinction, we should be call'd *The Society of the Free and Easy*: free, as being, by the general practice and habit of the virtues, free from the dominion of vice; and particularly by the practice of industry and frugality, free from debt, which exposes a man to confinement, and a species of slavery to his creditors.

This is as much as I can now recollect of the project, except that I communicated it in part to two young men, who adopted it with some enthusiasm; but my then narrow circumstances, and the necessity I was under of sticking close to my business, occasion'd my postponing the further prosecution of it at that time; and my multifarious occupations, public and private, induc'd me to continue postponing, so that it has been omitted till I have no longer strength or activity left sufficient for such an enterprise; tho' I am still of opinion that it was a practicable scheme, and might have been very useful, by forming a great number of good citizens; and I was not discourag'd by the seeming magnitude of the undertaking, as I have always thought that one man of tolerable abilities may work great changes, and accomplish great affairs among mankind, if he first forms a good plan, and, cutting off all amusements or other employments that would divert his attention, makes the execution of that same plan his sole study and business. . . .

Letter to Ezra Stiles[1]
March 9, 1790

REVEREND AND DEAR SIR,

I received your kind Letter of Jan'y 28, and am glad you have at length received the portrait of Gov'r Yale from his Family, and deposited it in the College Library. He was a great and good Man, and had the Merit of doing infinite Service to your Country by his Munificence to that Institution. The Honour you propose doing me by placing mine in the same Room with his, is much too great for my Deserts; but you always had a Partiality for me, and to that it must be ascribed. I am however too much obliged to Yale College, the first learned Society that took Notice of me and adorned me with its Honours[2] to refuse a Request that comes from it thro' so esteemed a Friend. But I do not think any one of the Portraits you mention, as in my Possession, worthy of the Place and Company you propose to place it in. You have an excellent Artist lately arrived. If he will undertake to make one for you, I shall cheerfully pay the Expence; but he must not delay setting about it, or I may slip thro' his fingers, for I am now in my eighty-fifth year, and very infirm.

I send with this a very learned Work, as it seems to me, on the ancient Samaritan Coins, lately printed in Spain, and at least curious for the Beauty of the Impression. Please to accept it for your College Library. I have subscribed for the Encylcopædia[3] now printing here, with the Intention of presenting it to the College. I shall probably depart before the Work is finished, but shall leave Directions for its Continuance to the End. With this you will receive some of the first numbers.

You desire to know something of my Religion. It is the first time I have been questioned upon it. But I cannot take your Curiosity amiss, and shall endeavour in a few Words to gratify it. Here is my Creed. I believe in one God, Creator of the Universe. That he governs it by his

Providence. That he ought to be worshipped. That the most acceptable Service we render to him is doing good to his other Children. That the soul of Man is immortal, and will be treated with Justice in another Life respecting its Conduct in this. These I take to be the fundamental Principles of all sound Religion, and I regard them as you do in whatever Sect I meet with them.

As to Jesus of Nazareth, my Opinion of whom you particularly desire, I think the System of Morals and his Religion, as he left them to us, the best the World ever saw or is likely to see; but I apprehend it has received various corrupting Changes, and I have, with most of the present Dissenters in England, some Doubts as to his Divinity; tho' it is a question I do not dogmatize upon, having never studied it, and think it needless to busy myself with it now, when I expect soon an Opportunity of knowing the Truth with less Trouble. I see no harm, however, in its being believed, if that Belief has the good Consequence, as probably it has, of making his Doctrines more respected and better observed: especially as I do not perceive, that the Supreme takes it amiss, by distinguishing the Unbelievers in his Government of the World with any peculiar Marks of his Displeasure.

I shall only add, respecting myself, that, having experienced the Goodness of that Being in conducting me prosperously thro' a long life, I have no doubt of its Continuance in the next, though without the smallest Conceit of meriting such Goodness. My Sentiments on this Head you will see in the Copy of an old Letter enclosed, which I wrote in answer to one from a zealous Religionist, whom I had relieved in a paralytic case by electricity, and who, being afraid I should grow proud upon it, sent me his serious though rather impertinent Caution. I send you also the Copy of another Letter, which will shew something of my Disposition relating to Religion. With great and sincere Esteem and Affection, I am, Your obliged old Friend and most obedient humble Servant.

B. FRANKLIN

Elizabeth Ashbridge
(1713–1755)

Elizabeth Ashbridge, an unusually spirited English girl who was raised as an Anglican, eloped at the age of fourteen, was widowed before she was nineteen, emigrated to America as an indentured servant before she was twenty, and, to escape the religious hypocrisy of her cruel master, then married again, this time a worldly schoolteacher named Sullivan who, as she reports, "fell in love with me for my dancing." The portion of her spiritual autobiography reprinted here tells of her initial attractions to the religion of the Quakers, the consequent tensions this produced with Sullivan, and her poignant struggle with guilt and fear as she attempted to live out the requirements of her new faith in the face of her husband's growing abuse. In addition to rendering a religious odyssey of marked candor and integrity, Some Account of the Early Part of the Life of Elizabeth Ashbridge, . . . Written by Herself—which was prepared for publication with the help of her third husband, Aaron Ashbridge, to whom she was happily married in 1746, two years after the death of Sullivan—provides an extraordinarily interesting picture of gender relations in eighteenth-century America.

from Some Account of the Early Part of the Life of Elizabeth Ashbridge, . . . Written by Herself (1807)

. . . I now began to think of my relations in Pennsylvania, whom I had not yet seen. My husband gave me liberty to visit them, and I obtained a certificate from the priest, in order that, if I made any stay, I might be received as a member of the church wherever I came. My husband accompanied me to the Blazingstar Ferry, saw me safely over, and then returned. In my way, I fell from my horse, and, for several days, was unable to travel. I abode at the house of an honest Dutchman, who, with his wife, paid me the utmost attention, and would have no recompence for their trouble. I left them with deep sentiments of gratitude for their extraordinary kindness, and they charged me, if ever I came that way again, to lodge with them. I mention this, because I shall have occasion to allude to it hereafter.

When I came to Trent-town Ferry, I felt no small mortification on hearing that my relations were all Quakers, and, what was worst of all, that my aunt was a preacher. I was exceedingly prejudiced against this people, and often wondered how they could call themselves Christians. I repented my coming, and was almost inclined to turn back; yet, as I was so far on my journey, I proceeded, though I expected but little comfort from my visit. How little was I aware it would bring me to the knowledge of the truth!

I went from Trent-town to Philadelphia by water, and from thence to my uncle's on horseback. My uncle was dead, and my aunt married again; yet, both she and her husband received me in the kindest manner. I had scarcely been three hours in the house, before my opinion of these people began to alter. I perceived a book lying upon the table, and, being fond of reading, took it up; my aunt observed me, and said, "Cousin, that is a Quaker's book." She saw I was not a Quaker, and supposed I would not like it. I made her no answer, but queried with myself, what can these people write about? I have heard that they deny the scriptures, and have no other bible than George Fox's Journal,[1] denying, also, all the holy ordinances. But, before I had read two pages, my heart burned within me, and, for fear I should be seen, I went into the garden. I sat down, and, as the piece was short, read it before I returned, though I was often obliged to stop to give vent to my tears. The fulness of my heart produced the involuntary exclamation of, "My God, must I, if ever I come to the knowledge of thy truth, be of this man's opinion, who has sought thee as I have done; and must I join this people, to whom, a few hours ago, I preferred the papists. O, thou God of my salvation, and of my life, who hath abundantly manifested thy long suffering and tender mercy, in redeeming me as from the lowest hell, I beseech thee to direct me in the right way, and keep me from error; so will I perform my covenant, and think nothing too near to part with for thy name's sake. O, happy people, thus beloved of God!" After having collected myself, I washed my face, that it might not be perceived I had been weeping. In the night I got but little sleep; the enemy of mankind haunted me

with his insinuations, by suggesting that I was one of those that wavered, and not steadfast in faith; and advancing several texts of scripture against me, as that, in the latter days, there should be those who
would deceive the very elect; that of such were the people I was among,
and that I was in danger of being deluded. Warned in this manner,
(from the right source as I thought,) I resolved to be aware of those
deceivers, and, for some weeks, did not touch one of their books. The
next day, being the first of the week, I was desirous of going to church,
which was distant about four miles; but, being a stranger, and having
no one to go with me, I gave up all thoughts of that, and, as most of
the family were going to meeting, I went there with them. As we sat
in silence, I looked over the meeting, and said to myself, "How like
fools these people sit; how much better would it be to stay at home,
and read the Bible, or some good book, than come here and go to
sleep." As for me I was very drowsy; and, while asleep, had nearly
fallen down. This was the last time I ever fell asleep in a meeting. I
now began to be lifted up with spiritual pride, and to think myself
better than they; but this disposition of mind did not last long. It may
seem strange that, after living so long with one of this society at Dub-
lin; I should yet be so much a stranger to them. In answer, let it be
considered that, while I was there, I never read any of their books,
nor went to one meeting; besides, I had heard such accounts of them,
as made me think that, of all societies, they were the worst. But he
who knows the sincerity of the heart, looked on my weakness with
pity; I was permitted to see my error, and shown that these were the
people I ought to join.

    A few weeks afterwards, there was an afternoon meeting at my
uncle's, at which a minister named William Hammans was present. I
was highly prejudiced against him when he stood up, but I was soon
humbled; for he preached the gospel with such power that I was
obliged to confess it was the truth. But, though he was the instrument
of assisting me out of many doubts, my mind was not wholly freed
from them. The morning before this meeting I had been disputing with
my uncle about baptism, which was the subject handled by this minister, who removed all my scruples beyond objection, and yet I seemed
loath to believe that the sermon I had heard proceeded from divine
revelation. I accused my aunt and uncle of having spoken of me to the
friend; but they cleared themselves, by telling me, that they had not
seen him, since my coming, until he came into the meeting. I then
viewed him as the messenger of God to me, and, laying aside my
prejudices, opened my heart to receive the truth; the beauty of which
was shown to me, with the glory of those who continued faithful to
it. I had also revealed to me the emptiness of all shadows and types,
which, though proper in their day, were now, by the coming of the

Son of God, at an end, and everlasting righteousness, which is a work in the heart, was to be established in the room thereof. I was permitted to see that all I had gone through was to prepare me for this day; and that the time was near, when it would be required of me, to go and declare to others what the God of mercy had done for my soul; at which I was surprised, and desired to be excused, lest I should bring dishonour to the truth, and cause his holy name to be evil spoken of.

Of these things I let no one know. I feared discovery, and did not even appear like a friend.

I now hired to keep school, and, hearing of a place for my husband, I wrote, and desired him to come, though I did not let him know how it was with me.

I loved to go to meetings, but did not love to be seen going on week-days, and therefore went to them, from my school, through the woods. Notwithstanding all my care, the neighbours, (who were not friends,) soon began to revile me with the name of Quaker; adding, that they supposed I intended to be a fool, and turn preacher. Thus did I receive the same censure, which, about a year before, I had passed on one of the handmaids of the Lord in Boston. I was so weak, that I could not bear the reproach. In order to change their opinion, I went into greater excess of apparel than I had freedom to do, even before I became acquainted with friends. In this condition I continued till my husband came, and then began the trial of my faith.

Before he reached me, he heard I was turned Quaker; at which he stamped, and said, "I had rather have heard she was dead, well as I love her; for, if it be so, all my comfort is gone." He then came to me; it was after an absence of four months; I got up and said to him, "My dear, I am glad to see thee." At this, he flew into a great rage, exclaiming, "The devil thee, thee, thee, don't thee me."[2] I endeavoured, by every mild means, to pacify him; and, at length, got him fit to speak to my relations. As soon after this as we were alone, he said to me, "And so I see your Quaker relations have made you one;" I replied, that they had not, (which was true,) I never told them how it was with me. He said he would not stay amongst them; and, having found a place to his mind, hired, and came directly back to fetch me, walking, in one afternoon, thirty miles to keep me from meeting the next day, which was first day.[3] He took me, after resting this day, to the place where he had hired, and to lodgings he had engaged at the house of a churchwarden. This man was a bitter enemy of Friends, and did all he could to irritate my husband against them.

Though I did not appear like a friend, they all believed me to be one. When my husband and he used to be making their diversions and reviling, I sat in silence, though now and then an involuntary sigh broke from me; at which he would say, "There, did not I tell you your wife was a Quaker, and she will become a preacher." On such an occasion as this, my husband once came up to me, in a great rage, and shaking his hand over me, said, "You had better be hanged in that day." I was seized with horror, and again plunged into despair, which continued nearly three months. I was afraid that, by denying the Lord, the heavens would be shut against me. I walked much alone in the woods, and there, where no eye saw, or ear heard me, lamented my miserable condition. Often have I wandered, from morning till night, without food. I was brought so low that my life became a burden to me; and the devil seemed to vaunt that, though the sins of my youth were forgiven me, yet now I had committed an unpardonable sin, and hell would inevitably be my portion, and my torments would be greater than if I had hanged myself at first.

In the night, when, under this painful distress of mind, I could not sleep, if my husband perceived me weeping, he would revile me for it. At length, when he and his friend thought themselves too weak to overset me, he went to the priest at Chester, to inquire what he could do with me. This man knew I was a member of the Church, for I had shown him my certificate. His advice was, to take me out of Pennsylvania, and settle in some place where there were no Quakers. My husband replied, he did not care where we went, if he could but restore me to my natural liveliness of temper. As for me, I had no resolution to oppose their proposals, nor much cared where I went. I seemed to have nothing to hope for. I daily expected to be made a victim of divine wrath, and was possessed with the idea that this would be by thunder.

When the time of removal came, I was not permitted to bid my relations farewell; and, as my husband was poor, and kept no horse, I was obliged to travel on foot. We came to Wilmington, fifteen miles, and from thence to Philadelphia by water. Here we stopt at a tavern, where I became the spectacle and discourse of the company. My husband told them his wife had become a Quaker, and he designed, if possible, to find out a place where there was none: (thought I,) I was once in a condition to deserve that name, but now it is over with me. O that I might, from a true hope, once more have an opportunity to confess the truth; though I was sure of all manner of cruelties, I would not regard them. Such were my concerns, while he was entertaining the company with my story, in which he told them that I had been a good dancer, but now he could get me neither to dance or sing. One of the company then started up, and said, "I'll fetch a fiddle, and we'll have a good dance;" a proposal with which my husband was pleased. When the fiddle was brought, my husband came and said to me, "My dear, shake off that gloom, and let us have a civil dance; you would, now and then, when you were a good churchwoman, and that's better than a stiff Quaker." I had taken up the resolution not to comply with his request, whatever might be the consequence; this I let him know, though I durst say little, for fear of his choleric temper. He pulled me round the room, till the tears fell from my eyes, at the sight of which the musician stopt, and said "I'll play no more; let your wife alone." There was a person in company that came from Freehold, in East Jersey, who said, "I see your wife's a Quaker, but, if you'll take my advice you need not go so far as you intend; come and live with us; we'll soon cure her of her Quakerism, and we want a schoolmaster and schoolmistress too." He consented, and a happy turn it was for me, as will shortly be seen. The answer of peace was afforded me, for refusing to dance; I rejoiced more than if I had been made mistress of much riches, and, with tears, prayed, "Lord, I dread to ask, and yet without thy gracious pardon, I am miserable. I therefore fall down before thy throne, imploring mercy at thy hand. O Lord, once more, I beseech thee, try my obedience, and then, in whatsoever thou commandest, I will obey thee, and not fear to confess thee before men." My cries were heard, and it was shown to me, that he delights not in the death of a sinner. My soul was again set at liberty, and I could praise him.

In our way to Freehold, we visited the kind Dutchman, whom I have mentioned in a former part of this narrative. He made us welcome, and invited us to pass a day or two with him. During our stay, we went to a large meeting of Presbyterians, held not only for worship, but business, in particular, the trial of one of their priests, who had been charged with drunkenness, was to come on. I perceived such great divisions among the people, respecting who should be their shepherd, that I pitied them. Some insisted on having the old offender restored; others wished to have a young man they had on trial for some weeks; others, again, were for sending to New England for a minister. In reply, one who addressed himself to the chief speaker observed, "Sir, when we have been at the expense (which will not be trifling) of fetching this gentleman from New England, perhaps he'll not stay with us." "Don't you know how to make him stay?" said another. "No Sir." "I'll tell you; give him a large salary, and I'll engage he'll stay." I listened attentively to the debate, and most plainly it appeared to me, that these mercenary creatures were all actuated by one and the same motive, which was, not the regard for souls, but the love of money. One of these men, called a reverend divine, whom these people almost adored, had, to my knowledge, left his flock in Long Island, and removed to Philadelphia, where he could get more money. I have myself heard some on the Island say that they had almost empoverished themselves in order to keep him; but, being unable to equal what he was offered at Philadelphia, he left them. Surely these are the shepherds who regard the fleece more than the flock, and in whose mouths are lies, when they say that they are the ambassadours of Christ, whose command it is, "Freely ye have received, freely give."

In our way to Freehold, as we came to Stony Brook, my husband turned towards me, and tauntingly said, "Here's one of Satan's synagogues, don't you long to be in it; I hope to see you cured of your new religion." A little further on, we came to a large run of water, over which there was no bridge, and, being strangers, we knew no way to avoid passing through it. He carried over our clothes, which we had in bundles; and, taking off my shoes, I walked through in my stockings. It was in the 12th month; the weather was very cold, and a fall of snow lay on the ground. It was the concern of my heart, that the Lord would sanctify all my afflictions to me, and give me patience to bear them. After walking nearly a mile, we came to a house, which proved to be a sort of tavern. My husband called for some spirituous liquors, and I got some weakened cider mulled, which rendered me extremely sick; so that, after we were a little past the house, being too faint to proceed, I fell down. "What's the matter now?" said my husband, "what, are you drunk? Where's your religion now?" He knew I was not drunk, and, at that time, I believe he pitied me, although he spoke in this manner. After I was a little recovered, we went on, and came to another tavern, where we lodged. The next day, as we journied, a young man, driving an empty cart, overtook us. We asked him to let us ride, and he readily granted the request. I had known the time when I would not have been seen in a cart, but my proud heart was humbled, and I did not now regard the look of it. This cart belonged to a man in Shrewsbury, and was to go through the place of our destination. We soon had the care of the team to ourselves, through a failure of the driver, and arrived with it at Freehold. My husband would have had me stay here, while he went to see the team safe home; I told him, No; since he had led me through the country like a vagabond, I would not stay behind him. We therefore went together, and lodged, that night, at the house of the owner of the cart. The next day, on our return to Freehold, we met a man riding full speed, who, stopping, said to my husband, "Sir, are you a schoolmaster?" He answered, "Yes." "I am come," replied the stranger, "to tell you of two new schoolhouses, two miles apart, each of which wants a master." How this person came to hear of us, who arrived but the night before, I never knew. I was glad he was not called a Quaker, lest it should have been thought a plot by my husband, to whom I turned and said,—"My dear, look on me with pity, if thou hast any affection left for me, which I hope thou hast, for I am not conscious of having done any thing to alienate it. Here is an opportunity to settle us both, and I am willing to do all in my power, towards getting an honest livelihood." After a short pause, he consented to go with the young man. In our way, we came to the house of a worthy Friend, who was a preacher, though we did not know it. I was surprised to see the people so kind to us. We had not been long in the house, till we were invited to lodge there for the night, being the last of the week. My husband accepted the invitation, saying, "My wife has had a tedious travel, and I pity her." These kind expressions affected me, for I heard them very seldom. The friend's kindness could not proceed from my appearing like a Quaker, because I had not yet altered my dress. The woman of the house, after we had concluded to stay, fixed her eyes upon me, and said, "I believe thou hast met with a deal of trouble," to which I made but little answer. My husband observing they were of that sort of people, whom he had so much endeavoured to shun, gave us no opportunity for discourse that night; but, the next morning, I let my friend know a little of my situation.

When meeting-time came, I longed to go, but dared not to ask my husband's leave. As the Friends were getting ready themselves, they asked him if he would accompany them, observing, that they knew those who were to be his employers, and, if they were at meeting, would speak to them. He consented. The woman Friend then said, "And wilt thou let thy wife go too;" which request he denied; but she answered his objections so prudently that he could not be angry, and at last consented. I went with joy, and a heavenly meeting it was. My spirit did rejoice in the God of my salvation. May I ever, in humility, preserve the remembrance of his tender mercies to me.

By the end of the week, we got settled in our new situation. We took a room, in a friend's house, one mile from each school, and eight from the meeting-house. I now deemed it proper to let my husband see I was determined to join with friends. When first day came, I directed myself to him in this manner: "My dear, art thou willing to let me go to meeting?" He flew into a rage, and replied "No you sha'n't." Speaking firmly, I told him, "That, as a dutiful wife, I was ready to obey all his lawful commands; but, when they imposed upon my conscience, I could not obey him. I had already wronged myself, in having done it too long; and though he was near to me, and, as a wife ought, I loved him, yet God, who was nearer than all the world to me, had made me sensible that this was the way in which I ought to go. I added, that this was no small cross to my own will; but I had given up my heart, and I trusted that He who called for it would enable me, for the remainder of my life, to keep it steadily devoted to his service; and I hoped I should not, on this account, make the worse wife." I spoke, however, to no purpose;—he continued inflexible.

I had now put my hand to the plough, and resolved not to draw back; I therefore went without leave. I expected he would immediately follow and force me back, but he did not. I called at the house of one of the neighbours, and, getting a girl to show me the way, I went on rejoicing, and praising God in my heart.

Thus, for some time, I had to go eight miles on foot to meeting, which I never thought hard. My husband had a horse, but he would not suffer me to ride on it; nor, when my shoes were worn out, would he let me have a new pair; but, though he hoped, on this account, to keep me from meeting, it did not hinder me:—I have tied them round with strings to keep them on.

Finding that all the means he had yet used could not alter my resolutions, he several times struck me with severe blows. I endeavoured to bear all with patience, believing that the time would come when he would see I was in the right. Once he came up to me, took out his penknife, and said, "If you offer to go to meeting to-morrow, with this knife I'll cripple you, for you shall not be a Quaker." I made him no answer. In the morning, I set out as usual; he did not attempt to harm me. Having despaired of recovering me himself, he fled, for help, to the priest, whom he told, that I had been a very religious woman, in the way of the Church of England, of which I was a member, and had a good certificate from Long Island; that I was now bewitched, and had turned Quaker, which almost broke his heart; and, therefore, he desired that, as he was one who had the care of souls, he would come and pay me a visit, and use his endeavours to reclaim me, which he hoped, by the blessing of God, would be done. The priest consented, and fixed the time for his coming, which was that day two weeks, as he said he could not come sooner. My husband came home extremely pleased, and told me of it. I replied, with a smile, I trusted I should be enabled to give a reason for the hope within me; yet I believed, at the same time, that the priest would never trouble himself about me, which proved to be the case. Before the day he appointed came, it was required of me, in a more public manner, to confess to the world what I was. I felt myself called to give up to prayer in meeting. I trembled, and would freely have given up my life to be excused. What rendered the required service harder on me was, that I was not yet taken under the care of friends; and was kept from requesting to be so, for fear I should bring a scandal on the society. I begged to be excused till I had joined, and then I would give up freely. The answer was, "I am a covenant-keeping God, and the word that I spake to thee, when I found thee in distress, even that I would never forsake thee, if thou wouldst be obedient to what I should make known unto thee, I will assuredly make good. If thou refusest, my spirit shall not always strive. Fear not, I will make way for thee through all thy difficulties, which shall be many, for my name's sake; but, be faithful, and I will give thee a crown of life." To this language

I answered "Thy will, O God, be done; I am in thy hand, do with me according to thy word;" and I then prayed.

This day, as usual, I had gone to meeting on foot. While my husband (as he afterwards told me) was lying on the bed, these words crossed his mind: "Lord, where shall I fly to shun thee," &c. upon which he arose, and, seeing it rain, got the horse and set off to fetch me, arriving just as the meeting broke up. I got on horseback as quickly as possible, lest he should hear I had been speaking; he did hear of it nevertheless, and, as soon as we were in the woods, began with saying, "Why do you mean thus to make my life unhappy? What, could you not be a Quaker, without turning fool in this manner?" I answered in tears, "My dear, look on me with pity, if thou hast any; canst thou think that I, in the bloom of my days, would bear all that thou knowest of, and much that thou knowest not of, if I did not feel it my duty." These words touched him, and, he said, "Well, I'll e'en give you up; I see it wont avail to strive; if it be of God I cannot overthrow it; and, if of yourself, it will soon fall." I saw the tears stand in his eyes, at which I was overcome with joy, and began already to reap the fruits of my obedience. But my trials were not yet over. The time appointed for the priest to visit me arrived, but no priest appeared. My husband went to fetch him, but he refused, saying he was busy, which so displeased my husband that he never went to hear him again, and, for some time, went to no place of worship.

My faith was now assaulted in another way, so strongly, that all my former trials were but trifling to it. This exercise came upon me unexpectedly, by hearing a woman speak of a book she had read, in which it was asserted that Christ was not the Son of God. A voice within me seemed to answer "No more he is, it's all a fancy, and the contrivance of men." Thus again was I filled with inexpressible trouble, which continued three weeks; and again did I seek desolate places, where I might make my moan. I have lain whole nights without sleep. I thought myself deserted of God, but did not let go my trust in him. I kept alive a hope that He who had delivered me as it were out of the paw of the bear, and the jaws of the lion, would in his own good time, deliver me from this temptation also. This was, at length, my experience; and I found the truth of his words, that all things shall work together for the good of those who love and fear him. My present exercises were to prepare me for further services in his cause; and it is necessary for his ministers to experience all conditions, that they may thereby be abler to speak to them.

This happened just after my first appearance as a minister, and friends had not been to talk with me. They did not well know what to do, till I had appeared again, which was not for some time, when the Monthly Meeting appointed four friends to pay me a visit. They left me well satisfied with the conference, and I joined the society. My husband still went to no place of worship. One day he said to me, "I would go to meeting, only I'm afraid I shall hear your clack, which I cannot bear." I used no persuasions. When meeting-time came, he got the horse, took me behind him, and went. For several months, if he saw me offer to rise, he went out; till, one day, I rose before he was aware and then, as he afterwards owned, he was ashamed to do it.

From this time, he left off the practice, and never hindered me from going to meeting. Though he did not take up the cross, yet his judgment was convinced; and, sometimes, melting into tears, he would say to me, "My dear, I have seen the beauty there is in the truth, and that thou hast followed the right way, in which I pray God to preserve thee." I told him, that I hoped He who had given me strength would also favour him, "O," said he, "I cannot bear the reproach thou dost, to be called turn-coat, and become a laughing-stock to the world; but I'll no longer hinder thee." This I considered a favour, and a little hope remained that my prayers, on his account, would be heard.

We lived in a small house by ourselves, which, though mean, and though we had little to put in it, our bed being no better than chaff, I was truly content. The only desires I had were for my own preservation, and to be blessed with the reformation of my husband. He was connected with a set of men whom he feared would make game of him, which indeed they already did; asking him when he designed to commence preacher, for they saw he intended to turn Quaker, and seemed to love his wife better since she became one than before. They used to come to our house, and provoked him to sit up and drink with them, sometimes till near day, while I have been sorrowing in a stable. Once, as I sat in this condition, I heard him say to his company, "I can't bear any longer to afflict my poor wife in this manner; for, whatever you may think of her, I do believe she's a good woman." He then came to me and said, "Come in, my dear, God has given thee a deal of patience: I'll put an end to this practice." This was the last time they sat up at night.

My husband now thought that if he was in any place where it was not known he had been so bitter against friends, he could do better. I objected to this, fearing it would not be for his benefit. Frequently, in a broken and affectionate manner, he condemned his ill usage of me. I answered, that I hoped it had been for my good, and therefore desired he would not be afflicted on that account. According to the measure of grace received, I did what I could, both by example and precept, for his good. My advice was for him to stay where he was, as I was afraid he would grow weaker in his good resolutions, if he removed.

All I could say would not avail. Hearing of a place at Bordentown, he went thither, but was not suited. He next removed to Mount Holly, where he settled. We had each of us a good school; we soon got our house pretty well furnished, and might have done very well. Nothing seemed wanting to complete my happiness, except the reformation of my husband, which I had much reason to doubt I should not see soon. It fell out according to my fears. He addicted himself much to drinking, and grew worse than before. Sorrow was again my lot, I prayed for patience to bear my afflictions, and to submit to the dispensations of Providence. I murmured not; nor do I recollect that I ever uttered any harsh expressions except on one occasion. My husband coming home a little intoxicated, (a state in which he was very fractious,) and, finding me at work by a candle, he put it out, fetching me, at the same time, a box on the ear, and saying, "You don't earn your light." At this unkind usage, which I had not been used to for the last two years, I was somewhat angry, and said, "Thou art a vile man." He struck me again; but my anger had cooled, and I received the blow without so much as a word in return. This also displeased him, and he went on in a distracted like manner, uttering such expressions of despair as, he believed he was predestined to damnation, and he did not care how soon God struck him dead. I said very little, till, at length, in the bitterness of my soul, I broke out into these expressions: "Lord, look down on my afflictions, and deliver me by some means or other." My prayer was granted, but in such a manner that I thought it would have killed me. He went to Burlington, where he got drunk, and inlisted to go as a common soldier to Cuba, in the year 1740. I had drunk many bitter cups, but this seemed the bitterest of them all. A thousand times I blamed myself for making such a request, which I was afraid had displeased God, who had, in displeasure, granted it for my punishment.

I have since had cause to believe that he was benefited by his rash act, as, in the army, he did what he could not at home;—he suffered for the testimony of truth. When they came to prepare for an engagement, he refused to fight; he was whipt, and brought before the general, who asked him, why he inlisted if he would not fight. "I did it," said he, "in a drunken frolic, when the devil had the better of me; but now my judgment is convinced I ought not to fight, neither will I, whatever I suffer. I have but one life, and you may take that if you please, for I'll never take up arms." He adhered to this resolution. By their cruel usage of him in consequence, he was so much disabled that the general sent him to Chelsea Hospital, near London. Within nine months afterwards, he died at this place, and I hope made a good end.

Having been obliged to say much of his ill usage to me, I have thought it my duty to say what I could in his favour. Although he was so bad, I never thought him the worst of men. If he had suffered religion to have had its perfect work, I should have been happy in the lowest situation of life. I have had cause to bless God, for enabling me, in the station of a wife, to do my duty, and now that I am a widow, I submit to his will. May I still be preserved by the arm of Divine Power; may I never forget the tender mercies of my God, the remembrance of which often boweth my soul in humility before his throne, and I cry, "Lord! what was I, that thou shouldst have revealed to my soul the knowledge of thy truth, and have done so much for one who deserved thy displeasure? Mayst thou, O God, be glorified, and I abased. It is thy own works that praise thee; and, of a truth, to the humble soul, thou makest every bitter thing sweet."

Jonathan Mayhew
(1720–1766)

Jonathan Mayhew, for almost twenty years pastor of Boston's West Church, was a religious and political thinker whose ideas were somewhat ahead of his time. A liberal Christian who repudiated the doctrine of the Trinity, affirmed the existence of free will, and defended the right of private judgment, Mayhew's views involved him in numerous controversies. The following selection, in which Mayhew establishes the grounds on which he saw civil disobedience as both legitimate and necessary, allies him with a later generation of American thinkers who were to frame the argument—at once civil, moral, and religious—for America's declaration of independence from English tyranny.

from A Discourse Concerning Unlimited Submission and Non-Resistance to the Higher Powers
(1750)

Thus it appears, that the common argument, grounded upon this passage [Romans 13:1–3], in favor of universal, and passive obedience, really overthrows itself, by proving too much, if it proves any thing at all; namely, that no civil officer is, in any case whatever, to be resisted, though acting in express contradiction to the design of his office; which no man, in his senses, ever did, or can assert.

If we calmly consider the nature of the thing itself, nothing can well be imagined more directly contrary to common sense, than to suppose that millions of people should be subjected to the arbitrary, precarious pleasure of one single man; (who has naturally no superiority over them in point of authority) so that their estates, and every thing that is valuable in life, and even their lives also, shall be absolutely at his disposal, if he happens to be wanton and capricious enough to demand them. What unprejudiced man can think, that God made ALL to be thus subservient to the lawless pleasure and phrenzy of ONE, so that it shall always be a sin to resist him! Nothing but the most plain and express revelation from heaven could make a sober impartial man believe such a monstrous, unaccountable doctrine, and, indeed, the thing itself, appears so shocking—so out of all proportion, that it may be questioned, whether all the miracles that ever were wrought, could make it credible, that this doctrine really came from God. At present, there is not the least syllable in scripture which gives any countenance to it. The hereditary, indefeasible, divine right of kings, and the doctrine of non-resistance, which is built upon the supposition of such a right, are altogether as fabulous and chimerical, as transubstantiation; or any of the most absurd reveries of ancient or modern visionaries. These notions are fetched neither from divine revelation, nor human reason; and if they are derived from neither of those sources, it is not much matter from whence they come, or whither they go. Only it is a pity that such doctrines should be propagated in society, to raise factions and rebellions, as we see they have in fact, been both in the last, and in the present, REIGN.

But then, if unlimited submission and passive obedience to the higher powers, in all possible cases, be not a duty, it will be asked, "How far are we obliged to submit? If we may innocently disobey and resist in some cases, why not in all? Where shall we stop? What is the measure of our duty? This doctrine tends to the total dissolution of civil government; and to introduce such scenes of wild anarchy and confusion, as are more fatal to society than the worst tyranny."

After this manner, some men object; and, indeed, this is the most plausible thing that can be said in favor of such an absolute submission as they plead for. But the worst (or rather the best) of it, is, that there is very little strength or solidity in it. For similar difficulties may be raised with respect to almost every duty of natural and revealed religion.—To instance only in two, both of which are near akin, and indeed exactly parallel, to the case before us. It is unquestionably the duty of children to submit to their parents; and of servants, to their masters. But no one asserts, that it is their duty to obey, and submit to them, in all supposeable cases; or universally a sin to resist them. Now does this tend to subvert the just authority of parents and masters? Or to introduce confusion and anarchy into private families? No. How then does the same principle tend to unhinge the government of that larger family, the body politic? We know, in general, that children and servants are obliged to obey their parents and masters respectively. We know also, with equal certainty, that they are not obliged to submit to them in all things, without exception; but may, in some cases, reasonably, and therefore innocently, resist them. These principles are acknowledged upon all hands, whatever difficulty there may be in fixing the exact limits of submission. Now there is at least as much difficulty in stating the measure of duty in these two cases, as in the case of rulers and subjects. So that this is really no objection, at least no reasonable one, against resistance to the higher powers: Or, if it is one, it will hold equally against resistance in the other cases mentioned.— It is indeed true, that turbulent, vicious-minded men, may take occasion from this principle, that their rulers may, in some cases, be lawfully resisted, to raise factions and disturbances in the state; and to make resistance where resistance is needless, and therefore, sinful. But is it not equally true, that children and servants of turbulent, vicious minds, may take occasion from this principle, that parents and masters may, in some cases be lawfully resisted, to resist when resistance is unnecessary, and therefore, criminal? Is the principle in either case false in itself, merely because it may be abused; and applied to legitimate disobedience and resistance in those instances, to which it ought not to be applied? According to this way of arguing, their will be no true principles in the world; for there are none but what may be wrested and perverted to serve bad purposes, either through the weakness or wickedness of men.[1]

A PEOPLE, really oppressed to a great degree by their sovereign, cannot well be insensible when they are so oppressed. And such a people (if I may allude to an ancient fable) have like the hesperian fruit, a *dragon* for their protector and guardian: Nor would they have any reason to mourn, if some *hercules* should appear to dispatch him—For a nation thus abused to arise unanimously, and to resist their prince, even to the dethroning him, is not criminal; but a reasonable way of vindicating their liberties and just rights; it is making use of the means, and the only means, which God has put into their power, for mutual and self-defence. And it would be highly criminal in them, not to make use of this means. It would be stupid tameness, and unaccountable folly, for whole nations to suffer one unreasonable, ambitious and cruel man, to wanton and riot in their misery. And in such a case it would, of the two, be more rational to suppose, that they that did NOT resist, than that they who did, would receive to themselves damnation.

John Woolman
(1720–1772)

The literary and religious reputation of John Woolman has often been overshadowed by those of some of his other eighteenth-century contemporaries, such as Jonathan Edwards and even Charles Chauncey, and he has never achieved the fame of his fellow Quaker and mystic John Greenleaf Whittier. Yet Charles Lamb confessed that Woolman's autobiographical Journal was the only American book he ever read twice, and Ralph Waldo Emerson declared that he found more wisdom in its pages than in "any other book written since the days of the apostles."

Woolman was a person of rare moral character. Among the first of his countrymen to confront the issue of poverty in the United States and to point out its degrading effects upon rich and poor alike, Woolman also anticipated Henry David Thoreau by almost a century in using nonpayment of taxes as a carefully considered act of civil disobedience. In addition, he was the first prominent American religious figure to work out a serious and compelling case against the institution of slavery. "Some Considerations on the Keeping of Negroes" challenges the moral and religious grounds on which others had defended their right to own slaves. The quiet dignity and compassion with which Woolman states his argument, together with the premises from which that argument springs, and the conclusions to which it leads, show that Woolman was exactly what Samuel Taylor Coleridge took him to be: a model of Christian charity.

from *Some Considerations on the Keeping of Negroes (1754)*

Forasmuch as ye did it to the least of these my Brethren, ye did it unto me, Matt. xxv. 40.

As Many Times there are different Motives to the same Actions; and one does that from a generous Heart, which another does for selfish Ends:——The like may be said in this Case.

There are various Circumstances amongst them that keep *Negroes*, and different Ways by which they fall under their Care; and, I doubt not, there are many well disposed Persons amongst them who desire rather to manage wisely and justly in this difficult Matter, than to make Gain of it.

But the general Disadvantage which these poor *Africans* lie under in an enlight'ned Christian Country, having often fill'd me with real Sadness, and been like undigested Matter on my Mind, I now think it my Duty, through Divine Aid, to offer some Thoughts thereon to the Consideration of others.

When we remember that all Nations are of one Blood, *Gen.* iii. 20. that in this World we are but Sojourners, that we are subject to the like Afflictions and Infirmities of Body, the like Disorders and Frailties in Mind, the like Temptations, the same Death, and the same Judgment, and, that the Alwise Being is Judge and Lord over us all, it seems to raise an Idea of a general Brotherhood, and a Disposition easy to be touched with a Feeling of each others Afflictions: But when we forget those Things, and look chiefly at our outward Circumstances, in this and some Ages past, constantly retaining in our Minds the Distinction betwixt us and them, with respect to our Knowledge and Improvement in Things divine, natural and artificial, our Breasts being apt to be filled with fond Notions of Superiority, there is Danger of erring in our Conduct toward them.

We allow them to be of the same Species with ourselves, the Odds is, we are in a higher Station, and enjoy greater Favours than they: And when it is thus, that our heavenly Father endoweth some of his Children with distinguished Gifts, they are intended for good Ends; but if those thus gifted are thereby lifted up above their Brethren, not considering themselves as Debtors to the Weak, nor behaving themselves as faithful Stewards, none who judge impartially can suppose them free from Ingratitude.

When a People dwell under the liberal Distribution of Favours from Heaven, it behoves them carefully to inspect their Ways, and consider the Purposes for which those Favours were bestowed, lest, through Forgetfulness of God, and Misusing his Gifts, they incur his heavy Displeasure, whose Judgments are just and equal, who exalteth and humbleth to the Dust as he seeth meet.

It appears by Holy Record that Men under high Favours have been apt to err in their Opinions concerning others. Thus *Israel*, according to the Description of the Prophet, *Isaih.* lxv. 5. when exceedingly corrupted and degenerated, yet remembred they were the chosen People of God and could say, *Stand by thyself, come not near me, for I am holier than thou.* That this was no chance Language, but their common Opinion of other People, more fully appears by considering the Circumstances which attended when God was beginning to fulfil his precious Promises concerning the Gathering of the *Gentiles.*

The Most High, in a Vision, undeceived *Peter*, first prepared his Heart to believe; and, at the House of *Cornelius*, shewed him of a Certainty that God was no Respecter of Persons.

The Effusion of the Holy Ghost upon a People with whom they, the *Jewish* Christians, would not so much as eat, was strange to them: All they of the Circumcision were astonished to see it; and the Apostles and Brethren of *Judea* contended with *Peter* about it, till he, having rehearsed the whole Matter, and fully shewn that the Father's Love was unlimited, they are thereat struck with Admiration, and cry out; *Then hath God also to the* Gentiles *granted Repentance unto Life*!

The Opinion of peculiar Favours being confined to them, was deeply rooted, or else the above Instance had been less strange to them, for these Reasons: *First*, They were generally acquainted with the Writings of the Prophets, by whom this Time was repeatedly spoken of, and pointed at. *Secondly*, Our Blessed Lord shortly before expressly said, *I have other Sheep, not of this Fold, them also must I bring*, &c. *Lastly*, His Words to them after his Resurrection, at the very Time of his Ascension, *Ye shall be Witnesses to me, not only in* Jerusalem, Judea, *and* Samaria, *but to the uttermost Parts of the Earth.*

Those concuring Circumstances, one would think, might have raised a strong Expectation of seeing such a Time; yet, when it came, it proved Matter of Offence and Astonishment.

To consider Mankind otherwise than Brethren, to think Favours are peculiar to one Nation, and exclude others, plainly supposes a Darkness in the Understanding: For as God's Love is universal, so where the Mind is inefficiently influenced by it, it begets a Likeness of itself, and the Heart is enlarged towards all Men. Again, to conclude a People froward, perverse, and worse by Nature than others (who ungratefully receive Favours, and apply them to bad Ends) this will excite a Behaviour toward them unbecoming the Excellence of true Religion.

To prevent such Error, let us calmly consider their Circumstance;

and, the better to do it, make their Case ours. Suppose, then, that our Ancestors and we had been exposed to constant Servitude in the more servile and inferior Employments of Life; that we had been destitute of the Help of Reading and good Company; that amongst ourselves we had had few wise and pious Instructors; that the Religious amongst our Superiors seldom took Notice of us; that while others, in Ease, have plentifully heap'd up the Fruit of our Labour, we had receiv'd barely enough to relieve Nature, and being wholly at the Command of others, had generally been treated as a contemptible, ignorant Part of Mankind: Should we, in that Case, be less abject than they now are? Again, If Oppression be so hard to bear, that a wise Man is made mad by it, *Eccl.* vii. 7. then a Series of those Things altering the Behaviour and Manners of a People, is what may reasonably be expected.

When our Property is taken contrary to our Mind, by Means appearing to us unjust, it is only through divine Influence, and the Enlargement of Heart from thence proceeding, that we can love our reputed Oppressors: If the *Negroes* fall short in this, an uneasy, if not a disconsolate Disposition, will be awak'ned, and remain like Seeds in their Minds, producing Sloth and many other Habits appearing odious to us, with which being free Men, they, perhaps, had not been chargeable. These, and other Circumstances, rightly considered, will lessen that too great Disparity, which some make between us and them.

Integrity of Heart hath appeared in some of them; so that if we continue in the Word of Christ (previous to Discipleship, *John* viii. 31.) and our Conduct towards them be seasoned with his Love, we may hope to see the good Effect of it: The which, in a good Degree, is the Case with some into whose Hands they have fallen: But that too many treat them otherwise, not seeming concious of any Neglect, is, alas! too evident.

When *Self-love* presides in our Minds, our Opinions are bias'd in our own Favour; in this Condition, being concerned with a People so situated, that they have no Voice to plead their own Cause, there's Danger of using ourselves to an undisturbed Partiality, till, by long Custom, the Mind becomes reconciled with it, and the Judgment itself infected.

To humbly apply to God for Wisdom, that we may thereby be enabled to see Things as they are, and ought to be, is very needful; hereby the hidden Things of Darkness may be brought to light, and the Judgment made clear: We shall then consider Mankind as Brethren: Though different Degrees and a Variety of Qualifications and Abilities, one dependant on another, be admitted, yet high Thoughts will be laid aside, and all Men treated as becometh the Sons of one Father, agreeable to the Doctrine of Christ Jesus.

He hath laid down the best Criterion, by which Mankind ought to judge of their own Conduct, and others judge for them of theirs, one towards another, *viz. Whatsoever ye would that Men should do unto you, do ye even so to them.* I take it, that all Men by Nature, are equally entitled to the Equity of this Rule, and under the indispensable Obligations of it. One Man ought not to look upon another Man, or Society of Men, as so far beneath him, but that he should put himself in their Place, in all his Actions towards them, and bring all to this Test, *viz.* How should I approve of this Conduct, were I in their Circumstance and they in mine? *A. Arscot*'s Considerations, Part III. Fol. 107.[1]

This Doctrine being of a moral unchangeable Nature, hath been likewise inculcated in the former Dispensation; *If a Stranger sojourn with thee in your Land, ye shall not vex him; but the Stranger that dwelleth with you, shall be as One born amongst you, and thou shalt love him as thyself. Lev.* xix. 33, 34. Had these People come voluntarily and dwelt amongst us, to have called them Strangers would be proper; and their being brought by Force, with Regret, and a languishing Mind, may well raise Compassion in a Heart rightly disposed: But there is Nothing in such Treatment, which upon a wise and judicious Consideration, will any Ways lessen their Right of being treated as Strangers. If the Treatment which many of them meet with, be rightly examined and compared with those Precepts, *Thou shalt not vex him nor oppress him; he shall be as one born amongst you, and thou shalt love him as thyself,* Lev. xix. 33. Deut. xxvii. 19. there will appear an important Difference betwixt them.

It may be objected there is Cost of Purchase, and Risque of their Lives to them who possess 'em, and therefore needful that they make the best Use of their Time: In a Practice just and reasonable, such Objections may have Weight; but if the Work be wrong from the Beginning, there's little or no Force in them. If I purchase a Man who hath never forfeited his Liberty, the natural Right of Freedom is in him; and shall I keep him and his Posterity in Servitude and Ignorance? How should I approve of this Conduct, were I in his Circumstances, and he in mine? It may be thought, that to treat them as we would willingly be treated, our Gain by them would be inconsiderable: And it were, in divers Respects, better that there were none in our Country.

We may further consider, that they are now amongst us, and those of our Nation the Cause of their being here; that whatsoever Difficulty accrues thereon, we are justly chargeable with, and to bear all Inconveniencies attending it, with a serious and weighty Concern of Mind to do our Duty by them, is the best we can do. To seek a Remedy by continuing the Oppression, because we have Power to do it, and see others do it, will, I apprehend, not be doing as we would be done by.

How deeply soever Men are involved in the most exquisite Difficulties, Sincerity of Heart, and upright Walking before God, freely submitting to his Providence, is the most sure Remedy: He only is able to relieve, not only Persons, but Nations, in their greatest Calamities. . . .

Francisco Palou

(1723–1789)

Fray Francisco Palou, born in Majorca, Spain, entered the Franciscan order in 1739 and ten years later came to Vera Cruz, Mexico, with Fray Junipero Serra to participate in missionary activities in the New World. When King Carlos III of Spain expelled Jesuit missionaries from Spanish dominions, the Franciscans sought to replace them in California and extend their activities. Reaching Lower California in 1768, Palou managed in five years to be reassigned to the missionary work in Upper California so that he could continue his association with Serra. Eventually assigned to the mission at San Francisco where he stayed until 1785, a year after Serra's death, he then returned to Mexico, now in ill health himself, and completed the life of Serra he had begun writing during his California years.

Fray Palou's life of Serra, Relacion historica (1787), contains much important information about the history of missions in early California, but it is primarily significant as a biography of the priest credited with the spiritual vision of founding and organizing many of them. As such it takes its place in a long tradition of American religious hagiography that includes such works as Cotton Mather's Magnalia Christi Americana and Jonathan Edwards's biographical fragment "Sarah Pierrepont."

from *Life of Junipero Serra* (1787)

CHAPTER XXII. THE ARRIVAL OF THE
EXPEDITIONS AT THE PORT OF
MONTEREY AND THE FOUNDING OF THE
MISSION AND GARRISON OF SAN
CARLOS.

I can best satisfy the requirements of this chapter by inserting here the
following letter which the Venerable Father wrote me and in which he
tells of their arrival at Monterey and of the activities of the expedition
in that port.

Long live Jesus, Mary and Joseph!—To the Reverend Father
Lector and President, Fr. Francisco Palou—Dearly Beloved
Friend and Respected Sir: On the 31st of May, with the favor
of God, our packet-boat, "San Antonio," under the command of Captain Don Juan Pérez, after a month and a half
of rather hard sailing and bad weather, anchored in this
beautiful harbor of Monterey, the very same harbor and un-
changed in substance and circumstances from what it was
when the expedition of Don Sebastian Vizcaino left it in the
year 1603.[1] To this comforting fact there has been added this
other one, that we found that just a week previously the land
expedition had also arrived and with it Father Fr. Juan, all
in good health. On the holy day of Pentecost, the 3d of June,
after having gathered together all the officers of sea and land
and all the rest of the people by the side of the little ravine
and oak where the Fathers of that other expedition had held
their celebration, an altar was erected, the bells were hung
up and rung, the hymn *Veni Creator* was sung and the water
blessed, and finally a large cross was erected and the royal
standard set up. I then sang the first Mass which we supposed
has been celebrated here since that long ago, and then we
sang the *Hail to Our Lady* before the image of our Most
Illustrious Queen which occupied the altar. After that I
preached a sermon to the assembled people. After the service
had been concluded with the *Te Deum* the officers performed
the ceremony of taking formal possession of the land in the
name of the King, our lord (whom may God keep). We afterwards ate our dinner together under a shade on the beach.

The whole service had been accompanied with much thunder of powder both on land and from the ship. To God alone be given all the honor and the glory. . . .

Another thing which I much desire to know is concerning the Missionaries from Spain. I earnestly entreat your Reverence that you secure two subjects for these Missions in order that with the four who are here we may complete the number (six) and equip the Mission of San Buenaventura in the channel of Santa Barbara, as the location is much more advantageous than that of San Diego or Monterey or any other point so far discovered. Provisions have already been sent twice for this Mission and now, since the failure to establish it could not be blamed in any way to the friars, I do not want the blame to fall upon us when the proper military protection is at hand for its inauguration. The truth is that as long as Father Fr. Juan and myself are in good health the founding will not be delayed because we shall separate and go each one to his own Mission, but it will be the greatest of all hardships for me to be located in a place from which the nearest friar is eighty leagues distant. I therefore beg your Reverence that you do what you can to shorten this period of cruel solitude. . . .

We are woefully lacking in wax for our Masses, both here and in San Diego; however, we are going to celebrate the feast and procession of Corpus Christi to-morrow, although with little ostentation, in order to frighten away how many soever little devils there may be lurking in this region. If there is any way to send the wax it would come very handy. Please send also the incense which I asked for on another occasion. You will not fail to inform His Excellency of the good news of the discovery of this port, and I am sure that you will also not fail to ever commend us to God. May He keep your Reverence many years in His holy love and grace. Mission of San Carlos of Monterey, June, on the feast of San Antonio of Padua, 1770. I kiss the hand of your Reverence.

Your affectionate Friend, Companion and Servant,
FR. JUNÍPERO SERRA.

On the same day in which possession was taken of the port, and the royal garrison of San Carlos was begun, the Mission was founded under the same name, and next to the garrison a little chapel was built with a stockade for a provisional church. A house was also erected with the necessary rooms for the dwelling-place of the Fathers and for the offices. Both establishments were surrounded with a stockade for defense. The pagans had not yet put in an appearance as they were greatly frightened by the discharge of the artillery and the rattle of the musketry of the troops; but little by little, they begun to draw near and the Venerable Father made them little presents in order to win them and to secure their entrance into the fold of Holy Church and the saving of their souls which was the principal object of all his plans. . . .

Don Pedro Fages, lieutenant of the volunteers from Cataluña, remained in command of the new garrison of San Carlos in Monterey; and as he considered that he was very short of troops, resolved, at the suggestion of the Venerable President, to suspend the founding of the Mission of San Buenaventura until a captain could arrive, with nineteen soldiers, who had gone down into Old California in the month of February to bring back the cattle. But the captain with the troop and cattle came up only as far as San Diego and sent us no further word until the following year when he communicated with us by ship, as we shall see later. Seeing that for these reasons the third Mission could not be begun, our Venerable Father, with his disciple Fr. Juan Crespi, devoted themselves to the conversion of the Indians of Monterey; but as there was no one who knew their language they encountered many difficulties at first, but finally God willed it that a door should be opened by means of a converted Indian boy whom they had brought from Old California, who, through the many conferences which the Venerable Fr. Junípero had him conduct with these pagans, began to understand them and to pronounce a few words in their language. When he could explain to them what was said he gave them to understand that the purpose of the Fathers in coming to their land was to direct their souls into the way of heaven.

It was on the 26th of December of the same year that the first baptism was celebrated among these gentile people and it was for the fervent and devoted heart of our Venerable Father a source of unbounded joy. Little by little others were won and the number of Christians increased so that three years later when I came up to that Mission there were in all one hundred and sixty-five; and when the Venerable Founder Junípero terminated his glorious career he left one thousand and fourteen baptized souls of whom many had already passed on to enjoy God and eternal life, as the fruitage of his incessant and Apostolic labors.

One of the things that had greatly helped in these conversions, or perhaps I had better say, that was the principal foundation of this most important Conquest, was the strange marvels and prodigies which God, our Lord, had wrought in the eyes of the gentiles that they might fear and also learn to love the Catholics: Fear, to restrain them so that in spite of their numbers far in excess of the little group of Christians,

they showed us no insolence; and Love, which brought them to hear
with affection the gospel doctrine which we had come to teach them,
and to embrace the gentle yoke of our holy law.

In his diary of the second land expedition to the port of Monterey,
Father Crespi writes, under the date of the 24th of May, as follows:

> After traveling about three leagues we arrived at one o'clock
> at the little salt water lakes near Pt. Pinos, toward the north-
> east, where in the first journey the second cross had been set
> up. Before making camp, the Governor, one of the soldiers
> and myself went on to see the cross in order to find out if
> there was any sign by which we might know if those of the
> vessel had already arrived, but nothing of the sort was found.
> We found the cross surrounded on all sides by arrows and
> little branches with many feathered crests, stuck up in the
> ground, which had been put there by the gentiles. There was
> also a string of sardines still somewhat fresh hanging from a
> branch by the side of the cross, on another was a piece of
> meat and at the foot of the cross there was a little pile of
> mussels.

All this excited great wonderment but as none could explain it
they suspended judgment.

As soon as the new converts who had been baptized could sufficiently make themselves understood in Spanish and when the Califor-
nian neophyte could understand their language they several times gave
us the following explanations. They said that the first time they saw
any of our people they noticed that *all of them wore upon the breast
a very brilliant cross*, and when they had gone away, leaving that large
cross standing on the shore, so great was the fear it inspired in them
that none of them dared to go near to that Sacred Symbol because
they saw it, after the sun had set and the shades of night had come
on, filled with the splendors of a great Light which seemed to them to
make it grow as it were until it reached up to the very heaven. But
when they drew near to it by day, when these strange appearances
were absent, and it was seen in its natural form they tried to win its
favor in order that it might not do them any harm, so they had brought
it this offering of meat, fish, and mussels, and when in wonderment
they noted that it did not eat anything they made the offering of the
arrows and the feathered crests as a sign that they wished to make
peace with the Holy Cross and with the people who had put it there.

This strange declaration was repeated by several of the Indians
(as I have said) on different occasions and last of all in the year 1774
when the Venerable Father President returned from Mexico. They told

him the same story that they had told me the previous year without the slightest variation. This the Servant of God communicated to His Excellency, the Viceroy, for his edification, in order to increase his fervor and activity in carrying out the plans of this spiritual enterprise. As a result of this prodigy and of many others which the Lord wrought, the conversion of the gentiles was accomplished most peacefully and without war's alarms. Blessed be God to whom be all the glory and praise.

Native American
Literature in the
Colonial Period

NORTH AMERICAN INDIAN ORATORY

The art of oratory was highly cultivated and refined by the Indians of North America. In many tribes it was essential to leadership. Decisions in the tribal council usually had to be unanimous, and the authority of the leader was often as dependent upon his powers of persuasion as upon his prowess as a warrior.

Since nearly all the surviving early Indian oratory was transcribed by whites, it is not surprising that the bulk of it is concerned with Indian-white relations. What is surprising, given the history of those relations, is that so much of it is not only dignified and restrained but also magnanimous. Even when Indian orators are protesting the enormous injustices, deceptions, betrayals, and violence committed against their people, their tone is never shrill, accusatory, or self-pitying. Their case is consistently based on universal grounds, and their appeal is always to the nobler side of their antagonists.

It has sometimes been countered that the eloquence and trenchancy of Indian oratory is attributable to the fact that the sympathetic whites who transcribed it wanted to put the Indian cause in its most attractive light. Fortunately, there are enough reliable translations of Indian oratory to leave little doubt as to the articulateness of its practitioners.

Chief Powhatan

Chief Powhatan presided over a confederacy of Algonguin tribes that roamed the territory of Virginia and Maryland at the time of the first English settlement at Jamestown in 1607. The generally amicable nature of early relations between Indians and whites appears to have been attributable to Powhatan's influence. His daughter Pocahontas actually married John Rolfe, one of the settlers. After Powhatan's death, however, hostilities broke out between the settlers and the natives, during which the Indians began a fourteen-year war to exterminate the whites. The following speech was given by Powhatan in 1609 at Werowcomico (Gloucester County) and reported by John Smith.

Why will you take by force what you may obtain by love? Why will you destroy us who supply you with food? What can you get by war? . . . We are unarmed, and willing to give you what you ask, if you come in a friendly manner. . . .

I am not so simple as not to know it is better to eat good meat, sleep comfortably, live quietly with my women and children, laugh and be merry with the English, and being their friend, trade for their copper and hatchets, than to run away from them. . . .

Take away your guns and swords, the cause of all our jealousy, or you may die in the same manner.

Chief Cannassatego

Canassatego, an Iroquois, delivered this speech during negotiations with whites in 1742 over land and goods. Canassatego is protesting what amounted to a breach of contract (actually, a failure to meet treaty obligations) on the part of the whites, but he is also forced to apologize for the poverty that white occupation and settlement of Indian lands has brought to his people, since it has prevented him from bringing as bountiful a gift of skins as is customary to begin new treaty negotiations. Therefore Canassatego has been obliged to plead that the white negotiators consider not the quantity of the skins presented so much as the spirit in which they have been given.

We received from the Proprietors yesterday, some goods in consideration of our release of the lands on the west side of Susquehanna. It is true, we have the full quantity according to agreement; but if the Proprietor had been here himself, we think, in regard of our numbers and poverty, he would have made an addition to them. If the goods were only to be divided amongst the Indians present, a single person would have but a small portion; but if you consider what numbers are left behind, equally entitled with us to a share, there will be extremely little. We therefore desire, if you have the keys of the Proprietor's chest, you will open it, and take out a little more for us.

We know our lands are now become more valuable: the white people think we do not know their value; but we are sensible that the land is everlasting, and the few goods we receive for it are soon worn out and gone. For the future we will sell no lands but when Brother

Onas[1] is in the country; and we will know beforehand the quantity of the goods we are to receive. Besides, we are not well used with respect to the lands still unsold by us. Your people daily settle on these lands, and spoil our hunting.—We must insist on your removing them, as you know they have no right to settle to the northward of *Kittoch-tinny-Hills.*—In particular, we renew our complaints against some people who are settled at *Juniata*, a branch of *Susquehanna*, and all along the banks of that river, as far as *Mahaniay*; and desire they may be forthwith made to go off the land; for they do great damage to our cousins the *Delawares*.

We have further to observe, with respect to the lands lying on the west side of *Susquehanna*, that though Brother *Onas* has paid us for what his people possess, yet some parts of that country have been taken up by persons whose place of residence is to the south of this province, from whom we have never received any consideration. This affair was recommended to you by our chiefs at our last treaty; and you then, at our earnest desire, promised to write a letter to that person who has the authority over those people, and to procure us his answer: as we have never heard from you on this head, we want to know what you have done in it. If you have not done anything, we now renew our request, and desire you will inform the person whose people are seated on our lands, that that country belongs to us, in right of conquest; we having bought it with our blood, and taken it from our enemies in fair war; and we expect, as owners of that land, to receive such a consideration for it as the land is worth. We desire you will press him to send us a positive answer: let him say *Yes* or *No*: if he says Yes, we will treat with him; if No, we are able to do ourselves justice; and we will do it, by going to take payment ourselves.

It is customary with us to make a present of skins whenever we renew our treaties. We are ashamed to offer our brethren so few; but your horses and cows have eat the grass our deer used to feed on. This has made them scarce, and will, we hope, plead in excuse for our not bringing a larger quantity: if we could have spared more we would have given more; but we are really poor; and desire you'll not consider the quantity, but, few as they are, accept them in testimony of our regard.

Chief Logan

In 1774 the colonial governor of Virginia, Lord Dunmore, called a council in an attempt to end an Indian war of revenge that had been provoked by white atrocities committed against the "Mingoes." The "Mingoes" constituted a band of friendly Iroquois who inhabited the upper Ohio River valley. Chief Logan's address to that council won him the admiration of Thomas Jefferson, who wrote in his Notes on the State of Virginia: *"I may challenge the whole orations of Demosthenes and Cicero, and of any more eminent orator, if Europe has furnished more eminent, to produce a single passage, superior to the speech of Logan." Logan reminded his white brothers that the senseless slaughter of all his living relations had compelled him to try to balance the scales of justice by avenging their deaths. But having recently accomplished his revenge and slaked his anger, Chief Logan declared that he was now prepared to embrace peace as eagerly as he had once sought retribution.*

I appeal to any white man to say, if ever he entered Logan's cabin hungry, and he gave him not meat; if ever he came cold and naked, and he clothed him not. During the course of the last long and bloody war, Logan remained idle in his cabin, an advocate for peace. Such was my love for the whites that my countrymen pointed as they passed, and said, "Logan is the friend of the white man." I had even thought to have lived with you, but for the injuries of one man, Colonel Cressap, who last spring, in cold blood and unprovoked, murdered all the relations of Logan, not even sparing my women and children.

There runs not a drop of my blood in the veins of any living creature. This called on me for revenge. I have sought it; I have killed many; I have fully glutted my vengeance. For my countrymen I rejoice at the beams of peace. But do not harbor a thought that mine is the joy of fear. Logan never felt fear! He will not turn on his heel to save his life. Who is there to mourn for Logan? Not one.

Chief Pachgantschilias

In 1787, Chief Pachgantschilias of the Delawares delivered this warning to a group of Christianized Indians at Gnadenhutten, Pennsylvania. It was taken down by a Moravian missionary who was among his listeners. The bitterness and cynicism of these words hold up a mirror to the double-dealing and treachery to which Indian peoples were so often exposed in their dealings with whites. Words of great candor and condemnation, Chief Pachgantschilias's phrases are also eloquent of suffering and disillusionment.

I admit that there are good white men, but they bear no proportion to the bad; the bad must be the strongest, for they rule. They do what they please. They enslave those who are not of their color, although created by the same Great Spirit who created them. They would make slaves of us if they could; but as they cannot do it, they kill us. There is no faith to be placed in their words. They are not like the Indians, who are only enemies while at war, and are friends in peace. They will say to an Indian, "My friend; my brother!" They will take him by the hand, and, at the same moment, destroy him. And so you will also be treated by them before long. Remember that this day I have warned you to beware of such friends as these. I know the Long-knives. They are not to be trusted.

Chief Tecumseh

The Shawnee Chief Tecumseh was outraged by the sale in 1810 of Indian lands to whites. In this particular case, he believed that there was special cause for resentment since the Indians involved were inebriated at the time and thus easily manipulated by their white brothers. Characteristically, his protest is not restricted to the specific offense but involves a larger issue having to do with the Indians' feeling for the land itself. "Sell a country!" Chief Tecumseh exclaims in disbelief: "Why not sell the air, the great sea, as well as the earth? Did not the Great Spirit make them all for the use of his children?"

Houses are built for you to hold councils in; Indians hold theirs in the open air. I am a Shawnee. My forefathers were warriors. Their son is a warrior. From them I take my only existence. From my tribe I take nothing. I have made myself what I am. And I would that I could make the red people as great as the conceptions of my own mind, when I think of the Great Spirit that rules over us all. . . . I would not then come to Governor Harrison to ask him to tear up the treaty. But I would say to him, "Brother, you have the liberty to return to your own country."

You wish to prevent the Indians from doing as we wish them, to unite and let them consider their lands as the common property of the whole. You take the tribes aside and advise them not to come into this measure. . . . You want by your distinctions of Indian tribes, in allotting to each a particular, to make them war with each other. You never see an Indian endeavor to make the white people do this. You are continually driving the red people, when at last you will drive them onto the great lake, where they can neither stand nor work.

Since my residence at Tippecanoe, we have endeavored to level all distinctions, to destroy village chiefs, by whom all mischiefs are done. It is they who sell the land to the Americans. Brother, this land that was sold, and the goods that was given for it, was only done by a few. . . . In the future we are prepared to punish those who propose to sell land to the Americans. If you continue to purchase them, it will make war among the different tribes, and, at last I do not know what will be the consequences among the white people. Brother, I wish you would take pity on the red people and do as I have requested. If you will not give up the land and do cross the boundary of our present settlement, it will be very hard, and produce great trouble between us.

The way, the only way to stop this evil is for the red men to unite in claiming a common and equal right in the land, as it was at first, and should be now—for it was never divided, but belongs to all. No tribe has the right to sell, even to each other, much less to strangers. . . . *Sell a country! Why not sell the air, the great sea, as well as the earth?* Did not the Great Spirit make them all for the use of his children?

How can we have confidence in the white people!

When Jesus Christ came upon the earth you killed Him and nailed Him to the cross. You thought He was dead, and you were mistaken. You have Shakers among you and you laugh and make light of their worship.

Everything I have told you is the truth. The Great Spirit has inspired me.

Literature of the
Early Republic

George Washington
(1732–1799)

First president of the United States (1789–1797) and before that commander in chief of the Continental Army during the Revolutionary
War, George Washington was in many respects a most improbable
leader. Born to wealth, he was raised from the age of ten, when his
father died, by his half-brother Lawrence, from whom he eventually
inherited the estate at Mount Vernon. Here he'd hoped to pursue the
settled life of a country gentleman, interrupted only by infrequent service in Virginia's House of Burgesses, but Washington was quickly
drawn into the widening colonial struggle and, because of his earlier
military experience against the French and Indians, was almost immediately placed in the role of command. As soon as the Revolutionary War was over in 1783, Washington attempted to retire to Mount
Vernon again but was quickly forced back into public life to assume
the presidency of the Constitutional Convention in 1787.

Elected president of the newly formed republic two years later,
Washington sided with the Federalists and particularly Alexander
Hamilton (1755–1804) by encouraging commerce and manufacturing.
In time these policies, together with the failure to support France in
the war against Great Britain, led to conflict with the more agrarian
orientation of Thomas Jefferson (1743–1826), who resigned from
Washington's administration and gave birth to the two-party system.
Despite the opposition Washington had to face during his second
term—particularly in relation to the treaty John Jay (1745–1829) ne-
gotiated with England in 1794, which seemed biased in favor of British
interests, and also to the tax that led to the Whiskey Rebellion of
1794—he did manage to stabilize the young country economically and

politically, to reduce the threat of Native American hostility, and to open up the Mississippi for navigation and trade.

Washington's Farewell Address is easily the most significant literary document he produced. Whether or not, as rumor has it, he was assisted in composing it by Hamilton and James Madison (1751–1836), there is no question but that the document expressed with some accuracy his hopes and his fears for his country.

from *The Farewell Address to the People of the United States* (September 17, 1796)

FRIENDS AND FELLOW-CITIZENS:

The period for a new election of a citizen, to administer the executive government of the United States, being not far distant, and the time actually arrived when your thoughts must be employed in designating the person who is to be clothed with that important trust, it appears to me proper, especially as it may conduce to a more distinct expression of the public voice, that I should now apprise you of the resolution I have formed, to decline being considered among the number of those out of whom a choice is to be made.

I beg you, at the same time, to do me the justice to be assured, that this resolution has not been taken without a strict regard to all the considerations appertaining to the relation which binds a dutiful citizen to his country; and that, in withdrawing the tender of service, which silence in my situation might imply, I am influenced by no diminution of zeal for your future interest; no deficiency of grateful respect for your past kindness; but am supported by a full conviction that the step is compatible with both. . . .

In looking forward to the moment which is intended to terminate the career of my public life, my feelings do not permit me to suspend the deep acknowledgment of that debt of gratitude which I owe to my beloved country for the many honors it has conferred upon me; still more for the steadfast confidence with which it has supported me; and for the opportunities I have thence enjoyed of manifesting my inviolable attachment by services faithful and persevering, though in usefulness unequal to my zeal. If benefits have resulted to our country from these services, let it always be remembered to your praise, and as an instructive example in our annals, that under circumstances in which the passions, agitated in every direction, were liable to mislead, amidst appearances sometimes dubious, vicissitudes of fortune often discouraging, in situations in which not unfrequently want of success has countenanced the spirit of criticism, the constancy of your support was the essential prop of the efforts, and a guaranty of the plans by which they were effected. Profoundly penetrated with this idea, I shall carry it with me to my grave, as a strong incitement to unceasing vows that Heaven may continue to you the choicest tokens of its beneficence; that your union and brotherly affection may be perpetual; that the free constitution, which is the work of your hands, may be sacredly maintained; that its administration in every department may be stamped with wisdom and virtue; that, in fine, the happiness of the people of these States, under the auspices of liberty, may be made complete, by so careful a preservation and so prudent a use of this blessing, as will acquire to them the glory of recommending it to the applause, the affection, and adoption of every nation which is yet a stranger to it.

Here, perhaps, I ought to stop. But a solicitude for your welfare, which cannot end but with my life, and the apprehension of danger natural to that solicitude, urge me, on an occasion like the present, to offer to your solemn contemplation, and to recommend to your frequent review, some sentiments, which are the result of much reflection, of no inconsiderable observation, and which appear to me all-important to the permanency of your felicity as a people. These will be offered to you with the more freedom, as you can only see in them the disinterested warnings of a parting friend, who can possibly have no personal motive to bias his counsel. Nor can I forget, as an encouragement to it, your indulgent reception of my sentiments on a former and not dissimilar occasion.

Interwoven as is the love of liberty with every ligament of your hearts, no recommendation of mine is necessary to fortify or confirm the attachment.

The unity of government, which constitutes you one people, is also now dear to you. It is justly so; for it is a main pillar in the edifice of your real independence, the support of your tranquillity at home, your peace abroad; of your safety; of your prosperity; of that very liberty which you so highly prize. But as it is easy to foresee that from different causes and from different quarters much pains will be taken, many artifices employed, to weaken in your minds the conviction of this truth; as this is the point in your political fortress against which the batteries of internal and external enemies will be most constantly and actively (though often covertly and insidiously) directed, it is of infinite moment that you should properly estimate the immense value of your national union to your collective and individual happiness; that you should cherish a cordial, habitual, and immovable attachment to it; accustoming yourselves to think and speak of it as of the palladium of your political safety and prosperity; watching for its preservation with jealous anxiety; discountenancing whatever may suggest even a suspicion that it can in any event be abandoned; and indignantly frowning upon the first dawning of every attempt to alienate any portion of our country from the rest, or to enfeeble the sacred ties which now link together the various parts.

For this you have every inducement of sympathy and interest. Citizens, by birth or choice of a common country, that country has a right to concentrate your affections. The name of America, which belongs to you, in your national capacity, must always exalt the just pride of patriotism, more than any appellation derived from local discriminations. With slight shades of difference, you have the same religion, manners, habits, and political principles. You have in a common cause fought and triumphed together; the independence and liberty you possess are the work of joint counsels and joint efforts, of common dangers, sufferings and successes.

But these considerations, however powerfully they address themselves to your sensibility, are greatly outweighed by those which apply more immediately to your interest. Here every portion of our country finds the most commanding motives for carefully guarding and preserving the union of the whole.

The North, in an unrestrained intercourse with the South, protected by the equal laws of a common government, finds in the productions of the latter great additional resources of maritime and commercial enterprise and precious materials of manufacturing industry. The South in the same intercourse, benefitting by the agency of the North, sees its agriculture grow and its commerce expand. Turning partly into its own channels the seamen of the North, it finds its particular navigation invigorated; and, while it contributes in different ways to nourish and increase the general mass of the national navigation, it looks forward to the protection of a maritime strength, to which itself is unequally adapted. The East, in a like intercourse with the West, already finds, and in the progressive improvement of interior communications by land and water will more and more find, a valuable vent for the commodities which it brings from abroad, or manufactures at home. The West derives from the East supplies requisite to its growth and comfort, and, what is perhaps of still greater consequence, it must of necessity owe the secure enjoyment of indispensable outlets for its own productions to the weight, influence, and the future maritime strength of the Atlantic side of the Union, directed by an indissoluble community of interest as one nation. Any other tenure by which the West can hold this essential advantage, whether derived from its own separate strength or from an apostate and unnatural connection with any foreign power, must be intrinsically precarious.

While, then, every part of our country thus feels an immediate and particular interest in union, all the parts combined cannot fail to find in the united mass of means and efforts greater strength, greater resource, proportionately greater security from external danger, a less frequent interruption of their peace by foreign nations, and, what is of inestimable value, they must derive from union an exemption from those broils and wars between themselves, which so frequently afflict neighboring countries not tied together by the same governments, which their own rivalships alone would be sufficient to produce, but which opposite foreign alliances, attachments, and intrigues would stimulate and embitter. Hence, likewise, they will avoid the necessity of those overgrown military establishments which, under any form of government, are inauspicious to liberty, and which are to be regarded as particularly hostile to republican liberty. In this sense it is that your union ought to be considered as a main prop of your liberty, and that the love of the one ought to endear to you the preservation of the other. . . .

In contemplating the causes which may disturb our Union, it occurs as a matter of serious concern, that any ground should have been furnished for characterizing parties by geographical discriminations Northern and Southern, Atlantic and Western; whence designing men may endeavor to excite a belief that there is a real difference of local interests and views. One of the expedients of party to acquire influence within particular districts is to misrepresent the opinions and aims of the other districts. You cannot shield yourselves too much against the jealousies and heart-burnings which spring from these misrepresentations; they tend to render alien to each other those who ought to be bound together by fraternal affection. The inhabitants of our western country have lately had a useful lesson on this head; they have seen, in the negotiation by the executive, and in the unanimous ratification by the senate, of the treaty with Spain, and in the universal satisfaction at that event throughout the United States, a decisive proof how unfounded were the suspicions propagated among them of a policy in the general government and in the Atlantic States unfriendly to their interests in regard to the Mississippi; they have been witnesses to the formation of two treaties, that with Great Britain and that with Spain, which secure to them everything they could desire, in respect to our foreign relations, towards confirming their prosperity. Will it not be their wisdom to rely for the preservation of these advantages on the Union by which they were procured? Will they not henceforth be deaf to those advisers if such there are, who would sever them from their brethren and connect them with aliens?

To the efficacy and permanency of your union, a government for the whole is indispensable. No alliances, however strict, between the parts can be an adequate substitute; they must inevitably experience the infractions and interruptions which all alliances in all times have experienced. Sensible of this momentous truth, you have improved upon your first essay, by the adoption of a constitution of government better calculated than your former for an intimate union, and for the efficacious management of your common concerns. This government, the offspring of our own choice, uninfluenced and unawed, adopted upon full investigation and mature deliberation, completely free in its principles, in the distribution of its powers, uniting security with energy, and containing within itself a provision for its own amendment, has a just claim to your confidence and your support. Respect for its authority, compliance with its laws, acquiescence in its measures, are duties enjoined by the fundamental maxims of true Liberty. The basis of our political systems is the right of the people to make and to alter their constitutions of government. But the constitution which at any time exists, till changed by an explicit and authentic act of the whole people, is sacredly obligatory upon all. The very idea of the power and the right of the people to establish government presupposes the duty of every individual to obey the established government.

All obstructions to the execution of the laws, all combinations and associations, under whatever plausible character, with the real design to direct, control, counteract, or awe the regular deliberation and action of the constituted authorities, are destructive of this fundamental principle, and of fatal tendency. They serve to organize faction, to give it an artificial and extraordinary force; to put in the place of the delegated will of the nation, the will of a party, often a small but artful and enterprising minority of the community; and, according to the alternate triumphs of different parties, to make the public administration the mirror of the ill-concerted and incongruous projects of fashion, rather than the organs of consistent and wholesome plans digested by common councils, and modified by mutual interests.

However combinations or associations of the above description may now and then answer popular ends, they are likely, in the course of time and things, to become potent engines, by which cunning, ambitious, and unprincipled men will be enabled to subvert the power of the people, and to usurp for themselves the reins of government; destroying afterwards the very engines which have lifted them to unjust dominion.

Towards the preservation of your government, and the permanency of your present happy state, it is requisite, not only that you steadily discountenance irregular oppositions to its acknowledged authority, but also that you resist with care the spirit of innovation upon its principles, however specious the pretexts. One method of assault may be to effect, in the form of the constitution, alterations, which will impair the energy of the system, and thus to undermine what cannot be directly overthrown. In all the changes to which you may be invited, remember that time and habit are at least as necessary to fix the true character of governments as of other human institutions; that experience is the surest standard by which to test the real tendency of the existing constitution of a country; that facility in changes, upon the credit of mere hypothesis and opinion, exposes to perpetual change, from the endless variety of hypothesis and opinion; and remember especially, that, for the efficient management of your common interests, in a country so extensive as ours, a government of as much vigor as is consistent with the perfect security of liberty is indispensable. Liberty itself will find in such a government, with powers properly distributed and adjusted, its surest guardian. It is, indeed, little else than a name, where the government is too feeble to withstand the enterprises of faction, to confine each member of the society within the limits prescribed by the laws, and to maintain all in the secure and tranquil enjoyment of the rights of person and property.

I have already intimated to you the danger of parties in the State, with particular reference to the founding of them on geographical discrimination. Let me now take a more comprehensive view, and warn you in the most solemn manner against the baneful effects of the spirit of party, generally.

This spirit, unfortunately, is inseparable from our nature, having its root in the strongest passions of the human mind. It exists under different shapes in all governments, more or less stifled, controlled, or repressed; but in those of the popular form it is seen in its greatest rankness, and is truly their worst enemy.

The alternate domination of one faction over another, sharpened by the spirit of revenge, natural to party dissension, which in different ages and countries has perpetrated the most horrid enormities, is itself a frightful despotism. But this leads at length to a more formal and permanent despotism. The disorders and miseries which result, gradually incline the minds of men to seek security and repose in the absolute power of an individual; and sooner or later the chief of some prevailing faction, more able or more fortunate than his competitors, turns this disposition to the purposes of his own elevation, on the ruins of public liberty.

Without looking forward to an extremity of this kind (which nevertheless ought not to be entirely out of sight), the common and continued mischiefs of the spirit of party are sufficient to make it the interest and duty of a wise people to discourage and restrain it.

It serves always to distract the public councils, and enfeeble the public administration. It agitates the community with ill-founded jealousies and false alarms; kindles the animosity of one part against another, foments occasionally riot and insurrection. It opens the doors to foreign influence and corruption, which find a facilitated access to the government itself through the channels of party passions. Thus the policy and the will of one country are subjected to the policy and will of another.

There is an opinion, that parties in free countries are useful checks upon the administration of the government, and serve to keep alive the spirit of liberty. This within certain limits is probably true, and in governments of a monarchical cast, patriotism may look with indulgence, if not with favor, upon the spirit of party. But in those of the popular character, in governments purely elective, it is a spirit not to be encouraged. From their natural tendency, it is certain there will always be enough of that spirit for every salutary purpose. And there being constant danger of excess, the effort ought to be, by force of public opinion to mitigate and assuage it. A fire not to be quenched, it demands a uniform vigilance to prevent its bursting into a flame lest instead of warming, it should consume.

It is important, likewise that the habits of thinking in a free country should inspire caution in those intrusted with its administration, to confine themselves within their respective constitutional spheres, avoiding in the exercise of the powers of one department to encroach upon another. The spirit of encroachment tends to consolidate the powers of all the departments in one, and thus to create, whatever the form of government, a real despotism. A just estimate of that love of power, and proneness to abuse it, which predominates in the human heart, is sufficient to satisfy us of the truth of this position. The necessity of reciprocal checks in the exercise of political power, by dividing and distributing it into different depositories, and constituting each the guardian of the public weal against invasions by the others, has been evinced by experiments ancient and modern, some of them in our country and under our own eyes. To preserve them must be as necessary as to institute them. If, in the opinion of the people, the distribution or modification of the constitutional powers be in any particular wrong, let it be corrected by an amendment in the way which the Constitution designates. But let there be no change by usurpation; for, though this, in one instance, may be the instrument of good, it is the customary weapon by which free governments are destroyed. The precedent must always greatly overbalance in permanent evil any partial or transient benefit which the use can at any time yield.

Of all the dispositions and habits which lead to political prosperity, religion and morality are indispensable supports. In vain would that man claim the tribute of patriotism, who should labor to subvert these great pillars of human happiness, these firmest props of the duties of men and citizens. The mere politician equally with the pious man ought to respect and to cherish them. A volume could not trace all their connections with private and public felicity. Let it simply be asked, Where is the security for property, for reputation, for life, if the sense of religious obligation desert the oaths, which are the instruments of investigation in courts of justice? And let us with caution indulge the supposition, that morality can be maintained without religion. Whatever may be conceded to the influence of refined education on minds of peculiar structure, reason and experience both forbid us to expect, that national morality can prevail in exclusion of religious principle.

It is substantially true that virtue or morality is a necessary spring of popular government. The rule, indeed, extends with more or less force to every species of free government. Who, that is a sincere friend to it, can look with indifference upon attempts to shake the foundation of the fabric?

Promote, then, as an object of primary importance, institutions for the general diffusion of knowledge. In proportion as the structure of a government gives force to public opinion, it is essential that public opinion should be enlightened.

As a very important source of strength and security, cherish public credit. One method of preserving it is, to use it as sparingly as possible; avoiding occasions of expense by cultivating peace, but remembering also that timely disbursements to prepare for danger frequently prevent much greater disbursements to repel it; avoiding likewise the accumulation of debt, not only by shunning occasions of expense, but by vigorous exertion in time of peace to discharge the debts, which unavoidable wars may have occasioned, not ungenerously throwing upon posterity the burden which we ourselves ought to bear. The execution of these maxims belongs to your representatives, but it is necessary that public opinion should co-operate. To facilitate to them the performance of their duty it is essential that you should practically bear in mind, that towards the payment of debts there must be revenue; that to have revenue there must be taxes; that no taxes can be devised which are not more or less inconvenient and unpleasant; that the intrinsic embarrassment, inseparable from the selection of the proper objects (which is always a choice of difficulties), ought to be a decisive motive for a candid construction of the conduct of the government in making it, and for a spirit of acquiescence in the measures for obtaining revenue which the public exigencies may at any time dictate.

Observe good faith and justice towards all nations; cultivate peace and harmony with all. Religion and morality enjoin this conduct; and can it be, that good policy does not equally enjoin it? It will be worthy of a free, enlightened, and at no distant period a great nation, to give to mankind the magnanimous and too novel example of a people always guided by an exalted justice and benevolence. Who can doubt that in the course of time and things, the fruits of such a plan would richly repay any temporary advantages, which might be lost by a steady adherence to it? Can it be that Providence has not connected the permanent felicity of a nation with its virtue? The experiment, at least, is recommended by every sentiment which ennobles human nature. Alas! is it rendered impossible by its vices?

In the execution of such a plan, nothing is more essential than that permanent, inveterate antipathies against particular nations, and passionate attachments for others, should be excluded; and that, in place of them, just and amicable feelings toward all should be cultivated. The nation which indulges towards another an habitual hatred, or an habitual fondness, is in some degree a slave. It is a slave to its animosity or to its affection, either of which is sufficient to lead it astray from its duty and its interest. Antipathy in one nation against another disposes each more readily to offer insult and injury, to lay hold of slight causes of umbrage, and to be haughty and intractable when accidental or trifling occasions of dispute occur. Hence, frequent collisions, obstinate, envenomed, and bloody contests. The nation, prompted by ill-will and resentment, some times impels to war the government, contrary to the best calculations of policy. The government sometimes participates in the national propensity, and adopts through passion what reason would reject; at other times, it makes the animosity of the nation subservient to projects of hostility instigated by pride, ambition, and other sinister and pernicious motives. The peace often, sometimes perhaps the liberty, of nations has been the victim.

So likewise, a passionate attachment of one nation for another produces a variety of evils. Sympathy for the favorite nation, facilitating the illusion of an imaginary common interest in cases where no real common interest exists, and infusing into one the enmities of the other, betrays the former into a participation in the quarrels and wars of the latter, without adequate inducement or justification. It leads also to concessions to the favorite nation of privileges denied to others, which is apt doubly to injure the nation making the concessions, by unnecessarily parting with what ought to have been retained, and by exciting jealousy, ill-will, and a disposition to retaliate, in the parties from whom equal privileges are withheld. And it gives to ambitious, corrupted, or deluded citizens (who devote themselves to the favorite nation), facility to betray or sacrifice the interests of their own country, without odium, sometimes even with popularity; gilding with the appearances of a virtuous sense of obligation, a commendable deference for public opinion, or a laudable zeal for public good, the base or foolish compliances of ambition, corruption, or infatuation.

As avenues to foreign influence in innumerable ways such attachments are particularly alarming to the truly enlightened and independent patriot. How many opportunities do they afford to tamper with domestic factions, to practise the arts of seduction, to mislead public opinion, to influence or awe the public councils! Such an attachment of a small or weak, towards a great and powerful nation, dooms the former to be the satellite of the latter.

Against the insidious wiles of foreign influence (I conjure you to believe me, fellow-citizens), the jealousy of a free people ought to be constantly awake, since history and experience prove that foreign influence is one of the most baneful foes of republican government. But that jealousy, to be useful, must be impartial; else it becomes the instrument of the very influence to be avoided, instead of a defence against it. Excessive partiality for one foreign nation, and excessive dislike of another, cause those whom they actuate to see danger only on one side, and serve to veil and even second the arts of influence on the other. Real patriots who may resist the intrigues of the favorite, are liable to become suspected and odious; while its tools and dupes usurp the applause and confidence of the purpose, to surrender their interests.

The great rule of conduct for us, in regard to foreign nations, is, in extending our commercial relations, to have with them as little political connection as possible. So far as we have already formed engagements, let them be fulfilled with perfect good faith. Here let us stop.

Europe has a set of primary interests, which to us have none, or a very remote relation. Hence she must be engaged in frequent controversies, the causes of which are essentially foreign to our concerns. Hence, therefore, it must be unwise in us to implicate ourselves, by artificial ties, in the ordinary vicissitudes of her politics, or the ordinary combinations and collisions of her friendships or enmities.

Our detached and distant situation invites and enables us to pursue a different course. If we remain one people, under an efficient government, the period is not far off when we may defy material injury from external annoyance; when we may take such an attitude as will cause the neutrality, we may at any time resolve upon, to be scrupulously respected; when belligerent nations, under the impossibility of making acquisitions upon us, will not lightly hazard the giving us provocation; when we may choose peace or war, as our interest, guided by justice, shall counsel.

Why forego the advantages of so peculiar a situation? Why quit our own to stand upon foreign ground? Why, by interweaving our destiny with that of any part of Europe, entangle our peace and prosperity in the toils of European ambition, rivalship, interest, humor, or caprice?

It is our policy to steer clear of permanent alliances with any portion of the foreign world; so far, I mean, as we are now at liberty to do it; for let me not be understood as capable of patronizing infidelity to existing engagements. I hold the maxim no less applicable to public than to private affairs, that honesty is always the best policy. I repeat it, therefore, let those engagements be observed in their genuine sense. But, in my opinion, it is unnecessary and would be unwise to extend them.

Taking care always to keep ourselves, by suitable establishments, on a respectable defensive posture, we may safely trust to temporary alliances for extraordinary emergencies.

Harmony, liberal intercourse with all nations, are recommended by policy, humanity, and interest. But even our commercial policy should hold an equal and impartial hand; neither seeking nor granting exclusive favors or preferences; consulting the natural course of things; diffusing and diversifying by gentle means the streams of commerce, but forcing nothing; establishing with powers so disposed, in order to give trade a stable course, to define the rights of our merchants, and to enable the government to support them, conventional rules of intercourse, the best that present circumstances and mutual opinion will permit, but temporary, and liable to be from time to time abandoned or varied, as experience and circumstances shall dictate; constantly keeping in view, that it is folly in one nation to look for disinterested favors from another; that it must pay with a portion of its independence for whatever it may accept under that character; that, by such acceptance, it may place itself in the condition of having given equivalents for nominal favors, and yet of being reproached with ingratitude for not giving more. There can be no greater error than to expect or calculate upon real favors from nation to nation. It is an illusion, which experience must cure, which a just pride ought to discard.

In offering to you, my countrymen, these counsels of an old and affectionate friend, I dare not hope they will make the strong and lasting impression I could wish; that they will control the usual current of the passions, or prevent our nation from running the course which has hitherto marked the destiny of nations. But, if I may even flatter myself that they may be productive of some partial benefit, some occasional good; that they may now and then recur to moderate the fury of party spirit, to warn against the mischiefs of foreign intrigue, to guard against the impostures of pretended patriotism; this hope will be a full recompense for the solicitude for your welfare, by which they have been dictated.

How far in the discharge of my official duties I have been guided by the principles which have been delineated, the public records and other evidences of my conduct must witness to you and to the world.

To myself, the assurance of my own conscience is, that I have at least believed myself to be guided by them. . . .

Though, in reviewing the incidents of my administration, I am unconscious of intentional error, I am nevertheless too sensible of my defects not to think it probable that I may have committed many errors. Whatever they may be, I fervently beseech the Almighty to avert or mitigate the evils to which they may tend. I shall also carry with me the hope that my country will never cease to view them with indulgence; and that, after forty-five years of my life dedicated to its service with an upright zeal, the faults of incompetent abilities will be consigned to oblivion, as myself must soon be to the mansions of rest.

Relying on its kindness in this as in other things, and actuated by that fervent love towards it, which is so natural to a man who views in it the native soil of himself and his progenitors for several generations, I anticipate with pleasing expectation that retreat, in which I promise myself to realize, without alloy, the sweet enjoyment of partaking, in the midst of my fellow-citizens, the benign influence of good laws under a free government, the ever favorite object of my heart, and the happy reward, as I trust, of our mutual cares, labors, and dangers.

Thomas Jefferson
(1734–1826)

The third president of the United States and chief author of the Declaration of Independence, Thomas Jefferson was one of the most gifted
statesmen in American history. In addition to his achievements in public life, Jefferson was an imaginative scientist and indefatigable inventor, a brilliant architect, an able naturalist, a skilled political tactician
as well as theorist, and a capable student of religion and ethics. Surely
no document besides the Constitution of the United States and the
attendant Bill of Rights has been more important in American history
than the Declaration of Independence, nor has any set out more clearly
and succinctly the social, ethical, and religious views of the Founding
Fathers. In its defense of the idea that a sovereign people may overthrow any government that systematically deprives them of their inalienable rights as human beings, the Declaration bases its argument
on an escalating series of offenses committed by the British Crown
that culminate (at least in the original version authored by Jefferson)
in the outrage committed against all humanity through the promotion
and participation of traffic in slaves. If there is no small irony in the
fact that this last and most serious charge brought against the English
king—indeed the indictment that seals the case for declaring independence—finally had to be removed from the document's final
draft because of the objections raised against it by two southern states,
there is also no small irony in the fact that the author of this clause
was the owner of nearly three hundred slaves himself and quite possibly the father of several slave children.

But Jefferson's literary reputation by no means rests on his au-
thorship of the Declaration alone. Another of the public documents

he composed, which he regarded as one of the three most important
public acts of his life (the other two being the drafting of the Decla-
ration itself and the founding of the University of Virginia at Char-
lottesville), was the Act for Establishing Religious Freedom in the State
of Virginia (1786). Virginia was also the subject of the one book Jef-
ferson published in his lifetime, called Notes on the State of Virginia
(1785). Notes *is a marvel of close observation and vivid sociological*
as well as naturalist description written to answer the questions put to
him about American customs and conditions by the secretary of the
French legation in Philadelphia that at the same time refuses to con-
front or engage the issue of Black slavery. Yet a third and more per-
sonal kind of writing at which Jefferson excelled was the letter,
sometimes occasioned by matters of state but more often, as here,
prompted by the inquiries of friends or admirers.

from *Autobiography*

[THE FRAMING OF THE DECLARATION OF INDEPENDENCE, 1776]

It appearing in the course of these debates, that the colonies of New
York, New Jersey, Pennsylvania, Delaware, Maryland, and South Carolina were not yet matured for falling from the parent stem, but that
they were fast advancing to that state, it was thought most prudent to
wait a while for them, and to postpone the final decision to July 1st;
but, that this might occasion as little delay as possible, a committee
was appointed to prepare a Declaration of Independence. The committee were John Adams, Dr. Franklin, Roger Sherman, Robert R.
Livingston, and myself. Committees were also appointed, at the same
time, to prepare a plan of confederation for the colonies, and to state
the terms proper to be proposed for foreign alliance. The committee
for drawing the Declaration of Independence, desired me to do it. It
was accordingly done, and being approved by them, I reported it to
the House on Friday, the 28th of June, when it was read, and ordered
to lie on the table. On Monday, the 1st of July, the House resolved
itself into a committee of the whole, and resumed the consideration of
the original motion made by the delegates of Virginia, which, being
again debated through the day, was carried in the affirmative by the
votes of New Hampshire, Connecticut, Massachusetts, Rhode Island,
New Jersey, Maryland, Virginia, North Carolina and Georgia. South

432   *Thomas Jefferson*

Carolina and Pennsylvania voted against it. Delaware had but two members present, and they were divided. The delegates from New York declared they were for it themselves, and were assured their constituents were for it; but that their instructions having been drawn near a twelve-month before, when reconciliation was still the general object, they were enjoined by them to do nothing which should impede that object. They, therefore, thought themselves not justifiable in voting on either side, and asked leave to withdraw from the question; which was given them. The committee rose and reported their resolution to the House. Mr. Edward Rutledge, of South Carolina, then requested the determination might be put off to the next day, as he believed his colleagues, though they disapproved of the resolution, would then join in it for the sake of unanimity. The ultimate question, whether the House would agree to the resolution of the committee, was accordingly postponed to the next day, when it was again moved, and South Carolina concurred in voting for it. In the meantime, a third member had come post from the Delaware counties, and turned the vote of that colony in favor of the resolution. Members of a different sentiment attending that morning from Pennsylvania also, her vote was changed, so that the whole twelve colonies who were authorized to vote at all, gave their voices for it; and, within a few days, the convention of New York approved of it, and thus supplied the void occasioned by the withdrawing of her delegates from the vote.

Congress proceeded the same day to consider the Declaration of Independence, which had been reported and lain on the table the Friday preceding, and on Monday referred to a committee of the whole. The pusillanimous idea that we had friends in England worth keeping terms with, still haunted the minds of many. For this reason, those passages which conveyed censures on the people of England were struck out, lest they should give them offence. The clause too, reprobating the enslaving the inhabitants of Africa, was struck out in complaisance to South Carolina and Georgia, who had never attempted to restrain the importation of slaves, and who, on the contrary, still wished to continue it. Our northern brethren also, I believe, felt a little tender under those censures; for though their people had very few slaves themselves, yet they had been pretty considerable carriers of them to others. The debates, having taken up the greater parts of the 2d, 3d, and 4th days of July, were, on the evening of the last, closed; the Declaration was reported by the committee, agreed to by the House, and signed by every member present, except Mr. Dickinson. As the sentiments of men are known not only by what they receive, but what they reject also, I will state the form of the Declaration as originally reported.[1]

A Declaration by the Representatives of the United States of America, in General Congress Assembled

When, in the course of human events, it becomes necessary for one people to dissolve the political bands which have connected them with another, and to assume among the powers of the earth the separate and equal station to which the laws of nature and of nature's God entitle them, a decent respect to the opinions of mankind requires that they should declare the causes which impel them to the separation.

We hold these truths to be self evident: that all men are created equal; that they are endowed by their Creator with CERTAIN [*inherent and*] inalienable rights; that among these are life, liberty, and the pursuit of happiness; that to secure these rights, governments are instituted among men, deriving their just powers from the consent of the governed; that whenever any form of government becomes destructive of these ends, it is the right of the people to alter or to abolish it, and to institute new government, laying its foundation on such principles, and organizing its powers in such form, as to them shall seem most likely to effect their safety and happiness. Prudence, indeed, will dictate that governments long established should not be changed for light and transient causes; and accordingly all experience hath shown that mankind are more disposed to suffer while evils are sufferable, than to right themselves by abolishing the forms to which they are accustomed. But when a long train of abuses and usurpations, [*begun at a distinguished period and*] pursuing invariably the same object, evinces a design to reduce them under absolute despotism, it is their right, it is their duty to throw off such government, and to provide such sufferance new guards for their future security. Such has been the patient sufferance of these colonies; and such is now the necessity which constrains them to ALTER [*expunge*] their former systems of government. The history of the present king of Great Britain is a history of REPEATED [*unremitting*] injuries and usurpations, ALL HAVING [*among which appears no solitary fact to contradict the uniform tenor of the rest, but all have*] in direct object the establishment of an absolute tyranny over these states. To prove this, let facts be submitted to a candid world [*for the truth of which we pledge a faith yet unsullied by falsehood*].

He has refused his assent to laws the most wholesome and necessary for the public good.

He has forbidden his governors to pass laws of immediate and pressing importance, unless suspended in their operation till his assent should be obtained; and, when so suspended, he has utterly neglected to attend to them.

He has refused to pass other laws for the accommodation of large districts of people, unless those people would relinquish the right of representation in the legislature, a right inestimable to them, and formidable to tyrants only.

He has called together legislative bodies at places unusual, uncomfortable, and distant from the depository of their public records, for the sole purpose of fatiguing them into compliance with his measures.

He has dissolved representative houses repeatedly [*and continually*] for opposing with manly firmness his invasions on the rights of the people.

He has refused for a long time after such dissolutions to cause others to be elected, whereby the legislative powers, incapable of annihilation, have returned to the people at large for their exercise, the state remaining, in the meantime, exposed to all the dangers of invasion from without and convulsions within.

He has endeavored to prevent the population of these states; for that purpose obstructing the laws for naturalization of foreigners, refusing to pass others to encourage their migrations hither, and raising the conditions of new appropriations of lands.

He has OBSTRUCTED [*suffered*] the administration of justice BY [*totally to cease in some of these states*] refusing his assent to laws for establishing judiciary powers.

He has made [*our*] judges dependent on his will alone for the tenure of their offices, and the amount and payment of their salaries.

He has erected a multitude of new offices [*by a self-assumed power*], and sent hither swarms of new officers to harass our people and eat out their substance.

He has kept among us in times of peace standing armies [*and ships of war*] without the consent of our legislatures.

He has affected to render the military independent of, and superior to, the civil power.

He has combined with others to subject us to a jurisdiction foreign to our constitutions and unacknowledged by our laws, giving his assent to their acts of pretended legislation for quartering large bodies of armed troops among us; for protecting them by a mock trial from punishment for any murders which they should commit on the inhabitants of these states; for cutting off our trade with all parts of the world; for imposing taxes on us without consent; for depriving us IN MANY CASES of the benefits of trial by jury; for transporting us beyond seas to be tried for pretended offences; for abolishing the free system of English laws in a neighboring province, establishing therein an arbitrary government, and enlarging its boundaries, so as to render it at once an example and fit instrument for introducing the same absolute rule into these COLONIES [*states*]; for taking away our charters, abolishing our most valuable laws, and altering fundamentally the forms of our governments; for suspending our own legislatures, and declaring themselves invested with power to legislate for us in all cases whatsoever.

He has abdicated government here BY DECLARING US OUT OF HIS PROTECTION, AND WAGING WAR AGAINST US [*withdrawing his governors, and declaring us out of his allegiance and protection*].

He has plundered our seas, ravaged our coasts, burnt our towns, and destroyed the lives of our people.

He is at this time transporting large armies of foreign mercenaries to complete the works of death, desolation and tyranny already begun with circumstances of cruelty and perfidy SCARCELY PARALLELED IN THE MOST BARBAROUS AGES, AND TOTALLY unworthy the head of a civilized nation.

He has constrained our fellow citizens taken captive on the high seas, to bear arms against their country, to become the executioners of their friends and brethren, or to fall themselves by their hands.

He has EXCITED DOMESTIC INSURRECTION AMONG US, AND HAS endeavored to bring on the inhabitants of our frontiers, the merciless Indian savages, whose known rule of warfare is an undistinguished destruction of all ages, sexes and conditions [*of existence*].

[*He has incited treasonable insurrections of our fellow citizens, with the allurements of forfeiture and confiscation of our property.*

He has waged cruel war against human nature itself, violating its most sacred rights of life and liberty in the persons of a distant people who never offended him, captivating and carrying them into slavery in another hemisphere, or to incur miserable death in their transportation hither. This piratical warfare, the opprobrium of INFIDEL *powers, is the warfare of the* CHRISTIAN *king of Great Britain. Determined to keep open a market where* MEN *should be bought and sold, he has prostituted his negative for suppressing every legislative attempt to prohibit or to restrain this execrable commerce. And that this assemblage of horrors might want no fact of distinguished die, he is now exciting those very people to rise in arms among us, and to purchase that liberty of which he has deprived them, by murding the people on whom he also obtruded them: thus paying off former crimes committed against the* LIBERTIES *of one people, with crimes which he urges them to commit against the* LIVES *of another.*]

In every stage of these oppressions we have petitioned for redress in the most humble terms: our repeated petitions have been answered only by repeated injuries.

A prince whose character is thus marked by every act which may define a tyrant is unfit to be the ruler of a FREE people [*who mean to be free. Future ages will scarcely believe that the hardiness of one man adventured, within the short compass of twelve years only, to lay a foundation so broad and so undisguised for tyranny over a people fostered and fixed in principles of freedom.*]

Nor have we been wanting in attentions to our British brethren. We have warned them from time to time of attempts by their legislature to extend AN UNWARRANTABLE [*a*] jurisdiction over US [*these our states*]. We have reminded them of the circumstances of our emigration and settlement here [*no one of which could warrant so strange a pretension: that these were effected at the expense of our own blood and treasure, unassisted by the wealth or the strength of Great Britain: that in constituting indeed our several forms of government, we had adopted one common king, thereby laying a foundation for perpetual league and amity with them: but that submission to their parliament was no part of our constitution, nor ever in idea, if history may be credited: and,*], we HAVE appealed to their native justice and magnanimity AND WE HAVE CONJURED THEM BY [*as well as to*] the ties of our common kindred to disavow these usurpations which WOULD INEVITABLY [*were likely to*] interrupt our connection and correspondence. They too have been deaf to the voice of justice and of consanguinity. WE MUST THEREFORE [*and when occasions have been given them, by the regular course of their laws, of removing from their councils the disturbers of our harmony, they have, by their free election, re-established them in power. At this very time too, they are permitting their chief magistrate to send over not only soldiers of our common blood, but Scotch and foreign mercenaries to invade and destroy us. These facts have given the last stab to agonizing affection, and manly spirit bids us to renounce forever these unfeeling brethren. We must endeavor to forget our former love for them, and hold them as we hold the rest of mankind, enemies in war, in peace friends. We might have a free and a great people together; but a communication of grandeur and of freedom, it seems, is below their dignity. Be it so, since they will have it. The road to happiness and to glory is open to us, too. We will tred it apart from them, and*] acquiesce in the necessity which denounces our [*eternal*] separation AND HOLD THEM AS WE HOLD THE REST OF MANKIND, ENEMIES IN WAR, IN PEACE FRIENDS.

We therefore the representatives of the United States of America in General Congress assembled, do in the name, and by the authority of the good people of these [*states reject and renounce all allegiance and subjection to the kings of Great Britain and all others who may hereafter claim by, through or under them; we utterly dissolve all political connection which may heretofore have substituted between us and the*

people or parliament of Great Britain: and finally we do as-
sert and declare these colonies to be free and independent
states,] and that as free and independent states, they have full
power to levy war, conclude peace, contract alliances, establish commerce, and to do all other acts and things which
independent states may of right do.

And for the support of this declaration, we mutually
pledge to each other our lives, our fortunes, and our sacred
honor.[2]

We, therefore, the representatives of the United States of America
in General Congress assembled, appealing to the supreme judge of the
world for the rectitude of our intentions, do in the name, and by the
authority of the good people of these colonies, solemnly publish and
declare, that these united colonies are, and of right ought to be free
and independent states; that they are absolved from all allegiance to
the British crown, and that all political connection between them and
the state of Great Britain is, and ought to be, totally dissolved; and
that as free and independent states, they have full power to levy war,
conclude peace, contract alliances, establish commerce, and to do all
other acts and things which independent states may of right do.

And for the support of this declaration, with a firm reliance on
the protection of divine providence, we mutually pledge to each other
our lives, our fortunes, and our sacred honor.

The Declaration thus signed on the 4th, on paper, was engrossed on
parchment, and signed again on the 2d of August.

from *Notes on the State of Virginia*
(1785)

FROM QUERY IV. A NOTICE OF ITS
MOUNTAINS?

. . . The passage of the Potomac through the Blue Ridge is, perhaps,
one of the most stupendous scenes in nature. You stand on a very high
point of land. On your right comes up the Shenandoah, having ranged
along the foot of the mountain an hundred miles to seek a vent. On
your left approaches the Potomac, in quest of a passage also. In the

moment of their junction, they rush together against the mountain, rend it asunder, and pass off to the sea. The first glance of this scene hurries our senses into the opinion, that this earth has been created in time, that the mountains were formed first, that the rivers began to flow afterwards, that in this place, particularly, they have been dammed up by the Blue Ridge of mountains, and have formed an ocean which filled the whole valley; that continuing to rise they have at length broken over at this spot, and have torn the mountain down from its summit to its base. The piles of rock on each hand, but particularly on the Shenandoah, the evident marks of their disrupture and avulsion from their beds by the most powerful agents of nature, corroborate the impression. But the distant finishing which nature has given to the picture, is of a very different character. It is a true contrast to the foreground. It is as placid and delightful as that is wild and tremendous. For the mountain being cloven asunder, she presents to your eye, through the cleft, a small catch of smooth blue horizon, at an infinite distance in the plain country, inviting you, as it were, from the riot and tumult roaring around, to pass through the breach and participate of the calm below. Here the eye ultimately composes itself; and that way, too, the road happens actually to lead. You cross the Potomac above the junction, pass along its side through the base of the mountain for three miles, its terrible precipices hanging in fragments over you, and within about twenty miles reach Fredericktown, and the fine country round that. This scene is worth a voyage across the Atlantic. Yet here, as in the neighborhood of the Natural Bridge, are people who have passed their lives within half a dozen miles, and have never been to survey these monuments of a war between rivers and mountains, which must have shaken the earth itself to its centre . . . in North America. From data, which may found a tolerable conjecture, we suppose the highest peak to be about four thousand feet perpendicular, which is not a fifth part of the height of the mountains of South America, nor one-third of the height which would be necessary in our latitude to preserve ice in the open air unmelted through the year. The ridge of mountains next beyond the Blue Ridge, called by us the North mountain, is of the greatest extent; for which reason they were named by the Indians the endless mountains.

A substance supposed to be Pumice, found floating on the Mississippi, has induced a conjecture that there is a volcano on some of its waters; and as these are mostly known to their sources, except the Missouri, our expectations of verifying the conjecture would of course be led to the mountains which divide the waters of the Mexican Gulf from those of the South Sea; but no volcano having ever yet been known at such a distance from the sea, we must rather suppose that this floating substance has been erroneously deemed Pumice.

FROM QUERY V.
ITS CASCADES AND CAVERNS?

. . . The *Natural Bridge*, the most sublime of nature's works, though not comprehended under the present head, must not be pretermitted.[1] It is on the ascent of a hill, which seems to have been cloven through its length by some great convulsion. The fissure, just at the bridge, is, by some admeasurements, two hundred and seventy feet deep, by others only two hundred and five. It is about forty-five feet wide at the bottom and ninety feet at the top; this of course determines the length of the bridge, and its height from the water. Its breadth in the middle is about sixty feet, but more at the ends, and the thickness of the mass, at the summit of the arch, about forty feet. A part of this thickness is constituted by a coat of earth, which gives growth to many large trees, The residue, with the hill on both sides, is one solid rock of lime-stone. The arch approaches the semi-elliptical form; but the larger axis of the ellipsis, which would be the cord of the arch, is many times longer than the transverse. Though the sides of this bridge are provided in some parts with a parapet of fixed rocks, yet few men have resolution to walk to them, and look over into the abyss. You involuntarily fall on your hands and feet, creep to the parapet, and peep over it. Looking down from this height about a minute, gave me a violent head-ache. If the view from the top be painful and intolerable, that from below is delightful in an equal extreme. It is impossible for the emotions arising from the sublime to be felt beyond what they are here; so beautiful an arch, so elevated, so light, and springing as it were up to heaven! the rapture of the spectator is really indescribable! The fissure continuing narrow, deep, and straight, for a considerable distance above and below the bridge, opens a short but very pleasing view of the North mountain on one side and the Blue Ridge on the other, at the distance each of them of about five miles. . . .

FROM QUERY XI.
A DESCRIPTION OF THE INDIANS
ESTABLISHED IN THAT STATE?

When the first effectual settlement of our colony was made, which was in 1607, the country from the sea-coast to the mountains, and from the Potomac to the most southern waters of James' river, was occupied by upwards of forty different tribes of Indians. Of these the *Powhatans*, the *Mannahoacs*, and *Monacans*, were the most powerful. Those between the seacoast and falls of the rivers, were in amity with one another, and attached to the *Powhatans* as their link of union. Those between the falls of the rivers and the mountains, were divided into two confederacies; the tribes inhabiting the head waters of Potomac and Rappahannock, being attached to the *Mannahoacs*; and those on the upper parts of James' river to the *Monacans*. But the *Monacans* and their friends were in amity with the *Mannahoacs* and their friends, and waged joint and perpetual war against the *Powhatans*. We are told that the *Powhatans, Mannahoacs,* and *Monacans,* spoke languages so radically different, that interpreters were necessary when they transacted business. Hence we may conjecture, that this was not the case between all the tribes, and, probably, that each spoke the language of the nation to which it was attached; which we know to have been the case in many particular instances. Very possibly there may have been anciently three different stocks, each of which multiplying in a long course of time, had separated into so many little societies. This practice results from the circumstance of their having never submitted themselves to any laws, any coercive power, any shadow of government. Their only controls are their manners, and that moral sense of right and wrong, which, like the sense of tasting and feeling in every man, makes a part of his nature. An offence against these is punished by contempt, by exclusion from society, or, where the case is serious, as that of murder, by the individuals whom it concerns. Imperfect as this species of coercion may seem, crimes are very rare among them, insomuch that were it made a question, whether no law, as among the savage Americans, or too much law, as among the civilized Europeans, submits man to the greatest evil, one who has seen both conditions of existence would pronounce it to be the last; and that the sheep are happier of themselves, than under care of the wolves. It will be said, that great societies cannot exist without government. The savages, therefore, break them into small ones. . . .

FROM QUERY XVII. RELIGION?

The error seems not sufficiently eradicated, that the operations of the mind, as well as the acts of the body, are subject to the coercion of the laws. But our rulers can have no authority over such natural rights, only as we have submitted to them. The rights of conscience we never submitted, we could not submit. We are answerable for them to our God. The legitimate powers of government extend to such acts only as are injurious to others. But it does me no injury for my neighbor to say there are twenty gods, or no God. It neither picks my pocket nor breaks my leg. If it be said, his testimony in a court of justice cannot be relied on, reject it then, and be the stigma on him. Constraint may make him worse by making him a hypocrite, but it will never make him a truer man. It may fix him obstinately in his errors, but will not cure them. Reason and free inquiry are the only effectual agents against error. Give a loose to them, they will support the true religion by bringing every false one to their tribunal, to the test of their investigation. They are the natural enemies of error, and of error only. Had not the Roman government permitted free inquiry, Christianity could never have been introduced. Had not free inquiry been indulged at the era of the reformation, the corruptions of Christianity could not have been purged away. If it be restrained now, the present corruptions will be protected, and new ones encouraged. Was the government to prescribe to us our medicine and diet, our bodies would be in such keeping as our souls are now. Thus in France the emetic was once forbidden as a medicine, and the potato as an article of food. Government is just as infallible, too, when it fixes systems in physics. Galileo was sent to the Inquisition for affirming that the earth was a sphere; the government had declared it to be as flat as a trencher, and Galileo was obliged to abjure his error. This error, however, at length prevailed, the earth became a globe, and Descartes declared it was whirled round its axis by a vortex. The government in which he lived was wise enough to see that this was no question of civil jurisdiction, or we should all have been involved by authority in vortices. In fact, the vortices have been exploded, and the Newtonian principle of gravitation is now more firmly established, on the basis of reason, than it would be were the government to step in, and to make it an article of necessary faith. Reason and experiment have been indulged, and error has fled before them. It is error alone which needs the support of government. Truth can stand by itself. Subject opinion to coercion: whom will you make your inquisitors? Fallible men; men governed by bad passions, by private as well as public reasons. And why subject it to coercion? To produce uniformity. But is uniformity of opinion desirable? No more than of face and stature. Introduce the bed of Procrustes then, and as there is danger that the large men may beat the small, make us all of a size, by lopping the former and stretching the latter. Difference of opinion is advantageous in religion. The several sects perform the office of a *censor morum* over such other. Is uniformity attainable? Millons of innocent men, women, and children, since the introduction of Christianity, have been burnt, tortured, fined, imprisoned; yet we have not advanced one inch towards uniformity. What has been the effect of coercion? To make one half the world fools, and the other half hypocrites. To support roguery and error all over the earth. Let us reflect that it is inhabited by a thousand millions of people. That these profess probably a thousand different systems of religion. That ours is but one of that thousand. That if there be but one right, and ours that one, we should wish to see the nine hundred and ninety-nine wandering sects gathered into the fold of truth. But against such a majority we cannot effect this by force. Reason and persuasion are the only practicable instruments. To make way for these, free inquiry must be indulged; and how can we wish others to indulge it while we refuse it ourselves. . . .

An Act for Establishing Religious Freedom in the State of Virginia (1786)

Well aware that Almighty God hath created the mind free; that all attempts to influence it by temporal punishments or burdens, or by civil incapacitations, tend only to beget habits of hypocrisy and meanness, and are a departure from the plan of the Holy Author of our religion, who being Lord both of body and mind, yet chose not to propagate it by coercions on either, as was in his Almighty power to do; that the impious presumption of legislators and rulers, civil as well as ecclesiastical, who, being themselves but fallible and uninspired men have assumed dominion over the faith of others, setting up their own opinions and modes of thinking as the only true and infallible, and as such endeavoring to impose them on others, hath established and maintained false religions over the greatest part of the world, and through all time; that to compel a man to furnish contributions of money for the propagation of opinions which he disbelieves, is sinful and tyrannical; that even the forcing him to support this or that teacher of his own religious persuasion, is depriving him of the comfortable liberty of giving his contributions to the particular pastor whose morals he would make his pattern, and whose powers he feels most persuasive to righteousness, and is withdrawing from the ministry those temporal rewards, which proceeding from an approbation of their personal conduct, are an additional incitement to earnest and unremitting labors for the instruction of mankind; that our civil rights have no dependence on our religious opinions, more than our opinions in physics or geometry; that, therefore, the proscribing any citizen as unworthy the public confidence by laying upon him an incapacity of being called to the offices of trust and emolument, unless he profess or renounce this or that religious opinion, is depriving him injuriously of those privileges and advantages to which in common with his fellow citizens he has a natural right; that it tends also to corrupt the principles of that very religion it is meant to encourage, by bribing, with a monopoly of worldly honors and emoluments, those who will externally profess and conform to it; that though indeed these are criminal who do not withstand such temptation, yet neither are those innocent who lay the bait in their way; that to suffer the civil magistrate to intrude his powers into the field of opinion and to restrain the profession or propagation of principles, on the supposition of their ill tendency, is a dangerous fallacy, which at once destroys all religious liberty, because he being of course judge of that tendency, will make his opinions the rule of judgment, and approve or condemn the sentiments of others only as they shall square with or differ from his own; that it is time enough for the rightful purposes of civil government, for its officers to interfere when principles break out into overt acts against peace and good order; and finally, that truth is great and will prevail if left to herself, that she is the proper and sufficient antagonist to error, and has nothing to fear from the conflict, unless by human interposition disarmed of her natural weapons, free argument and debate, errors ceasing to be dangerous when it is permitted freely to contradict them.

Be it therefore enacted by the General Assembly, That no man shall be compelled to frequent or support any religious worship, place or ministry whatsoever, nor shall be enforced, restrained, molested, or burthened in his body or goods, nor shall otherwise suffer on account of his religious opinions or belief; but that all men shall be free to profess, and by argument to maintain, their opinions in matters of religion, and that the same shall in nowise diminish, enlarge, or affect their civil capacities.

And though we well know this Assembly, elected by the people for the ordinary purposes of legislation only, have no power to restrain the acts of succeeding assemblies, constituted with the powers equal to our own, and that therefore to declare this act irrevocable, would be of no effect in law, yet we are free to declare, and do declare, that the rights hereby asserted are of the natural rights of mankind, and that if any act shall be hereafter passed to repeal the present or to narrow its operation, such act will be an infringement of natural right.

First Inaugural Address
(March 4, 1801)

Friends and Fellow Citizens:—Called upon to undertake the duties of the first executive office of our country, I avail myself of the presence of that portion of my fellow-citizens which is here assembled, to express my grateful thanks for the favor with which they have been pleased to look toward me, to declare a sincere consciousness that the task is above my talents, and that I approach it with those anxious and awful presentiments which the greatness of the charge and the weakness of my powers so justly inspire. A rising nation, spread over a wide and fruitful land, traversing all the seas with the rich productions of their industry, engaged in commerce with nations who feel power and forget right, advancing rapidly to destinies beyond the reach of mortal eye—when I contemplate these transcendent objects, and see the honor, the happiness, and the hopes of this beloved country committed to the issue and the auspices of this day, I shrink from the contemplation, and humble myself before the magnitude of the undertaking. Utterly indeed, should I despair, did not the presence of many whom I here see remind me, that in the other high authorities provided by our constitution, I shall find resources of wisdom, of virtue, and of zeal, on which to rely under all difficulties. To you, then, gentlemen, who are charged with the sovereign functions of legislation, and to those associated with you, I look with encouragement for that guidance and support which may enable us to steer with safety the vessel in which we are all embarked amid the conflicting elements of a troubled world.

During the contest of opinion through which we have passed, the animation of discussion and of exertions has sometimes worn an aspect which might impose on strangers unused to think freely and to speak and to write what they think; but this being now decided by the voice of the nation, announced according to the rules of the constitution, all will, of course, arrange themselves under the will of the law, and unite in common efforts for the common good. All, too, will bear in mind this sacred principle, that though the will of the majority is in all cases to prevail, that will, to be rightful, must be reasonable; that the minority possess their equal rights, which equal laws must protect, and to violate which would be oppression. Let us, then, fellow-citizens, unite with one heart and one mind. Let us restore to social intercourse that harmony and affection without which liberty and even life itself are but dreary things. And let us reflect that having banished from our land that religious intolerance under which mankind so long bled and suffered, we have yet gained little if we countenance a political intolerance as despotic, as wicked, and capable of as bitter and bloody persecutions. During the throes and convulsions of the ancient world, during the agonizing spasms of infuriated man, seeking through blood and slaughter his long-lost liberty, it was not wonderful that the agitation of the billows should reach even this distant and peaceful shore; that this should be more felt and feared by

some and less by others; that this should divide opinions as to measures of safety. But every difference of opinion is not a difference of
principle. We have called by different names brethren of the same principle. We are all republicans—we are federalists. If there be any among
us who would wish to dissolve this Union or to change its republican
form, let them stand undisturbed as monuments of the safety with
which error of opinion may be tolerated where reason is left free to
combat it. I know, indeed, that some honest men fear that a republican
government cannot be strong; that this government is not strong
enough. But would the honest patriot, in the full tide of successful
experiment, abandon a government which has so far kept us free and
firm, on the theoretic and visionary fear that this government, the
world's best hope, may by possibility want energy to preserve itself? I
trust not. I believe this, on the contrary, the strongest government on
earth. I believe it is the only one where every man, at the call of the
laws, would fly to the standard of the law, and would meet invasions
of the public order as his own personal concern. Sometimes it is said
that man cannot be trusted with the government of himself. Can he,
then, be trusted with the government of others? Or have we found
angels in the forms of kings to govern him? Let history answer this
question.

Let us, then, with courage and confidence pursue our own federal
and republican principles, our attachment to our union and representative government. Kindly separated by nature and a wide ocean from
the exterminating havoc of one quarter of the globe; too high-minded
to endure the degradations of the others; possessing a chosen country,
with room enough for our descendants to the hundredth and thousandth generation; entertaining a due sense of our equal right to the
use of our own faculties, to the acquisitions of our industry, to honor
and confidence from our fellow-citizens, resulting not from birth but
from our actions and their sense of them; enlightened by a benign
religion, professed, indeed, and practised in various forms, yet all of
them including honesty, truth, temperance, gratitude, and the love of
man; acknowledging and adoring an overruling Providence, which by
all its dispensations proves that it delights in the happiness of man
here and his greater happiness hereafter; with all these blessings, what
more is necessary to make us a happy and prosperous people? Still
one thing more, fellow citizens—a wise and frugal government, which
shall restrain men from injuring one another, which shall leave them
otherwise free to regulate their own pursuits of industry and improvement, and shall not take from the mouth of labor the bread it has
earned. This is the sum of good government, and this is necessary to
close the circle of our felicities.

About to enter, fellow citizens, on the exercise of duties which comprehend everything dear and valuable to you, it is proper that you should understand what I deem the essential principles of our government, and consequently those which ought to shape its administration. I will compress them within the narrowest compass they will bear, stating the general principle, but not all its limitations. Equal and exact justice to all men, of whatever state or persuasion, religious or political; peace, commerce, and honest friendship, with all nations—entangling alliances with none; the support of the state governments in all their rights, as the most competent administrations for our domestic concerns and the surest bulwarks against anti-republican tendencies; the preservation of the General Government in its whole constitutional vigor, as the sheet-anchor of our peace at home and safety abroad; a jealous care of the right of election by the people—a mild and safe corrective of abuses which are lopped by the sword of the revolution where peaceable remedies are unprovided; absolute acquiescence in the decisions of the majority—the vital principle of republics, from which there is no appeal but to force the vital principle and immediate parent of despotism; a well-disciplined militia—our best reliance in peace and for the first moments of war, till regulars may relieve them; the supremacy of the civil over the military authority; economy in the public expense, that labor may be lightly burdened; the honest payment of our debts and sacred preservation of the public faith; encouragement of agriculture, and of commerce as its handmaid; the diffusion of information and the arraignment of all abuses at the bar of public reason; freedom of religion; freedom of the press; freedom of person under the protection of the *habeas corpus*; and trial by juries impartially selected—these principles form the bright constellation which has gone before us, and guided our steps through an age of revolution and reformation. The wisdom of our sages and the blood of our heroes have been devoted to their attainment. They should be the creed of our political faith—the text of civil instruction—the touchstone by which to try the services of those we trust; and should we wander from them in moments of error or alarm, let us hasten to retrace our steps and to regain the road which alone leads to peace, liberty, and safety.

I repair, then, fellow-citizens, to the post you have assigned me. With experience enough in subordinate offices to have seen the difficulties of this, the greatest of all, I have learned to expect that it will rarely fall to the lot of imperfect man to retire from this station with the reputation and the favor which bring him into it. Without pretensions to that high confidence reposed in our first and great revolutionary character, [George Washington] whose preëminent services had entitled him to the first place in his country's love, and destined for him the fairest page in the volume of faithful history, I ask so much confidence only as may give firmness and effect to the legal administration of your affairs. I shall often go wrong through defect of judgment. When right, I shall often be thought wrong by those whose positions will not command a view of the whole ground. I ask your indulgence for my own errors, which will never be intentional; and your support against the errors of others, who may condemn what they would not if seen in all its parts. The approbation implied by your suffrage is a consolation to me for the past; and my future solicitude will be to retain the good opinion of those who have bestowed it in advance, to conciliate that of others by doing them all the good in my power, and to be instrumental to the happiness and freedom of all.

Relying, then, on the patronage of your good-will, I advance with obedience to the work, ready to retire from it whenever you become sensible how much better choice it is in your power to make. And may that Infinite Power which rules the destinies of the universe, lead our councils to what is best, and give them a favorable issue for your peace and prosperity.

Letter to James Madison
(December 20, 1787)

. . . I like much the general idea of framing a government, which should go on of itself peaceably, without needing continual recurrence to the State legislatures. I like the organization of the government into legislative, judiciary and executive. I like the power given the legislature to levy taxes, and for that reason solely, I approve of the greater House being chosen by the people directly. For though I think a House so chosen will be very far inferior to the present Congress, will be very ill qualified to legislate for the Union, for foreign nations, &c. yet this evil does not weigh against the good, of preserving inviolate the fundamental principle, that the people are not to be taxed but by representatives chosen immediately by themselves. I am captivated by the compromise of the opposite claims of the great and little States, of the latter to equal, and the former to proportional influence. I am much pleased too, with the substitution of the method of voting by persons, instead of that of voting by States; and I like the negative given to the Executive, conjointly with a third of either House; though I should have liked it better, had the judiciary been associated for that purpose, or invested separately with a similar power. There are other good things of less moment. I will now tell you what I do not like. First, the omission of a bill of rights, providing clearly, and without the aid of sophism, for freedom of religion, freedom of the press, protection against standing armies, restriction of monopolies, the eternal and unremitting force of the habeas corpus laws, and trials by jury in all matters of fact triable by the laws of the land, and not by the laws of nations. To say, as Mr. Wilson does, that a bill of rights was not necessary, because all is reserved in the case of the general government which is not given, while in the particular ones, all is given which is not reserved, might do for the audience to which it was addressed; but it is surely a *gratis dictum*, the reverse of which might just as well be said; and it is opposed by strong inferences from the body of the instrument, as well as from the omission of the clause of our present Confederation, which had made the reservation in express terms. It was hard to conclude, because there has been a want of uniformity among the States as to the cases triable by jury, because some have been so incautious as to dispense with this mode of trial in certain cases; therefore, the more prudent States shall be reduced to the same level of calamity. It would have been much more just and wise to have concluded the other way, that as most of the States had preserved with jealousy this sacred palladium of liberty, those who had wandered should be brought back to it; and to have established general right rather than general wrong. For I consider all the ill as established, which may be established. I have a right to nothing, which another has a right to take away; and Congress will have a right to take away trials by jury in all civil cases. Let me add, that a bill of rights is what the people are entitled to against every government on earth, general or particular; and what no just government should refuse, or rest on inference.

The second feature I dislike, and strongly dislike, is the abandonment, in every instance, of the principle of rotation in office, and most particularly in the case of the President. Reason and experience tell us, that the first magistrate will always be re-elected if he may be re-elected. He is then an officer for life. This once observed, it becomes of so much consequence to certain nations, to have a friend or a foe at the head of our affairs, that they will interfere with money and with arms. A Galloman, or an Angloman, will be supported by the nation he befriends. If once elected, and at a second or third election outvoted by one or two votes, he will pretend false votes, foul play, hold possession of the reins of government, be supported by the States voting for him, especially if they be the central ones, lying in a compact body themselves, and separating their opponents; and they will be aided by one nation in Europe, while the majority are aided by another. The election of a President of America, some years hence, will be much more interesting to certain nations of Europe, than ever the election of a King of Poland was. Reflect on all the instances in history, antient and modern, of elective monarchies, and say, if they do not give foundation for my fears; the Roman Emperors, the Popes while they were of any importance, the German Emperors till they became hereditary in practice, the Kings of Poland, the Deys of the Ottoman dependencies. It may be said, that if elections are to be attended with these disorders, the less frequently they are repeated the better. But experience says, that to free them from disorder, they must be rendered less interesting by a necessity of change. No foreign power, nor domestic party, will waste their blood and money to elect a person, who must go out at the end of a short period. The power of removing every fourth year by the vote of the people, is a power which they will not exercise, and if they were disposed to exercise it, they would not be permitted. The King of Poland is removable every day by the diet. But they never remove him. Nor would Russia, the Emperor, &c. permit them to do it. Smaller objections are, the appeals on matters of fact as well as law; and the binding all persons, legislative, executive and judiciary by oath, to maintain that constitution. I do not pretend to decide, what would be the best method of procuring the establishment of the manifold good things in this constitution, and of getting rid of the bad. Whether by adopting it, in hopes of future amendment; or, after it shall have been duly weighed and canvassed by the people, after seeing the parts they generally dislike, and those they generally approve, to say to them, "We see now what you wish. You are willing to give to your federal government such and such powers: but you wish, at the same time, to have such and such fundamental rights secured to you, and certain sources of convulsion taken away. Be it so. Send together your deputies again. Let them establish your fundamental rights by a sacrosanct declaration, and let them pass the parts of the constitution you have approved. These will give powers to your federal government sufficient for your happiness."

This is what might be said, and would probably produce a speedy, more perfect and more permanent form of government. At all events, I hope you will not be discouraged from making other trials, if the present one should fail. We are never permitted to despair of the commonwealth. I have thus told you freely what I like, and what I dislike, merely as a matter of curiosity; for I know it is not in my power to offer matter of information to your judgment, which has been formed after hearing and weighing every thing which the wisdom of man could offer on these subjects. I own, I am not a friend to a very energetic government. It is always oppressive. It places the governors indeed more at their ease, at the expense of the people. The late rebellion in Massachusetts [Shay's Rebellion] has given more alarm, than I think it should have done. Calculate that one rebellion in thirteen States in the course of eleven years, is but one for each State in a century and a half. No country should be so long without one. Nor will any degree of power in the hands of government, prevent insurrections. In England, where the hand of power is heavier than with us, there are seldom half a dozen years without an insurrection. In France, where it is still heavier, but less despotic, as Montesquieu supposes, than in some other countries, and where there are always two or three hundred thousand men ready to crush insurrections, there have been three in the course of the three years I have been here, in every one of which greater numbers were engaged than in Massachusetts, and a great deal more blood was spilt. In Turkey, where the sole nod of the despot is death, insurrections are the events of every day. Compare again the ferocious depredations of their insurgents, with the order, the moderation and the almost self-extinguishment of ours. And say, finally, whether peace is best preserved by giving energy to the government, or information to the people. This last is the most certain, and the most legitimate engine of government. Educate and inform the whole mass of the people. Enable them to see that it is their interest to preserve peace and order, and they will preserve them. And it requires no very high degree of education to convince them of this. They are the only sure reliance for the preservation of our liberty. After all, it is my principle that the will of the majority should prevail. If they approve the proposed constitution in all its parts, I shall concur in it cheerfully, in hopes they will amend it, whenever they shall find it works wrong. This reliance cannot deceive us, as long as we remain virtuous; and I think we shall be so, as long as agriculture is our principal object, which will be the case, while there remain vacant lands in any part of America. When we get piled upon one another in large cities, as in Europe, we shall become corrupt as in Europe, and go to eating one another as they do there. I have tired you by this time with disquisitions which you have already heard repeated by others, a thousand and a thousand times; and therefore, shall only add assurances of the esteem and attachment, with which I have the honor to be,

Dear Sir, your affectionate friend and servant,

TH: JEFFERSON.

P.S. The instability of our laws is really an immense evil. I think it would be well to provide in our constitutions, that there shall always be a twelvemonth between the engrossing a bill and passing it: that it should then be offered to its passage without changing a word: and that if circumstances should be thought to require a speedier passage, it should take two-thirds of both Houses, instead of a bare majority.

Letter to Dr. Benjamin Rush
(April 21, 1803)

DEAR SIR,

In some of the delightful conversations with you, in the evenings of 1798–99, and which served as an anodyne to the afflictions of the crisis through which our country was then labouring, the Christian religion was sometimes our topic; and I then promised you, that one day, or other, I would give you my views of it. They are the result of a life of inquiry and reflection, and very different from that anti-Christian system imputed to me by those who know nothing of my opinions. To the corruptions of Christianity I am, indeed, opposed, but not to the genuine precepts of Jesus himself. I am a Christian in the only sense in which he wished any one to be; sincerely attached to his doctrines, in preference to all others; ascribing to himself every *human* excellence, and believing he never claimed any other. At the short intervals since these conversations, when I could justifiably abstract my mind from public affairs, the subject has been under my contemplation; but the more I considered it, the more it expanded beyond the measure of either my time or information. In the moment of my late departure from Monticello, I received from Doctor Priestley[1] his little treatise of 'Socrates and Jesus compared.' This being a section of the general view I had taken of the field, it became a subject of reflection while on the road, and unoccupied otherwise. The result was, to arrange in my mind a syllabus, or outline, of such an estimate of the comparative merits of Christianity, as I wished to see executed by some one of more leisure and information for the task than myself. This I now send you, as the only discharge of my promise I can probably ever execute. And in confiding it to you, I know it will not be exposed to the malignant perversions of those who make every word from me a text for new misrepresentations and calumnies. I am moreover averse to the communication of my religious tenets to the public; because it would countenance the presumption of those who have endeavoured to draw them before that tribunal, and to seduce public opinion to erect itself into that inquisition over the rights of conscience, which the laws have so justly proscribed. It behoves every man who values liberty of conscience for himself, to resist invasions of it in the case of others; or their case may, by change of circumstances, become his own. It behoves him, too, in his own case, to give no example of concession, betraying the common right of independent opinion, by answering questions of faith, which the laws have left between God and himself. Accept my affectionate salutations.

TH. JEFFERSON.

Syllabus of an estimate of the merit of the doctrines of Jesus, compared with those of others.

In a comparative view of the Ethics of the enlightened nations of antiquity, of the Jews, and of Jesus, no notice should be taken of the corruptions of reason among the antients, to wit, the idolatry and superstition of the vulgar, nor of the corruptions of Christianity by the learned among its professors.

Let a just view be taken of the moral principles inculcated by the most esteemed of the sects of antient philosophy, or of their individuals; particularly Pythagoras, Socrates, Epicurus, Cicero, Epictetus, Seneca, Antoninus.

I. Philosophers. 1. Their precepts related chiefly to ourselves, and the government of those passions which, unrestrained, would disturb our tranquillity of mind. In this branch of philosophy they were really great.

2. In developing our duties to others, they were short and defective. They embraced, indeed, the circles of kindred and friends, and inculcated patriotism, or the love of our country in the aggregate, as a primary obligation; towards our neighbours and countrymen they taught justice, but scarcely viewed them as within the circle of benevolence. Still less have they inculcated peace, charity, and love to our fellow men, or embraced with benevolence the whole family of mankind.

II. Jews. 1. Their system was Deism; that is, the belief in one only God. But their ideas of him and of his attributes were degrading and injurious.

2. Their Ethics were not only imperfect, but often irreconcilable with the sound dictates of reason and morality, as they respect intercourse with those around us; and repulsive and anti-social, as respecting other nations. They needed reformation, therefore, in an eminent degree.

III. Jesus. In this state of things among the Jews, Jesus appeared. His parentage was obscure; his condition poor; his education null; his natural endowments great; his life correct and innocent: he was meek, benevolent, patient, firm, disinterested, and of the sublimest eloquence.

The disadvantages under which his doctrines appear are remarkable.

1. Like Socrates and Epictetus, he wrote nothing himself.

2. But he had not, like them, a Xenophon or an Arrian to write for him. I name not Plato, who only used the name of Socrates to cover the whimsies of his own brain. On the contrary, all the learned of his country, entrenched in its power and riches, were opposed to him, lest his labours should undermine their advantages; and the committing to writing his life and doctrines fell on unlettered and ignorant men; who wrote, too, from memory, and not till long after the transactions had passed.

3. According to the ordinary fate of those who attempt to enlighten and reform mankind, he fell an early victim to the jealousy and combination of the altar and the throne, at about thirty-three years of age, his reason having not yet attained the *maximum* of its energy, nor the course of his preaching, which was but of three years at most, presented occasions for developing a complete system of morals.

4. Hence the doctrines which he really delivered were defective as a whole, and fragments only of what he did deliver have come to us, mutilated, misstated, and often unintelligible.

5. They have been still more disfigured by the corruptions of schismatising followers, who have found an interest in sophisticating and perverting the simple doctrines he taught, by engrafting on them the mysticisms of a Grecian sophist, frittering them into subtleties, and obscuring them with jargon, until they have caused good men to reject the whole in disgust, and to view Jesus himself as an impostor.

Notwithstanding these disadvantages, a system of morals is presented to us, which, if filled up in the style and spirit of the rich fragments he left us, would be the most perfect and sublime that has ever been taught by man.

The question of his being a member of the Godhead, or in direct communication with it, claimed for him by some of his followers, and denied by others, is foreign to the present view, which is merely an estimate of the intrinsic merit of his doctrines.

1. He corrected the Deism of the Jews, confirming them in their belief of one only God, and giving them juster notions of his attributes and government.

2. His moral doctrines, relating to kindred and friends, were more pure and perfect than those of the most correct of the philosophers, and greatly more so than those of the Jews; and they went far beyond both in inculcating universal philanthropy, not only to kindred and friends, to neighbours and countrymen, but to all mankind, gathering all into one family, under the bonds of love, charity, peace, common wants, and common aids. A development of this head will evince the peculiar superiority of the system of Jesus over all others.

3. The precepts of philosophy, and of the Hebrew code, laid hold

of actions only. He pushed his scrutinies into the heart of man; erected his tribunal in the region of his thoughts, and purified the waters at the fountain head.

4. He taught, emphatically, the doctrine of a future state, which was either doubted or disbelieved by the Jews; and wielded it with efficacy, as an important incentive, supplementary to the other motives to moral conduct.

Letter to Peter Carr
(August 19, 1785)

DEAR PETER,—I received, by Mr. Mazzei, your letter of April the 20th. I am much mortified to hear that you have lost so much time; and that, when you arrived in Williamsburg, you were not at all advanced from what you were when you left Monticello. Time now begins to be precious to you. Every day you lose will retard a day your entrance on that public stage whereon you may begin to be useful to yourself. However, the way to repair the loss is to improve the future time. I trust, that with your dispositions, even the acquisition of science is a pleasing employment. I can assure you, that the possession of it is, what (next to an honest heart) will above all things render you dear to your friends, and give you fame and promotion in your own country. When your mind shall be well improved with science, nothing will be necessary to place you in the highest points of view, but to pursue the interests of your country, the interests of your friends, and your own interests also, with the purest integrity, the most chaste honor. The defect of these virtues can never be made up by all the other acquirements of body and mind. Make these, then, your first object. Give up money, give up fame, give up science, give up the earth itself and all it contains, rather than do an immoral act. And never suppose, that in any possible situation, or under any circumstances, it is best for you to do a dishonorable thing, however slightly so it may appear to you. Whenever you are to do a thing, though it can never be known but to yourself, ask yourself how you would act were all the world looking at you, and act accordingly. Encourage all your virtuous dispositions, and exercise them whenever an opportunity arises; being assured that they will gain strength by exercise, as a limb of the body does, and that exercise will make them habitual. From the practice of the purest virtue, you may be assured you will derive the most sublime comforts in every moment of life, and in the moment of death. If ever you find yourself environed with difficulties and perplexing circumstances, out of which you are at a loss how to extricate yourself, do what is right, and be assured that that will extricate you the best out of the worst situations. Though you cannot see, when you take one step, what will be the next, yet follow truth, justice, and plain dealing, and never fear their leading you out of the labyrinth, in the easiest manner possible. The knot which you thought a Gordian one, will untie itself before you. Nothing is so mistaken as the supposition, that a person is to extricate himself from a difficulty, by intrigue, by chicanery, by dissimulation, by trimming, by an untruth, by an injustice. This increases the difficulties tenfold; and those, who pursue these methods, get themselves so involved at length, that they can turn no way but their infamy becomes more exposed. It is of great importance to set a resolution, not to be shaken, never to tell an untruth. There is no vice so mean, so pitiful, so contemptible; and he who permits himself to tell a lie once, finds it much easier to do it a second and third time, till at length it becomes habitual; he tells lies without attending to it, and truths without the world's believing him. This falsehood of the tongue leads to that of the heart, and in time depraves all its good dispositions.

An honest heart being the first blessing, a knowing head is the second. It is time for you now to begin to be choice in your reading; to begin to pursue a regular course in it; and not to suffer yourself to be turned to the right or left by reading anything out of that course. I have long ago digested a plan for you, suited to the circumstances in which you will be placed. This I will detail to you, from time to time, as you advance. For the present, I advise you to begin a course of ancient history, reading everything in the original and not in translations. First read Goldsmith's history of Greece. This will give you a digested view of that field. Then take up ancient history in the detail, reading the following books, in the following order: Herodotus, Thucydides, Xenophontis Anabasis, Arrian, Quintus Curtius, Diodorus Siculus, Justin. This shall form the first stage of your historical reading, and is all I need mention to you now. The next will be of Roman history.[1] From that, we will come down to modern history. In Greek and Latin poetry, you have read or will read at school, Virgil, Terence, Horace, Anacreon, Theocritus, Homer, Euripides, Sophocles. Read also Milton's "Paradise Lost," Shakspeare, Ossian, Pope's and Swift's works, in order to form your style in your own language. In morality, read Epictetus, Xenophontis Memorabilia, Plato's Socratic dialogues, Cicero's philosophies, Antoninus, and Seneca. In order to assure a certain progress in this reading, consider what hours you have free from the school and the exercises of the school. Give about two of them, every day, to exercise; for health must not be sacrificed to learning. A strong body makes the mind strong. As to the species of exercise, I advise the gun. While this gives a moderate exercise to the body, it gives boldness, enterprise, and independence to the mind. Games played with the ball, and others of that nature, are too violent for the body, and stamp no character on the mind. Let your gun, therefore, be the constant companion of your walks. Never think of taking a book with you. The object of walking is to relax the mind. You should therefore not permit yourself even to think while you walk; but divert yourself by the objects surrounding you. Walking is the best possible exercise. Habituate yourself to walk very far. The Europeans value themselves on having subdued the horse to the uses of man; but I doubt whether we have not lost more than we have gained, by the use of this animal. No one has occasioned so much the degeneracy of the human body. An Indian goes on foot nearly as far in a day, for a long journey, as an enfeebled white does on his horse; and he will tire the best horses. There is no habit you will value so much as that of walking far without fatigue. I would advise you to take your exercise in the afternoon: not because it is the best time for exercise, for certainly it is not; but because it is the best time to spare from your studies; and habit will soon reconcile it to health, and render it nearly as useful as if you gave to that the more precious hours of the day. A little walk of half an hour, in the morning, when you first rise, is advisable also. It shakes off sleep, and produces other good effects in the animal economy. Rise at a fixed and an early hour, and go to bed at a fixed and early hour also. Sitting up late at night is injurious to the health, and not useful to the mind. Having ascribed proper hours to exercise, divide what remain (I mean of your vacant hours) into three portions. Give the principal to History, the other two, which should be shorter, to Philosophy and Poetry. Write to me once every month or two, and let me know the progress you make. Tell me in what manner you employ every hour in the day. The plan I have proposed for you is adapted to your present situation only. When that is changed, I shall propose a corresponding change of plan. I have ordered the following books to be sent to you from London, to the care of Mr. Madison: Herodotus, Thucydides, Xenophon's Hellenics, Anabasis and Memorabilia, Cicero's works, Baretti's Spanish and English Dictionary, Martin's Philosophical Grammar, and Martin's Philosophia Britannica. I will send you the following from hence: Bezout's Mathematics, De la Lande's Astronomy, Muschenbrock's Physics, Quintus Curtius, Justin, a Spanish Grammar, and some Spanish books. You will observe that Martin, Bezout, De la Lande, and Muschenbrock, are not in the preceding plan. They are not to be opened till you go to the University. You are now, I expect, learning French. You must push this; because the books which will be put into your hands when you advance into Mathematics, Natural philosophy, Natural history, &c., will be mostly

French, these sciences being better treated by the French than the English writers. Our future connection with Spain renders that the most necessary of the modern languages, after the French. When you become a public man, you may have occasion for it, and the circumstance of your possessing that language, may give you a preference over other candidates. I have nothing further to add for the present, but husband well your time, cherish your instructors, strive to make everybody your friend; and be assured that nothing will be so pleasing as your success to, Dear Peter,

> Yours affectionately.

Letter to Thomas Law, Esq.
(June 13, 1814)

DEAR SIR,—The copy of your Second Thoughts on Instinctive Impulses, with the letter accompanying it, was received just as I was setting out on a journey to this place, two or three days distant from Monticello. I brought it with me and read it with great satisfaction, and with the more as it contained exactly my own creed on the foundation of morality in man. It is really curious that on a question so fundamental, such a variety of opinions should have prevailed among men and those, too, of the most exemplary virtue and first order of understanding. It shows how necessary was the care of the Creator in making the moral principle so much a part of our constitution as that no errors of reasoning or of speculation might lead us astray from its observation in practice. Of all the theories on this question, the most whimsical seems to have been that of Wollaston, who considers *truth* as the foundation of morality. The thief who steals your guinea does wrong only inasmuch as he acts a lie in using your guinea as if it were his own. Truth is certainly a branch of morality, and a very important one to society. But presented as its foundation, it is as if a tree taken up by the roots, had its stem reversed in the air, and one of its branches planted in the ground. Some have made the love of God the foundation of morality. This, too, is but a branch of our moral duties, which are generally divided into duties to God and duties to man. If we did a good act merely from the love of God and a belief that it is pleasing to Him, whence arises the morality of the Atheist? It is idle to say, as some do, that no such being exists. We have the same evidence of the fact as of most of those we act on, to wit: their own affirmations, and their reasonings in support of them. I have observed, indeed, generally, that while in Protestant countries the defections from the Platonic

Thomas Jefferson

Christianity of the priests is to Deism, in Catholic countries they are to Atheism. Diderot, D'Alembert, D'Holbach, Condorcet, are known to have been among the most virtuous of men. Their virtue, then, must have had some other foundation than the love of God.

The Το καλου [the beautiful] of others is founded in a different faculty, that of taste, which is not even a branch of morality. We have indeed an innate sense of what we call beautiful, but that is exercised chiefly on subjects addressed to the fancy, whether through the eye in visible forms, as landscape, animal figure, dress, drapery, architecture, the composition of colors, etc., or to the imagination directly, as imagery, style, or measure in prose or poetry, or whatever else constitutes the domain of criticism or taste, a faculty entirely distinct from the moral one. Self-interest, or rather self-love, or *egoism*, has been more plausibly substituted as the basis of morality. But I consider our relations with others as constituting the boundaries of morality. With ourselves we stand on the ground of identity, not of relation, which last, requiring two subjects, excludes self-love confined to a single one. To ourselves, in strict language, we can owe no duties, obligation requiring also two parties. Self-love, therefore, is no part of morality. Indeed it is exactly its counterpart. It is the sole antagonist of virtue, leading us constantly by our propensities to self-gratification in violation of our moral duties to others. Accordingly, it is against this enemy that are erected the batteries of moralists and religionists, as the only obstacle to the practice of morality. Take from man his selfish propensities, and he can have nothing to seduce him from the practice of virtue. Or subdue those propensities by education, instruction or restraint, and virtue remains without a competitor. Egoism, in a broader sense, has been thus presented as the source of moral action. It has been said that we feed the hungry, clothe the naked, bind up the wounds of the man beaten by thieves, pour oil and wine into them, set him on our own beast and bring him to the inn, because we receive ourselves pleasure from these acts. So Helvetius, one of the best men on earth, and the most ingenious advocate of this principle, after defining "interest" to mean not merely that which is pecuniary, but whatever may procure us pleasure or withdraw us from pain, [*de l'esprit*, or, "of the spirit," 2, 1,] says, [ib. 2, 2,] "the humane man is he to whom the sight of misfortune is insupportable, and who to rescue himself from this spectacle, is forced to succor the unfortunate object." This indeed is true. But it is one step short of the ultimate question. These good acts give us pleasure, but how happens it that they give us pleasure? Because nature hath implanted in our breasts a love of others, a sense of duty to them, a moral instinct, in short, which prompts us irresistibly to feel and to succor their distresses, and protests against the language of Helvetius, [ib. 2, 5,] "what other motive than self-interest could determine a man to generous actions? It is as impossible for him to love what is good for the sake of good, as to love evil for the sake of evil." The Creator would indeed have been a bungling artist, had he intended man for a social animal, without planting in him social dispositions. It is true they are not planted in every man, because there is no rule without exceptions; but it is false reasoning which converts exceptions into the general rule. Some men are born without the organs of sight, or of hearing, or without hands. Yet it would be wrong to say that man is born without these faculties, and sight, hearing, and hands may with truth enter into the general definition of man.

The want or imperfection of the moral sense in some men, like the want or imperfection of the senses of sight and hearing in others, is no proof that it is a general characteristic of the species. When it is wanting, we endeavor to supply the defect by education, by appeals to reason and calculation, by presenting to the being so unhappily conformed, other motives to do good and to eschew evil, such as the love, or the hatred, or rejection of those among whom he lives, and whose society is necessary to his happiness and even existence; demonstrations by sound calculation that honesty promotes interest in the long run; the rewards and penalties established by the laws; and ultimately the prospects of a future state of retribution for the evil as well as the good done while here. These are the correctives which are supplied by education, and which exercise the functions of the moralist, the preacher, and legislator; and they lead into a course of correct action all those whose disparity is not too profound to be eradicated. Some have argued against the existence of a moral sense, by saying that if nature had given us such a sense, impelling us to virtuous actions, and warning us against those which are vicious, then nature would also have designated, by some particular ear-marks, the two sets of actions which are, in themselves, the one virtuous and the other vicious. Whereas, we find, in fact, that the same actions are deemed virtuous in one country and vicious in another. The answer is, that nature has constituted *utility* to man, the standard and test of virtue. Men living in different countries, under different circumstances, different habits and regimens, may have different utilities; the same act, therefore, may be useful, and consequently virtuous in one country which is injurious and vicious in another differently circumstanced. I sincerely, then, believe with you in the general existence of a moral instinct. I think it the brightest gem with which the human character is studded, and the want of it as more degrading than the most hideous of the bodily deformities. I am happy in reviewing the roll of associates in this principle which you present in your second letter, some of which I had not before met with. To these might be added Lord Kaims, one of the ablest of our advocates, who goes so far as to say, in his Principles of Natural Religion, that a man owes no duty to which he is not urged by some impulsive feeling. This is correct, if referred to the standard of general feeling in the given case, and not to the feeling of a single individual. Perhaps I may misquote him, it being fifty years since I read his book.

The leisure and solitude of my situation here has led me to the indiscretion of taxing you with a long letter on a subject whereon nothing new can be offered you. I will indulge myself no farther than to repeat the assurances of my continued esteem and respect.

John Adams
(1735–1826)

*Elected the first vice president of the United States in 1788 and the
second president in 1796, John Adams lost the 1800 election to Thomas Jefferson and retired immediately to private life in Quincy, Massachusetts. But this retirement from public service by no means
represented a withdrawal from the public realm. If John Adams had
accomplished no more in the years remaining to him, he had, with his
extraordinary wife, Abigail, founded one of the most remarkable families in American history: Their son John Quincy Adams became the
sixth president of the United States in 1825; their grandson Charles
Francis Adams served as minister to Britain during the War between
the States; and their great-grandson Henry Adams became a famous
historian, autobiographer, and novelist. But Adams's later years were
spent gathering his papers (his* Works *have been collected in ten volumes), carrying on a vigorous correspondence, and writing an autobiography that described a man who was strong in opposition to the
Stamp Act, who served as a delegate to both Continental Congresses
(proposing George Washington as military commander at the second),
who helped draft the Declaration of Independence and was, according
to Jefferson, "the pillar of its support on the floor of Congress," who
was appointed commissioner to France from 1777 to 1779, and who
then served as envoy to Britain from 1785 to 1788. His preface to his
three-volume* Defense of the Constitutions of Government of the
United States of America against the Attack of Mr. Turgot *was written
during his residence in England and published in 1787.*

from the Preface to *A Defense of the Constitutions of Government (1787)*

The arts and sciences, in general, during the three or four last centuries, have had a regular course of progressive improvement. The inventions in mechanic arts, the discoveries in natural philosophy, navigation, and commerce, and the advancement of civilization and humanity, have occasioned changes in the condition of the world, and the human character, which would have astonished the most refined nations of antiquity. A continuation of similar exertions is every day rendering Europe more and more like one community, or single family. Even in the theory and practice of government, in all the simple monarchies, considerable improvements have been made. The checks and balances of republican governments have been in some degree adopted at the courts of princes. By the erection of various tribunals, to register the laws, and exercise the judicial power—by indulging the petitions and remonstrances of subjects, until by habit they are regarded as rights—a control has been established over ministers of state, and the royal councils, which, in some degree, approaches the spirit of republics. Property is generally secure, and personal liberty seldom invaded. The press has great influence, even where it is not expressly tolerated; and the public opinion must be respected by a minister, or his place becomes insecure. Commerce begins to thrive; and if religious toleration were established, personal liberty a little more protected, by giving an absolute right to demand a public trial in a certain reasonable time, and the states were invested with a few more privileges, or rather restored to some that have been taken away, these governments would be brought to as great a degree of perfection, they would approach as near to the character of governments of laws and not of men, as their nature will probably admit of. In so general a refinement, or more properly a reformation of manners and improvement in science, is it not unaccountable that the knowledge of the principles and construction of free governments, in which the happiness of life, and even the further progress of improvement in education and society, in knowledge and virtue, are so deeply interested, should have remained at a full stand for two or three thousand years?

According to a story in Herodotus,[1] the nature of monarchy, aristocracy, and democracy, and the advantages and inconveniences of each, were as well understood at the time of the neighing of the horse of Darius,[2] as they are at this hour. A variety of mixtures of these simple species were conceived and attempted, with various success, by the Greeks and Romans. Representations, instead of collections, of the people; a total separation of the executive from the legislative power, and of the judicial from both; and a balance in the legislature, by three independent, equal branches, are perhaps the only three discoveries in the constitution of a free government, since the institution of Lycurgus.[3] Even these have been so unfortunate, that they have never spread: the first has been given up by all the nations, excepting one, which had once adopted it; and the other two, reduced to practice, if not invented, by the English nation, have never been imitated by any other, except their own descendants in America.

While it would be rash to say, that nothing further can be done to bring a free government, in all its parts, still nearer to perfection, the representations of the people are most obviously susceptible of improvement. The end to be aimed at, in the formation of a representative assembly, seems to be the sense of the people, the public voice. The perfection of the portrait consists in its likeness. Numbers, or property, or both, should be the rule; and the proportions of electors and members an affair of calculation. The duration should not be so long that the deputy should have time to forget the opinions of his constituents. Corruption in elections is the great enemy of freedom. Among the provisions to prevent it, more frequent elections, and a more general privilege of voting, are not all that might be devised. Dividing the districts, diminishing the distance of travel, and confining the choice to residents, would be great advances towards the annihilation of corruption. The modern aristocracies of Holland, Venice, Bern, &c., have tempered themselves with innumerable checks, by which they have given a great degree of stability to that form of government; and though liberty and life can never be there enjoyed so well as in a free republic, none is perhaps more capable of profound sagacity. We shall learn to prize the checks and balances of a free government, and even those of the modern aristocracies, if we recollect the miseries of Greece, which arose from its ignorance of them. The only balance attempted against the ancient kings was a body of nobles; and the consequences were perpetual alternations of rebellion and tyranny, and the butchery of thousands upon every revolution from one to the other. When kings were abolished, aristocracies tyrannized; and then no balance was attempted but between aristocracy and democracy. This, in the nature of things, could be no balance at all, and therefore the pendulum was forever on the swing.

It is impossible to read in Thucydides,[4] his account of the factions and confusions throughout all Greece, which were introduced by this want of an equilibrium, without horror. "During the few days that Eurymedon, with his troops, continued at Corcyra, the people of that city extended the massacre to all whom they judged their enemies. The crime alleged was, their attempt to overturn the democracy. Some perished merely through private enmity; some, by the hands of the bor-rower, on account of the money they had lent. Every kind of death, every dreadful act, was perpetrated. Fathers slew their children; some were dragged from altars, some were butchered at them; numbers, immured in temples, were starved. The contagion spread through the whole extent of Greece; factions raged in every city; the licentious many contending for the Athenians, and the aspiring few for the La-cedæmonians. The consequence was, seditions in cities, with all their numerous and tragical incidents."

"Such things ever will be," says Thucydides, "so long as human nature continues the same." But if this nervous historian had known a balance of three powers, he would not have pronounced the dis-temper so incurable, but would have added—*so long as parties in cities remain unbalanced.* He adds,—"Words lost their signification; brutal rashness was fortitude; prudence, cowardice; modesty, effeminacy; and being wise in every thing, to be good for nothing: the hot temper was manly valor; calm deliberation, plausible knavery; he who boiled with indignation, was trustworthy; and he who presumed to contradict, was ever suspected. Connection of blood was less regarded than transient acquaintance; associations were not formed for mutual advantage, consistent with law, but for rapine against all law; trust was only communication of guilt; revenge was more valued, than never to have suffered an injury; perjuries were master-pieces of cunning; the dupes only blushed, the villains most impudently triumphed."

"The source of all these evils was a thirst of power, from rapa-cious and ambitious passions. The men of large influence, some con-tending for the just equality of the democratical, and others for the fair decorum of aristocratical government, by artful sounds, embar-rassed those communities, for their own private lucre, by the keenest spirit, the most daring projects, and most dreadful machinations. Re-venge, not limited by justice or the public welfare, was measured only by such retaliation as was judged the sweetest; by capital condemna-tions, by iniquitous sentences, and by glutting the present rancor of their hearts with their own hands. The pious and upright conduct was on both sides disregarded; the moderate citizens fell victims to both. Seditions introduced every species of outrageous wickedness into the Grecian manners. Sincerity was laughed out of countenance; the whole order of human life was confounded; the human temper, too apt to transgress in spite of laws, now having gained the ascendant over law, seemed to glory that it was too strong for justice, and an enemy to all superiority."

Mr. Hume[5] has collected, from Diodorus Siculus[6] alone, a few massacres which happened in only sixty of the most polished years of

Greece:—"From Sybaris, 500 nobles banished; of Chians, 600 citizens; at Ephesus, 340 killed, 1000 banished; of Cyrenians, 500 nobles killed, all the rest banished; the Corinthians killed 120, banished 500; Phæbidas banished 300 Bœotians. Upon the fall of the Lacedæmonians, democracies were restored in many cities, and severe vengeance taken of the nobles; the banished nobles returning, butchered their adversaries at Phialæ, in Corinth, in Megara, in Phliasia, where they killed 300 of the people; but these again revolting, killed above 600 of the nobles, and banished the rest. In Arcadia, 1400 banished, besides many killed; the banished retired to Sparta and Pallantium; the latter were delivered up to their countrymen, and all killed. Of the banished from Argos and Thebes, there were 500 in the Spartan army. The people, before the usurpation of Agathocles, had banished 600 nobles; afterwards that tyrant, in concurrence with the people, killed 4000 nobles, and banished 6000; and killed 4000 people at Gela; his brother banished 8000 from Syracuse. The inhabitants of Ægesta, to the number of 40,000, were killed, man, woman, and child, for the sake of their money; all the relations of the Libyan army, fathers, brothers, children, killed; 7000 exiles killed after capitulation. These numbers, compared with the population of those cities, are prodigious; yet Agathocles was a man of character, and not to be suspected of wanton cruelty, contrary to the maxims of his age."[7]

Such were the fashionable outrages of unbalanced parties. In the name of human and divine benevolence, is such a system as this to be recommended to Americans, in this age of the world? Human nature is as incapable now of going through revolutions with temper and sobriety, with patience and prudence, or without fury and madness, as it was among the Greeks so long ago. The latest revolution that we read of was conducted, at least on one side, in the Grecian style, with laconic energy; and with a little Attic salt, at least, without too much patience, foresight, and prudence, on the other. Without three orders, and an effectual balance between them, in every American constitution, it must be destined to frequent unavoidable revolutions; though they are delayed a few years, they must come in time. The United States are large and populous nations, in comparison with the Grecian commonwealths, or even the Swiss cantons; and they are growing every day more disproportionate, and therefore less capable of being held together by simple governments. Countries that increase in population so rapidly as the States of America did, even during such an impoverishing and destructive war as the last was, are not to be long bound with silken threads; lions, young or old, will not be bound by cobwebs. It would be better for America, it is nevertheless agreed, to ring all the changes with the whole set of bells, and go through all the revolutions of the Grecian States, rather than establish an absolute monarchy among them, notwithstanding all the great and real improvements which have been made in that kind of government.

The objection to it is not because it is supported by nobles, and a subordination of ranks; for all governments, even the most democratical, are supported by a subordination of offices, and of ranks too. None ever existed without it but in a state of anarchy and outrage, in a contempt of law and justice, no better than no government. But the nobles, in the European monarchies, support them more by opposing than promoting their ordinary views. The kings are supported by their armies; the nobles support the crown, as it is in full possession of the gift of all employments; but they support it still more by checking its ministers, and preventing them from running into abuses of power and wanton despotism; otherwise the people would be pushed to extremities and insurrections. It is thus that the nobles reconcile the monarchical authority to the obedience of the subjects; but take away the standing armies, and leave the nobles to themselves, and in a few years, they would overturn every monarchy in Europe, and erect aristocracies.

It is become a kind of fashion among writers, to admit, as a maxim, that if you could be always sure of a wise, active, and virtuous prince, monarchy would be the best of governments. But this is so far from being admissible, that it will forever remain true, that a free government has a great advantage over a simple monarchy. The best and wisest prince, by means of a freer communication with his people, and the greater opportunities to collect the best advice from the best of his subjects, would have an immense advantage in a free state over a monarchy. A senate consisting of all that is most noble, wealthy, and able in the nation, with a right to counsel the crown at all times, is a check to ministers, and a security against abuses, such as a body of nobles who never meet, and have no such right, can never supply. Another assembly, composed of representatives chosen by the people in all parts, gives free access to the whole nation, and communicates all its wants, knowledge, projects, and wishes to government; it excites emulation among all classes, removes complaints, redresses grievances, affords opportunities of exertion to genius, though in obscurity, and gives full scope to all the faculties of man; it opens a passage for every speculation to the legislature, to administration, and to the public; it gives a universal energy to the human character, in every part of the state, such as never can be obtained in a monarchy.

There is a third particular which deserves attention both from governments and people. In a simple monarchy, the ministers of state can never know their friends from their enemies; secret cabals undermine their influence, and blast their reputation. This occasions a jealousy ever anxious and irritated, which never thinks the government safe without an encouragement of informers and spies, throughout every part of the state, who interrupt the tranquillity of private life, destroy the confidence of families in their own domestics and in one another, and poison freedom in its sweetest retirements. In a free government, on the contrary, the ministers can have no enemies of consequence but among the members of the great or little council, where every man is obliged to take his side, and declare his opinion, upon every question. This circumstance alone, to every manly mind, would be sufficient to decide the preference in favor of a free government. Even secrecy, where the executive is entire in one hand, is as easily and surely preserved in a free government, as in a simple monarchy; and as to despatch, all the simple monarchies of the whole universe may be defied to produce greater or more numerous examples of it than are to be found in English history. An Alexander, or a Frederic,[8] possessed of the prerogatives only of a king of England, and leading his own armies, would never find himself embarrassed or delayed in any honest enterprise. He might be restrained, indeed, from running mad, and from making conquests to the ruin of his nation, merely for his own glory; but this is no argument against a free government.

There can be no free government without a democratical branch in the constitution. Monarchies and aristocracies are in possession of the voice and influence of every university and academy in Europe. Democracy, simple democracy, never had a patron among men of letters. Democratical mixtures in government have lost almost all the advocates they ever had out of England and America. Men of letters must have a great deal of praise, and some of the necessaries, conveniences, and ornaments of life. Monarchies and aristocracies pay well and applaud liberally. The people have almost always expected to be served gratis, and to be paid for the honor of serving them; and their applauses and adorations are bestowed too often on artifices and tricks, on hypocrisy and superstition, on flattery, bribes, and largesses. It is no wonder then that democracies and democratical mixtures are annihilated all over Europe, except on a barren rock, a paltry fen, an inaccessible mountain, or an impenetrable forest. The people of England, to their immortal honor, are hitherto an exception; but, to the humiliation of human nature, they show very often that they are like other men. The people in America have now the best opportunity and the greatest trust in their hands, that Providence ever committed to so small a number, since the transgression of the first pair; if they betray their trust, their guilt will merit even greater punishment than other nations have suffered, and the indignation of Heaven. If there is one certain truth to be collected from the history of all ages, it is this; that the people's rights and liberties, and the democratical mixture in a constitution, can never be preserved without a strong executive, or, in other words, without separating the executive from the legislative power. If the executive power, or any considerable part of it, is left in the hands either of an aristocratical or a democratical assembly, it will corrupt the legislature as necessarily as rust corrupts iron, or as arsenic poisons the human body; and when the legislature is corrupted, the people are undone.

The rich, the well-born, and the able, acquire an influence among the people that will soon be too much for simple honesty and plain sense, in a house of representatives. The most illustrious of them must, therefore, be separated from the mass, and placed by themselves in a senate; this is, to all honest and useful intents, an ostracism. A member of a senate, of immense wealth, the most respected birth, and transcendent abilities, has no influence in the nation, in comparison of what he would have in a single representative assembly. When a senate exists, the most powerful man in the state may be safely admitted into the house of representatives, because the people have it in their power to remove him into the senate as soon as his influence becomes dangerous. The senate becomes the great object of ambition; and the richest and the most sagacious wish to merit an advancement to it by services to the public in the house. When he has obtained the object of his wishes, you may still hope for the benefits of his exertions, without dreading his passions; for the executive power being in other hands, he has lost much of his influence with the people, and can govern very few votes more than his own among the senators.

It was the general opinion of ancient nations, that the Divinity alone was adequate to the important office of giving laws to men. The Greeks entertained this prejudice throughout all their dispersions; the Romans cultivated the same popular delusion; and modern nations, in the consecration of kings, and in several superstitious chimeras of divine right in princes and nobles, are nearly unanimous in preserving remnants of it. Even the venerable magistrates of Amersfort devoutly believe themselves God's vicegerents. Is it that obedience to the laws can be obtained from mankind in no other manner? Are the jealousy of power, and the envy of superiority, so strong in all men, that no considerations of public or private utility are sufficient to engage their submission to rules for their own happiness? Or is the disposition to imposture so prevalent in men of experience, that their private views of ambition and avarice can be accomplished only by artifice? It was a tradition in antiquity that the laws of Crete were dictated to Minos by the inspiration of Jupiter. This legislator and his brother Rhadamanthus were both his sons; once in nine years they went to converse with their father, to propose questions concerning the wants of the people; and his answers were recorded as laws for their government.

The laws of Lacedæmon were communicated by Apollo to Lycurgus; and, lest the meaning of the deity should not have been perfectly comprehended, or correctly expressed, they were afterwards confirmed by his oracle at Delphos. Among the Romans, Numa was indebted for those laws which procured the prosperity of his country to his conversations with Egeria. The Greeks imported these mysteries from Egypt and the East, whose despotisms, from the remotest antiquity to this day, have been founded in the same solemn empiricism; their emperors and nobles being all descended from their gods. Woden and Thor were divinities too; and their posterity ruled a thousand years in the north by the strength of a like credulity. Manco Capac was the child of the sun, the visible deity of the Peruvians; and transmitted his divinity, as well as his earthly dignity and authority, through a line of incas. And the rudest tribes of savages in North America have certain families from which their leaders are always chosen, under the immediate protection of the god War. There is nothing in which mankind have been more unanimous; yet nothing can be inferred from it more than this, that the multitude have always been credulous, and the few are always artful.

The United States of America have exhibited, perhaps, the first example of governments erected on the simple principles of nature; and if men are now sufficiently enlightened to disabuse themselves of artifice, imposture, hypocrisy, and superstition, they will consider this event as an era in their history. Although the detail of the formation of the American governments is at present little known or regarded either in Europe or in America, it may hereafter become an object of curiosity. It will never be pretended that any persons employed in that service had interviews with the gods, or were in any degree under the inspiration of Heaven, more than those at work upon ships or houses, or laboring in merchandise or agriculture; it will forever be acknowledged that these governments were contrived merely by the use of reason and the senses, as Copley painted Chatham; West, Wolf; and Trumbull,[9] Warren and Montgomery; as Dwight, Barlow, Trumbull, and Humphries[10] composed their verse, and Belknap and Ramsay[11] history; as Godfrey invented his quadrant, and Rittenhouse his planetarium; as Boylston[12] practised inoculation, and Franklin electricity; as Paine exposed the mistakes of Raynal, and Jefferson those of Buffon, so unphilosophically borrowed from the despicable dreams of De Pau. Neither the people, nor their conventions, committees, or subcommittees, considered legislation in any other light than as ordinary arts and sciences, only more important. Called without expectation, and compelled without previous inclination, though undoubtedly at the best period of time, both for England and America, suddenly to erect new systems of laws for their future government, they adopted the method of a wise architect, in erecting a new palace for the residence of his sovereign. They determined to consult Vitruvius, Palladio, and all other writers of reputation in the art; to examine the most celebrated buildings, whether they remain entire or in ruins; to compare these with the principles of writers; and to inquire how far both the theories and models were founded in nature, or created by fancy; and when this was done, so far as their circumstances would allow, to adopt the advantages and reject the inconveniences of all. Unembarrassed by attachments to noble families, hereditary lines and successions, or any considerations of royal blood, even the pious mystery of holy oil had no more influence than that other one of holy water. The people were universally too enlightened to be imposed on by artifice; and their leaders, or more properly followers, were men of too much honor to attempt it. Thirteen governments thus founded on the natural authority of the people alone, without a pretence of miracle or mystery, and which are destined to spread over the northern part of that whole quarter of the globe, are a great point gained in favor of the rights of mankind. The experiment is made, and has completely succeeded; it can no longer be called in question, whether authority in magistrates and obedience of citizens can be grounded on reason, morality, and the Christian religion, without the monkery of priests, or the knavery of politicians. As the writer was personally acquainted with most of the gentlemen in each of the states, who had the principal share in the first draughts, the following work was really written to lay before the public a specimen of that kind of reading and reasoning which produced the American constitutions.

It is not a little surprising that all this kind of learning should have been unknown to any illustrious philosopher and statesman, and especially one who really was, what he has been often called, "a well of science." But if he could be unacquainted with it, or it could have escaped his memory, we may suppose millions in America have occasion to be reminded of it. The writer has long seen with anxiety the facility with which philosophers of greatest name have undertaken to write of American affairs, without knowing any thing of them, and have echoed and reëchoed each other's visionary language. Having neither talents, leisure, nor inclination to meet such champions in the field of literary controversy, he little thought of venturing to propose to them any questions. Circumstances, however, have lately occurred which seem to require that some notice should be taken of one of them. If the publication of these papers should contribute any thing to turn the attention of the younger gentlemen of letters in America to this kind of inquiry, it will produce an effect of some importance to their country. The subject is the most interesting that can engage the understanding or the heart; for whether the end of man, in this stage of his existence, be enjoyment, or improvement, or both, it can never be attained so well in a bad government as a good one. . . .

The institutions now made in America will not wholly wear out for thousands of years. It is of the last importance, then, that they should begin right. If they set out wrong, they will never be able to return, unless it be by accident, to the right path. After having known the history of Europe, and of England in particular, it would be the height of folly to go back to the institutions of Woden and of Thor, as the Americans are advised to do. If they had been counselled to adopt a single monarchy at once, it would have been less mysterious.

Robertson, Hume, and Gibbon have given such admirable accounts of the feudal institutions and their consequences, that it would have been, perhaps, more discreet to have referred to them, without saying any thing more upon the subject. To collect together the legislation of the Indians would take up much room, but would be well worth the pains. The sovereignty is in the nation, it is true, but the three powers are strong in every tribe; and their royal and aristocratical dignities are much more generally hereditary, from the popular partiality to particular families, and the superstitious opinion that such are favorites of the God of War, than late writers upon this subject have allowed.

J. Hector St. Jean
de Crevecoeur
(1737–1818)

Frenchman Michel-Guillaume Jean de Crevecoeur emigrated to Canada and served under Montcalm in the last of the French and Indian wars. After the war, Crevecoeur, a trained cartographer, explored the vast wilderness of the Great Lakes region and eventually settled in New York State. In 1765 he became an American citizen under the assumed name of J. Hector St. Jean de Crevecoeur, took up farming, and began writing his celebrated Letters *(1782). Despite his idealization of the self-reliant American husbandman, whom he pictured as continually regenerated by the land from which he wrests his living, Crevecoeur apparently found his loyalties divided on the eve of the American Revolution and during the War of Independence was forced to return to France. When he came back to America at the war's end, he found his farm destroyed, his wife dead, and his children separated, but he slowly put back together again the remaining pieces of his life, and before his permanent return to France in 1790, he even served for a time with distinction as the French consul in New York.*

Crevecoeur's famous question "What then is the American, this new man?" has been asked from the earliest years of Renaissance discovery to the present. Crevecoeur's own answer—that the American is one who derives new manners and morals, not to say a new metaphysics, from the new mode of life he has been obliged to adopt in the New World—has also had its echo down through the years, especially among those who conceive of the American environment as somehow decisive in the development of the American character and consciousness. But as the second selection indicates, this definition of the American was not only idealized but selective, inasmuch as it left out of account all those nonwhite peoples who were already settled on the land before European immigration began or those hundreds of thousands of others who were brought forcibly to the New World in chains and sold as slaves. Crevecoeur was honest enough with himself to include a portrait of one among those many less fortunate inhabitants of the New World who were excluded from this definition of the "American."

from *Letters from an American Farmer* (1782)

FROM LETTER III.
WHAT IS AN AMERICAN?

I wish I could be acquainted with the feelings and thoughts which must agitate the heart and present themselves to the mind of an enlightened Englishman, when he first lands on this continent. He must greatly rejoice that he lived at a time to see this fair country discovered and settled; he must necessarily feel a share of national pride, when he views the chain of settlements which embellishes these extended shores. When he says to himself, this is the work of my countrymen, who, when convulsed by factions, afflicted by a variety of miseries and wants, restless and impatient, took refuge here. They brought along with them their national genius, to which they principally owe what liberty they enjoy, and what substance they possess. Here he sees the industry of his native country displayed in a new manner, and traces in their works the embrios of all the arts, sciences, and ingenuity which flourish in Europe. Here he beholds fair cities, substantial villages, extensive fields, an immense country filled with decent houses, good roads, orchards, meadows, and bridges, where an hundred years ago all was wild, woody and uncultivated! What a train of pleasing ideas this fair spectacle must suggest; it is a prospect which must inspire a good citizen with the most heartfelt pleasure. The difficulty consists in the manner of viewing so extensive a scene. He is arrived on a new continent; a modern society offers itself to his contemplation, different from what he had hitherto seen. It is not composed, as in Europe, of great lords who possess every thing, and of a herd of people who have nothing. Here are no aristocratical families, no courts, no kings, no bishops, no ecclesiastical dominion, no invisible power giving to a few a very visible one; no great manufacturers employing thousands, no great refinements of luxury. The rich and the poor are not so far removed from each other as they are in Europe. Some few towns ex-

cepted, we are all tillers of the earth, from Nova Scotia to West
Florida. We are a people of cultivators, scattered over an immense
territory, communicating with each other by means of good roads and
navigable rivers, united by the silken bands of mild government, all
respecting the laws, without dreading their power, because they are
equitable. We are all animated with the spirit of an industry which is
unfettered and unrestrained, because each person works for himself.
If he travels through our rural districts he views not the hostile castle,
and the haughty mansion, contrasted with the clay-built hut and miserable cabin, where cattle and men help to keep each other warm, and
dwell in meanness, smoke, and indigence. A pleasing uniformity of
decent competence appears throughout our habitations. The meanest
of our log-houses is a dry and comfortable habitation. Lawyer or merchant are the fairest titles our towns afford; that of a farmer is the
only appellation of the rural inhabitants of our country. It must take
some time ere he can reconcile himself to our dictionary, which is but
short in words of dignity, and names of honour. There, on a Sunday,
he sees a congregation of respectable farmers and their wives, all clad
in neat homespun, well mounted, or riding in their own humble wag-
gons. There is not among them an esquire, saving the unlettered magistrate. There he sees a parson as simple as his flock, a farmer who
does not riot on the labour of others. We have no princes, for whom
we toil, starve, and bleed: we are the most perfect society now existing
in the world. Here man is free as he ought to be; nor is this pleasing
equality so transitory as many others are. Many ages will not see the
shores of our great lakes replenished with inland nations, nor the unknown bounds of North America entirely peopled. Who can tell how
far it extends? Who can tell the millions of men whom it will feed and
contain? for no European foot has as yet travelled half the extent of
this mighty continent!

The next wish of this traveller will be to know whence came all
these people? they are a mixture of English, Scotch, Irish, French,
Dutch, Germans, and Swedes. From this promiscuous breed, that race
now called Americans have arisen. The eastern provinces must indeed
be excepted, as being the unmixed descendants of Englishmen. I have
heard many wish that they had been more intermixed also: for my
part, I am no wisher, and think it much better as it has happened.
They exhibit a most conspicuous figure in this great and variegated
picture; they too enter for a great share in the pleasing perspective
displayed in these thirteen provinces. I know it is fashionable to reflect
on them, but I respect them for what they have done; for the accuracy
and wisdom with which they have settled their territory; for the decency of their manners; for their early love of letters; their ancient
college,[1] the first in this hemisphere; for their industry; which to me

who am but a farmer, is the criterion of everything. There never was a people, situated as they are, who with so ungrateful a soil have done more in so short a time. Do you think that the monarchical ingredients which are more prevalent in other governments, have purged them from all foul stains? Their histories assert the contrary.

In this great American asylum, the poor of Europe have by some means met together, and in consequence of various causes; to what purpose should they ask one another what countrymen they are? Alas, two thirds of them had no country. Can a wretch who wanders about, who works and starves, whose life is a continual scene of sore affliction or pinching penury; can that man call England or any other kingdom his country? A country that had no bread for him, whose fields procured him no harvest, who met with nothing but the frowns of the rich, the severity of the laws, with jails and punishments; who owned not a single foot of the extensive surface of this planet? No! urged by a variety of motives, here they came. Every thing has tended to regenerate them; new laws, a new mode of living, a new social system; here they are become men: in Europe they were as so many useless plants, wanting vegitative mould, and refreshing showers; they withered, and were mowed down by want, hunger, and war; but now by the power of transplantation, like all other plants they have taken root and flourished! Formerly they were not numbered in any civil lists of their country, except in those of the poor; here they rank as citizens. By what invisible power has this surprising metamorphosis been performed? By that of the laws and that of their industry. The laws, the indulgent laws, protect them as they arrive, stamping on them the symbol of adoption; they receive ample rewards for their labours; these accumulated rewards procure them lands; those lands confer on them the title of freemen, and to that title every benefit is affixed which men can possibly require. This is the great operation daily performed by our laws. From whence proceed these laws? From our government. Whence the government? It is derived from the original genius and strong desire of the people ratified and confirmed by the crown. This is the great chain which links us all, this is the picture which every province exhibits, Nova Scotia excepted.[2] There the crown has done all; either there were no people who had genius, or it was not much attended to: the consequence is, that the province is very thinly inhabited indeed; the power of the crown in conjunction with the musketos has prevented men from settling there. Yet some parts of it flourished once, and it contained a mild harmless set of people. But for the fault of a few leaders, the whole were banished. The greatest political error the crown ever committed in America, was to cut off men from a country which wanted nothing but men!

What attachment can a poor European emigrant have for a coun-

try where he had nothing? The knowledge of the language, the love
of a few kindred as poor as himself, were the only cords that tied him:
his country is now that which gives him land, bread, protection, and
consequence: *Ubi panis ibi patria*,[3] is the motto of all emigrants. What
then is the American, this new man? He is either an European, or the
descendant of an European, hence that strange mixture of blood,
which you will find in no other country. I could point out to you a
family whose grandfather was an Englishman, whose wife was Dutch,
whose son married a French woman, and whose present four sons have
now four wives of different nations. *He* is an American, who leaving
behind him all his ancient prejudices and manners, receives new ones
from the new mode of life he has embraced, the new government he
obeys, and the new rank he holds. He becomes an American by being
received in the broad lap of our great *Alma Mater*. Here individuals
of all nations are melted into a new race of men, whose labours and
posterity will one day cause great changes in the world. Americans are
the western pilgrims, who are carrying along with them that great mass
of arts, sciences, vigour, and industry which began long since in the
east; they will finish the great circle. The Americans were once scattered all over Europe; here they are incorporated into one of the finest
systems of population which has ever appeared, and which will hereafter become distinct by the power of the different climates they inhabit. The American ought therefore to love this country much better
than that wherein either he or his forefathers were born. Here the
rewards of his industry follow with equal steps the progress of his
labour; his labour is founded on the basis of nature, *self-interest*; can
it want a stronger allurement? Wives and children, who before in vain
demanded of him a morsel of bread, now, fat and frolicsome, gladly
help their father to clear those fields whence exuberant crops are to
arise to feed and to clothe them all; without any part being claimed,
either by a despotic prince, a rich abbot, or a mighty lord. Here religion demands but little of him; a small voluntary salary to the minister,
and gratitude to God; can he refuse these? The American is a new
man, who acts upon new principles; he must therefore entertain
new ideas, and form new opinions. From involuntary idleness, servile
dependence, penury, and useless labour, he has passed to toils of a
very different nature, rewarded by ample subsistence.—This is an
American.

•   •   •

He who would wish to see America in its proper light, and have a true
idea of its feeble beginnings and barbarous rudiments, must visit our

extended line of frontiers where the last settlers dwell, and where he
may see the first labours of settlement, the mode of clearing the earth,
in all their different appearances; where men are wholly left dependent
on their native tempers, and on the spur of uncertain industry, which
often fails when not sanctified by the efficacy of a few moral rules.
There, remote from the power of example, and check of shame, many
families exhibit the most hideous parts of our society. They are a kind
of forlorn hope, preceding by ten or twelve years the most respectable
army of veterans which come after them. In that space, prosperity will
polish some, vice and the law will drive off the rest, who uniting again
with others like themselves will recede still farther; making room for
more industrious people, who will finish their improvements, convert
the loghouse into a convenient habitation, and rejoicing that the first
heavy labours are finished, will change in a few years that hitherto
barbarous country into a fine fertile, well regulated district. Such is
our progress, such is the march of the Europeans toward the interior
parts of this continent. In all societies there are off-casts; this impure
part serves as our precursors or pioneers; my father himself was one
of that class, but he came upon honest principles, and was therefore
one of the few who held fast; by good conduct and temperance, he
transmitted to me his fair inheritance, when not above one in fourteen
of his contemporaries had the same good fortune.[4]

Forty years ago this smiling country was thus inhabited; it is now
purged, a general decency of manners prevails throughout, and such
has been the fate of our best countries.

Exclusive of those general characteristics, each province has its
own, founded on the government, climate, mode of husbandry, customs, and peculiarity of circumstances. Europeans submit insensibly
to these great powers, and become, in the course of a few generations,
not only Americans in general, but either Pensylvanians, Virginians, or
provincials under some other name. Whoever traverses the continent
must easily observe those strong differences, which will grow more
evident in time. The inhabitants of Canada, Massachuset, the middle
provinces, the southern ones will be as different as their climates; their
only points of unity will be those of religion and language.

•   •   •

But to return to our back settlers. I must tell you, that there is something in the proximity of the woods, which is very singular. It is with
men as it is with the plants and animals that grow and live in the
forests; they are entirely different from those that live in the plains. I
will candidly tell you all my thoughts but you are not to expect that

I shall advance any reasons. By living in or near the woods, their actions are regulated by the wildness of the neighbourhood. The deer often come to eat their grain, the wolves to destroy their sheep, the bears to kill their hogs, the foxes to catch their poultry. This surrounding hostility, immediately puts the gun into their hands; they watch these animals, they kill some; and thus by defending their property, they soon become professed hunters; this is the progress; once hunters, farewell to the plough. The chase renders them ferocious, gloomy, and unsociable; a hunter wants no neighbour, he rather hates them, because he dreads the competition. In a little time their success in the woods makes them neglect their tillage. They trust to the natural fecundity of the earth, and therefore do little; carelessness in fencing, often exposes what little they sow to destruction; they are not at home to watch; in order therefore to make up the deficiency, they go oftener to the woods. That new mode of life brings along with it a new set of manners, which I cannot easily describe. These new manners being grafted on the old stock, produce a strange sort of lawless profligacy, the impressions of which are indelible. The manners of the Indian natives are respectable, compared with this European medley. Their wives and children live in sloth and inactivity; and having no proper pursuits, you may judge what education the latter receive. Their tender minds have nothing else to contemplate but the example of their parents; like them they grow up a mongrel breed, half civilized, half savage, except nature stamps on them some constitutional propensities. That rich, that voluptuous sentiment is gone that struck them so forcibly; the possession of their freeholds no longer conveys to their minds the same pleasure and pride. To all these reasons you must add, their lonely situation, and you cannot imagine what an effect on manners the great distances they live from each other has! Consider one of the last settlements in its first view: of what is it composed? Europeans who have not that sufficient share of knowledge they ought to have, in order to prosper; people who have suddenly passed from oppression, dread of government, and fear of laws, into the unlimited freedom of the woods. This sudden change must have a very great effect on most men, and on that class particularly. Eating of wild meat, whatever you may think, tends to alter their temper: though all the proof I can adduce, is, that I have seen it: and having no place of worship to resort to, what little society this might afford, is denied them. The Sunday meetings, exclusive of religious benefits, were the only social bonds that might have inspired them with some degree of emulation in neatness. Is it then surprising to see men thus situated, immersed in great and heavy labours, degenerate a little? It is rather a wonder the effect is not more diffusive. The Moravians and the

Quakers are the only instances in exception to what I have advanced. The first never settle singly, it is a colony of the society which emigrates; they carry with them their forms, worship, rules, and decency: the others never begin so hard, they are always able to buy improvements, in which there is a great advantage, for by that time the country is recovered from its first barbarity. Thus our bad people are those who are half cultivators and half hunters; and the worst of them are those who have degenerated altogether into the hunting state. As old ploughmen and new men of the woods, as Europeans and new made Indians, they contract the vices of both; they adopt the moroseness and ferocity of a native, without his mildness, or even his industry at home. If manners are not refined, at least they are rendered simple and inoffensive by tilling the earth; all our wants are supplied by it, our time is divided between labour and rest, and leaves none for the commission of great misdeeds. As hunters it is divided between the toil of the chase, the idleness of repose, or the indulgence of inebriation. Hunting is but a licentious idle life, and if it does not always pervert good dispositions; yet, when it is united with bad luck, it leads to want: want stimulates that propensity to rapacity and injustice, too natural to needy men, which is the fatal gradation. After this explanation of the effects which follow by living in the woods, shall we yet vainly flatter ourselves with the hope of converting the Indians? We should rather begin with converting our back-settlers; and now if I dare mention the name of religion, its sweet accents would be lost in the immensity of these woods. Men thus placed, are not fit either to receive or remember its mild instructions; they want temples and ministers, but as soon as men cease to remain at home, and begin to lead an erratic life, let them be either tawny or white, they cease to be its disciples.

FROM LETTER IX. DESCRIPTION OF CHARLES-TOWN; THOUGHTS ON SLAVERY; ON PHYSICAL EVIL; A MELANCHOLY SCENE.

Charles-town is, in the north, what Lima[5] is in the south; both are Capitals of the richest provinces of their respective hemispheres: you may therefore conjecture, that both cities must exhibit the appearances necessarily resulting from riches. Peru abounding in gold, Lima is filled with inhabitants who enjoy all those gradations of pleasure, refinement, and luxury, which proceed from wealth. Carolina produces

commodities, more valuable perhaps than gold, because they are
gained by greater industry; it exhibits also on our northern stage, a
display of riches and luxury, inferior indeed to the former, but far
superior to what are to be seen in our northern towns. . . .

While all is joy, festivity, and happiness in Charles-Town, would
you imagine that scenes of misery overspread in the country? Their
ears by habit are become deaf, their hearts are hardened; they neither
see, hear, nor feel for the woes of their poor slaves, from whose painful
labours all their wealth proceeds. Here the horrors of slavery, the hardship of incessant toils, are unseen; and no one thinks with compassion
of those showers of sweat and of tears which from the bodies of Africans, daily drop, and moisten the ground they till. The cracks of the
whip urging these miserable beings to excessive labour, are far too
distant from the gay Capital to be heard. The chosen race eat, drink,
and live happy, while the unfortunate one grubs up the ground, raises
indigo, or husks the rice; exposed to a sun full as scorching as their
native one; without the support of good food, without the cordials of
any chearing liquor. This great contrast has often afforded me subjects
of the most afflicting meditation. On the one side, behold a people
enjoying all that life affords most bewitching and pleasurable, without
labour, without fatigue, hardly subjected to the trouble of wishing.
With gold, dug from Peruvian mountains, they order vessels to the
coasts of Guinea; by virtue of that gold, wars, murders, and devasta-
tions are committed in some harmless, peaceable African neighbourhood, where dwelt innocent people, who even knew not but that all
men were black. The daughter torn from her weeping mother, the child
from the wretched parents, the wife from the loving husband; whole
families swept away and brought through storms and tempests to this
rich metropolis! There, arranged like horses at a fair, they are branded
like cattle, and then driven to toil, to starve, and to languish for a few
years on the different plantations of these citizens. And for whom must
they work? For persons they know not, and who have no other power
over them than that of violence; no other right than what this accursed
metal has given them! Strange order of things! Oh, Nature, where art
thou?—Are not these blacks thy children as well as we? On the other
side, nothing is to be seen but the most diffusive misery and wretchedness, unrelieved even in thought or wish! Day after day they drudge
on without any prospect of ever reaping for themselves; they are
obliged to devote their lives, their limbs, their will, and every vital
exertion to swell the wealth of masters; who look not upon them with
half the kindness and affection with which they consider their dogs
and horses. Kindness and affection are not the portion of those who
till the earth, who carry the burdens, who convert the logs into useful

boards. This reward, simple and natural as one would conceive it, would border on humanity; and planters must have none of it!

•   •   •

The history of the earth! doth it present any thing but crimes of the most heinous nature, committed from one end of the world to the other? We observe avarice, rapine, and murder, equally prevailing in all parts. History perpetually tells us, of millions of people abandoned to the caprice of the maddest princes, and of whole nations devoted to the blind fury of tyrants. Countries destroyed; nations alternately buried in ruins by other nations; some parts of the world beautifully cultivated, returned again to the pristine state; the fruits of ages of industry, the toil of thousands in a short time destroyed by a few! If one corner breathes in peace for a few years, it is, in turn subjected, torne, and levelled; one would almost believe the principles of action in man, considered as the first agent of this planet, to be poisoned in their most essential parts. We certainly are not that class of beings which we vainly think ourselves to be; man an animal of prey, seems to have rapine and the love of bloodshed implanted in his heart; nay, to hold it the most honourable occupation in society: we never speak of a hero of mathematics, a hero of knowledge of humanity; no, this illustrious appellation is reserved for the most successful butchers of the world. If Nature has given us a fruitful soil to inhabit, she has refused us such inclinations and propensities as would afford us the full enjoyment of it. Extensive as the surface of this planet is, not one half of it is yet cultivated, not half replenished; she created man, and placed him either in the woods or plains, and provided him with passions which must for ever oppose his happiness; every thing is submitted to the power of the strongest; men, like the elements, are always at war; the weakest yield to the most potent; force, subtilty, and malice, always triumph over unguarded honesty, and simplicity. Benignity, moderation, and justice, are virtues adapted only to the humble paths of life: we love to talk of virtue and to admire its beauty, while in the shade of solitude, and retirement; but when we step forth into active life, if it happen to be in competition with any passion or desire, do we observe it to prevail? Hence so many religious impostors have triumphed over the credulity of mankind, and have rendered their frauds the creeds of succeeding generations, during the course of many ages; until worne away by time, they have been replaced by new ones. Hence the most unjust war, if supported by the greatest force, always succeeds; hence the most just ones, when supported only by their justice, as often fail. Such is the ascendancy of power; the supreme arbiter of all the revolutions which we observe in this planet: so irresistible is power, that it often thwarts the tendency of the most forcible causes, and prevents their subsequent salutary effects, though ordained for the good of man by the Governor of the universe. Such is the perverseness of human nature; who can describe it in all its latitude?

• • • •

The following scene will I hope account for these melancholy reflections, and apologize for the gloomy thoughts with which I have filled this letter: my mind is, and always has been, oppressed since I became a witness to it. I was not long since invited to dine with a planter who lived three miles from ——, where he then resided. In order to avoid the heat of the sun, I resolved to go on foot, sheltered in a small path, leading through a pleasant wood. I was leisurely travelling along, attentively examining some peculiar plants which I had collected, when all at once I felt the air strongly agitated; though the day was perfectly calm and sultry. I immediately cast my eyes toward the cleared ground, from which I was but at a small distance, in order to see whether it was not occasioned by a sudden shower; when at that instant a sound resembling a deep rough voice, uttered, as I thought, a few inarticulate monosyllables. Alarmed and surprized, I precipitately looked all round, when I perceived at about six rods distance something resembling a cage, suspended to the limbs of a tree; all the branches of which appeared covered with large birds of prey, fluttering about, and anxiously endeavouring to perch on the cage. Actuated by an involuntary motion of my hands, more than by any design of my mind, I fired at them; they all flew to a short distance, with a most hideous noise: when, horrid to think and painful to repeat, I perceived a negro, suspended in the cage, and left there to expire! I shudder when I recollect that the birds had already picked out his eyes, his cheek bones were bare; his arms had been attacked in several places, and his body seemed covered with a multitude of wounds. From the edges of the hollow sockets and from the lacerations with which he was disfigured, the blood slowly dropped, and tinged the ground beneath. No sooner were the birds flown, than swarms of insects covered the whole body of this unfortunate wretch, eager to feed on his mangled flesh and to drink his blood. I found myself suddenly arrested by the power of affright and terror; my nerves were convulsed; I trembled, I stood motionless, involuntarily contemplating the fate of this negro, in all its dismal latitude. The living spectre, though deprived of his eyes, could still distinctly hear, and in his uncouth dialect begged me to give him some water to allay his thirst. Humanity herself would have recoiled back with horror; she would have balanced whether to lessen such reliefless distress, or mercifully with one blow to end this dreadful scene of agonizing torture! Had I had a ball in my gun, I certainly should have despatched him; but finding myself unable to perform so kind an office, I sought, though trembling, to relieve him as well as I could. A shell ready fixed to a pole, which had been used by some negroes, presented itself to me; filled it with water, and with trembling hands I guided it to the quivering lips of the wretched sufferer. Urged by the irresistible power of thirst, he endeavoured to meet it, as he instinctively guessed its approach by the noise it made in passing through the bars of the cage. "Tankè, you whitè man, tankè you, putè somè poy- son and givè me." How long have you been hanging there? I asked him. "Two days, and me no die; the birds, the birds; aaah me!" Oppressed with the reflections which this shocking spectacle afforded me, I mustered strength enough to walk away, and soon reached the house at which I intended to dine. There I heard that the reason for this slave being thus punished, was on account of his having killed the overseer of the plantation. They told me that the laws of self-preservation rendered such executions necessary; and supported the doctrine of slavery with the arguments generally made use of to justify the practice; with the repetition of which I shall not trouble you at present.

Adieu.

Thomas Paine
(1737–1809)

Thomas Paine emigrated to America from England in 1774 with the help of Benjamin Franklin, who had been impressed by Paine's knowledge and interests. He is best known as a political pamphleteer, and his broadsides against tyranny and oppression, as in the "Introduction" to Common Sense *(1776), which sold almost a half million copies, encouraged the American rebellion. Paine's polemical and candid style, together with his outspoken social and religious views, frequently got him into trouble with authorities in England and France as well as in America. Barely escaping arrest for treason in England when the first part of his* The Rights of Man *(1790) was published, he was eventually imprisoned in France and narrowly missed execution by the guillotine before his release at the time of Robespierre's fall. Returning to an America that had by that time grown far more conservative after the American Revolution and the Constitutional crisis as it attempted to consolidate the gains of independence, Paine quickly found himself forsaken by most of his former friends and admirers and died in poverty. Regarded by many of his contemporaries, in the words of one of them, as "a loathsome reptile," his reputation was to continue to suffer from the general opinion voiced a century later by Theodore Roosevelt that he was "a filthy little atheist."*

As it happens, nothing could be further from the truth, nor less just to the diversity of Paine's mind. As he stated in The Age of Reason *(1797), his great work in defense of Deism, he found the most compelling argument for the existence of God "in the immensity of the creation" and "the unchangeable order by which the incomprehensible whole is governed." Words such as these could have easily won assent from most of the Founding Fathers, though they would no doubt have*

experienced considerably more difficulty accepting the sentiments con-
tained in his "Occasional Letter on the Female Sex." Here, as in so
much of his writing, Paine was carrying forward his belief in the ne-
cessity of an emancipation that must begin with liberation from re-
pressive institutions but that could only be completed with liberation
from repressive ideas.

An Occasional Letter on the Female Sex (1775)

O Woman! lovely Woman!
Nature made thee to temper man,
We had been Brutes without you.
                    Otway.[1]

If we take a survey of ages and of countries, we shall find the women, almost—without exception—at all times and in all places, adored and oppressed. Man, who has never neglected an opportunity of exerting his power, in paying homage to their beauty, has always availed himself of their weakness. He has been at once their tyrant and their slave.

Nature herself, in forming beings so susceptible and tender, appears to have been more attentive to their charms than to their happiness. Continually surrounded with griefs and fears, the women more than share all our miseries, and are besides subjected to ills which are peculiarly their own. They cannot be the means of life without exposing themselves to the loss of it; every revolution which they undergo, alters their health, and threatens their existence. Cruel distempers attack their beauty—and the hour, which confirms their release from those, is perhaps the most melancholy of their lives. It robs them of the most essential characteristic of their sex. They can then only hope for protection from the humiliating claims of pity, or the feeble voice of gratitude.

Society, instead of alleviating their condition, is to them the source of new miseries. More than one half of the globe is covered with savages; and among all these people women are completely wretched. Man, in a state of barbarity, equally cruel and indolent, active by necessity, but naturally inclined to repose, is acquainted with little more than the physical effects of love; and, having none of those moral ideas which only can soften the empire of force, he is led to consider it as his supreme law, subjecting to his despotism those whom reason had made his equal, but whose imbecility betrayed them to his strength. "Nothing" (says Professor Miller, speaking of the women of barbarous nations) "can exceed the dependence and subjection in which they are kept, or the toil and drudgery which they are obliged to undergo. The husband, when he is not engaged in some warlike exercise, indulges himself in idleness, and devolves upon his wife the whole burden of his domestic affairs. He disdains to assist her in any of those servile employments. She sleeps in a different bed, and is seldom permitted to have any conversation or correspondence with him."

The women among the Indians of America are what the Helots were among the Spartans, a vanquished people, obliged to toil for their conquerors. Hence on the banks of the Oroonoko,[2] we have seen mothers slaying their daughters out of compassion, and smothering them in the hour of their birth. They consider this barbarous pity as a virtue.

> "The men (says Commodore Byron, in his account of the inhabitants of South-America) exercise a most despotic authority over their wives, whom they consider in the same view they do any other part of their property, and dispose of them accordingly: Even their common treatment of them is cruel; for though the toil and hazard of procuring food lies entirely on the women, yet they are not suffered to touch any part of it till the husband is satisfied; and then he assigns them their portion, which is generally very scanty, and such as he has not a stomach for himself."

Among the nations of the East we find another kind of despotism and dominion prevail—the Seraglio,[3] and the domestic servitude of woman, authorised by the manners and established by the laws. In Turkey, in Persia, in India, in Japan, and over the vast empire of China, one half of the human species is oppressed by the other.

The excess of oppression in those countries springs from the excess of love.

All Asia is covered with prisons, where beauty in bondage waits the caprices of a master. The multitude of women there assembled have no will, no inclinations but his: Their triumphs are only for a moment; and their rivalry, their hate, and their animosities, continue till death. There the lovely sex are obliged to repay even their servitude with the most tender affections; or, what is still more mortifying, with the counterfeit of an affection, which they do not feel: There the most gloomy tyranny has subjected them to creatures, who, being of neither sex, are a dishonour to both: There, in short, their education tends only to debase them; their virtues are forced; their very pleasures are involuntary and joyless; and after an existence of a few years—till the bloom of youth is over—their period of neglect commences, which is long and dreadful. In the temperate latitude where the climates, giving less ardour to passion, leave more confidence in virtue, the women have not been deprived of their liberty, but a severe legislation has, at all times, kept them in a state of dependence. One while, they were confined to their own apartments, and debarred at once from business and amusement; at other times, a tedious guardianship defrauded their hearts, and insulted their understandings. Affronted in one country by polygamy, which gives them their rivals for their inseparable companions; inslaved in another by indissoluble ties, which often join the gentle to the rude, and sensibility to brutality: Even in countries where they may be esteemed most happy, constrained in their desires in the disposal of their goods, robbed of freedom of will by the laws, the slaves of opinion, which rules them with absolute sway, and construes the slightest appearances into guilt; surrounded on all sides by judges, who are at once tyrants and their seducers, and who, after having prepared their faults, punish every lapse with dishonour—nay, usurp the right of degrading them on suspicion! Who does not feel for the tender sex? Yet such, I am sorry to say, is the lot of woman over the whole earth. Man with regard to them, in all climates, and in all ages, has been either an insensible husband or an oppressor; but they have sometimes experienced the cold and deliberate oppression of pride, and sometimes the violent and terrible tyranny of jealousy. When they are not beloved they are nothing; and, when they are, they are tormented. They have almost equal cause to be afraid of indifference and of love. Over three quarters of the globe nature has placed them between contempt and misery.

"The melting desires, or the fiery passions," says Professor Ferguson,[4] "which in one climate take place between the sexes, are, in another, changed into a sober consideration, or a patience of mutual disgust. This change is remarked in crossing the Mediterranean, in following the course of the Mississippi, in ascending the mountains of Caucasus, and in passing from the Alps and the Pyrenees to the shores of the Baltic.

"The burning ardours and torturing jealousies of the Seraglio and Harem, which have reigned so long in Asia and Africa, and which, in the southern parts of Europe, have scarcely given way to the differences of religion and civil establishments, are found, however, with an abatement of heat in the climate, to be more easily changed, in one latitude, into a temporary passion, which engrosses the mind without infeebling it, and which excites to romantic atchievments. By a farther progress to the north it is changed into a spirit of gallantry, which employs the wit and fancy more than the heart, which prefers intrigue to enjoyment, and substitutes affection and vanity where sentiment and desire have failed. As it departs from the sun, the same passion is farther composed into a habit of domestic connection, or frozen into a state of insensibility, under which the sexes at freedom scarcely choose to unite their society."

Even among people where beauty received the highest homage, we find men who would deprive the sex of every kind of reputation: "The most virtuous woman," says a celebrated Greek,[5] "is she who is least talked of." That morose man, while he imposes duties upon women, would deprive them of the sweets of public esteem, and in exacting virtues from them, would make it a crime to aspire at honour.

If a woman were to defend the cause of her sex, she might address him in the following manner:

"How great is your injustice? If we have an equal right with you to virtue, why should we not have an equal right to praise? The public esteem ought to wait upon merit. Our duties are different from yours, but they are not therefore less difficult to fulfil, or of less consequence to society: They are the fountains of your felicity, and the sweetness of life. We are wives and mothers. 'T is we who form the union and the cordiality of families: 'T is we who soften that savage rudeness which considers everything as due to force, and which would involve man with man in eternal war. We cultivate in you that humanity which makes you feel for the misfortunes of others, and our tears forewarn you of your own danger. Nay, you cannot be ignorant that we have need of courage not less than you: More feeble in ourselves, we have perhaps more trials to encounter. Nature assails us with sorrow, law and custom press us with constraint, and sensibility and virtue alarm us with their continual conflict. Sometimes also the name of citizen demands from us the tribute of fortitude. When you offer your blood to the State think that it is ours. In giving it our sons and our husbands we give more than ourselves. You can only die on the field of battle, but we have the misfortune to survive those whom we love most. Alas! while your ambitious vanity is unceasingly labouring to cover the earth with statues, with monuments, and with inscriptions to eternize, if possible, your names, and give yourselves an existence, when this body is no more, why must we be condemned to live and to die unknown? Would that the grave and eternal forgetfulness should be our lot. Be not our tyrants in all: Permit our names to be sometimes pronounced

beyond the narrow circle in which we live: Permit friendship, or at
least love, to inscribe its emblems on the tomb where our ashes repose;
and deny us not that public esteem which, after the esteem of one's
self, is the sweetest reward of well doing."

All men, however, it must be owned, have not been equally unjust
to their fair companions. In some countries public honours have been
paid to women. Art has erected them monuments. Eloquence has celebrated their virtues, and History has collected whatever could adorn
their character.

from *the Introduction to Common Sense (1776)*

Perhaps the sentiments contained in the following pages, are not *yet*
sufficiently fashionable to procure them general Favor; a long Habit
of not thinking a Thing *wrong*, gives it a superficial appearance of
being *right*, and raises at first a formidable outcry in defence of Custom. But the Tumult soon subsides. Time makes more Converts than
Reason.

As a long and violent abuse of power is generally the means of
calling the right of it in question, (and in matters too which might
never have been thought of, had not the sufferers been aggravated into
the inquiry,) and as the King of England hath undertaken in his *own
right*, to support the Parliament in what he calls *Theirs*, and as the
good People of this Country are grievously oppressed by the Combination, they have an undoubted privilege to enquire into the Pretensions of both, and equally to reject the Usurpation of *either*.

In the following Sheets, the Author hath studiously avoided every
thing which is personal among ourselves. Compliments as well as censure to individuals make no part thereof. The wise and the worthy
need not the triumph of a Pamphlet; and those whose sentiments are
injudicious or unfriendly will cease of themselves, unless too much
pains is bestowed upon their conversions.

The cause of America is in a great measure the cause of all mankind. Many circumstances have, and will arise, which are not local,
but universal, and through which the principles of all lovers of mankind are affected, and in the event of which their affections are interested. The laying a country desolate with fire and sword, declaring
war against the natural rights of all mankind, and extirpating the de-
fenders thereof from the face of the earth, is the concern of every man

to whom nature hath given the power of feeling; of which class, re-
gardless of party censure, is

THE AUTHOR.

from *Of the Religion of Deism*[1]
Compared with the Christian Religion,
and the Superiority of the Former over
the Latter (1804)

Every person, of whatever religious denomination he may be, is a DE-
IST in the first article of his Creed. Deism, from the Latin word *Deus*,
God, is the belief of a God, and this belief is the first article of every
man's creed.

It is on this article, universally consented to by all mankind, that
the Deist builds his church, and here he rests. Whenever we step aside
from this article, by mixing it with articles of human invention, we
wander into a labyrinth of uncertainty and fable, and become exposed
to every kind of imposition by pretenders to revelation.

The Persian shows the Zend-Avesta of Zoroaster, the lawgiver of
Persia, and calls it the divine law; the Bramin shows the *Shaster*, revealed, he says, by God to Brama, and given to him out of a cloud;
the Jew shows what he calls the Law of Moses, given, he says, by God,
on the Mount Sinai; the Christian shows a collection of books and
epistles, written by nobody knows who, and called the New Testament; and the Mahometan shows the Koran, given, he says, by God
to Mahomet: each of these calls itself *revealed religion*, and the *only*
true Word of God, and this the followers of each profess to believe
from the habit of education, and each believes the others are imposed
upon.

But when the divine gift of reason begins to expand itself in the
mind and calls man to reflection, he then reads and contemplates God
and His works, and not in the books pretending to be revelation. The
creation is the Bible of the true believer in God. Everything in this vast
volume inspires him with sublime ideas of the Creator. The little and
paltry, and often obscene, tales of the Bible sink into wretchedness
when put in comparison with this mighty work.

The Deist needs none of those tricks and shows called miracles to
confirm his faith, for what can be a greater miracle than the creation
itself and his own existence?

There is a happiness in Deism, when rightly understood, that is not to be found in any other system of religion. All other systems have something in them that either shock our reason, or are repugnant to it, and man, if he thinks at all, must stifle his reason in order to force himself to believe them.

But in Deism our reason and our belief become happily united. The wonderful structure of the universe, and everything we behold in the system of the creation, prove to us, far better than books can do, the existence of a God, and at the same time proclaim His attributes.

It is by the exercise of our reason that we are enabled to contemplate God in His works, and imitate Him in His way. When we see His care and goodness extended over all His creatures, it teaches us our duty toward each other, while it calls forth our gratitude to Him. It is by forgetting God in His works, and running after the books of pretended revelation, that man has wandered from the straight path of duty and happiness, and become by turns the victim of doubt and the dupe of delusion.

Except in the first article in the Christian creed, that of believing in God, there is not an article in it but fills the mind with doubt as to the truth of it, the instant man begins to think. Now every article in a creed that is necessary to the happiness and salvation of man ought to be as evident to the reason and comprehension of man as the first article is, for God has not given us reason for the purpose of confounding us, but that we should use it for our own happiness and His glory.

The truth of the first article is proved by God Himself, and is universal; for *the creation is of itself demonstration of the existence of a Creator.* But the second article, that of God's begetting a son, is not proved in like manner, and stands on no other authority than that of a tale.

Certain books in what is called the New Testament tell us that Joseph dreamed that the angel told him so (Matthew i. 20): "And behold the angel of the Lord appeared to Joseph, in a dream, saying, Joseph, thou son of David, fear not to take unto thee Mary thy wife, for that which is conceived in her is of the Holy Ghost."

The evidence upon this article bears no comparison with the evidence upon the first article, and therefore is not entitled to the same credit, and ought not to be made an article in a creed, because the evidence of it is defective, and what evidence there is is doubtful and suspicious. We do not believe the first article on the authority of books, whether called Bibles or Korans, nor yet on the visionary authority of dreams, but on the authority of God's own visible works in the creation.

The nations who never heard of such books, nor of such people as Jews, Christians or Mahometans, believe the existence of God as fully as we do, because it is self-evident. The work of man's hands is a proof of the existence of man as fully as his personal appearance would be.

When we see a watch, we have as positive evidence of the existence of a watchmaker, as if we saw him; and in like manner the creation is evidence to our reason and our senses of the existence of a Creator. But there is nothing in the works of God that is evidence that He begat a son, nor anything in the system of creation that corroborates such an idea, and, therefore, we are not authorized in believing it. . . .

The four books called the Evangelists, Matthew, Mark, Luke and John, which give, or pretend to give, the birth, sayings, life, preaching, and death of Jesus Christ, make no mention of what is called the fall of man; nor is the name of Adam to be found in any of those books, which it certainly would be if the writers of them believed that Jesus was begotten, born and died for the purpose of redeeming mankind from the sin which Adam had brought into the world. Jesus never speaks of Adam himself, of the Garden of Eden, nor of what is called the fall of man.

But the Church of Rome having set up its new religion, which it called Christianity, invented the creed which it named the Apostles's Creed, in which it calls Jesus the *only son of God, conceived by the Holy Ghost, and born of the Virgin Mary*; things of which it is impossible that man or woman can have any idea, and consequently no belief but in words; and for which there is no authority but the idle story of Joseph's dream in the first chapter of Matthew, which any designing impostor or foolish fanatic might make.

It then manufactured the allegories in the book of Genesis into fact, and the allegorical tree of life and the tree of knowledge into real trees, contrary to the belief of the first Christians, and for which there is not the least authority in any of the books of the New Testament; for in none of them is there any mention made of such place as the Garden of Eden, nor of anything that is said to have happened there.

But the Church of Rome could not erect the person called Jesus into a Savior of the world without making the allegories in the book of Genesis into fact, though the New Testament, as before observed, gives no authority for it. All at once the allegorical tree of knowledge became, according to the Church, a real tree, the fruit of it real fruit, and the eating of it sinful.

As priestcraft was always the enemy of knowledge, because priestcraft supports itself by keeping people in delusion and ignorance, it was consistent with its policy to make the acquisition of knowledge a real sin.

The Church of Rome having done this, it then brings forward Jesus the son of Mary as suffering death to redeem mankind from sin, which Adam, it says, had brought into the world by eating the fruit of the tree of knowledge. But as it is impossible for reason to believe such a story, because it can see no reason for it, nor have any evidence of it, the Church then tells us we must not regard our reason, but must *believe*, as it were, and that through thick and thin, as if God had given man reason like a plaything, or a rattle, on purpose to make fun of him. . . .

The dogma of the redemption is the fable of priestcraft invented since the time the New Testament was compiled, and the agreeable delusion of it suited with the depravity of immoral livers. When men are taught to ascribe all their own crimes and vices to the temptations of the devil, and to believe that Jesus, by his death, rubs all off, and pays their passage to heaven gratis, they become as careless in morals as a spendthrift would be of money were he told that his father had engaged to pay off all his scores.

It is a doctrine not only dangerous to morals in this world, but to our happiness in the next world, because it holds out such a cheap, easy, and lazy way of getting to heaven, as has a tendency to induce men to hug the delusion of it to their own injury.

But there are times when men have serious thoughts, and it is at such times, when they begin to think, that they begin to doubt the truth of the Christian religion; and well they may, for it is too fanciful and too full of conjecture, inconsistency, improbability and irrationality to afford consolation to the thoughtful man. His reason revolts against his creed. He sees that none of its articles are proved, or can be proved.

He may believe that such a person as is called Jesus (for Christ was not his name) was born and grew to be a man, because it is no more than a natural and probable case. But who is to prove he is the son of God, that he was begotten by the Holy Ghost? Of these things there can be no proof; and that which admits not of proof, and is against the laws of probability and the order of nature, which God Himself has established, is not an object for belief. God has not given man reason to embarrass him, but to prevent his being imposed upon.

He may believe that Jesus was crucified, because many others were crucified, but who is to prove he was crucified *for the sins of the world*? This article has no evidence, not even in the New Testament; and if it had, where is the proof that the New Testament, in relating things neither probable nor probable, is to be believed as true?

When an article in a creed does not admit of proof nor of probability, the salvo is to call it revelation; but this is only putting one difficulty in the place of another, for it is as impossible to prove a thing to be revelation as it is to prove that Mary was gotten with child by the Holy Ghost.

Here it is that the religion of Deism is superior to the Christian religion. It is free from all those invented and torturing articles that shock our reason or injure our humanity, and with which the Christian religion abounds. Its creeds is pure, and sublimely simple. It believes in God, and there it rests.

It honors reason as the choicest gift of God to man, and the faculty by which he is enabled to contemplate the power, wisdom and goodness of the Creator displayed in the creation: and reposing itself on His protection, both here and hereafter, it avoids all presumptuous beliefs, and rejects, as the fabulous inventions of men, all books pretending to relevation.

William Bartram
(1739–1823)

William Bartram, son of America's first native botanist, John Bartram, was a naturalist who brought much of his Quaker spirituality to the observation of external details rather than of internal feelings. Delighting in the variety and plentitude of the natural world lying, so to speak, at his doorstep, Bartram's fame rests on the autobiographical account of his Travels Through North and South Carolina, Georgia, East and West Florida, the Cherokee Country, the Extensive Territories of the Muscogulges, or Creek Confederacy, and the Country of the Choctaws *(1791). Regarded by Samuel Taylor Coleridge as a work of "high merit," one can see why it would have appealed to Romantic writers like Coleridge, Wordsworth, and Chateaubriand, from this description of himself that Bartram placed toward the beginning of the book:*

> *Continuously impelled by a restless spirit of curiosity, in pursuit of new productions of nature, my chief happiness consisted in tracing and admiring the infinite power, majesty, and perfection of the great almighty Creator, and in the contemplation, that through divine aid and permission, I might be instrumental in discovering, and introducing into my native country, some original productions of nature, which might become useful to society.*

from *Travels Through North and South Carolina, Georgia, East and West Florida (1791)*

The evening was temperately cool and calm. The crocodiles[1] began to roar and appear in uncommon numbers along the shores and in the river. I fixed my camp in an open plain, near the utmost projection of the promontory, under the shelter of a large Live Oak, which stood on the highest part of the ground and but a few yards from my boat. From this open, high situation, I had a free prospect of the river, which was a matter of no trivial consideration to me, having good reason to dread the subtle attacks of the allegators, who were crouding about my harbour. Having collected a good quantity of wood for the purpose of keeping up a light and smoke during the night, I began to think of preparing my supper, when, upon examining my stores, I found but a scanty provision, I thereupon determined, as the most expeditious way of supplying my necessities, to take my bob and try for some trout. About one hundred yards above my harbour, began a cove or bay of the river, out of which opened a large lagoon. The mouth or entrance from the river to it was narrow, but the waters soon after spread and formed a little lake, extending into the marshes, its entrance and shores within I observed to be verged with floating lawns of the Pistia and Nymphea[2] and other aquatic plants; these I knew were excellent haunts for trout.

The verges and islets of the lagoon were elegantly embellished with flowering plants and shrubs; the laughing coots with wings half spread were tripping over the little coves and hiding themselves in the tufts of grass; young broods of the painted summer teal, skimming the still surface of the waters, and following the watchful parent unconscious of danger, were frequently surprised by the voracious trout, and he in turn, as often by the subtle, greedy alligator. Behold him rushing forth from the flags and reeds. His enormous body swells. His plaited tail brandished high, floats upon the lake. The waters like a cataract descend from his opening jaws. Clouds of smoke issue from his dilated nostrils. The earth trembles with his thunder. When immediately from the opposite coast of the lagoon, emerges from the deep his rival champion. They suddenly dart upon each other. The boiling surface of the lake marks their rapid course, and a terrific conflict commences. They now sink to the bottom folded together in horrid wreaths. The water becomes thick and discoloured. Again they rise, their jaws clap together, re-echoing through the deep surrounding forests. Again they sink, when the contest ends at the muddy bottom of the lake, and the vanquished makes a hazardous escape, hiding himself in the muddy turbulent waters and sedge on a distant shore. The proud victor exulting returns to the place of action. The shores and forests resound his dreadful roar, together with the triumphing shouts of the plaited tribes around, witnesses of the horrid combat.

My apprehensions were highly alarmed after being a spectator of so dreadful a battle; it was obvious that every delay would but tend to encrease my dangers and difficulties, as the sun was near setting, and the alligators gathered around my harbour from all quarters; from these considerations I concluded to be expeditious in my trip to the lagoon, in order to take some fish. Not thinking it prudent to take my fusee[3] with me, lest I might lose it overboard in case of a battle, which I had every reason to dread before my return, I therefore furnished myself with a club for my defence, went on board, and penetrating the first line of those which surrounded my harbour, they gave way; but being pursued by several very large ones, I kept strictly on the watch, and paddled with all my might towards the entrance of the lagoon, hoping to be sheltered there from the multitude of my assailants; but ere I had half-way reached the place, I was attacked on all sides, several endeavouring to overset the canoe. My situation now became precarious to the last degree: two very large ones attacked me closely, at the same instant, rushing up with their heads and part of their bodies above the water, roaring terribly and belching floods of water over me. They struck their jaws together so close to my ears, as almost to stun me, and I expected every moment to be dragged out of the boat and instantly devoured, but I applied my weapons so effectually about me, though at random, that I was so successful as to beat them off a little; when, finding that they designed to renew the battle, I made for the shore, as the only means left me for my preservation, for, by keeping close to it, I should have my enemies on one side of me only, whereas I was before surrounded by them, and there was a probability, if pushed to the last extremity, of saving myself, by jumping out of the canoe on shore, as it is easy to outwalk them on land, although comparatively as swift as lightning in the water. I found this last expedient alone could fully answer my expectations, for as soon as I gained the shore they drew off and kept aloof. This was a happy relief, as my confidence was, in some degree, recovered by it. On recollecting myself, I discovered that I had almost reached the entrance of the lagoon, and determined to venture in, if possible to take a few fish and then return to my harbour, while day-light continued; for I could now, with caution and resolution, make my way with safety along shore, and indeed there was no other way to regain my camp, without leaving my boat and making my retreat through the marshes and reeds, which, if I could even effect, would have been in a manner throwing myself away, for then there would have been no hopes of ever recovering my bark, and returning in safety to any settlements of men. I accordingly proceeded and made good my entrance into the lagoon, though not without opposition from the alligators, who formed a line across the entrance, but did not pursue me into it, nor was I molested by any there, though there were some very large ones in a cove at the upper end. I soon caught more trout than I had present occasion for, and the air was too hot and sultry to admit of their being kept for many hours, even though salted or barbecued. I now prepared for my return to camp, which I succeeded in with but little trouble, by keeping close to the shore, yet I was opposed upon re-entering the river out of the lagoon, and pursued near to my landing (though not closely attacked) particularly by an old daring one, about twelve feet in length, who kept close after me, and when I stepped on shore and turned about, in order to draw up my canoe, he rushed up near my feet and lay there for some time, looking me in the face, his head and shoulders out of water; I resolved he should pay for his temerity, and having a heavy load in my fusee, I ran to my camp, and returning with my piece, found him with his foot on the gunwale of the boat, in search of fish, on my coming up he withdrew sullenly and slowly into the water, but soon returned and placed himself in his former position, looking at me and seeming neither fearful or any way disturbed. I soon dispatched him by lodging the contents of my gun in his head, and then proceeded to cleanse and prepare my fish for supper, and accordingly took them out of the boat, laid them down on the sand close to the water, and began to scale them, when, raising my head, I saw before me, through the clear water, the head and shoulders of a very large alligator, moving slowly towards me; I instantly stepped back, when, with a sweep of his tail, he brushed off several of my fish. It was certainly most providential that I looked up at that instant, as the monster would probably, in less than a minute, have seized and dragged me into the river. This incredible boldness of the animal disturbed me greatly, supposing there could now be no reasonable safety for me during the night, but by keeping continually on the watch; I therefore, as soon as I had prepared the fish, proceeded to secure myself and effects in the best manner I could: in the first place, I hauled my bark upon the shore, almost clear out of the water, to prevent their oversetting or sinking her, after this every moveable was taken out and carried to my camp, which was but a few yards off; then ranging some dry wood in such order as was the most convenient, cleared the ground round about it, that there might be no impediment in my way, in case of an attack in the night, either from the water or the land; for I discovered by this time, that this small isthmus, from its remote situation and fruitfulness, was resorted to by bears and wolves. Having prepared myself in the best manner I could, I charged my gun and proceeded to reconnoitre my camp and the adjacent grounds; when I discovered that the peninsula and grove, at the distance of about two hundred yards from my encampment, on the land side, were invested by a Cypress swamp, covered with water, which below was joined to the shore of the little lake, and above to the marshes surrounding the lagoon, so that I was confined to an islet exceedingly circumscribed, and I found there was no other retreat for me, in case of an attack, but by either ascending one of the large Oaks, or pushing off with my boat.

It was by this time dusk, and the alligators had nearly ceased their roar, when I was again alarmed by a tumultuous noise that seemed to be in my harbour, and therefore engaged my immediate attention. Returning to my camp I found it undisturbed, and then continued on to the extreme point of the promontory, where I saw a scene, new and surprising, which at first threw my senses into such a tumult, that it was some time before I could comprehend what was the matter; however, I soon accounted for the prodigious assemblage of crocodiles at this place, which exceeded every thing of the kind I had ever heard of.

How shall I express myself so as to convey an adequate idea of it to the reader, and at the same time avoid raising suspicions of my want of veracity. Should I say, that the river (in this place) from shore to shore, and perhaps near half a mile above and below me, appeared to be one solid bank of fish, of various kinds, pushing through this narrow pass of St. Juans[4] into the little lake, on their return down the river, and that the alligators were in such incredible numbers, and so close together from shore to shore, that it would have been easy to have walked across on their heads, had the animals been harmless. What expressions can sufficiently declare the shocking scene that for some minutes continued, whilst this mighty army of fish were forcing the pass? During this attempt, thousands, I may say hundreds of thousands of them were caught and swallowed by the devouring alligators. I have seen an alligator take up out of the water several great fish at a time, and just squeeze them betwixt his jaws, while the tails of the great trout flapped about his eyes and lips, ere he had swallowed them. The horrid noise of their closing jaws, their plunging amidst the broken banks of fish, and rising with their prey some feet upright above the water, the floods of water and blood rushing out of their mouths, and the clouds of vapour issuing from their wide nostrils, were truly frightful. This scene continued at intervals during the night, as the fish came to the pass. After this sight, shocking and tremendous as it was, I found myself somewhat easier and more reconciled to my situation, being convinced that their extraordinary assemblage here, was owing to this annual feast of fish, and that they were so well

employed in their own element, that I had little occasion to fear their
paying me a visit. . . .

The alligator when full grown is a very large and terrible creature,
and of prodigious strength, activity and swiftness in the water. I have
seen them twenty feet in length, and some are supposed to be twenty-
two or twenty-three feet; their body is as large as that of a horse; their
shape exactly resembles that of a lizard, except their tail, which is flat
or cuniform, being compressed on each side, and gradually diminishing
from the abdomen to the extremity, which, with the whole body is
covered with horny plates or squamae, [scales] impenetrable when on
the body of the live animal, even to a rifle ball, except about their head
and just behind their fore-legs or arms, where it is said they are only
vulnerable. The head of a full grown one is about three feet, and the
mouth opens nearly the same length, the eyes are small in proportion
and seem sunk deep in the head, by means of the prominency of the
brows; the nostrils are large, inflated and prominent on the top, so
that the head in the water, resembles, at a distance, a great chunk of
wood floating about. Only the upper jaw moves, which they raise
almost perpendicular, so as to form a right angle with the lower one.
In the fore part of the upper jaw, on each side, just under the nostrils,
are two very large, thick, strong teeth or tusks, not very sharp, but
rather the shape of a cone, these are as white as the finest polished
ivory, and are not covered by any skin or lips, and always in sight,
which gives the creature a frightful appearance; in the lower jaw are
holes opposite to these teeth, to receive them; when they clap their
jaws together it causes a surprising noise, like that which is made by
forcing a heavy plank with violence upon the ground, and may be
heard at a great distance.

But what is yet more surprising to a stranger, is the incredible
loud and terrifying roar, which they are capable of making, especially
in the spring season, their breeding time; it most resembles very heavy
distant thunder, not only shaking the air and waters, but causing the
earth to tremble; and when hundreds and thousands are roaring at the
same time, you can scarcely be persuaded, but that the whole globe is
violently and dangerously agitated.

An old champion, who is perhaps absolute sovereign of a little
lake or lagoon (when fifty less than himself are obliged to content
themselves with swelling and roaring in little coves round about) darts
forth from the reedy coverts all at once, on the surface of the waters,
in a right line; at first seemingly as rapid as lightning, but gradually
more slowly until he arrives at the center of the lake, when he stops;
he now swells himself by drawing in wind and water through his
mouth, which causes a loud sonorous rattling in the throat for near a
minute, but it is immediately forced out again through his mouth and

nostrils, with a loud noise, brandishing his tail in the air, and the vapour ascending from his nostrils like smoke. At other times, when swollen to an extent ready to burst, his head and tail lifted up, he spins or twirls round on the surface of the water. He acts his part like an Indian chief when rehearsing his feats of war, and then retiring, the exhibition is continued by others who dare to step forth, and strive to excel each other, to gain the attention of the favourite female. . . .

Abigail Adams
(1744–1818)

Abigail Adams was not only the wife of John Adams, the second president of the United States (1797–1801); and the mother of John Quincy Adams, the sixth president of the United States; the grandmother of Charles Francis Adams, the Republican minister to England appointed by Abraham Lincoln who helped prevent the British from siding with the Confederacy; and the great-grandmother of Henry Adams, the distinguished autobiographer, historian, and novelist; she was also a woman of independent intelligence and rare wit who carried on an extensive correspondence, particularly with her husband, during long absences enforced by his public service. These letters, later published in two volumes by her grandson Charles Francis Adams, testify not only to the loving and spirited relationship John and Abigail enjoyed but also to her deep and thoughtful involvement in the affairs of the emergent republic as well as in the lives of family and friends. A strong advocate for the reform of consciousness during the Revolutionary era, she nonetheless most often pressed her case with levity as well as force.

Abigail Adams to John Adams

March 31, 1776

I wish you would ever write me a Letter half as long as I write you; and tell me if you may where your Fleet are gone? What sort of Defence Virginia can make against our common Enemy? Whether it is so situated as to make an able Defence? Are not the Gentery Lords and the common people vassals, are they not like the uncivilized Natives Brittain represents us to be? I hope their Riffel Men who have shewen themselves very savage and even Blood thirsty; are not a specimen of the Generality of the people.

I am willing to allow the Colony great merrit for having produced a Washington but they have been shamefully duped by a Dunmore.[1]

I have sometimes been ready to think that the passion for Liberty cannot be Eaquelly Strong in the Breasts of those who have been accustomed to deprive their fellow Creatures of theirs. Of this I am certain that it is not founded upon that generous and christian principal of doing to others as we would that others should do unto us.

Do not you want to see Boston; I am fearfull of the small pox, or I should have been in before this time. I got Mr. Crane[2] to go to our House and see what state it was in. I find it has been occupied by one of the Doctors of a Regiment, very dirty, but no other damage has been done to it. The few things which were left in it are all gone. Cranch[3] has the key which he never deliverd up. I have wrote to him for it and am determined to get it cleand as soon as possible and shut it up. I look upon it a new acquisition of property, a property which one month ago I did not value at a single Shilling, and could with pleasure have seen it in flames.

The Town in General is left in a better state than we expected, more oweing to a percipitate flight than any Regard to the inhabitants, tho some individuals discoverd a sense of honour and justice and have left the rent of the Houses in which they were, for the owners and the furniture unhurt, or if damaged sufficient to make it good.

Others have committed abominable Ravages. The Mansion House of your President is safe and the furniture unhurt whilst both the House and Furniture of the Solisiter General have fallen a prey to their own merciless party. Surely the very Fiends feel a Reverential awe for Virtue and patriotism, whilst they Detest the paricide and traitor.

I feel very differently at the approach of spring to what I did a month ago. We knew not then whether we could plant or sow with safety, whether when we had toild we could reap the fruits of our own industery, whether we could rest in our own Cottages, or whether we should not be driven from the sea coasts to seek shelter in the wilderness, but now we feel as if we might sit under our own vine and eat the good of the land.

I feel a gaieti de Coar[4] to which before I was a stranger. I think the Sun looks brighter, the Birds sing more melodiously, and Nature puts on a more chearfull countanance. We feel a temporary peace, and the poor fugitives are returning to their deserted habitations.

Tho we felicitate ourselves, we sympathize with those who are trembling least the Lot of Boston should be theirs. But they cannot be in similar circumstances unless pusilanimity and cowardise should take possession of them. They have time and warning given them to see the Evil and shun it. (I long to hear that you have declared an independancy—and by the way in the new Code of Laws[5] which I suppose it will be necessary for you to make I desire you would Remember the Ladies, and be more generous and favourable to them than your ancestors.) Do not put such unlimited power into the hands of the Husbands. Remember all Men would be tyrants if they could. (If perticuliar care and attention is not paid to the Laidies we are determined to foment a Rebelion, and will not hold ourselves bound by any Laws in which we have no voice, or Representation.)

That your Sex are Naturally Tyrannical is a Truth so thoroughly established as to admit of no dispute, but such of you as wish to be happy willingly give up the harsh title of Master for the more tender and endearing one of Friend. Why then, not put it out of the power of the vicious and the Lawless to use us with cruelty and indignity with impunity. Men of Sense in all Ages abhor those customs which treat us only as the vassals of your Sex. Regard us then as Beings placed by providence under your protection and in immitation of the Supreem Being make use of that power only for our happiness.

April 5

Not having an opportunity of sending this I shall add a few lines more; tho not with a heart so gay. I have been attending the sick chamber of our Neighbour Trot whose affliction I most sensibly feel but cannot discribe, striped of two lovely children in one week. Gorge the Eldest died on wedensday and Billy the youngest on fryday, with the Canker fever, a terible disorder so much like the thr[o]at distemper, that it differs but little from it. Betsy Cranch has been very bad, but upon the recovery. Becky Peck they do not expect will live out the day. Many grown person[s] are now sick with it, in this [street?] 5. It rages much in other Towns. The Mumps too are very frequent. Isaac is now confined with it. Our own little flock are yet well. My Heart trembles with anxiety for them. God preserve them.

I want to hear much oftener from you than I do. March 8 was the last date of any that I have yet had.—You inquire of whether I am making Salt peter. I have not yet attempted it, but after Soap making believe I shall make the experiment. I find as much as I can do to manufacture cloathing for my family which would else be Naked. I know of but one person in this part of the Town who has made any, that is Mr. Tertias Bass as he is calld who has got very near an hundred weight which has been found to be very good. I have heard of some others in the other parishes. Mr. Reed of Weymouth has been applied to, to go to Andover to the mills which are now at work, and has gone. I have lately seen a small Manuscrip de[s]cribing the proportions for the various sorts of powder, fit for cannon, small arms and pistols. If it would be of any Service your way I will get it transcribed and send it to you.—Every one of your Friend[s] send their Regards, and all the little ones. Your Brothers youngest child lies bad with convulsion fitts. Adieu. I need not say how much I am Your ever faithfull Friend.

Boston, 13 July, 1776.

I must begin with apologizing to you for not writing since the 17th of June. I have really had so many cares upon my hands and mind, with a bad inflammation in my eyes, that I have not been able to write. I now date from Boston, where I yesterday arrived and was with all of our little ones inoculated for the small-pox. . . .

As to news, we have taken several prizes since I wrote you, as you will see by the newspapers. The present report is of Lord Howe's[6] coming with unlimited powers. However, suppose it is so, I believe he little thinks of treating with us as Independent States. How can any person yet dream of a settlement, accommodations, etc.? They have neither the spirit nor the feeling of men. Yet I see some who never were called Tories gratified with the idea of Lord Howe's being upon his passage with such powers!

14 August, 1776.

Your letter of August 3 came by this day's post. I find it very convenient to be so handy. I can receive a letter at night, sit down and reply to it, and send it off in the morning.

You remark upon the deficiency of education in your countrymen. It never, I believe, was in a worse state, at least for many years. The college is not in the state one could wish. The scholars complain that their professor in philosophy is taken off by public business, to their great detriment. In this town I never saw so great a neglect of education. The poorer sort of children are wholly neglected, and left to range the streets, without schools, without business, given up to all evil. The town is not, as formerly, divided into wards. There is either too much business left upon the hands of a few, or too little care to do it. We daily see the necessity of a regular government.

You speak of our worthy brother. I often lament it, that a man so peculiarly formed for the education of youth, and so well qualified as he is in many branches of literature, excelling in philosophy and the mathematics, should not be employed in some public station. I know not the person who would make half so good a successor to Dr. Winthrop.[7] He has a peculiar, easy manner of communicating his ideas to youth; and the goodness of his heart and the purity of his morals, without an affected austerity, must have a happy effect upon the minds of pupils.

If you complain of neglect of education in sons, what shall I say with regard to daughters, who every day experience the want of it? With regard to the education of my own children, I find myself soon out of my depth, destitute and deficient in every part of education.

I most sincerely wish that some more liberal plan might be laid and executed for the benefit of the rising generation, and that our new Constitution may be distinguished for encouraging learning and virtue. If we mean to have heroes, statesmen, and philosophers, we should have learned women. The world perhaps would laugh at me and accuse me of vanity, but you, I know, have a mind too enlarged and liberal to disregard the sentiment. If much depends, as is allowed, upon the early education of youth, and the first principles which are instilled take the deepest root, great benefit must arise from literary accomplishments in women.

Excuse me. My pen has run away with me. I have no thoughts of coming to Philadelphia. The length of time I have and shall be detained here would have prevented me, even if you had no thoughts of returning till December; but I live in daily expectation of seeing you here. Your health, I think, requires your immediate return. I expected Mr. G——[8] would have set off before now, but he perhaps finds it very hard to leave his mistress. I won't say harder than some do to leave their wives. Mr. Gerry stood very high in my esteem. What is meat for one is not for another. No accounting for fancy. She is a queer dame and leads people wild dances.

But hush! Post, don't betray your trust and lose my letter.

PORTIA.

April 10th. 1782

MY DEAREST FRIEND

How great was my joy to see the well known Signature of my Friend after a Melancholy Solicitude of many months in which my hopes and fears alternately preponderated.

It was January when Charles arrived. By him I expected Letters, but found not a line; instead of which the heavy tidings of your illness reachd me. I then found my Friends had been no strangers of what they carefully conceald from me. Your Letter to Charles dated in November[2] was the only consolation I had; by that I found that the most dangerous period of your illness was pass'd, and that you considered yourself as recovering tho feeble. My anxiety and apprehensions from that day untill your Letters arrived, which was near 3 months, conspired to render me unhappy. Capt. Trowbridge in the Fire Brand arrived with your favours of October and December and in some measure dispeld the Gloom which hung heavy at my heart. How did it leap for joy to find I was not the misirable Being I sometimes feared I was. I felt that Gratitude to Heaven which great deliverences both demand and inspire. I will not distrust the providential Care of the supreem disposer of events, from whose Hand I have so frequently received distinguished favours. Such I call the preservation of my dear Friend and children from the uncertain Element upon which they have frequently embarked; their preservation from the hands of their enimies I have reason to consider in the same view, especially when I reflect upon the cruel and inhumane treatment experienced by a Gentleman of Mr. Laurences[9] age and respectable character.

The restoration of my dearest Friend from so dangerous a Sickness, demands all my gratitude, whilst I fail not to supplicate Heaven for the continuance of a Life upon which my temporal happiness rests, and deprived of which my own existance would become a burden. Often has the Question which you say staggerd your philosophy occured to me, nor have I felt so misirable upon account of my own personal Situation, when I considerd that according to the common course of Nature, more than half my days were allready passt, as for those in whom our days are renewed. Their hopes and prospects would vanish, their best prospects, those of Education, would be greatly diminished—but I will not anticipate those miseries which I would shun. Hope is my best Friend and kindest comforter; she assures me that the pure unabated affection, which neither time or absence can allay or abate, shall e'er long be crowned with the completion of its fondest wishes, in the safe return of the beloved object; the age of romance has long ago past, but the affection of almost Infant years has matured and strengthened untill it has become a vital principle, nor has the world any thing to bestow which could in the smallest degree compensate for the loss. Desire and Sorrow were denounced upon our Sex; as a punishment for the transgression of Eve. I have sometimes thought that we are formed to experience more exquisite Sensations than is the Lot of your Sex. More tender and susceptable by Nature of those impression[s] which create happiness or misiry, we Suffer and enjoy in a higher degree. I never wonderd at the philosopher who thanked the Gods that he was created a Man rather than a Woman.

I cannot say, but that I was dissapointed when I found that your return to your native land was a still distant Idea. I think your Situation cannot be so dissagreable as I feared it was, yet that dreadfull climate is my terror.—You mortify me indeed when you talk of sending Charles to Colledge, who it is not probable will be fit under three or four years. Surely my dear Friend fleeting as time is I cannot reconcile myself to the Idea of living in this cruel State of Seperation for [4?] or even three years to come. Eight years have already past, since you could call yourself an Inhabitant of this State. I shall assume the Signature of Penelope,[10] for my dear Ulysses has already been a wanderer from me near half the term of years that, that Hero was encountering Neptune, Calipso, the Circes and Syrens. In the poetical Language of Penelope I shall address you

> "Oh! haste to me! A Little longer Stay
> Will ev'ry grace, each fancy'd charm decay:
> Increasing cares, and times resistless rage
> Will waste my bloom, and wither it to age."[11]

You will ask me I suppose what is become of my patriotick virtue? It is that which most ardently calls for your return. I greatly fear that the climate in which you now reside will prove fatal to your Life, whilst your Life and usefullness might be many years of Service to your Country in a more Healthy climate. If the Essentials of her political system are safe, as I would fain hope they are, yet the impositions and injuries, to which she is hourly liable, and daily suffering, call for the exertions of her wisest and ablest citizens. You know by many years experience what it is to struggle with difficulties—with wickedness in high places—from thence you are led to covet a private Station as the post of Honour, but should such an Idea generally prevail, who would be left to stem the torrent?

Should we at this day possess those invaluable Blessings transmitted us by our venerable Ancestors, if they had not inforced by their example, what they taught by their precepts?

> "While pride, oppression and injustice reign
> the World will still demand her Catos presence."[12]

Why should I indulge an Idea, that whilst the active powers of my Friend remain, they will not be devoted to the Service of his country?

Can I believe that the Man who fears neither poverty or dangers, who sees not charms sufficient either in Riches, power or places to tempt him in the least to swerve from the purest Sentiments of Honour and Delicacy; will retire, unnoticed, Fameless to a Rustick cottage there by dint of Labour to earn his Bread. I need not much examination of my Heart to say I would not willing[ly] consent to it.

Have not Cincinnatus and Regulus[13] been handed down to posterity, with immortal honour?

Without fortune it is more than probable we shall end our days, but let the well earned Fame of having Sacrificed those prospects, from a principal of universal Benevolence and good will to Man, descend as an inheritance to our ofspring. The Luxery of Foreign Nations may possibly infect them but they have not before them an example of it, so far as respects their domestick life. They are not Bred up with an Idea of possessing Hereditary Riches or Grandeur. Retired from the Capital, they see little of the extravagance or dissipation, which prevails there, and at the close of day, in lieu of the Card table, some usefull Book employs their leisure hours. These habits early fixed, and daily inculcated, will I hope render them usefull and ornamental Members of Society.—But we cannot see into futurity.—With Regard to politicks, it is rather a dull season for them, we are recruiting for the Army.

The Enemy make sad Havock with our Navigation. Mr. Lovell is appointed continental Receiver of taxes and is on his way to this State.

It is difficult to get Gentlemen of abilities and Integrity to serve in congress, few very few are willing to Sacrifice their Interest as others have done before them.

Your favour of december 18th came by way of Philadelphia, but all those Letters sent by Capt. Reeler were lost, thrown over Board. Our Friends are well and desire to be rememberd to you. Charles will write if he is able to, before the vessel sails, but he is sick at present, threatned I fear with a fever. I received one Letter from my young Russian to whom I shall write—and 2 from Mr. Thaxter. If the vessel gives me time I shall write. We wait impatiently for the result of your demand. These slow slugish wheels move not in unison with our feelings.

Adieu my dear Friend. How gladly would I visit you and partake of your Labours and cares, sooth you to rest, and alleviate your anxieties were it given me to visit you even by moon Light, as the faries are fabled to do.

I cheer my Heart with the distant prospect. All that I can hope for at present, is to hear of your welfare which of all things lies nearest the Heart of Your ever affectionate

PORTIA.

Gustavus Vassa
[Olaudah Equiano]
(1745–1797)

Olaudah Equiano was a young African kidnapped into slavery at the age of eleven who was fortunate enough, upon his arrival in the New World, to be purchased by a British sea captain and placed in service at sea. Having escaped some of the restrictions that awaited virtually all slaves destined for the plantations, Equiano was also, through his extensive travels, able to acquire a sense of the wider world and within ten years to earn enough money to purchase his freedom in 1766. Remaining at sea for the next twenty years and even assisting in the transport of slaves (for which he was roundly criticized), he was eventually persuaded by abolitionist agitation in Parliament to join the antislavery cause and composed his two-volume autobiography in partial contribution to it.

His Narrative found an immediate and admiring audience that included John Wesley, the founder of Methodism, who asked that Equiano's book be read to him on his deathbed. A precursor of the slave narratives of the nineteenth century, Equiano's work also draws on the rich tradition of spiritual autobiography that descends from the Puritan era.

from The Interesting Narrative of the Life of Olaudah Equiano, or Gustavus Vassa, the African, Written by Himself (1789)

I hope the reader will not think I have trespassed on his patience in introducing myself to him, with some account of the manners and customs of my country. They had been implanted in me with great care, and made an impression on my mind, which time could not erase, and which all the adversity and variety of fortune I have since experienced, served only to rivet and record; for, whether the love of one's country be real or imaginary, or a lesson of reason, or an instinct of nature, I still look back with pleasure on the first scenes of my life, though that pleasure has been for the most part mingled with sorrow.

I have already acquainted the reader with the time and place of my birth. My father, besides many slaves, had a numerous family, of which seven lived to grow up, including myself and a sister, who was the only daughter. As I was the youngest of the sons, I became, of course, the greatest favorite with my mother, and was always with her; and she used to take particular pains to form my mind. I was trained up from my earliest years in the art of war: my daily exercise was shooting and throwing javelins; and my mother adorned me with emblems, after the manner of our greatest warriors. In this way I grew up till I was turned the age of eleven, when an end was put to my happiness in the following manner:—generally when the grown people in the neighborhood were gone far in the fields to labor, the children assembled together in some of the neighboring premises to play; and commonly some of us used to get up a tree to look out for any assailant, or kidnapper, that might come upon us—for they sometimes took those opportunities of our parents' absence, to attack and carry off as many as they could seize. One day as I was watching at the top of a tree in our yard, I saw one of those people come into the yard of our next neighbor but one to kidnap, there being many stout young people in it. Immediately on this I gave the alarm of the rogue, and he was surrounded by the stoutest of them, who entangled him with cords, so that he could not escape till some of the grown people came and secured him. But, alas! ere long it was my fate to be thus attacked, and to be carried off, when none of the grown people were nigh. One day, when all our people were gone out to their works as usual, and only I and my dear sister were left to mind the house, two men and a woman got over our walls, and in a moment seized us both, and, without giving us time to cry out, or make resistance, they stopped

our mouths, and ran off with us into the nearest wood. Here they tied
our hands, and continued to carry us as far as they could, till night
came on, when we reached a small house, where the robbers halted
for refreshment, and spent the night. We were then unbound, but were
unable to take any food; and, being quite overpowered by fatigue and
grief, our only relief was some sleep, which allayed our misfortune for
a short time. The next morning we left the house, and continued travelling all the day. For a long time we had kept the woods, but at last
we came into a road which I believed I knew. I had now some hopes
of being delivered; for we had advanced but a little way before I discovered some people at a distance, on which I began to cry out for
their assistance; but my cries had no other effect than to make them
tie me faster and stop my mouth, and then they put me into a large
sack. They also stopped my sister's mouth, and tied her hands; and in
this manner we proceeded till we were out of sight of these people.
When we went to rest the following night, they offered us some victuals, but we refused it; and the only comfort we had was in being in
one another's arms all that night, and bathing each other with our
tears. But alas! we were soon deprived of even the small comfort of
weeping together. The next day proved a day of greater sorrow than
I had yet experienced; for my sister and I were then separated, while
we lay clasped in each other's arms. It was in vain that we besought
them not to part us; she was torn from me, and immediately carried
away, while I was left in a state of distraction not to be described. I
cried and grieved continually; and for several days did not eat any
thing but what they forced into my mouth. At length, after many days
travelling, during which I had often changed masters, I got into the
hands of a chieftain, in a very pleasant country. This man had two
wives and some children, and they all used me extremely well, and did
all they could to comfort me; particularly the first wife, who was something like my mother. Although I was a great many days' journey from
my father's house, yet these people spoke exactly the same language
with us. This first master of mine, as I may call him, was a smith, and
my principal employment was working his bellows, which were the
same kind as I had seen in my vicinity. They were in some respects
not unlike the stoves here in gentlemen's kitchens, and were covered
over with leather; and in the middle of that leather a stick was fixed,
and a person stood up, and worked it in the same manner as is done
to pump water out of a cask with a hand pump. I believe it was gold
he worked, for it was of a lovely bright yellow color, and was worn
by the women on their wrists and ancles. I was there I suppose about
a month, and they at last used to trust me some little distance from
the house. This liberty I used in embracing every opportunity to inquire the way to my own home; and I also sometimes, for the same

purpose, went with the maidens, in the cool of the evenings, to bring pitchers of water from the springs for the use of the house. I had also remarked where the sun rose in the morning, and set in the evening, as I had travelled along; and I had observed that my father's house was towards the rising of the sun. I therefore determined to seize the first opportunity of making my escape, and to shape my course for that quarter; for I was quite oppressed and weighed down by grief after my mother and friends; and my love of liberty, ever great, was strengthened by the mortifying circumstance of not daring to eat with the free-born children, although I was mostly their companion. While I was projecting my escape one day, an unlucky event happened, which quite disconcerted my plan, and put an end to my hopes. I used to be sometimes employed in assisting an elderly slave to cook and take care of the poultry; and one morning, while I was feeding some chickens, I happened to toss a small pebble at one of them, which hit it on the middle, and directly killed it. The old slave, having soon after missed the chicken, inquired after it; and on my relating the accident, (for I told her the truth, for my mother would never suffer me to tell a lie,) she flew into a violent passion, and threatened that I should suffer for it; and, my master being out, she immediately went and told her mistress what I had done. This alarmed me very much, and I expected an instant flogging, which to me was uncommonly dreadful, for I had seldom been beaten at home. I therefore resolved to fly; and accordingly I ran into a thicket that was hard by, and hid myself in the bushes. Soon afterwards my mistress and the slave returned, and, not seeing me, they searched all the house, but not finding me, and I not making answer when they called to me, they thought I had run away, and the whole neighborhood was raised in the pursuit of me. In that part of the country, as in ours, the houses and villages were skirted with woods, or shrubberies, and the bushes were so thick that a man could readily conceal himself in them, so as to elude the strictest search. The neighbors continued the whole day looking for me, and several times many of them came within a few yards of the place where I lay hid. I expected every moment, when I heard a rustling among the trees, to be found out, and punished by my master; but they never discovered me, though they were often so near that I even heard their conjectures as they were looking about for me; and I now learned from them that any attempts to return home would be hopeless. Most of them supposed I had fled towards home; but the distance was so great, and the way so intricate, that they thought I could never reach it, and that I should be lost in the woods. When I heard this I was seized with a violent panic, and abandoned myself to despair. Night, too, began to approach, and aggravated all my fears. I had before entertained hopes of getting home, and had determined when it should be dark to make the attempt; but I was now convinced it was fruitless, and began to consider that, if possibly I could escape all other animals, I could not those of the human kind; and that, not knowing the way, I must perish in the woods. Thus was I like the hunted deer—

> ——'Every leaf and every whisp'ring breath,
> Convey'd a foe, and every foe a death.'

I heard frequent rustlings among the leaves, and being pretty sure they were snakes, I expected every instant to be stung by them. This increased my anguish, and the horror of my situation became now quite insupportable. I at length quitted the thicket, very faint and hungry, for I had not eaten or drank any thing all the day, and crept to my master's kitchen, from whence I set out at first, which was an open shed, and laid myself down in the ashes with an anxious wish for death, to relieve me from all my pains. I was scarcely awake in the morning, when the old woman slave, who was the first up, came to light the fire, and saw me in the fire place. She was very much surprised to see me, and could scarcely believe her own eyes. She now promised to intercede for me, and went for her master, who soon after came, and, having slightly reprimanded me, ordered me to be taken care of, and not ill treated.

Soon after this, my master's only daughter, and child by his first wife, sickened and died, which affected him so much that for some time he was almost frantic, and really would have killed himself, had he not been watched and prevented. However, in short time afterwards he recovered, and I was again sold. I was now carried to the left of the sun's rising, through many dreary wastes and dismal woods, amidst the hideous roarings of wild beasts. The people I was sold to used to carry me very often, when I was tired, either on their shoulders or on their backs. I saw many convenient well built sheds along the road, at proper distances, to accommodate the merchants and travellers, who lay in those buildings along with their wives, who often accompany them; and they always go well armed.

From the time I left my own nation, I always found somebody that understood me till I came to the sea coast. The languages of different nations did not totally differ, nor where they so copious as those of the Europeans, particularly the English. They were therefore, *easily learned*; and, while I was journeying thus through Africa, I acquired two or three different tongues. In this manner I had been travelling for a considerable time, when, one evening, to my great surprise, whom should I see brought to the house where I was but my dear sister! As soon as she saw me, she gave a loud shriek, and ran into my arms—I was quite overpowered: neither of us could speak; but, for a considerable time, clung to each other in mutual embraces, unable to do any thing but weep. Our meeting affected all who saw us; and, indeed, I must acknowledge, in honor of those sable destroyers of human rights, that I never met with any ill treatment, or saw any offered to their slaves, except tying them, when necessary, to keep them from running away. When these people knew we were brother and sister, they indulged us to be together; and the man, to whom I supposed we belonged, lay with us, he in the middle, while she and I held one another by the hands across his breast all night; and thus for a while we forgot our misfortunes, in the joy of being together; but even this small comfort was soon to have an end; for scarcely had the fatal morning appeared when she was again torn from me forever! I was now more miserable, if possible, than before. The small relief which her presence gave me from pain, was gone, and the wretchedness of my situation was redoubled by my anxiety after her fate, and my apprehensions lest her sufferings should be greater than mine, when I could not be with her to alleviate them. Yes, thou dear partner of all my childish sports! thou sharer of my joys and sorrows! happy should I have ever esteemed myself to encounter every misery for you and to procure your freedom by the sacrifice of my own.—Though you were early forced from my arms, your image has been always rivetted in my heart, from which neither time nor fortune have been able to remove it; so that, while the thoughts of your sufferings have damped my prosperity, they have mingled with adversity and increased its bitterness. To that Heaven which protects the weak from the strong, I commit the care of your innocence and virtues, if they have not already received their full reward, and if your youth and delicacy have not long since fallen victims to the violence of the African trader, the pestilential stench of a Guinea ship, the seasoning in the European colonies, or the lash and lust of a brutal and and unrelenting overseer.

I did not long remain after my sister. I was again sold, and carried through a number of places, till after travelling a considerable time, I came to a town called Tinmah, in the most beautiful country I had yet seen in Africa. It was extremely rich, and there were many rivulets which flowed through it, and supplied a large pond in the centre of the town, where the people washed. Here I first saw and tasted cocoa nuts, which I thought superior to any nuts I had ever tasted before; and the trees which were loaded, were also interspersed among the houses, which had commodious shades adjoining, and were in the same manner as ours, the insides being neatly plastered and whitewashed. Here I also saw and tasted for the first time, sugar-cane. Their money consisted of little white shells, the size of the finger nail. I was sold here for one hundred and seventy-two of them, by a merchant who lived and brought me there. I had been about two or three days at his house, when a wealthy widow, a neighbor of his, came there one evening, and brought with her an only son, a young gentleman about my own age and size. Here they saw me; and, having taken a fancy to me, I was bought of the merchant, and went home with them. Her house and premises were situated close to one of those rivulets I have mentioned, and were the finest I ever saw in Africa: they were very extensive, and she had a number of slaves to attend her. The next day I was washed and perfumed, and when meal time came, I was led into the presence of my mistress, and ate and drank before her with her son. This filled me with astonishment; and I could scarce help expressing my surprise that the young gentleman should suffer me, who was bound, to eat with him who was free; and not only so, but that he would not at any time either eat or drink till I had taken first, because I was the eldest, which was agreeable to our custom. Indeed, every thing here, and all their treatment of me, made me forget that I was a slave. The language of these people resembled ours so nearly, that we understood each other perfectly. They had also the very same customs as we. There were likewise slaves daily to attend us, while my young master and I, with other boys, sported with our darts and bows and arrows, as I had been used to do at home. In this resemblance to my former happy state, I passed about two months; and I now began to think I was to be adopted into the family, and was beginning to be reconciled to my situation, and to forget by degrees my misfortunes, when all at once the delusion vanished; for, without the least previous knowledge, one morning early, while my dear master and companion was still asleep, I was awakened out of my reverie to fresh sorrow, and hurried away even amongst the uncircumcised.[1]

Thus, at the very moment I dreamed of the greatest happiness, I found myself most miserable; and it seemed as if fortune wished to give me this taste of joy only to render the reverse more poignant.— The change I now experienced, was as painful as it was sudden and unexpected. It was a change indeed, from a state of bliss to a scene which is inexpressible by me, as it discovered to me an element I had never before beheld, and till then had no idea of, and wherein such instances of hardship and cruelty continually occurred, as I can never reflect on but with horror.

All the nations and people I had hitherto passed through, resembled our own in their manners, customs, and language: but I came at length to a country, the inhabitants of which differed from us in all those particulars. I was very much struck with this difference, especially when I came among a people who did not circumcise, and ate without washing their hands. They cooked also in iron pots, and had European cutlasses and cross bows, which were unknown to us, and fought with their fists among themselves. Their women were not so modest as ours, for they ate, and drank, and slept with their men. But above all, I was amazed to see no sacrifices or offerings among them. In some of those places the people ornamented themselves with scars, and likewise filed their teeth very sharp. They wanted sometimes to ornament me in the same manner, but I would not suffer them; hoping that I might some time be among a people who did not thus disfigure themselves, as I thought they did. At last I came to the banks of a large river which was covered with canoes, in which the people appeared to live with their household utensils, and provisions of all kinds. I was beyond measure astonished at this, as I had never before seen any water larger than a pond or a rivulet: and my surprise was mingled with no small fear when I was put into one of these canoes, and we began to paddle and move along the river. We continued going on thus till night, and when we came to land, and made fires on the banks, each family by themselves; some dragged their canoes on shore, others stayed and cooked in theirs, and laid in them all night. Those on the land had mats, of which they made tents, some in the shape of little houses; in these we slept; and after the morning meal, we embarked again and proceeded as before. I was often very much astonished to see some of the women, as well as the men, jump into the water, dive to the bottom, come up again, and swim about.—Thus I continued to travel, sometimes by land, sometimes by water, through different countries and various nations, till, at the end of six or seven months after I had been kidnapped, I arrived at the sea coast. It would be tedious and uninteresting to relate all the incidents which befel me during this journey, and which I have not yet forgotten; of the various hands I passed through, and the manners and customs of all the different people among whom I lived—I shall therefore only observe, that in all the places where I was, the soil was exceedingly rich; the pumpkins, eadas, plaintains, yams, &c. &c. were in great abundance, and of incredible size. There were also vast quantities of different gums, though not used for any purpose, and every where a great deal of tobacco. The cotton even grew quite wild, and there was plenty of redwood. I saw no mechanics whatever in all the way, except such as I have mentioned. The chief employment in all these countries was agriculture, and both the males and females, as with us, were brought up to it, and trained in the arts of war.

The first object which saluted my eyes when I arrived on the coast, was the sea, and a slave ship, which was then riding at anchor, and waiting for its cargo. These filled me with astonishment, which was soon converted into terror, when I was carried on board. I was immediately handled, and tossed up to see if I were sound, by some of the crew; and I was now persuaded that I had gotten into a world of bad spirits, and that they were going to kill me. Their complexions, too, differing so much from ours, their long hair, and the language they spoke, (which was very different from any I had ever heard) united to confirm me in this belief. Indeed, such were the horrors of my views and fears at the moment, that, if ten thousand worlds had been my own, I would have freely parted with them all to have exchanged my condition with that of the meanest slave in my own country. When I looked round the ship too, and saw a large furnace of copper boiling, and a multitude of black people of every description chained together, every one of their countenances expressing dejection and sorrow, I no longer doubted of my fate; and, quite overpowered with horror and anguish, I fell motionless on the deck and fainted. When I recovered a little, I found some black people about me, who I believed were some of those who had brought me on board, and had been receiving their pay; they talked to me in order to cheer me, but all in vain. I asked them if we were not to be eaten by those white men with horrible looks, red faces, and long hair. They told me I was not: and one of the crew brought me a small portion of spirituous liquor in a wine glass, but, being afraid of him, I would not take it out of his hand. One of the blacks, therefore, took it from him and gave it to me, and I took a little down my palate, which, instead of reviving me, as they thought it would, threw me into the greatest consternation at the strange feeling it produced, having never tasted any such liquor before. Soon after this, the blacks who brought me on board went off, and left me abandoned to despair.

I now saw myself deprived of all chance of returning to my native country, or even the least glimpse of hope of gaining the shore, which I now considered as friendly; and I even wished for my former slavery in preference to my present situation, which was filled with horrors of every kind, still heightened by my ignorance of what I was to undergo. I was not long suffered to indulge my grief; I was soon put down under the decks, and there I received such a salutation in my nostrils as I had never experienced in my life: so that, with the loathsomeness of the stench, and crying together, I became so sick and low that I was not able to eat, nor had I the least desire to taste any thing. I now wished for the last friend, death, to relieve me; but soon, to my grief, two of the white men offered me eatables; and, on my refusing to eat, one of them held me fast by the hands, and laid me across, I think the windlass, and tied my feet, while the other flogged me severely. I had never experienced any thing of this kind before, and although not being used to the water, I naturally feared that element the first time I saw it, yet, nevertheless, could I have got over the nettings, I would have jumped over the side, but I could not; and besides, the crew used to watch us very closely who were not chained down to the decks, lest we should leap into the water; and I have seen some of these poor

African prisoners most severely cut, for attempting to do so, and hourly whipped for not eating. This indeed was often the case with myself. In a little time after, amongst the poor chained men, I found some of my own nation, which in a small degree gave ease to my mind. I inquired of these what was to be done with us? they gave me to understand, we were to be carried to these white people's country to work for them. I then was a little revived, and thought, if it were no worse than working, my situation was not so desperate; but still I feared I should be put to death, the white people looked and acted, as I thought, in so savage a manner; for I had never seen among any people such instances of brutal cruelty; and this not only shown towards us blacks, but also to some of the whites themselves. One white man in particular I saw, when we were permitted to be on deck, flogged so unmercifully with a large rope near the foremast, that he died in consequence of it; and they tossed him over the side as they would have done a brute. This made me fear these people the more; and I expected nothing less than to be treated in the same manner. I could not help expressing my fears and apprehensions to some of my countrymen; I asked them if these people had no country, but lived in this hollow place? (the ship) they told me they did not, but came from a distant one. 'Then,' said I, 'how comes it in all our country we never heard of them?' They told me because they lived so very far off. I then asked where were their women? had they any like themselves? I was told they had. 'And why,' said I, 'do we not see them?' They answered, because they were left behind. I asked how the vessel could go? they told me they could not tell; but that there was cloth put upon the masts by the help of the ropes I saw, and then the vessel went on; and the white men had some spell or magic they put in the water when they liked, in order to stop the vessel. I was exceedingly amazed at this account, and really thought they were spirits. I therefore wished much to be from amongst them, for I expected they would sacrifice me; but my wishes were vain—for we were so quartered that it was impossible for any of us to make our escape.

While we stayed on the coast I was mostly on deck; and one day, to my great astonishment, I saw one of these vessels coming in with the sails up. As soon as the whites saw it, they gave a great shout, at which we were amazed; and the more so, as the vessel appeared larger by approaching nearer. At last, she came to an anchor in my sight, and when the anchor was let go, I and my countrymen who saw it, were lost in astonishment to observe the vessel stop—and were now convinced it was done by magic. Soon after this the other ship got her boats out, and they came on board of us, and the people of both ships seemed very glad to see each other.—Several of the strangers also shook hands with us black people, and made motions with their hands, signifying I suppose, we were to go to their country, but we did not understand them.

At last, when the ship we were in, had got in all her cargo, they made ready with many fearful noises, and we were all put under deck, so that we could not see how they managed the vessel. But this disappointment was the least of my sorrow. The stench of the hold while we were on the coast was so intolerably loathsome, that it was dangerous to remain there for any time, and some of us had been permitted to stay on the deck for the fresh air; but now that the whole ship's cargo were confined together, it became absolutely pestilential. The closeness of the place, and the heat of the climate, added to the number in the ship, which was so crowded that each had scarcely room to turn himself, almost suffocated us. This produced copious perspirations, so that the air soon became unfit for respiration, from a variety of loathsome smells, and brought on a sickness among the slaves, of which many died—thus falling victims to the improvident avarice, as I may call it, of their purchasers. This wretched situation was again aggravated by the galling of the chains, now became insupportable; and the filth of the necessary tubs, into which the children often fell, and were almost suffocated. The shrieks of the women, and the groans of the dying, rendered the whole a scene of horror almost inconceivable. Happily perhaps, for myself, I was soon reduced so low here that it was thought necessary to keep me almost always on deck; and from my extreme youth I was not put in fetters. In this situation I expected every hour to share the fate of my companions, some of whom were almost daily brought upon deck at the point of death, which I began to hope would soon put an end to my miseries. Often did I think many of the inhabitants of the deep much more happy than myself. I envied them the freedom they enjoyed, and as often wished I could change my condition for theirs. Every circumstance I met with, served only to render my state more painful, and heightened my apprehensions, and my opinion of the cruelty of the whites.

One day they had taken a number of fishes; and when they had killed and satisfied themselves with as many as they thought fit, to our astonishment who were on deck, rather than give any of them to us to eat, as we expected, they tossed the remaining fish into the sea again, although we begged and prayed for some as well as we could, but in vain; and some of my countrymen, being pressed by hunger, took an opportunity, when they thought no one saw them, of trying to get a little privately; but they were discovered, and the attempt procured them some very severe floggings. One day, when we had a smooth sea and moderate wind, two of my wearied countrymen who were chained together, (I was near them at the time,) preferring death to such a life of misery, somehow made through the nettings and jumped into the sea: immediately, another quite dejected fellow, who, on account of his illness, was suffered to be out of irons, also followed their example; and I believe many more would very soon have done the same, if they had not been prevented by the ship's crew, who were instantly alarmed. Those of us that were the most active, were in a moment put down under the deck, and there was such a noise and confusion amongst the people of the ship as I never heard before, to stop her, and get the boat out to go after the slaves. However, two of the wretches were drowned, but they got the other, and afterwards flogged him unmercifully, for thus attempting to prefer death to slavery. In this manner we continued to undergo more hardships than I can now relate, hardships which are inseparable from this accursed trade. Many a time we were near suffocation from the want of fresh air, which we were often without for whole days together. This, and the stench of the necessary tubs, carried off many.

During our passage, I first saw flying fishes, which surprised me very much; they used frequently to fly across the ship, and many of them fell on the deck. I also now first saw the use of the quadrant; I had often with astonishment seen the mariners make observations with it, and I could not think what it meant. They at last took notice of my surprise; and one of them, willing to increase it, as well as to gratify my curiosity, made me one day look through it. The clouds appeared to me to be land, which disappeared as they passed along. This heightened my wonder; and I was now more persuaded than ever, that I was in another world, and that every thing about me was magic. At last, we came in sight of the island of Barbadoes, at which the whites on board gave a great shout, and made many signs of joy to us. We did not know what to think of this; but as the vessel drew nearer, we plainly saw the harbor, and other ships of different kinds and sizes, and we soon anchored amongst them, off Bridgetown. Many merchants and planters now came on board, though it was in the evening. They put us in separate parcels, and examined us attentively. They also made us jump, and pointed to the land, signifying we were to go there. We thought by this, we should be eaten by these ugly men, as they appeared to us; and, when soon after we were all put down under the deck again, there was much dread and trembling among us, and nothing but bitter cries to be heard all the night from these apprehensions, insomuch, that at last the white people got some old slaves from the land to pacify us. They told us we were not to be eaten, but to work, and were soon to go on land, where we should see many of our country people. This report eased us much. And sure enough, soon after we were landed, there came to us Africans of all languages.

We were conducted immediately to the merchant's yard, where we were all pent up together, like so many sheep in a fold, without regard to sex or age. As every object was new to me, every thing I saw filled me with surprise. What struck me first, was, that the houses were built with bricks and stories, and in every other respect different from those I had seen in Africa; but I was still more astonished on seeing people on horseback. I did not know what this could mean; and, indeed, I thought these people were full of nothing but magical arts. While I was in this astonishment, one of my fellow-prisoners spoke to a countryman of his, about the horses, who said they were the same kind they had in their country. I understood them, though they were from a distant part of Africa; and I thought it odd I had not seen any horses there; but afterwards, when I came to converse with different Africans, I found they had many horses amongst them, and much larger than those I then saw.

We were not many days in the merchant's custody, before we were sold after their usual manner, which is this:—On a signal given, (as the beat of a drum,) the buyers rush at once into the yard where the slaves are confined, and make choice of that parcel they like best. The noise and clamor with which this is attended, and the eagerness visible in the countenances of the buyers, serve not a little to increase the apprehension of terrified Africans, who may well be supposed to consider them as the ministers of that destruction to which they think themselves devoted. In this manner, without scruple, are relations and friends separated, most of them never to see each other again. I remember, in the vessel in which I was brought over, in the men's apartment, there were several brothers, who, in the sale, were sold in different lots; and it was very moving on this occasion, to see and hear their cries at parting. O, ye nominal Christians! might not an African ask you—Learned you this from your God, who says unto you, Do unto all men as you would men should do unto you? Is it not enough that we are torn from our country and friends, to toil for your luxury and lust of gain? Must every tender feeling be likewise sacrificed to your avarice? Are the dearest friends and relations, now rendered more dear by their separation from their kindred, still to be parted from each other, and thus prevented from cheering the gloom of slavery, with the small comfort of being together, and mingling their sufferings and sorrows? Why are parents to lose their children, brothers their sisters, or husbands their wives? Surely, this is a new refinement in cruelty, which, while it has no advantage to atone for it, thus aggravates distress, and adds fresh horrors even to the wretchedness of slavery.

Hugh Henry Brackenridge
(1748–1816)

Hugh Henry Brackenridge was a Scot who emigrated to the United States at the age of five and eventually wound up, years later, as a classmate of James Madison and Philip Freneau at Princeton. Collaborating with the latter on a Commencement Day poem titled "The Rising Glory of America" (1771), Brackenridge spent many years in literary experimentation before he found the comic, satirical, picaresque form that he would turn into his six-volume novel, Modern Chivalry (1792–1815). During these years he would move from teacher and playwright to chaplain before settling on a career in the law, which took him, at age thirty-three, to what at that time was the frontier village of Pittsburgh.

Brackenridge's political insight was more acute than his common touch. Equipped with a sharp tongue and a savage wit, his inability to suffer fools gladly did little for his political ambitions, even if it eventually guaranteed his literary achievement. After a variety of false starts—A Poem on Divine Revelation (1774), the plays The Battle of Bunkers-Hill (1776) and The Death of General Montgomery (1777), and his collection of sermons titled Six Political Discourses (1778)—he found his stride with the creation of Captain Farrago, the testy, opinionated, shrewd, but still idealistic yeoman farmer who, like Don Quixote, makes his way through the American countryside on his plow horse, accompanied by his opportunistic Irish servant, Teague O'Regan. His travels give Brackenridge the opportunity to comment on local foibles and conditions, while also enabling him to raise many of the complex issues defining the nature and cost of democracy.

from *Modern Chivalry* (1792)

FROM CHAPTER I

John Farrago, was a man of about fifty-three years of age, of good natural sense, and considerable reading; but in some things whimsical, owing perhaps to his greater knowledge of books than of the world; but, in some degree, also, to his having never married, being what they call an old bachelor, a characteristic of which is, usually, singularity and whim. He had the advantage of having had in early life, an academic education; but having never applied himself to any of the learned professions, he had lived the greater part of his life on a small farm, which he cultivated with servants or hired hands, as he could conveniently supply himself with either. The servant that he had at this time, was an Irishman, whose name was Teague O'Regan. I shall say nothing of the character of this man, because the very name imports what he was.

A strange idea came into the head of Captain Farrago about this time; for, by the bye, I had forgot to mention that having being chosen captain of a company of militia in the neighborhood, he had gone by the name of Captain ever since; for the rule is, once a captain, and always a captain; but, as I was observing, the idea had come into his head, to saddle an old horse that he had, and ride about the world a little, with his man Teague at his heels, to see how things were going on here and there, and to observe human nature. For it is a mistake to suppose, that a man cannot learn man by reading him in a corner, as well as on the widest space of transaction. At any rate, it may yield amusement. . . .

CHAPTER III

The Captain rising early next morning, and setting out on his way, had now arrived at a place where a number of people were convened, for the purpose of electing persons to represent them in the legislature of the state. There was a weaver who was a candidate for this appointment, and seemed to have a good deal of interest among the people. But another, who was a man of education, was his competitor. Relying on some talent of speaking which he thought he possessed, he addressed the multitude.

Said he, "Fellow citizens, I pretend not to any great abilities; but am conscious to myself that I have the best good will to serve you.

But it is very astonishing to me, that this weaver should conceive himself qualified for trust. For though my acquirements are not great, yet his are still less. The mechanical business which he pursues, must necessarily take up so much of his time, that he cannot apply himself to political studies. I should therefore think it would be more answerable to your dignity, and conducive to your interest, to be represented by a man at least of some letters, than by an illiterate handicraftsman like this. It will be more honorable for himself, to remain at his loom and knot threads, than to come forward in a legislative capacity: because, in the one case, he is in the sphere where God and nature has placed him; in the other, he is like a fish out of water, and must struggle for breath in a new element.

"Is it possible he can understand the affairs of government, whose mind has been concentrated to the small object of weaving webs; to the price by the yard, the grist of the thread, and such like matters as concern a manufacturer of cloths? The feet of him who weaves, are more occupied than the head, or at least as much; and therefore the whole man must be, at least, but in half accustomed to exercise his mental powers. For these reasons, all other things set aside, the chance is in my favor, with respect to information. However, you will decide, and give your suffrages to him or to me, as you shall judge expedient."

The Captain hearing these observations, and looking at the weaver, could not help advancing, and undertaking to subjoin something in support of what had been just said. Said he, "I have no prejudice against a weaver more than another man. Nor do I know any harm in the trade; save that from the sedentary life in a damp place, there is usually a paleness of the countenance: but this is a physical, not moral evil. Such usually occupy subterranean apartments; not for the purpose, like Demosthenes, of shaving their heads, and writing over eight times the history of Thucydides, and perfecting a style of oratory; but rather to keep the thread moist; or because this is considered but as an inglorious sort of trade, and is frequently thrust away into cellars, and damp outhouses, which are not occupied for a better use.

"But to rise from the cellar to the senate-house, would be an unnatural hoist. To come from counting threads, and adjusting them to the splits of a reed, to regulate the finances of a government, would be preposterous; there being no congruity in the case. There is no analogy between knotting threads and framing laws. It would be a reversion of the order of things. Not that a manufacturer of linen or woolen, or other stuff, is an inferior character, but a different one, from that which ought to be employed in affairs of state. It is unnecessary to enlarge on this subject; for you must all be convinced of the truth and propriety of what I say. But if you will give me leave to take the manufacturer aside a little, I think I can explain to him my ideas on the subject; and very probably prevail with him to withdraw his pretensions."

The people seeming to acquiesce, and beckoning to the weaver, they drew aside, and the Captain addressed him in the following words:

"Mr. Traddle," said he, for that was the name of the manufacturer, "I have not the smallest idea of wounding your sensibility; but it would seem to me, it would be more your interest to pursue your occupation, than to launch out into that of which you have no knowledge. When you go to the senate-house, the application to you will not be to warp a web; but to make laws for the commonwealth. Now, suppose that the making these laws, requires a knowledge of commerce, or of the interests of agriculture, or those principles upon which the different manufacturers depend, what service could you render. It is possible you might think justly enough; but could you speak? You are not in the habit of public speaking. You are not furnished with those commonplace ideas, with which even ignorant men can pass for knowing something. There is nothing makes a man so ridiculous as to attempt what is above his sphere. You are no tumbler for instance; yet should you give out that you could vault upon a man's back; or turn head over heels, like the wheel of a cart; the stiffness of your joints would encumber you; and you would fall upon your backside to the ground. Such a squash as that would do you damage. The getting up to ride on the state is an unsafe thing to those who are not accustomed to such horsemanship. It is a disagreeable thing for a man to be laughed at, and there is no way of keeping one's self from it but by avoiding all affectation."

While they were thus discoursing, a bustle had taken place among the crowd. Teague hearing so much about elections, and serving the government, took it into his head, that he could be a legislator himself. The thing was not displeasing to the people, who seemed to favor his pretensions; owing, in some degree, to there being several of his countrymen among the crowd; but more especially to the fluctuation of the popular mind, and a disposition to what is new and ignoble. For though the weaver was not the most elevated object of choice, yet he was still preferable to this tatterdemalion, who was but a menial servant, and had so much of what is called the brogue on his tongue, as to fall far short of an elegant speaker.

The Captain coming up, and finding what was on the carpet, was greatly chagrined at not having been able to give the multitude a better idea of the importance of a legislative trust; alarmed also, from an apprehension of the loss of his servant. Under these impressions he resumed his address to the multitude. Said he, "This is making the matter still worse, gentlemen: this servant of mine is but a bog-trotter; who can scarcely speak the dialect in which your laws ought to be written; but certainly has never read a single treatise on any political subject; for the truth is, he cannot read at all. The young people of the lower class, in Ireland, have seldom the advantage of a good education; especially the descendants of the ancient Irish, who have most of them a great assurance of countenance, but little information, or literature. This young man, whose family name is O'Regan, has been my servant for several years. And, except a too great fondness for women, which now and then brings him into scrapes, he has demeaned himself in a manner tolerable enough. But he is totally ignorant of the great principles of legislation; and more especially, the particular interests of the government.

"A free government is a noble possession to a people: and this freedom consists in an equal right to make laws, and to have the benefit of the laws when made. Though doubtless, in such a government, the lowest citizen may become chief magistrate; yet it is sufficient to possess the right; not absolutely necessary to exercise it. Or even if you should think proper, now and then, to show your privilege, and exert, in a signal manner, the democratic prerogative, yet is it not descending too low to filch away from me a hireling, which I cannot well spare, to serve your purposes? You are surely carrying the matter too far, in thinking to make a senator of this hostler; to take him away from an employment to which he has been bred, and put him to another, to which he has served no apprenticeship: to set those hands which have been lately employed in currying my horse, to the draughting-bills, and preparing business for the house."

The people were tenacious of their choice, and insisted on giving Teague their suffrages; and by the frown upon their brows, seemed to indicate resentment at what had been said; as indirectly charging them with want of judgment; or calling in question their privilege to do what they thought proper.

"It is a very strange thing," said one of them, who was a speaker for the rest, "that after having conquered Burgoyne and Cornwallis, and got a government of our own, we cannot put in it whom we please. This young man may be your servant, or another man's servant; but if we choose to make him a delegate, what is that to you. He may not be yet skilled in the matter, but there is a good day a-coming. We will impower him; and it is better to trust a plain man like him, than one of your high flyers, that will make laws to suit their own purposes."

Said the Captain, "I had much rather you would send the weaver, though I thought that improper, than to invade my household, and thus detract from me the very person that I have about to brush my boots, and clean my spurs." The prolocutor of the people gave him to understand that his surmises were useless, for the people had determined on the choice, and Teague they would have for a representative.

Finding it answered no end to expostulate with the multitude, he requested to speak a word with Teague by himself. Stepping aside, he said to him, composing his voice, and addressing him in a soft manner, "Teague, you are quite wrong in this matter they have put into your head. Do you know what it is to be a member of a deliberative body? What qualifications are necessary? Do you understand any thing of geography? If a question should be, to make a law to dig a canal in some part of the state, can you describe the bearing of the mountains, and the course of the rivers? Or if commerce is to be pushed to some new quarter, by the force of regulations, are you competent to decide in such a case? There will be questions of law, and astronomy on the carpet. How you must gape and stare like a fool, when you come to be asked your opinion on these subjects? Are you acquainted with the abstract principles of finance; with the funding public securities; the ways and means of raising the revenue; providing for the discharge of the public debts, and all other things which respect the economy of the government? Even if you had knowledge, have you a facility of speaking. I would suppose you would have too much pride to go to the house just to say, Ay, or No. This is not the fault of your nature, but of your education; having been accustomed to dig turf in your early years, rather than instructing yourself in the classics, or common school books.

"When a man becomes a member of a public body, he is like a raccoon, or other beast that climbs up the fork of a tree; the boys pushing at him with pitchforks, or throwing stones, or shooting at him with an arrow, the dogs barking in the meantime. One will find fault with your not speaking; another with your speaking, if you speak at all. They will have you in the newspapers, and ridicule you as a perfect beast. There is what they call the caricature; that is, representing you with a dog's head, or a cat's claw. As you have a red head, they will very probably make a fox of you, or a sorrel horse, or a brindled cow, or the like. It is the devil in hell to be exposed to the squibs and crackers of the gazette wits and publications.

"You know no more about these matters than a goose; and yet you would undertake rashly, without advice, to enter on the office; nay, contrary to advice. For I would not for a thousand guineas, though I have not the half of it to spare, that the breed of the O'Regans should come to this; bringing on them a worse stain than stealing sheep; to which they are addicted. You have nothing but your character, Teague, in a new country to depend upon. Let it never be said, that you quitted an honest livelihood, the taking care of my horse, to follow the newfangled whims of the times, and to be a statesman."

Teague was moved chiefly with the last part of the address, and consented to give up the object.

The Captain, glad of this, took him back to the people, and announced his disposition to decline the honor which they had intended him.

Teague acknowledged that he had changed his mind, and was willing to remain in a private station.

The people did not seem well pleased with the Captain; but as nothing more could be said about the matter, they turned their attention to the weaver, and gave him their suffrages.

CHAPTER V

A democracy is beyond all question the freest government: because under this, every man is equally protected by the laws, and has equally a voice in making them. But I do not say an equal voice; because some men have stronger lungs than others, and can express more forcibly their opinions of public affairs. Others, though they may not speak very loud, yet have a faculty of saying more in a short time; and even in the case of others, who speak little or none at all, yet what they do say containing good sense, comes with greater weight; so that all things considered, every citizen, has not, in this sense of the word, an equal voice. But the right being equal, what great harm if it is unequally exercised? is it necessary that every man should become a statesman? No more than that every man should become a poet or a painter. The sciences, are open to all; but let him only who has taste and genius pursue them. If any man covets the office of a bishop, says St. Paul, he covets a good work. But again, he adds this caution, Ordain not a novice, lest being lifted up with pride, he falls into the condemnation of the devil. It is indeed making a devil of a man to lift him up to a state to which he is not suited. A ditcher is a respectable character, with his overalls on, and a spade in his hand; but put the same man to those offices which require the head, whereas he has been accustomed to impress with his foot, and there appears a contrast between the man and the occupation.

There are individuals in society, who prefer honor to wealth; or cultivate political studies as a branch of literary pursuits; and offer themselves to serve public bodies, in order to have an opportunity of discovering their knowledge, and exercising their judgment. It must be chagrining to these, and hurtful to the public, to see those who have no talent this way, and ought to have no taste, preposterously obtrude themselves upon the government. It is the same as if a bricklayer should usurp the office of a tailor, and come with his square and perpendicular, to take the measure of a pair of breeches.

It is proper that those who cultivate oratory, should go to the house of orators. But for an Ay and No man to be ambitious of that place, is to sacrifice his credit to his vanity.

I would not mean to insinuate that legislators are to be selected from the more wealthy of the citizens, yet a man's circumstances ought to be such as afford him leisure for study and reflection. There is often wealth without taste or talent. I have no idea, that because a man lives in a great house, and has a cluster of bricks or stones about his back-side, that he is therefore fit for a legislator. There is so much pride and arrogance with those who consider themselves the first in a government, that it deserves to be checked by the populace, and the evil most usually commences on this side. Men associate with their own persons, the adventitious circumstances of birth and fortune: So that a fellow blowing with fat and repletion, conceives himself superior to the poor lean man, that lodges in an inferior mansion. But as in all cases, so in this, there is a medium. Genius and virtue are independent of rank and fortune; and it is neither the opulent, nor the indigent, but the man of ability and integrity that ought to be called forth to serve his country: and while, on the one hand, the aristocratic part of the government, arrogates a right to represent; on the other hand, the democratic contends the point; and from this conjunction and opposition of forces, there is produced a compound resolution, which carries the object in an intermediate direction. When we see, therefore, a Teague O'Regan lifted up, the philosopher will reflect, that it is to balance some purse-proud fellow, equally as ignorant, that comes down from the sphere of the aristocratic interest.

But every man ought to consider for himself, whether it is his use to be this drawback, on either side. For as when good liquor is to be distilled, you throw in some material useless in itself to correct the effervescence of the spirit; so it may be his part to act as a sedative. For though we commend the effect, yet still the material retains but its original value.

But as the nature of things is such, let no man, who means well to the commonwealth, and offers to serve it, be hurt in his mind when someone of meaner talents is preferred. The people are a sovereign, and greatly despotic; but, in the main, just.

I have a great mind, in order to elevate the composition, to make quotations from the Greek and Roman history. And I am conscious to myself, that I have read over the writers on the government of Italy and Greece, in ancient, as well as modern times. But I have drawn a great deal more from reflection on the nature of things; than from all the writings I have ever read. Nay, the history of the election, which I have just given, will afford a better lesson to the American mind, than all that is to be found in other examples. We have seen here, a weaver a favored candidate, and in the next instance, a bog-trotter superseding him. Now it may be said, that this is fiction; but fiction, or no fiction, the nature of the thing will make it a reality. But I return to the adventure of the Captain, whom I have upon my hands; and who, as far as I can yet discover, is a good honest man; and means what is benevolent and useful; though his ideas may not comport with the ordinary manner of thinking, in every particular.

John Trumbull
(1750–1831)

Trained in the law that he practiced in New Haven and Hartford for more than fifty years, John Trumbull first developed his literary interests, along with many of the other Connecticut Wits, while a student at Yale University. In a valedictory address titled An Essay on the Uses and Advantages of the Fine Arts, *he took pleasure in attacking neoclassical standards that he himself could exemplify perfectly. Several years later, he composed a satire on university education called* The Progress of Dulness *(1772–1773). But it was not until ten years later, when asked by members of the first Congress to write something favorable to the revolutionary cause, that he hit his literary stride in the mock epic* M'Fingal *(1782). He was also to contribute to the mock epic produced collaboratively with other Connecticut Wits, such as David Humphreys, Lemuel Hopkins, Timothy Dwight, and Joel Barlow, known as* The Anarchiad *(1786–1787).*

from *M'Fingal* (1782)

THE LIBERTY POLE

Now arm'd with ministerial ire,
Fierce sallied forth our loyal squire,
And on his striding steps attends
His desp'rate clan of Tory friends;
When sudden met his angry eye

A pole,[1] ascending through the sky,
Which num'rous throngs of Whiggish race
Were raising in the market-place:
Not higher schoolboys' kites aspire
Or royal mast or country spire,
Like spears at Brobdignagian[2] tiltin'
Or Satan's walking staff in Milton;[3]
And on its top the flag unfurl'd
Wav'd triumph o'er the prostrate world,
Inscrib'd with inconsistent types
Of liberty and thirteen stripes.
 . . . Our squire, yet undismay'd,
Call'd forth the constable to aid
And bade him read in nearer station
The riot act and proclamation;
Who, now advancing toward the ring,
Began, "Our sov'reign lord, the King—"
When thousand clam'rous tongues he hears
And clubs and stones assail his ears.
To fly was vain, to fight was idle,
By foes encompass'd in the middle;
In stratagem his aid he found
And fell right craftily to ground,
Then crept to seek an hiding place,
'Twas all he could, beneath a brace;
Where soon the conqu'ring crew espi'd him,
And where he lurk'd, they caught and ti'd him.
 At once, with resolution fatal,
Both Whigs and Tories rush'd to battle.
Instead of weapons, either band
Seiz'd on such arms as came to hand.
And as fam'd Ovid paints th'adventures
Of wrangling Lapithae and Centaurs[4]
Who at their feast, by Bacchus[5] led,
Threw bottles at each other's head
And, these arms failing in their scuffles,
Attack'd with hand-irons, tongs, and shovels:
So clubs and billets, staves and stones,
Met fierce, encount'ring ev'ry sconce,
And cover'd o'er with knobs and pains
Each void receptacle for brains.
Their clamors rend the hills around,
And earth rebellows with the sound;
And many a groan increas'd the din

From broken nose and batter'd shin.
M'Fingal, rising at the word,
Drew forth his old militia sword,
Thrice cri'd, "King George," as erst in distress
Romancing heroes did their mistress,
And, brandishing the blade in air,
Struck terror through th'opposing war.
The Whigs, unsafe within the wind
Of such commotion, shrunk behind.
With whirling steel around address'd,
Fierce through their thickest throng he press'd
(Who roll'd on either side in arch
Like Red Sea waves in Israel's march)
And, like a meteor rushing through,
Struck on their pole a vengeful blow.
Around, the Whigs of clubs and stones
Discharg'd whole volleys in platoons
That o'er in whistling terror fly,
But not a foe dares venture nigh.

    Meanwhile, beside the pole the guard
A bench of justice had prepar'd,
Where sitting round in awful sort
The grand committee hold their court;
While all the crew, in silent awe,
Wait from their lips the lore of law.
Few moments with deliberation
They hold the solemn consultation,
When soon in judgment all agree,
And clerk declares the dread decree:
"That Squire M'Fingal, having grown
The vilest Tory in the town,
And now, on full examination,
Convicted by his own confession,
Finding no tokens of repentance,
The Court proceed to render sentence;
That first the mob a slip-knot single
Tie round the neck of said M'Fingal
And in due form do tar him next
And feather, as the law directs;
Then through the town, attendant, ride him,
In cart with constable beside him,
And, having held him up to shame,
Bring to the pole from whence he came."

Forthwith the crowd proceed to deck
With halter'd noose M'Fingal's neck,
While he, in peril of his soul,
Stood tied, half-hanging, to the pole,
Then, lifting high the pond'rous jar,
Pour'd o'er his head the smoking tar.
With less profusion erst was spread
   The Jewish oil on royal head,
     That down his beard and vestments ran
     And cover'd all his outward man. . . .
So from the high-rais'd urn the torrents
Spread down his side their various currents.
His flowing wig, as next the brim,
First met and drank the sable stream;
Adown his visage, stern and grave,
Roll'd and adher'd the viscid wave;
With arms depending as he stood,
Each cuff, capacious, holds the flood;
From nose and chin's remotest end
The tarry icicles depend;
Till, all o'erspread, with colors gay
He glitter'd to the western ray
Like sleet-bound trees in wintry skies
Or Lapland idol carv'd in ice.
And now the feather bag, display'd,
Is wav'd in triumph o'er his head
And spreads him o'er with feathers missive
And down upon the tar adhesive:
Not Maia's son,[6] with wings for ears,
Such plumes around his visage wears,
Nor Milton's six-wing'd angel[7] gathers
Such superfluity of feathers;
Till, all complete, appears our squire
Like Gorgon or Chimera[8] dire,
Nor more could boast, on Plato's plan,
To rank amid the race of man
Or prove his claim to human nature
As a two-legg'd, unfeather'd creature.[9]
   Then on a two-wheel'd car of state
They rais'd our grand duumvirate.[10]
And as at Rome a like committee
That found an owl within their city
With solemn rites and sad processions
At ev'ry shrine perform'd lustrations.[11]

And, lest infection should abound
From prodigy with face so round,
All Rome attends him through the street
In triumph to his country seat;
With like devotion all the choir
Paraded round our feather'd squire;
In front the martial music comes
Of horns and fiddles, fifes and drums,
With jingling sound of carriage bells
And treble creak of rusted wheels,
Behind, the crowd, in lengthen'd row,
With grave procession clos'd the show,
And at fit period ev'ry throat
Combined in universal shout
And hail'd great Liberty in chorus,
Or bawl'd: Confusion to the Tories! . . .
    Thus, having borne them round the town,
Last at the pole they set them down
And toward the tavern take their way
To end in mirth the festal day.

The Federalist Papers
(1787–1788)

First published as letters to the New York Independent Journal, Packet, and Daily Advertiser in 1787 and 1788, the Federalist Papers were essays written in support of the Constitution by Alexander Hamilton (1755–1804), James Madison (1751–1836), and John Jay (1745–1829). Though Hamilton is known to have written fifty-one, Madison fifteen, and Jay at least five (the rest written by Hamilton or Madison or the two together), these three Federalists signed themselves as "Publius" and argued for the importance of a central government with checks and balances because they feared the possibilities of factionalism and demogoguery. They were opposed by Anti-Federalists who were convinced that a strong federal government with no limits on the re-electability of the president would threaten the powers and rights of individual states. Strong objection to the ratification of the Constitution was also registered by those concerned about the absence of a Bill of Rights guaranteeing freedom of religion, of speech, of the press, and of assembly. With the assistance of the lucid, powerful arguments of the eighty-five essays that make up the Federalist Papers—Jefferson said of them that they make "the best commentary on the principles of government which was ever written"—the nine states required had approved the Constitution by June 1788, and most of the rest were willing to grant provisional approval if a Bill of Rights was adopted. That Bill of Rights was, of course, provided as the first ten amendments to the Constitution.

NO. I (1787). ON THE PURPOSE OF THE
WRITER [ALEXANDER HAMILTON]

After an unequivocal experience of the inefficacy of the subsisting fed-eral government, you are called upon to deliberate on a new Consti-tution for the United States of America. The subject speaks its own importance, comprehending in its consequences nothing less than the existence of the UNION, the safety and welfare of the parts of which it is composed, the fate of an empire, in many respects, the most in-teresting in the world. It has been frequently remarked that it seems to have been reserved to the people of this country by their conduct and example to decide the important question whether societies of men are really capable or not of establishing good government from reflec-tion and choice, or whether they are forever destined to depend, for their political constitutions, on accident and force. If there be any truth in the remark, the crisis at which we are arrived may with propriety be regarded as the era in which that decision is to be made; and a wrong election of the part we shall act may in this view deserve to be considered as the general misfortune of mankind.

This idea will add the inducements of philanthropy to those of patriotism to heighten the solicitude which all considerate and good men must feel for the event. Happy will it be if our choice should be directed by a judicious estimate of our true interests, unperplexed and unbiassed by considerations not connected with the public good. But this is a thing more ardently to be wished than seriously to be ex-pected. The plan offered to our deliberations affects too many partic-ular interests, innovates upon too many local institutions, not to involve in its discussion a variety of objects foreign to its merits, and of views, passions, and prejudices little favorable to the discovery of truth.

Among the most formidable of the obstacles which the new Con-stitution will have to encounter, may readily be distinguished the ob-vious interest of a certain class of men in every State to resist all changes which may hazard a diminution of the power, emolument, and consequence of the offices they hold under the State estab-lishments—and the perverted ambition of another class of men, who will either hope to aggrandize themselves by the confusions of their country or will flatter themselves with fairer prospects of elevation from the subdivision of the empire into several partial confederacies, than from its union under one government.

It is not, however, my design to dwell upon observations of this nature. I am well aware that it would be disingenuous to resolve indiscriminately the opposition of any set of men (merely because their situations might subject them to suspicion) into interested or ambitious views: Candor will oblige us to admit, that even such men may be actuated by upright intentions; and it cannot be doubted that much of the opposition which has made its appearance, or may hereafter make its appearance, will spring from sources blameless at least, if not respectable; the honest errors of minds led astray by preconceived jealousies and fears. So numerous, indeed, and so powerful are the causes, which serve to give a false bias to the judgment, that we, upon many occasions, see wise and good men on the wrong as well as on the right side of questions of the first magnitude to society. This circumstance, if duly attended to, would furnish a lesson of moderation to those who are ever so much persuaded of their being in the right in any controversy. And a further reason for caution in this respect might be drawn from the reflection that we are not always sure that those who advocate the truth are influenced by purer principles than their antagonists. Ambition, avarice, personal animosity, party opposition, and many other motives not more laudable than these, are apt to operate as well upon those who support, as upon those who oppose, the right side of a question. Were there not even these inducements to moderation, nothing could be more ill-judged than that intolerant spirit, which has at all times characterized political parties. For, in politics as in religion, it is equally absurd to aim at making proselytes by fire and sword. Heresies in either can rarely be cured by persecution.

And yet however just these sentiments will be allowed to be, we have already sufficient indications that it will happen in this as in all former cases of great national discussion. A torrent of angry and malignant passions will be let loose. To judge from the conduct of the opposite parties, we shall be led to conclude that they will mutually hope to evince the justness of their opinions and to increase the number of their converts by the loudness of their declamations and the bitterness of their invectives. An enlightened zeal for the energy and efficiency of government will be stigmatized, as the offspring of a temper fond of despotic power, and hostile to the principles of liberty. An over-scrupulous jealousy of danger to the rights of the people, which is more commonly the fault of the head than of the heart, will be represented as mere pretence and artifice; the stale bait for popularity at the expense of public good. It will be forgotten, on the one hand, that jealousy is the usual concomitant of violent love, and that the noble enthusiasm of liberty is too apt to be infected with a spirit of narrow and illiberal distrust. On the other hand, it will be equally forgotten that the vigor of government is essential to the security of liberty; that in the contemplation of a sound and well-informed judgment their interests can never be separated; and that a dangerous ambition more often lurks behind the specious mask of zeal for the rights of the people than under the forbidding appearance of zeal for the firmness and efficiency of government. History will teach us that the former has been found a much more certain road to the introduction of despotism than the latter; and that of those men who have overturned the liberties of republics the greatest number have begun their career by paying an obsequious court to the people; commencing demagogues, and ending tyrants.

In the course of the preceding observations I have had an eye, my fellow-citizens, to putting you upon your guard against all attempts, from whatever quarter, to influence your decision in a matter of the utmost moment to your welfare by an impressions other than those which may result from the evidence of truth. You will, no doubt, at the same time, have collected from the general scope of them that they proceed from a source not unfriendly to the new Constitution. Yes, my countrymen, I own to you that after having given it an attentive consideration I am clearly of opinion it is your interest to adopt it. I am convinced that this is the safest course for your liberty, your dignity, and your happiness. I affect not reserves, which I do not feel. I will not amuse you with an appearance of deliberation, when I have decided. I frankly acknowledge to you my convictions, and I will freely lay before you the reasons on which they are founded. The consciousness of good intentions disdains ambiguity. I shall not, however, multiply professions on this head. My motives must remain in the depository of my own breast; my arguments will be open to all, and may be judged of by all. They shall at least be offered in a spirit which will not disgrace the cause of truth.

I propose, in a series of papers, to discuss the following interesting particulars: The utility of the UNION to your political prosperity; the insufficiency of the present confederation to preserve that Union; the necessity of a government at least equally energetic with the one proposed, to the attainment of this object; the conformity of the proposed Constitution to the true principles of republican government; its analogy to your own State Constitution; and, lastly, the additional security, which its adoption will afford to the preservation of that species of government, to liberty and to property.

In the progress of this discussion I shall endeavor to give a satisfactory answer to all the objections which shall have made their appearance, that may seem to have any claim to your attention.

It may, perhaps, be thought superfluous to offer arguments to prove the utility of the UNION, a point, no doubt, deeply engraved on the hearts of the great body of the people in every State, and one which, it may be imagined, has no adversaries. But the fact is that we already hear it whispered in the private circles of those who oppose

the new Constitution, that the Thirteen States are of too great extent
for any general system, and that we must of necessity resort to separate
confederacies of distinct portions of the whole. This doctrine will, in
all probability, be gradually propagated, till it has votaries enough to
countenance an open avowal of it. For nothing can be more evident,
to those who are able to take an enlarged view of the subject, than
the alternative of an adoption of the new Constitution or a dismem-
berment of the Union. It will, therefore, be of use to begin by examining the advantages of that Union, the certain evils, and the probable
dangers, to which every State will be exposed from its dissolution. This
shall accordingly constitute the subject of my next address.

PUBLIUS.

NO. 10 (1787) [JAMES MADISON]

November 22, 1787

TO THE PEOPLE OF THE STATE OF NEW YORK.

Among the numerous advantages promised by a well constructed
Union, none deserves to be more accurately developed than its tendency to break and control the violence of faction. The friend of popular governments, never finds himself so much alarmed for their
character and fate, as when he contemplates their propensity to this
dangerous vice. He will not fail therefore to set a due value on any
plan which, without violating the principles to which he is attached,
provides a proper cure for it. The instability, injustice and confusion
introduced in the public councils, have in truth been the mortal diseases under which popular governments have every where perished; as
they continue to be the favorite and fruitful topics from which the
adversaries to liberty derive their most specious declamations. The valuable improvements made by the American Constitutions on the popular models, both ancient and modern, cannot certainly be too much
admired; but it would be an unwarrantable partiality, to contend that
they have as effectually obviated the danger on this side as was wished
and expected. Complaints are every where heard from our most considerate and virtuous citizens, equally the friends of public and private
faith, and of public and personal liberty; that our governments are too
unstable; that the public good is disregarded in the conflicts of rival
parties; and that measures are too often decided, not according to the
rules of justice, and the rights of the minor party; but by the superior
force of an interested and overbearing majority. However anxiously
we may wish that these complaints had no foundation, the evidence
of known facts will not permit us to deny that they are in some degree

true. It will be found indeed, on a candid review of our situation, that some of the distresses under which we labor, have been erroneously charged on the operation of our governments; but it will be found, at the same time, that other causes will not alone account for many of our heaviest misfortunes; and particularly, for that prevailing and increasing distrust of public engagements, and alarm for private rights, which are echoed from one end of the continent to the other. These must be chiefly, if not wholly, effects of the unsteadiness and injustice, with which a factious spirit has tainted our public administrations.

By a faction I understand a number of citizens, whether amounting to a majority or minority of the whole, who are united and actuated by some common impulse of passion, or of interest, adverse to the rights of other citizens, or to the permanent and aggregate interests of the community.

There are two methods of curing the mischiefs of faction: the one, by removing its causes; the other, by controling its effects.

There are again two methods of removing the causes of faction: the one by destroying the liberty which is essential to its existence; the other, by giving to every citizen the same opinions, the same passions, and the same interests.

It could never be more truly said than of the first remedy, that it is worse than the disease. Liberty is to faction, what air is to fire, an aliment [nutriment] without which it instantly expires. But it could not be a less folly to abolish liberty, which is essential to political life, because it nourishes faction, than it would be to wish the annihilation of air, which is essential to political life, because it nourishes faction, than it would be to wish the annihilation of air, which is essential to animal life, because it imparts to fire its destructive agency.

The second expedient is as impracticable, as the first would be unwise. As long as the reason of man continues fallible, and he is at liberty to exercise it, different opinions will be formed. As long as the connection subsists between his reason and his self-love, his opinions and his passions will have a reciprocal influence on each other; and the former will be objects to which the latter will attach themselves. The diversity in the faculties of men from which the rights of property originate, is not less an insuperable obstacle to a uniformity of interests. The protection of these faculties is the first object of Government. From the protection of different degrees and kinds of property immediately results; and from the influence of these on the sentiments and views of the respective proprietors, ensues a division of the society into different interests and parties.

The latent causes of faction are thus sown in the nature of man; and we see them every where brought into different degrees of activity, according to the different circumstances of civil society. A zeal for different opinions concerning religion, concerning Government and many other points, as well of speculation as of practice; an attachment to different leaders ambitiously contending for pre-eminence and power; or to persons of other descriptions whose fortunes have been interesting to the human passions, have in turn divided mankind into parties, inflamed them with mutual animosity, and rendered them much more disposed to vex and oppress each other, than to cooperate for their common good. So strong is this propensity of mankind to fall into mutual animosities, that where no substantial occasion presents itself, the most frivolous and fanciful distinctions have been sufficient to kindle their unfriendly passions, and excite their most violent conflicts. But the most common and durable source of factions, has been the various and unequal distribution of property. Those who hold, and those who are without property, have ever formed distinct interests in society. Those who are creditors, and those who are debtors, fall under a like discrimination. A landed interest, a manufacturing interest, a mercantile interest, a monied interest, with many lesser interests, grow up of necessity in civilized nation, and divide them into different classes, actuated by different sentiments and views. The regulation of these various and interfering interests forms the principal task of modern Legislation, and involved the spirit of party and faction in the necessary and ordinary operations of Government.

No man is allowed to be a judge in his own cause; because his interest would certainly bias his judgment, and, not improbably, corrupt his integrity. With equal, nay with greater reason, a body of men, are unfit to be both judges and parties, at the same time; yet, what are many of the most important acts of legislation, but so many judicial determinations, not indeed concerning the rights of single persons, but concerning the rights of large bodies of citizens; and what are the different classes of legislators, but advocates and parties to the causes which they determine? Is a law proposed concerning private debts? It is a question to which the creditors are parties on one side, and the debtors on the other. Justice ought to hold the balance between them. Yet the parties are and must be themselves the judges; and the most numerous party, or in other words, the most powerful faction must be expected to prevail. Shall domestic manufactures be encouraged, and in what degree, by restrictions on foreign manufactures? are questions which would be differently decided by the landed and the manufacturing classes; and probably by neither, with a sole regard to justice and the public good. The apportionment of taxes on the various descriptions of poverty, is an act which seems to require the most exact impartiality; yet, there is perhaps no legislative act in which greater opportunity and temptation are given to a predominant party, to trample on the rules of justice. Every shilling with which they over-burden the inferior number, is a shilling saved to their own pockets.

It is in vain to say, that enlightened statesmen will be able to adjust these clashing interests, and render them all subservient to the public good. Enlightened statesmen will not always be at the helm: Nor, in many cases, can such an adjustment be made at all, without taking into view indirect and remote considerations, which will rarely prevail over the immediate interest which one party may find in disregarding the rights of another, or the good of the whole.

The inference to which we are brought, is, that the causes of faction cannot be removed; and that relief is only to be sought in the means of controling its effects.

If a faction consists of less than a majority, relief is supplied by the republican principle, which enables the majority to defeat its sinister views by regular vote: it may clog the administration, it may convulse the society; but it will be unable to execute and mask its violence under the forms of the Constitution. When a majority is included in a faction, the form of popular government on the other hand enables it to sacrifice to its ruling passion or interest, both the public good and the rights of other citizens. To secure the public good, and private rights, against the danger of such a faction, and at the same time to preserve the spirit and the form of popular government, is then the great object to which our enquiries are directed: Let me add that it is the great desideratum, by which alone this form of government can be rescued from the opprobrium under which it has so long labored, and be recommended to the esteem and adoption of mankind.

By what means is this object attainable? Evidently by one of two only. Either the existence of the same passion or interest in a majority at the same time, must be prevented; or the majority, having such coexistent passion or interest, must be rendered, by their number and local situation, unable to concert and carry into effect schemes of oppression. If the impulse and the opportunity be suffered to coincide, we well know that neither moral nor religious motives can be relied on as an adequate control. They are not found to be such on the injustice and violence of individuals, and lose their efficacy in proportion to the numbers combined together; that is, in proportion as their efficacy becomes needful.

From this view of the subject, it may be concluded, that a pure Democracy, by which I mean, a Society, consisting of a small number of citizens, who assemble and administer the Government in person, can admit of no cure for the mischiefs of faction. A common passion or interest will, in almost every case, be felt by a majority of the whole; a communication and concern results from the form of Government itself; and there is nothing to check the inducements to sacrifice the weaker party, or an obnoxious individual. Hence it is, that such Democracies have ever been spectacles of turbulence and contention; have ever been found incompatible with personal security, or the rights of property; and have in general been as short in their lives, as they have been violent in their deaths. Theoretic politicians, who have patronized this species of Government, have erroneously supposed, that by reducing mankind to a perfect equality in their political rights, they would at the same time, be perfectly equalized and assimilated in their possessions, their opinions, and their passions.

A Republic, by which I mean a Government in which the scheme of representation takes place, opens a different prospect, and promises the cure for which we are seeking. Let us examine the points in which it varies from pure Democracy, and we shall comprehend both the nature of the cure, and the efficacy which it must derive from the Union.

The two great points of difference between a Democracy and a Republic are, first, the delegation of the Government, in the latter, to a small number of citizens elected by the rest: secondly, the greater number of citizens, and greater sphere of country, over which the latter may be extended.

The effect of the first difference is, on the one hand to refine and enlarge the public views, by passing them through the medium of a chosen body of citizens, whose wisdom may best discern the true interest of their country, and whose patriotism and love of justice, will be least likely to sacrifice it to temporary or partial considerations. Under such a regulation, it may well happen that the public voice pronounced by the representatives of the people, will be more consonant to the public good, than if pronounced by the people themselves convened for the purpose. On the other hand, the effect may be inverted. Men of factious tempers, of local prejudices, or of sinister designs, may by intrigue, by corruption or by other means, first obtain the suffrages, [the voters' support in election] and then betray the interests of the people. The question resulting is, whether small or extensive Republics are most favorable to the election of proper guardians of the public wealth and it is clearly decided in favor of the latter by two obvious considerations.

In the first place it is to be remarked that however small the Republic may be, the Representatives must be raised to a certain number, in order to guard against the cabals of a few; and that however large it may be, they must be limited to a certain number, in order to guard against the confusion of a multitude. Hence the number of Representatives in the two cases, not being in proportion to that of the Constituents, and being proportionally greatest in the small Republic, it follows, that if the proportion of fit characters, be not less, in the large than in the small Republic, the former will present a greater option, and consequently a greater probability of a fit choice.

In the next place, as each Representative will be chosen by a greater number of citizens in the large than in the small Republic, it will be more difficult for unworthy candidates to practise with success the vicious arts, by which elections are too often carried; and the suffrages of the people being more free, will be more likely to centre on men who possess the most attractive merit, and the most diffusive and established characters.

It must be confessed, that in this, as in most other cases, there is a mean, on both sides of which inconveniencies will be found to lie. By enlarging too much the number of electors, you render the representative too little acquainted with all their local circumstances and lesser interests; as by reducing it too much, you render him unduly attached to these, and too little fit to comprehend and pursue great and national objects. The Federal Constitution forms a happy combination in this respect; the great and aggregate interests being referred to the national, the local and particular, to the state legislatures.

The other point of difference is, the greater number of citizens and extent of territory which may be brought within the compass of Republican, than of Democratic Government; and it is this circumstance principally which renders factious combinations less to be dreaded in the former, than in the latter. The smaller the society, the fewer probably will be the distinct parties and interests composing it; the fewer the distinct parties and interests, the more frequently will a majority be found of the same party; and the smaller the numbers of individuals composing a majority, and the smaller the compass within which they are placed, the more easily will they concert and execute their plans of oppression. Extend the sphere, and you take in a greater variety of parties and interests; you make it less probable that a majority of the whole will have a common motive to invade the rights of other citizens; or if such a common motive exists, it will be more difficult for all who feel it to discover their own strength, and to act in unison with each other. Besides other impediments, it may be remarked, that where there is a consciousness of unjust or dishonorable purposes, communication is always checked by distrust, in proportion to the number whose concurrence is necessary.

Hence it clearly appears, that the same advantage, which a Republic has over a Democracy, in controling the effects of faction, is enjoyed by a large over a small Republic—is enjoyed by the Union over the States composing it. Does this advantage consist in the substitution of Representatives, whose enlightened views and virtuous sentiments render them superior to local prejudices, and to schemes of injustice? It will not be denied, that the Representation of the Union will be most likely to possess these requisite endowments. Does it consist in the greater security afforded by a greater variety of parties, against the event of any one party being able to outnumber and oppress the rest? In an equal degree does the encreased variety of parties, comprised within the Union, encrease this security? Does it, in fine, consist in the greater obstacles opposed to the concert and accomplishment of the secret wishes of an unjust and interested majority? Here, again, the extent of the Union gives it the most palpable advantage.

The influence of factious leaders may kindle a flame within their particular States but will be unable to spread a general conflagration through the other States: a religious sect, may degenerate into a political faction in a part of the confederacy: but the variety of sects dispersed over the entire face of it, must secure the national Councils against any danger from that source: a rage for paper money, for an abolition of debts, for an equal division of property, or for any other improper or wicked project, will be less apt to pervade the whole body of the Union, than a particular member of it; in the same proportion as such a malady is more likely to taint a particular county or district, than an entire State.

In the extent and proper structure of the Union, therefore, we behold a Republican remedy for the diseases most incident to Republican Government. And according to the degree of pleasure and pride, we feel in being Republicans, ought to be our zeal in cherishing the spirit, and supporting the character of Federalists.

PUBLIUS.
1787.

Judith Sargent Murray
(1751–1820)

Usually known as the wife of John Murray, an Englishman who emigrated to America in 1770 and began preaching the doctrine of Universalism, or the possible salvation of all people, Judith Sargent Murray was the author of two plays, The Medium, or Virtue Triumphant and The Traveller Returned, a novel titled The Story of Margaretta, and a variety of prose pieces and poems that were published in two series, The Repository and The Gleaner. It was in the second of these series, which ran in the Massachusetts Magazine from 1792 to 1794, that Murray began to take up and explore some of the more pressing issues of late eighteenth-century American life that would interest her, from the domestic education of children to the creation of a national theatre, federalism, and the universalist gospel. But what most distinguished Murray from many of her contemporaries was the seriousness with which she took the Republican virtues of liberty, patriotism, and, above all, equality. Thus she was to insist, as in the most famous of her essays reprinted here, that sexual egalitarianism was crucial not only to the development of women but also to the development of a new republic.

On the Equality of the Sexes (1790)

That minds are not alike, full well I know,
This truth each day's experience will show;
To heights surprising some great spirits soar,

With inborn strength mysterious depths explore;
Their eager gaze surveys the path of light,
Confest it stood to Newton's piercing sight.[1]
    Deep science, like a bashful maid retires,
And but the *ardent* breast her worth inspires;
By perserverance the coy fair is won.
And Genius, led by Study, wears the crown.
    But some there are who wish not to improve,
Who never can the path of knowledge love,
Whose souls almost with the dull body one,
With anxious care each mental pleasure shun;
Weak is the level'd, enervated mind,
And but while here to vegetate design'd.
The torpid spirit mingling with its clod,
Can scarcely boast its origin from God;
Stupidly dull—they move progressing on—
They eat, and drink, and all their work is done.
While others, emulous of sweet applause,
Industrious seek for each event a cause,
Tracing the hidden springs whence knowledge flows,
Which nature all in beauteous order shows.
    Yet cannot I their sentiments imbibe,
Who this distinction to the sex ascribe,
As if a woman's form must needs enrol,
A weak, servile, an inferiour soul;
And that the guise of man must still proclaim,
Greatness of mind, and him, to be the same:
Yet as the hours revolve fair proofs arise,
Which the bright wreath of growing fame supplies;
And in past times some men have *sunk so low*,
That female records nothing *less* can show.
But imbecility is still confin'd,
And by the lordly sex to us consign'd;
They rob us of the power t' improve,
And then declare we only trifles love;
· Yet haste the era, when the world shall know,
That such distinctions only dwell below;
The soul unfetter'd, to no sex confin'd,
Was for the abodes of cloudless day design'd.
    Mean time we emulate their manly fires,
Though erudition all their thoughts inspires,
Yet nature with *equality* imparts,
And *noble passions*, swell e'en *female hearts*.

Is it upon mature consideration we adopt the idea, that nature is thus partial in her distributions? Is it indeed a fact, that she hath yielded to one half of the human species so unquestionable a mental superiority? I know that to both sexes elevated understandings, and the reverse, are common. But, suffer me to ask, in what the minds of females are so notoriously deficient, or unequal. May not the intellectual powers be ranged under these four heads—imagination, reason, memory and judgment. The province of imagination hath long since been surrendered up to us, and we have been crowned undoubted sovereigns of the regions of fancy. Invention is perhaps the most arduous effort of the mind; this branch of imagination hath been particularly ceded to us, and we have been time out of mind invested with that creative faculty. Observe the variety of fashions (here I bar the contemptuous smile) which distinguish and adorn the female world; how continually are they changing, insomuch that they almost render the wise man's assertion problematical, and we are ready to say, *there is something new under the sun.*[2] Now what a playfulness, what an exuberance of fancy, what strength of inventive imagination, doth this continual variation discover? Again, it hath been observed, that if the turpitude of the conduct of our sex, hath been ever so enormous, so extremely ready are we, that the very first thought presents us with an apology, so plausible, as to produce our actions even in an amiable light. Another instance of our creative powers, is our talent for slander; how ingenious are we at inventive scandal? What a formidable story can we in a moment fabricate merely from the force of a prolifick imagination? how many reputations, in the fertile brain of a female, have been utterly despoiled? how industrious are we at improving a hint? suspicion how easily do we convert into conviction, and conviction, embellished by the power of eloquence, stalks abroad to the surprise and confusion of unsuspecting innocence. Perhaps it will be asked if I furnish these facts as instances of excellency in our sex. Certainly not; but as proofs of a creative faculty, of a lively imagination. Assuredly great activity of mind is thereby discovered, and was this activity properly directed, what beneficial effects would follow. Is the needle and kitchen sufficient to employ the operations of a soul thus organized? I should conceive not. Nay, it is a truth that those very departments leave the intelligent principle vacant, and at liberty for speculation. Are we deficient in reason? we can only reason from what we know, and if an opportunity of acquiring knowledge hath been denied us, the inferiority of our sex cannot fairly be deduced from thence. Memory, I believe, will be allowed us in common, since every one's experience must testify, that a loquacious old woman is as frequently met with, as a communicative old man; their subjects are alike drawn from the fund of other times, and the transactions of their youth, or of maturer life, entertain, or perhaps fatigue you, in the evening of their lives. "But our judgment is not so strong—we do not distinguish so well."—Yet it may be questioned, from what doth this superiority, in this determining faculty of the soul, proceed. May we not trace its source in the difference of education, and continued advantages? Will it be said that the judgment of a male of two years old, is more sage than that of a female's of the same age? I believe the reverse is generally observed to be true. But from that period what partiality! how is the one exalted, and the other depressed, by the contrary modes of education which are adopted! the one is taught to aspire, and the other is early confined and limitted. As their years increase, the sister must be wholly domesticated, while the brother is led by the hand through all the flowery paths of science. Grant that their minds are by nature equal, yet who shall wonder at the *apparent* superiority, if indeed custom becomes *second nature*; nay if it taketh place of nature, and that it doth the experience of each day will evince. At length arrived at womanhood, the uncultivated fair one feels a void, which the employments allotted her are by no means capable of filling. What can she do? to books she may not apply; or if she doth, *to those only of the novel kind*, lest she merit the appellation of a *learned lady*; and what ideas have been affixed to this term, the observation of many can testify. Fashion, scandal, and sometimes what is still more reprehensible, are then called in to her relief; and who can say to what lengths the liberties she takes may proceed. Meantime she herself is most unhappy; she feels the want of a cultivated mind. Is she single, she in vain seeks to fill up time from sexual employments or amusements. Is she united to a person whose soul nature made equal to her own, education hath set him so far above her, that in those entertainments which are productive of such rational felicity, she is not qualified to accompany him. She experiences a mortifying consciousness of inferiority, which embitters every enjoyment. Doth the person to whom her adverse fate hath consigned her, posses a mind incapable of improvement, she is equally wretched, in being so closely connected with an individual whom she cannot but despise. Now, was she permitted the same instructors as her brother, (with an eye however to their particular departments) for the employment of a rational mind an ample field would be opened. In astronomy she might catch a glimpse of the immensity of the Deity, and thence she would form amazing conceptions of the august and supreme Intelligence. In geography she would admire Jehovah in the midst of his benevolence; thus adapting this globe to the various wants and amusements of its inhabitants. In natural philosophy she would adore the infinite majesty of heaven, clothed in condescension; and as she traversed the reptile world, she would hail the goodness of a creating God. A mind, thus filled, would have little room for the trifles with which our sex are, with too much justice, accused of amusing themselves, and they would thus be rendered fit companions for those, who should one day wear them as their crown. Fashions, in their variety, would then give place to conjectures, which might perhaps conduce to the improvement of the literary world, and there would be no leisure for slander or detraction. Reputation would not then be blasted, but serious speculations would occupy the lively imaginations of the sex. Unnecessary visits would be precluded, and that custom would only be indulged by way of relaxation, or to answer the demands of consanguinity and friendship. Females would become discreet, their judgments would be invigorated, and their partners for life being circumspectly chosen, an unhappy Hymen[3] would then be as rare, as is now the reverse.

Will it be urged that those acquirements would supersede our domestick duties. I answer that every requisite in female economy is easily attained; and, with truth I can add, that when once attained, they require no further *mental attention*. Nay, while we are pursuing the needle, or the superintendency of the family, I repeat, that our minds are at full liberty for reflection; that imagination may exert itself in full vigor; and that if a just foundation is early laid, our ideas will then be worthy of rational beings. If we were industrious we might easily find time to arrange them upon paper, or should avocations press too hard for such an indulgence, the hours allotted for conversation would at least become more refined and rational. Should it still be vociferated, "Your domestick employments are sufficient"—I would calmly ask, is it reasonable, that a candidate for immortality, for the joys of heaven, an intelligent being, who is to spend an eternity in contemplating the works of Deity, should at present be so degraded, as to be allowed no other ideas, than those which are suggested by the mechanism of a pudding, or the sewing the seams of a garment? Pity that all such censurers of female improvements do not go one step further, and deny their future existence; to be consistent they surely ought.

Yes, ye lordly, ye haughty sex, our souls are by nature *equal* to yours; the same breath of God animates, enlivens, and invigorates us; and that we are not fallen lower than yourselves, let those witness who have greatly towered above the various discouragements by which they have been so heavily oppressed; and though I am unacquainted with the list of celebrated characters on either side, yet from the observations I have made in the contracted circle in which I have moved, I dare confidently believe, that from the commencement of time to the present day, there hath been as many females, as males, who, by the *mere force of natural powers*, have merited the crown of applause; who, *thus unassisted*, have seized the wreath of fame. I know there are who assert, that as the animal powers of the one sex are superiour, of course their mental faculties also must be stronger; thus attributing strength of mind to the transient organization of this earth born tenement. But if this reasoning is just, man must be content to yield the palm to many of the brute creation, since by not a few of his brethren of the field, he is far surpassed in bodily strength. Moreover, was this argument admitted, it would prove too much, for occular demonstration evinceth, that there are many robust masculine ladies, and effeminate gentlemen. Yet I fancy that Mr. Pope[4] though clogged with an enervated body, and distinguished by a diminutive stature, could nevertheless lay claim to greatness of soul; and perhaps there are many other instances which might be adduced to combat so unphilosophical an opinion. Do we not often see, that when the clay built tabernacle is well nigh dissolved, when it is just ready to mingle with the parent soil, the immortal inhabitant aspires to, and even attaineth heights the most sublime, and which were before wholly unexplored. Besides, were we to grant that animal strength proved any thing, taking into consideration the accustomed impartiality of nature, we should be induced to imagine, that she had invested the female mind with superiour strength as an equivalent for the bodily powers of man. But waving this however palpable advantage, for *equality only*, we wish to contend.

I am aware that there are many passages in the sacred oracles which seem to give the advantage to the other sex; but I consider all these as wholly metaphorical. Thus David was a man after God's own heart, yet see him enervated by his licentious passions! behold him following Uriah to the death,[5] and shew me wherein could consist the immaculate Being's complacency. Listen to the curses which Job bestoweth upon the day of his nativity, and tell me where is his perfection, where his patience—*literally* it existed not. David and Job were types of him who was to come; and the superiority of man, as exhibited in scripture, being also emblematical, all arguments deduced from thence, of course fall to the ground. The exquisite delicacy of the female mind proclaimeth the exactness of its texture, while its nice sense of honour announceth its innate, its native grandeur. And indeed, in one respect, the preeminence seems to be tacitly allowed us, for after an education which limits and confines, and employments and recreations which naturally tend to enervate the body, and debilitate the mind; after we have from early youth been adorned with ribbons, and other gewgaws, dressed out like the ancient victims previous to a sacrifice, being taught by the care of our parents in collecting the most showy materials that the ornamenting our exteriour ought to be the principal object of our attention; after, I say, fifteen years thus spent, we are introduced into the world, amid the united adulation of every beholder. Praise is sweet to the soul; we are immediately intoxicated by large draughts of flattery, which being plentifully administered, is to the pride of our hearts the most acceptable incense. It is expected that with the other sex we should commence immediate war, and that we should triumph over the machinations of the most artful. We must be constantly upon our guard; prudence and discretion must be our characteristicks; and we must rise superiour to, and obtain a complete victory over those who have been long adding to the native strength of their minds, by an unremitted study of men and books, and who have, moreover, conceived from the loose characters which they have been portrayed in the extensive variety of their reading, a most contemptible opinion of the sex. Thus unequal, we are, notwithstanding, forced to the combat, and the infamy which is consequent upon the smallest deviation in our conduct, proclaims the high idea which was formed of our native strength; and thus, indirectly at least, is the preference acknowledged to be our due. And if we are allowed an equality of acquirement, let serious studies equally employ our minds, and we will bid our souls arise to equal strength. We will meet upon even ground, the despot man; we will rush with alacrity to the combat, and, crowned by success, we shall then answer the exalted expectations which are formed. Though sensibility, soft compassion, and gentle commiseration, are inmates in the female bosom, yet against every deep laid art, altogether fearless of the event, we will set them in array; for assuredly the wreath of victory will encircle the spotless brow. If we meet an equal, a sensible friend, we will reward him with the hand of amity, and through life we will be assiduous to promote his happiness; but from every deep laid scheme for our ruin, retiring into ourselves, amid the flowery paths of science, we will indulge in all the refined and sentimental pleasures of contemplation. And should it still be urged, that the studies thus inlisted upon would interfere with our more peculiar department, I must further reply, that *early hours*, and close application, will do wonders; and to her who is from the first dawn of reason taught to fill up time rationally, both the requisites will be easy. I grant that niggard fortune is too generally unfriendly to the mind; and that much of that valuable treasure, time, is necessarily expended upon the wants of the body; but it should be remembered, that in embarrassed circumstances our companions have as little leisure for literary improvement, as is afforded to us; for most certainly their provident care is at least as requisite as our exertions. Nay, we have even more leisure for sedentary pleasures, as our avocations are more retired, much less laborious, and, as hath been observed, by no means require that avidity of attention which is proper to the employments of the other sex. In high life, or, in other words, where the parties are in possession of affluence, the objection respecting time is wholly obviated, and of course falls to the ground; and it may also be repeated, that many of those hours which are at present swallowed up in fashion and scandal, might be redeemed, were we habituated to useful reflections. But in one respect, O ye arbiters of our fate! we confess that the superiority is indubitably yours; you are by nature formed for our protectors; we pretend not to vie with you in bodily strength; upon this point we will never contend for victory. Shield us then, we beseech you, from external evils, and in return we will transact *your* domestick affairs. Yes, *your*, for are you not equally interested in those matters with ourselves? Is not the elegancy of neatness as agreeable to your sight as to ours; is not the well favoured viand equally delightful to your taste; and doth not your sense of hearing suffer as much, from the discordant sounds prevalent in an ill regulated family, produced by the voices of children and many *et ceteras*?

CONSTANTIA.

Timothy Dwight
(1752–1817)

A grandson of Jonathan Edwards and a future president of Yale University from 1795 until the time of his death, Timothy Dwight also helped organize the group of what later came to be called the Connecticut Wits, when he and John Trumbull, a fellow classmate at Yale, attempted to introduce modern literature into the curriculum. Though the arc of Dwight's career was more decisively shaped by his religious interests than by his literary preoccupations, the two are not easily separated. If his most famous literary production was the discursive, semipastoral poem "Greenfield Hill" (1794), some of his more important religious works included the poems The Conquest of Canaan (1785) and The Triumph of Infidelity (1788), as well as the five-volume collection of sermons he delivered at Yale, Theology, Explained and Defended (1818–1819). In America he captured much of the celebrationist vision of the country shared by all the Connecticut Wits in verse modeled on the poetry of Alexander Pope. The balanced couplets, the generalizing diction, the heroic historical perspective, all conventions of eighteenth-century English verse, were an attempt to create a literary sense of nationhood to complement the emergent sense of political nationhood.

from America (1790)

As in a lonely vale with glooms o'erspread,
Retir'd I rov'd where guiding fancy led.

Deep silence reign'd; a sudden stream of light
Flam'd through the darksome grove and cheer'd the night.
An awful[1] form advanc'd along the ground,
And circling glories cast a radiance round:
Her face divine with sparkling brightness shone
Like the clear splendor of the mid-day sun;
Robes of pure white her heav'nly limbs enfold,
and on her scepter FREEDOM blaz'd in gold.
"Mortal, attend!" she said and smil'd sublime.
"Borne down the stream of ever-rolling time,
View the bright scenes which wait this happy shore,
Her virtue, wisdom, arts, and glorious power. . . .
    "See Hist'ry all the scenes of time unveil
And bid my sons attend her wondrous tale!
Led by her voice, behold them mount the throne
And stretch their sway to regions yet unknown! . . .
    "Hail, land of light and joy! Thy power shall grow
Far as the seas which round the regions flow.
Through earth's wide realms thy glory shall extend,
And savage nations at thy scepter bend.
Around the frozen shores thy sons shall sail
Or stretch their canvas to the Asian gale,
Or like Columbus steer their course unknown,
Beyond the regions of the flaming zone[2]
To worlds unfound beneath the southern pole,
Whose native hears Antarctic oceans roll;
Where artless nature rules with peaceful sway,
And where no ship e'er stemmed the untri'd way.
    "For thee proud India's spicy isles shall blow,
Bright silks be wrought and sparkling diamonds glow;
Earth's richest realms their treasures shall unfold,
And op'ning mountains yield the flaming gold.
Round thy broad fields more glorious Romes arise,
With pomp and splendor bright'ning all the skies;
Europe and Asia with surprise behold
Thy temples starr'd with gems and roof'd with gold.
From realm to realm broad Appian ways[3] shall wind
and distant shores by long canals be join'd,
The ocean hear thy voice, the waves obey,
And through green valleys trace their wat'ry way.
No more shall war her fearful horrors sound,
Nor strew her thousands on th'embattled ground;
No more on earth shall rage and discord dwell,
but sink, with envy, to their native hell.

"Then, then an heav'nly kingdom shall descend[4]
And light and glory through the world extend,
Th'almighty Saviour His great power display
From rising morning to the setting day,
Love reign triumphant, fraud and malice cease,
And every region smile in endless peace;
Till the last trump the slumb'ring dead inspire,
Shake the wide heav'ns and set the world on fire;
Thron'd on a flaming cloud, with brightness crown'd,
The Judge descend, and angels shine around,
The mountains melt, the moon and stars decay,
The sun grow dim, and nature melt away;
God's happy children mount to worlds above,
Drink streams of purest joys and taste immortal love."

Philip Freneau
(1752–1832)

Philip Freneau cuts a touching as well as impressive figure in colonial American literary history. In literary terms a precursor of the nineteenth-century Romantics as well as a skillful satirist of British folly; in political terms an ardent anti-Federalist and Jeffersonian described by Yale President Timothy Dwight as a "mere incendiary, or rather as a despicable tool of bigger incendiaries" and dismissed by George Washington simply as "that rascal Freneau," Philip Freneau was in biographical terms an early version of Ralph Waldo Emerson's "American Scholar" seeking to find the appropriate intellectual vocation in an age moving too fast for him to quite manage to define himself. Starting out after college as a teacher; then at the outbreak of the Revolution turning to poetry; after discovering that poetry does not pay, quickly shifting to the role of personal secretary to a prominent planter in the West Indies; eventually captured by the British, not once but twice, before being exchanged on the point of death as a prisoner of war; then taking to the sea for six years as master of a small brig; later marrying upon his return to America and assuming the editorship of several short-lived magazines, during which he also held a minor government appointment as translating clerk in the State Department; subsequently driven by poverty to return to sea again as a master of coastal freighters, all the while writing no less than five volumes of poetry during his lifetime, Freneau was a writer whose large and varied talent, despite the attention it attracted in its time, always remained somehow homeless in his world. Frustrated at almost every turn in his career, Freneau found in poetry not only a kind of consolation for his troubles but also a place to wait out the death of one age and the beginning of another.

On the Emigration to America
(1784)

To western woods, and lonely plains,
Palemon[1] from the crowd departs,
Where Nature's wildest genius reigns,
To tame the soil, and plant the arts—
What wonders there shall freedom show,
What mighty states successive grow!

From Europe's proud, despotic shores
Hither the stranger takes his way,
And in our new found world explores
A happier soil, a milder sway,
Where no proud despot holds him down,
No slaves insult him with a crown.

What charming scenes attract the eye,
On wild Ohio's savage stream!
There Nature reigns, whose works outvie
The boldest pattern art can frame;
There ages past have rolled away,
And forests bloomed but to decay.

From these fair plains, these rural seats,
So long concealed, so lately known,
The unsocial Indian far retreats,
To make some other clime his own,
When other streams, less pleasing, flow,
And darker forests round him grow.

Great Sire[2] of floods! whose varied wave
Through climes and countries takes its way,
To whom creating Nature gave
Ten thousand streams to swell thy sway!
No longer shall they useless prove,
Nor idly through the forests rove;

Nor longer shall your princely flood
From distant lakes be swelled in vain,
Nor longer through a darksome wood
Advance, unnoticed, to the main,

Far other ends, the heavens decree—
And commerce plans new freights for thee.

While virtue warms the generous breast,
There heaven-born freedom shall reside,
Nor shall the voice of war molest,
Nor Europe's all-aspiring pride—
There Reason shall new laws devise,
And order from confusion rise.

Forsaking kings and regal state,
With all their pomp and fancied bliss,
The traveller owns, convinced though late,
No realm so free, so blest as this—
The east is half to slaves consigned,
Where kings and priests enchain the mind.

O come the time, and haste the day,
When man shall man no longer crush,
When Reason shall enforce her sway,
Nor these fair regions raise our blush,
Where still the African complains,
And mourns his yet unbroken chains.

Far brighter scenes a future age,
The muse predicts, these States will hail,
Whose genius may the world engage,
Whose deeds may over death prevail,
And happier systems bring to view,
Than all the eastern sages knew.

The Wild Honey Suckle (1786)

Fair flower, that dost so comely grow,
Hid in this silent, dull retreat,
Untouched thy honied blossoms blow,
Unseen thy little branches greet:
    No roving foot shall crush thee here,
    No busy hand provoke a tear.

By Nature's self in white arrayed,
She bade thee shun the vulgar eye,
And planted here the guardian shade,
And sent soft waters murmuring by;
    Thus quietly thy summer goes,
    Thy days declining to repose.

Smit with those charms, that must decay,
I grieve to see your future doom;
They died—nor were those flowers more gay,
The flowers that did in Eden bloom;
    Unpitying frosts, and Autumn's power
    Shall leave no vestige of this flower.

From morning suns and evening dews
At first thy little being came:
If nothing once, you nothing lose,
For when you die you are the same;
    The space between, is but an hour,
    The frail duration of a flower.

The Indian Burying Ground (1787)

In spite of all the learned have said,
   I still my old opinion keep;
The posture, that we give the dead,
   Points out the soul's eternal sleep.

Not so the ancients of these lands—
   The Indian, when from life released,
Again is seated with his friends,
   And shares again the joyous feast.[1]

His imaged birds, and painted bowl,
   And venison, for a journey dressed,
Bespeak the nature of the soul,
   Activity, that knows no rest.

His bow, for action ready bent,
   And arrows, with a head of stone,

Can only mean that life is spent,
    And not the old ideas gone.

Thou, stranger, that shalt come this way,
    No fraud upon the dead commit—
Observe the swelling turf, and say
    They do not lie, but here they sit.

Here still a lofty rock remains,
    On which the curious eye may trace
(Now wasted, half, by wearing rains)
    The fancies of a ruder race.

Here still an aged elm aspires,
    Beneath whose far-projecting shade
(And which the shepherd still admires)
    The children of the forest played!

There oft a restless Indian queen
    (Pale Shebah,⁷ with her braided hair)
And many a barbarous form is seen
    To chide the man that lingers there.

By midnight moons, o'er moistening dews;
    In habit for the chase arrayed,
The hunter still the deer pursues,
    The hunter and the deer, a shade!

And long shall timorous fancy see
    The painted chief, and pointed spear,
And Reason's self shall bow the knee
    To shadows and delusions here.

On Mr. Paine's Rights of Man
(1791)

Thus briefly sketched the sacred RIGHTS OF MAN,
How inconsistent with the ROYAL PLAN!¹
Which for itself exclusive honour craves,
Where some are masters born, and millions slaves.
With what contempt must every eye look down

On that base, childish bauble called a *crown*,
The gilded bait, that lures the crowd, to come,
Bow down their necks, and meet a slavish doom;
The source of half the miseries men endure,
The quack that kills them, while it seems to cure.
    Roused by the REASON of his manly page,
Once more shall PAINE a listening world engage:
From Reason's source, a bold reform he brings,
In raising up *mankind*, he pulls down *kings*,
Who, source of discord, patrons of all wrong,
On blood and murder have been fed too long:
Hid from the world, and tutored to be base,
The curse, the scourge, the ruin of our race,
Their's was the task, a dull designing few,
To shackle beings that they scarcely knew,
Who made this globe the residence of slaves,
And built their thrones on systems formed by knaves
—Advance, bright years, to work their final fall,
And haste the period that shall crush them all.
    Who, that has read, and scann'd the historic page
But glows, at every line, with kindling rage,
To see by them the rights of men aspersed,
Freedom restrain'd, and Nature's law reversed,
Men, ranked with beasts, by monarchs *will'd* away,
And bound young fools, or madmen to obey:
Now driven to wars, and now oppressed at home,
Compelled in crowds o'er distant seas to roam,
From India's climes the plundered prize to bring
To glad the strumpet, or to glut the king.
    COLUMBIA[2] hail! immortal be thy reign:
Without a king, we till the smiling plain;
Without a king, we trace the unbounded sea,
And traffic round the globe, through each degree;
Each foreign clime our honour'd flag reveres,
Which asks no monarch, to support the STARS:
Without a *king* the laws maintain their sway,
While honour bids each generous heart obey.
Be ours the task the ambitious to restrain,
And this great lesson teach—that kings are vain;
That warring realms to certain ruin haste,
That kings subsist by war, and wars are waste:
So shall our nation, form'd on Virtue's plan,
Remain the guardian of the Rights of Man,
A vast Republic, famed through every clime,
Without a king, to see the end of time.

Phillis Wheatley
(1753?–1784)

Phillis Wheatley was brought to America as a slave at the age of seven
and sold to a wealthy tailor from Boston named John Wheatley. Once
installed in the Wheatley household, Phillis Wheatley's precocious intelligence was almost immediately recognized by Wheatley's wife, Susanna, who, in addition to encouraging Phillis's voracious appetite for
education, began to treat her almost as a member of the family. Under
such circumstances, it took very little time for Phillis Wheatley's literary gifts to display themselves. Reading some of the most difficult
passages of the Bible within sixteen months and the English as well as
ancient classics soon thereafter, she had published her first poem by
the time she was thirteen and become an author by the age of nineteen,
when her Poems on Various Subjects, Religious and Moral (1773)
appeared in London, attributed to a young woman describing herself
on the title page as "Negro Servant to Mr. John Wheatley." So remarkable an identification of an author of a book of poems written
in the prevailing Augustan mode required the prefatory testimony of
eighteen distinguished citizens, including the governor of Massachusetts and John Hancock, merely to certify that these poems in fact
"were written by Phillis . . . who was but a few years since, brought
an uncultivated barbarian from Africa."

Notwithstanding Thomas Jefferson's dismissal of her verse, Phillis
Wheatley's achievement was, and is, no less than astonishing, inasmuch as we can still hear in the "clear, bell-like limpid cadence" of
her lines, despite their stylistic idiom, what the modern African-
American novelist Richard Wright described as "the hope of freedom
in the New World." But recognition of her achievement was tragically
short-lived. Sent to England to meet her patron, the Countess of Hun-

*tingdon, and to receive the attentions of an extremely admiring English
literary public, she was almost immediately called back to America to
attend her dying mistress. And even though she received her freedom
when the Wheatleys died and then went on to marry a free black
named John Peters, two of her three children preceded her in death,
her husband turned out to be a business failure, and her last years
were spent in poverty and obscurity.*

On Being Brought from Africa to America (1773)

'TWAS mercy brought me from my pagan land,
Taught my benighted soul to understand
That there's a God—that there's a Saviour too;
Once I redemption neither sought nor knew.
Some view our sable race with scornful eye—
'Their color is a diabolic dye.'
Remember, Christians, Negroes black as Cain
May be refined, and join the angelic train.

On the Death of the Rev. Mr. George Whitefield (1770)

HAIL, happy saint! on thine immortal throne,
Possest of glory, life, and bliss unknown:
We hear no more the music of thy tongue;
Thy wonted auditories cease to throng.
Thy sermons in unequalled accents flowed,
And ev'ry bosom with devotion glowed;
Thou didst, in strains of eloquence refined,
Inflame the heart, and captivate the mind.
Unhappy, we the setting sun deplore,
So glorious once, but ah! it shines no more.

Behold the prophet in his towering flight!
He leaves the earth for heaven's unmeasured height,
And worlds unknown receive him from our sight.
There Whitefield wings with rapid course his way,

And sails to Zion through vast seas of day.
Thy prayers, great saint, and thine incessant cries,
Have pierced the bosom of thy native skies.
Thou, moon, hast seen, and all the stars of light,
How he has wrestled with his God by night.
He prayed that grace in ev'ry heart might dwell;
He longed to see America excel;
He charged its youth that ev'ry grace divine
Should with full lustre in their conduct shine.
That Saviour, which his soul did first receive,
The greatest gift that ev'n a God can give,
He freely offered to the numerous throng,
That on his lips with list'ning pleasure hung.

    "Take him, ye wretched for your only good,
"Take him, ye starving sinners, for your food;
"Ye thirsty, come to this life-giving stream,
"Ye preachers, take him for your joyful theme;
"Take him, my dear Americans, he said,
"Be your complaints on his kind bosom laid:
"Take him, ye Africans, he longs for you;
"Impartial Saviour is his title due:
"Washed in the fountain of redeeming blood,
"You shall be sons, and kings, and priests to God."

    Great Countess,¹ we Americans revere
Thy name, and mingle in thy grief sincere;
New-England deeply feels, the orphans mourn,
Their more than father will no more return.

    But though arrested by the hand of death,
Whitefield no more exerts his lab'ring breath,
Yet let us view him in the eternal skies,
Let ev'ry heart to this bright vision rise;
While the tomb, safe, retains its sacred trust,
Till life divine reanimates his dust.

To S. M.,¹ A Young African Painter, On Seeing His Works (1773)

    To show the lab'ring bosom's deep intent,
And thought in living characters to paint,
When first thy pencil did those beauties give,
And breathing figures learnt from thee to live,

How did those prospects give my soul delight,
A new creation rushing on my sight!
Still, wondrous youth! each noble path pursue;
On deathless glories fix thine ardent view:
Still may the painter's and the poet's fire,
To aid thy pencil and thy verse conspire!
And may the charms of each seraphic theme
Conduct thy footsteps to immortal fame!
High to the blissful wonders of the skies
Elate thy soul, and raise thy wishful eyes.
Thrice happy, when exalted to survey
That splendid city, crowned with endless day,
Whose twice six gates[2] on radiant hinges ring:
Celestial Salem[3] blooms in endless spring.
Calm and serene thy moments glide along,
And may the muse inspire each future song!
Still, with the sweets of contemplation blessed,
May peace with balmy wings your soul invest!
But when these shades of time are chased away,
And darkness ends in everlasting day,
On what seraphic pinions shall we move,
And view the landscapes in the realms above!
There shall thy tongue in heavenly murmurs flow,
And there my muse with heavenly transport glow;
No more to tell of Damon's[4] tender sighs,
Or rising radiance of Aurora's eyes;
For nobler themes demand a nobler strain,
And purer language on the etherial plain.
Cease, gentle Muse! the solemn gloom of night
Now seals the fair creation from my sight.

To His Excellency General
Washington (1776)

Celestial choir! enthron'd in realms of light,
Columbia's[1] scenes of glorious toils I write.
While freedom's cause her anxious breast alarms,
She flashes dreadful in refulgent arms.
See mother earth her offspring's fate bemoan,
And nations gaze at scenes before unknown!
See the bright beams of heaven's revolving light

Involv'd in sorrows and the veil of night!
The goddess comes, she moves divinely fair,
Olive and laurel bind her golden hair:
Wherever shines this native of the skies,
Unnumber'd charms and recent graces rise.

Muse! bow propitious, while my pen relates
How pour her armies through a thousand gates;
As when Eolus[2] heaven's fair face deforms,
Enwrap'd in tempest, and a night of storms;
Astonish'd ocean feels the wild uproar,
The refluent surges beat the sounding shore;
Or thick as leaves in autumn's golden reign,
Such, and so many, moves the warrior train.
In bright array they seek the work of war,
Where high unfurl'd the ensign waves in air.
Shall I to Washington their praise recite?
Enough thou know'st them in the fields of fight.
Thee, first in place and honours,—we demand
The grace and glory of thy martial band.
Fam'd for thy valour, for thy virtues more,
Hear every tongue thy guardian aid implore!

One century scarce perform'd its destin'd round,
When Gallic powers Columbia's fury found;[3]
And so may you, whoever dares disgrace
The land of freedom's heaven-defended race!
Fix'd are the eyes of nations on the scales,
For in their hopes Columbia's arm prevails.
Anon Britannia droops the pensive head,
While round increase the rising hills of dead.
Ah! cruel blindness to Columbia's state!
Lament thy thirst of boundless power too late.

Proceed, great chief, with virtue on thy side,
Thy every action let the goddess guide.
A crown, a mansion, and a throne that shine,
With gold unfading, WASHINGTON! be thine.

Joel Barlow
(1754–1812)

Best known for his mock-heroic poem "The Hasty Pudding" (1793, 1796), celebrating his memories of the blessings of New England cooking and living, which had been evoked by the smell of cornmeal mush at an inn where he had stopped in the Alps during the Reign of Terror, Joel Barlow was a member of a literary generation that included Philip Freneau, John Trumbull, Timothy Dwight, and Royall Tyler. And like several of them, Barlow spent much of his life trying out different vocations: poet, army chaplain, schoolteacher, newspaper editor, printer and stationer, lawyer, diplomat, land speculator, political advisor, pamphleteer, and revolutionary consultant. In the course of an extraordinarily varied career, Barlow exchanged his early conservative Federalism, first for Jeffersonian Republicanism, then for English and Parisian radicalism. If his first important poem, the patriotic "The Vision of Columbus" (1787), was originally dedicated to King Louis XVI, his last, "Advise to a Raven in Russia," composed in Poland on a mission to Napoleon, is a bitter protest over the devastation of war.

Advise to the Privileged Orders (1792) *was written during a seventeen-year sojourn in Europe, where Barlow not only deepened his friendship with Tom Paine and became a supporter of the French Revolution (after becoming a French citizen, he even attempted without success to get elected to the National Assembly) but subsequently amassed a considerable fortune. His target in this radically republican treatise is the critique of the revolutionary politics produced by Edmund Burke (1729–1797) in his* Reflections on the Revolution in France *(1790), and he wastes no time in mounting a vigorous counterattack against, among other things, "monarchy, aristocracy, the clergy, and growing trans-Atlantic militarism."*

In "The Hasty Pudding" Barlow adopts an entirely different critical mode that is by turns comic, idealizing, satirical, and sentimental. The mock-heroic form is, as with Hugh Henry Brackenridge, a wonderfully appropriate vehicle for enabling the "provincial" American to display his mastery of a form that is supposed to be European, while at the same time celebrating the virtues of the ordinary American by puncturing European pretentions.

from *Advise to the Privileged Orders in the Several States of Europe, Resulting from the Necessity and Propriety of a General Revolution in the Principle of Government (1792)*

The French Revolution is at last not only accomplished, but its accomplishment universally acknowledged, beyond contradiction abroad, or the power of retraction at home. It has finished its work, by organizing a government, on principles approved by reason; an object long contemplated by different writers, but never before exhibited, in this quarter of the globe. The experiment now in operation will solve a question of the first magnitude in human affairs: Whether *Theory* and *Practice*, which always agree together in things of slighter moment, are really to remain eternal enemies in the highest concerns of men?

The change of government in France is, properly speaking, a renovation of society; an object peculiarly fitted to hurry the mind into a field of thought; which can scarcely be limited by the concerns of a nation, or the improvements of an age. As there is a tendency in human nature to imitation; and, as all the apparent causes exist in most of the governments of the world, to induce the people to wish for a similar change, it becomes interesting to the cause of humanity, to take a deliberate view of the real nature and extent of this change, and find what are the advantages and disadvantages to be expected from it.

There is not that necromancy in politics, which prevents our foreseeing, with tolerable certainty, what is to be the result of operations so universal, in which all the people concur. Many truths are as perceptible when first presented to the mind, as an age or a world of experience could make them; others require only an indirect and collateral experience; some demand an experience direct and positive.

It is happy for human nature, that in morals we have much to do with this first class of truths, less with the second, and very little with the third; while in physics we are perpetually driven to the slow process of patient and positive experience.

The Revolution in France certainly comes recommended to us under one aspect which renders it at first view extremely inviting: it is the work of argument and rational conviction, and not of the sword. The *ultima ratio regum*[1] had nothing to do with it. It was an operation designed for the benefit of the people; it originated in the people, and was conducted by the people. It has therefore a legitimate origin, and this circumstance entitles it to our serious contemplation, on two accounts: because there is something venerable in the idea, and because other nations, in similar circumstances, will certainly be disposed to imitate it. . . .

Philosophers and contemplative men, who may think themselves disinterested spectators of so great a political drama, will do well to consider how far the catastrophe is to be beneficial or detrimental to the human race; in order to determine whether in conscience they ought to promote or discourage, accelerate or retard it, by the publication of their opinions. It is true, the work was set on foot by this sort of men; but they have not all been of the same opinion relative to the best organization of the governing power, nor how far the reform of abuses ought to extend. Montesquieu,[2] Voltaire,[3] and many other respectable authorities, have accredited the principle, that republicanism is not convenient for a great state. Rousseau[4] and others take no notice of the distinction between great and small states, in deciding, that this is the only government proper to ensure the happiness, and support the dignity of man. Of the former opinion was a great majority of the constituting national assembly of France. Probably not many years will pass, before a third opinion will be universally adopted, never to be laid aside: That the republican principle is not only proper and safe for the government of any people; but, that its propriety and safety are in proportion to the magnitude of the society and the extent of the territory.

Among sincere enquirers after truth, all general questions on this subject reduce themselves to this: Whether men are to perform their duties by an easy choice or an expensive cheat; or, whether our reason be given us to be improved or stifled, to render us greater or less than brutes, to increase our happiness or aggravate our misery.

Among those whose anxieties arise only from interest, the enquiry is, how their privileges or their professions are to be affected by the new order of things. These form a class of men respectable both for their numbers and their sensibility; it is our duty to attend to their case. I sincerely hope to administer some consolation to them in the course of this essay. And though I have a better opinion of their philanthrophy, than political opponents generally entertain of each other, yet I do not altogether rely upon their presumed sympathy with their fellow-citizens, and their supposed willingness to sacrifice to the public good; but I hope to convince them, that the establishment of general liberty will be less injurious to those who now live by abuses, than is commonly imagined; that protected industry will produce effects far more astonishing than have ever been calculated; that the increase of enjoyments will be such, as to ameliorate the condition of every human creature.

To persuade this class of mankind that it is neither their duty nor their interest to endeavour to perpetuate the ancient forms of government, would be a high and holy office; it would be the greatest act of charity to them, as it might teach them to avoid a danger that is otherwise unavoidable; it would preclude the occasion of the people's indulging what is sometimes called a ferocious disposition, which is apt to grow upon the revenge of injuries, and render them less harmonious in their new station of citizens; it would prevent the civil wars, which might attend the insurrections of the people, where there should be a great want of unanimity,—for we are not to expect in every country that mildness and dignity which have uniformly characterized the French, even in their most tumultuous movements: it would remove every obstacle and every danger that may seem to attend that rational system of public felicity to which the nations of Europe are moving with rapid strides, and which in prospect is so consoling to the enlightened friends of humanity.

To induce the men who now govern the world to adopt these ideas, is the duty of those who now possess them. I confess the task at first view appears more than Herculean; it will be thought an object from which the eloquence of the closet must shrink in despair, and which prudence would leave to the more powerful argument of events. But I believe at the same time that some success may be expected; that though the harvest be great, the laborers may not be few; that prejudice and interest cannot always be relied on to garrison the mind against the assaults of truth. This belief, ill-grounded as it may appear, is sufficient to animate me in the cause; and to the venerable host of republican writers, who have preceded me in the discussions occasioned by the French revolution, this belief is my only apology for offering to join the fraternity, and for thus practically declaring my opinion, that they have not exhausted the subject.

Two very powerful weapons, the force of reason and the force of numbers, are in the hands of the political reformers. While the use of the first brings into action the second, and ensures its co-operation, it remains a sacred duty, imposed on them by the God of reason, to wield with dexterity this mild and beneficent weapon, before recurring to the use of the other; which, though legitimate, may be less harmless; though infallible in operation, may be less glorious in victory.

The tyrannies of the world, whatever be the appellation of the government under which they are exercised, are all aristocratical tyrannies. An ordinance to plunder and murder, whether it fulminate from the Vatican, or steal silently forth from the Harem; whether it come clothed in the *certain science* of a Bed of Justice, or in the legal solemnities of a bench of lawyers; whether it be purchased by the caresses of a woman, or the treasures of a nation,—never confines its effects to the benefit of a single individual; it goes to enrich the whole combination of conspirators, whose business it is to dupe and to govern the nation. It carries its own bribery with itself through all its progress and connexions,—in its origination, in its enaction, in its vindication, in its execution; it is a fertilizing stream, that waters and vivifies its happy plants in the numerous channels of its communication. Ministers and secretaries, commanders of armies, contractors, collectors and tide-waiters, intendants, judges and lawyers,—whoever is permitted to drink of the salutary stream,—are all interested in removing the obstructions and in praising the fountain from whence it flows.

The state of human nature requires that this should be the case. Among beings so nearly equal in power and capacity as men of the same community are, it is impossible that a solitary tyrant should exist. Laws that are designed to operate unequally on society, must offer an exclusive interest to a considerable portion of its members, to ensure their execution upon the rest. Hence has arisen the necessity of that strange complication in the governing power, which has made of politics an inexplicable science hence the reason for arming one class of our fellow creatures with the weapons of bodily destruction, and another with the mysterious artillery of the vengeance of heaven; hence the cause of what in England is called the independence of the judges, and what on the continent has created a judiciary nobility, a set of men who purchase the privilege of being the professional enemies of the people, of selling their decisions to the rich, and of distributing individual oppression; hence the source of those Draconian[5] codes of criminal jurisprudence which enshrine the idol Property in a bloody sanctuary, and teach the modern European, that his life is of less value than the shoes on his feet; hence the positive discouragements laid upon agriculture, manufactures, commerce, and every method of improving the condition of men; for it is to be observed, that in every country the shackles imposed upon industry are in proportion to the degree of general despotism that reigns in the government. This arises not only from the greater debility and want of enterprise in the people, but from the superior necessity that such governments are under, to prevent their subjects from acquiring that ease and information, by which they could discern the evil and apply the remedy.

To the same fruitful source of calamities we are to trace that perversity of reason, which, in governments where men are permitted to discuss political subjects, has given rise to those perpetual shifts of sophistry by which they vindicate the prerogative of kings. In one age it is the *right of conquest*, in another the *divine right*, then it comes to be a *compact between king and people*, and last of all, it is said to be founded on general convenience, *the good of the whole community*. In England these several arguments have all had their day; though it is astonishing that the two former could ever have been the subjects of rational debate: the first is the logic of the musquet, and the second of the chalice; the one was buried at Rennimede on the signature of Magna Charta,[6] the other took its flight to the continent with James the Second.[7] The compact of king and people has lain dormant the greater part of the present century; till it was roused from slumber by the French revolution, and came into the service of Mr. Burke.[8]

Hasty men discover their errors when it is too late. It had certainly been much more consistent with the temperament of that writer's mind, and quite as serviceable to his cause, to have recalled the fugitive claim of the divine right of kings. It would have given a mystic force to his declamation, afforded him many new epithets, and furnished subjects perfectly accordant with the copious charges of *sacrilege, atheism, murders, assassinations, rapes* and *plunders* with which his three volumes abound. He then could not have disappointed his friends by his total want of argument, as he now does in his two first essays; for on such a subject no argument could be expected; and in his third, where it is patiently attempted, he would have avoided the necessity of showing that he has none, by giving a different title to his book; for the "appeal," instead of being "from the new to the old whigs," would have been *from the new whigs to the old tories*; and he might as well have appealed to Caesar[9]; he could have found at this day no court to take cognizance of his cause.

But the great advantage of this mode of handling the subject would have been, that it could have provoked no answers; the gauntlet might have been thrown, without a champion to have taken it up; and the last solitary admirer of chivalry have retired in negative triumph from the field.

Mr. Burke, however, in his defence of royalty, does not rely on this argument of the compact. Whether it be, that he is conscious of its futility, or that in his rage he forgets that he has used it, he is perpetually recurring to the last ground that has yet been heard of, on which we are called upon to consider kings even as a tolerable nuisance, and to support the existing forms of government: this ground is *the general good of the community*. It is said to be dangerous to pull down systems that are already formed, or even to attempt to improve them; and it is likewise said, that, were they peaceably destroyed, and we had society to build up anew, it would be best to create hereditary kings, hereditary orders, and exclusive privileges.

These are sober opinions, uniting a class of reasoners too numerous and too respectable to be treated with contempt. I believe however that their number is every day diminishing, and I believe the example which France will soon be obliged to exhibit to the world on this subject, will induce every man to reject them, who is not personally and exclusively interested in their support.

The inconsistency of the constituting assembly, in retaining an hereditary king, armed with an enormous civil list, to wage war with a popular government, has induced some persons to predict the downfall of their constitution. But this measure had a different origin from what is commonly assigned to it, and will probably have a different issue. It was the result rather of local and temporary circumstances, than of any general belief in the utility of kings, under any modifications or limitations that could be attached to the office.

It is to be observed, *first*, that the French had a king upon their hands. This king had always been considered as a well-disposed man; so that, by a fatality somewhat singular, though not unexampled in *regal history*, he gained the love of the people, almost in proportion to the mischief which he did them. *Secondly*, their king had very powerful family connexions, in the sovereigns of Spain, Austria, Naples and Sardinia; besides his relations within the kingdom, whom it was necessary to attach, if possible, to the interests of the community. *Thirdly*, the revolution was considered by all Europe as a high and dangerous experiment. It was necessary to hide as much as possible the appearance of its magnitude from the eye of the distant observer. The reformers considered it as their duty to produce an internal regeneration of society, rather than an external change in the appearance of the court; to set in order the counting-house and the kitchen, before arranging the drawingroom. This would leave the sovereigns of Europe totally without a pretext for interfering; while it would be consoling to that class of philosophers, who still believed in the compatibility of royalty and liberty. *Fourthly*, this decree, That *France should have a king*, and that he *could do no wrong*, was passed at an early period of their operations; when the above reasons were apparently more urgent than they were afterwards, or probably will ever be again.

From these considerations we may conclude, that royalty is preserved in France for reasons which are fugitive; that a majority of the constituting assembly did not believe in it, as an abstract principle; that a majority of the people will learn to be disgusted with so unnatural and ponderous a deformity in their new edifice, and will soon hew it off.

After this improvement shall have been made, a few years experience in the face of Europe, and on so great a theatre as that of France, will probably leave but one opinion in the minds of honest men, relative to the republican principle, or the great simplicity of nature applied to the organization of society.

The example of America would have had great weight in producing this conviction; but it is too little known to the European reasoner, to be a subject of accurate investigation. Besides, the difference of circumstances between that country and the states of Europe has given occasion for imagining many distinctions which exist not in fact, and has prevented the application of principles which are permanently founded in nature, and follow not the trifling variations in the state of society.

But I have not prescribed to myself the talk of entering into arguments on the utility of kings, or of investigating the meaning of Mr. Burke, in order to compliment him with an additional refutation. My subject furnishes a more extensive scope. It depends not on me, or Mr. Burke, or any other writer, or description of writers, to determine the question, whether a change of government shall take place, and extend through Europe. It depends on a much more important class of men, the class that cannot write; and in a great measure, on those who cannot read. It is to be decided by men who reason better without books, than we do with all the books in the world. Taking it for granted, therefore, that a general revolution is at hand, whose progress is *irresistible*, my object is to contemplate its probable effects, and to comfort those who are afflicted at the prospect.

The Hasty Pudding[1]
A Poem, in Three Cantos

WRITTEN AT CHAMBERY,
IN SAVOY,[2]
JANUARY, 1793

Omne tulit punctum qui miscuit utile dulci.[3]
He makes a good breakfast who mixes pudding with molasses.

PREFACE

A simplicity in diet, whether it be considered with reference to the happiness of individuals or the prosperity of a nation, is of more consequence than we are apt to imagine. In recommending so important an object to the rational part of mankind, I wish it were in my power to do it in such a manner as would be likely to gain their attention. I am sensible that it is one of those subjects in which example has infinitely more power than the most convincing arguments or the highest charms of poetry. Goldsmith's *Deserted Village*,[4] though possessing these two advantages in a greater degree than any other work of the kind, has not prevented villages in England from being deserted. The apparent interest of the rich individuals, who form the taste as well as the laws in that country, has been against him; and with that interest it has been vain to contend.

The vicious habits which in this little piece I endeavor to combat, seem to me not so difficult to cure. No class of people has any interest in supporting them, unless it be the interest which certain families may feel in vying with each other in sumptuous entertainments. There may indeed be some instances of depraved appetites, which no arguments will conquer; but these must be rare. There are very few persons but what would always prefer a plain dish for themselves, and would prefer it likewise for their guests, if there were no risk of reputation in the case. This difficulty can only be removed by example; and the example should proceed from those whose situation enables them to take the lead in forming the manners of a nation. Persons of this description in America, I should hope, are neither above nor below the influence of truth and reason, when conveyed in language suited to the subject.

Whether the manner I have chosen to address my arguments to them be such as to promise any success is what I cannot decide. But I certainly had hopes of doing some good, or I should not have taken the pains of putting so many rhymes together. The example of domestic virtues has doubtless a great effect. I only wish to rank simplicity of diet among the virtues. In that case I should hope it will be cherished and more esteemed by others than it is at present.

THE AUTHOR

CANTO I

Ye Alps audacious, through the heavens that rise,
To cramp the day and hide me from the skies;
Ye Gallic flags,[5] that o'er their heights unfurled,
Bear death to kings, and freedom to the world,
I sing not you. A softer theme I choose,
A virgin theme, unconscious of the muse,
But fruitful, rich, well suited to inspire
The purest frenzy of poetic fire.

Despise it not, ye bards to terror steeled,
Who hurl your thunders round the epic field;
Nor ye who strain your midnight throats to sing
Joys that the vineyard and the stillhouse[6] bring;
Or on some distant fair your notes employ,
And speak of raptures that you ne'er enjoy.
I sing the sweets I know, the charms I feel,
My morning incense, and my evening meal,
The sweets of Hasty Pudding. Come, dear bowl,
Glide o'er my palate, and inspire my soul.
The milk beside thee, smoking from the kine,[7]
Its substance mingled, married in with thine,
Shall cool and temper thy superior heat,
And save the pains of blowing while I eat.
    Oh! could the smooth, the emblematic song
Flow like thy genial juices o'er my tongue,
Could those mild morsels in my numbers chime,
And, as they roll in substance, roll in rhyme,
No more thy awkward unpoetic name
Should shun the muse, or prejudice thy fame;
But rising grateful to the accustomed ear,
All bards should catch, and all realms revere!
    Assist me first with pious toil to trace
Through wrecks of time thy lineage and thy race;
Declare what lovely squaw, in days of yore,
(Ere great Columbus sought thy native shore)
First gave thee to the world; her works of fame
Have lived indeed, but lived without a name.
Some tawny Ceres,[8] goddess of her days,
First learned with stones to crack the well-dried maize,
Through the rough sieve to shake the golden shower,
In boiling water stir the yellow flour:
The yellow flour, bestrewed and stirred with haste,
Swells in the flood and thickens to a paste,
Then puffs and wallops,[9] rises to the brim,
Drinks the dry knobs that on the surface swim;
The knobs at last the busy ladle breaks,
And the whole mass its true consistence takes.
    Could but her sacred name, unknown so long,
Rise, like her labors, to the son of song,
To her, to them, I'd consecrate my lays,
And blow her pudding with the breath of praise.
If 'twas Oella,[10] whom I sang before,[11]
I here ascribe her one great virtue more.

Not through the rich Peruvian realms alone
The fame of Sol's[12] sweet daughter should be known,
But o'er the world's wide climes should live secure,
Far as his rays extend, as long as they endure.
    Dear Hasty Pudding, what unpromised joy
Expands my heart, to meet thee in Savoy!
Doomed o'er the world through devious paths to roam,
Each clime my country, and each house my home,
My soul is soothed, my cares have found an end,
I greet my long-lost, unforgotten friend.
    For thee through Paris, that corrupted town,
How long in vain I wandered up and down,
Where shameless Bacchus,[13] with his drenching hoard,
Cold from his cave usurps the morning board.
London is lost in smoke and steeped in tea;
No Yankee there can lisp the name of thee;
The uncouth word, a libel on the town,
Would call a proclamation from the crown.[14]
For climes oblique, that fear the sun's full rays,
Chilled in their fogs, exclude the generous maize;
A grain whose rich luxuriant growth requires
Short gentle showers, and bright ethereal fires.
    But here, though distant from our native shore,
With mutual glee we meet and laugh once more.
The same! I know thee by that yellow face,
That strong complexion of true Indian race,
Which time can never change, nor soil impair,
Nor Alpine snows, nor Turkey's morbid air;
For endless years, through every mild domain,
Where grows the maize, there thou art sure to reign.
    But man, more fickle, the bold incense claims,
In different realms to give thee different names.
Thee the soft nations round the warm Levant[15]
Polanta call, the French of course *polenta*;[16]
Ev'n in thy native regions, how I blush
To hear the Pennsylvanians call thee *mush*!
On Hudson's banks, while men of Belgic spawn[17]
Insult and eat thee by the name *suppawn*.[18]
All spurious appellations, void of truth;
I've better known thee from my earliest youth,
Thy name is *Hasty Pudding*! thus our sires
Were wont to greet thee fuming from their fires;
And while they argued in thy just defense

With logic clear, they thus explained the sense:
"In *haste* the boiling cauldron, o'er the blaze,
Receives and cooks the ready-powdered maize;
In *haste* 'tis served, and then in equal *haste*,
With cooling milk, we make the sweet repast.
No carving to be done, no knife to grate
The tender ear, and wound the stony plate;
But the smooth spoon, just fitted to the lip,
And taught with art the yielding mass to dip,
By frequent journeys to the bowl well stored,
Performs the hasty honors of the board."
Such is thy name, significant and clear,
A name, a sound to every Yankee dear,
But most to me, whose heart and palate chaste
Preserve my pure hereditary taste.

    There are who strive to stamp with disrepute
The luscious food, because it feeds the brute;
In tropes of high-strained wit, while gaudy prigs
Compare thy nursling, man, to pampered pigs;
With sovereign scorn I treat the vulgar jest,
Nor fear to share thy bounties with the beast.
What though the generous cow gives me to quaff
The milk nutritious; am I then a calf?
Or can the genius of the noisy swine,
Though nursed on pudding, thence lay claim to mine?
Sure the sweet song, I fashion to thy praise,
Runs more melodious than the notes they raise.

    My song resounding in its grateful glee,
No merit claims; I praise myself in thee.
My father loved thee through his length of days;
For thee his fields were shaded o'er with maize;
From thee what health, what vigor he possessed,
Ten sturdy freemen from his loins attest;
Thy constellation ruled my natal morn,
And all my bones were made of Indian corn.
Delicious grain! whatever form it take,
To roast or boil, to smother or to bake,
In every dish 'tis welcome still to me,
But most, my Hasty Pudding, most in thee.

    Let the green succotash with thee contend,
Let beans and corn their sweetest juices blend,
Let butter drench them in its yellow tide,
And a long slice of bacon grace their side;

Not all the plate, how famed soe'er it be,
Can please my palate like a bowl of thee.
  Some talk of hoe-cake, fair Virginia's pride,
Rich johnny-cake this mouth has often tried;
Both please me well, their virtues much the same;
Alike their fabric, as allied their fame,
Except in dear New England, where the last
Receives a dash of pumpkin in the paste,
To give it sweetness and improve the taste.
But place them all before me, smoking hot,
The big round dumpling rolling from the pot;
The pudding of the bag, whose quivering breast,
With suet lined, leads on the Yankee feast;
The charlotte brown,[19] within whose crusty sides
A belly soft the pulpy apple hides;
The yellow bread, whose face like amber glows,
And all of Indian that the bakepan knows
You tempt me not—my favorite greets my eyes,
To that loved bowl my spoon by instinct flies.

CANTO II

  To mix the food by vicious rules of art,
To kill the stomach and to sink the heart,
To make mankind to social virtue sour,
Cram o'er each dish, and be what they devour;
For this the kitchen muse first framed her book,
Commanding sweat to stream from every cook;
Children no more their antic gambols tried,
And friends to physic wondered why they died.
  Not so the Yankee—his abundant feast,
With simples furnished, and with plainness dressed,
A numerous offspring gathers round the board,
And cheers alike the servant and the lord;
Whose well-bought hunger prompts the joyous taste,
And health attends them from the short repast.
  While the full pail rewards the milkmaid's toil,
The mother sees the morning cauldron boil;
To stir the pudding next demands their care,
To spread the table and the bowls prepare;

To feed the children, as their portions cool,
And comb their heads, and send them off to school.
      Yet may the simplest dish some rules impart,
For nature scorns not all the aids of art.
Ev'n Hasty Pudding, purest of all food,
May still be bad, indifferent, or good,
As sage experience the short process guides,
Or want of skill, or want of care presides,
Who'er would form it on the surest plan,
To rear the child and long sustain the man;
To shield the morals while it mends the size,
And all the powers of every food supplies,
Attend the lessons that the muse shall bring.
Suspend your spoons, and listen while I sing.
      But since, O man! thy life and health demand
Not food alone, but labor from thy hand,
First in the field, beneath the sun's strong rays,
Ask of thy mother earth the needful maize;
She loves the race that courts her yielding soil,
And gives her bounties to the sons of toil.
      When now the ox, obedient to thy call,
Repays the loan that filled the winter stall,
Pursue his traces o'er the furrowed plain,
And plant in measured hills the golden grain.
But when the tender germs begins to shoot,
And the green spire declares the sprouting root,
Then guard your nursling from each greedy foe,
The insidious worm, the all-devouring crow.
A little ashes, sprinkled round the spire,
Soon steeped in rain, will bid the worm retire;
The feathered robber with his hungry maw
Swift flies the field before your man of straw,
A frightful image, such as schoolboys bring
When met to burn the Pope or hang the King.[20]
      Thrice in the season, through each verdant row
Wield the strong plowshare and the faithful hoe;
The faithful hoe, a double task that takes,
To till the summer corn, and roast the winter cakes.
      Slow springs the blade, while checked by chilling rains,
Ere yet the sun the seat of Cancer[21] gains;
But when his fiercest fires emblaze the land,
Then start the juices, then the roots expand;
Then, like a column of Corinthian mold,[22]

The stalk struts upward, and the leaves unfold;
The busy branches all the ridges fill,
Entwine their arms, and kiss from hill to hill.
Here cease to vex them, all your cares are done;
Leave the last labors to the parent sun;
Beneath his genial smiles the well-dressed field,
When autumn calls, a plenteous crop shall yield.

    Now the strong foliage bears the standards high,
And shoots the tall top-gallants to the sky;
The suckling ears their silky fringes bend,
And pregnant grown, their swelling coats distend;
The loaded stalk, while still the burden grows,
O'erhangs the space that runs between the rows;
High as a hop-field waves the silent grove,
A safe retreat for little thefts of love,
When the pledged roasting ears invite the maid,
To meet her swain beneath the new-formed shade;
His generous hand unloads the cumbrous hill,
And the green spoils her ready basket fill;
Small compensation for the two-fold bliss,
The promised wedding and the present kiss.

    Slight depredations these; but now the moon
Calls from his hollow tree the sly raccoon;
And while by night he bears his prize away,
The bolder squirrel labors through the day.
Both thieves alike, but provident of time,
A virtue rare, that almost hides their crime.
Then let them steal the little stores they can,
And fill their granaries from the toils of man;
We've one advantage where they take no part,
With all their wiles they ne'er have found the art
To boil the Hasty Pudding; here we shine
Superior far to tenants of the pine;
This envied boon to man shall still belong,
Unshared by them in substance or in song.

    At last the closing season browns the plain,
And ripe October gathers in the grain;
Deep loaded carts the spacious corn-house fill,
The sack distended marches to the mill;
The laboring mill beneath the burden groans,
And showers the future pudding from the stones;
Till the glad housewife greets the powdered gold,
And the new crop exterminates the old.

CANTO III

The days grow short; but though the falling sun
To the glad swain proclaims his day's work done,
Night's pleasing shades his various task prolong,
And yield new subjects to my various song.
For now, the corn-house filled, the harvest home,
The invited neighbors to the husking come;
A frolic scene, where work, and mirth, and play,
Unite their charms, to chase the hours away.

Where the huge heap lies centered in the hall,
The lamp suspended from the cheerful wall,
Brown corn-fed nymphs, and strong hard-handed beaux,
Alternate ranged, extend in circling rows,
Assume their seats, the solid mass attack;
The dry husks rustle, and the corncobs crack;
The song, the laugh, alternate notes resound,
And the sweet cider trips in silence round.

The laws of husking every wight²³ can tell;
And sure no laws he ever keeps so well:
For each red ear a general kiss he gains,
With each smut ear he smuts the luckless swains;²⁴
But when to some sweet maid a prize is cast,
Red as her lips, and taper as her waist,
She walks the round, and culls one favored beau,
Who leaps the luscious tribute to bestow.
Various the sport, as are the wits and brains
Of well-pleased lasses and contending swains;
Till the vast mound of corn is swept away,
And he that gets the last ear wins the day.

Meanwhile the housewife urges all her care,
The well-earned feast to hasten and prepare.
The sifted meal already waits her hand,
The milk is strained, the bowls in order stand,
The fire flames high; and, as a pool (that takes
The headlong stream that o'er the milldam breaks)
Foams, roars, and rages with incessant toils,
So the vexed cauldron rages, roars, and boils.

First with clean salt she seasons well the food,
Then strews the flour, and thickens all the flood.
Long o'er the simmering fire she lets it stand;

To stir it well demands a stronger hand;
The husband takes his turn; and round and round
The ladle flies: at last the toil is crowned;
When to the board the thronging huskers pour,
And take their seats as at the corn before.

     I leave them to their feast. There still belong
More copious matters to my faithful song.
For rules there are, though ne'er unfolded yet,
Nice[25] rules and wise, how pudding should be ate.

     Some with molasses line the luscious treat,
And mix, like bards, the useful with the sweet.
A wholesome dish, and well deserving praise,
A great resource in those bleak wintry days,
When the chilled earth lies buried deep in snow,
And raging Boreas[26] drives the shivering cow.

     Blessed cow! thy praise shall still my notes employ,
Great source of health, the only source of joy;
Mother of Egypt's God[27]—but sure, for me,
Were I to leave my God, I'd worship thee.
How oft thy teats these pious hands have pressed!
How oft thy bounties proved my only feast!
How oft I've fed thee with my favorite grain!
And roared, like thee, to find thy children slain!

     Ye swains who know her various worth to prize,
Ah! house her well from winter's angry skies.
Potatoes, pumpkins, should her sadness cheer,
Corn from your crib, and mashes from your beer;
When spring returns she'll well acquaint the loan,
And nurse at once your infants and her own.

     Milk then with pudding I should always choose;
To this in future I confine my muse,
Till she in haste some further hints unfold,
Well for the young, nor useless to the old.
First in your bowl the milk abundant take,
Then drop with care along the silver lake
Your flakes of pudding; these at first will hide
Their little bulk beneath the swelling tide;
But when their growing mass no more can sink,
When the soft island looms above the brink,
Then check your hand; you've got the portion's due,
So taught our sires, and what they taught is true.

     There is a choice in spoons. Though small appear
The nice distinction, yet to me 'tis clear.
The deep-bowled Gallic spoon, contrived to scoop

In ample draughts the thin diluted soup,
Performs not well in those substantial things,
Whose mass adhesive to the metal clings;
Where the strong labial muscles must embrace,
The gentle curve, and sweep the hollow space.
With ease to enter and discharge the freight,
A bowl less concave but still more dilate,
Becomes the pudding best. The shape, the size,
A secret rests unknown to vulgar eyes.
Experienced feeders can alone impart
A rule so much above the lore of art.
These tuneful lips that thousand spoons have tried,
With just precision could the point decide,
Though not in song; the must but poorly shines
In cones, and cubes, and geometric lines;
Yet the true form, as near as she can tell,
Is that small section of a goose-egg shell,
Which in two equal portions shall divide
The distance from the center to the side.
     Fear not to slaver; 'tis no deadly sin.
Like the free Frenchman, from your joyous chin
Suspend the ready napkin; or, like me,
Poise with one hand your bowl upon your knee;
Just in the zenith your wise head project,
Your full spoon, rising in a line direct,
Bold as a bucket, heeds no drops that fall,
The wide-mouthed bowl will surely catch them all.

Royall Tyler
(1757–1826)

Royall Tyler is known to literary history chiefly as the author of the first American comedy to have been publicly produced, The Contrast *(1787), though he also published a novel,* The Algerine Captive *(1797), and, in association with the Federalist critic Joseph Dennie, wrote plays, essays, and satirical poetry. But Tyler was also a distinguished jurist who eventually became chief justice of the Supreme Court of Vermont. As a lawyer and man of letters, Tyler was representative of a somewhat isolated but active literary culture in the late eighteenth century, including Governor Thomas Hutchinson, Hugh Henry Brackenridge, and Joel Barlow, that would, in form at least, extend to a modern writer like Wallace Stevens.*

Choice of a Wife (1796)

Fluttering lovers, giddy boys,
Sighing soft for Hymen's[1] joys,
Would you shun the tricking arts,
Beauty's traps for youthful hearts,
Would you treasure in a wife,
Riches, which shall last through life;
Would you in your choice be nice,
Hear Minerva's[2] sage advice.

Be not caught with shape, nor air,
Coral lips, nor flowing hair;
Shape and jaunty air may cheat,
Coral lips may speak deceit.
Girls unmask'd would you descry,
Fix your fancy on the eye;
NATURE there has truth design'd,
'Tis the eye, that speaks the mind.
Shun the proud, disdainful eye,
Frowning fancied dignity,
Shun the eye with vacant glare;
COLD INDIFFERENCE WINTERS THERE.

Shun the eager orb of fire
Gloating with impure desire;
Shun the wily eye of prude,
Looking coy to be pursued.
From the jilting eye refrain,
Glancing love, and now disdain.
Fly the fierce, satiric eye,
Shooting keen severity;
For Nature thus, her truth design'd
And made the eye proclaim the mind.

The Prologue to *The Contrast*

Written by a young gentleman of New-York, and spoken by Mr. Wignell.[1]

Exult, each patriot heart!—this night is shewn
A piece, which we may fairly call our own;
Where the proud titles of "My Lord! Your Grace!"
To humble *Mr.* and plain *Sir* give place.
Our Author pictures not from foreign climes
The fashions or the follies of the times;
But has confin'd the subject of his work
To the gay scenes—the circles of New-York.
On native themes his Muse displays her pow'rs;
If ours the faults, the virtues too are ours.

Why should our thoughts to distant countries roam,
When each refinement may be found at home?
Who travels now to ape the rich or great,
To deck an equipage and roll in state;
To court the graces, or to dance with ease,
Or by hypocrisy to strive to please?
Our free-born ancestors such arts despis'd;
Genuine sincerity alone they priz'd;
Their minds, with honest emulation fir'd,
To solid good—not ornament—aspir'd;
Or, if ambition rous'd a bolder flame,
Stern virtue throve, where indolence was shame.

But modern youths, with imitative sense,
Deem taste in dress the proof of excellence;
And spurn the meanness of your homespun arts,
Since homespun habits would obscure their parts;
Whilst all, which aims at splendour and parade,
Must come from Europe, *and be ready made.*
Strange! we should thus our native worth disclaim,
And check the progress of our rising fame.
Yet *one*, whilst imitation bears the sway,
Aspires to nobler heights, and points the way.
Be rous'd, my friends! his bold example view;
Let your own Bards be proud to copy *you*!
Should rigid critics reprobate our play,
At least the patriotic heart will say,
"Glorious our fall, since in a noble cause.
"The bold *attempt alone* demands applause."
Still may the wisdom of the Comic Muse
Exalt your merits, or your faults accuse.
But think not, 'tis her aim to be severe;—
We all are mortals, and as mortals err.
If candour pleases, we are truly blest;
Vice trembles, when compell'd to stand confess'd.
Let not light Censure on your faults offend,
Which aims not to expose them, but amend.
Thus does our Author to your candour trust;
Conscious, the *free* are generous, as just.

Hannah Webster Foster
(1758–1840)

*Hannah Foster was born and raised in Massachusetts before being sent
to a boarding school that provided the material for one of her two
books,* The Boarding School; or, Lessons of a Preceptress to Her Pupils
*(1798). Some years later, after settling in Boston, she was married to
the Rev. John Foster and bore him six children during the forty-five
years he served as pastor of the First Church in Brighton, Massachusetts.*

The Coquette; or, The Life and Letters of Eliza Wharton *(1797)
was an immediate success upon its publication and, along with Susanna Rowson's* Charlotte Temple *(1794) and William Hill Brown's
earlier* The Power of Sympathy *(1789), became one of the three best-
sellers of the 1790s. Utilizing the epistolary method Samuel Richardson had first developed in* Pamela *(1740), Foster based her novel of
temptation, seduction, confusion, and death in childbirth on the trag-
edy of a woman from Hartford, Connecticut, named Elizabeth Whitman, a distant cousin of her husband's, whose sad story was well
known by the time Foster published her novel. Unlike other sentimental novels, however, Foster does not moralize her tale by furnishing
her heroine with a suitable mate whom she rejects for a rake. Because
both of Eliza's marital choices are unsatisfactory, Foster lifts her story
above the tale of a fallen woman who must pay the price of her disgrace by confronting the dilemma experienced by so many women in
the eighteenth and nineteenth centuries, who found themselves echoing*

Eliza's lament that "Marriage is the tomb of friendship. It appears to me a very selfish state" (Letter 12).

from *The Coquette; or, The Life and Letters of Eliza Wharton.*

LETTER I.[1]

New Haven. To Miss Lucy Freeman.

An unusual sensation possesses my breast—a sensation which I once thought could never pervade it on any occasion whatever. It is *pleasure*, pleasure, my dear Lucy, on leaving my paternal roof. Could you have believed that the darling child of an indulgent and dearly-beloved mother would feel a gleam of joy at leaving her? But so it is. The melancholy, the gloom, the condolence which surrounded me for a month after the death of Mr. Haly had depressed my spirits, and palled every enjoyment of life. Mr. Haly was a man of worth—a man of real and substantial merit. He is, therefore, deeply and justly regretted by *his* friends. He was chosen to be a future guardian and companion for me, and was, therefore, beloved by *mine*. As their choice, as a good man, and a faithful friend, I esteemed him; but no one acquainted with the disparity of our tempers and dispositions, our views and designs, can suppose my heart much engaged in the alliance. Both nature and education had instilled into my mind an implicit obedience to the will and desires of my parents. To them, of course, I sacrificed my fancy in this affair, determined that my reason should concur with theirs, and on that to risk my future happiness. I was the more encouraged, as I saw, from our first acquaintance, his declining health, and expected that the event would prove as it has. Think not, however, that I rejoice in his death. No; far be it from me; for though I believe that I never felt the passion of love for Mr. Haly, yet a habit of conversing with him, of hearing daily the most virtuous, tender, and affectionate sentiments from his lips, inspired emotions of the sincerest friendship and esteem.

He is gone. His fate is unalterably, and I trust happily, fixed. He lived the life, and died the death, of the righteous. O that my last end may be like his! This event will, I hope, make a suitable and abiding impression upon my mind, teach me the fading nature of all sublunary enjoyments, and the little dependence which is to be placed on earthly felicity. Whose situation was more agreeable, whose prospects more flattering, than Mr. Haly's? Social, domestic, and connubial joys were fondly anticipated, and friends and fortune seemed ready to crown every wish; yet, animated by still brighter hopes, he cheerfully bade them all adieu. In conversation with me but a few days before his exit, "There is," said he, "but one link in the chain of life undissevered; that, my dear Eliza, is my attachment to you. But God is wise and good in all his ways; and in this, as in all other respects, I would cheerfully say, His will be done."

You, my friend, were witness to the concluding scene; and, therefore, I need not describe it.

I shall only add on the subject, that if I have wisdom and prudence to follow his advice and example, if his prayers for my temporal and eternal welfare be heard and answered, I shall be happy indeed.

The disposition of mind which I now feel I wish to cultivate. Calm, placid, and serene, thoughtful of my duty, and benevolent to all around me, I wish for no other connection than that of friendship.

This letter is all an egotism. I have even neglected to mention the respectable and happy friends with whom I reside, but will do it in my next. Write soon and often; and believe me sincerely yours,

ELIZA WHARTON.

LETTER II.

New Haven. To the same.

Time, which effaces every occasional impression, I find gradually dispelling the pleasing pensiveness which the melancholy event, the subject of my last, had diffused over my mind. Naturally cheerful, volatile, and unreflecting, the opposite disposition I have found to contain sources of enjoyment which I was before unconscious of possessing.

My friends here are the picture of conjugal felicity. The situation is delightful—the visiting parties perfectly agreeable. Every thing tends to facilitate the return of my accustomed vivacity. I have written to my mother, and received an answer. She praises my fortitude, and admires the philosophy which I have exerted under what she calls my heavy bereavement. Poor woman! she little thinks that my heart was untouched; and when that is unaffected, other sentiments and passions make but a transient impression. I have been, for a month or two, excluded from the gay world, and, indeed, fancied myself soaring above it. It is now that I begin to descend, and find my natural propensity for mixing in the busy scenes and active pleasures of life returning. I have received your letter—your moral lecture rather; and be assured, my dear, your monitorial lessons and advice shall be attended to. I believe I shall never again resume those airs which you term *coquettish*, but which I think deserve a softer appellation, as they proceed from an innocent heart, and are the effusions of a youthful and cheerful mind. We are all invited to spend the day to-morrow at Colonel Farington's, who has an elegant seat in this neighborhood. Both he and his lady are strangers to me; but the friends by whom I am introduced will procure me a welcome reception. Adieu.

ELIZA WHARTON.

LETTER III.

New Haven. To the same.

Is it time for me to talk again of conquests? or must I only enjoy them in silence? I must write to you the impulses of my mind, or I must not write at all. You are not so morose as to wish me to become a nun, would our country and religion allow it. I ventured, yesterday, to throw aside the habiliments of mourning, and to array myself in those more adapted to my taste. We arrived at Colonel Farington's about one o'clock. The colonel handed me out of the carriage, and introduced me to a large company assembled in the hall.

My name was pronounced with an *emphasis*, and I was received with the most flattering tokens of respect. When we were summoned to dinner, a young gentleman in a clerical dress offered me his hand, and led me to a table furnished with an elegant and sumptuous repast, with more gallantry and address than commonly fall to the share of students. He sat opposite me at table; and whenever I raised my eye, it caught his. The ease and politeness of his manners, with his particular attention to me, raised my curiosity, and induced me to ask Mrs. Laiton who he was. She told me that his name was Boyer; that he was descended from a worthy family; had passed with honor and applause through the university where he was educated; had since studied divinity with success; and now had a call to settle as a minister in one of the first parishes in a neighboring state.

The gates of a spacious garden were thrown open at this instant, and I accepted with avidity an invitation to walk in it. Mirth and hilarity prevailed, and the moments fled on downy wings, while we traced the beauties of Art and Nature, so liberally displayed and so happily blended in this delightful retreat. An enthusiastic admirer of scenes like these, I had rambled some way from the company, when I was followed by Mrs. Laiton to offer her condolence on the supposed loss which I had sustained in the death of Mr. Haly. My heart rose against the woman, so ignorant of human nature as to think such conversation acceptable at such a time. I made her little reply, and waved the subject, though I could not immediately dispel the gloom which it excited.

The absurdity of a custom authorizing people at a first interview to revive the idea of griefs which time has lulled, perhaps obliterated, is intolerable. To have our enjoyments arrested by the empty compliments of unthinking persons for no other reason than a compliance with fashion, is to be treated in a manner which the laws of humanity forbid.

We were soon joined by the gentlemen, who each selected his partner, and the walk was prolonged.

Mr. Boyer offered me his arm, which I gladly accepted, happy to be relieved from the impertinence of my female companion. We returned to tea; after which the ladies sung, and played by turns on the piano forte; while some of the gentlemen accompanied with the flute, the clarinet, and the violin, forming in the whole a very decent concert. An elegant supper, and half an hour's conversation after it, closed the evening; when we returned home, delighted with our entertainment, and pleased with ourselves and each other. My imagination is so impressed with the festive scenes of the day that Morpheus waves his ebon wand in vain. The evening is fine beyond the power of description; all Nature is serene and harmonious, in perfect unison with my present disposition of mind. I have been taking a retrospect of my past life, and, a few juvenile follies excepted, which I trust the recording angel has blotted out with a tear of charity, find an approving conscience and a heart at ease. Fortune, indeed, has not been very liberal of her gifts to me; but I presume on a large stock in the bank of friendship, which, united with health and innocence, give me some pleasing anticipations of future felicity. Whatever my fate may be, I shall always continue your

ELIZA WHARTON.

LETTER IV.

New Haven. To Mr. Selby.

You ask me, my friend, whether I am in pursuit of truth, or a lady. I answer, Both. I hope and trust they are united, and really expect to find Truth, and the Virtues and Graces besides, in a fair form. If you mean by the first part of your question whether I am searching into the sublimer doctrines of religion,—to these I would by no means be inattentive; but, to be honest, my studies of that kind have been very much interrupted of late. The respectable circle of acquaintances with which I am honored here has rendered my visits very frequent and numerous. In one of these I was introduced to Miss Eliza Wharton—a young lady whose elegant person, accomplished mind, and polished manners have been much celebrated. Her fame has often reached me; but, as the Queen of Sheba said to Solomon, the half was not told me. You will think that I talk in the style of a lover I confess it; nor am I ashamed to rank myself among the professed admirers of this lovely fair one. I am in no danger, however, of becoming an enthusiastic devotee. No; I mean I act upon just and rational principles. Expecting soon to settle in an eligible situation, if such a companion as I am persuaded she will make me may fall to my lot, I shall deem myself as happy as this state of imperfection will admit. She is now resident at General Richman's. The general and his lady are her particular friends; they are warm in her praises. They tell me, however, that she is naturally of a gay disposition. No matter for that; it is an agreeable quality, where there is discretion sufficient for its regulation. A cheerful friend, much more a cheerful wife, is peculiarly necessary to a person of a studious and sedentary life. They dispel the gloom of retirement, and exhilarate the spirits depressed by intense application. She was formerly addressed by the late Mr. Haly, of Boston. He was not, it seems, the man of her choice; but her parents were extremely partial to him, and wished the connection to take place. She, like a dutiful child, sacrificed her own inclination to their pleasure so far as to acquiesce in his visits. This she more easily accomplished, as his health, which declined from their first acquaintance, led her to suppose, as the event has proved, that he would not live to enter into any lasting engagements. Her father, who died some months before him, invited him to reside at his house for the benefit of a change of air, agreeably to the advice of his physicians. She attended him during his last illness with all the care and assiduity of a nurse and with all the sympathizing tenderness of a sister.

I have had several opportunities of conversing with her. She discovers an elevated mind, a ready apprehension, and an accurate knowledge of the various subjects which have been brought into view. I have not yet introduced the favorite subject of my heart. Indeed, she seems studiously to avoid noticing any expression which leads towards it; but she must hear it soon. I am sure of the favor and interest of the friends with whom she resides. They have promised to speak previously in my behalf. I am to call, as if accidentally, this afternoon just as they are to ride abroad. They are to refer me to Miss Wharton for entertainment till their return. What a delightful opportunity for my purpose! I am counting the hours—nay, the very moments. Adieu. You shall soon again hear from your most obedient,

J. BOYER.

LETTER V.

New Haven. To Miss Lucy Freeman.

These bewitching charms of mine have a tendency to keep my mind in a state of perturbation. I am so pestered with these admirers! Not that I am so very handsome neither; but, I don't know how it is, I am certainly very much the taste of the other sex. Followed, flattered, and caressed, I have cards and compliments in profusion. But I must try to be serious; for I have, alas! one serious lover. As I promised you to be particular in my writing, I suppose I must proceed methodically. Yesterday we had a party to dine. Mr. Boyer was of the number. His attention was immediately engrossed; and I soon perceived that every word, every action, and every look was studied to gain my approbation. As he sat next me at dinner, his assiduity and politeness were pleasing; and as we walked together afterwards, his conversation was improving. Mine was sentimental and sedate—perfectly adapted to the taste of my gallant. Nothing, however, was said particularly expressive of his apparent wishes. I studiously avoided every kind of discourse which might lead to this topic. I wish not for a declaration from any one, especially from one whom I could not repulse and do not intend to encourage at present. His conversation, so similar to what I had often heard from a similar character, brought a deceased friend to mind, and rendered me somewhat pensive. I retired directly after supper. Mr. Boyer had just taken leave.

Mrs. Richman came into my chamber as she was passing to her own. "Excuse my intrusion, Eliza," said she. "I thought I would just step in and ask you if you have passed a pleasant day."

"Perfectly so, madam; and I have now retired to protract the enjoyment by recollection." "What, my dear, is your opinion of our favorite, Mr. Boyer?" "Declaring him your favorite, madam, is sufficient to render me partial to him; but to be frank, independent of that, I think him an agreeable man." "Your heart, I presume, is now free." "Yes, and I hope it will long remain so." "Your friends, my dear, solicitous for your welfare, wish to see you suitably and agreeably connected." "I hope my friends will never again interpose in my concerns of that nature. You, madam, who have ever known my heart, are sensible that, had the Almighty spared life in a certain instance, I must have sacrificed my own happiness or incurred their censure. I am young, gay, volatile. A melancholy event has lately extricated me from those shackles which parental authority had imposed on my mind. Let me, then, enjoy that freedom which I so highly prize. Let me have opportunity, unbiased by opinion, to gratify my natural disposition in

a participation of those pleasures which youth and innocence afford."
"Of such pleasures, no one, my dear, would wish to deprive you; but
beware, Eliza! Though strewed with flowers, when contemplated by
your lively imagination, it is, after all, a slippery, thorny path. The
round of fashionable dissipation is dangerous. A phantom is often
pursued, which leaves its deluded votary the real form of wretchedness." She spoke with an emphasis, and, taking up her candle, wished
me a good night. I had not power to return the compliment. Something
seemingly prophetic in her looks and expressions cast a momentary
gloom upon my mind; but I despise those contracted ideas which confine virtue to a cell. I have no notion of becoming a recluse. Mrs.
Richman has ever been a beloved friend of mine; yet I always thought
her rather prudish. Adieu.

ELIZA WHARTON.

LETTER VIII.

New Haven. To Mr. Charles Deighton.

We had an elegant ball, last night, Charles; and what is still more
to the taste of your old friend, I had an elegant partner; one exactly
calculated to please my fancy—gay, volatile, apparently thoughtless
of every thing but present enjoyment. It was Miss Eliza Wharton—a
young lady whose agreeable person, polished manners, and refined
talents have rendered her the toast of the country around for these
two years; though for half that time she has had a clerical lover imposed on her by her friends; for I am told it was not agreeable to her
inclination. By this same clerical lover of hers she was for several
months confined as a nurse. But his death has happily relieved her;
and she now returns to the world with redoubled lustre. At present
she is a visitor to Mrs. Richman, who is a relation. I first saw her on
a party of pleasure at Mr. Frazier's, where we walked, talked, sang,
and danced together. I thought her cousin watched her with a jealous
eye; for she is, you must know, a prude; an immaculate—more so
than you or I—must be the man who claims admission to her society.
But I fancy this young lady is a coquette; and if so, I shall avenge my
sex by retaliating the mischiefs she meditates against us. Not that I
have any ill designs, but only to play off her own artillery by using a
little unmeaning gallantry. And let her beware of the consequences. A
young clergyman came in at General Richman's yesterday, while I was
waiting for Eliza, who was much more cordially received by the general and his lady than was your humble servant; but I lay that up.
When she entered the room, an air of mutual embarrassment was

evident. The lady recovered her assurance much more easily than the gentleman. I am just going to ride, and shall make it in my way to call and inquire after the health of my dulcinea. Therefore, adieu for the present.

PETER SANFORD.

LETTER XII.

New Haven. To Miss Lucy Freeman.

The heart of your friend is again besieged. Whether it will surrender to the assailants or not I am unable at present to determine. Sometimes I think of becoming a predestinarian, and submitting implicitly to fate, without any exercise of free will; but, as mine seems to be a wayward one, I would counteract the operations of it, if possible.

Mrs. Richman told me this morning that she hoped I should be as agreeably entertained this afternoon as I had been the preceding; that she expected Mr. Boyer to dine and take tea, and doubted not but he would be as attentive and sincere to me, if not as gay and polite, as the gentleman who obtruded his civilities yesterday. I replied that I had no reason to doubt the sincerity of the one or the other, having never put them to the test, nor did I imagine I ever should. "Your friends, Eliza," said she, "would be very happy to see you united to a man of Mr. Boyer's worth, and so agreeably settled as he has a prospect of being." "I hope," said I, "that my friends are not so weary of my company as to wish to dispose of me. I am too happy in my present connections to quit them for new ones. Marriage is the tomb of friendship. It appears to me a very selfish state. Why do people in general, as soon as they are married, centre all their cares, their concerns, and pleasures in their own families? Former acquaintances are neglected or forgotten; the tenderest ties between friends are weakened or dissolved; and benevolence itself moves in a very limited sphere." "It is the glory of the marriage state," she rejoined, "to refine by circumscribing our enjoyments. Here we can repose in safety.

> 'The friendships of the world are oft
> Confed'racies in vice, or leagues in pleasure:
> Ours has the purest virtue for its basis;
> And such a friendship ends not but with life.'

True, we cannot always pay that attention to former associates which we may wish; but the little community which we superintend is quite as important an object, and certainly renders us more beneficial to the public. True benevolence, though it may change its objects, is not limited by time or place. Its effects are the same, and, aided by a second self, are rendered more diffusive and salutary."

Some pleasantry passed, and we retired to dress. When summoned to dinner, I found Mr. Boyer below. If what is sometimes said be true, that love is diffident, reserved, and unassuming, this man must be tinctured with it. These symptoms were visible in his deportment when I entered the room. However, he soon recovered himself, and the conversation took a general turn. The festive board was crowned with sociability, and we found in reality "the feast of reason and the flow of soul." After we rose from table, a walk in the garden was proposed—an amusement we are all peculiarly fond of. Mr. Boyer offered me his arm. When at a sufficient distance from our company, he begged leave to congratulate himself on having an opportunity, which he had ardently desired for some time, of declaring to me his attachment, and of soliciting an interest in my favor; or, if he might be allowed the term, affection. I replied, "That, sir, is indeed laying claim to an important interest. I believe you must substitute some more indifferent epithet for the present." "Well, then," said he, "if it must be so, let it be esteem or friendship." "Indeed, sir," said I, "you are entitled to them both. Merit has always a share in that bank; and I know of none who has a larger claim on that score than Mr. Boyer." I suppose my manner was hardly serious enough for what he considered a weighty cause. He was a little disconcerted, but, soon regaining his presence of mind, entreated me, with an air of earnestness, to encourage his suit, to admit his addresses, and, if possible, to reward his love. I told him that this was rather a sudden affair to me, and that I could not answer him without consideration. "Well, then," said he, "take what time you think proper; only relieve my suspense as soon as may be. Shall I visit you again to-morrow?" "O, not so soon," said I; "next Monday, I believe, will be early enough. I will endeavor to be at home." He thanked me even for that favor, recommended himself once more to my kindness, and we walked towards the company, returned with them to the house, and he soon took leave. I immediately retired to write this letter, which I shall close without a single observation on the subject until I know your opinion.

Eliza Wharton.

LETTER XIII.

Hartford. To Miss Eliza Wharton.

And so you wish to have my opinion before you know the result of your own.

This is playing a little too much with my patience; but, however, I will gratify you this once, in hopes that my epistle may have a good effect. You will ask, perhaps, whether I would influence your judgment. I answer, No, provided you will exercise it yourself; but I am a little apprehensive that your fancy will mislead you. Methinks I can gather from your letters a predilection for this Major Sanford. But he is a rake, my dear friend; and can a lady of your delicacy and refinement think of forming a connection with a man of that character? I hope not; nay, I am confident you do not. You mean only to exhibit a few more girlish airs before you turn matron; but I am persuaded, if you wish to lead down the dance of life with regularity, you will not find a more excellent partner than Mr. Boyer. Whatever you can reasonably expect in a lover, husband, or friend, you may perceive to be united in this worthy man. His taste is undebauched, his manners not vitiated, his morals uncorrupted. His situation in life is, perhaps, as elevated as you have a right to claim. Forgive my plainness, Eliza. It is the task of friendship, sometimes, to tell disagreeable truths. I know your ambition is to make a distinguished figure in the first class of polished society, to shine in the gay circle of fashionable amusements, and to bear off the palm amidst the votaries of pleasure. But these are fading honors, unsatisfactory enjoyments, incapable of gratifying those immortal principles of reason and religion which have been implanted in your mind by Nature, assiduously cultivated by the best of parents, and exerted, I trust, by yourself. Let me advise you, then, in conducting this affair,—an affair big, perhaps, with your future fate,—to lay aside those coquettish airs which you sometimes put on; and remember that you are not dealing with a fop, who will take advantage of every concession, but with a man of sense and honor, who will properly estimate your condescension and frankness. Act, then, with that modest freedom, that dignified unreserve, which bespeak conscious rectitude and sincerity of heart.

I shall be extremely anxious to hear the process and progress of this business. Relieve my impatience as soon as possible; and believe me yours with undissembled affection.

LUCY FREEMAN.

LETTER XVIII.

New Haven. To Mr. Charles Deighton.

Do you know, Charles, that I have commenced lover? I was always a general one, but now I am somewhat particular. I shall be the more interested, as I am likely to meet with difficulties; and it is the glory of a rake, as well as of a Christian, to combat obstacles. This same Eliza, of whom I have told you, has really made more impression on my heart than I was aware of, or than the sex, take them as they rise, are wont to do. But she is besieged by a priest—a likely lad though. I know not how it is, but they are commonly successful with the girls, even the gayest of them. This one, too, has the interest of all her friends, as I am told. I called yesterday at General Richman's, and found this pair together, apparently too happy in each other's society for my wishes. I must own that I felt a glow of jealousy, which I never experienced before, and vowed revenge for the pain it gave me, though but momentary. Yet Eliza's reception of me was visibly cordial; nay, I fancied my company as pleasing to her as that which she had before. I tarried not long, but left him to the enjoyment of that pleasure which I flatter myself will be but shortlived. O, I have another plan in my head—a plan of necessity, which, you know, is the mother of invention. It is this: I am very much courted and caressed by the family of Mr. Lawrence, a man of large property in this neighborhood. He has only one child—a daughter, with whom I imagine the old folks intend to shackle me in the bonds of matrimony. The girl looks very well; she has no soul, though, that I can discover; she is heiress, nevertheless, to a great fortune, and that is all the soul I wish for in a wife. In truth, Charles, I know of no other way to mend my circumstances. But lisp not a word of my embarrassments for your life. Show and equipage are my hobby horse; and if any female wishes to share them with me, and will furnish me with the means of supporting them, I have no objection. Could I conform to the sober rules of wedded life, and renounce those dear enjoyments of dissipation in which I have so long indulged, I know not the lady in the world with whom I would sooner form a connection of this sort than with Eliza Wharton. But it will never do. If my fortune or hers were better, I would risk a union, but as they are, no idea of the kind can be admitted. I shall endeavor, notwithstanding, to enjoy her company as long as possible. Though I cannot possess her wholly myself, I will not tamely see her the property of another.

I am now going to call at General Richman's, in hopes of an opportunity to profess my devotion to her. I know I am not a welcome visitor to the family; but I am independent of their censure or esteem, and mean to act accordingly.

PETER SANFORD.

LETTER LXV.[2]

Hartford. To Mr. Charles Deighton.

Good news, Charles, good news! I have arrived to the utmost bounds of my wishes—the full possession of my adorable Eliza. I have heard a quotation from a certain book, but what book it was I have forgotten, if I ever knew. No matter for that; the quotation is, that "stolen waters are sweet, and bread eaten in secret is pleasant." If it has reference to the pleasures which I have enjoyed with Eliza, I like it hugely, as Tristram Shandy's father said of Yorick's sermon; and I think it fully verified.

I had a long and tedious siege. Every method which love could suggest, or art invent, was adopted. I was sometimes ready to despair, under an idea that her resolution was unconquerable, her virtue impregnable. Indeed, I should have given over the pursuit long ago, but for the hopes of success I entertained from her parleying with me, and, in reliance upon her own strength, endeavoring to combat and counteract my designs. Whenever this has been the case, Charles, I have never yet been defeated in my plan. If a lady will consent to enter the lists against the antagonist of her honor, she may be sure of losing the prize. Besides, were her delicacy genuine, she would banish the man at once who presumed to doubt, which he certainly does who attempts to vanquish it. But far be it from me to criticize the pretensions of the sex. If I gain the rich reward of my dissimulation and gallantry, that, you know, is all I want.

To return, then, to the point. An unlucky, but not a miraculous accident has taken place which must soon expose our amour. What can be done? At the first discovery, absolute distraction seized the soul of Eliza, which has since terminated in a fixed melancholy. Her health, too, is much impaired. She thinks herself rapidly declining, and I tremble when I see her emaciated form.

My wife has been reduced very low of late. She brought me a boy a few weeks past, a dead one though.

These circumstances give me neither pain nor pleasure. I am too much engrossed by my divinity to take an interest in any thing else. True, I have lately suffered myself to be somewhat engaged here and there by a few jovial lads who assist me in dispelling the anxious thoughts which my perplexed situation excites. I must, however, seek

some means to relieve Eliza's distress. My finances are low; but the
last fraction shall be expended in her service, if she need it.

Julia Granby is expected at Mrs. Wharton's every hour. I fear that
her inquisitorial eye will soon detect our intrigue and obstruct its continuation. Now, there's a girl, Charles, I should never attempt to seduce; yet she is a most alluring object, I assure you. But the dignity of
her manners forbids all assaults upon her virtue. Why, the very expression of her eye blasts in the bud every thought derogatory to her
honor, and tells you plainly that the first insinuation of the kind would
be punished with eternal banishment and displeasure. Of her there is
no danger. But I can write no more, except that I am, &c.,

PETER SANFORD.

LETTER LXVIII.[3]

Tuesday. To Mrs. M. Wharton.

My honored and dear mamma: In what words, in what language
shall I address you? What shall I say on a subject which deprives me
of the power of expression? Would to God I had been totally deprived
of that power before so fatal a subject required its exertion. Repentance comes too late, when it cannot prevent the evil lamented: for
your kindness, your more than maternal affection towards me, from
my infancy to the present moment, a long life of filial duty and un-
erring rectitude could hardly compensate. How greatly deficient in
gratitude must I appear, then, while I confess that precept and example, counsel and advice, instruction and admonition, have been all
lost upon me!

Your kind endeavors to promote my happiness have been repaid
by the inexcusable folly of sacrificing it. The various emotions of
shame and remorse, penitence and regret, which torture and distract
my guilty breast, exceed description. Yes, madam, your Eliza has
fallen, fallen indeed. She has become the victim of her own indiscretion, and of the intrigue and artifice of a designing libertine, who is
the husband of another. She is polluted, and no more worthy of her
parentage. She flies from you, not to conceal her guilt, (that she humbly and penitently owns,) but to avoid what she has never experienced,
and feels herself unable to support—a mother's frown; to escape the
heartrending sight of a parent's grief, occasioned by the crimes of her
guilty child.

I have become a reproach and disgrace to my friends. The consciousness of having forfeited their favor and incurred their disappro-
bation and resentment induces me to conceal from them the place of

my retirement; but lest your benevolence should render you anxious for my comfort in my present situation, I take the liberty to assure you that I am amply provided for.

I have no claim even upon your pity; but from my long experience of your tenderness, I presume to hope it will be extended to me. O my mother, if you knew what the state of my mind is, and has been for months past, you would surely compassionate my case. Could tears efface the stain which I have brought upon my family, it would long since have been washed away; but, alas! tears are in vain; and vain is my bitter repentance; it cannot obliterate my crime, nor restore me to innocence and peace. In this life I have no ideas of happiness. These I have wholly resigned. The only hope which affords me any solace is that of your forgiveness. If the deepest contrition can make an atonement,—if the severest pains, both of body and mind, can restore me to your charity,—you will not be inexorable. O, let my sufferings be deemed a sufficient punishment, and add not the insupportable weight of a parent's wrath. At present I cannot see you. The effect of my crime is too obvious to be longer concealed, to elude the invidious eye of curiosity. This night, therefore, I leave your hospitable mansion. This night I become a wretched wanderer from my paternal roof. O that the grave were this night to be my lodging! Then should I lie down and be at rest. Trusting in the mercy of God, through the mediation of his Son, I think I could meet my heavenly Father with more composure and confidence than my earthly parent.

Let not the faults and misfortunes of your daughter oppress your mind. Rather let the conviction of having faithfully discharged your duty to your lost child support and console you in this trying scene.

Since I wrote the above, you have kindly granted me your forgiveness, though you knew not how great, how aggravated was my offence. You forgive me, you say. O, the harmonious, the transporting sound! It has revived my drooping spirits, and will enable me to encounter, with resolution, the trials before me.

Farewell, my dear mamma![4] Pity and pray for your ruined child; and be assured that affection and gratitude will be the last sentiments which expire in the breast of your repenting daughter,

ELIZA WHARTON.

Susanna Haswell Rowson
(1762?–1824)

Though born in England, Susanna Haswell Rowson was raised in America and then returned to England where she published five novels, including Charlotte Temple *(1791), to little critical acclaim. It was only after she re-emigrated to the United States in 1793 and arranged for* Charlotte Temple's *publication here that the book, like her career, took off. Though* Charlotte Temple *was but one of ten novels Rowson produced in a busy writing life, along with six theatrical works, two volumes of poetry, six textbooks for her "Young Ladies Academy" in Boston, and a host of songs, it was phenomenally successful. The best-selling book in America before the publication of Harriet Beecher Stowe's* Uncle Tom's Cabin *(1852), it had gone into more than 200 editions by the twentieth century and shows no signs of losing its interest. Though the novel is much too long to reprint here, its "Author's Preface" may explain some of the sources of that interest. Setting itself the task—like other works in the tradition of sentimental fiction initiated by Samuel Richardson's* Clarissa—*of warning its readers about the ways of the world and particularly of the wiles of men, it helped create, even as it found, an immense and grateful audience composed primarily of women who discovered in the book's cautionary intent and sympathetic understanding some of the terms of a new sisterhood.*

The Author's Preface to Charlotte: A Tale of Truth (1794)

For the perusal of the young and thoughtless of the fair sex, this Tale of Truth is designed; and I could wish my fair readers to consider it as not merely the effusion of Fancy, but as a reality. The circumstances on which I have founded this novel were related to me some little time since by an old lady who had personally known Charlotte, though she concealed the real names of the characters, and likewise the place where the unfortunate scenes were acted: yet as it was impossible to offer a relation to the public in such an imperfect state, I have thrown over the whole a slight veil of fiction, and substituted names and places according to my own fancy. The principal characters in this little tale are now consigned to the silent tomb: it can therefore hurt the feelings of no one; and may, I flatter myself, be of service to some who are so unfortunate as to have neither friends to advise, or understanding to direct them, through the various and unexpected evils that attend a young and unprotected woman in her first entrance into life.

While the tear of compassion still trembled in my eye for the fate of the unhappy Charlotte, I may have children of my own, said I, to whom this recital may be of use, and if to your own children, said Benevolence, why not to the many daughters of Misfortune who, deprived of natural friends, or spoilt by a mistaken education, are thrown on an unfeeling world without the least power to defend themselves from the snares not only of the other sex, but from the more dangerous arts of the profligate of their own.

Sensible as I am that a novel writer, at a time when such a variety of works are ushered into the world under that name stands but a poor chance for fame in the annals of literature, but conscious that I wrote with a mind anxious for the happiness of that sex whose morals and conduct have so powerful an influence on mankind in general; and convinced that I have not wrote a line that conveys a wrong idea to the head or a corrupt wish to the heart, I shall rest satisfied in the purity of my own intentions, and if I merit not applause, I feel that I dread not censure.

If the following tale should save one hapless fair one from the error which ruined poor Charlotte, or rescue from impending misery the heart of one anxious parent, I shall feel a much higher gratification in reflecting on this trifling performance, than could possibly result from the applause which might attend the most elegant finished piece of literature whose tendency might deprave the heart or mislead the understanding.

EXPLANATORY NOTES

How the World Was Made

1. In the Cherokee belief system, the world consists of several levels, including earth, an underworld, and heaven. Gălûn'lătĭ is between earth and heaven.

How the Spaniards Came to Shung-opovi

1. Coronado, in 1540, was the first Spaniard to visit the Hopi.
2. The Hopi believed that the Bahana, a fair-skinned hero exiled in the east, would return to them, bringing peace and prosperity.
3. The exact identity of this priest is unknown; most likely he is a conflated figure representing the wrongs of several individuals.
4. On August 13, 1680, the Pueblo Indian communities successfully revolted, ending Spanish control of the region until 1692.

The Saga of Eric the Red

1. Olaf was king of Norway from 995 to 1000.
2. Most likely maple.

A Letter to Lord Raphael Sanchez

1. Actually thirty-three days; the error probably arises from a misprint.
2. Columbus thought it was a province of China.
3. Puerto Gibara.
4. Tenerife, one of the Canary Islands.
5. *Castellanos* are worth about $7.50; *blancas* are copper coins worth less than a penny.

6. Twenty-five pounds.
7. A long rowboat.
8. The island of Dominica, whose Carib name is Charis or Caire.
9. Martinique.
10. The Genoan government.

The Narrative of
Alvar Nuñez Cabeza de Vaca

1. The sweet-gum tree.
2. An opossum.
3. Tescuco is better known as Tezcoco, in Mexico City. Don Pedro is thought to be an Aztec prince, the brother of the heir to the throne who was dispossessed by his father. Allied with his brother and Cortés, he commanded the army against the Aztecs in the final battle for Mexico City.
4. The reference is to eastern Texas.
5. Ambushes.
6. An early handgun.
7. Passages so narrow people can only pass in single file.

Narrative of the Expedition of Coronado

1. "Red house," in Aztec, located in what is now southern Arizona.
2. San Miguel Culiacan in central Sinaloa, in northwestern Mexico.
3. The Zuni River in Arizona.
4. A war cry invoking Saint James.

Of Cannibals

1. Brazil, where Villegaigon landed in 1557.
2. "The ivy grows best spontaneously; the arbutus best in shady caves; and the wild notes of birds are sweeter than art can teach" (Propertius, i.2, 10).
3. "Men fresh from the gods" (Seneca, *Epistles* 90).
4. "These were the manners first taught by nature" (Virgil, *Georgics*, ii.20).
5. "No victory is complete, which the conquered do not admit to be so" (Claudius, *De Sexto Consulatu Honorii*, v.248).

To the Virginian Voyage

1. Female deer.
2. Aeolius, the god of the winds.
3. Seeing, with the sense of "knowing."

A Modell of Christian Charity

1. Matthew 5:43 and 19:19.
2. In Genesis 18:1–2, Abraham entertains the angels. The "old man of Gibea" is from Judges 19:16–21.
3. Galatians 6:10.
4. Luke 18:22.
5. Actually 2 Corinthians 8:1–4.
6. These were followers of Pater Valdes, who, rejecting the authority of the Pope, taught that the Bible was the sole source of authority in religion.
7. Pope Pius II, who reigned from 1458 to 1464.
8. Micah 6:8.
9. Ephesians 4:3–4.
10. Matthew 5:14–15.

John Winthrop's Christian Experience

1. Winthrop entered Trinity College at age fourteen, where he remained, apparently, for two years.
2. William Perkins, author of *A Declaration of the State of Grace and Condemnation* and celebrated among the Puritans.

Of Plymouth Plantation

1. Officials in the Church of England who enforced religious conformity.
2. An allusion to Proverbs 24:34.
3. Leyden, in the Netherlands.
4. This truce, signed in 1609, was to expire in 1621.
5. See Ruth 1:14.
6. An allusion to Lamentations 3:27.
7. Now Provincetown Harbor.
8. A Roman Stoic philosopher and statesman.
9. The mountain from which God showed Moses the Promised Land (Gilead). See Deuteronomy 33:34, 34:1–4.
10. A small, single-masted boat.
11. Psalms 107:1–5, 8.
12. The Mayflower Compact.
13. The Phillistines' false idol in I Samuel 5.

The New English Canaan

1. The year of our prosperity.
2. A laurel tree into which Daphne, according to the Greek myth, was supposed to have been transformed.
3. The "little neck of land" of the Massachusetts Indians, located below Boston.
4. Morton's settlement was at Mount Wollaston, sometimes called Merry Mount. To please himself, Morton changed the name to Mare Mount, suggesting among other things a place by the sea.
5. This is May 1, or May Day, a blend of the spring festivals of ancient cultures and of the feast of Saint Philip and Saint James, whose name is Jacob in Latin.
6. Morton refers to himself throughout the work in the third person, as "mine host."
7. A name for the Puritans of Plymouth colony.
8. See Exodus 32 and Deuteronomy 9:13–21. The golden calf made by the Israelites at Mount Horeb was subsequently destroyed by Moses.
9. The cupbearer to Jupiter/Zeus.
10. The god of marriage.
11. Latin for "hail."
12. An allusion to Matthew 23:23.
13. The box Aphrodite gave to Phaon for ferrying her from Lesbos to Chios, which contained an elixir that restored his youth.
14. A counterfeit coin.
15. Captain Miles Standish, who was short and stout.
16. A red liqueur.
17. One of the giants in Greek mythology who fought with the gods.
18. A judge of the underworld in Greek mythology.

The Examination of Mrs. Ann Hutchinson

1. Thomas Shephard, a colonial leader, was a minister at Cambridge and author of "The Covenant of Grace" (see pages 170–74).
2. An assistant to the synod.
3. An assistant to the synod.
4. An assistant to the synod.
5. An assistant to the synod.
6. A minister of Roxbury.
7. A minister of Roxbury.
8. Mr. Hugh Peters, a minister of Salem.
9. A deputy, probably of Ipswich.

The Prologue

1. Guillaume du Bartas (1544–1599), a French poet much admired by the Puritans.
2. Demosthenes (384–322 B.C.), an orator and statesman in Athens who overcame a speech impediment.

The Author to Her Book

1. Common people.

Before the Birth of One of Her Children

1. Stepmother's.
2. Body, corpse.

Contemplations

1. Decorated.
2. Acorn.
3. An allusion to Psalms 19:5.
4. Circumstances.
5. A place of judgment.
6. From Genesis 4:16, the land east of Eden where Cain lived after killing Abel.
7. The sea.
8. From time to time.
9. Roman god of the ocean.
10. A nightingale.
11. Painful.
12. An allusion to Revelation 2:17.

To My Dear and Loving Husband

1. Then pronounced "per-SEver," to rhyme with "ever."

A Letter to Her Husband, Absent Upon Public Employment

1. Ipswich, Massachusetts, north of Boston, where the Bradstreets lived for approximately ten years.
2. The tenth zodiacal sign, signaling winter.
3. The fourth zodiacal sign, signifying summer.
4. An allusion to Genesis 2:23.

In Memory of My Dear Grand-child
Elizabeth Bradstreet

1. Since.

Here Follows Some Verses upon the Burning
of Our House

1. Possessions or wealth somewhat ill-gotten.

A Brief Recognition

1. Engrafted.
2. An allusion to the Antinomians, as Ann Hutchinson, Roger Williams, and others were known.
3. The supposed source of human affections.
4. Probably a reference to, among other events, the founding of the Third Church in Boston, in 1669, by unhappy members of the First Church
5. Numbers 17:31–32.

God's Controversy with New-England

1. Enemies of the Israelites.
2. An allusion to Psalms 146:8.
3. Pitched, like a tent.
4. Overcast skies.
5. In Puritan terms, aids to worship.
6. Savage spirits.
7. A reference to the manna given to the Israelites in Exodus 16:32, which was later interpreted as a prefiguration of Christ as the living bread (John 6:51).
8. An allusion to Revelation 6:14, in which it is predicted that heaven will deport as a scroll rolled-up.
9. An allusion to Amos 2:12–13.
10. Irresponsible behavior.
11. Despite.

A Narrative of the Captivity

1. Because of changes to the calendar, Rowlandson's date is our Thursday, February 20, 1676.
2. John Ball and his family.
3. Projections for fortification.
4. Psalms 46:8.

5. Ephraim Roper, though, unknown to Rowlandson, three children of the Kettle family also escaped.
6. Massachusetts Bay.
7. On August 22, 1675, the Nashaway Indians, led by Monoco or One-Eyed John, attacked Lancaster.
8. The group moved to Princeton, Massachusetts, on February 11 (Rowlandson's dates).
9. Between February 12 and February 27, the group moved to camp at a stronghold of the Quabaug Indians, Wenimesset or Meminimisset, now New Braintree, Massachusetts.
10. On September 4, 1675, Captain Richard Beers and his company, attempting to save the Northfield Garrison, were waylaid by over one hundred native warriors; of the 37 men, Beers and 19 others were killed and Pepper taken captive.
11. Job 16:1–2.
12. Rowlandson became a servant to Quinnapin's wife, Weetamoo, otherwise known as the Queen of Pocasset.
13. Jacob's lament in Genesis 42:36.
14. Psalms 27:14.
15. Between Monday, February 28, and Friday, March 3, the group moved to the Native American village of Nichewaug.
16. The group moved to Squakeag, near Northfield.
17. Proverbs 27:7.
18. The group moved to Princeton, Massachusetts, from Friday, April 28, to Tuesday, May 2.
19. Amos 3:6.
20. Amos 6:6–7.
21. On the road to Marlborough; all the houses in Lancaster had been burned.
22. Ecclesiastes 10:19.
23. Actually Psalms 6:6.

God's Determinations Concerning His Elect

1. Grooved.
2. An allusion to Job 38:4–8.
3. Girded.
4. Emerald green.
5. A ball of wool yarn.
6. To measure out or apportion.
7. A species of couch-grass or weed. A wand is a stick used for whipping.
8. Stick used for whipping.
9. To fetch.
10. To scold or rebuke.
11. An allusion to Song of Solomon 2:10–14, 5:2, and 6:9.

12. An allusion to George Herbert's "The Search."
13. To torture by exerting pressure.
14. A tuning peg on a stringed instrument, which can also be associated with a torture rack.
15. An allusion to Genesis 3:15.
16. See Daniel 3.
17. See Exodus 17:6.

Preparatory Meditations

1. Discerning.
2. On a decaying body.
3. A lawyer.
4. Witnesses.
5. Dismisses.
6. "According to the form of poverty," a legal procedure that allows an impoverished person to sue without fear of court costs if he loses.
7. Pustules.
8. Bit on a horse's bridle.

Occasional Poems

1. *Occasional Poems* constitute a section of eight numbered poems copied on a torn fragment in the manuscript of Taylor's "Poetical Works." These poems, probably copied in the early 1680s, are preceded by the heading "occurrants [or allegorizations of natural events] occasioning what follow."
2. The whorlepin holds the whorle, a small flywheel used to regulate the speed of a spinning wheel's spindle.
3. Peevish.
4. The part of a spinning wheel that holds the raw wool.
5. The wheel of the spinning wheel, which twists fibers into thread or yarn.
6. The spool of a spinning wheel, on which thread or yarn is wound.
7. Bobbins or spools.
8. Mills where the cloth is cleaned with fuller's earth or soap.
9. Ornamented by cutting.
10. A receptacle for burning incense.
11. "Foolish fire": a Latin term for the natural phosphorescence over swamps, which could lead unwary travelers astray.

The Diary of Samuel Sewall

1. Giles Corey, about eighty years old according to contemporary witnesses, was executed by having heavy stones laid on his chest until he suffocated.
2. At this point, confession insured immunity from trial, imprisonment, or execution.
3. Cotton Mather's *The Wonders of the Invisible World*.
4. Massachusetts set this day aside as a day of atonement and fasting for the execution of the witches; Sewall was the only public official involved who made a public confession of his error.
5. The court the governor instituted in May 1692 "to enquire, hear, and determine all manner of crimes and offenses."
6. Hannah Hull Sewall died on October 19, 1717; Sewall married Abigail Tilley on October 29, 1719, who died within a year. A few months after her death, Sewall began courting Mary Winthrop but married instead Mary Gibbs on March 29, 1722, who survived him.
7. A week later.
8. Madam Mico was Madam Winthrop's sister, Mary, who had been a widow since 1718.
9. Prison.
10. Wine from the Canary Islands.
11. The book's title is *Bowels Opened: Or a Discovery of the Neere and Deere Love . . . Between Christ and the Church*.
12. "The Lord will provide."
13. Madam Winthrop.
14. Foolish.
15. In not refueling the fire, she is signaling for Sewall to leave.

The Selling of Joseph

1. This story is found in Genesis, chaps. 37–50, and tells of the resentment Joseph aroused in his brothers because of the special favor he found in their father's heart. Cast into a pit to die, he was found by traveling merchants who sold him into slavery. Though Joseph pleased his master, he was falsely accused by his master's wife and thrown into prison, where he became famous as an interpreter of dreams. Eventually released, Joseph then prospered and was soon approached by his brothers, now unaware of his identity, for assistance. When Joseph made himself known to them, he forgave them and was reconciled with his father in his old age.
2. Paul Baynes, *A Commentary Upon the First Chapter of the Epistle of Saint Paul to the Ephesians* (1618).
3. Any dark-skinned person.

4. "More precious than all the gold in the world."
5. "Let the purchaser beware!"
6. Blood that seeps out of normal vessels and into nearby tissues.
7. Europeans held in slavery in Africa.

Magnalia Christi Americana

1. "This I say for the benefit of those who may happen to read the book"—Theodoret, (393?–457) a Greek Orthodox bishop and church historian.
2. An allusion to George Herbert's "The Church Militant."
3. Harvard University.
4. Creoles, that is, people of European or African descent naturalized in America.
5. Ancient Greek author (430?–355? B.C.).
6. Pierre de la Ramee (1515–1572), a French philosopher and eventual convert to Protestantism whose logic became the standard method of disputation for several generations of New England divines.
7. Matthew 25:30.
8. The second shield-bearer; Bradford was the second governor of the Plymouth colony.
9. "His watchfulness guards others' sleep; his labor, their rest; his diligence, their enjoyments; his constancy, their leisure."
10. John Bradford (1510?–1555), an English essayist and theologian who was burned at the stake during the religious persecutions of Mary Tudor's reign (1553–1558).
11. Boston, England.
12. Luke 4:4.
13. A reference to the Edict of Nantes (1598), which allowed freedom of worship in France while preserving the authority of the Crown.
14. After Robert Browne (c.1550–1633), who believed that discipline was an essential element of the true church.
15. A Protestant sect that held infant baptism invalid and argued for the separation of church and state.
16. See Acts 9:3–5.
17. "If only I might reach a similar end to life!"
18. The Greek epitaph from Plato, included by Mather, translates, "The shepherd is the provider of the human flock."

The Sot-Weed Factor

1. A plant that makes one besotted, or drunk; the reference here is to tobacco.
2. By the *Cape*, is meant the *Capes of Virginia*, the first Land on the

Coast of *Virginia and Maryland*. [Cook's own annotation from the
original publication; hereafter so designated]

3. To *Cove* is to lie at Anchor safe in Harbour. [Cook]

4. The Bay of *Piscato-way*, the usual place where our Ships come to
Anchor in *Mary-Land*. [Cook]

5. The Planters generally wear Blue *Linnen*. [Cook]

6. The gallows.

7. A *Canoo* is an *Indian* Boat, cut out of the body of a Popler-Tree.
[Cook]

8. Wolves are very numerous in *Mary-Land*. [Cook]

9. 'Tis supposed by the Planters, that all unknown Persons are run away
from some Master. [Cook]

10. Syder-pap is a sort of Food made of Syder and small Homine, like
our Oatmeal. [Cook]

11. Pon is bread made of *Indian Corn*. [Cook]

12. Mush is a sort of Hasty-Pudding made with Water and *Indian*
Flower. [Cook]

13. Homine is a Dish that is made of boiled *Indian* Wheat, eaten with
Molossus, or Bacon-Fat. [Cook]

14. Pipe.

15. 'Tis the Custom of Servants to be obliged for four Years to very
servile Work, after which time they have their Freedom. [Cook]

16. These are the general Excuses made by *English* Women, which are
sold, or sell themselves to *Mary-Land*. [Cook]

17. Beds stand in the Chimney-corner in this Country. [Cook]

18. Frogs are called *Virginea* Bells, and make, (both in that Country and
in *Mary-Land*) during the Night, a very hoarse ungrateful noise.
[Cook]

19. A reference to one of Aesop's fables.

20. A reference to the French romance "Valentine and Orson," in which
the abandoned infant Orson is suckled by a bear.

21. Cockerouse, is a Man of Quality. [Cook]

22. Musmilleon Vines are what we call Muskmilleon Plants. [Cook]

23. Ælthon is one of the Poetical Horses of the Sun. [Cook]

24. Chinces are a sort of Vermin like our Bugs in England. [Cook]

25. Wild Turkies are very good Meat, and prodigiously large in *Mary-
land*. [Cook]

26. A card game.

27. The highest card.

28. Prostitution.

29. Succahana is Water. [Cook]

30. A Goad grows upon as Indian Vine, resembling a Bottle, when ripe
is hollow; this the Planters make use of to drink Water out of. [Cook]

31. A medicine.

32. This Fellow was an Apothecary, and turn'd an Attorney at Law.
[Cook]

33. The *Yaws* is the *Pox*. [Cook]
34. The Chief of *Mary-land* containing about twenty four *Houses*. [Cook]
35. There is a Law in this Country, the Plantiff may pay his Debt in Country pay, which consists in the produce of his Plantation. [Cook]
36. The homeward bound fleet meets here. [Cook]
37. The Author does not intend by this, any of the *English* Gentlemen resident there. [Cook]

Report Made by Reverend Father
Fray Carlos Delgado

1. Guardianship.
2. In northern Mexico.
3. Official hearing on the conduct of officials.
4. In the eighteenth century, a town just north of Mexico City.

Personal Narrative

1. An allusion to Proverbs 26:11.
2. An allusion to Romans 9:18.
3. Canticles, another name for the Song of Solomon.
4. An allusion to Song of Solomon 5:10.

Sinners in the Hands of an Angry God

1. From Deuteronomy 32:28.
2. Job 38:11.
3. An allusion to Psalms 91:5.
4. The three believing captives who emerged unharmed from a fiery furnace in Daniel 3:12–27.
5. From Psalms 90:11.
6. A nearby town.
7. A paraphrase of Matthew 3:10.
8. Genesis 19:17.

The Nature of True Virtue

1. Deists believe that God is revealed in nature rather than in the Bible.

Information to Those Who Would
Remove to America

1. In his own note, Franklins quotes Watts: ". . . born merely to eat up the corn."

Remarks Concerning the Savages of North America

1. The league of Iroquois tribes that included the Cayuga, Mohawk, Oneida, Onondaga, Seneca, and Tuscarora, united under the leadership of Dekanawida; formerly, until the admission of the Tuscarora, the Confederacy of the Five Nations.
2. College of William and Mary.
3. Yell.
4. Franklin's note: "It is remarkable that in all Ages and Countries, Hospitality has been allow'd as the Virtue of those whom the civiliz'd were pleas'd to call Barbarians. The Greeks celebrated the Scythians for it. The Saracens possess'd it eminently, and it is to this day the reigning Virtue of the wild Arabs. St. Paul, too, in the Relation of his Voyage and Shipwreck on the Island of Melita says, 'The Barbarous People shewed us no little kindness; for they kindled a fire, and received us every one, because of the present Rain, and because of the Cold.' " He quotes Acts 28:2.

The Autobiography of Benjamin Franklin

1. Philippians 4:8.
2. A Greek mathematician and philosopher living in the sixth century B.C. The advice, which Franklin's notes indicate that he intended to insert, is: "Let sleep not close your eyes till you have thrice examined the transactions of the day: where have I strayed, what have I done, what good have I omitted?"

Letter to Ezra Stiles

1. Edward Stiles was the grandson of Edward Taylor and president of Yale College. He had written to Franklin asking about Franklin's religious "sentiments."
2. Yale awarded Franklin an honorary degree in 1753.
3. The third edition of the *Encyclopædia Britannica*, being printed in America for the first time.

Some Account . . . of the Life of Elizabeth Ashbridge.

1. George Fox (1624–1691) founded the Society of Friends (the "Quakers") and authored their doctrine of "inner light." His journal was published in 1694.
2. The use of "thee" and "thou" in personal exchanges was a Quaker trait; Ashbridge's husband is afraid she has become a Quaker.

3. Avoiding pagan names, Quakers designate months and days of the week with numbers.

A Discourse Concerning Unlimited Submission

1. Here Mayhew appends a long footnote, arguing, "We may very safely assert these two things in general, without undermining government: One is, that no civil rulers are to be obeyed when they enjoin things that are inconsistent with the commands of God. . . . Another thing that may be asserted with equal truth and safety, is, That no government is to be submitted to, at the expence of that which is the sole end of all government,—the common good and safety of society."

Some Considerations on the Keeping of Negroes

1. This is a slightly altered quotation from Alexander Arscott's *Some Considerations Relating to the Present State of the Christian Religion*, Part III (1734).

Life of Junipero Serra

1. Despite voyages farther north, the Spanish did not discover Monterey Bay until 1602, and although plans were made at that time to settle the area, the first Spanish settlement was Father Serra's mission.

Canassatego

1. Brother Onas was the proprietor of Pennsylvania.

Jefferson's Autobiography

1. The parts Congress rejected are printed in italics and enclosed in brackets; those added by Congress are printed in capitals.
2. This is the conclusion Jefferson drafted; the following paragraph is the version Congress finally accepted.

Notes on the State of Virginia

1. In other words, although the natural bridge is not a cascade, it can't be left out of Jefferson's account.

Letter to Dr. Benjamin Rush

1. Joseph Priestley (1733–1804) was a Unitarian clergyman and chemist.

Letter to Peter Carr

1. Jefferson's footnote: "Livy, Sallust, Caesar, Cicero's epistles, Suetonius, Tacitus, Gibbon."

A Defense of the Constitutions of Government

1. Herodotus, who lived in the fifth century B.C., was honored by Cicero and others as "the father of history."
2. Darius (521–486 B.C.) consolidated and expanded the Persian empire.
3. Lycurgus was an Attic orator who excelled at finance and who carried out many important public works.
4. The historian (460–400 B.C.) of the Peloponnesian wars.
5. David Hume (1711–1776), a Scottish philosopher and political economist.
6. A first-century B.C. Sicilian historian.
7. From "On the Populousness of Ancient Nations," found in Hume's *Essays*, Volume I.
8. Alexander III of Macedon (356–323 B.C.) and Frederick William II of Prussia (1744–1797).
9. American painters John Singleton Copley (1738–1815), Benjamin West (1738–1820), and John Trumbull (1756–1843).
10. American poets Timothy Dwight (1752–1817), Joel Barlow (1754–1812), and David Humphreys.
11. American historians Jeremy Belknap and David Ramsay.
12. American scientists Thomas Godfrey (1704–1749), David Rittenhouse (1732–1796), and Zabdiel Boyston.

Letters from an American Farmer

1. Harvard, founded in 1636.
2. Britain had banished thousands of French settlers from Nova Scotia in 1755.
3. Latin: "Where there is bread, there is one's fatherland."
4. Part of Crevecoeur's disguise, as his father was never in America.
5. Lima, Peru.

An Occasional Letter on the Female Sex

1. From Thomas Otway's play *Venice Preserved* (1682), I.337.
2. The Orinoco, a river in southeastern Venezuela.
3. A sultan's harem.
4. Adam Ferguson (1723–1816), professor of moral philosophy at the University of Edinburgh.
5. Sophocles (c. 496–406 B.C.); the quotation is from his *Ajax*.

Of the Religion of Deism

1. For his argument's sake, Paine begins by generalizing deism. More specifically, "deism" describes a belief in a God who rules natural phenomena by established laws, not by miracles, and in the inherent rationality of human beings.

Travels Through North and South Carolina

1. Bartram uses "crocodiles" and "alligators" interchangeably.
2. Water lettuce and water chestnut, respectively.
3. A type of light musket.
4. The St. Johns River.

Letters of Abigail Adams to John Adams

1. The earl of Dunmore, the colonial governor of Virginia, was a Loyalist who later seized the arsenal at Williamsburg.
2. Adams's agent in Boston.
3. Probably a slip for "Crane," although Richard Cranch was Adams's brother-in-law.
4. *Gaiete du coeur* means "lightheartedness" in French.
5. Adams's anticipation of the Constitution.
6. Admiral Richard Howe (1726–1799) was commissioned by Britain to attend the Continental Congress.
7. Dr. John Winthrop (1714–1779), Hollis Professor of Mathematics and Natural Philosophy at Harvard College.
8. Elbridge Gerry (1744–1814), a delegate to the Continental Congress from Massachusetts who signed the Declaration of Independence and later served as vice president of the United States (1813–1814).
9. John Laurance, a judge who later became a senator.
10. Ulysses's (Odysseus's) faithful wife, who held off other suitors for twenty years, waiting for him to return.
11. Adams's own verse.
12. The source of this verse is unknown.

Acknowledgments

In the preparation of this book, I have received invaluable assistance from several people: Robin Craig, who worked for me from the beginning of this project until almost the end and was particularly helpful in locating texts, tracking down references, and compiling footnotes; Nancy Plooster, who then took over as my assistant and aided me with proofreading; and the staff of the Department of English at the University of California, Santa Barbara (specifically Chris Nelson, Delta Giordano, and Laura Baldwin), which facilitated so many of the small tasks involved in collating, reproducing, and mailing versions of a manuscript of this size. The labors of several of these individuals was supported by a grant from the General Research Fund of the Academic Senate of the University of California, Santa Barbara.

I also wish to thank my wife, Professor Deborah Sills, for her generous interest in this project, and her patience with the occasional frustrations that attended its completion.

Permission Acknowledgments and Source Notes

"This Newly Created World" translated by Paul Radin from *The Road of Life and Death: A Ritual Drama of American Indians* by Paul Radin.

"How the Spanish Came to Shung-Opovi" from *Truth of a Hopi: Stories Relating to the Origin, Myth, and Clan Histories of the Hopi* by Edmund Nequatewa. Flagstaff, Arizona: Northland Publishing Company in cooperation with the Museum of Northern Arizona, 1967.

"Letter on Discovery: Lofty Lands Most Beautiful" from *Christopher Columbus, Mariner* by Samuel Eliot Morison. Copyright 1942, © 1955 by Samuel Eliot Morison. Copyright © renewed 1983 by Emily Morison Beck. By permission of Little, Brown and Company.

Excerpts from "A Model of Christian Charity" from *The Winthrop Papers*, Volume II: 1623–1630. Courtesy Massachusetts Historical Society.

"John Winthrop's Christian Experience" from *The Winthrop Papers*, Volume I: 1498–1628. Courtesy Massachusetts Historical Society.

Excerpts from "The Examination of Mrs. Anne Hutchinson at the Court of Newton" from *The History of the Colony and Province of Massachusetts-Bay*, Volume II, Appendix II, by Thomas Hutchinson, edited by Lawrence Shaw Mayo, Cambridge, Mass.: Harvard University Press. Copyright © 1936 by the President and Fellows of Harvard College. Reprinted by permission of the publishers.

"To My Dear Children" from *The Works of Anne Bradstreet* edited by Jeannine Hensley, Cambridge, Mass.: Harvard University Press. Copyright © 1967 by the President and Fellows of Harvard College. Reprinted by permission of the publishers.

Excerpts from "Narrative of the Captivity and Restauration of Mrs. Mary Rowlandson" from *Original Narratives of Early American History*, Volume 19: *Narratives of the Indian Wars, 1675–1699* edited by Charles H. Lincoln, 1913, Barnes and Noble Books.

"Upon a Spider Catching a Fly," "Huswifery," "Meditation One," "Meditation Eight," and "Meditation Thirty-Eight" from *The Poetical Works of Edward*

   Sanford, meanwhile, marries a rich young lady but continues to pursue Eliza, eventually seducing her.
3. Eliza becomes pregnant and leaves home secretly with Sanford.
4. Eliza dies in childbirth, alone and unknown in Boston. H
   and family discover her death through an article in
   newspaper.

13. Two ancient Romans who behaved with extraordinary honor. Cincinnatus voluntarily resigned his dictatorship. Regulus, captured in Carthage but allowed to return to Rome on parole, honored his parole and returned to Carthage, where presumably he was tortured to death.

The Interesting Narration

1. In other words, he was treated as a person of very low esteem.

M'Fingal

1. The tradition of the Liberty Pole began in 1766, when the Sons of Liberty in New York, the associated patriots opposed to the Stamp Act, erected a tall pole near City Hall that was inscribed, "To his most gracious majesty, George the Third, Wm. Pitt and Liberty."
2. In Jonathan Swift's *Gulliver's Travels*, Brobdignagians are giants living in the land of Brobdignag.
3. In Book I of *Paradise Lost*, Milton describes Satan's spear as being so large that the tallest pine "were but a wand."
4. Hostile tribes of Thessaly.
5. The god of wine, here initiating a drunken brawl.
6. Mercury, who wore wings on his shoes, not ears.
7. A seraph from Book V of *Paradise Lost*.
8. Horrible mythological monsters extremely dangerous to humans.
9. Plato defined a human being as a "two-legged animal without feathers."
10. In ancient Rome, the joint government by two men.
11. Roman religious ceremonies to clean public places.

On the Equality of the Sexes

1. Sir Isaac Newton's work *Opticks* (1704), dealing with the phenomena of light and color, was generally the best known of his works in the eighteenth century.
2. A paraphrase and inversion of Ecclesiastes 1:9.
3. The god of marriage.
4. Alexander Pope, an eighteenth-century English poet and among the first to support himself solely through his literary productions, had been stunted and deformed in childhood by tuberculosis of the spine.
5. David sent Uriah to his death in battle so that he might have Uriah's wife, Bathsheba.

America

1. Awe-inspiring.
2. The equatorial zone.
3. The Appian Way was the main highway through Italy to Rome. Dwight not only compares America to the Republic of Rome, a common trope in his day, but implies through the plural, "ways," that America will be greater.
4. Dwight draws some of his apocalyptic imagery from the Book of Revelation.

On the Emigration to America

1. A character from Chaucer's "Knight's Tale," from *The Canterbury Tales*, who can represent any person setting out on a journey.
2. Freneau's note identifies this reference as the Mississippi River.

The Indian Burying Ground

1. Freneau's note: "The North American Indians bury their dead in a sitting posture; decorating the corpse with wampum, the images of birds, quadrupeds, &c: And (if that of a warrior) with bows, arrows, tomhawks, and other military weapons."
2. The Queen of Sheba, from 1 Kings 10.

On Mr. Paine's Rights of Man

1. Thomas Paine had supported the French Revolution, against the French monarchy, in *The Rights of Man* (1791).
2. A poetic name for America.

On the Death of the
Rev. Mr. George Whitefield

1. Selina Shirley Hastings, the Countess of Huntingdon, her patron.

To S. M., A Young African Painter

1. Probably Scipio Moorhead, a slave of the Reverend John Moorhead of Boston.
2. The heavenly city of Jerusalem has twelve gates.
3. Jerusalem.
4. In classical mythology, Damon, a shepherd and singer, offered his life for his condemned friend Pythias.

To His Excellency General Washington

1. A poetic name for America.
2. God of the winds in Roman mythology.
3. Wheatley refers to the French and Indian War, also known as the Seven Years War (1756–1763), in which the English and American colonists triumphed over the French.

Advise to the Privileged Classes

1. Latin for "the final argument of Kings."
2. Baron Charles Louis de Secondat de Montesquieu (1689–1755), French political philosopher and author of *Spirit of Laws*.
3. Voltaire was the pen name of Francois Marie Arouet (1694–1778), a French novelist, dramatist, essayist, and philosopher.
4. Jean Jacques Rousseau (1712–1778), French author and political theorist.
5. The code of laws prepared by Draco for Athens (c. 621 B.C.) was particularly severe; most offenses were punishable with death.
6. The Magna Charta was the "great charter" of English liberties that the English barons were able to force King John to sign at Runnymede on June 15, 1215.
7. James II, king of England (1685–1688).
8. Edmund Burke (1729–1799), British statesman and author of, among other important works, *Reflections on the Revolution in France* (1790), to which Barlow is here taking exception.
9. Gaius Julius Caesar (c. 104–44 B.C.), Roman statesman, general, orator, historian, and ruler.

The Hasty Pudding

1. A breakfast dish made in America from Indian corn and water.
2. France.
3. Barlow's translation of this famous line from Horace's *Ars Poetica* is in part a joke, since the line should read "He who combines the useful with the pleasing [or sweet and agreeable] wins the approval of all."
4. A poem by Oliver Goldsmith (1728–1774) that idealizes English rural life.
5. In 1792 the French had annexed Savoy from Sardinia.
6. Distillery.
7. Cattle.
8. Roman goddess of grain.
9. Bubbles.
10. A legendary Inca Indian, Oella was thought to be the Sun's daughter and the originator of spinning.

11. He is referring to his *Vision of Columbus* (1787).
12. The sun.
13. God of wine.
14. Barlow's note: "A certain king [George III of England], at the time when this was written, was publishing proclamations to prevent American principles from being propagated in his country."
15. Coastlands of the eastern Mediterranean.
16. Italian and French words for "cooked cereal."
17. Dutch ancestry.
18. Approximation of the word for "cornmeal mush" in one American Indian language.
19. A kind of pie or cake.
20. On Guy Fawkes Day, November 5, English and American Protestants celebrate the discovery of the Gunpowder Plot of 1605, an unsuccessful Roman Catholic scheme to blow up Parliament and assassinate the king.
21. When the sun reaches the Tropic of Cancer, on June 21, the summer solstice begins.
22. The top of a Corinthian column bears a resemblance to the tassles and green leaves of corn stalks.
23. Individual.
24. Young men are marked with an ear of corn that is fungus-infected.
25. Exact.
26. The coldest north wind in Greek mythology.
27. The mother of Osiris was sometimes depicted as a cow.

Choice of a Wife

1. The god of marriage.
2. The goddess of wisdom.

The Prologue to The Contrast

1. Thomas Wignell played the role of Jonathan, a character in the play.

The Coquette

1. As the novel opens, Eliza's former fiancé, an elderly clergyman named Mr. Haly, has died before they could marry, leaving Eliza happily free to re-enter society. She visits General and Mrs. Richman.
2. Returning home, Eliza becomes engaged to Boyer but continues to see Sanford. Boyer warns her that she is risking her reputation, and he breaks off their engagement when he catches Eliza and Sanford in an intimate conversation. Eliza tries to regain his affections, but fails.